Gettysburg

Baltimore.

Area of Operations
ARMY of the POTOMAC
1862~1865

Washington

Alexandria

POTOMAC RIVER

Chesapeake Bay

ATLANTIC OCEAN

MATTAPONI RIVER

RAPPAHANNOCK RIVER

bor
s Mill

ale
alvern Hill

YORK RIVER

Williamsburg

JAMES RIVER

GRAPE AND CANISTER

GRAPE AND CANISTER

THE STORY OF THE FIELD ARTILLERY

OF THE ARMY OF THE POTOMAC, 1861-1865

L. Van Loan Naisawald

Reprinted by

Olde Soldier Books, Inc.

18779 B North Frederick Rd.
Gaithersburg, Maryland 20879
(301) 963-2929

*To that loyal, devoted, and frequently too much maligned
body of men who, from the birth of this Republic, have given their
years, even their lives, in the protection of this Nation —
the officers and men of the Regular Army of the United States —
this book is respectfully dedicated.*

PREFACE

THE ROLE of field artillery in the American Civil War is all too often beclouded by the names of great commanders — Lee, Grant, Sherman, Longstreet, and Jackson — or by the picture of rolling waves of infantry symbolized by such names as the Iron Brigade, Hood's Texans, A. P. Hill's Light Division, the Irish Brigade, and many others. Virtually forgotten are the batteries which backed up the infantry. Jennings Wise has told the story of the Confederate artillery in *The Long Arm of Lee,* but the names of such Federal artillerymen as Cushing, Cowan, Hazard, Hall, Dilger, or even Generals Hunt and Barry, are seldom mentioned in accounts of the war.

The Army of the Potomac was saved several times because of this arm and these men. It escaped probable defeat and destruction at Malvern Hill by the massed fire of its artillery. So it was at Fairview during Chancellorsville; and the enfilading fire of Meade's artillery took the weight out of the last desperate attack against his lines at Gettysburg. The mention of the exploits of the artillery is usually relegated to generalizations, with the individual commanders and their batteries lost in collective terminology.

The purpose of this work is twofold. I have endeavored to tell the story of the field artilleryman of the Union Army of the Potomac, and second, to show the part this arm played: its capabilities and limitations, its equipment and organization. This study treats only the operations of the Army of the Potomac and its predecessors, from 1861 till the final campaign in April 1865. I have dealt only with the field batteries except as it became necessary to incorporate the activities of some of the heavy batteries in front of Petersburg. The heavy artillery units of the Army saw little action except as infantry, and this only in the closing months of the war. As such their role as artillery per se was a minor one.

The point should become evident as the story unfolds that field artillery of that day was a potent force — but only defensively. No offensive operation of either side was decisively affected by the offensive use of artillery; it was beyond the capabilities of the matériel and fire control systems of that era. A great principle did evolve, though, the principle of divisional massed artillery, with additional massed guns available to corps commanders. It was a crude system, a system that was to a great extent only a vague theory superimposed on infantry command channels and organization. But the beginnings of the present-day tactics of massing fires can be seen through the battle haze of the American Civil War.

In the opening chapter of this narrative the reader may become confused by the technical terms used in describing the Federal weapons as they rolled into firing positions. The author hopes, however, that the reader will bear with the story until the second chapter in which the description of the various weapons is covered in detail. To have begun this saga with a dull and dry treatise on the ordnance matériel then in use might have prevented some readers from ever reaching the action chapters which are the true heart of the book. For this reason the narrative begins with the first major action of the war, the First Bull Run.

While I have covered the life of the artillery of the Union Army of the Potomac, the story would be somewhat similar for the Western armies, though it would appear on the basis of limited research that these armies had a slightly wider variety of matériel and fewer cannon per thousand men, and lagged a bit behind Hunt's theories of centralized control. A veteran of the Army of the Potomac, however, would not have felt himself an utter stranger in the artillery camps of the Western armies.

In writing this book the principal source was of course the standard published volumes of the *Official Records of the Union and Confederate Armies in the War of the Rebellion,* usually referred to as the *Official Records* or 'OR's.' To catch the human interest angle, the little personal items that never reached the official reports, the unofficial histories were referred to. Unfortunately, few artillery units ever put their sagas into print. Of the many Regular Army batteries which served throughout the war only one, Battery B, 4th U.S. Artillery, seems to have published its story. Of the Volunteer units, only a half-dozen were found to be rich in detail and narrative. Of inestimatable value has been the monographic material done by the National Park personnel at the various National Battlefield Parks. Joseph Mills Hanson did some helpful research on the First and Second Bull Run actions and on the artillery engaged at Antietam.

There were a few manuals in existence at the time (of which copies exist today), and these were absolutely necessary for the technical detail. Of primary importance were the editions of *Instruction for Field Artillery,* all of which remained basically unchanged throughout the war; Benton's *Ordnance and Gunnery,* and John Gibbon's *Artillerist's Manual.* Also of great assistance in getting a feel for the subject were Gen. Hunt's series of articles on 'Artillery in the Great Rebellion,' which appeared in the *Journal of the Military Service Institute,* a military magazine of the postwar era. It is most regrettable that Gen. Hunt left no memoirs and that no scholarly biography of the man exists. Gen. Hunt is buried with other members of his family in the National Cemetery of the U.S. Soldiers Home, Washington, D.C.

The manuscript material which the author examined unfortunately had little that could be used in this rather specialized story of the war. Diaries and letters of artillery soldiers were extremely scarce.

L.V.N.

Manassas, Virginia
March 1960

ACKNOWLEDGMENTS

THE PROCESS of writing a book can rarely be done without considerable help from persons who willingly give of their time and knowledge to assist an author in his goal. The full worth of such persons is rarely realized by the general reader, so it is hoped that these few lines of grateful recognition will call attention to the contribution these individuals have made to this project.

Mr. Marshall Andrews of Sterling, Va., a noted authority on the American Civil War, stimulated my interest in that conflict. Brig. Gen. Carl Baehr, U.S. Army (Ret.), of Bethesda, Md., answered numerous questions on organization and matériel which confronted a beginner in this subject.

In an effort to prevent any gross errors in the over-all stories of the various battles, I requested and graciously received the help of the historians of the National Park Service at the various National Battlefield Parks. The following Park Historians reviewed and made useful comments on the chapters indicated: In the two Manassas (Bull Run) chapters I received the enthusiastic assistance of Mr. Frank Sarles and Mr. Robert Sanner; the splendid review of the Antietam phase was done by Mr. Louis Tuckerman and Mr. R. L. Lagemann, and Superintendent Harry W. Doust of that Park aided by making available data on artillery in that engagement; Mr. Albert Delahunty and Mr. Ralph Happel assisted greatly by reviewing the chapters covering Fredericksburg, Wilderness, and Spotsylvania, and Chancellorsville; Mr. Harry Pfanz willingly gave of his off-duty time to join me in tramping the fields of Gettysburg in efforts to come up with the picture of artillery in that fighting; and to Mr. Tom Harrison who added a number of worthy suggestions to the final chapter of the saga.

Mr. Harvey Sniteker of New York, N.Y., did a superb job of research for me in the unit histories.

To my friend, Mr. R. Jackson Ratcliffe of Manassas, Va., go my thanks for the cartographic work in this volume.

To the staffs of the Library of Congress and of the Civil War Branch of the National Archives I am most grateful for their patient efforts in my behalf.

In the tedious job of typing I was ably assisted by Mrs. Mary Crohan of Levittown, N.Y., and by my sister-in-law Miss Gertrude Rust of Washington, D.C.

I owe much to Mr. Bruce Catton for his over-all guidance and stimulus to my morale when at times I despaired of ever putting this project into a publishable manuscript.

Last, but far from least, I must acknowledge the patience of my wife Mary Lou, who willingly trudged the battlefields with me though thoroughly distracted by our two young children. Only her patience and courage enabled her to be an author's participating wife.

L.V.N.

CONTENTS

GRAPE AND CANISTER

1

THAT WAS THE END OF US

First Bull Run

A NATION was at war, not with an alien power but against itself. The crack in the union of the United States, plastered and patched many times, had parted too wide for minor repair. The American Civil War had begun with the shelling of Fort Sumter in April 1861. President Lincoln prepared to take drastic action to repair the break.

It was now early July 1861. The city of Washington sweltered under humid, oppressive heat. For weeks the Virginia heights across the Potomac from the city had bristled with stacks of bayoneted muskets. Regiment after regiment of volunteers, many clad in gaudy red and blue Zouave-type uniforms, pitched their tents in response to the President's call for 75,000 volunteers. No one expected to be there for more than ninety days — that was the length of service imposed by the President's call; the 'war' certainly would be over before then.

Brig. Gen. Irvin McDowell, an able but ill-starred Regular, was struggling to ready a force of 35,000 Federals to move on Brig. Gen. G. T. Beauregard's Confederate troops encamped near Centerville, about twenty-five miles to the west. When that battle was over, the Confederacy would be through and everyone could go home.

Ill-trained and unconditioned, McDowell's troops eagerly struck their tents on July 16, 1861, and began the move-

3

ment westward. The Federal general did not feel that his men were ready, but his opinion had little weight in a nation where political authority overweighed military authority. The cry was 'On to Richmond,' so McDowell obeyed.

The Federals reached Centerville on July 18 and found that their foe had fallen back south and west of a high-banked little stream that few men in either army had ever heard of, known locally as Bull Run. One of McDowell's generals, Dan Tyler, wandered southward toward Manassas to make a reconnaissance in force of the Confederate right. Tyler found Rebels there — in force. McDowell decided to turn the enemy's left instead. The plans were drawn; the Federals would strike at dawn July 21.

H-hour was set for 2 a.m., at which time three of McDowell's four divisions began to move (down what is now U.S. Highway 29 and 211) westward from Centerville. It was an annoying as well as tiring march, for newly raised armies do not mesh gears with the best of rhythm and timing.

Bumping along in the darkness with the lead division, Tyler's, was a monstrous 30-pounder Parrott rifle dragged by ten untrained horses — the term '30-pounder' describing the weight of the projectile it fired. Two wagons carrying ammunition followed in the gun's dusty wake.

In command of this weapon was a newly graduated West Point lieutenant, Peter C. Hains, and this was his first duty assignment. His unit consisted of six cannoneers and five drivers, plus the wagon drivers and those ten balky, untrained beasts hauling the 6000-pound weapon. Hains had originally been attached to Lt. John Edwards's Company G, 2nd U.S. Artillery, but Edwards's two-gun battery had been assigned to cover the Blackburn's Ford area while Hains moved west with the main column. Fresh from the Academy, Lt. Hains had, in late June, received orders to go to what is now Fort Myer, Virginia, and organize this detachment of men and animals into a military unit.

Hains's crew had begun to expect great things of their huge

cannon and displayed an open affection for it. Hains would hear his men pat the big breech and mutter, 'Good old boy, you'll make 'em sit up — just wait a bit.'[1] They apparently regarded this cannon with the same awe and respect as C. S. Forester's characters of his novel *The Gun* were later to look upon theirs.

Dawn found Tyler deploying his division across the Warrenton Turnpike about three-quarters of a mile east of Bull Run. His mission was to feint at the Stone Bridge while McDowell took two divisions on a circuitous flanking march to the north. McDowell's divisions would cross the stream at a ford two miles above the bridge and come down on the Confederate left rear.

It was now about 4:45 a.m., Sunday July 21, 1861. Hains's big gun unlimbered in the turnpike[2] and the crew prepared to open fire. The signal for the Federal Army to start shooting was to be given by three shots in succession by the big Parrott — since it was the biggest and loudest weapon on either side. Hains ordered the Parrott loaded with a percussion shell and trained its sights on the Van Pelt house on a rise, a quarter-mile west of the bridge, which appeared to be a Confederate command post — as indeed it was, being the location of one of their three signal stations.

It was about 5 a.m. when Gen. Tyler gave Hains the nod, and the lieutenant barked the fateful command, 'Fire!' A sharp, heavy concussion shattered the early morning quiet. The 30-pounder, shrouded in smoke, was pushed back into battery from its recoiled position, and the eager crew rammed home a second round. Another crash reverberated across the creek valley.[3]

A motley collection of artillery pieces began to take up firing positions on the slopes with Tyler's infantry. Capt. J. Howard Carlisle's Battery E, 2nd U.S. Artillery, with two 13-pounder James rifles, two old 6-pounder smoothbores, and two 12-pounder howitzers rolled into line to the right of the road. The rifled section opened fire. Coming in behind these was Capt. Romeyn B. Ayres's four-gun collection of 10-pounder Parrott rifles and 6-pounder guns of Battery E, 3rd U.S. Artillery.

So far the Confederates made no reply to the angry barks of the Federal cannon. The Rebel artillery behind the bridge, two out-ranged old 6-pounders, remained discreetly silent.[4]

A Federal soldier, sitting astride a limb of a tall oak near Tyler's position, kept him apprised of the progress of the Federal flanking column, which was marked by dust and occasional reflections of sun on burnished metal. The column was nearing Sudley Springs, about two miles to the northwest, when Tyler pushed a regiment down to the banks of the stream. Now the enemy's artillery came to life, snapping viciously at the cautiously advancing regiment. The Federal batteries moved forward a short distance to try to get their smoothbores into range of the Rebel guns. A noisy but harmless cannonading ensued as Tyler shuffled his regiments about in a vain effort to deceive the Confederates.

On the other side of the stream, Rebel Capt. John D. Imboden alerted his battery when the first dull boom of the big Parrott reached his tent. Teams were harnessed eagerly, and four ancient 6-pounders soon stood ready. Imboden rode forward with Gen. Barnard E. Bee to the heights where the Lewis house, 'Portici,' stood. The two officers could see plainly the great clouds of dust far to the north. Already from Capt. Alexander's wig-wag system had come the intelligence that a heavy Federal force was splashing across Bull Run near Sudley Springs, two miles to the north and in the rear of the Confederate left flank. A courier from the picket to the north galloped up with similar news.[5]

Col. Nathan George Evans, commanding the Confederate troops opposite the Stone Bridge, already had concluded that Tyler's efforts were bluff and that the main attack would fall elsewhere. A message from Alexander, 'Look out for your left; you are turned,' confirmed his suspicions. Evans began shifting the troops in front of the bridge to the high ground near the Matthews house, half a mile north of the turnpike and east of the Manassas-Sudley Road.

With sound military judgment, Gen. Bee began to build up a second line across the north face of the Henry house hill. Imboden was ordered to ride back and bring his battery forward. Twenty minutes later the four 6-pounders came bouncing down the rutted road past the Lewis house to an admirable position selected by Bee about a hundred yards north of Mrs. Henry's little one-story frame cottage.

The position Bee had picked was excellent: the ground just north of the house dropped away into a soft hollow before rising again to a low crest, and it was just behind this sheltering crest that Imboden unlimbered his weapons. Some 500 yards directly to the front, in a valley, was the Warrenton Turnpike-Sudley Road intersection and the now famous Old Stone House. The advancing Federals were on the high ground north of the turnpike, some 1200 yards range from Imboden's position. This was about maximum range for 6-pounder guns, but Imboden ordered his battery to open fire.[6]

Lurching and lumbering along with the Federal turning force were the three Regular batteries of James B. Ricketts, Charles Griffin, and Richard Arnold; a Rhode Island battery of six 13-pounder James rifles; and two 12-pounder Dahlgren boat howitzers dragged by men of the 71st New York Infantry.[7] It was close to 10 a.m. when the leading brigade, commanded by Col. Ambrose E. Burnside of Hunter's division, shook itself into line north of the Matthews house and east of the Manassas-Sudley Road. The Rhode Island battery, led by Capt. William H. Reynolds, and accompanied by the state's governor, William Sprague, trotted forward to a knoll near the Matthews house. Gray skirmishers in a declivity of a hill and in a shallow valley to the front began popping away at the battery. One of the cannoneers was sure those skirmishers were confused fellow 'Yanks,' and he proceeded to walk forward, shouting at them to quit firing and threatening to fling a round from his gun in their direction. The 'Rebs' corrected his mistake.

The sniping continued. A colonel's horse and then the Governor's were killed by the harassing fire. The Governor was given a second horse, only to have some clear-eyed Southerner knock it down too. Then Sprague was given the last spare mount in the battery. Maj. George Sykes, commanding a battalion of Regular infantry, saw that the battery's guns were badly exposed; he promptly slipped his command to the left into supporting position. The threat to the guns was canceled.

Shortly, the 71st New York with its two boat howitzers wheeled into line on the left. Minutes later the four 10-pounder Parrotts and two old howitzers of Battery D, 5th U.S. Artillery, known as the West Point Battery because it had been recruited from old Regulars at that station, Capt. Charles Griffin commanding, came in on a gallop to a ridge just west of Sudley Road. Col. Andrew Porter's brigade, to which Griffin was attached, went into line of battle to back up Burnside. Griffin estimated the range to the enemy batteries on the Henry house plateau at 1000 yards. Imboden's Rebel battery was the target, and the six pieces opened fire. Immediately Griffin lost the use of one of his Parrott rifles as a round became wedged in the tube.

Imboden's battery presented a difficult mark in a defiladed position. As the guns fired, their recoil rocked them farther back behind a sheltering slope. There they were reloaded, run forward till their tubes barely cleared the ground in front, and fired again. Although the Federal fire was accurate, only the howitzer shells seemed to inflict any damage. The rifled projectiles appeared to strike the ground at an angle of fifteen to twenty degrees and to burrow into the ground before blowing; and Imboden remarked that easily a hundred such projectiles had hit about his battery, exploding harmlessly underground, though the field about his position looked as if it had been rooted up by hogs.

A regiment from Heintzelman's division filed onto the field. The small Confederate brigade of Evans and those of Bee and Francis S. Bartow, which had crossed the turnpike to aid Evans, were hard pressed. Thirty minutes after Griffin had opened fire, Ricketts's Battery I, 1st U.S. Artillery, unlimbered its six 10-pounder Parrott rifles 500 yards to Griffin's left rear. A flurry of ordered activity, a raised arm, and six lanyards were jerked in unison. Sixty pounds of Parrott shells buzzed over the 1500-yard course to the Rebel batteries on the far heights.

The Confederate infantry was strung out along the turnpike from a house and haystacks on the Federal right to the Robinson house beyond the left of Burnside's brigade. A Southern battery near the Robinson house sought to stay the Union advance.[8] Their efforts brought little beyond the 'intimidation' of some of the more nervous Yankee units. A grove of trees in front of the Rebel right gave the defenders some protection, while shrubbery and fences along the road screened their left.

The Gray forces began to fall back across Young's Branch onto the Robinson house hill as the mass of committed Blue troops pushed forward. The Federal brigades of Cols. William T. Sherman and Erasmus D. Keyes found a ford 500 yards north of the Stone Bridge, crossed, and came in on the left of the advancing Union line. Maj. William F. Barry, McDowell's chief-of-artillery, ordered the Rhode Island battery to displace 500 yards forward as the enemy line fell back. Ricketts and Griffin were now firing over the heads of the Federal infantry — a technique that infantry of that time never liked; poor fuzes often rendered the projectiles more harmful to friend than foe.

The Confederate artillery on the east edge of Henry house hill, coupled with Imboden near the west edge, bellowed back. Two pieces from Capt. H. Grey Latham's battery had been firing at the Federals from north of the turnpike but had now pulled back to the hill. Two Napoleons of the famed Washing-

ton Artillery had joined the fracas, and the batteries of Col.
William Nelson Pendleton and Capt. Ephraim G. Alburtis were
now arriving.

The Union lines reached the Stone House, which still stands
at the junction of the turnpike and the Manassas-Sudley Road.
Imboden watched as Blue officers straightened their lines and
pointed menacingly with their swords at his battery. The
Rebel battery, its ammunition almost gone and half its horses
down, was a ripe target. Imboden ordered his unit to retire.
As the sections pulled back, Imboden chose the route that
passed behind the widow Henry's white frame house, a rise
of ground there giving him a screening for some 200–300
yards.

The Federal gunners tracked their fleeing quarry. As their
target passed behind the small white house, Yankee shells
slammed into the building, scattering boards, shingles, and
splinters. A rifled projectile from one of the Federal pieces
shattered the axle of one of Imboden's guns, forcing its
abandonment. Blue infantry let fly a distant and harmless
volley as the harassed battery passed into the safety of Thomas
J. Jackson's Confederate brigade, already nearing the pine
woods on the southeast face of the plateau.

It looked as if the day had been all but won by the Federals.
The Confederate brigades north of the turnpike had fled in
disorder across the road where they were rallied behind
Jackson's regiments. Still, this was not much of a force to
oppose some 8000 Federals if McDowell began to push
vigorously. He failed to do so! From noon until about 2 p.m.
there was a lull; only then did McDowell determine to drive
the Confederates from the high ground south of the turnpike. Blue infantry already was preparing to cross that road
and push up the slopes toward the Robinson and Henry houses.
McDowell planned to move some artillery up the ridge to
finish off the Southerners. The commanding general turned
to Maj. Barry, his artillery chief, and ordered him to get two
batteries up on the plateau and direct them into position

near the Rebel battery. Barry made the fateful selection —
Griffin's and Ricketts's Regulars. The artillery commander
dispatched Lt. Henry W. Kingsbury of McDowell's staff to
carry the order to Ricketts and Barry personally rode across
the fields to Griffin's position.

Griffin received Barry's orders coldly; the two men had
not been on friendly terms for some time. The battery commander scanned the far hill where Barry said he was to go.
Griffin protested; there was no Blue infantry up there; he'd
be a sitting duck in that open field without any support. Barry
replied that the 11th New York — Ellsworth's Fire Zouaves
— would support him. Griffin was skeptical; this group,
though famed in newsprint, had no recorded deeds to their
credit; moreover, they had showed a decided lack of discipline. Barry insisted. Reluctantly, the battery captain ordered
his five usable pieces limbered, and the small column started
forward.

Lt. Kingsbury found Capt. Ricketts and his battery in process
of moving forward to a new position; the lieutenant delivered
Barry's order. The exact spot to which the battery was to go
was not clear to Ricketts. He questioned Kingsbury, insistent
that there must be no mistake about the place. The order was
clarified, and Ricketts studied the distant terrain for a moment.
It was a dangerous spot to send a battery. There was no
Federal force near, the area had not been scouted, and the
enemy line was within easy musket range. But this was an
order, and Ricketts would carry it out.

Griffin's battery began the descent toward the turnpike and
Young's Branch. There was no sign of any friendly infantry
moving along to support the battery. Griffin rode after Barry
to protest again, and Barry assured him that the Zouaves were
about ready to go into action and would follow. Griffin
suggested that they precede the battery, arguing that the
regiment could retire to a supporting position behind the
battery after the guns were in position on the hill. Barry disagreed. The battery commander then suggested that a better

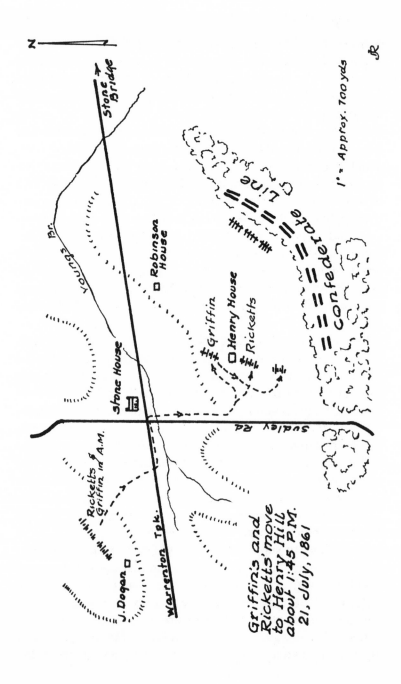

N

Stone Bridge

Young's Br.

Robinson House

Confederate Line

Stone House

Griffin

Henry House

Ricketts

Sudley Rd

Ricketts &
Griffin in A.M.

J. Dogan

Warrenton Tpk.

Griffin's and
Ricketts' move
to Henry Hill
about 1:45 P.M.
21, July, 1861

1" = Approx. 700 yds

position would be another hill 500 yards in the rear of that designated. But this was contrary to Gen. McDowell's order, which was to go to the Henry house hill, said Barry. Disgusted, Griffin protested a last time that the contemplated infantry support was worthless. 'I will go; but mark my words, they will not support us,' said Griffin bitterly as he went to rejoin his command.

Griffin's and Ricketts's batteries moved independently toward the Henry house hill. Enemy artillery began to search out the range to Ricketts's battery as it approached a small ravine. Lt. Douglas Ramsay, the first lieutenant of the battery, expressed doubt to Ricketts that the guns could cross at this point. The Confederates' searching artillery fire told Ricketts to try; to countermarch could bring confusion, disorder, and disaster. One by one the vehicles crossed; one wheel broke but was quickly replaced. The column began the pull up the hill, in the process passing Griffin's unit, which had erroneously turned off into a field to the right and now was trying to correct the mistake.

Ricketts's pieces were hurriedly put into battery in a slight depression just south of the Henry house. Immediately, musket fire bit into the little group, killing horses and wounding men. It appeared that much of this damaging fire was coming from the Henry house itself. Ricketts, determined to end it, swung his tubes on the little dwelling. With an ear-splitting crash the house was riddled and shattered by the salvo from the Parrotts. The battery then turned its attention to the enemy's main position — some 300 yards to the east. Griffin's five pieces now rolled in on the north side of the house, raising to eleven the number of Federal cannon on the plateau.[9]

The enemy's line could be traced by the flicks of flame and the low, wispy clouds of grayish smoke that billowed above, swinging in a great concave arc from the northeast to southwest across the back face of the open plateau. Behind the center of the Rebel line and running along the southern edge of the plateau was a low pine and oak woods. Up to this time the fighting had been slow, methodical, and orderly. There had been little close-range action and no local surprises occasioning panic or disorder. But at this moment the tempo changed. The Rebels had built up a strong line about Jackson's brigade which stood, as Bee said, 'like a stone wall.' Some thirteen Confederate cannon were in that line now — at a range where their smoothbore pieces were actually at an advantage over rifled guns.

Ricketts and Griffin concentrated on trying to beat down the enemy's artillery fire. In turn, the Gray infantry and artillery concentrated on them. A sleet of shell, case shot, canister, and musket slugs converged on the two Union batteries. Men began to drop, and wounded horses screamed in pain. A Minié ball shattered the right thigh of Lt. Adelbert Ames, who was commanding a section of Griffin's battery. Two men quickly wrapped a tourniquet about the wounded officer's leg and obeyed his command to lift him onto a nearby limber. From his exposed perch Lt. Ames resumed command of his section. Immediately, a solid shot from an enemy smoothbore hit a few feet in front of one of Ames's pieces, bounced once, and crushed a wheel of the piece. Ames bellowed from the limber to pull the extra wheel from the caisson. A corporal and several men responded; the wheel was replaced and the gun reopened. For his conduct here Lt. Ames was awarded the Medal of Honor.

Griffin then made a tragic mistake; he switched some of his pieces to the right of Ricketts to try to get a better shot at one of the annoying Rebel batteries. This brought the right flank of the line of cannon into tempting range of Southern infantry. The guns had fired two rounds when suddenly a line of advancing infantry appeared through the smoke to the right front. The line was beyond a rail fence, which the men promptly scaled. When they had re-formed their ranks, a lone figure stepped out in front and faced the line; he appeared to be making a speech.

Griffin shot a quick glance and ordered canister — that

was a Rebel regiment. Maj. Barry, having accompanied the 11th New York onto the field, rode up to Griffin and cautioned him to refrain from firing. According to Barry they were Federals sent by Heintzelman as battery support. Griffin again argued with Barry, who was convinced this unit was Federal. Unconvinced, Griffin reluctantly switched his guns back to their original target. But the battery commander watched that ominous line as his cannoneers were swinging back to the orginal target.

The speech apparently over, the line suddenly faced to the left and marched about fifty yards toward the woods. Then it faced right and headed for the Yankee gun position. The advancing line came to an abrupt halt about seventy yards from the batteries.[10] A Federal staff officer on the hill watched this movement and raised his field glasses to get a better look. A twist of the thumb on the adjusting screw and the horrified officer found himself peering into the barrels of leveled muskets. There was a loud command. A roar and a cloud of smoke punctuated their movement. It seemed as if 'every man and horse . . . just laid right down and died right off,' the stunned officer recalled later,[11] and, as Griffin subsequently put it, 'that was the last of us.' [12] Ricketts went to the earth badly wounded and apparently dead. His first lieutenant, Ramsay, a conspicuous mark since he was the only officer wearing a fancy dress uniform, turned to run and was shot dead by a young Confederate who quickly confiscated the officer's personal equipment.

Actually that blast of musketry effected more shock than physical damage. At first it appeared as if the units had been obliterated, but it later turned out that actual casualties for both units for the entire day amounted to only thirty-two.[13] But the horse teams, which represented the batteries' mobility, had been cut to shreds, and the shock of that volley destroyed those two commands as effective units. And for the rest of the day the Yankee guns stood silent and helpless in the open field. The Zouaves and a small battalion of newly en-

listed marines had come up into supporting position behind
the batteries, but both units seemed stunned by the suddenness
and thoroughness of the Confederate volley. Griffin rode back
and pleaded for them to come forward and engage the enemy
— the 33rd Virginia which now charged and took at least
part of Griffin's battery, the two or three guns he had shifted.
The dazed men just stood there. A few heard the commands of
their officers and fired one or two ragged volleys. Then the
much-vaunted Zouaves and the marines turned and fled.

Suddenly there was a thundering of many hoofs. Down
a little road emerging from the woods on the Federal right
galloped two companies of Col. James E. B. Stuart's cavalry.
The horsemen rode smack into, and through, the fleeing
Zouaves, who scattered, suffering a few casualties. The two
reserve companies of the Zouave regiment held their formation long enough to empty a few of Stuart's saddles, but
this ended the effective contribution of the 11th New York and
the marines for the day.

A column of Union infantry, moving toward the left of
the batteries when the bolt struck, now made a rush to save
the guns. The 33rd Virginia, the regiment that had fired the
murderous volley, reached the guns first. A fierce melee raged
over the debris of the shattered batteries and over the prostrate
form of the wounded Ricketts. The 33rd Virginia was driven
off. The Southerners got reinforcements and lashed back,
driving off their enemy. Gray-clad figures attempted to turn
captured pieces back on their erstwhile owners.

The 38th New York Infantry tangled with the Rebs for
a few minutes, then retired. Its colonel reported that since
Griffin had been driven from the field, he felt his regiment was
no longer needed. More Yankee infantry poured onto the
field. Once more the Confederates gave up their prize, falling
back to the safety of the nearby pine woods. The 38th New
York, ordered back into the fray, dragged three of Ricketts's
rifles 300 yards to the supposed safety of the high-banked

Manassas-Sudley Road. A charge by Hampton's Legion swept past the Henry house and again seized parts of the crippled batteries, and the course of battle swayed to and fro for about an hour.

Finally, about 3:45 p.m., McDowell's last brigade, Col. Oliver O. Howard's, came onto the field. These troops double-timed forward across the turnpike and up the slopes of Chinn Ridge — 700 yards to the west. There was a battery hard pressed up on the heights, Howard was told; he was to support it if he could. The Blue column, nearly exhausted from its long march under a brutal sun, thrashed its way through a thicket below the crest of the hill. Emerging on the far side, Col. Howard met Lt. Edmund Kirby of Ricketts's battery, his face scarcely recognizable through a froth of blood from his mount's bullet-pierced nose. Kirby had one of the battery's caissons with him, all that he had been able to haul off the field up to that time.

Howard's men swept past Kirby and his caisson. They reached the crest. Before them was a Rebel line, visible through the sulphurous smoke. The Federals halted and fired. The Confederates volleyed back. More cannon to the front, being worked by shirt-sleeved Southerners, spat canister. The Federal infantry fired twenty to thirty rounds per man before the collapse came. About 4 p.m. the Confederate reserve brigades of Kirby Smith and Jubal Early poured across the Manassas-Sudley Road from the south and extended to the left of the Rebel line. These troops began to curl about McDowell's right flank — Howard's troops. Then a Gray battery opened up from that quarter. A regiment somewhere along the right of the Union line decided it had had enough and turned about. At the same time Beauregard loosed his whole line in a final assault, and the entire Blue line collapsed like a sand castle before an onrushing wave.

A bitter and enraged Griffin extricated two of his pieces from that death-swept hill. Down the slope toward the turn-

pike he led them. As he neared Young's Branch, Griffin
noticed an officer watering his horse in the trickling flow.
On closer look the the officer turned out to be Barry.

Griffin dug his spurs into his mount and turned its head
in Barry's direction. The Captain rode up to the Chief-of-
Artillery, 'Major, do you think the Zouaves will support
us?'

An embarrassed Barry winced under the biting sarcasm;
'I was mistaken,' he admitted quietly.

Griffin was not through: 'Do you think that was our support?'

'I was mistaken,' replied Barry.

'Yes,' cut back Griffin, 'you were mistaken all around.'
With that he pulled his horse's head up from the stream
and turned back to rejoin the remnants of his command.[14]

There was confusion and disorder as the Federals pulled
back off that body-strewn plateau into the valley by the
turnpike, but as yet there was no panic. Capt. Richard
Arnold's Battery D, 2nd U.S. Artillery, had come up late
but now was firing rapidly from a position just northwest of
the Stone House — about 800 yards from the enemy line.
Union infantry about Arnold melted away; in a hurried con-
ference, Arnold and his officers decided that a retreat was in
order for them too. His personnel losses had been light, but
fifteen or twenty of his horses were out of action. The guns,
two James rifles and two 6-pounders, were limbered, and
Battery D wound its way down the slope.

Arnold tried to find his division commander, Heintzelman,
but with no success. Maj. Fry of McDowell's staff hailed him,
and ordered him to cover the retreat. McDowell wanted a
rally made on the Matthews hill. Arnold brought over his four
pieces and opened fire. But the proposed stand never materialized. The Federals were beaten and wanted no more that day.
Semiorganized units and disorganized groups straggled back
over the routes by which they had advanced that morning,
the only way they knew to leave the field. Maj. George Sykes's

Regulars stubbornly gave ground as they covered the rear of McDowell's retreating and demoralized army.

The Federal artillery had been hard hit by the loss on the hill of all six of Ricketts's rifles and three of Griffin's pieces. This was over 37 per cent of the tubes in McDowell's main effort. But still intact were the Rhode Island battery, Arnold's, and the two New York boat howitzers. East of the Stone Bridge were the two batteries with Tyler's division, those of Capt. R. B. Ayres and J. Howard Carlisle. These had not crossed the stream and had been only lightly engaged. Ayres had made an attempt to follow Sherman's brigade over the stream, but had found the banks too high.

Four more batteries had been lightly engaged at Blackburn's Ford, and one battery of old 6-pounders rested inactive on the hills about Centerville. The men who had comprised the original battery of these 6-pounders had gone home the day before, their term of enlistment having expired. They were now manned by a makeshift battery of Germans who had had some experience with this arm in their native country.

Near Blackburn's Ford, Capt. Henry J. Hunt, who had a distinguished career in the Mexican War, had answered the enemy's demonstration with a furious burst from his new 12-pounder Napoleon guns — the only guns of this type on the field. Three other Regular batteries — the combined A and G of the 2nd U.S. Artillery, and the 20-pounder Parrotts of G, 1st U.S. Artillery, under Lts. John C. Tidball, Oliver D. Greene, and John Edwards — broke in with Hunt. The Federal left retired unharmed and unmolested when word was received of the retreat. There was a brief show of panic among some of the nearby Blue infantry, which Hunt allayed by walking his battery calmly to the rear.

As the force which had stormed the Henry house hill retreated, word spread to other parts of the field. Tyler's brigades in front of the bridge, with Ayres's and Carlisle's batteries and Hains's big 30-pounder, got the order to retire to Centerville. Ayres's command took up a rear guard mission as the Federal troops turned into a long dark ribbon moving east on the turnpike.

Lt. Hains cleared his ponderous weapon from the fields overlooking Bull Run, though a disabled ammunition wagon had to be left behind. Joining the stream of fleeing soldiery, the gun detachment moved slowly down the road. Shortly they reached a house with a well, around which were gathered what Hains estimated as a crowd of about 1000 exhausted and dehydrated Union soldiers. Since Hains and his men were in a like condition he authorized the detachment to pause for water.[15] Hains himself had just consumed about half a bucketful of the refreshing water when he noticed some lines of cavalry forming in the fields across the road. Curious, the lieutenant watched them; their leader, a man with a large black beard, was dressing their lines with great care. At this point Ayres's battery pulled abreast of the house.

Apparently the realization hit Ayres and Hains simultaneously — that mounted force was Confederate cavalry! Hains screamed at the men about the well to form ranks, but these green troops were unimpressed by the commands of a strange baby-faced lieutenant, and only three of them showed any inclination to obey. Lt. Hains yelled again that Rebel cavalry was getting ready to charge, only to be told that what he saw was friendly troops. He continued to plead and, as the mounted line began to move toward the road, two or three of the Federal soldiers did raise their muskets and fire.

In the meantime Ayres swung his guns from column into line facing the oncoming cavalry, and his loud command 'Canister — double charges — load!' rang out. Then the large black-bearded enemy officer was heard yelling, 'Charge!'

Ayres let the black line of galloping cavalry reach almost to the road before he yelled the command to fire; the guns crashed, and through the smoke of the discharges the Federals could see terrible carnage. Wounded and dismembered men and animals were thrown into a tangle of wreckage and confusion, while surviving troopers and riderless horses were running to the rear, harassed by a scattered flurry of musket fire of nearby Union infantry who now realized Hains had been right.

The Confederate officer could be heard yelling to his men to re-form and charge the guns. His cries were drowned out as Ayres's guns discharged their powerful loads a second time and the wrecked cavalry force fled the field.

Some distance ahead of Hains's detachment, which was probably one of the last units to clear the battle area, was Carlisle's battery; and from his position in their rear Lt. Hains and his men saw another cavalry detachment wade into Carlisle's column. Two of that unit's sections were caught in a tight column on the road, which at that point passed through a fringe of woods. A loud racket ensued: wild yells, shouts, clang of saber steel, pistol shots, shrieks of wounded animals; cannoneers, drivers, and cavalrymen tumbled to earth. Carlisle yelled the order to gallop.

Tired horses lunged at traces as the harassed little command began to pick up speed. Then a loud crack and a noise of splintering wood gave notice that the wheel of one piece had come off. The crew tried to drag it, but the tired horses were not up to it, so the gun was abandoned. The strain was too great on the wheels and one after another they gave way. Only the third section, coming up late, saved itself by tying in with Ayres.

Hains and his gun passed safely through the wreckage of Carlisle's battery, and about 6 p.m. he reached and crossed Cub Run some two and a half miles east of Bull Run. On the other side, however, things came to a halt; the turnpike was jammed with stalled and abandoned wagons and a share of overturned ones. The lieutenant glanced around quickly for a way to bypass the snarl, and decided to try to haul his piece up the steep wooded hill just north of the clogged road. The attempt failed; the gun became stuck halfway up. As he and his men struggled futilely with the monster, Hains spotted some

infantry waiting at the top of the hill. He rode up and begged
for help.

'All right, all right; I'll let you have men,' said their general.
'How many do you need? Don't leave it behind.'

'I'll need a whole regiment to haul it up,' replied the lieutenant, 'and the sooner the better.' With the general promising
to send the men immediately, the young officer returned to
his gun.[16]

Hains and his detachment waited by the Parrott. Five
minutes went by, ten, fifteen. Hains looked to the west where
the sun was beginning to set, and saw a column of infantry
which he recognized as Sykes's Regular Army battalion moving up the road — but there was nothing behind them! He
quickly spurred up the hill in search of his promised help
just as a sputtering of rearguard fire broke loose at some
Rebels moving in from the right of the road. On reaching
the crest he found the general, who was beginning to move
his command in a continuance of his retreat.

'Can I have the men?' cried Hains.

'Too late, now — too late,' came the terse reply, and
with his next breath the general put his command under way.

Dejected and grim-lipped, Hains returned to his command,
determined to fight his little detachment to the last in defense
of that huge gun. From his sergeant he was able to get fresh
loads for his revolver, but only five others besides himself
carried pistols — the other six men were armed with nothing
but whips! Realizing this, he decided to spike the gun and save
the lives of his men.

The team was uncoupled from the limber and started to
the rear. Then, securing a priming iron, the officer rammed
it in the vent hole and drove it in hard with a rock, so that
the Rebels would have trouble before they made the weapon
usable again. And with that the gun which had opened the
battle was abandoned to the Rebels, who proudly added it
to their rich booty of captured war matériel.[17]

In the meantime what had been confusion and disorder

on the turnpike became sheer panic. About 6:30 p.m. a pursuing Rebel battery had plunked a shell smack into a Yankee wagon crossing the little Cub Run bridge. With that the span had collapsed, and the terrified men threw away rifles and equipment and began to run in terror. Capt. Ayres had sent his caissons, wagons, and forge on ahead of his guns, which were being used to keep pursuing Rebels at a distance. From these vehicles panic-stricken soldiers cut out individual horses, mounted them, and fled the area.

As the elements which had comprised the flanking column neared Cub Run, they found the western approach blocked and choked with crowds of fleeing men and horseless equipment. The road and the fields on either side looked like a dumping ground. Wheeled vehicles of all description had been either deserted in the road or left in the fields west of the stream. There appeared to be no other way to cross that stream.

Lt. Kirby, carefully nursing along the remnants of Ricketts's battery — six caissons, three limbers, a wagon, and a forge — had to abandon his charges. Griffin tried to get his exhausted teams to pull his three salvaged cannon through the fields and over the stream. Only one Parrott rifle and a 12-pounder limber made it. Arnold's battery, still intact, reined to a halt, unable to get close to the debris-strewn approaches to Cub Run. The commander ordered his guns spiked and the teams cut from the traces. Similarly five of the Rhode Island battery's rifles were left behind, as were the two boat howitzers of the 71st New York.[18]

The beaten Army — or rather parts of it — rested for a few hours at Centerville. Other elements and individuals kept going till they reached the supposed sanctuary of the Washington defenses. There would be no more fighting of any consequence in the Eastern theater until early the next summer. Both sides were disorganized, and each knew now that the war would be no brief chivalrous tournament.

The Federal artillery had been badly handled. McDowell's decision to send Griffin and Ricketts forward was not sound, and Barry had erred in letting them go up before the support was formed. As it developed, the two batteries were performing an infantry mission, not the role of artillery then or now. Griffin, too, had committed a costly error when he shifted his forces too close to the Confederate line.[19] He later stated that he believed Ricketts's battery should have been permitted to remain north of the turnpike and his own should have been allowed to go into position on that hill he had suggested to Barry — probably the front slopes of Chinn Ridge about 700 yards west of the Henry house. One of his opposing battery commanders, Imboden, agreed after the war that one of the two batteries should have been left north of Young's Branch; that battery could then have swept the upper reaches of the plateau when Beauregard was re-forming his shaken brigades.

But it is hard to conceive that batteries left north of the turnpike would have had much effect. The range would have been great — upwards of 1200 yards — and the amount of damage rifled cannon could do at that range was very small. Psychologically perhaps, this might have had some effective influence on green troops. Yet the Rhode Island battery with its James rifles, firing from north of Young's Branch, apparently had little effect on the long Gray lines.

McDowell had taken a small but progressive step in appointing a chief-of-artillery, but his chief did not exercise tactical control over the batteries. In this fight batteries were assigned to brigades and even regiments — a tactic that belonged to the vanishing era of the smoothbore musket. Barry had been a channel through which McDowell had passed many of his orders to the artillery; only during the retreat did Barry have a free hand to manage the guns covering the rear.

Complete separation of artillery command channels as well as its tactical control from the infantry's would be a long time coming — not until after this and several subsequent wars had ended. Throughout the Civil War the tragic practice of senior infantry officers' judging themselves to be competent artillery commanders as well would endure. While the role of artillery, then as now, was to support infantry or cavalry (armor), the mechanics of its operation should have rested with the artillery commanders. In reality, the capabilities and limitations of field artillery in this war were outside the grasp of all but a few officers on both sides.

During the night of July 22, a sleepy telegraph operator in the War Department in Washington was handed a message that was to have lasting effect on the artillery arm of the Yankee establishment. The telegraph operator was told to get the wire off quickly. The message read:

GENERAL GEORGE B. MCCLELLAN, BEVERLY, VA.
    CIRCUMSTANCES MAKE YOUR PRESENCE HERE NECESSARY. CHARGE ROSECRANS OR SOME OTHER GENERAL WITH YOUR PRESENT DEPARTMENT AND COME HITHER WITHOUT DELAY.
                        L. THOMAS
                    ADJUTANT-GENERAL [20]

]]

AN ARMY IS BORN

IT WAS LATE in the afternoon of Friday, July 26, 1861, just
ten days after McDowell's forces had left the Washington
area for what became the First Battle of Bull Run. The air
was as heavy and humid as it had been that earlier day. Four
days had passed since the sleepy operator had dispatched the
telegram to Gen. McClellan. Now the train from the West
carrying the general was pulling into the old Washington
B. & O. station.

The city of Washington was already accustomed to seeing
its streets, restaurants, hotels, and terminals thronged with
blue-uniformed men. A youthful looking officer stepping from
a car of the newly arrived train thus attracted little attention.
Short but sturdy looking, his mouth hidden by a drooping
reddish moustache, and effusing a magnetic air of confidence,
George Brinton McClellan arrived in the nation's capital. The
handsome hero of recent victories in what is now West
Virginia, soon to be popularly and somewhat reverently
referred to as the 'Little Napoleon,' called on the aged Gen.
Winfield Scott, the Army's commanding general, that same
evening. The next morning McClellan reported to the adjutant
general and received instructions to pay a prompt visit to
the President.

Mr. Lincoln, we are told, received this vain thirty-five-year-
old general cordially. When McClellan departed from the
White House he had received oral orders from the President

to assume command of the city of Washington and all of the troops in its vicinity.

Disorder and confusion irked McClellan. The multitudinous conglomeration of troops which cluttered up the streets, hotels, and saloons of the city lacked, to McClellan's mind, order and discipline, and scarcely deserved the honor of being referred to as an army. His second general order — the first had announced his assumption of command — was designed to bring some semblance of military discipline to this uniformed mob. The order announced that a Provost Guard of Regulars had been established; there would be no more loitering and loafing about Washington's fleshpots by officers or their men; brigade commanders were to be held responsible for their troops' compliance with the new order. The first step had been taken toward the creation of the powerful Army of the Potomac.

In answer to a request from the President for the general's ideas on required forces, McClellan submitted, on August 2, 1861, his 'hasty' estimate of the forces required to defeat the Confederacy. For what he called the 'main army of operations,' the one which eventually became the Army of the Potomac, he envisaged 250 infantry regiments of 225,000 men and 100 field batteries of 600 guns and 15,000 men, plus necessary cavalry and engineers.

With this as his guide McClellan began the task of providing for defense of the capital while simultaneously building an army out of this hodgepodge of uniforms. The veteran troops were organized into permanent infantry brigades and stationed on the enemy side of the river. New units were to be thrown into provisional brigades, trained and equipped in suburban Maryland camps, and then assigned to the other side of the river. Sometimes the scheme failed to work as planned, as Durell's Pennsylvania battery discovered. The battery reached Washington on November 7th, a completely raw and unequipped outfit. Three weeks later the men received their horses, ten days after that harness arrived. And on December

12th, four rifled guns and two smoothbores were dragged into Durell's camp. 'Boots and saddles' sounded on the morning of December 18th, and Durell's battery found itself leaving its camp of instruction for the Virginia hills without so much as a day of training with horses and cannon.

McClellan hoped to be able to create permanent divisions and eventually corps. The creation of the latter he intended to delay until the troops were battle-tested and officers had shown their worthiness for high command. Furthermore, the forces should be organized, he thought, not as a geographical division but as an over-all army. On August 20, 1861, McClellan's headquarters issued orders decreeing that henceforth all troops comprising various departments and commands under his control would be combined and known as the Army of the Potomac.

For the most part the men McClellan picked for the big jobs turned out to be good choices. When he organized his personal staff he selected Maj. William F. Barry as chief-of-artillery. While Barry had been guilty of a tragic blunder on the field of Bull Run, he was a graduate of West Point and a distinguished veteran of the Mexican War, and was regarded highly in the old service. In 1860 Barry, along with Henry J. Hunt and William H. French, had written the manual for artillery service which was used with only minor modification throughout the war.[1] Although Barry was never to receive the recognition and fame of his colleague Hunt, he deserves much of the credit for building what many regarded as the most powerful arm of the Union service.

In addition to Barry, McClellan acquired the talents of the man whose name was later to become the symbol of this army's artillery — Henry J. Hunt. At this time a major of artillery, Hunt had already acquired considerable experience and reputation. A graduate of West Point, class of 1839, he had twice been breveted for gallantry in the Mexican War, and twice wounded. In that war he had served with Duncan's Battery, whose exploits were still a topic of conversation in 1861.

Promoted to major shortly after Bull Run, he was in charge of the artillery defenses south of the Potomac when McClellan took command. The commanding general selected him to head the Artillery Reserve of the Army.

The problems facing McClellan that hot summer were legion. One small one was to procure appropriate rank for some of his officers — a task complicated by law and politics. An *ad hoc* solution was obtained by procuring passage of an act authorizing appointment of additional aides-de-camp to general officers — to be from military or civil life, but to have no higher rank than colonel. By this device he promoted Barry and Hunt to colonels.

The headache of organizing the artillery for the army was given to Col. Barry. Like his superior, Barry appears to have been very capable at this task — which proved fortunate, as it was necessary to organize the forces that summer quickly and effectively. Fear of a lightning assault by the Confederates against Washington demanded that some sort of usable force be trained and ready at once. Also, the stream of new levies had begun to arrive, some as batteries, some as whole regiments, most without any equipment other than uniforms, and almost all totally devoid of training. McClellan's scheme envisaged each division being broken down into three infantry brigades of four regiments each, one regiment of cavalry, and four light field batteries — a total of some 14,000 men. Barry drew up a set of principles to be used in creating the army's field artillery organization. These principles, which McClellan adopted, were: [2]

1. There should be at least two and one-half and preferably three pieces for every 1000 men.

2. Matériel should be restricted to the system of the U.S. Ordnance Department, of Parrott's, and of smoothbores, the latter to be exclusively the 12-pounder, model 1857, variously called the 'gun-howitzer,' the 'light 12-pounder,' or the 'Napoleon.' A limited number of smoothbore howitzers would be authorized for special service.

3. Each field battery should, if practicable, be composed of six guns, never less than four, all to be of uniform caliber.[3]

4. Field batteries would be assigned to divisions in lieu of brigades — four per division. One of the four batteries was to be a battery of Regulars, whose captain would also be the division chief-of-artillery. If divisions were combined into corps, at least one-half the division artillery was to constitute the reserve artillery of the corps.

5. There would be an artillery reserve for the whole army of 100 guns. This reserve would contain light field batteries, all guns of position, and all horse artillery until such time as the cavalry units were organized into major size units.

6. The amount of ammunition to accompany the field batteries would not be less than 400 rounds per gun.

7. There would be a siege train of 50 pieces.

8. Instruction in theory, practice of gunnery, and tactics would be given all officers and noncommissioned officers of Volunteer batteries. This would be accomplished by the use of texts and recitation in each division, under the direction of the Regular Army officer commanding the division artillery.

9. As frequently as possible, personal inspection would be made by the Army chief-of-artillery. He was to insure the strict observance of the established organization and drill, regulations and orders, and to note improvement and readiness for active service of both Regular and Volunteer batteries.

One question still remained: What authority should the position of artillery chief carry? A board of officers was assembled to consider the problem; they reported that practices varied in different armies — scarcely an enlightening finding. McClellan, against Barry's arguments, determined to make the functions of his artillery chief purely administrative. He published his decision in General Orders No. 110, on March 26, 1862, just before embarkation for the Peninsula. The chief-of-artillery could inspect, and was responsible for equipping and supplying (but without provision for a staff to carry out this prodigious task), but he could not exercise command without specific orders from the commanding general.

Similarly, the division artillery chiefs were limited in their authority. The reasoning behind this stand had some degree of validity. There were too few trained field-grade Regular artillerymen to fill all these positions. McClellan's scheme, therefore, provided that the Regular officer in command of the Regular battery would also be the division chief-of-artillery. Few of the junior-grade Regular officers, however, had had any instruction in mounted field battery duty, as in the decade prior to the war there had been only two such batteries from each of the four twelve-company Regular regiments equipped for this duty; the rest had served as foot artillery or infantry.[4]

In addition, under the Volunteer system as initially set up, a state could send in its quota, either a number of independent batteries, or full twelve-battery artillery regiments complete with field-grade officers. McClellan's organization did not take into consideration such units, so that when these regiments were added, the batteries were treated as individual units and ordered where needed. There still remained the question of what to do with the field-grade officers who were virtually ignorant in military matters, having attained their rank by political influence. Their rank entitled them to positions of command over the battery commanders, including the Regular captains. The logical solution for these people then was staff jobs, where they could learn the routine and where they would have administrative authority only. Thus, McClellan withheld command authority from his artillery staff officers and division chiefs until experience proved them worthy.

In the top echelon, though, limitations on rank imposed by law were to plague the Army for the duration of the war. Barry, on McClellan's initiative, sought to have the Adjutant General of the Army authorize the appointment of two brigadier generals of artillery — one to command the artillery proper and the other to command the reserve. The Adjutant General, however, replied that the law would not allow it. The law authorized only one brigadier general for each brigade, and each brigade was to have not less than four regiments, which in turn would cover forty companies. Barry pointed out that McClellan's organization called for some sixty companies or batteries. It made no difference; the answer was still no. Barry then switched the angle of attack: a battery was equivalent to an infantry battalion, and on that basis the artillery was entitled to five generals. But the Adjutant General remained adamant, obtained the backing of the Secretary of War, and ruled a company was a company, regardless of its branch.

Later, in 1862, when Halleck arrived as chief-of-staff, the reasoning became even more fantastic. McClellan, hoping to receive more sympathetic treatment tried again, only to be amazed by Halleck's reply. A battery, said Halleck, was the equivalent of a regiment! Then came more double talk: since a battery was commanded by a captain, it had no need for field officers. In essence then, the War Department ruled that a battery was a company and so could not have generals, and a battery was a regiment and so could not have field officers! Halleck backed up this ruling by directing in orders that henceforth artillery should be taken into service by single batteries, thus rendering field and staff officers unnecessary.

Another problem facing McClellan was that in the early part of the war a number of Regular officers wanted to accept commissions in the Volunteer service. Under existing law such action required resignation from the Regular Army. Fortunately for the Union, the War Department, led by old Scott, was not disposed for some months to grant many releases for this purpose. Scott wanted the Regular establishment kept intact. This was hard on the individuals, but it probably saved the efficiency of the artillery arm at a time when it could have been virtually wrecked by the wholesale jumping to the Volunteers of the trained Regulars. So the majority of the young Regular artillery officers, hoping to emulate the fame and glory of Ringgold and Duncan in the Mexican

War, chose to stay with the Regular arm. But there were many others who saw the ladder of rapid promotion in the Volunteer Army. Because of the limited opportunity for advancement in the Regular Army, it is small wonder that men like Gibbon, Reynolds, Griffin, and Ricketts resigned early in the war to accept eagled colonelcies of Volunteer infantry regiments or the stars of a general officer of Volunteers.

McClellan's task in organizing his army was made easier by certain inherent advantages the North had in its struggle with the South, advantages which were to play no small part in the eventual outcome. Among these was the superiority in manpower, in wealth, and in manufacturing capacity. But there were several which applied directly to the artillery and gave that arm an initial superiority which could never be beaten down. First, there was a small but efficient base of Regular Army artillery on which to build — a factor of great significance in the early campaigns. And second, the skills required by the artillery service were more widely common in the industrial North. (This same matter of special skills gave the Confederate cavalry a decided advantage at the war's start.) The artillery manual prescribed that artillerymen should be intelligent, active, muscular, not less than five feet seven, and that a large proportion of the force should be mechanics — the last requirement was easily met, as the industrial North abounded with mechanics.

Barry proposed that maximum use be made of the Regular Army artillery. Late in August 1861 he had advised McClellan that the Army of the Potomac should have an overwhelming force of field artillery. In order for this overwhelming force to be an efficient one, Barry believed that as many of the batteries as possible should be Regular Army — the Volunteers having limitations in experience and training. Therefore, all of the Regular artillery companies (the term 'battery' was not used officially until Congress approved the raising of the 5th U.S. Regiment of Artillery in July 1861) should be withdrawn from the seaboards as well as the interior and ordered to Washington, where they would be mounted as field artillery. This was feasible, Barry believed, since the Confederacy was not a maritime power the need of coastal defense was negligible.

This idea McClellan accepted. At first the Commanding General nibbled at the Secretary of War by asking for the 3rd Artillery. Then, in addition, he asked for one-half of the companies forming the artillery school at Fort Monroe. When these requests were well received, McClellan fired his big bolt, asking for the whole of the Regular artillery, both old and new units; the only exceptions would be mounted batteries actually serving in other departments and a minimum number of companies for garrison duty. The result was that the Army of the Potomac received as field batteries one-half of the Regular artillery of the United States Army.

The foundation on which McClellan planned to base his artillery was not an imposing one. On July 28, 1861, only nine imperfectly equipped batteries stood in front of Washington, and these comprised but 30 guns, 400 horses, and 650 men. McDowell, in command of all the troops on the Virginia side, reported that he had but one battery ready for action as of July 30.[5]

Maj. Henry Hunt, however, had rendered an informal report the day before which was not quite so pessimistic. Some of the field batteries, Hunt said, were in sad shape, but three and perhaps a fourth were in good condition, each having four pieces and a fair complement of men. Two others had only three pieces between them, and a third had none at all. Hunt, in charge of the artillery south of the Potomac, was struggling to refit all the batteries up to six guns as fast as the Washington Arsenal could get the equipment.

Out on the old Bladensburg Road, a few miles east of the Capitol, an artillery training camp was set up and named Camp Barry. Here during the entire course of the war, artillery units were assembled, equipped, and trained, and battle-shattered batteries refitted. Obtaining sufficient manpower was not at this time a problem; the major problem was getting equipment for the units already available and due to arrive. Even the Regular batteries were not ready for field duty. Some came in with horses and harness but with a heterogeneous mixture of 6-pounder guns, the old model 12-pounder gun, and the 12-pounder howitzer.

The Volunteer units presented even greater problems. About one-fourth of the batteries brought a few guns and carriages from their states, but they were nearly all lacking in uniformity of caliber or were otherwise unserviceable, and only about one-sixth came with horses and harness. Apparently less than one-tenth were fully equipped for field duty when they reached Washington, and every one of these needed extensive training.

At an early stage in the training and organization of the Army, McClellan made an important decision in respect to the matériel of his artillery. He rightly concluded that the country in which his Army was most likely to operate was so cluttered by woods and forests as to present few favorable opportunities for long-range artillery. Therefore the short-range, light 12-pounder smoothbore — the Napoleon — was to be the backbone of his artillery; two-thirds of the field batteries were to be equipped with this weapon, and the remaining one-third with rifled cannon — a new innovation in warfare.

McClellan's recommendations did not at first materialize, however. The facilities for the construction of Napoleon guns were extremely limited, and those for iron guns were comparatively great. But this was only a part of the problem. Since the American Revolution there had been considerable controversy, both in and out of the Army, as to the most efficient metal for use in cannon, particularly field pieces. Brass was preferred during the Revolution, but in the years following the trend was toward iron. Iron was considerably cheaper, the necessary raw materials were close at hand, and the iron industry in America was growing rapidly. However, in 1835 the Ordnance Board swung back to brass, or, as it became known, bronze, which retained its official preferred position until 1861.

The 1850's saw a growing number of converts to the theory of the rifled cannon, though. In 1857 the Army had commenced the rifling of its smoothbore muskets, but the rifling of cannon was slow to follow. Not until 1860 did the Ordnance Board recommend that 50 per cent of the bronze guns then in service be rifled. This was done, but the results were discouraging: the bronze gun could not stand the additional strain. It was at this point that the proponents of iron as the best metal joined with the believers in the rifled system to bring pressure on the War Department, and on June 22, 1861, the day following the disaster at Bull Run, Secretary Cameron placed the first order for some 300 iron guns, 200 of which were to be rifles, with private contractors. The die was cast.

Hunt regarded the adoption of the iron rifled gun as a great mistake. 'Unfortunately we adopted a rifle gun of 3-inch caliber, the feeblest in the world,' wrote Hunt, 'and our ammunition, of which there was no fixed system, was not good.' [6] The Napoleon gun had been adopted in 1857 as a means of decreasing the variety of field guns then in use. The rifled guns, with their many varied systems — Parrott, Schenkl, James, Hotchkiss, and others — greatly complicated the ammunition supply problem. But it is probable that, had the War Department decided that only the bronze gun would be issued, sufficient quantities would not have been available to permit the Army to take the field in the spring of 1862. When McClellan finally moved that spring, less than one-third of his pieces were smoothbore Napoleons.

The Civil War put the North's great mechanical skill to work in a way profitable both to the Union cause and to the manufacturers and their employees. The manufacture of all kinds of matériel was given immediate impetus with the direct result that private manufacturers alone, unaided by the military authorities, gave the Army its first system of rifled ordnance. Into the batteries of the Union armies went James rifles, Wiard steel rifles, and other systems. But the basic field artillery weapons throughout the war were the 12-pounder light gun or Napoleon, the 10-pounder Parrott rifle, and the 3-inch ordnance rifle. All three were muzzle-loaders.

The Napoleon, the weapon favored by McClellan, and later proclaimed by many as the most efficient and easily maintained gun, was made of bronze — 90 parts copper to 10 parts tin; it was a copy of the piece designed by Napoleon III. Its design was intended to increase the power of the light artillery, and at the same time reduce the weight and make only one type of field gun necessary for the batteries. The Napoleon was a muzzle-loading smoothbore, 4.62 inches in bore diameter, and weighed 1227 pounds. It was theoretically capable, with a standard charge of two and a half pounds of black powder and elevated to five degrees, of throwing a 12-pound solid shot some 1680 yards. Actually, it was seldom used over 1200 yards. When firing canister under 300 yards it was a deadly effective weapon. Solid shot, shell, spherical case or shrapnel, and canister were the primary loadings used in the Napoleon.

A companion to the Napoleon was the 10-pounder Parrott, a cast-iron rifled gun, with a reinforcing jacket of wrought iron shrunk around the breech. Parrott guns began to appear during the winter of 1860–61, and were the first iron rifled guns purchased for the Army. Parrott guns were made in a variety of calibers, but the 10-pounder found the widest use, with a scattering of 20-pounders in the Artillery Reserve. The 10-pounder weighed 900 pounds, and had a theoretical range, with a standard one-pound load of black powder and an elevation of thirty-five degrees, of 6200 yards. Its bore was 2.9 inches (later, models were enlarged to 3.0 inches to permit interchange of ammunition with the 3-inch rifled gun) and its projectile weighed, as its name indicated, ten pounds.

The 20-pounder Parrott was a half-breed gun, neither light field artillery nor siege artillery. Its 1800 pounds made it a cumbersome weapon for field use, and its range was approximately the same as the 10-pounder. It was used, however, by both sides, principally in the Reserve. Because of its brittleness, by 1863 this type of gun had largely disappeared from the field batteries of the Army of the Potomac.

The long, sleek, slender-barreled 3-inch iron rifle was the third party to this triumvirate of cannon. This gun soon acquired the title of the 'ordnance gun.' It was made of wrought iron, manufactured on a plan developed by the Phoenixville Iron Works of Pennsylvania. It was made by wrapping boiler plate around a mandril, heating it, and rolling it. This was the lightest gun used — 820 pounds, 3-inch bore, and a theoretical range of some 4000 yards. The loadings for the ordnance gun were the same as those for the Parrott and the Napoleon.

In addition to these basic weapons, a few odd varieties crept into the batteries of the Army of the Potomac. This was particularly true during the first year of the war when federal and state arsenals were stripped clean of weapons that could be made to fire. Thus, one finds a few batteries in 1861–62 equipped either partially or wholly with old 6-pounder bronze smoothbores, 12-pounder howitzers, and even a few 12-pounder mountain howitzers. As the production of the North caught up with demand, the majority of these pieces — particularly the 6-pounders — vanished in favor of one of the three basic types.

The howitzer was a weird breed of cannon. (Gibbon's *Manual* described it as 'a *gun* with a *chamber* in it.') It had first been put into general use by the French about 1800, and was designed to fire the hollow explosive type of projectile — shell and spherical case. Since it was believed that these projectiles were more fragile than the solid rounds then commonly used in field guns, the manuals said that less powder should be used as a propellant. In order to use less powder and yet obtain all the power to which it was susceptible, the howitzer contained a chamber at the base of the tube.

Other physical characteristics which distinguished it from its big brother, the old model 12-pounder gun, and even from the new Napoleon gun, were the lack of swell or bulge at the muzzle and its comparative light weight: 778 pounds against 1757 for the old 12-pounder gun and 1227 for the Napoleon. Unlike the modern howitzer, it was not designed for high angle fire.

The mountain howitzer was an extremely light cannon, 220 pounds, just a little over a yard long. This weapon and its carriage could be dismantled and carried on muleback for operations in difficult terrain. Since it was a specialized weapon, there were very few of them in service, and these were gradually replaced by the heavier field pieces.

All of these weapons would go into the field with their ammunition chests filled with four types of rounds: solid shot, shell, case shot or shrapnel, and canister. Solid shot was, as the name implies, a solid iron projectile; shell was an explosive iron projectile activated by a crude time fuze, or, in the case of the rifled guns, percussion or point detonating fuzes; case shot was a thin-walled iron projectile filled with musket balls and a small explosive charge activated in the same manner as the shell; canister was a tin container filled with balls slightly larger than those in the case shot, with the container rupturing as it moved down the bore. The canister round was used at ranges under 400 yards, and was the only really effective killer in the 1861–65 ammunition chests. It turned a field gun into a huge shotgun.

For smoothbore cannon all projectiles except canister were spherical, and those for the rifled guns were cylindro-conoidal. While the rifled weapons were capable of greater accuracy and range, they were not feared by opposing infantry as much as the Napoleon gun, since the smaller bore of the rifles greatly reduced the size of the canister round.

In the siege train which McClellan organized for his Peninsula campaign and several other operations, the Army of the Potomac used some of the heavier and more cumber-

some cannon. At Malvern Hill, for example, Col. R. O. Tyler's
1st Connecticut Heavy Artillery Regiment operated 4.5-inch
iron rifles — the big brother to the 3-inch ordnance rifle —
some 30-pounder Parrotts, 8-inch howitzers, and two English
Whitworth 10-pounder rifles. At Petersburg virtually all
artillery became siege artillery, and Blue gunners struggled
with huge mortars like the 13-inch 'Dictator,' small portable
cohern mortars, etc. But these pieces were not in reality field
artillery and in fact were not then so-termed.

Handicapped in the early months by a lack of virtually
everything, including good weather, the Volunteers struggled
to train. The area around the capital had become the armed
camp and training ground for the embryonic Army of the
Potomac. The Volunteer artillery officers and noncoms received training in the basic rudiments of their new trade from
the few Regular officers. The Volunteers then passed on their
learning to their ignorant but willing subordinates. Congress
appropriated funds for the purchase of books of tactics and
instruction for Volunteers, but the 'books' appear to have
been limited to a few copies of the artillery manual.

Some of their officers proved to be hopelessly unqualified.
In order to eliminate these unfit officers in all branches of the
Volunteer service, Congress empowered the President in
July 1861 through military boards to examine the qualifica-
tions of all officers appointed by the governors, and to remove
the unfit. However, if the unfit were eliminated, the vacancy
could be filled by popular election. Although these boards
weeded out many incompetents in the artillery as elsewhere,
they had their limitations. The supply of good officers was
shallow because of a lack of an officer-training program, and
replacements were frequently little or no better than their
predecessors.

Amid continual inspections and jittery apprehensions of
a Rebel attack on Washington, McClellan watched his army
grow. By the end of August the President's calls for volunteers had brought in seven complete field artillery regiments.

McClellan himself reported that he had eighty guns on August 20th, and by October 15th he had twenty-seven batteries of divisional artillery — seventeen of which were Regular and the balance Volunteer. But since some of these batteries were still 4-gun units, he had no more than 140 pieces, more than two-thirds of which were rifled.

The North had tooled up, and as fast at the matériel had come in it was issued to the units. But the flow did not reach the desired level until early winter. By mid-November the total had risen to 228 guns. It would be April 1862, before a sufficient number of equipped batteries would be available to fill out the reserve and divisional artillery. But when the Army of the Potomac finally struck its tents about Washington that spring, it owned 30 Regular and 62 Volunteer batteries, totaling 520 guns, 11,000 horses, and 12,500 men.

McClellan, with Barry's and Hunt's stern assistance, turned out a large and well-drilled artillery force. That drill and conduct of fire were limited to the level of the individual battery did not detract from the positive fact that the Federal batteries could now maneuver in the field and execute firing missions with eager precision. The field artillery of the Army of the Potomac, when it landed on the Peninsula, comprised some 274 guns, organized into 49 usable batteries. It reached a maximum strength of 57 batteries of 318 tubes.[7]

On March 17, 1862, Hamilton's division of the III Corps clambered aboard the transports at Alexandria, Virginia. Five days later Fitz John Porter's division followed, and the Army of the Potomac was embarking on its long and gory route toward destiny and immortality.

lll

A PRACTICE BATTLE

Williamsburg

THE FLEDGLING Army of the Potomac, eager under its vain but popular commander, disembarked at Fort Monroe, Virginia, during the closing weeks of March 1862. The trip down the Potomac on ship had been cramped and stuffy; the men were glad to have firm earth under foot again. The troops anxiously awaited word to begin moving up the Peninsula toward Richmond.

April 4, 1862 was the day McClellan set his host in motion toward the enemy capital and the long Blue columns began to move slowly, for nothing McClellan ever touched rang of speed. The next day the advance elements of the Army of the Potomac bumped into the first weak belt of defenses across the lower Peninsula. A Rhode Island battery and Griffin's old battery exchanged fire with Rebel defenders.

The way was open if McClellan chose to push. But the self-styled little Napoleon allowed his fears to counsel him, and the Army sat down before the little colonial village of Yorktown. To McClellan the enemy works seemed strong and Rebel strength great. The situation reminded him of the Crimea and made him think about siege operations. Since a siege train had been an original part of McClellan's artillery scheme he already had his ponderous weapon forged. And so the Army waited while the engineers and the heavy artillerymen of the siege train dug gun positions, hauled ammunition, and then dug some more. At last it appeared that the great weapons would be ready to open a gigantic pounding of the Confederate works; the bombardment would begin on May 4th.

The Rebel commander, Gen. Joseph E. Johnston, was too clever to be trapped in such an indefensible position, however. The Southerners silently evacuated Yorktown during the night of May 3rd, leaving McClellan's iron monsters with a hollow and effortless victory. When the enemy's departure was reported to McClellan, his columns slowly took up the dusty march again.

The rasping call of bugles sent the horse batteries of Tidball, Robertson, Benson, and Gibson from Hunt's Reserve slogging through the gummy mud on the road out of Yorktown. They were to support Brig. Gen. George Stoneman and his cavalry division, now starting a delayed pursuit of the Rebels. The column had just cleared the town when Capt. Horatio Gibson, commanding the combined battery C and G, 3rd U.S. Artillery, received orders to send one section to the head of the column. Gen. Cooke, leading the advance guard, felt that the presence of artillery well to the front, might facilitate the rapid reduction of enemy-delaying parties. Lt. Fuller, with two 3-inch iron rifles, pulled out of the battery and picked up a fast trot toward his new position with the advance guard.

All four batteries were armed with six 3-inch rifled guns, soon to be called the 'ordnance gun.' This type of gun was ideally suited for the role of horse artillery because of its light weight — everyone in the horse artillery batteries rode his own mount, so that it was vital that the pulled weight be reduced to an absolute minimum. Stoneman thus had twenty-four guns capable of keeping up with the cavalry and, should they catch up with the Rebs, capable of pouring considerable fire into a retreating infantry column. There was no surer way of forcing the enemy infantry to shake itself out of a marching column and into line of battle. All the Federals had to do was to catch up with the Rebel column and then fight their guns into range of the rear of Johnston's infantry.

The job of catching Johnston was handicapped by the fact that the last elements of the Confederate Army had filed out of the forts sometime before dawn May 4th. At about 3 o'clock, some three hours after the artillery had joined his force, Cooke was fired on as his little command neared Williamsburg. A short flurry of firing ensued, and then the small enemy force melted away to the west. But everyone in the Yankee column knew this fracas meant only one thing: they had at last bumped into the rearmost elements of Joe Johnston's force. The opposition had probably come from Stuart's command, which had been sent to delay the Yankees. The mounted column was now within sparring range. Their next job was to get within slugging distance.

Stoneman pushed his command; his aides had told him that Joe Hooker with his supporting infantry division was close behind. The cavalry commander detached Brig. Gen. Emory, with the 3rd Pennsylvania Cavalry under Averill, Barker's squadron, and Benson's Battery M, 2nd U.S. Artillery. This force was sent clanking southward in the direction of the Lee's Mill Road in the vain hope of snapping off straggling Confederate elements, falling back from the oncoming infantry division of Union Gen. W. F. 'Baldy' Smith. Two miles farther along the road the same process was repeated, the Federals being held up for about fifteen minutes as they drove away a second nest of Rebel cavalry. The signs indicated that the Yanks were now getting close to the enemy's rearguard.

The advance continued, somewhat more cautiously now, since they had entered heavy woods. Maj. Palmer, commanding the lead cavalry squadron debouched his command onto an open plain. On the far side manned earthworks were visible. The emergence of the Federal cavalrymen from the woods was the signal for the Rebels in those works to open fire with both rifle and artillery. Palmer sent word to Gen.

Cooke that he was being held up by about a brigade of infantry, at least one cavalry regiment, and some 300 artillerymen with six to eight guns. Cooke came quickly forward over the narrow muddy road, sized this force up as a small rearguard, and determined to show such boldness as to intimidate the enemy into withdrawing. He would make a big show to the front, and hit them on their left flank as well, the latter by means of another road which reportedly turned that flank.

His plan decided upon, Cooke again bellowed for the guns. The leading section, Fuller's again, went into battery along the road on the skirt of the timber. The fire from the Rebels was increasing, and a battery in a redoubt about 1000 yards to Fuller's left front began to find the range. Cooke's position was not good — he was in a bottleneck. In order to get his full weight into action he had to clear the road and put his cavalry squadrons out into the open where they could maneuver. Cooke told Gibson to bring Fuller's section forward into the field to the right of the road and to put the other pieces in on the opposite side. As the battery was changing position Gibson watched the Rebel lines for targets. Through the smoke he was able to see a considerable force moving from their work in front toward another to his right. Cooke's shouts to his gunners quickly brought the fire of the Rebel battery to bear on his from its new position.

Indeed, the Rebels were far from being intimidated — they were thoroughly provoked. The volume of their fire reached a roar, and Gibson found himself under a cross-fire from two works. His left section was ordered to direct its fire at the one in front, while the rest attempted to beat down the fire from the newly occupied redoubt to the right. The battery's horses and caissons were beginning to take a terrific beating. Left at the edge of the timber, the caissons had begun to settle in soggy mud, several of them up to the axle. A lieutenant in charge of the line of caissons was hit twice but stayed at his position. One shell made a direct hit on a caisson, blowing it up, and killing its six horses.

It soon became evident to everyone that Cooke had taken on more than he could comfortably handle. Forty-five minutes had passed since the flanking column had departed. If there were going to be any effects from that movement, they would have made themselves felt by now. The Federal cavalry was taking a severe hammering, and Gibson's battery was rapidly reaching the point where it would become immobilized — its teams shot to shreds. Cooke sent a courier flogging his horse back down the sloppy road to find Stoneman and ask what to do. The courier returned; Stoneman ordered Cooke to pull back to a clearing about a half-mile behind where the rest of the division would be re-formed. If the Rebels kept pressing, the whole command would have to fall back until supporting infantry arrived, and right now Joe Hooker's force was nowhere in sight.

Cooke gave the order to retire. Gibson began to pull his guns out, section by section. The Rebs made menacing motions in the direction of the battery's small covering force. But it appeared that Gibson was going to extricate his battery. Then trouble struck in the form of a boggy hole at the edge of the road. As the last gun came out of the field and turned onto the road, its wheels lost traction and it slid into the hole. Frantic efforts of sweating, cursing drivers and straining horses were fruitless. Gibson sent a lieutenant running down the road to catch the rest of the battery and bring back some teams; not only was one gun in danger of being lost but some of the caissons were also blocked in the field behind it. The officer, his horse down from a shell fragment, carried out his mission afoot. The one gun, the caissons, and one small cavalry squadron covering the battery's withdrawal were the only targets left on the field. The Confederate gunners were now pouring in shell and spherical case at this concentrated target area.

It seemed as if Gibson's lieutenant would never arrive. Finally he was seen coming with extra horses. Ten powerful artillery horses lurched and heaved in the traces, but the gun stayed in the hole. Seeing the helpless condition of the battery's caissons unable to get out with the piece blocking the road, an officer gave the order to unhitch and save their teams.

As the last elements of the battery reached the heavy timber, a party of Stuart's troopers crashed into the rear of the column. A Federal cavalry captain turned his 60-man cavalry force about, and in the resulting melee one cannoneer snatched a standard from a Confederate as the fight raged close to the battery. An overly zealous Yank cavalryman sabered the cannoneer, forcing him to relinquish his prize.

When the Southerners gave up the pursuit the battery took stock of its losses. Gibson had to report with extreme regret (for no artilleryman likes to lose a gun) the abandonment of one piece, along with three caissons and one caisson chest. Enemy fire had played havoc with his horses — seventeen killed and five wounded. A lieutenant was out of action, suffering from two severe wounds, and four enlisted men would carry wound scars as the result of this little scrap. Furthermore, the battery was now short of ammunition. At least seven chests of ammunition had been lost, and they had shot up 250 rounds during the hour's fighting.[1] Gibson clearly needed resupply in horses and ammunition.

So far the day's operations had disclosed an aggressive, if somewhat delayed, pursuit by Stoneman of the elusive Joe Johnston. The Yankees had moved faster than was expected, and Johnston had become worried: Stuart had reported that his pickets were being driven in, and that Yankee infantry was close behind; and Johnston's own trains had made sluggish progress through the slime. The line of unoccupied earthworks in front of Williamsburg had to be manned and the Federals delayed till the Confederate Army's sprawling wagon train was safe. First one, then a second brigade of Rebel infantry, together with two batteries and some cavalry, halted their retreat, about-faced, and tramped back to these works. These were the men who had bumped Cooke so rudely.

Two of the batteries with the cavalry division had been in action, but only Gibson's had done much shooting. The effects, however, had not been great. Gen. Lafayette McLaws, commanding the forces opposing Cooke and Stoneman, reported his loss as slight, probably not in excess of ten casualties to all causes.

At about 5:30 that afternoon Stoneman's exhausted troopers were buoyed by the sight of massed infantry bayonets, carried by regiment after regiment of Baldy Smith's division, which was now swinging into view. Increasing darkness, combined with snarled undergrowth, frustrated Smith's attempts to attack. The infantry found the going over sloppy roads in driving rain and in the dark too much; their commander decided to halt about 10 o'clock, and planned to resume the march at dawn.

Hooker's columns, which finally reached the field at dawn, swung into action at 7 o'clock. Infantry skirmishers needled their way northward toward the main Confederate position, Fort Magruder. This fort was at the head of the junction of the Yorktown and Hampton Roads, coming into Williamsburg from the south. On either side of the fort were a number of lesser redoubts. Immediately to the front, the Confederates had cleared the ground to a depth of 600–700 yards. Beyond the cleared area the timber had been felled for about a half-mile on both sides of the roads.

To support his infantry, Hooker had at his disposal one Regular battery, H, 1st U.S. Artillery, under a newly arrived commander, Capt. Webber, and three New York Volunteer batteries under Capts. Bramhall, Osborn, and Smith. Hooker commanded chief-of-artillery, Maj. Wainwright, to put Webber and Bramhall into position in the cleared field to the right of the Hampton Road, slightly in advance of the felled timber. The range to target would be about 700 yards.

Webber's Regulars dug their spurs, and horses strained the traces. Four 10-pounder Parrott and two 12-pounder Napoleon guns moved slowly toward the clearing. The going was tough; a cold drizzle was falling and the ground under foot was like grease.

The slow emergence of the battery gave the Confederates a chance to get set. As Webber's first section began to unlimber in the road, the air overhead became filled with smoke, flame, and shirring metal; a battery officer was knocked from his horse at the first salvo. The Confederate gunners were cutting their fuzes just right. A minute later a second salvo exploded. One shell exploded right over the number two gun, leaving a lieutenant and two of the gun crew bleeding in the mud. Panic hit the men; drivers and cannoneers streamed toward the cover of the woods. Webber and his first sergeant aided Maj. Wainwright in the vain attempt to drive the men back to their guns. Only a handful showed any indication of obeying.

Wainwright, realizing the gravity of the situation, reined his horse to a halt in front of Osborn's four-gun battery, now coming forward. He demanded to know who would man the guns of the abandoned battery in the roadway. With the naïve eagerness of that May day, Osborn's entire battery volunteered. Webber rounded up about eighteen of his men, and these now joined Osborn's in manhandling the guns into firing position. Then the drizzle turned into a blinding, driving rain. The vision of gunners on both sides was impaired. Through the haze Webber picked out the orange darts of Rebel artillery firing from Fort Magruder and from a redoubt to the left front. The number four men slipped primers into the vents of their pieces,[2] gunners checked their sights, and the battery opened fire.

Thirty minutes later Capt. Bramhall brought his battery bumping through the slop. Wainwright directed him into the field to the right of Webber's guns. That ground was now a quagmire. Horses and men together were able to get in only five of the battery's six 3-inchers. The battery commander picked out his targets, as gunners and cannoneers opened ammunition

chests and prepared for action. Then the reverberations of
Bramhall's 6th New York Battery joined Webber's, and for
thirty minutes the two replied to the enemy fire.

It was about 9:30 a.m. when the Rebels ceased their concerted fire, but sporadic outbursts from guns in redoubts farther
to the left enfiladed Bramhall's sections. Wainwright accordingly ordered the battery's right elements moved forward in
echelon, thereby lessening the target. Occasional angry sputtering between the artillery of both sides kept up till 1 p.m.

During one lull in the firing, Corp. George Westcott of
Osborn's command strolled over toward the timber to the
left front. Suddenly he heard voices speaking with the unmistakable Southern accent. He grabbed a musket lying on
the ground in front of him and crouched behind a felled tree.
Cautiously he peered over, and saw three Rebels walking
unsuspectingly back toward their lines. At his call to surrender
and the sight of a leveled rifle, the three Southerners dropped
their weapons and raised their hands. Corp. Westcott paraded
his catch back to the battery position. The captives were dispatched to the rear and Westcott became the center of attention. Questions, jokes, and congratulations were suddenly
jarred by the stark revelation that Westcott's musket was
unloaded.

Meanwhile, in the woods to the left, the fight had been
growing in intensity all morning. Hooker shoved in his last
reserves about noon. Vicious Confederate attacks were stopped
short of the Union line, but now many of the regiments were
reduced to scrounging ammunition from the cartridge boxes
of the fallen. Aid did not appear to be forthcoming; Hooker
and his boys would have to go it alone. Taking a long gamble,
Hooker shifted the regiments supporting the batteries. The
5th New Jersey and 2nd New Hampshire were pulled back
from their advanced position in front of the pieces. Hooker
placed them in on the left, a short distance away from the
artillery, and ordered the men to watch both the front and
the left.

The men manning the eleven Federal guns had been under artillery and sniper fire for some seven hours. Casualties were light, but this experience had been tiring for new troops. Wainwright headed for the rear to hurry Capt. James E. Smith's 4th New York Battery forward. When last seen, this unit had been floundering about in sloppy fields trying to get clear of division baggage trains jamming up the roads. Wainwright, the division's chief-of-artillery, was thus performing an orderly's job when the bolt struck.

The Rebels came forward, red battle flags snapping over their lines. Over the roar of the Yankee rifle volleys came the piercing screech of the Rebel yell. Their whole line was advancing — Longstreet's entire division was in action now. The eleven available guns of Hooker's division spat shell at the oncoming lines. When the range dropped to 300 yards the two batteries switched to canister — frightful stuff when fired at close range. The Rebel infantry poured into the space between the batteries' left and their infantry support. Webber's battery was overrun. There had been no time to save the guns. The situation was hopeless anyway, for the guns were bemudded a third of the way up their spokes, and the teams had been decimated.

Bramhall continued to fire his guns until Webber's battery was almost in enemy hands. As if they had not trouble enough to the front, Bramhall's men found themselves in the line of fire of the 26th Pennsylvania Infantry to their right rear. Blue cannoneers and gunners began to stagger, pitch, and drop as the fire from Longstreet's men blanketed the area. The position was clearly no longer defensible by his handful of artillerymen. The battery commander ordered the men to fall back. Bramhall's guns, too, were hub-deep in adhesive mud, and a quick glance at the limber positions told of great carnage there. The Federal gunners fell back. Twelve guns stood silent in the field and road as yelling Rebels swarmed gleefully through the abandoned positions.

The retreating artillerymen reached the woods as Maj. Wain-

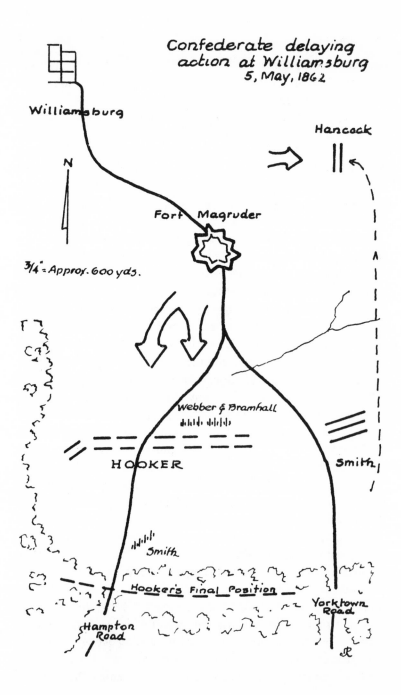

Confederate delaying
action at Williamsburg
5, May, 1862

Williamsburg

N

3/4" = Approx. 600 yds.

Fort Magruder

Hancock

Webber & Bramhall

HOOKER

Smith

Smith

Hooker's Final Position

Hampton
Road

Yorktown
Road

wright rode up, followed by the leading section of Smith's battery. A huge gap had been opened in the Federal line. To plug it, Wainwright used Smith's 10-pounder Parrotts. Under the urging of the chief-of-artillery and the battery officers, four pieces were dragged into position on a small knoll to the right of the road, just within the woods.[3] Smith roared the order to load canister. Rifled guns were not the most suitable weapon for this loading, but they would do the job. Hooker rode around, madly exhorting his men to stand. Old Gen. Heintzelman succeeded in rallying some fleeing regimental musicians shouting, 'Play! Play! It's all you're good for. Play damn it! Play some marching tune! Play *Yankee Doodle* or any doodle you can think of, only play something!' The frightened musicians bleated out discordant and nervous versions of *Hail Columbia* and *Yankee Doodle*.[4]

The Southerners paused after overrunning the two abandoned batteries. But there was no assurance that they would not at any moment come charging down the road toward the wood. The crews stood by their pieces, canister charges rammed home — each charge of 27 cast-iron balls about the size of a hickory nut. In a smoothbore or a rifled gun it could hurt massed infantry at less than 300 yards. Primers in the vents, the number four men stood with lanyards in hand. Tense, the men watched the enemy works and the silent timber to their left front. Behind the guns, drivers were struggling to turn their teams about and head rearward. The decision had been made: if the enemy struck, the guns would either beat them back or they would have to be spiked and surrendered. With the road in terrible shape, they could not hope to extricate the pieces in time.

They had not long to wait — thirty minutes perhaps. Then the cry went up: Here they come! Every nerve was taut, awaiting the command to open fire. On they came. The range began to drop; 300 yards, 250, 200, 175. Gunners tracked their target. The Confederate line reached a point 150 yards distant. Smith looked anxiously at Wainwright; the latter nodded. Smith shouted the orders to fire by piece. The battery was instantly transformed into frenzied activity. Acrid clouds of gray smoke rose from its position. Number one men drove their rammers on new charges. Gunners checked the sights; a second clouded crash rent the air. That was enough. The Rebels broke for cover to the rear. The cease fire came down.

The lull was short-lived. The thump of a musket echoed from the felled trees to the front; a dozen or so more followed in rapid succession. Two cannoneers at the right piece collapsed. The Confederate guns in the works to the front and left front now added their bass notes to the tune. Smith's battery reopened fire, dividing its attention between the crouching infantry in the timber and the Confederate cannon. Three more of the battery's cannoneers were dumped by this annoying musket fire before they were run off by Col. Orlando Poe's 2nd Michigan Infantry of Kearny's division, now taking over from Hooker's pummeled regiments.

At sundown the relief of Hooker's infantry by Kearny was about completed. Capt. James Thompson, the chief-of-artillery of Kearny's division, rode up to Wainwright and saluted. The presence of this division's three fresh batteries was now assured. The relief of Hooker's depleted batteries began at sunset. Thompson, profiting by Hooker's sad experience, chose not to bog his guns down in the muddy obstructed fields, but kept them available on firmer ground a little to the rear.

Hooker's artillery was in bad shape. Three Parrotts and one Napoleon gun of Webber's Regular battery had been gleefully hauled off by the Rebs, along with one caisson. Only the mud, playing no favorites, prevented them from absconding with Bramhall's as well. Over eighty horses were dead, wounded, captured, or missing. Webber had been hardest hit — his guns gone, two men killed, two officers and six men in the hands of the medics. Osborn's men, those who joined with the residue of Webber's, lost one killed and seven wounded. All told, the division's artillery found itself with four men dead, two officers and eighteen men wounded. Only

Osborn's and Smith's batteries were still in fighting condition.[5]

Simultaneously with Hooker's effort in front of Fort Magruder, another attack was taking place against the Confederate left flank. Shortly after Hooker's force left, sixteen Negro slaves arrived at Gen. Sumner's headquarters. By virtue of seniority Sumner was in command of the forces in front of Williamsburg while McClellan remained at Yorktown to supervise the movement of Franklin's division by water.

A questioning of the contrabands netted a multitude of wild-eyed tales. But there was one thread which seemed to be woven throughout all their chatterings: Some of the works on the Rebel left flank were unoccupied. A hurried reconnaissance gave credence to the story. Old Bull Sumner, never one to shirk a fight, gave a direct order to Brig. Gen. Hancock to take four or five regiments and one battery, move to the right and cross Cub Dam Creek, and, if possible, take possession of the enemy earthworks there.

Capt. Romeyn B. Ayres, the chief-of-artillery of Baldy Smith's division, ordered the 1st New York Battery, Capt. Andrew Cowan commanding, to accompany the five regiments preparing to move out. The column hit the road, and six 3-inch ordnance guns bounced along behind the second regiment. One and a half miles later the little force halted, as a frowning redoubt came into view on the far side of the creek. The 5th Wisconsin and the 6th Maine Infantry Regiments crossed to find out if it was occupied. Cowan unlimbered on a ridge 600 yards from the fort, covering the infantry. The fort was empty. Hancock shoved a small holding force into the redoubt, and with the rest of his command, deployed in a field to the front, Cowan's battery remained in the center of the line.

A courier flogged an exhausted horse into Smith's headquarters, carrying the good news from Hancock. Hancock wanted reinforcements, though, to cover his rear and right flank. There were two additional forts within his striking distance, and a great opportunity seemed in the making. On his own, Ayres promptly ordered Capt. Charles C. Wheeler,

commanding Battery E, 1st New York Artillery, to support
Hancock. The battery, one of the few units in the Army which
proudly boasted of a hired civilian cook,[6] set off at a gallop,
fearful lest Ayres's order be countermanded. Four infantry
regiments were also ordered to go.

With reinforcements promised, Hancock moved forward,
occupying a second unmanned redoubt, two-thirds of a mile
to the front. From this position the Federals clearly saw
Confederate troops lining the parapets of two more works.
Quickly, Hancock determined to advance and drive the Rebels
out if possible, or at least make a diversion to assist Hooker.

The position then held by the little flanking column was
on a crest, with a natural glacis on either flank, extending to
heavy woods on the right and left. In front was a gradually
widening plain, stretching to Fort Magruder. Every Confederate position on the plain between Fort Magruder and the crest
was visible. Hancock stretched his force in a thin line, in front
of the captured redoubt. Cowan unlimbered on the right of
the newly occupied fort. A slow rhythmic fire was opened on
Rebel works 1200 yards to the left front. Some twenty rounds
of shell and case were fired by the battery. Cowan concluded
the range excessive, and moved forward 600 yards, near some
frame farm buildings. He now switched targets, picking on
the two smaller forts from which fire was coming. The ranges
were much more appropriate — 350 yards to the left, 500
to the right.

The Confederates, extremely sensitive to this jab in their
flanks, were rushing aid. Cowan's shelling provoked return fire
from several pieces. The enemy's ranging was good, but the
old bugaboo of Civil War artillery — poor fuzing — reduced
their effect. Many of the Rebel shell projectiles failed to
explode. Cowan accepted the challenge. One section swung its
tubes to engage the enemy guns. Casualties in the duel that
followed were light — one man killed, one man wounded.
A 6-pounder shot dumped one private lifeless to the still-
soggy ground, as he was preparing to sponge out his piece. A

spent 12-pounder shot bounced into another cannoneer's shoulder, rendering him painfully but not seriously *hors de combat.*

As this cannonading was going on Wheeler arrived. It was now about 4 p.m. Hancock, operating within the command system that rarely permitted a battery commander even to select the ground for his pieces, ordered Wheeler's four 3-inch ordnance rifles into battery in the farmyard. The position was to thc right of Cowan, behind a slight rise in the ground, and some 1700 yards from Fort Magruder. The guns, with their limbers, moved in; the caissons stayed behind the redoubt. Calmly, Wheeler's men went into action. The command went down the line to load case shot. Number five men stepped to the limber chests, received a round, and handed it to the number two. Charges were rammed home, primers inserted, and the reports 'Ready' echoed from the chiefs of piece. 'Fire by piece,' called Wheeler; the command was repeated by the chiefs. 'Number one, Fire,' yelled Wheeler, and one by one his four rifles joined the argument.

A second Rebel battery at the corner of the woods near Fort Magruder received special attention, then the fort itself was fired upon. Wheeler expended sixty rounds of case and seventeen of shell on the enemy's artillery and infantry. The fort received nine percussion shells, five of which fell short, four exploding within the position. But the Federals, too, were troubled with poor fuzes, Wheeler reporting that two-thirds of his case and shell failed to explode. The only damage to his unit was the loss of one gun whose axle was broken from high angle firing on the fort.

Hancock had hoped his promised infantry support would arrive in time to permit an all-out attack. As late afternoon approached and the opportunity appeared to be slipping away, a message arrived from Sumner to fall back to the first redoubt. Hancock pondered the order. He decided to stall awhile. A series of messages, however, between himself, Smith, his division commander, and Sumner forced Hancock to conclude

that reinforcements were not coming and he had better fall
back from his exposed position.

It was about 5 p.m., and rain began to fall again. Hancock
prepared to retire. Then it happened. A flurry of activity in
the forts to the front; enemy infantry poured in. Gray cavalry
trotted out from the woods near the right redoubt. The Federal
skirmish line broke out in little puffs of smoke, as the riflemen
picked out targets. A messenger took off in a gallop to Smith;
the enemy was making menacing gestures, and it appeared as
if it meant to back them up, for lines of infantry were beginning to form on the plain. Crews speedily loaded their guns.
Cowan and Wheeler shouted for case shot. The two batteries
poured it on as the enemy line advanced. Out of the woods to
the right burst two yelling Rebel infantry regiments, headed
directly for the Federal batteries. Hancock began to pull in
his widely scattered infantry. When the Rebel riflemen reached
a fence line 300 yards away, the two batteries switched to
canister. It was every gun for itself now. They were firing as
fast as crews could load, which meant three rounds of canister
a minute.

Hancock sent word to the guns to withdraw by piece to
the second line, which was already forming on the ridge behind. Cowan and his upstate New York farm boys pulled out
first. Back to the ridge they went, two of the men acquiring bullet
wounds en route. A team horse caught a slug, stumbled, but
kept going. Lt. Wright's horse foamed blood. Up the ridge and
into battery to the right of the earthwork they went, followed
by Wheeler. The disabled gun was sent first; then as the
enemy line closed to 150 yards, the left piece, its field of fire
now masked, was hurriedly limbered up and hauled out. The
limbers of the remaining guns moved up to the pieces, ready to
hook on when ordered. The oncoming infantry was now twenty
yards from the house fence. Wheeler bellowed the order over
the roar of action, and the last two pieces started back. Immediately, Corp. James Bryant's gun became tangled in the
smashed fencing. Ten pairs of hands frantically pulled at the

debris. Supposing the piece now freed, the cannoneers ran for the new position. Drivers booted the team, but the gun resnagged. Bryant hauled the drivers from the saddles; more pushing, tugging, sweating, and swearing, and the gun was freed. Back to the ridge it went, Bryant hanging onto the tube. (Corp. Bryant survived this action only to be killed six weeks later by a freak bolt of lightning which stunned the entire battery.) Wheeler shoved his battery into action on the ridge, to the left of the earthwork.

Both batteries began flinging canister at the enemy infantry, now lying down behind the fence enclosing the farm buildings. Hancock's infantry hung on grimly. Wheeler's battery had trouble finding targets, as the Rebels at the fence line were masked from its fire. A part of the Gray line immediately in front of Wheeler rose up and slammed a volley into the battery and the 7th Maine Infantry.

A second line of Southern infantry now appeared, coming to the support of the shattered first. Wheeler's guns were in danger of being captured; a small force of Graybacks had wedged in between the guns and the 7th Maine. Wheeler shouted to his section chiefs to limber up, then turned his horse into the dazed left wing of the 7th Maine. Led by this artilleryman, a former school principal, the infantry coiled, then lashed out, restoring the line. The battery was safe, and the guns unlimbered again.

The crisis passed. The enemy, D. H. Hill's and Jubal Early's men, had received no supporting artillery fire, and their infantry strength was not enough to break through the Federal line. Hancock looked at his guns. Their presence now, while beneficial, was no longer peremptory. Moreover, the rain had deepened the mud; several of the guns were imbedded to their axles, their trails submerged in the slime. Concluding it was wise to get the batteries free while the chance existed, Hancock ordered both units back 200 yards to a third position on a plain between their present one and the dam. The Gray line, decimated and unsupported, began to withdraw. Wheeler's rifles flung a few final rounds, then slowly limbered up and walked off the ridge, followed by Cowan's.

At Williamsburg, the artillery of three divisions and several of the horse batteries of Col. Hunt's Artillery Reserve had seen action. All four of Hooker's batteries had been in — two of them, Webber's and Bramhall's, coming out in unusable condition. The other two, Osborn's and Smith's, had lost eight and six men respectively, but otherwise were in good shape. During the night, part of the damage was remedied when Federal infantry recovered Bramhall's abandoned guns. This left Webber's battery as the only serious loss. Two men had been killed, and two officers and six men wounded, in addition to the loss of its guns. This was the Regular battery, and supposedly the nucleus of the division artillery.

The artillery of the Army of the Potomac had fought its first fight — though it had been only a small one in comparison with things to come. McClellan's organization had had its shakedown; basically it was sound, but division and corps commanders had tried to be artillery commanders as well. Hooker had shoved batteries into swampy fields with exuberant carelessness, impetuosity, and ignorance. It must be said, though, in fairness to Hooker, that he accepted full responsibility for the beating his batteries took.

As the war progressed, the artillerymen learned fast, but the system of 1862 had made its dent, and in this war seldom would a battery commander or a division artillery chief have the right even to select his own firing position. The difficulties which this system made had become evident both at Bull Run and Williamsburg; but much greater trouble lay ahead.

IV

WE WERE NOT EXPECTING

SO SEVERE A BATTLE

Seven Pines and Fair Oaks

THE FIGHT at Williamsburg had bloodied McClellan's none-too-aggressive nose. The Confederate Army then continued its retreat toward the Richmond defenses, unhindered except for a readily handled flanking effort by Franklin's division at Eltham's Landing. The Army of the Potomac followed leisurely after its adversary.

On May 17th, from White House, McClellan resumed his advance on Richmond. The Army was now composed of five corps under Sumner, Heintzelman, Keyes, Porter, and Franklin. Keyes's corps, the IV, led the advance, and on May 20th his leading brigade crossed the muddy Chickahominy at Bottom's Bridge. Three days later the remainder of the corps and its commander followed. One other corps, Heintzelman's, crossed behind Keyes, but the rest of the Army stretched itself out in an arc north of the river. Keyes, following McClellan's orders, selected and fortified a strong position on the Williamsburg Road, near Savage Station.

McClellan, worried about the road junction at Seven Pines, directed the Army's engineer officer, Gen. Barnard, to construct a line there. On May 28th the thudding of axes and grating of shovels indicated that work on Barnard's line had begun. About a mile and a half west of Seven Pines rifle pits were dug across the Williamsburg Road and earth was thrown up to form a pentagonal redoubt just south of the road, a few yards west of twin houses that resembled shoe-boxes standing on end. Constructing and manning this still-unfinished line were the young men of Brig. Gen. Silas Casey's division — mostly New York regiments. The digging of earthworks, clearing of timber, and construction of abatis were to continue through the morning of May 31st.

Casey's advanced picket line had its hands full during the 29th and 30th of May, as Gray regiments prodded, poked, and exchanged fire all along the line. Confederate Gen. Joe Johnston was feeling for a soft spot in the Yankee line, and he soon found one. Quickly, he determined to strike McClellan before the Federals were reinforced by McDowell's corps from Fredericksburg, and while those two advance corps of the Army of the Potomac were still south of the Chickahominy River. At noon on the 30th, Johnston ordered the concentration of twenty-three of the twenty-seven Confederate brigades for a cataclysmic crushing of the two Union corps — Keyes's and Heintzelman's. The attack was set for dawn of the 31st.

Keyes's corps, composed of Casey's and Couch's divisions, held the lines about Seven Pines and Fair Oaks. Casey's boys were out front: four regiments manned the still-unfinished pits and redoubt; some 400 yards closer to the Rebel lines were six more regiments; and 1000 yards beyond these was Casey's picket line. Couch's men dug in around Seven Pines, astride the Williamsburg Road.

The ground to the west of Seven Pines was cleared and open for a distance of about one mile, extending approximately a quarter of a mile on each side of the Williamsburg Road. Two belts of abatis had been felled across this area. The first of these was just at the westernmost edge of the cleared area north of the road, and the second was directly in front of Crouch's position at Seven Pines, extending on both sides of the road. Torrential rains and violent flashings of lightning harassed the tired troops during the night of May 30th. But the skies cleared with the dawn, and soon the area was blotched with the smoke of damp wood breakfast fires. Down in the camps of the Yankee artillery batteries, drivers followed the age-old military rule of caring for horse before man. Work parties from Casey's division marched out to improve the far belt of abatis.

During the morning of the 31st, musket fire sputtered continually along the length of Casey's picket line. Up near the Nine Mile Road, Lt. Washington, an aide of Gen. Johnston, was snapped up by Casey's outposts, and hauled before the stern, big-nosed Keyes. Washington, while he maintained silence, appeared to be quite nervous, frequently casting anxious glances in the direction of the Confederate lines. The very presence of an officer known to be on Johnston's staff boded no good. The Federal pickets had reported Rebel railroad activity all through the night from the same general area where this officer had been captured. The signs foretold trouble; the Yankees became alert for a 'big thing.'

Casey's division had a full complement of four batteries of artillery. The chief-of-artillery, a fine former Regular, Col. Guilford D. Bailey, had resigned from the Regular Army to raise a 12-battery artillery regiment for the state of New York. Two of those batteries were with him now — A and H, 1st New York Light Artillery. The balance of the division's artillery was filled out by the 7th and 8th Independent New York batteries.

Shortly before noon, a mounted Federal vedette came in to report that a body of Rebels was coming down the Williamsburg Road. Moments later, a second courier reined to a halt in front of Casey with the news that Rebels in force were coming through the swampy woods in front of the pickets. Two dull booms away to the west were quickly followed by the whistling of two shells as they passed over Casey's camp. Rebel signal guns, without doubt. Casey's headquarters group bustled with activity; couriers left at a gallop for various parts of the field.

The work parties were called back to their regiments. Casey hurried an orderly to the artillery bivouac with orders to harness up and get ready for action.

Up front, the staggered and intermittent popping along the picket line took on a more ominous volume. More orders sent more couriers and orderlies running for their horses. An infantry regiment hurried by at the double-quick, moving to support the hard-pressed pickets. Enemy artillery fire began to search out targets.

Casey sent for a battery. He wanted some artillery to move forward to a position about halfway between his line of entrenchments and his pickets; four infantry regiments would go as support. Col. Bailey complied with the order. Capt. Spratt's four 3-inch rifles of Battery H, 1st New York, trundled down the muddy road and wheeled into position about a hundred yards in the rear of the first line of abatis. Gun crews stood their positions, charges were made ready, and the battery waited tensely for a target. It would not be long in coming, nor one easily missed. Casey now positioned three additional batteries along his entrenched line. Battery A, 1st New York's six Napoleon guns, Lt. Hart commanding, were rolled into the crude redoubt; Regan's 7th New York, six 3-inchers, were in the rear and on the right of the Nine Mile Road; Fitch's six rifles of the 8th New York were manhandled into battery directly behind the redoubt.

Then it happened. As the men of Spratt's battery watched the woods to the front, the foliage seemed suddenly to disgorge blue-clad figures running toward the battery. The picket line was being driven in. Now the Pennsylvania regiment, sent to support the picket line, streamed by in panic. Teamsters, camp followers, and skulkers joined in the flight. A few minutes later, with a rending yell, Confederate infantry burst from the woods on both sides of the road. The four Union regiments in front of Spratt stood fast and discharged a volley at the oncoming mass. Spratt's four rifles, loaded with canister, coughed their charges through the gaps in the Blue line. The

Rebels north of the road, Garland's brigade, were slammed back by this heavy fire. The two Federal regiments south of the road were also holding, but the pressure was building up fast as Confederate Gen. Rodes put more regiments into line.

Back at Seven Pines, Keyes was now convinced that a heavy Confederate attack was falling on his corps, not from the suspected northwest area but directly down the Williamsburg Road. Every man in his corps was under arms; Casey's division was now completely committed, and Couch's men were checking their muskets as they moved into rifle pits astride the road junction at Seven Pines. Casey called for help. What infantry could be spared was sent forward, and Keyes, fearing he would need help, sent to Heintzelman for aid. He ordered Couch to create a diversion north of the Williamsburg Road in order to take some of the pressure off Casey. It failed. Micah Jenkins's South Carolinians drove the Bluecoats back across the Nine Mile Road.

The pressure on the Federals holding the advanced line increased. But a new threat developed. Skillfully, Rains side-slipped his Confederate brigade through the woods south of the clearing. The Union troops in the advanced line and now those in the entrenched line, came under a galling flank fire. Rebel marksmen found a fine target in Spratt's battery, sitting in an open field facing west. In a minute Spratt himself was sprawling in the clay, his shoulder a welter of bloody flesh. Lt. Howell succeeded to the command; he lasted some fifteen minutes. Lt. Mink then took over the hazardous job.

Spratt's guns were in danger, and Casey saw it. His troops south of the road were being pushed back to the redoubt line. An orderly carried the word to the four infantry regiments north of the road to attack, in order to cover Spratt's withdrawal. With a roar, the thin Blue line swept forward. The Southerners recoiled under this sudden blow. This was Mink's chance, and he yelled for his limbers. Three units responded — the forth, its horses all casualties, was being manhandled to the rear. But the Rebels, now reinforced with another brigade,

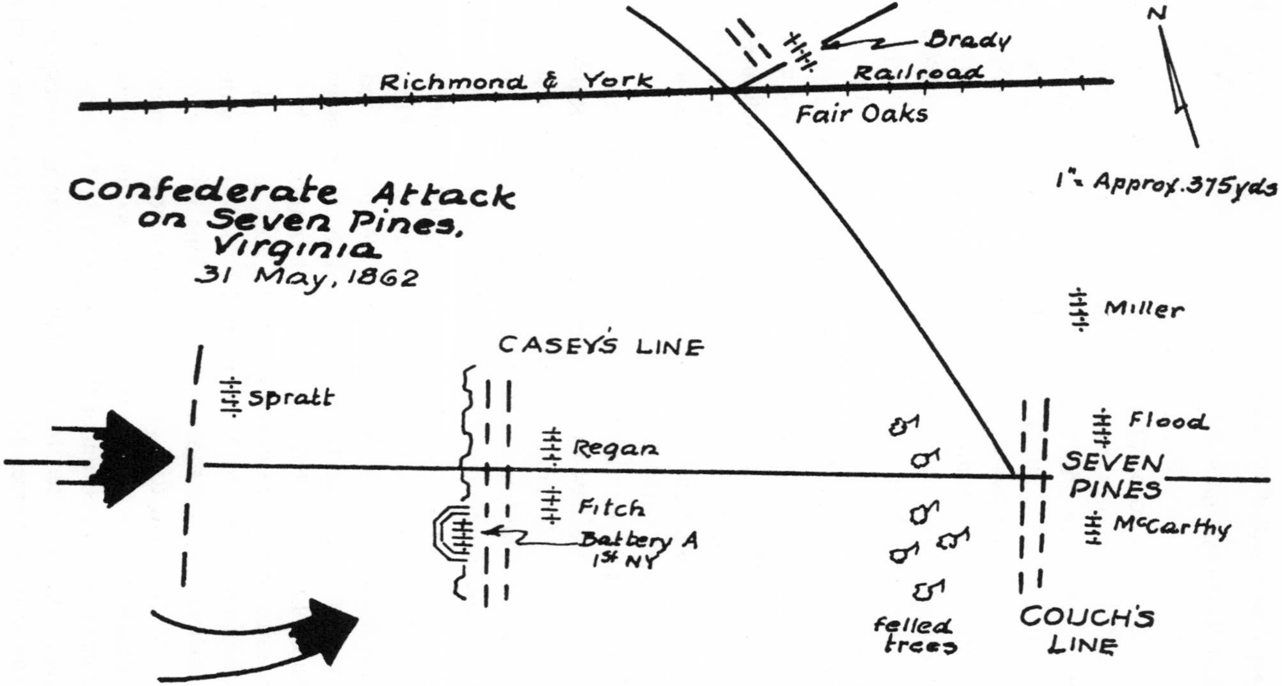

Confederate Attack
on Seven Pines,
Virginia,
31 May, 1862

N

1" Approx. 375yds

Richmond & York

Railroad

Brady

Fair Oaks

Miller

Flood

SEVEN
PINES

McCarthy

COUCH'S
LINE

felled
trees

CASEY'S LINE

Regan

Fitch

Battery A
1st NY

Spratt

started forward anew. It was a race, and Spratt's men won. One gun, with no limber, had to be left behind.

As the retreating Federals fell back into the line of entrenchments, they uncovered the fields of fire of Fitch's and Hart's guns. Col. Bailey gave the order. The twelve rifles set up a constant booming as they flung case shot at the advancing forces.[1] The Confederate brigades attacking frontally were hit hard. But the situation south of the road was critical.

From vantage points high in trees and from the cover of heavy timber, Confederate rifle fire took a frightful toll. It appeared that unless reinforcements came in soon the corps' first line, Casey's, would have to be abandoned. Maj. Van Valkenburgh of Col. Bailey's staff rode over to where Capt. Peter Regan's battery stood, harnessed and ready to move. From their masked position to the right of the Nine Mile Road, Van Valkenburgh ordered the battery into action astride the Williamsburg Road, just in the rear of the rifle pits. Regan's cannon swung into position. One section unlimbered in the road, and the other two in the field just north of the road. Regan gave orders to load canister and fire by piece. Eighteen guns now concentrated their fire on the enemy to the front. The Southerners were temporarily stopped.

But south of the redoubt, Rain's tawny men were volleying and sniping from the cover of the woods. Many Rebels took to the trees. From their positions aloft, they brought every point on the field under their fire. The Federal infantry line began to waver. It appeared just a matter of minutes before the works would fall.

Guilford Bailey prepared for the worst; the teams of Battery A in the redoubt no longer existed. Bailey roared orders to prepare to spike the guns. The words were scarcely out of his mouth when he dropped to the floor of the redoubt dead, a bullet through his head. Another bullet cut down his adjutant. Like a flood of water from a breaking wave, the Gray horde swept into the position. Battery A's guns fell silent. It was the battery's first and last fight.

Regan's battery, to the right rear of the redoubt, was now directly hit. This battery was to suffer the severest personnel losses — eleven — of any Federal battery that day. The enemy line was barely thirty yards distant when Regan grabbed a flag and rode in front of his battery. It was a silly effort designed to give the illusion of reinforcements. The shaft nicked twice, and his mount shot from under him, Regan gave up this foolish venture, fortunate to be still alive.

With coincident timing, Van Valkenburgh shouted to Regan to get the four pieces in the field to the rear. He was to use the section in the road to cover the withdrawal. Fitch's sections were already wheeling off.[2] Horses heaved and lunged in their traces as the teams strove to extricate the four guns from the boggy field. Regan turned to Van Valkenburgh to ask for the battery's next position just as that officer fell dead from the saddle.

One of Casey's brigadiers appeared at this point. He ordered them to fix their prolonges and retire while firing. Sweaty, grimy hands hurriedly attached the long hemp rope to the trail of one gun — there was room in the road now for only one piece. Lt. McIntyre jumped over the trail and took on the number one's duties; a corporal served the ammunition, and Regan acted as gunner. The remainder of the crew held the far end of the rope, and following each discharge pulled the piece a short distance to the rear. Then the gun was reloaded, fired, and the pulling process repeated. The three men were able to fire a few rounds before they began to run out of primers. Then their only lanyard snapped. In a desperate effort to save the guns, the New York Garde Lafayette regiment charged past them, stalling the enemy advance, and enabling Regan to roll his still-smoking piece down the road to join the rest of the retiring battery.

Regan had saved all of his guns, but two of his men were dead and eight wounded; still another was missing. Two of his caissons, their horses down, were left behind. The battery was also to lose its battery wagon and rolling forge before the day was out. Prior to the fight, Regan had received orders to harness one section to accompany a reconnaissance party. Then Casey's hurried order had come. 'We were not expecting so severe a battle so soon,' wrote Regan afterwards.[3]

Keyes's first line collapsed altogether. The Federal infantry, under fire from the lost guns in the redoubt now manned by Rodes's men, gave ground. Casey had held some three hours before his battered regiments began to fall away to the east and northeast. The corps commander, aware that a breakthrough of his second line at Seven Pines would be disastrous, had attempted to beef up the defenses there. Two batteries of Couch's artillery, McCarthy's and Flood's, C and D, 1st Pennsylvania Light Artillery, were ordered into position near the junction of the Williamsburg and Nine Mile Roads. A third, Miller's Battery E, of the same regiment, put its trails down to the right rear of Couch's infantry pits. The remaining battery of the division's artillery, Brady's Battery H, also of the 1st Pennsylvania, was getting into position near Fair Oaks Station — the right flank of Couch's line.

Flood and McCarthy cut loose at the Rebels on Keyes's command about 2:30 p.m., in an effort to break up the attack on Casey's earthworks. The ten 10-pounder Parrotts hurled percussion and then case shot over the heads of the friendly infantry into the enemy masses some 1500 yards distant. For two hours this cannonade roared unabated.

About 3 p.m. the Southerners, having carried the first Yankee line, set sail for the second — Couch's. The Federal artillery positions there immediately began to catch both Rebel rifle and cannon fire. Gray infantry were trying to work to the left of McCarthy's battery. That officer, fearing his guns might be seized by a sudden rush, hooked his pieces to their limbers. Back fifty yards they went, and into action again.

McCarthy started to direct his fire into the woods to the south, but choruses of hurrahs, overlapping with eerie yells of Rebels, indicated men of both sides were contesting that area.

Instead, the battery shifted its tubes, picking now on an annoying enemy battery to the front. One Rebel gun, firing from the road, received a percussion round, blowing it out of action. McCarthy switched to case shot as the enemy gunners strove to haul their damaged weapon back; his salvo blew all about them, and McCarthy looked for another target.

McCarthy's men had not been in the new location fifteen minutes when counter-battery fire commenced to hammer them. But the Yankee gunners concentrated on the more immediate threat — the enemy's advancing infantry. Incoming shell fire was violent and profuse: a solid shot smashed the lunette of the number four piece to bits; a rammer was knocked from the hands of a crewman preparing to swab out his piece; whirring pieces of fractured iron slapped and thudded the ground, the guns, and the limbers about the men. Surprisingly, the battery lost but one man killed and three wounded during the day's fighting.

The exhausted men were now working in their shirt sleeves, for the intense heat of the gun tubes was making their work difficult. Number three men, who covered the vent during the loading process with a leather device worn on the thumb called a thumbstall, saw these sizzle as they touched the hot metal. So hot were the tubes now that the cloth powder cases were singed as the men rammed them home.

The order to cease fire came from McCarthy; he had concluded it was no longer safe to work the guns. Three of his 10-pounder Parrotts were promptly limbered up and sent bouncing to a vacant field in the rear. The remaining gun, its lunette or towing ring smashed, had to be left behind. The fighting ended for the men of Battery C, with McCarthy estimating he had fired some 500 rounds during the four or five hours he was in action.

Over on the north side of the road, Flood was receiving the same treatment. Rebel artillery fire pounded his position. With a deafening roar one shell blew along side the limber of his right piece, smashing its wheel, wounding a driver, and ripping the canteen from the hip of the number seven man. For two hours the battery stuck to its work. A cannoneer caught a piece of shell and dropped dead; two more wheels were reduced to splinters. The tubes of Flood's cannon, too, became so hot that it was only with great difficulty that they were reloaded. Under such conditions it is no wonder that the crews welcomed the order to cease fire and move back some hundred yards.[4]

At the new location, number six and seven men took up their posts by the limber chests and prepared case shot. The gunners stooped over their tubes and checked the bubbles on their sighting device, called a pendulum-hausse. Grimy hands placed charges in the mouths of the guns. Over and over, they repeated the monotonous process of loading, firing, swabbing, loading, firing, and swabbing. At last Heintzelman sent word to cease fire, and pull back behind the woods in the rear of the camp.

Farther to the right, near the Nine Mile Road, Miller was fighting his guns as if they were pistols. From his original position in advance and to the right of Flood and McCarthy, he had been able to spot the initial assault of the Southerners as they burst from the boggy woods. Picking out enemy infantry masses to his right front, his four Napoleons let go with a boom — spherical case bursting over the heads of the attackers some 900 yards away.

Quick and vicious came the enemy's reaction. Some keen-eyed Rebel battery commander picked up Miller's location; immediately 12-pounder howitzer shells began to explode within Battery E's position. Miller yelled for his limbers. The guns were hooked on, and four teams of horses splattered their way across the muddy field, halting some 200 yards to the right. Once more the four smoothbores roared and recoiled as they resumed battle with Confederate infantry. For some twenty minutes they fired, stopping only when the supply of ammunition on the limbers — the manual called for thirty-two rounds of all types per gun — was exhausted.

Again Miller limbered (the process of fastening the gun trail to the horse drawn limber so that the piece might be pulled at reasonable speed) his guns and returned to his original position, 200 yards to the left. The Rebel counter-battery fire had pounded that smoke-shrouded spot for about fifteen minutes after Miller had vacated it, but now the fire had ceased. Taking advantage of the lull, the battery commander called up the caisson limbers with their fresh ammunition chests, sending the gun limbers back in their stead. The latter each replenished its supply by exchanging its empty chest for one of the two full ones carried by the caissons. The gun limbers then became the caisson limbers until another exchange took place.

Capt. Miller was following the book here, which said that the limber chests should be kept full at the expense of the caissons. The caisson of that era was heavy and awkward, loaded down with two ammunition chests, an extra wheel, and other impedimenta. As such, they were usually kept to the rear of the line of battle, only the guns and their limbers were sent forward. Since field artillery batteries were likely to be shunted about the field, battery commanders always tried to keep their limber chests filled, running a limber shuttle system back to the line of caissons to replenish or exchange chests.

The lull at Battery E's guns was suddenly cracked by a shriek from the direction of the woods to the south. Regiments of bronzed Southerners were pouring out of the thicket, screaming and volleying. The distance from battery to target was a scant 350 yards — canister range. Number five men ran to the limbers, snatched a round, and ran back to the guns. The long rammers clunked home the charges; primers were slid into the vents, and the four guns exploded with a crash as the number four men jerked their lanyards. Before the echo of the blast had vanished, crewmen were sponging out the tubes, and the loading process was ready to be repeated. As the dense pillar of acrid, gray smoke shifted slowly upward, the Blue gunners saw only a field strewn with bodies. The survivors were nowhere to be seen.

Again, counter-battery fire started to explode about Battery E's position. Confederate infantry over in the woods took the battery under fire. Lead slugs splattered against limbers, carriages, and chests; wheels and spokes were chipped and shattered and the ominous buzz of Minié balls churned the air about the crews. Miller called to limber up, and once more the unit shifted position, this time setting its trails down a hundred yards to the left rear. Again the ammunition chests were exchanged, and the guns reopened fire. They were now close to Flood and McCarthy, and the three batteries flung their iron spit at the oncoming hordes of infantry. For another hour the three batteries kept at it; the cease fire finally came at about 6 p.m.

Battery E was reaching the bottom of its ammunition supply. Miller was firing solid shot toward the end — all that remained in his chests.[5] This was a favored round for use against infantry or cavalry in column, but it was not very effective against deployed troops. The standard loading for the 12-pounder ammunition chest called for twelve rounds of solid shot, twelve of spherical case, four of shell, and four of canister. All rounds came fixed — the projectile fastened by thin metal straps to a wooden board or sabot, and the cloth powder sack fastened to the other face of this sabot. Miller's total expenditure for his four guns was 192 rounds of spherical case, forty rounds of shell, six of canister, and ten of solid shot — sixty-two rounds per gun. Miraculously, the battery lost but five horses, and suffered no serious personnel casualties.

By the time the three batteries quit firing, all of their supporting infantry regiments had been committed, and the infantry on the right flank was giving ground. If they gave way completely, the flood of enemy would probably cause the loss of all or part of the batteries. They were commanded to retire beyond the woods and await further orders. Maj. Robert M.

West, chief of Couch's artillery, rode off to to inform Keyes.[6]

Up near Fair Oaks Station, the situation was even more confused. Couch had part of Abercrombie's brigade posted near the station to protect his right flank. This little force comprised Brady's four guns of Battery H, 1st Pennsylvania, and at first two and later four regiments of infantry. Couch's efforts earlier in the day to relieve the pressure on Casey by a counterattack from the area just south of Fair Oaks had failed. The Bluecoats had been driven back across the Nine Mile Road, and Rebel infantry, D. H. Hill's men, poured over in close pursuit. Thus, a great gap had been ripped in Couch's line, his elements at Fair Oaks cut off.

Brady's battery and two Federal regiments were soon involved in a jumbled, confused fight in the wood- and field-patched area about Fair Oaks Station. Increasing numbers of Gray infantrymen lowered their rifle barrels in the direction of this shabby little Federal line. More enemy, crimson flags snapping defiantly, were spotted working their way around Abercrombie's right.

Couch himself, with two infantry regiments, had also been cut off from the main Federal body by the Confederate plunge across the Nine Mile Road. The general and the two regiments retired toward Fair Oaks Station and joined forces with Abercrombie. Couch gave the order to fall back northeast along the road to the Grapevine Bridge; the forces would go into position on a small rise near the Adams house, about 800 yards from Fair Oaks Station. A staff officer spurred his horse along the muddy road, headed for Bull Sumner's headquarters across the Chickahominy for help.

Then the Rebels' numerical advantage, already great, was about to be increased again. Down the Nine Mile Road came a full fresh Confederate division, Whiting's — their destination to reinforce their companions in front of Seven Pines. As the head of the leading brigade reached the railroad tracks at Fair Oaks, Whiting halted the column; there were Federals in unknown force north of the tracks, in a position to slam their way into the division's flank or rear. The Confederate commanding general, Joe Johnston, riding with Whiting's division, decried his caution and demanded that Whiting push on. Suddenly Whiting's caution was vindicated by the unmistakable explosion of artillery from the threatened direction. Dimly visible off on the Rebels' left flank were two separate sections of Yankee guns, their crews now furiously reloading. James Brady's four 10-pounder Parrotts were snapping at the Rebel flank.

Brady was fighting his battery by sections — Lt. Fagan handling one and Brady the other. Part of a Confederate brigade turned to meet this annoyance. The Southerners burst howling from the cover of woods to knock out or capture the battery. The crews worked rapidly, often so fast that they did not even stop to swab the tubes between rounds. Fagan's section ran out of canister and resorted to the novel trick of firing case and shell without fuze, bursting the projectiles as they left the tubes. The battery's canister and the Minié balls of the Blue infantry slashed and ripped at the attacking ranks. The Rebels fell back. Couch's men watched as the Gray lines reformed for another try; the Blue line would try to hold here until Sumner could come to their aid from the far side of the flooded Chickahominy.

On the other side of that river, McClellan, appraised of the Confederate attack on his left wing, had alerted Sumner about 1 p.m. to be ready to move. Old Bull had already heard the firing, and armed with this warning order he put his regiments in motion toward the bridges. His division commanders, Sedgwick and Richardson, were told to wait at the north side for further orders.

At 2:30 p.m. Sumner received word, and cries of 'forward' rang out along the length of his waiting regiments. Sedgwick's division led the way, with Battery I, 1st U.S. Artillery, Ricketts's old battery now under Lt. Edmund Kirby, well to the front. Three other batteries brought up the division rear. Only Kirby's guns were destined to reach the field before darkness ended the fighting.

The rains of the preceding days had caused the Chicka-

hominy to flood its banks and had turned the soil everywhere into a gummy slime. As the columns approached the
bridges, the going became increasingly bad. For the infantry
it was hard, but for the artillery it was a nightmare. Horses
sank in the slime, at times up to their girths. Drivers and
cannoneers unharnessed teams and tried to pull their guns,
limbers, and caissons through by use of the prolonges and
muscle, the men standing at times in waist-deep water.

The ground at the west end of the bridges was flooded to a
depth of eighteen inches for a width of 200 yards. Huge
logs from the corduroy road that previously existed here
floated two-thirds submerged in the murky water — drifting
into wheels, banging horses' legs, and bruising the shins of the
men struggling on foot to push the guns through. Men and
horses hauled and heaved at the ends of the ropes which
snapped as if they had been but pack-thread. Traces parted,
dumping animals and men into the water. Two ambulances
which had somehow strayed into the column stood bogged and
abandoned, blocking the west exit from the morass.

Sedgwick's division successfully crossed the Grapevine
Bridge and reached the field in time to stem the tide. It was
about 4:30 p.m. when Kirby trotted up to the Federal position near the Adams house, three Napoleons and one caisson
bouncing along behind him. The rest of his battery was still
struggling to extricate itself. Sumner ordered Kirby to put
his guns in battery about seventy yards from the Adams house,
facing south toward Fair Oaks, their right resting on a strip
of woods. Brady, with two pieces from his battery, shifted
across the road to bolster the growing Union line. Kirby's guns
had barely been unhooked before the woods 1000 yards distant disgorged advancing regiments of enemy infantry. Kirby
opened fire. The Confederates headed for the woods to the
battery's right flank.

Kirby and Fagan were now firing to the right oblique into
the woods across the road. At that instant Lt. Woodruff
arrived with two more of the Battery I's pieces. The battery

commander ordered Woodruff to move in on the left and open on the woods through which the Rebels were advancing. The five guns began a rhythmic fire, only to have the trail of the number two piece snap at the fourth discharge. This unfortunate stroke of luck was quickly remedied when another of Kirby's lieutenants reined up with the remaining Napoleon of the battery splashing through the slop behind him. Once more, five guns boomed case and shell. In short time the supply of spherical case and shell gave out and Kirby switched to solid shot, the enemy being beyond effective canister range, while two limbers careened down the road to replenish from the mired caissons.

The limbers returned and the guns switched back to the fragmenting projectiles. The Rebel infantry tightened its ranks and went after the battery again. At 500 yards range, Kirby calmly called for canister. The Confederates halted and let go a volley which killed one of Kirby's men and wounded four others. But the fire of the guns and the supporting infantry proved too costly and the attackers fell back.

A moment later there was a flurry of movement on the right flank, and the battery saw another column of infantry move down a wood road, heading for the general direction of the battery's right flank. Kirby shifted his alignment, throwing his left guns forward and turning the axis of fire toward this unidentified column. Then they saw the red, starred battle flags of the Confederacy. The long column was still pouring out of the woods as Kirby called for canister. The tin containers and their powder charges were rammed home. Kirby gave the command to fire, and the five Napoleons recoiled as one. Fire at will was now the order. The shiny smoothbores banged out an uneven staccato.

The Southerners kept coming. The 62nd New York Infantry lying in support of the guns displayed nervousness and their line wavered. Their colonel dashed out in front of the ranks to rally their lagging courage by example, only to drop lifeless, a Rebel musket ball through his brain. The division

commander, Couch, rode up and with stern words stayed a
break in the line.

The attacking ranks were hewn hard by lead and iron. Some
Rebels were struck down only fifteen yards from the gun tubes,
but the hail was too heavy. The Southerners broke for the
cover of the road banks and the woods and from here they
kept up an annoying fire. Darkness was fast approaching as
Sumner prepared to send his infantry to the attack. Kirby
ordered his guns forward. He wanted to get in a few more blows
before Sumner's infantry masked his fire. Crews strained and
heaved, but only two guns could be budged from their muddy
ruts — and these only with the assistance of nearby infantry.
These two pieces fired a few defiant shots, and the action
closed for the battery. Everywhere in the woods and fields
north of the railroad the attacking Confederates had been
fought to a standstill. Darkness ended the fighting.

The men of Battery I had probably been in action for not
more than three hours. Their expenditure was 343 rounds of
all types: 70 shell, 210 spherical case, 48 canister, and 15
solid shot. Considering that there were never more than five
guns in action at any one time, this averaged about 23 rounds
per gun per hour — about one shot every two and a half
minutes, sustained rate. Their casualties had been but five
men.

Meanwhile, down at Seven Pines, the three batteries which
had been supporting the infantry there had, in accordance with
orders, pulled out of action. Maj. West advised Keyes of this,
and the general promptly sent them back into action. West
spurred his horse in pursuit of the batteries. A short distance
to the rear he found Flood and ordered him to move his
battery back to its last position. The exhausted men turned
their teams about and headed back.

The enemy was about 700 yards away when Flood's battery
set its trails down at its old position behind Couch's line.
The Rebels were still pressing Couch, though some of their
force seemed to have been dissipated. The Federals were still

stubbornly giving up ground, though, inch by inch. The line fell back toward Flood's line of guns. The gunners twisted at the elevating screws, leveled the tubes at two degrees, and let go with case shot, firing just over the heads of the friendly infantry. Then it was over; the Blue ranks were so close to his guns that Flood ordered the battery into column of pieces, and the six Parrotts rolled slowly to the rear again, their action really ended now for this day.

The fighting that day about Seven Pines and Fair Oaks ended around 7:30 p.m. The Federal line was still intact 1000 yards east of Seven Pines. The next day Longstreet made a feeble attack on Richardson's division, which had crossed over during the night, but the attackers were beaten off handily by the Blue ranks, aided by the remainder of the corps' artillery which had been pulled over the river by dawn of June 1st. But the true decision had been reached the previous day.

The Federal Army had suffered a partial defeat. One of its divisions had been roughly handled, and Keyes had given up ground. But the Confederates had failed to destroy any portion of the Army of the Potomac. And the Blue gunners had lent a conspicuous hand in saving the Army from what might have been more serious losses.

The brigades of D. H. Hill and Longstreet had suffered frightful losses — over 6000 — in ghastly frontal attacks on Casey's and Couch's artillery-supported infantry lines. Only the flanking effort of Rains had given the Southerners any success. Toward the end of the day, the Confederate division under Whiting, coming down the Nine Mile Road, might have landed on the flank of Couch's heavily engaged troops near Seven Pines had it not been for Brady's and Kirby's below-strength batteries.

The Federal artillery had been hurt but not crippled. One complete battery had fallen with the redoubt, and others had lost individual pieces. At least eight and perhaps ten guns had fallen into enemy hands.[7] Personnel losses were reported as light, no battery suffering greater than eleven casualties.

But battery commanders, and the Army as a whole, had still to learn that any loss in an artillery battery would ultimately be a heavy one; replacements for artillery units had a very low priority in the unsystematic replacement scheme of the Union armies.

V

HEROIC AND GRAND SLAUGHTER

Mechanicsville and Gaines Mill

THE CONFEDERATE troops were much dispirited by the in-
decisive results of the fighting about Seven Pines and Fair
Oaks, not knowing that that battle had brought them an
unexpected blessing. Little did anyone in the Rebel Army
realize the significance of the appointment to army command,
the day after the fighting, of Robert Edward Lee to replace
the wounded Joe Johnston.

On the night of June 1st, Lee pulled the Confederate forces
back to their former positions close to Richmond. While his
men dug deeper and more extensive fortifications in the face
of their numerically superior foe, Lee planned an offensive.

McClellan, for his part, continued his exchange of notes
and demands with Washington, and moved slowly back onto
the ground from which the Blue Army had just been driven.
Stonewall Jackson's dust and smoke in the Shenandoah Valley
to the west had all but precluded the probability that Mc-
Dowell's Federal corps at Fredericksburg would be released
to McClellan. Still the Union commander hoped and begged
for more help. Just in case, the newly formed V Corps
under Brig. Gen. Fitz John Porter was left north of the
Chickahominy River as a linking force with McDowell, should
the latter be ordered to march overland to cooperate or join
with the main Army. The rest of McClellan's massive host

was marched to the south side of that river, with its base of supply at White House on the York River.

Thursday, June 26, 1862, dawned clear and bright. About 2 p.m. Fitz John Porter, sitting by the telegraph operator at his headquarters, heard the boom of a single gun from the direction of Mechanicsville. This was the prearranged Federal signal that Confederate troops were crossing the Chickahominy in force. With one distant boom from one lone gun began the blood-letting of the Seven Days campaign — a campaign which closed to the thunder of some one hundred-tiered Union guns massed on Malvern Hill.

McClellan's right flank, Fitz John Porter's V Corps, lay north of the Chickahominy River. The rest of the Federal Army rested south of the river and peered across rifle pits at the Rebel defenses, as the Federal commander hesitatingly prepared to order an advance for the next day. But the former captain of the U.S. Engineers, R. E. Lee, stole the march on his young adversary. Once more the Confederate battle plan envisaged the destruction of an isolated member of the Federal Army — this time Porter's V Corps.

It was about 3:30 p.m. when the long Gray columns could be seen filing down the two roads leading eastward from the hamlet of Mechanicsville. The Federal pickets had done their job well; adequate warning had been given Porter. His troops, some of the best the Federals were ever to put in the field, were ready with capped muskets and shotted cannon. His position on the east slopes of Beaver Dam Creek was masterfully developed. The waist-deep, swamp-fringed creek ran roughly north-south, through a steep-banked valley. Confederate columns attacking the position had two access roads, each of which approached the creek at an angle; Yankee infantry and artillery would be able to concentrate flanking fire as the Rebels moved in. At one point, in front of Ellerson's Mill, the lower road ran exactly parallel to the Union position.

McCall's division, Pennsylvania troops, held the infantry

pits along the creek banks — this was to be their first battle. Reynold's brigade held the right, Seymour's the left, and Meade's was in reserve. McCall's infantry was backed up by six batteries of artillery — some thirty-two guns. Reynolds and Seymour supervised the positioning of the batteries, and all were well sited.

The lower road out of Mechanicsville and the sloping fields leading down to where this road crossed the creek at Ellerson's Mill could be swept by one section — two guns, of Cooper's Battery B, 1st Pennsylvania, and one section of Smead's Battery K, 5th U.S. The two sections were emplaced on either side of the road as it debouched onto the east bank. A little farther north were the four 12-pounders of Easton's Battery A, 1st Pennsylvania. The center of the line was covered by DeHart's six Napoleons of Battery C, 5th U.S., whose tubes could be brought to bear on either road. Later, Reynolds slid a section of Kerns's G, 1st Pennsylvania, in on DeHart's right front with orders to cover the bridge at Ellerson's Mill. The upper road was straddled by the remaining section of Smead's battery and the other four guns from Cooper's battery. The last two sections of Battery G, 1st Pennsylvania, Capt. Kerns commanding, were subsequently ordered to support this flank.

It was close to 4 p.m. when A. P. Hill's leading Rebel elements came in range and began to deploy. Hill was to earn the reputation as a slugging, impetuous fighter. This day was to be no exception. On the heels of his infantry came five batteries of artillery, each gun pulled by two extra horses to insure its presence on the field; these now began to unlimber on the opposite slopes.

The Blue gunners cut loose when their opponents were about halfway down the banks of the valley. Cooper's four 10-pounder Parrotts near the upper road belched solid shot and shell as Archer's brigade attempted to cross the field in front. The 'Johnnies' struck back quickly as a battery of their rifled pieces opened on Cooper from a concealed position on the right. The Pennsylvanians concentrated on the enemy infantry. Not until the Gray lines were thrown back from the bridge area did Cooper switch his target to the annoying Rebel battery. The Southerners then changed positions, moving farther to the Federal left. At this instant, a battery of smoothbores opened on Cooper from the cover of the woods in front. There was a tense few seconds for Cooper's men; where would the Rebel salvo hit? The shells fell way short. The range was too great for the smoothbores.

Smead's section joined with Cooper. The two Napoleons flung shell and spherical case at 700 yards range. Lt. Piper, commanding the section, fell wounded in the first few minutes; one of his men was fatally hit, and three of the gun limber's horses were badly wounded.

A. P. Hill had begun his advance impetuously, but caution seized him momentarily in front of Beaver Dam Creek. An assault on this position, he knew, would bring heavy losses. Jackson, who had secretly marched his forces from the valley on June 17th to reinforce Lee, had reached Ashland some twenty miles north of Richmond on June 25th. He was now supposed to be coming down on the Union right flank, so Hill delayed his full assault till the roar of gunfire from that quarter signified Stonewall's arrival.

As A. P. Hill strove to shake his brigades into line of battle, the Union batteries on the far slopes inflicted casualties and brought confusion into his ranks. The Confederates were severely shaken by this fire. Hill, tired of waiting on Jackson's guns (which never opened that day), abandoned caution at twilight and struck hard at the Federal right flank. McCall promptly strengthened that point, running in two sections of Kerns's battery and an infantry regiment to support it. The third section of the battery was detached into a crude earthwork to the right front of DeHart's guns; these two weapons were to cover the road down to Ellerson's Mill. From this spot they could hit the flank or rear of any column trying to use the road to the lower bridge.

The fight at the upper bridge was a furious slaughter house for the Gray lines. Yankee infantrymen, lying in shallow rifle pits, and the supporting guns on the slopes behind chopped the Gray regiments to shreds. One rush toward Kerns's guns was broken up by two pieces firing double charges of canister. The Confederate repulse in this quarter was complete.

The enemy turned his attention toward the lower road and the bridge at Ellerson's Mill. McCall shuttled reserves to that point. Down the road advanced the Southern columns. The crackle of musket fire broke out along the Federal infantry line. Up on the banks behind them some eighteen tubes were brought to bear on the attackers. A deep, sonorous overtone of artillery fire was now added to the melody as the Yankee guns fired case shot and shell. A lieutenant commanding the two Parrotts of Cooper's battery close to the bridge estimated that four successive assaults were thrown back before the Confederate attack spent itself and darkness halted further fighting. As the action was sputtering to a close, one of Hunt's Artillery Reserve batteries, L/M, 3rd U.S., under Capt. John Edwards, pulled in behind the Federal left and opened fire. But the Confederate attempt to force a crossing on this day had already failed.

The Confederate repulse here was achieved at a loss of but 363 of the approximate 5000 Union troops engaged. The Southerners had lost about 1400 men, with two regiments virtually destroyed. Most of these casualties probably resulted from Federal infantry fire. Even though Confederate reports refer to the intensity of the incoming artillery, most of the ammunition expended by the Yankee gunners was shell and case shot, and these two types of ammunition were not the great killers of that war. The most effective charge was canister, and only 6 per cent of the approximately 2800 artillery rounds fired were of this type.[1] Caustic D. H. Hill remarked after the war, that attacks like that made against Beaver Dam Creek were heroic and grand, but of a grandeur the South could not afford.

McClellan himself arrived at Fitz John Porter's tent as the action was drawing to a close. The firing sputtered out, and exhausted Federals slept where they had fought. All evening reports coming to McClellan corroborated the suspicions about Jackson's movements. His presence on the Federal right flank was certain. Thus as dawn came up fiery red the next day, Friday, June 27th, Porter's columns in dirtied blue began to fall back to Gaines Mill. They plodded the dusty road from Mechanicsville toward New Cold Harbor accompanied by the V Corps batteries. Two horse batteries, Tidball's and Robertson's, from Hunt's Reserve covered the infantry's rear.

Through New Cold Harbor the Federal columns passed, wound their way down the open fields north of Boatswains Creek, and disappeared into the dense woods bordering both banks of the swampy bottom. The Blue lines waded across and up the far slopes. They halted on the far side; the V Corps would stand and fight. Borrowing a handful of axes and shovels from the artillerymen to augment their tin cups, pointed sticks, and bayonets, the infantrymen scooped out rifle pits, felled trees, and piled up packs to form a crude breastwork amid the heavy timber south of the swamp. Tiered from bottom to top of the pine-covered slopes the men of Morell's and Sykes's divisions prepared to give their following foe a nasty greeting.

The V Corps line was a long convex arc, its right hanging astride the road south from Old Cold Harbor, its left terminus the swampy fringes of the Chickahominy. Porter, aware that Jackson's valley legions had added their weight to the Confederate forces north of the river, had chosen a fine defensive position. Attacking infantry would have to advance across much open ground, pass through woods, descend into a boggy ravine, cross the creek, and climb the twenty-to-forty-foot banks on the far side to come to grips with the protected lines of the V Corps. The Confederates would be wide-open targets as they moved across the open ground. Then the confusion,

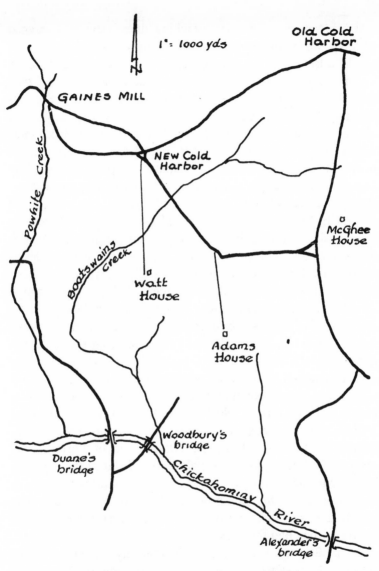

1" = 1000 yds

Old Cold Harbor

GAINES MILL

New Cold Harbor

Powhite Creek

Boatswains Creek

Watt House

McGhee House

Adams House

Duane's bridge

Woodbury's bridge

Chickahominy River

Alexander's bridge

AREA OF Porter's STAND
BELOW GAINES MILL

JR

which always accompanies attacking lines moving in rugged country while under heavy fire from a protected enemy, would offset much of the Confederate numerical superiority. The Federal batteries hauled by sweating horses rolled past the infantry regiments onto the open ground beyond the woods south of the creek. Before the sun would set that day some twenty Federal batteries would smell burned powder from their own tubes; but as the noon sun baked the dry fields there were but elements of eleven batteries deployed along the line or in immediate reserve. Down in the low ground on Porter's extreme left, behind Butterfield's brigade, stood Battery E, Massachusetts Light Artillery. Nearby was Weeden's Rhode Island battery, in sections between the gaps in Martindale's line. Between Morell and Sykes were the six Napoleons of Martin's Battery C, Massachusetts Light Artillery. Sykes's men could glance over their shoulders and glimpse through the foliage the frowning tubes of a Regular battery — L/M, 3rd U.S., also dispersed by sections along the length of Sykes's front. In reserve, there being no available firing position, was Kingsbury's D, 5th U.S., six 10-pounder Parrott rifles.

It was nearly noon when another Regular battery, I, 5th U.S., Capt. Weed commanding, got its barrels into position to sweep the road from Old Cold Harbor. Thirty minutes later Tidball, from Hunt's Artillery Reserve, unlimbered his 3-inchers on Weed's right — the extreme end of Porter's line, several hundred yards to the right and in front of the McGhee house. McCall's division, blooded at Mechanicsville, was in corps reserve on the open ground behind the Watt house. The four batteries of this division were not destined to come off as lightly as they had the previous day.

At 12:30 p.m. rifle fire grew in intensity on the northeast side of Boatswains Swamp, in the direction of New Cold Harbor. Porter's rearguard was bitterly contesting A. P. Hill's advance. But back at the artillery positions the battle had not yet begun. In little groups the Yankee crews sat about their guns, gnawed hardtack, sipped hot stale water from sun-heated canteens, and puffed well-chewed pipes. A man in Edwards's battery leaned against a gun wheel and stared anxiously in the direction of the firing. Earlier that day mail had reached the troops, and now dirty hands pawed letters that had already been read many times during those brief hours. Newsboys hawked New York and Philadelphia papers, also recently arrived.

The firing came closer. In increasing numbers, spent rifle slugs flicked up little spurts of dust about the gun positions. A twig of a tree nearby snapped and fluttered to the ground as the angry buzz of a Minié ball searched the air above. Patient horses, tragic sufferers in this war, pricked their ears, shook their heads, gently rustling harness and traces, and then lowered them to munch on scarce blades of grass. From the woods in front, Federal infantry commanders could be heard alerting their men; Gray columns could be seen coming down the road from New Cold Harbor. Battery commanders took up the cue. Crews got up, stretched, knocked the ashes from their pipes, and calmly took their battle stations.

A solid crash from the center of the Federal line announced that the Rebels had come into range. From this moment until sunset Porter's lines were ablaze from flank to flank as long lines of yelling Confederates hurled themselves at the tiered Union ranks.

The first assault was made by Gregg's brigade of A. P. Hill's command, which drove hard at the center of the Union line. Martin's six Napoleons, in the interval between Sykes and Morell, roared and recoiled as two and one-half pounds of black powder thundered each round of spherical case on its way. Confederate cannon fire began to slap ineffectively about a section of Edwards's battery posted in advance of the brigade's right flank. The two guns returned the fire with case shot. Gregg's men reached the ravine, though Yankee fire was taking a huge toll. The section switched to double canister. Sykes ordered the two guns to move back behind the infantry lest they be lost.

The fight at Gaines Mill was like a leaf fire in a fickle breeze, blazing fiercely at this point, flickering to an ember at that, only to burst anew as fresh fuel fed its fury. First A. P. Hill's front sputtered and crackled as his brigades beat against the Federal lines. The flame subsided, to roar again as Ewell's men sought to punch their way through where Hill's had failed. Then the line flamed in front of Morell, as Pickett of Longstreet's command tried a diversionary attack. But it was sundown before the Confederate line was set to punch in concert, with D. H. Hill's and Jackson's men filling out the eastern end of the Confederate line.

The Federal batteries above the crest let go with shell and case shot as the Gray regiments tramped across the open ground headed for the wooded ravine. Their fire was annoying but scarcely effective.[2] Not until the enemy entered the woods did the artillery make its weight felt. Then, firing double canister in shotgun like blasts, the guns churned the air with lead and iron. The Confederates, struggling in the foliage in an effort to reach the south bank of the swamp, were shattered. The din was terrific. One Yankee battery's fire was so effective that A. P. Hill ordered six companies to take it. The attack got nowhere. Men could not stand, let alone move forward, under the rain of rifle and cannon fire. The Rebel commanders sent their men to the prone position.

The Southerners, handicapped by the lack of heavy metal and scarcity of good firing positions, tried to bring their own artillery to bear. Their efforts harvested little fruit; A. P. Hill could bring but eight tubes to bear. Confederate Capt. Crenshaw brought his battery into an opening in the woods. For two hours he dueled with the Yankee batteries. The Blue gunners got his range and hammered with a vengeance. With five men and eleven horses down, no room to maneuver, and two guns out with broken axles, Crenshaw pulled out of the fight.

At about 2 o'clock D. H. Hill's division turned south from Old Cold Harbor, its regiments beginning to deploy in the more open ground east of A. P. Hill's now stalled and shaken brigades. Back near the McGhee house, on the right of Porter's line, Weed's and Tidball's men could see the Rebel regiments forming in line. Cannoneers grabbed handspikes to swing the tubes to bear as gunners squinted along their sights. Eager hands twisted at elevating screws. A hard crash, another, and dense smoke obscured the target from the crews. The twelve 3-inch rifles were quickly rolled back into position, swabbed, and reloaded. The two Regular batteries began a steady hammering at the enemy's columns. Then Kingsbury's D, 5th U.S. unlimbered alongside Weed, and the weight of a third battery tilted the scale even further.

D. H. Hill had more open ground than his namesake on his right, but advancing his artillery was still another matter. There was only one road down from Old Cold Harbor, and the Union's rifled guns could hammer it for virtually the length of its course. But D. H. Hill tried. Capt. John Pelham of the Stuart Horse Artillery had run up a Blakely and a Napoleon and opened on the Yankee batteries. The Blakely was disabled after the first discharge, but since the Napoleon was still working, it might be used as a base of fire.

One of D. H. Hill's batteries needled its way into position on the west side of a road leading toward the Federal line. The Federal fire splashed about the Gray battery. Case and shell blew to all sides, in front, and overhead. As was so often the case in this war, the brunt of the casualties was taken by the horses. Twenty-eight of the enemy's animals were killed or disabled. Ten crew members were nursing wounds and three others were dead. Hill pulled the battery out, splintered evidence of the superiority of the Federal artillery — 'always the most effective arm of his [Federal] service,' Hill later remarked.

If the Union lines were to be broken, only Gray infantry could do it, with little help from the few Rebel batteries able to find firing positions. It was close to 4 o'clock when D. H. Hill turned his men loose. The Confederate lines splashed,

thrashed, and stumbled through the tangled swamp. Yankee
muskets sought to stay the advance, and booms of the guns
on the line echoed over the racket in the ravine. The Gray
wave reached the southern edge of the swamp and some
regiments fought their way up through the underbrush onto
cleared ground. In front was an open plain some 400 yards
deep. On the far side a low, wispy cloud of smoke marked
the new Federal line. There were cannon there too — in
great number; the deep reverberations of their explosions
were quite distinguishable to the oncoming Confederates.

At that moment, though, those guns were not as annoying
as a battery on the Confederate left flank. D. H. Hill made a
quick decision. That battery had to be taken or driven off;
it could enfilade Hill's entire line as it crossed the plain.
Five regiments were sent in a pincers to trap those troublesome guns. Four of the regiments ran afoul in the woods. The
fifth, the 20th North Carolina, crossed open ground, taking
frightful casualties, and waded into the battery. A furious
fight milled about the guns as bayonets clashed with rammer
staffs, musket barks mixed with pistol cracks, and cries of pain
with victorious shouts. Then a surging hurrah surmounted the
clamor as a Federal infantry regiment piled into the melee and
saved the battery.[3]

In the brief ten minutes that those guns were silent the
entire Rebel line rose from the swamp. The divisions of
Jackson, D. H. Hill, Ewell, and the shattered remnants of
A. P. Hill's moved forward. The Federal line drew itself in
toward the center. The last of Porter's reserves were in action
now. Reports reaching Porter next told of massed bayonets
approaching from the west — Longstreet's men. The fate of
the V Corps and perhaps the whole Army hung fatefully on the
outnumbered muzzles of its muskets and the tubes of its
artillery. The reserve line of guns tried to take up the slack.

McCall's division was committed and so were its four
batteries. Twice, Battery G, 1st Pennsylvania, drove back
enemy assaults with waist-high blasts of double canister.

Again the Confederates struck. A Rebel color bearer and his red banner were knocked to earth eighty yards away by a canister round from the right section. The Southern line discharged a volley. Lead slugs splattered about the position, bowling over crewmen and splintering the wood on the carriages.

The battery commander, Capt. Kerns, tried to move his guns back. Two of his pieces were hopelessly immobilized, every horse in their teams a casualty. Eighteen of his crewmen were disabled. Kerns ran to the center section, reduced to a handful of men, and took personal command. He would cover the retirement of the other two still-mobile pieces with this section, and then trust to luck to move it out. Feverishly, Kerns loaded the two guns. The enemy was coming forward at a run; Kerns held his fire. The advancing Gray swarm was within a hundred yards. Kerns jerked the lanyard of one piece, and the roar of the second rocked the air an instant later. Struggling hands latched the lunettes to the limbers and the two guns galloped rearward, Kerns bleeding profusely from a nasty bullet wound in his calf. Dense smoke covered his vacated position, but a loud cheer went up moments after, indicating that the Rebels had reached the spot and had taken the two abandoned guns.

A battery of the same regiment, Captain Easton's, was posted on a hill to the left of what was probably the Adams house, facing the dense woods 700–800 yards away. The Rebel attack found this unit unsupported by infantry as the dusty Gray ranks opened fire from the front and left flank. The battery's four Napoleons thundered back with shell and spherical case. The Southerners tried to close with the battery. For nearly thirty minutes it was rifle bullet against cannon. Then with a wild yell the Southerners came running. Easton's men rammed in two of those gray tin containers which made up the double canister charge and stepped back. 'Fire!' the cry rang out. The attackers, gaps hewn in their ranks, were temporarily stopped.

Egged on by the shouts of Easton, who was loudly proclaiming that the Rebs would have his battery only over his dead body, the crews reloaded without swabbing. The Confederates were not long in verifying Easton's boast, as they let fly another volley which wreaked havoc about the guns. Easton dropped dead instantly; two of the lieutenants felt the sickening splat of Minié balls biting into their flesh, and six of the enlisted men fell to the earth. In an instant the tips of the attacking bayonets were probing over the gun tubes. The four guns fell silent.

The other two batteries of McCall's division were likewise hotly engaged. DeHart's C, 5th U.S. hung on grimly against fierce infantry assaults, finally losing its commander and three of its Napoleons. Cooper's Battery B alone escaped with all its guns. Martin's battery, in the center of the V Corps line, saw the Federal infantry ahead begin to melt toward the rear as the pressure increased. The hedge of Southern muskets was 150 yards distant when Martin bellowed the command to fire. Double canister from the six Napoleons slammed into the oncoming ranks. Six times the battery fired. The attackers paused to realign their battered ranks. Martin seized the opportunity to flee his precarious and unsupported position, leaving only three horseless caissons as spoils of war to the enemy.

On the left end of the Yankee line the scene was much the same. Swarms of bayonet-wielding Rebels were yelling themselves hoarse as they pressed the thin line of Morell's division. Two sections of Weeden's Rhode Island battery, their trails dug in the dirt behind Griffin's brigade, bellowed and boomed. The first line of Yankee infantry began to fall back onto the second. Another salvo swished from the four guns. But the Rebs kept coming. Weeden sent his sections back a hundred yards, in line with some other Federal batteries barely distinguishable through the dirty haze. The Rhode Islanders opened fire again.

Somewhere to the left of Weeden's position was Battery E,

Massachusetts Light Artillery. This unit had little to do during the early part of that afternoon. One gun had been ordered forward from the battery location in a peach orchard behind Morell's lines in the woods. This gun had barked loudly at Pickett's diversionary raid earlier in the day. When the attempt ended, the gun retired to battery.

When the call came from Butterfield's and Martindale's brigades that Longstreet's men were coming forward in heavy force in what appeared to be a major Rebel effort, Battery E's bugler pierced the air with his calls. Drivers dug in spurs, harness and traces tightened, and the left and center sections trotted toward the line of battle. From their location just behind the line of battle the artillerymen could dimly discern through the smoke and foliage parts of a Rebel line. The four 3-inch rifles cut loose. At the first blast, small saplings in front were blown or cut down by the swath from the tubes, and dense smoke and dust saturated the sultry air. From the south bank of the Chickahominy two heavy 20-pounder Parrott batteries fired at long range at the advancing Southerners' right flank.

The badly thinned Federal infantry line was wavering. The third section of Battery E under Lt. Hyde was sent rolling forward to the edge of the woods. The roar of battle seemed to reach the length of the corps line. The men of Battery E could hear the distinctive detonation of artillery pieces at work from the area where Weeden and Martin were supposed to be. But so dense was the acrid cloud of smoke and dust that the men of one section could not see their friends in the adjoining one. Then the volume of artillery fire dropped noticeably on Martindale's front as charging Rebels, their battle blood fully aroused, tore into a section of Weeden's battery and reduced it to shambles.

Lt. Phillips, commanding Battery E's center section, felt his horse wince as a slug imbedded in the animal's flank. A sergeant's horse dropped like a plummet — its brain neatly holed by a Minié ball. The deadly buzzing of searching Rebel bullets increased. Then out of the woods came dirtied blue figures, some carrying muskets, others empty-handed. In frightened reckless disorder the men from Morell's division began to hurry to the rear. Phillips tried to rally some in front of his tubes, but they would not obey. Wild-eyed, the stunned men brushed their way past Phillips's outstretched arms, ignored his pleas and commands, and ran down the slope to the rear.

The wild Rebel yell rose piercingly above the din of battle. Their advancing line was now 200 yards from Phillips's section. The lieutenant ordered canister. The sharp bark of the two rifles rang out. Phillips ordered his pieces limbered back to an open field. Unlimbering again the section banged away at a flag-waving enemy regiment 300 yards away. But rifled guns firing canister were not the potent force of similarly loaded Napoleons, and the Southerners kept coming. Reluctantly Phillips continued his retreat.

Lt. Scott, commanding the left section, had run his pieces in on the left of Phillips. His men joined in the furious process of loading, swabbing, and firing. Through the stifling screen of smoke came grimy-faced Federals from Morell's infantry, struggling to the rear. 'What's the trouble below?' called Scott. 'Trouble enough,' snarled one hatless corporal. 'The Rebels are crossing the ditch on our right!' Scott received the order to fall back; Phillips was to lead. Anxious men moved their guns hurriedly. Down the slope the two sections galloped, headed for the spot where they had left the third or right section.

Phillips, leading the column, approached the stray section. The men watched in anticipation for his arm to go up in the signal to halt. But the lieutenant veered off from the unlimbered section and passed it by a hundred or so yards. The mystery quickly cleared. Phillips had spotted strange uniforms about those guns. Another look convinced him that the section was in the hands of Rebels. Confusion and Confederate exuberance let Phillips and Scott go by, temporarily unnoticed.

Phillips and the head of the little column passed around the right side of a small foothill. Scott, riding at the head of his section, turned in his saddle to make sure that his two pieces were closed up behind him. To his utter astonishment only one piece was following — the other under Sgt. Spear was just disappearing around the other side of the hill. Scott shouted for a sergeant to take over and he galloped after his erring gun. Reaching the far side of the hill Scott found a small hollow, and there in a ditch was his missing gun. A worse predicament could scarcely be conceived; the stalled gun was in full range and view of the Rebs who were busily engaged in swinging the tubes of Hyde's captured section about. Atop the rise, on their other flank was the last line of Federal guns, flinging their loads dangerously low overhead.

The men struggled to get the gun out; horses lunged and heaved. The piece refused to budge. Scott shot a glance toward the Rebels; they could blow this crew sky high. But they made no move to fire. Finally a concerted heave by man and horse freed the wheels. There was no stopping the dismounted men from running after the rolling carriages and leaping on. Up the slope toward the safety of that artillery line they went. There the gun was unlimbered and the little 3-inch rifle sassily mocked the enemy who, for some reason, had let it escape. The job was now to find the rest of the battery. Scott left the firing gun under its sergeant and rode off to find Phillips. Some distance to the rear he found him and Lt. Hyde. Both officers had sorry tales to tell.

Hyde said that the enemy had slipped down through the peach orchard under cover of the smoke. The crews discovered their approach in time to fire one round of canister. There was not time to reload. Muskets barked sharply. Corp. Milliken was shot clean through the head and Pvt. Gustine's jacket turned a soggy red on its left side. Hyde yelled for the survivors to grab the rammer staffs and fall back. He and most of his men got away, only five falling into Southern hands — three of these badly wounded.

Phillips's section, with Scott's other gun tagging along, had passed close to a small woods thought to have been held by Federal infantry. A blast of fire and the Rebel yell indicated otherwise. Phillips's horse went down; so did two team horses of the lead piece. The Southerners rushed the section. Phillips, a handful of his men, and Scott's gun under the sergeant got away.

Battery E had been thoroughly battered, losing four of its guns, thirty horses, but fortunately only eight men. The grimy-faced corporal's prediction to Lt. Scott came true.

Morell's line had snapped. Smoke and noise were everywhere. Confederates jauntily climbed over the crude barricades and breastworks vacated by their fleeing foe. The Yankee left was being ripped apart, their infantry was retreating, and much of their artillery was in the hands of the victorious Southerners.

Daylight was running out, which meant that Lee's force would have to move fast if they were to complete their rout of the V Corps. On again came the realigned and adjusted Confederate regiments. Atop a low hill near the left of Porter's line a battery from Hunt's Reserve had been sitting quietly. The men of the unit, Lt. Robertson's B/L, 2nd U.S. Artillery, suddenly caught sight of running figures in scattered groups fleeing down a far slope. The men were wearing blue. Robertson's men readied their pieces. The Federals reached the bottom of the slope; out of the distant haze where moments before these figures had appeared another body of men came into sight, also running but in a long wavering line.

A gunner pointed to the oncoming line of Longstreet's infantry. Robertson made a hurried check; he could fire over the heads of his friends now in the low ground to front. There might be a premature burst, not an uncommon event with the time fuzes of those days, but that was a chance everyone would have to take. He dropped his right hand and six 3-inch rifles coughed shell, smoke, and orange flame.

The fleeing Federals poured up the slope and between the pieces of the battery. Robertson pleaded with them to stand and fight. But his words were useless.

That ominous Gray hedge kept coming. Robertson bellowed for canister, and the crews switched loads. The guns shot furiously. The enemy ran for some nearby woods. From this cover his riflemen sniped at the gun crews. The battery's horses, their ponderous frames making ideal targets, caught the fury of the Rebel fire. Robertson looked about for some Union infantry; there was none to be seen. Under these conditions there was only one thing to do — fall back to the next hill. And this he did, though not without losing two guns whose teams were dead.

The two remaining sections of Weeden's Rhode Island battery had opened when the first line had retired. They were only able to fire a few rounds before it was obvious they, too, should fall back, for the enemy was turning their left flank. The guns had fallen back a hundred yards, unlimbered again, and opened fire. Foul-smelling smoke was everywhere, blinding and stifling. But through the sulphurous haze the artillerymen saw what appeared to be Gray lines again working toward their left flank. Visibility, an absolute prerequisite for artillery fire in those days of direct fire, was only sporadic. Officers found it difficult to fire at positive enemy targets in that eye-smarting haze. The batteries began to retire to a second rise of ground, closer to the bridges over the Chickahominy. Porter had ordered a line of batteries established to the rear of the Union center and left, ready for an emergency.

Weeden's sections began retiring in good order. Suddenly, a thundering moving dust cloud bore down on Weeden's men from behind. With a roar five troops of the 5th U.S. Cavalry charged through the battery position toward the oncoming regiments of Longstreet's command.[4] The cavalry attack was promptly shot apart and scattered, and wild-eyed, frothing horses, with bits in their teeth, some with riders, others without, wheeled back through the battery position. For a moment Weeden's men were thrown into confusion as his team horses sensed the panic and fought their drivers. The artillerymen made the best of the bad moment and took their teams to the rear at a fast trot, saving all but one mired piece.

It was about this time, too, that Capt. H. V. DeHart's Regulars, the extreme right flank battery of McCall's division, ran into trouble. When the guns first rolled into battery the mass of fleeing Federal infantry had prevented DeHart from opening fire. At last he got a clear field and began flinging out first case then canister, keeping the enemy at a distance. But by now the smoke was so thick that the gunners lost sight of their targets and were simply firing blind. Taking advantage of this smoke cover, some Rebels slipped into a gap on DeHart's left, and with a whooping rush quickly overran the three left-most guns and mortally wounded De-Hart. The three remaining pieces somehow escaped and retreated three-quarters of a mile before turning about and going into action again.

The picture was indeed a bleak one for the Federals on the field. It was obvious to everyone that the enemy had broken through on the left. Porter had no more reserves, though help had been asked for. At last, late in the day, loud cheering in the rear of the V Corps position told of reinforcements arriving. The men of the Irish Brigade, their green flag snapping, had crossed the river and were filing into line. Other brigades were coming in their wake.

A New Jersey battery, Hexamer's, crossed the river with elements of Taylor's brigade, and reached an open field about 200 yards from a woods where a severe infantry fight was being waged. The guns waited. The French Prince de Joinville, an aide of McClellan serving that day with Porter, rode up to Hexamer and ordered him to move forward fifty yards to the edge of the field and to break up the Rebel line some 1400 yards away. The six guns banged away with case. The great noise was good for the morale of the men on its side, but, although it sometimes hit a few men, case was not really very effective.

Another battery opened up to the left of the New Jerseymen. Somewhere to the front of the two batteries another Rebel column was supposed to be forming for a charge. The two units fired case and canister furiously for fifteen minutes before they got the cease fire. There was a momentary silence on the field. It was too smoky to see over much of the area. Suddenly a loud crash of an infantry volley shook the stillness. Rebels were on the left flank. A wild yell went up; running figures emerged from the smoke. A Confederate raised his musket over his head and brought it down full force on the skull of one of the gunners at the adjoining battery. In an instant the position was full of milling men, nearly all in other than blue dress.

Hexamer appeared to be next on their list. He moved fast. With no friendly infantry in sight to support him, Hexamer ordered his limbers up. Just in time the command was given; the Gray host was now turning its attention toward the New Jersey battery. A chance-fired volley bowled over a driver and two horses. Another volley knocked down three horses pulling the caissons. Another horse fell, and four men were hit before the battery got out of range. But even the New Jerseymen had left a gun behind for the usual reason — no horses.

It was now almost dark. Rebel commanders, listening carefully to the growing chorus of cheers from the Federal rear, restrained their panting men. Many of them had believed that the whole of McClellan's Army was directly in front of them, but now those cheers could mean only one thing — Yankee reinforcements coming on the field; and with the infantry, no doubt more cannon. A few of the newly arrived batteries got into position to throw a few rounds, but darkness and Confederate caution ended the fighting for the day.

At the far right of Porter's line, the breaking of Morell's

line had become apparent so the Blue infantry of Sykes and McCall shifted position rearward. The three Yankee batteries of Tidball, Weed, and Kingsbury kept firing and shifting about. These Regular batteries were particularly annoying to the Rebels in the eastern quarter, as any sign of movement by the Southern columns that smacked of an advance brought forth the full fury of their eighteen guns. Stonewall Jackson found them obnoxious and asked for more artillery. When the break in the left end of the line came, the batteries changed front to the west for a time. But three rifled batteries and a handful of infantry could scarcely hold off the might of three Confederate divisions. When the enemy reached the open ground in front of the guns and began to hit them with rifle fire, the batteries withdrew to the new line now forming in the smoky twilight.

The battle of Gaines Mill was ended.

VI

A SWAMP AND A FARM

White Oak Swamp and Frayser's Farm (Glendale)

FITZ JOHN PORTER had fought his corps so well at Gaines Mill that the Confederates believed they had faced the bulk of the Yankee Army. A good part of the Army of the Potomac was still fresh and uncommitted at the end of the battle. Even so, when night fell McClellan made his decision to fall back to the James River. For the next four days it would be the Army of the Potomac which would fight for its very existence; Robert E. Lee, still new to Confederate high command, struggled to mold a Cannae for the Yankee Army.

The Union corps began their retreat during the night of June 27th. All night the narrow dirt roads were jammed with marching men, supply wagons, artillery batteries, and ambulance trains. The sky took on a reddish glow as the Federals began to destroy whatever they could not carry with them. Deafening explosions jarred the ground underfoot, signifying the destruction of carloads of ammunition. All through the night the holocaust continued. By morning the leading elements of the Yankee Army were on their way toward the bridges over White Oak Swamp.

Elements of Sumner's and Heintzelman's corps were in a nasty scrap on the morning of June 29th at Allen's Farm, south of the Chickahominy near the old Fair Oaks battlefield. Battery B, 1st New York Light Artillery, under Capt. Rufus Pettit, and Lt. George Washington Hazzard's Regular

battery helped drive off Rebel Gen. Magruder's assaults, but
not before Hazzard's caissons had to be called back from
Savage Station to replenish empty limbers.

The Union Army had to fight rearguard actions continually as the Confederate command strove to cut off,
trap, and destroy their elements. Late in the morning of
the 29th a determined group of Southerners banged into
Franklin's corps at Savage Station, and soon some of Sumner's
men were also in the skirmish. Six Yankee batteries opened
fire before the attacks were stemmed. Meanwhile, Porter's
and Keyes's corps, the Reserve Artillery, and the immense
5000-vehicle wagon train were rumbling safely southward
over White Oak Swamp Bridge.

The morning of June 30th found the Federal Army on
the south side of the morass, battered but still intact. In a
cleared tract on the south edge of the swamp, Franklin's
corps had paused to rest; the batteries of one of the divisions
covered the bridge site. The roads and fields leading away
from the south bank were speckled with wagons, troops,
and ambulances. As the sun climbed, the Federals began to
take to the road again.

It was now about noon. With a thundering roar part of the
far height north of the swamp erupted in grayish smoke.
Seconds later the air and earth about the relaxing men of
Franklin's division seemed to explode. The Confederates had
found an advantageous rise of ground, partly screened from
enemy view by heavy timber. In a draw behind the rise they
had assembled twenty-eight of Stonewall Jackson's cannon,
loaded them, and with a sudden rush ran them forward to
the crest and opened fire.

The Federals were stunned by the suddenness and fierce accuracy of the fire. Panic hit some units and they bolted for the
cover of woods on the south edge of their field. Capt. Romeyn
Ayres, chief-of-artillery of one of Franklin's divisions, moved his
own and Mott's 3rd New York Independent Battery into position to return fire. But the Confederate artillerists had a perfect

position, and they gave the Yankee batteries, caught by surprise in an open field, an immediate pounding. Mott's battery was instantly thrown into confusion and became useless; Ayres ordered it from the field. Another division battery, Wheeler's, was so undermanned that it could field but two pieces; Ayres sent it to the edge of the woods in the rear of the field.[1] The remaining battery, Cowan's, in a disadvantageous position, was given the same order.[2] Ayres tried to get his own battery into action. All told, it was a very uneven fight — six guns against twenty-eight. The Yankee gunners shot only four rounds before they were ordered to withdraw across the field. Confederate riflemen, firing from the cover of woods just across the swamp, accentuated the urgency of the order. Back the battery went though a rapidly emptying dust-clouded field.

Ayres looked back at the field once more. Scarcely visible through the screen of parching dust stood a deserted gun, complete with limber and five horses. Mott had been in that position, but his outfit had left the scene in a state of great disorder. Ayres collared a stray corporal from Mott's battery as he was riding past and ordered him to hitch up the gun team and drive the gun off the field. One of Mott's lieutenants rode by; he, too, was commanded to assist in saving the piece. Thinking the job would now be done, Ayres turned toward his own unit. Later that afternoon he discovered Mott's gun still in the field, unmoved.[3]

Capt. Ayres wheeled his battery about at the edge of the woods and unlimbered. Dust was everywhere; exploding shells, the racket of equipment and teams bouncing across the plain, and the loud yells of officers and noncoms made it seem as if war had never known any order or discipline. The battery prepared to open fire. Then, through the dirt clouds Ayres's gunners watched another Federal battery unlimber directly ahead of them — Lt. Hazzard's battery A & C, 4th U.S. Ayres slipped his guns to the right and took up the fight again.

The men of Hazzard's battery, one of several such Regular units organized by combining the personnel of two under-strength batteries of a regiment, had had a narrow escape earlier that morning. In the evening following their fight about Allen's Farm and Savage Station the tired artillery-men had slept in a woods on the ground where they had fought — the Federal lines having held fast against Magruder's attacks. A heavy storm pelted the exhausted Federals for most of the night, but fatigue was a narcotic for these men. Dawn came quiet and clear. Then sleeping batterymen were awakened by the noise of drums and bugles — Rebel music, and not too distant! Hazzard jumped to his feet; a hurried scanning of the surrounding area revealed that the battery was apparently the sole occupant of the previous day's battle-field.

The battery commander quickly roused his men. With every effort to maintain quiet the battery was hurriedly limbered. The caissons went out first, followed by two gun sections. Hazzard with two loaded Napoleons covered the rear. To keep noise at a minimum and to allay suspicion they walked for nearly a mile. Then, the road being in good shape despite the night's rain, the commander gave the order to trot.

Sometime between 9 and 10 a.m. the battery reached the site of the bridge over White Oak Swamp. But Hazzard found the wooden structure burned by the retreating Federal Army, now south of that swamp. The only thing to do was to try to cross at some shallow point. Hazzard rode down close to the ruined bridge, walked his horse into the swamp, and finding the bottom fairly solid, turned, and ordered his command forward. Crowds of amazed Bluecoats gathered on the crest overlooking the crossing, watched as the battery heaved and lunged across, and then trotted toward the back edge of a bordering field. They were resting at the rear of the field when Jackson's guns let go.

Hazzard's men were engulfed in a storm of artillery missiles. The enemy fire was rapid, accurate, and varied: Armstrong rifled projectiles, 6-pounder rifled bolts, 6-pounder balls, and pieces of railroad iron six to twelve inches long were claimed to have been seen.[4] Lt. Hazzard calmly ordered his men to prepare for action. The men mounted and the column started forward. A shell exploded overhead; a sergeant doubled up and grabbed his leg, and the battery guidon flopped to earth, its staff cut in half. A Federal general pointed out a position to Hazzard and ordered him there.

The Federal gunners could see no target. To their front only a dense pall of smoke hanging over a distant ridge indicated the apparent enemy gun positions. The smoke and dust grew thicker, until both sides were firing blind. The torrent of Rebel rounds continued, and Hazzard, indifferent to the fire, walked from piece to piece. At one position three horses and two wounded drivers of an overturned limber were entangled in traces. Hazzard coolly cut them free. He carried ammunition to one gun whose crew was short, and with another lieutenant took turns at the duties of the number one of the piece.

The battery had been in action almost thirty minutes when Hazzard walked over to a limber to watch the cutting of fuzes for readied shells. With a flash and a bang an enemy round exploded and Hazzard collapsed on the ground, his leg cut in half. Lt. King took command as the wounded officer was lifted to a stretcher; Hazzard, who had been offered a colonelcy in the Indiana Volunteers but had chosen to fight as an artillery lieutenant, died of his wound some months later.

No part of the battery position was spared that converging fire. The unit was overstrength with eight guns manned by about 175 men, so it presented a good-sized target. King kept the men pouring out return fire at the Confederate batteries and at the ruined bridge site, to prevent any attempts to ford there. The lieutenant rode from gun to gun urging the gunners to keep up the fire. A clanking caught his ear. Turning, King was astounded to see one decimated crew led by a noncom, pulling their weapon out of the fight. With a shout the lieutenant jammed his spurs to his horse and quickly caught up with the crew, swore at them, and sent the gun back into action. So excellent was King's performance that day that he was awarded the Congressional Medal of Honor.

Lt. King hurriedly saluted as Gen. Meagher, famed leader of the Irish Brigade, rode up to watch the battery at work. Seeing the crew of one piece having difficulty rolling it forward after recoil, the general dismounted and put his weight to the wheel. But now the battery's ammunition was running low. Meagher, so informed, volunteered to advise King's division commander.

Capt. Rufus Pettit's battery was ordered to relieve the Regulars under King. As the New Yorkers rode on the field Hazzard's old battery was pulling back; King stopped and carefully pointed out to Pettit the supposed location of every enemy target. Armed with this intelligence Pettit's six 10-pounder Parrott rifles opened fire. Pettit drew his pipe from his pocket as he watched his gunners adjust their pieces. After filling his pipe the captain stooped to pick up an ember from a nearby fire; a sudden swishing noise, a dull thud, a swirl of dust, and a solid shot from the far ridge bounced harmlessly between Pettit's legs. The captain vowed prompt repayment.

The guns had opened at 1200 yards. The range was too short; Pettit raised it 300. Still short; gunners turned their elevating screws till they estimated 1800 yards. Another salvo — a sheet of orange flame on the far ridge, a tremendous boom, and what had apparently been an enemy caisson or limber took a direct hit. Having found the range, the battery poured in round after round.

It was almost entirely an artillery fight at White Oak Swamp. The Federal infantry lay in long parallel lines behind the batteries or waited in the woods and fields to the rear. Rebel infantry never got within musket range. The Confederates sent a cavalry regiment across the boggy bottom to feel out the opposition, but Yankee sharpshooters hidden in the woods up front hurled them back. A Rebel battery tried unsuccessfully to drive off these riflemen.

Toward sundown the Confederates slackened their rate and fired only at intervals. Pettit adopted the tactic of holding fire until the enemy would fling a round, then firing his whole battery in return. Now the New Yorkers' ammunition supply began to dwindle, as they had expended nearly 1600 rounds.

Late in the afternoon another Regular battery came into action — Battery I, 5th U.S., under Capt. Stephen Weed. Another New York unit, the 4th Independent Battery, also joined the fray — much to Weed's disgust, as he contended that they killed more Federals than enemy, a charge vigorously denied by the New Yorkers.

Like a ponderous anaconda, the slowly moving Army of the Potomac stretched across half the peninsula, its tail at the edge of White Oak Swamp, its head on the rising ground of Malvern Hill overlooking the James River. McClellan or his commanders had done a masterful job in shifting much of the Army and its supplies across his own rear. Now south of the great swamp, the Army slithered slowly southward over two narrow roads.

Lee hoped to catch his adversary in this vulnerable position, with Jackson pushing down from the north on McClellan's rear, Huger hitting from the northwest, and A. P. Hill and Longstreet coming in from the west, thus cutting the strung-out Yankee Army in half. But Jackson had failed at White Oak Swamp. His efforts late in the afternoon of June 30th dwindled to rebuilding the bridge over the swamp, while the distant sound of gunfire to the southwest swelled. Likewise, Huger's attack failed to get under way. Lee then hurled Longstreet and A. P. Hill forward on a desperate chance that they could break the Yankee column. The collision occurred near a country crossroad known as Glendale on the gently rolling acres about Frayser's Farm.

McClellan had wisely covered his western flank. He placed

McCall's division of Pennsylvanians to protect the important road junction at Glendale. These troops took up position astride the Long Bridge or New Market Road just west of its junction with the Quaker or Willis Church Road leading south to Malvern Hill. Northeast of McCall, on the Charles City Road, was Kearny's division, and on his right were Slocum's men.

McCall put his batteries in front of his infantry line, as the country was dotted with clearings in his immediate front. Randol's six Napoleons of E, 1st U.S., temporarily attached to McCall from Hunt's Reserve, the general put just north of the New Market Road. Just south of the road were his own Pennsylvania batteries commanded by Cooper and Amsden, and on the division's left were Knieriem's and Diederich's batteries of 20-pounder Parrotts from the Artillery Reserve. The 20-pounder guns faced an open field some 600 yards square. These latter two units were made up of first and second generation New York Germans and were known, as were all German units in the Blue armies, as 'Dutchmen.'

Close to the right of Lt. Alanson Randol's Napoleons was the Regular Battery G, 2nd U.S., of Capt. James Thompson. This unit, one of Kearny's batteries, covered the interval between McCall and Kearny. Thompson's men lowered a fence 150 yards in front of their position and cleared several small patches of brush and scrub growth from the probable field of fire. Gen. Kearny rode up to check the position of this battery. It seemed to him that Thompson's tubes were not pointed to give maximum cover to his division; he ordered Thompson to shift his battery to the right till its line lay nearly in the rear of and almost perpendicular to Randol. The captain obeyed. The racket of the fight up at White Oak Swamp was plainly audible to the Federals guarding the Army's flank. Tired men in blue sat on the ground and chewed hardtack and wondered how it was going to the north of them.

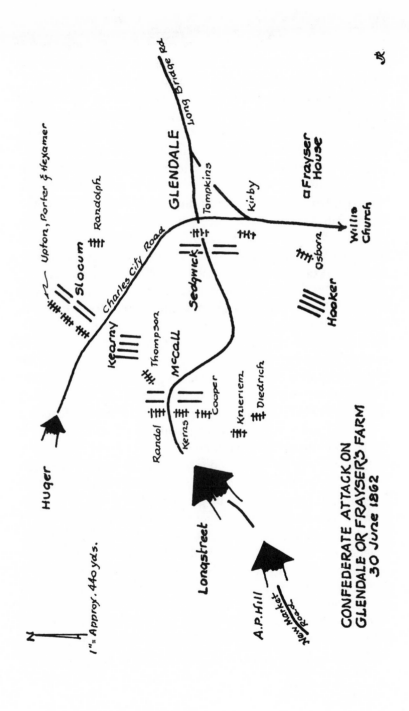

N

1" = Approx. 440 yds.

Huger

Upton, Porter & Hexamer

Slocum

Randolph

Charles City Road

GLENDALE

Long Bridge Rd

Kearny

Thompson

Tompkins

Kirby

Frayser House

Randol

McCall

Sedgwick

Osborn

Willis Church

Kerns

Cooper

Knieriem

Diedrich

Hooker

Longstreet

A.P. Hill

New Market Road

CONFEDERATE ATTACK ON
GLENDALE OR FRAYSER'S FARM
30 June 1862

About 2 o'clock their thoughts were abruptly interrupted.
Kearny had just departed when a loud noise broke out. Incoming artillery fire and the familiar thump-thump of musketry indicated something was happening along the Charles
City Road. A few minutes later there was another burst of
firing along New Market Road. If an attack came down New
Market Road Thompson saw it would catch him in flank and
rear; he promptly deployed his pieces forward in echelon on
a line nearly parallel to Randol's again — roughly where he
had been before Kearny moved him. In this position he could
more readily fire in either direction.

This sudden outburst of gunfire on the New Market Road
was occasioned by the firing of several of Longstreet's batteries. That officer had heard the blast of a cannon up near the
Charles City Road and had erroneously believed this was
Huger's signal that he was attacking. Longstreet had run
some of his own guns forward to acknowledge it with a few
rounds. Several of the Yankee batteries, interpreting these
enemy rounds as precursors of an immediate Confederate
assault, began a furious cannonading of the distant woods.
Unknown to the Northern gunners some of their rounds
narrowly missed the most lucrative target in the Confederacy
— a small gathering of horsemen made up of Jefferson Davis,
James Longstreet, A. P. Hill, and Robert E. Lee.

Lee, hoping for some coordination of attacks, delayed
loosing Longstreet until nearly 5 o'clock. Then seeing that
coordination was impossible, he gave the order to attack.
Longstreet's brigades spread their lines across the New Market
Road. With a yell, they swept forward across fields, through
patches of woods, down a small ravine, and then up onto
the clearing-dotted plateau where the Yankee lines were.

On the south edge of the road a Rebel brigade made such
rapid progress that it moved far ahead of its associates. A
regiment of Federals deployed in line of skirmishers bolted
rearward. The two German batteries opened fire. More
Federal infantry in a barricaded house and in log breastworks

nearby fled. The Germans manning the two 20-pounder batteries turned and ran to the rear. Powder-smeared Alabama troops streamed into the position. The yelling attackers kept coming forward. When Yankee infantry in the woods behind the lost batteries counter-attacked, though, the Rebel brigade retreated across the field to a copse bordering the road. Cooper's battery interrupted its argument with some Rebel guns to join Amsden's in flinging iron into the Rebels retreating obliquely across their front.

More Confederates advanced on the south side of the road, obviously intent on taking the two Pennsylvania batteries. Randol could now bring his tubes to bear as the action came close to his left flank. The lieutenant swung his battery front ninety degrees to the left, and his first salvo caught the Gray ranks in flank. The attackers were shaken, but the fire of the Yankee artillery did not halt them. A Confederate regiment delivered a vicious volley which cut down many of the horses about the position. In the face of the follow-up charge by the 9th and 10th Alabama regiments, the Yankee gunners south of the road fled to the woods in rear.

On the north side of the New Market Road, Randol's tubes had been firing south and southwest across the road. Then, with the distinctive Rebel yell, enemy infantry appeared across the open field on the battery's right flank. Randol ordered a change front to the rear on his left piece; this brought his guns back to their original position facing west. The range was 300 yards; Randol yelled for canister. At a hundred yards the Gray line broke, then quickly rallied.

Randol's guns, now aided by the fire of Thompson's Napoleons, dug into the enemy attackers. One of Randol's gunners, watching the oncoming Rebels, grimly muttered, 'I ain't goin' to git from no such ragged fellars as they be.' [5] At fifty yards the charging line halted. The 4th Pennsylvania Infantry, Randol's support which was lying down between his line of limbers and that of the caissons, rose up and eagerly rushed the supposedly demoralized Rebel line. But the Southerners, the 11th Alabama Regiment, received the charge of the 4th and then shot them to shreds. Now with a wild yell the Alabamians plunged for Randol's guns.

The battery commander stood, arm raised, ready to fire. But the fleeing remnants of his support came straight back toward the gun positions. Randol frantically yelled and waved his arms to try to get the fleeing Federals to retire by the battery's flanks. Wild-eyed, and many without weapons, the Blue infantrymen quickly fled through the battery position. With the enemy at thirty yards Randol's gunners finally had a clear field to fire. But it was too late.

About fifty musket-wielding Rebel infantrymen rushed into Randol's position. The Federal Regulars fought grimly with handspike and rammer staff to hold the battery's ground. The artillerymen, armed with more courage than weapons, had to give ground, and fell back to the woods. Lt. Randol rounded up a few companies of frightened infantry, rallied his own survivors, who had now picked up muskets of the fallen, and charged back into his position. Then followed a vicious hand-to-hand fight. Men fired muskets in each other's faces; officers discharged pistols into opponents' chests with one hand and with the other hand used a sword. Clubbed muskets banged against bayonets and skulls. Two Federal officers fell before a Rebel captain's sword, and the captain in turn collapsed from three bayonet wounds and a bullet-pierced leg. The Alabama troops gave ground and took shelter in a strip of woods edging the road.

A short distance north of Randol's position Thompson's six Napoleons were hard pressed too. The battery had loaded with spherical case as the Gray lines came into sight 400 yards away. As had happened in front of Randol, the Rebels came forward, ducking under the artillery barrage and pausing to fire. The guns switched to canister and this together with the supporting infantry fire began to have an effect on the attackers. At the site of the demolished fence line the Federal fire halted them.

The repulse was brief, as the Southerners closed their gaps and charged the battery again. Thompson's Napoleons coughed canister, then double canister. On their left the enemy stormed into Randol's position. The crews fired without sponging — a dangerous stunt and done only in dire emergency. A spark in the chamber, a burning piece of cloth from the powder bag of a discharged round, could easily ignite a new charge as it was being rammed home.

A scythe-like volley from the supporting 63rd Pennsylvania Regiment stopped the Rebels cold and forced them to withdraw their assault line to the fence rails again. With the battery's supply of canister nearly exhausted, some guns began loading with spherical case set to burst at a half-second. The enemy ranks fell away to the woods to the right.

McCall's thin line — his division strength was down to 6000 following its severe fighting at Mechanicsville and Gaines Mill — had had two holes punched in it, but the Confederates had not yet been able to exploit them. Union commanders strove to shore up the creaky defenses in that quarter.

North of McCall's twice-punctured lines the divisions of Kearny and Slocum were only sporadically engaged. Slocum's men had spotted prying Rebels about 11 a.m. that morning. There was a burst of firing as the three division batteries commenced shelling a narrow belt of timber across their front. Shortly after, the enemy was seen sliding to the south, toward Kearny's and McCall's front. Slocum pushed a brigade forward in an attempt to flank the enemy. A heavy line of Southerners met the fleeing Federals and hurled them back. Upton's battery had to be hurriedly brought forward to help extricate the brigade. The rest of the day Slocum's front reverberated to the booming of cannon fire as Hexamer's, Upton's, and Porter's batteries dueled at long range. Later in the day DeRussy's Regular battery from the Artillery Reserve and Randolph's Rhode Island battery joined in, shelling the woods to the front — largely a waste of ammunition in those days, if effectiveness is to be measured by lethal effect.

The attacking brigades of Longstreet had spent their strength, and if anything further was to be gained, A. P. Hill's men would have to do it. The order was given, and Hill's fresh brigades loaded their muskets and grimly moved forward. Their division had been nearly wrecked in the slaughter at Gaines Mill.

Cooper's battery in the clearing south of the road had not been re-manned after its loss. Confederate infantry in the woods nearby would have made it extremely difficult to attempt it. The other battery, Amsden's G, 1st Pennsylvania, had expended its ammunition and withdrawn, after three fruitless attempts by Amsden to locate his caissons which had been foolishly ordered to the rear by a Federal general. Gen. McCall personally encountered the cowering crews of the deserted German batteries and ordered them back to their guns.

It was nearly sundown when A. P. Hill's men moved into action. The Dutchmen, just returned to their positions by McCall, fled again, some on battery horses, riding blindly into and scattering Blue infantry, which was escorting prisoners to the rear. Enemy infantry laid eager hands on the big 20-pounder rifles and swung them about. But the field was now a jumbled mass of friend and foe; to fire those monsters into the woodland just to the east might wound friend as well as foe. The idea was dropped. Two Virginia regiments seized Cooper's abandoned battery again and pressed on, bent on cracking the Federal infantry line.

On the other side of the road Randol, too, became a target again. Another savage melee raged about the position. The action was critical. Gen. George Meade, who about a year later inherited command of this army, was cut down near the battery, badly wounded. An officer ran on foot to Gen. Kearny and asked for help. The general promised aid; it came, but too late. The Bluecoats were forced out and Randol's six Napoleons became a permanent Confederate prize.

Thompson's crews were again firing without sponging.

Three times the enemy was hurled back by the battery and the fire of friendly infantry. The supply of canister having been exhausted earlier, the entire battery had taken to firing spherical case set to explode soon after leaving the muzzle. Then the supply of case rounds gave out. All that remained in the chests was solid shot. Crewmen took to loading the 12-pound balls of iron into the reeking gun barrels. But the effect from the solids was negligible. Thompson gave the order to retreat. Hurriedly the guns were hooked to the limbers, and the sections began pulling out. The traces of one gun snapped. There was a frantic effort to exchange teams as the Blue gunners could see Rebel infantry moving forward again. A loud crash of a volley followed by shrieks and screams of wounded horses ended the effort to rescue the gun.

McCall's division was thoroughly beaten, and its right flank appeared to have collapsed. Kearny's division was hit so hard that it had to send to Slocum for help. Kearny had watched the fire of Thompson's guns sweep the field in front but destructive as it was, he remarked, it 'ceased to be a calculation.' From Slocum's division came a brigade of infantry and a section of 12-pounder howitzers of a Rhode Island battery under Lt. Pardon S. Jastram. As the section of guns rolled onto the darkening and sulphurous-smelling field, one of Kearny's aides urged Jastram to hurry up. When Jastram asked where he should go, the aide could not tell him. When Jastram asked for the target, the aide again said he did not know, but finally directed Jastram to 'fire toward the sun.'

It was a bad beginning for Jastram, but the ending was even worse. The lieutenant gave the order, 'Action front, spherical case, two seconds time.' The undermanned, inexperienced crews — the little section was operating with but three men per piece, the lead driver serving as number one at one of the guns — got the order confused and loaded with canister. Under these conditions, all Jastram could do was to order the tubes raised to maximum elevation so that the canister would be discharged into the air, thus preventing the deadly pellets from being thrown into some friendly unit in the smoky blackness to the front.

Then retreating Blue infantry repeated the error made at Randol's position and fled into and through Jastram's position. (This unfortunate habit later evoked a bitter denunciation from Hunt, who pleaded with the Army high command to take steps to have the practice stopped.) Jastram gave the order to limber up. The first piece cleared the field, but the wheel horse of the second was hit and collapsed across the pole. Frantic efforts to get the gun free failed, so the lieutenant ordered it spiked.

Stern, humorless Kearny viewed Jastram's conduct on the field severely and later ordered a court of inquiry. The court found the lieutenant derelict of duty on four counts but recommended no action other than its administrative reprimand.

McCall and Kearny tried to build a new line in the darkness. McCall got his directions mixed and rode into the Confederate lines. Luckily for the Federals some of their infantry which had been up at White Oak now marched into Glendale. Sedgwick's full division with Kirby's and Tompkins's batteries hurriedly went into position astride the New Market Road behind McCall's crumbling line. Burn's brigade, supported by heavy fire from Kirby and Tompkins, rushed forward and collided with the advancing but disorganized Confederates. The attacking Confederate waves held briefly, wavered, then fell back into the night. Another Confederate attempt to break the Union Army in half had been thwarted.

At one time or another some fourteen Federal batteries, about eighty pieces, were involved in fending off Confederate attacks or supposed attacks west of the Glendale area. The brunt had been taken by McCall's and Kearny's artillery; the batteries had no doubt inflicted heavy casualties with their canister but, isolated as they were, many were singled out and overrun. The guns of at least one battery, Randol's, were lost *en toto* and probably all six of Cooper's. One gun each from Thompson's and Jastram's commands had been lost, but the Federals recovered six of the eight 20-pounder Parrott rifles of Knieriem's and Diederich's batteries.[6] Nonetheless, at Glendale, Union artillery had played a major role in saving the Army.

The Confederate command had correctly concluded that McClellan's legions were tramping down the Willis Church Road toward Malvern Hill and the James River. However, they erred in believing reports of widespread confusion among the Blue columns. Late in the afternoon of June 30th a Confederate column under Gen. Holmes, moving along a road close to the river, tried to capitalize on the assumed Blue confusion. But up on that bluff were some 20,000 men of Fitz John Porter's redoubtable V Corps. And Col. Henry Jackson Hunt was there, too, with part of his Artillery Reserve. Hunt had divided his Reserve, which was in reality an artillery division, into brigades. Under his command were some fourteen light batteries — all but two of which were Regular — three batteries of 20-pounder Parrotts, one battery of 32-pounder howitzers, and the siege train of twenty-five monsters of various sizes.

When Rebel Gen. Holmes began his attack, there were already two batteries of 20-pounder Parrotts and probably five light batteries in position to cover the river road. The cloud of dust stirred up by the marching Rebel feet had alerted the Bluecoats to watch this flank carefully. Holmes ran forward a battery of six rifled pieces, which was supposed to cause further 'confusion' in the already 'disordered' Federal ranks. The Confederate infantry began to form for the fight. The Gray regiments reached an open field facing the steep slope of the western face of Malvern Hill. Holmes's men, completely inexperienced, were suddenly stunned by a deafening crash as a heavy shell exploded overhead. This was followed by a second, then a third, and finally the explosions came so fast as to be an almost uninterrupted din. Some of the Southerners panicked.

Eight heavy 20-pounder Parrott rifles boomed distinctively over the racket of the ten smaller caliber rifles of Edward's and Osborn's batteries firing from the heights. Out in the James River a distant resonant boom gave audible evidence that the Federal gunboats were getting the range, too. Martin's Napoleons down in the lowlands with Warren's Brigade brought the total to some twenty tubes playing on Holmes's command. Other batteries were at hand — Smead's and Weed's Regulars, and Bramhall's New Yorkers — if the action warranted it.

One lone enemy battery attempted to reply to this iron-flecked thunderstorm. The result was pitiful. From their advantageous position on the heights the massed Federal cannon poured a withering fire. The Blue batteries, lined along the western crest in somewhat of an arc, decimated the Gray battery. So fast and furious was the fire from the heights that the Confederate artillery commander could only guess through the dense pall of smoke that twenty-five or thirty pieces were hammering his command. Everywhere on the plain below there was chaos. Another Gray battery tried to come to the aid of the beleaguered battery, but took to the woods, became entangled in the brush, and ended by deserting two of their pieces and caissons. Holmes concluded that an attack by his 6000 men would be sheer suicide, and retired his shot-up columns out of range.

Everywhere, from White Oak Swamp, to Glendale, to Turkey Bridge, the day had been costly for the Gray legions. But undoubtedly the most critical moment for McClellan's Army and for the Union was at Glendale. The absence of Thompson's or Randol's batteries or their failure to perform at utmost efficiency could well have ended the career of the Federal Army.

The Confederacy was just reaching its military manhood

by the end of June 1862. One can but speculate about the final outcome had A. P. Hill's regiments broken through the thin Blue line at Frayser's Farm. Gen. E. P. Alexander, a much respected Confederate commander, wrote years later:

I have often thought that in his [Lee's] retrospect of the war no one day of the whole four years would seem to him more unfortunate than June 30, 1862. It was, undoubtedly, the opportunity of his life, for the Confederacy was then in its prime, with more men available than ever before or after, and at no other period would the moral or physical effect of a victory have been so great as upon this occasion.[7]

VII

IT WAS NOT WAR — IT WAS MURDER

Malvern Hill

WHILE parts of several of McClellan's corps had held Lee's
followers in check at White Oak Swamp and at Glendale, the
rest of his army had marched to the consoling shelter of the
gunboat-guarded riverside. Earlier some one in the Yankee
Army had realized the tremendous defensive position available on the heights called Malvern Hill. Here on the morning
and afternoon of June 30th Fitz John Porter had begun
deploying two of his blooded divisions of the V Corps. The
rest of the Army was to withdraw to the river under the cover
of Porter's command.

Rumbling along a dirt road, sandwiched between some of
Porter's infantry, came the remaining two guns of Hyde's
Massachusetts battery. This unit had lost four of its pieces
at Gaines Mill, and the battery commander was worrying
about the future of his little band. As they clanked southward
up the straight road, rising almost imperceptibly toward the
crest of the hill, the men could see neat, cultivated fields on
either side of them. On their right was a wheatfield, some
of the grain cut and stacked; on the other side a cornfield,
the stalks already four feet high. The keen-eyed country-
raised boys in the battery quickly spotted blackberry vines
intermixed with the corn.

A three-day steady diet of water and hard bread, the forerunner of the hardtack of World War I, had sharpened

appetites. The battery reined to a halt, and a brief rest was ordered. Scavenging cannoneers scaled the typical Virginia rail fence and descended like locusts on the fields. Keenly sensible to the needs of their horses as well, the artillerymen carried armfuls of wheat and piled them on top of the caissons. From the other field, hungry men stuffed their pockets with ears of fresh corn, pulled up the stalks for fodder, and filled their stained blue caps with sweet berries. Someone spied a cherry tree and its branches were soon fair game. Then an officer cried out: 'Mount up,' and Battery E resumed its march.

The distant rumbling of the cannon fire which raged about Glendale that afternoon was plainly audible to the weary Blue troops as they methodically prepared positions on the north and west faces of the hill. One Federal general solemnly cautioned his men that this was as far back as they could go; there was no Washington to run to, no Chickahominy to protect their retreat, only the muddy waters of the James River lay behind them.

The powerful ward of Col. Hunt, the Army's Artillery Reserve — in reality an artillery division with its fourteen light batteries, mostly Regulars, and a scattering of heavy 20- and 30-pounder units — had reached Malvern Hill by late afternoon of June 30th. Tirelessly, thoroughly, Hunt had positioned his batteries. Some of them had helped beat down that Rebel attempt to invade the Federal flank via the river road. A small grizzly man with a high-pitched voice, Hunt had already demonstrated that his knowledge and reputation as a skilled artillerist was not without raw fact. By sundown July 1st Henry Hunt and his Artillery Reserve would be the talk of both armies.

During the night of June 30th the final elements of the exhausted Federal Army plodded down the Quaker Road and up onto the elevated and cleared lands of Malvern Hill. McCall's battered and powder-blackened regiments arrived from Glendale and went into reserve just in front of the

quaint, early eighteenth-century, red-brick Malvern house.
Col. Robert O. Tyler had saved twenty-five of the twenty-
six pieces of his siege train which had begun the retreat from
the Chickahominy three days before. Late in the afternoon
of June 30th, Tyler's command, the siege train manned by
men of the 1st Connecticut Heavy Artillery, had just reached
its destination of Turkey Island, a mile south of Malvern
Hill. Then the orders came to haul some of their monsters up
the steep south face to positions near the Malvern house.
Five companies of Tyler's regiment heaved and tugged all
night to put in position, just in front of the house, five 4.5
inch Rodman rifles, five 30-pounder Parrotts, two 8-inch
howitzers, and two 10-pounder English Whitworth rifles.
Tyler's siege guns were placed under Porter's orders.

The sun rose cheerfully that July 1st. The day promised to
be clear and warm, and the soft blueness of the sky was
undiluted by the presence of clouds. It appeared to be just
another lazy July morning. But the men in Union blue along
the crest of that hill were not so naïve. When last seen Lee's
men had been yelling and sniping in the fading light at
Glendale; there was no reason to believe that those men had
now given up their openly avowed purpose of destroying the
invaders. While they had not appeared yet, the men in blue
suspected that it would not be long before they would catch
sight of those red flags and hear the shrill Rebel battle yell.
Breakfast then, in many of the regimental camps was meager;
apprehensive, lest any effort to cook a meal be starkly
interrupted, some units ate what had been the customary
breakfast for the past few days — water and hard bread.

As the sun rose over the eastern horizon the Blue lines were
readied. The Union position ran along the cleared crest of
the north face of Malvern Hill, from Western Run on the
east flank to the steep western edge of the hill, the line was
about a mile in length from flank to flank. Couch's division
held the right half of the line and Morell's the left. Near the
western edge of the Union line stood a low white frame house

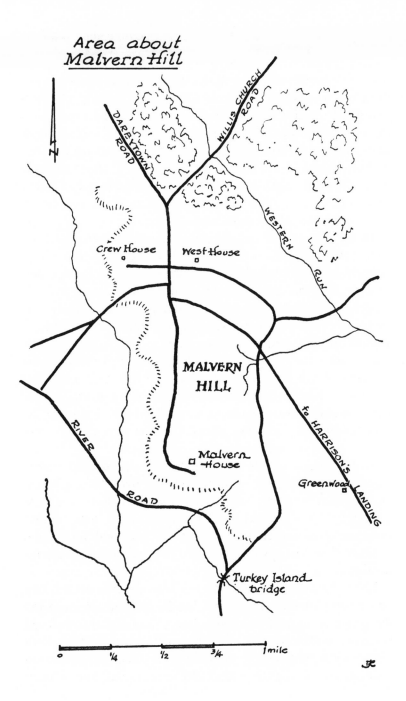

Area about
Malvern Hill

N

DARBYTOWN ROAD

WILLIS CHURCH ROAD

WESTERN RUN

Crew House □   West House □

MALVERN
HILL

RIVER

Malvern □
House

to HARRISON'S LANDING

Greenwood □

ROAD

✗ Turkey Island
bridge

0   ¼   ½   ¾   1 mile

— the residence of Dr. Mellert, more often referred to as the Crew house. Here the Federal line turned south a short distance, covering the low wheat-shocked meadow that bordered the western edge of Malvern Hill and the approaches from the river road. Sykes's brigade of Regular infantry lowered their muskets to cover this area. Within reinforcing distance of Porter's lines were the troops of Sumner's, Heintzelman's, and Franklin's corps, on the right and to the rear of Couch. The bulk of Col. Hunt's Artillery Reserve batteries were in reserve near the Malvern house.

In the past few days before that morning there had been some criticism in the Army of the Potomac that the Artillery Reserve command had not been doing its share of the fighting. But the batteries' performance on the field that day refuted this report. For every available battery of the Artillery Reserve was engaged in action, many having gone forward a second time after replenishing exhausted ammunition chests. Hunt met every request for additional artillery, and his batteries, which were but one-third of the Army's total, suffered one-half of the Union artillery casualties in this action. One outspoken critic of Hunt's Reserve, when informed of its accomplishments that day, stated that his opposition would cease.

With Fitz John Porter that day, as a brigade commander, was a former Regular artillery captain, Brig. Gen. Charles Griffin. This was the same officer who had taken his little battery up onto the hell of Henry house hill almost a year earlier. Porter placed under Griffin's command all of the artillery then occupying positions in and around Morell's division.

Early that Tuesday morning the Blue generals made final adjustments in their lines, and McClellan himself inspected the Union position. The division fronts were slightly advanced to make maximum use of the ground, with the artillery batteries just behind the crest. The infantry lines were arranged between the batteries to protect and be protected. The infantry could also be thrown forward from its positions, if the opportunity arose, without interfering with the artillery fire. The batteries of Morell's division were four in number, but two of them, Hyde's Massachusetts and Weeden's Rhode Island, had only two and three pieces respectively.[1] To beef up the front here Hunt sent two Regular batteries, Livingston's and Ames's, from his Reserve.

It was shortly after 7 a.m.; the arena was ready. One determined contestant waited atop advantageous ground, with plenty of support at hand; the other contestant was already marching toward the spacious cleared fields. Confederate Gen. D. H. Hill, a staunch fighter and an utter realist, on learning of the strength of the Yankee position toward which his troops were marching, cautioned Lee, 'If Gen. McClellan is there in force, we had better let him alone.'[2] The remark was discounted.

About 7:30 a.m. the leading elements of the advancing Confederate host bumped into the Union pickets. A ripple of firing broke out. Several Yankee batteries, catching sight of Gray columns coming down the road from Willis Church, began firing at long range. Sporadic bursts of gunfire drowned out the intermittent crackling and popping of the outpost and skirmish line muskets. Griffin and Hunt had deliberately placed the artillery batteries on the north face so that with only minor shifting of positions they could sweep the earth in front of either Morell or Couch. From this rise then, every enemy movement detected on the far edge of the open fields in front, in the woods beyond, or in cleared areas anywhere in gun range evoked a thunderous pounding from the Yankee batteries.

It was mid-morning when the Bluecoats caught sight of what they estimated as two enemy brigades forming on the east side of Quaker Road in front of Couch's division. The Federal troops believed this was only the first of a long series of piecemeal attacks against their lines. Actually, the enemy never made any attempt to storm the distant slope until mid-afternoon. But the grim Federals working those guns, recalling the fury of the Gray assaults against a somewhat similar position at Gaines Mill, determined to use all their effort to break up anything which looked like a Rebel attack before it could get started.

Four Union batteries now swung their tubes to point at this threat on Couch's front. Savagely the guns snapped. The cleared ground in front of the Confederates was plowed and churned by Yankee shellfire. In the woods behind, where D. H. Hill's and Winder's men were halted, there was continuous banging of exploding shells, snapping and crashing of shattered and broken tree limbs, and an occasional scream of a Confederate hit by one of the jagged fragments. Some of the Rebels sought shelter by ducking behind the larger trees. But this helped little. D. H. Hill saw one of his men seated comfortably behind a large tree, apparently feeling very secure. While the general watched, a rifled shell passed completely through the trunk of the tree, carrying the man's head with it when it emerged on the other side.

It became obvious to most of the Confederate high command that the Yankee position was another masterful defensive position. The swampy creek to the east made assault from that quarter extremely difficult; and the steepness of the west face militated against sending waves of attacking infantry up those bluffs. But the ground to the front was open. The main factor to be considered before attacking over these fields was the apparent concentration of Union firepower on the top of the slope just east of the Crew house. The defending fire from this rise would necessarily be divergent, but the Confederates could concentrate their fire on this strong point. The attackers would first have to knock out those Yankee batteries. Therefore, the Gray commanders ordered their artillery forward.

The order was more easily given than executed. Confederate commanders strove to establish two bases of artillery fire, one just east of Quaker Road in a cleared field near Western

Run, and a second in a clearing up Darbytown Road about one-half mile northwest of its junction with Quaker Road. Even the redoubtable Stonewall Jackson personally stopped to help a North Carolina battery push through the heavy tangle. In one of Jackson's batteries, as it came forward, was a light 6-pounder section. Outgunned before they started, the men of the section were quickly reduced to a skeleton number, unable to continue to fire the guns. Their battery commander sent the survivors and their little guns off the field.

Fierce, accurate, and profuse came the rain of Federal missiles. That Confederate personnel casualties in their batteries were not higher was only due to their finding defiladed positions. Often this advantage meant little, for the mile-long Union front could bring a cross-fire to bear on the Gray cannoneers from almost any position. During the entire day Jackson was able to get but eighteen guns into position to support his troops, and most of these were hammered out of action or had to be withdrawn.

The Gray artillery was hopelessly handicapped. The batteries of one of their divisions had been sent to the rear the day before to refit; their Army Reserve artillery commander failed to learn of the needs; and the roads and trails by which available batteries could get to the firing positions were few. Furthermore, most of those Yankee guns on the hill were rifles with greater range than the smoothbores which comprised the bulk of the Southern ordnance. A Gray commander who complained that his battery had but two pieces capable of reaching the Yankee position was not unusual that day. Rifled artillery was limited when used against infantry, but against the bulky target presented by an opposing enemy battery it was an excellent weapon. The Yankee rifles could hold off their opponents at long range and methodically batter them to splinters.

The Confederates were able to get a few batteries into action. The increase in shelling from their lines only caused a proportionate increase in the fire from the Federal batteries. Up on the forward Union position the racket was frightful. Some seven Yank batteries were filling the air with successive and simultaneous explosion, sulphur smoke, and whirling pieces of iron.

About 12:30 p.m. Capt. Weeden, commanding the remnants of his own and Hyde's batteries, put the five rifles in position facing west near Dr. Mellert's house. From their position on the brow of the hill they could sweep the meadow that intervened between the woods on the far side and the Union position. Searching rounds of enemy artillery fire whirred and buzzed overhead. Weeden's men could not return the fire, as it was coming in from their right and right rear. But the enemy's range was off, and the rounds burst harmlessly beyond. But then shells originating from the battery's left flank increased the crews' discomfort; some heavy caliber Federal batteries were firing. This time the range was unfortunately in greater error than the enemy's, as the banging of exploding shells — big ones, 32-pounders, the Massachusetts men thought — ripped the air about the gun positions. A flash of flame, a stunning roar, and a blast of one short round knocked six of the batterymen down. Gladly Weeden's command shortly received the order to move over to the right to relieve another battery.

Battery A, 5th U.S., under Lt. Adelbert Ames — the same Ames who had been decorated for his bravery while wounded at First Bull Run — was already well on its way to expending the staggering total of 1392 rounds that day. Ames was dispatching his caissons to the rear as soon as they were emptied, getting them refilled at the ammunition train, and sending them back to position. Somewhat remorsefully, Ames remarked in his report of the action, that if the ammunition train had not subsequently been removed from the hill his battery would not have lacked ammunition at any time. Such was the quality and quantity of the Union artillery fire which crashed from that hillside.

Kingsbury's Regular Battery D, 5th U.S., Griffin's old battery, began to run low on ammunition. Capt. Weeden, acting as Morell's chief-of-artillery, received orders to move his composite battery from the position on the left over to the center to replace Kingsbury. Amid a flurry of Confederate fire which wounded two of its men, the battery crossed the crest. As they came into line behind Kingsbury, that battery was preparing to expend its final rounds at another infantry mass which had appeared on its front.

Kingsbury had been firing at some of the Rebel batteries with case shot, or shrapnel as it was even then beginning to be called. Then, 500 yards to the front there appeared shining reflections off burnished steel of Rebel musket barrels. Enemy infantry was preparing to charge. Ames's battery, just across the road on Kingsbury's left, apparently had not spotted the threat yet; Kingsbury yelled to Ames and pointed emphatically in the threatening direction. A look and a wave of the hand indicated the message was understood. There was a flurry of activity about the handspikes of both batteries as the gunners hurried to fire on the new target. Nearby the men of the 22nd Massachusetts Infantry, a unit badly depleted at Gaines Mill, were loudly singing *John Brown's Body* and 'We'll hang Jeff Davis on a sour apple tree.'

So rapid was the fire that one battery could scarcely see the unit on its flank through the dense clouds of filthy smoke. Shrapnel rounds burst over the attacking lines, but still they came. The battery commanders ordered canister and put the pieces under the charge of the sergeants' chiefs-of-piece as the guns began firing at will. Even the troops in reserve caught a share of the Union artillery's anger. One Confederate brigade commander moved his regiments rearward twice in efforts to escape the flailing of iron fragments and balls. Many of the Gray commanders ordered their men prone on the ground until it was actually time to move. As far back as the Willis Church, Southern columns were being hit by the vigorous pounding of the Union rifled guns.

At 150 yards the Gray ranks were stopped. Kingsbury's ammunition chests were almost empty. Since his caissons had been blown up to prevent capture on June 28th, he had entered this fight with less than 600 rounds. He had received 150 additional rounds of shell which he had used on massed targets, and as the battery prepared to pull out, sixteen rounds per piece remained — reserved on orders for dire emergency.

There was, for all the Confederate difficulties, incoming fire, too; the enemy had established a few batteries in those clearings. One of Hyde's lieutenants leaned against a limber watching the furious cannonade. A shell burst a short distance in front of him, and the lieutenant plainly saw the fragments slap the ground twenty feet away. But one piece, which the lieutenant in that fleeting second thought to be about one inch square, bounced off the ground and headed straight for his shoulder. With a quick and graceful right oblique the young officer evaded the flying missile.

A deeper sound now added its chorus to the deadly theme; Hunt's heavy 20-pounder batteries and Tyler's siege pieces back near Porter's headquarters in the Malvern house began to fling their noisy rounds out over the western flank in front of Sykes. And distant but heavy reverberations out on the river indicated that the Yankee gunboats were adding their fire to the maelstrom. The struggle for artillery fire superiority had been a one-sided affair from the start. Some of the Federal gunners even felt a little sympathetic toward their opponents. One Gray battery gallantly trotted into position only to be reduced to shambles in fifteen minutes. D. H. Hill termed the duel 'farcical.' [3]

It was now after 4 o'clock. The Confederate command, usually extremely accurate in its estimate of Yankee intentions, erred again in believing the enemy might be shifting off the hill. Rebel officers had seen some of Sumner's men pulling into defilade and misunderstood the move. More Confederates, Magruder's men, went over to the attack. More

Union batteries were brought up onto that smoking inferno. Capt. Edwards with the combined Battery L/M, 3rd U.S., reported to Griffin and was immediately shoved into line to relieve Livingston's Regulars. The range to the far woods where clouds of smoke indicated a Rebel battery was firing was 900 yards. The battery opened on the Confederate position. A snapping and buzzing about the cannoneers indicated Rebel infantry was within musket range someplace. There now appeared in a wooded ravine 250 yards away, snipers; Edwards switched to canister to drive them out.

This had been the most serious attack so far, and while it appeared to the Blue commanders that it had been readily handled, they were not so confident of any follow-up assault — which appeared in the making. Hunt, asked for more guns, sent Wolcott's Maryland battery and two of the 20-pounder German batteries clattering down the dirt and rock trail to reinforce Sumner, who was holding the far right. Snow's Maryland, Seeley's Regular, and Frank's New York batteries trotted rapidly down the lane to support Couch's lines on the right of Quaker Road. Just in case, Hunt ordered three of the last remaining available batteries into position to sweep the road by which the Rebels would debouch onto the plateau, should they break the Union left. Porter, too, apparently decided that the issue could be in doubt, for he ordered the heavy siege pieces to withdraw; ponderous, immobile, these would be easy pickings if the Confederates broke the line. Hunt, continually riding about checking his batteries, sending ammunitionless trains off the plain, had three horses shot out from under him.

Snow's Marylanders went into position in an oatfield on the right of the Union front. An enemy battery in a wheatfield welcomed their arrival with a salvo of shell. The Rebel gunners were taking advantage of the standing and stacked grain which partially obscured them from Yankee view. But in thirty minutes the Gray unit pulled out, one piece with its entire team destroyed. Another battery appeared in the

same field only 200 yards closer to the Blue lines. Similar
action ensued. Crouching Rebel riflemen, working their way
up a wooded ravine to the front took Snow's position under
fire. Pleas for Federal infantry to go forward and clean them
out went unanswered — a frequent complaint of battery commanders this day; they failed to understand the necessities
of keeping the infantry intact and in hand for the major effort.

The sun was beginning to slip more rapidly toward the
western horizon now. The sky began to take on the faint
sunset tinges of orange and red. With a crescendo of yells
the last desperate Confederate attack began. The Union line
blazed from flank to flank as every gun tube on the line
boomed. The air over the heads of the advancing lines was
filled with the smoke of bursting shells. By the time their
ranks had traversed half the distance gaps in the lines appeared
and streams of individuals — the wounded and the shirkers
— straggled off to the rear. So rapid did the rate of fire become, that some of the batteries took to piling the fresh rounds
alongside the guns and sending their limbers searching rearward for more.[4] One battery had to turn in its Parrott rifles
for replacement the next day — the rifles ruined as a result
of their heavy work that day.

The attacking ranks, yelling loudly, marched on through
the withering fire. The principal attack came straight up both
sides of Quaker Road, directly toward the heart of the Union
position. Another assault was trying to break in from the
northwest through a ravine in front of the Crew house. Capt.
Snow over on the right flank received a hurry-up order to send
help to the left. Two sections were hurriedly limbered and
sent cantering toward the threatened flank. The Yankee crews
stopped swabbing as the long wavering lines came into
canister range. Then some batteries began shoving in double
canister. At 200 yards most of the attacking regiments were
brought to a halt.

One of D. H. Hill's brigades had moved halfway across
that 900-yard shell-swept field when the bloody fire drove

the survivors to the earth. Here, taking what cover they could find in plow furrows and behind tiny mounds of earth, they began returning the fire. Unable to get the men to go farther, the commander sent word back that he did not think he could hold them even this far forward much longer.

Not far away, in front of Edwards's Regulars, the enemy appeared extremely reckless and determined. So close did the ragged ranks get that some of the noncoms in the battery fired effectively at the oncoming masses with their pistols. Edwards yelled for the infantry in his rear to come forward. With a loud cheer a regiment rose up and advanced into Edwards's limbers. Here the riflemen halted, crouched, and opened fire. The battery commander yelled and waved his arms; their firing was endangering their friends. The regiment ceased fire and moved forward and Edwards hurriedly ordered his guns limbered fifty yards to the rear. At this point, for the first time during the day, the Federal infantry took over the primary role, rushing forward to fling scathing volleys into the faces of their decimated foe. 'It was not war, it was murder,' wrote one Southern general.[5]

The attack was broken. But well into the evening hours the flash and bark of gunfire sputtered along the front. Gradually, under the covering of darkness, the bleeding Southern regiments withdrew from their positions in front of that awful hill. Several Confederate divisions had been wrecked before the fire of the twenty-five-odd Blue batteries and the infantry which here supported the artillery. Their losses, over 5000, were almost as great as those for Gaines Mill; but here the slaughter had been primarily by artillery. 'More than half the casualties were from field pieces — an unprecedented thing in warfare,' said embittered D. H. Hill. This battle only helped to convince Hill that 'Confederate infantry and Federal artillery, side by side on the same field, need fear no foe on earth.'[6]

The next morning the Confederates found that hill quiet and unoccupied. Gone too were many of the trees whose foliage had shaded and beautified the gentle slopes. Where green fields had been, there were now rutted tracks of wheeled vehicles, and the debris left behind by an army which gives up the battlefield. McClellan had slipped away during the night and pulled down close to the river. Here, backed up by the awesome-sounding cannon of the naval vessels in the river, the Army of the Potomac went into camp, to remain virtually idle. Lee thereupon felt free to turn his full strength on a second Federal Army which had taken the field against him — Pope's Army of Virginia, which was moving down the line of the Orange and Alexandria Railroad toward Gordonsville, approximately forty miles northwest of Richmond.

VIII

EXPERIMENT ON THOSE FELLOWS OVER THERE

Second Battle of Bull Run

THICK choking clouds of white powdery dust hung heavily over the sandy roads. As far as the eye could see endless columns of Union soldiers in worn and sweat-stained blue plodded and shuffled along the narrow sand roads of the Virginia Peninsula. It was August 13, 1862, and the Army of the Potomac was headed back down the Peninsula to Fort Monroe. There waited the schooners, barges, and transports that were to carry the troops back to northern Virginia. The Lincoln administration had decided that better use could be made of this Army if it were brought north and perhaps united with Pope's forces then operating in northern Virginia.

Until now the Army of the Potomac still believed that McClellan would lead it into Richmond, even though in the Seven Days battles Little Mac had caused it to give up ground. To many the retreats that followed these battles were difficult to understand — particularly that following Malvern Hill; it seemed that five months of hardships and losses had been wasted.

A voluminous exchange of letters and telegrams had passed between McClellan and Washington before that officer acquiesced to orders to bring his army northward. He had protested vehemently, pleadingly, that if the administration would give him another army corps, or even one more division, he would deliver the city of Richmond. He had suddenly marched back on August 5th and re-occupied Malvern Hill, a move that startled the Confederate high command. Alarmed at this new burst of activity, the Rebels had hurriedly shifted troops back to watch him. From those heights Little Mac continued to utter optimistic statements, to emit vague and profuse promises of early advances on Richmond, to continue his petty head counting, and all in all to continue to be McClellan. The Confederates, satisfied that their old antagonist had not changed his habits, turned toward the Rappahannock.

McClellan's threat to the Confederate capital was over, but there was another Blue army that had been of growing concern to Lee. It was made up of the old independent commands of Frémont, Banks, and McDowell — the first two old Shenandoah Valley acquaintances of Stonewall Jackson. These forces had been combined in mid-June under a single field commander and given the name of the Army of Virginia. The best that can be said of its commander, Maj. Gen. John Pope, is that he was not afraid to attack Lee. The life of Pope's Army was short. His troops for the most part later found themselves members of a reorganized Army of the Potomac, and many of his old units marched behind Meade in the great victory parade along Washington's Pennsylvania Avenue in May 1865.

Maj. Gen. John Pope had been given a threefold mission: to protect Washington, to safeguard the Shenandoah Valley, and to operate against the enemy lines of communications in the direction of Charlottesville and Gordonsville. The latter mission was designed to draw off troops facing McClellan on the Peninsula. The new Union commander had moved in mid-July toward Gordonsville, and Lee had countered by sending Jackson to meet the new threat. At Cedar Mountain, on August 9th, Stonewall found it difficult to hold the field against the leading corps of Pope's Army. One of Pope's three missions had been successful.

It was about this time, though, that the decision was made

to withdraw the veteran Army of the Potomac from the malarial swamps east of Richmond. It then became a race — Lee to crush the Army of Virginia before McClellan's Army reached Pope, and the Federals to join forces ere the sharpest sword of the Confederacy landed a mortal blow. Lee moved up to the line of the Rappahannock in mid-August, sparred with Pope, and looked for an opening through which to throw his bayonets. Pope, with the help of captured orders, gave a fair account of himself in these initial operations. But when Lee sent Jackson's gaunt regiments hurrying toward the valley and the Yankee right flank, John Pope's luck and skill ran out.

While Pope's pickets were covering the crossings of the Rappahannock, the first of the lumbering vessels hauling the Army of the Potomac began to disgorge its cargo at Aquia Creek Landing, a Union supply depot just south of the present U.S. Marine base at Quantico. Others continued up the Potomac, tying up at the wharves of the old port town of Alexandria, six miles south of the capital. Apparently neither McClellan nor his quartermaster had been advised or anticipated any need to combat load the Army of the Potomac, though a more aggressive officer might have foreseen the wisdom of such a move. The infantry was loaded for the most part with their unit integrity retained. But not so the artillery and supply echelons of the commands. Guns were rolled onto one schooner, horses and drivers on a second, cannoneers on a third, and rarely did one ship sail simultaneously with the rest, or the battery with the division to which it had been attached.

By August 26th all of the infantry of the Army of the Potomac had been shipped from the Peninsula, but the artillery was strung out from Alexandria to Fort Monroe. Porter's and Franklin's batteries had sailed about the same time as their infantry, as had three each of Sumner's and Heintzelman's. The rest of the divisional and Reserve batteries were in various stages of loading and shipment.

Porter's battle-proven V Corps reached Aquia on August 21st with six batteries accompanying the infantry, though the corps' reserve ammunition was somewhere in its wake. Nevertheless, orders were given to hasten to Pope's aid all of McClellan's units as fast as they could be unloaded. Accordingly, whatever batteries were available were attached to whatever divisions came through Aquia with no regard to previous assignment. When Porter's corps tramped north to join Pope, it had no transport and its infantry had only the ammunition in their boxes — forty rounds, not much, those veterans knew, when a tangle with Lee was expected.

This state of unreadiness was bad enough, but if we can accept the opinion of one Regular officer of McClellan's army as being typical, then Pope's forces were an even more disheartening sight to the men of the Army of the Potomac. Capt. Alanson Randol, the same officer whose battery was overrun at Frayser's Farm, had disembarked at Aquia with four new Napoleons in his refitted command. He joined with Stephen Weed's battery and the two units were ordered to join Porter at Warrenton Junction. Enroute Randol bumped into elements of Pope's Army for the first time. He was stunned; according to him, they were 'undisciplined, disorganized and demoralized.' He tried to procure supplies from some of Pope's quartermasters, 'but such was the confusion that it was found to be impossible.' There was disorder everywhere; abandoned wagons and plundering stragglers littered the fields, and the roads were choked with crawling columns apathetic about their destination. In disgust Weed and Randol unslung their axes from their caissons and hacked their own bypasses around snarled columns and jammed fords.

Late in the afternoon of August 26th an empty Union supply train rattled northward out of Bristoe Station, some three miles south of Manassas Junction. Minutes later a distant whistle heralded the approach of another train moving north from Warrenton to Bristoe. The train neared Bristoe, and the engineer, leaning from the cab of the engine *Secretary*, roused himself as he saw in the sunset distant figures hurriedly piling debris across the tracks.

The little woodburner chugged closer. A thump of a musket quickly followed by a volley dispersed any doubts the engineer may have had. To stop his train, to reverse it to escape capture was impossible; the trainman instantly opened his throttle all the way and the rattling cars picked up speed. The engineer and fireman threw themselves to the floor of the cab. The train clattered down the tracks, and the wide cow-catcher on the front of the *Secretary* banged into the pilings, scattering them. Muskets in the hands of lean men in Rebel dress spit at the escaping train as it sped to spread the alarm that Confederate infantry was behind Pope, and set loose the rapid events which characterized the days of the Second Manassas, or Second Battle of Bull Run, as it was usually styled in the North. A few hours later Stonewall Jackson's men were feasting off the lavishly stocked Yankee railhead at Manassas Junction.

The cunning Jackson was now trapped, so thought John Pope. Couriers streaked away from Army headquarters with plans and orders calculated to destroy that portion of the Rebel Army which had contemptuously dared Pope's rear. Jackson, for his part, gleaned the pickings from the vast stores at the junction, burned the rest, then set his host marching north via several routes toward the Warrenton Turnpike. The Gray columns on reaching the Warrenton Turnpike then turned away from Centerville and headed west, a move that was to cause the Federals no end of confusion.

In heavy woods, 1500 yards north of a tiny hamlet of Groveton on the turnpike about two miles west of the ground of the First Bull Run, Jackson hid his regiments. All morning on August 28th the ragged and exhausted brigades massed behind an abandoned railroad bed that cut across the woodland from southwest to northeast. In the cool woods the tired men would rest until late that afternoon.

It was nearly 5 o'clock that afternoon of August 28th when

Federal Gen. King's division appeared, tramping eastward along the pike headed for Centerville. The long swaying column neared Groveton, flankers well out. The leading brigade passed over a small rise and disappeared. Brig. Gen. John Gibbon's brigade followed in closed columns, with Battery B, 4th U.S. Artillery, following in its wake. The day had been hot and humid; the olive drab carriages and caissons and the faded blue uniforms of the men were filmed in powdery dust. The division was bringing up the rear of McDowell's corps, now ordered to Centerville whence Pope believed Jackson had been chased.

Gibbon's men reached a rise, and the leading regiment passed over. A lone horseman appeared for a short time in the field north of the turnpike; then the rider turned toward the woods on the northern edge of the field and disappeared. Those Federals who noticed this rider probably never learned that he was the famed Stonewall himself, deliberating an attack on the marching column. Jackson, flecked with military genius, made his decision; he sternly ordered two of his deadly divisions turned loose at the Federals. Now a Gray battery trotted forward into the field, swung about with its muzzles leveled at the Yankee columns, and the hot lazy world about the tired Federals exploded in flame, smoke, and iron.

Gibbon reacted quickly. It looked as if this was merely a battery of Rebel horse artillery; a regiment of infantry could easily chase it off. Gibbon sent most of his men prone against the road bank, as he prepared to move a regiment out to remove the annoyance. Then up from the rear of the brigade came Battery B, Gibbon's own command of Regular Army days. The prone infantrymen covered their faces from flying stones and dirt as the six gun sections came up at a gallop. Gunners sprang from the seats on the ammunition chests and tore down a rail fence to the left of the turnpike, and the battery went onto a little knoll. Two Gray batteries were firing now, and long sinister lines of enemy infantry dispelled any misapprehension that this might be merely Rebel cavalry enjoying their favorite sport of worrying Blue infantry. Battery B unlimbered and in drill time the first salvo of six shells screamed from the Napoleons toward the oncoming Gray ranks.

Gibbon's brigade became perhaps the most famed and certainly one of the best units in the Union armies. It was made up at this time of one Indiana and three Wisconsin regiments. The men wore the wide-brimmed black felt hat in contrast to the small kepi or forage cap used by most of the Eastern regiments. Their hat gave them their first nickname of the 'Black Hat Brigade,' which held until their valor earned them the sobriquet of the 'Iron Brigade.' Quite a bond was to grow between the Black Hat boys and Battery B which usually supported them. In fact many of the vacancies in the battery's ranks were filled by men detached from the brigade. McClellan, aware that his Regular batteries had nearly all fallen far below authorized strength, sought to remedy the situation. To get recruits to join Regular units when the Volunteers offered bonuses, alleged lighter discipline, and greater informality, was almost impossible. Therefore McClellan authorized recruiting of Regular batteries from Volunteer regiments of commands to which they were attached.

This was the first action of any size for both battery and brigade; and it would be remembered by the survivors as long as they lived. Until nearly 9:00 p.m. without respite, both sides loaded and fired. The opposing infantry lines stood within easy stone's throw of each other, Jackson's own division and Ewell's volleying with Gibbon's and one other Blue brigade.

A lieutenant in Battery B flinched and his mount lunged as a shell burst overhead. The officer turned to see his horse's flowing tail, neatly severed, lying in the dust. The horse survived this humiliating wound and during a later review elicited the corny remark from Mr. Lincoln that this horse reminded him of a tale.[1]

Behind Gibbon's brigade was Doubleday's brigade, and some distance behind this command was Patrick's. One of the division batteries had pulled off the road for a meal break when the match was struck. Gen. King himself had accepted an invitation to eat with Capt. Monroe's Battery D, 1st Rhode Island Light Artillery. Cannoneers had gathered bunches of dry leaves, twigs, and sticks, and the smoke from dozens of tiny fires could be seen in the still air. Drivers had dismounted and were hanging feed bags on their still-harnessed animals, who were shifting and pawing and swishing their tails at worrying flies. The men were at ease, a banter of light chatter rippled back and forth, and the smell of coffee hovered about the fires.

Then the boom of cannon fire caught Monroe with his fork halfway to his mouth. Gen. King dropped his mess gear, hurried to his horse, and galloped down the pike, Monroe threw the remnants of his unfinished meal behind a nearby bush, wiped his hands on a red handkerchief, and bade his bugler blow *Boots and Saddles*. The Battery commander then led the way back onto the pike, and the little column moved at a walk toward the firing. Monroe spurred his mount to a gallop as he pushed out ahead of his command. At a little rise Monroe was able to view the field where Gibbon's Black Hat boys, partially hidden in the fresh gunsmoke, were beginning their argument with Jackson. The captain hurried back to the guns, raised his hand high overhead, and loudly bellowed 'Trot — Heeo!'

The battery neared a small hillock to the left of the rise where Monroe had seen the fighting, and where he had concluded he would emplace his guns. Just as the column reached the base, a panting staff officer came running over the top wildly waving his sword and calling for the battery to turn back. No sooner had the officer yelled his warning than the lead horses of a Rebel battery appeared near the brow of the hill — coming after the same position. The Gray gunners got there first.[2]

Monroe halted his command and ordered it counter-marched, a difficult maneuver in cramped road space. At that instant the first salvo roared from the enemy guns. The turning column wound itself free and galloped back to a low spot in the road fringed on both sides with timber and out of enemy sight. The Reb gunners shot several salvos, but their aim was poor. The Rhode Islanders clattered to a halt in the hollow, and the captain looked about for another possible firing position. There, about 125 yards away, was a low hill; the battery would try for it, though the column would be exposed to enemy fire for about a hundred yards of the way. Monroe gave the order.

Drivers whacked their teams and yelled loudly. The powerful beasts lunged forward in the traces, and Battery D was soon trotting. The guns picked up speed as hoofs beat at the earth with a gallop. But alert Gray gunners had been waiting and now opened fire. The first salvo missed, and the column raced on. Another flurry of booms, then a loud crack — a solid shot splintered the stock of one of the caissons, causing the vehicle to swerve back and forth. There was the threat that it would hurl itself and the cannoneers astride it into a gulley. Drivers heaved back on the reins and brought the pounding teams to a halt.

Monroe galloped back to take a look; the caisson could not be repaired here; it would have to be destroyed. A lieutenant volunteered to stay behind and do the job. A length of slow match was taken from one of the ammunition chests; the lieutenant tied one end to a powder bag in the chest, and closed the lid, lit the other end, mounted his horse, and galloped clear. As the officer reached the battery, now going into position on the little hill, a flash of orange flame and a deafening roar shook the earth as the ammunition on the disabled caisson exploded.

Battery D came into position, but only two of its pieces could be brought to bear on the enemy line. These guns boomed only a few rounds before night began to fall on the field. Jackson ordered a column out to turn the flank of Gibbon's line, but darkness assisted its failure, and a deadly quiet hovered over the body-strewn field.

Both sides slept on the ground where they had fought. Then about midnight Yankee officers and noncoms quietly wakened the sleeping men. All orders were given in whispers, and back at the artillery bivouacs cannoneers tied pieces of cloth around trace chains and other metal parts that might clink. Slowly King pulled his division out onto the road to Manassas, the blackness of night covering the move.

John Pope was sure that this fight had been occasioned by King's division's bumping into Jackson fleeing westward for the cover of Thoroughfare Gap and the mountains. Jackson, he now thought, had been cornered. By dim candlelight Pope's harried headquarters clerks penned orders: the Army of Virginia would concentrate and annihilate Stonewall's command.

That there was no artillery organization in Pope's Army comparable to that of the Army of the Potomac is soon evident to a student of that arm in the respective campaigns. Gallant and splendid batteries there were, led by such men as 'Leather-britches' Dilger, Sam Benjamin, Jim Hall, and others. But the firm guiding hands of Barry and Hunt were conspicuously absent in the wasteful dissipation of Pope's artillery effort. The number of instances in which Pope's batteries ran out of ammunition and had to withdraw because they could not get resupplied was appalling. Were these instances confined to the skeleton-provisioned batteries of the Army of the Potomac there might have been some excuse, but for Pope's batteries it is hard to justify.

Organization and administration were not among Pope's few abilities. His Army was an army on paper — by decree, but hardly much more. Why Pope failed to create an artillery

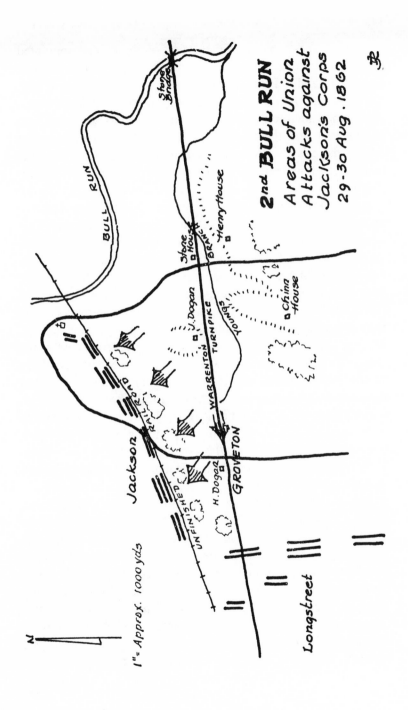

2nd **BULL RUN**
Areas of Union
Attacks against
Jackson's Corps
29-30 Aug. 1862

reserve or make more efficient use of an officer appointed
to care for the artillery arm is unexplained in the records.
Capt. Alexander Piper, a Regular of the 3rd U.S. Artillery,
had been appointed chief-of-artillery at Pope's headquarters,
but beyond mention of his name in the orders assigning him
to this post and the appearance of his name in Pope's final
report, there is absolutely no evidence in the *Official Records*
to indicate that this officer actively participated in the campaign.

It was now an accepted fact that the Artillery Reserve
of the Army of the Potomac was formidable not only because of its guns but because of the hundreds of wagons that
made up its own ammunition train. At Malvern Hill many of
the Federal batteries had been resupplied from the Reserve
train — a number of the division wagons having gone on to
Harrison's Landing with the baggage train. Later, at Gettysburg when the artillery ammunition supply became critical
because the brigade wagons arrived late, fortunately for
Meade those of the Reserve were available to Meade. Artillery
supply superimposed on infantry supply channels, as was
the case for the division batteries, rarely received prompt,
sympathetic, or understanding consideration. The Artillery
Reserve train time and again was the unintended bulwark
for all of the batteries of the Army of the Potomac. Pope
had created no such reserve, and Halleck had ordered Hunt's
to Alexandria.

Pope's Army alone had over thirty batteries comprising
about 175 pieces. Their armament was largely the same as
McClellan's batteries, though there were a few more odd
breeds about — some Wiard steel rifles, 12-pounder howitzers,
one battery of 6-pounders, and a battery of mountain guns.
To this was added some twelve batteries from the Army of the
Potomac which actually joined the Army of Virginia. The
tragedy was not the variety but that so few batteries were
committed in mass. The Army of Virginia clung to the
obsolete tactic of attaching batteries to brigades, usually

on a one-for-one basis. There was no gun line as there had been at Malvern Hill, where flaming blasts of canister had built a lead and iron wall through which the enemy could not pass. A complete lack of understanding by the high command in this Army of the capabilities of the artillery arm was conspicuous; their opponent, it will soon be seen, gave them an exemplary lesson in the power of massed artillery fire on the defensive.

With much marching and counter-marching, Pope's divisions began to concentrate, as Jackson was finally located near Groveton. At dawn August 29th Sigel's corps and Reynolds's Pennsylvania division were readying to attack westward from the vicinity of the Manassas-Sudley Road. Siegel had Schurz's division on the right, Milroy's independent brigade in the center, and Schenck's division on the left near the turnpike. It was around 6 a.m. when a Federal battery fired with a roar that echoed through the quiet woodland; the Blue infantry lines began to move forward slowly. Unknowingly they were tramping into an American Balaclava. In the left rear of Jackson's line stood sixteen Confederate cannon, and twenty-four more pieces were arrayed behind his right center. Moreover, the Rebel strength here ran about five muskets per yard of front. The enemy position was somewhat reminiscent of those taken by the Federals on the Peninsula, only now the Gray legions would enjoy the benefit of position.

The fields of fire for both the Rebel infantry and artillery were fairly clear except at a point on their left where the woods ran up to the Confederate line. If the Yankee cannon chose to duel with the enemy batteries on the ridge behind their infantry, then the Confederate riflemen would be spared that annoyance. Should the Federal gunners elect to fire on the enemy infantry behind the cuts and fills and in the heavy woods — hardly a profitable target with the matériel available — the Rebel batteries would be free to choose their own targets at will.

Doctrine of that day prescribed that on the attack artillery should concentrate on the enemy's cannon; on the defensive it should hit his infantry. Mass, the book said, was the key to real effectiveness in either case. Despite the theory that said the Yankee guns should in this case hit the enemy batteries — since by theory they should neutralize the enemy's most potent defensive weapon — it made practical sense to shoot at a target they had more chance of hitting and hurting — a bulky artillery battery whose target area was nearly as deep as it was wide. But most of the Blue commanders had apparently never read the book nor perceived the practicalities of artillery fire; their artillery effort as a whole was totally inept.

A thin line of Federal skirmishers came over the low rise of ground just east of the Groveton-Sudley Road as the attack got under way. Little puffs of smoke popped from the woods in front as the Confederate picket line opened fire. With steady step the Blue riflemen closed the gap, a man pausing here and there to return the fire. The screen of Gray riflemen fell back toward their main line. A sheet of flame streaked across the slope in front of the Yanks; the Rebel line had been developed, and it was now up to the massed regiments to break it with their fire power.

From dawn till nearly midday the Federals made much noise, covered the countryside with smoke, but failed to develop any serious threat. Every time Blue infantry ventured out in threatening force Jackson's two groups of guns hammered at it and his infantry sent forth crashing volleys; with no lush infantry targets to shoot at, his cannon picked on the covering Yankee batteries. Bitter and sharp skirmishes flamed all along the line, but the Bluecoats could not put together a coordinated effort. Rebel infantry ventured a move toward the Groveton woods, and Sigel shifted a regiment and two guns of Schirmer's New York battery opposite the threatened point. The two pieces opened with canister. The enemy reacted by swinging a battery over in counter-battery fire, but the two pieces had already completed their mission of driving off the intruders.

Some of Schenck's artillery got into action in the morning as Siegel pushed that division westward toward Groveton. Battery K, 1st Ohio Light Artillery, claimed they dismounted one of the enemy guns, blew up a caisson, and drove their antagonist off the field. But there was an ominous sign which should have been recognized by the battery commander as he removed his men from action shortly after: his ammunition was exhausted, a situation which would hit most of Pope's artillery before the next two days were over.

A blazing noonday sun beat down on the farmland. The Federal attacks now became more determined; a German brigade of Schurz's division stormed into the Groveton woods just east of the Groveton-Sudley Road. The Southerners bitterly contested their advance. Milroy's brigade found the going difficult as Gray guns atop the ridge to his left front took him under fire. A battery accompanying Milroy returned the fire. The waving line reached the open ground in front of the woods. A thunderous banging and rattling shook the field as the Confederate infantry flung their volleys into their marching targets. Some of the Blue regiments broke, were rallied, and the line charged. A bloody repulse was the result.

The enemy swarmed out after the retreating Federals just as a second Yank battery, Dieckman's New Yorkers, came into action behind the pummeled Blue regiments. Six guns rolled into line — the last one being manhandled into position, its horses already down. The Blue ranks steadied to the comforting booming of their own cannon and the visible effects of canister on the enemy lines. As Confederate gunners swung onto Dieckman, there was a crash of splintering wood, and a solid shot wrecked the carriage of one piece. Then horses went down, screaming and thrashing, their hoofs in the air. In a few minutes a complete section was disabled. The battery commander gave the order to pull back, and the five guns rolled back — the tube of the sixth slung by the prolonge under a limber.

The Yankee attacks still failed to make much progress. Schenck's assault had been greatly weakened at the expense of plugging gaps along Sigel's entire front. Three gun batteries — Haskins's Ohio, Schirmer's New York, and Buell's West Virginians — had attempted to support Schenck. Buell had promptly dueled with Jackson's batteries on the ridge and soon was pounded off the field. DeBeck, and then Schirmer, had run out of ammunition, leaving the division for a time without artillery support.

Behind Schenck's thinned ranks a dust cloud billowed along the pike, as a Yankee battery, horses at full gallop, headed for an elevation on the left of the road. Astride a powerful mare, leading the battery into position, rode a Federal captain in non-regulation doeskin britches. Hubert Dilger, commanding Battery I, 1st Ohio Light Artillery, who became known throughout the Army as 'Leather-britches' Dilger, was bringing his guns into action. Dilger's feats became oft-told tales of the Union armies. He had come to this country when the war broke out, leaving a commission in the Baden Mounted Artillery to serve in the Federal ranks. An intrepid man who fought his guns at times as if they were pistols, Dilger earned a conspicuous niche in history of the Union artillery.

Up on the far ridge what appeared to be ten Reb guns saluted Dilger's arrival. For two hours the batteries shot at each other. A distant roar shook the ridge; a dense grayish ball of smoke rose lazily over the far tree tops. Apparently an enemy caisson or limber had been hit. Then a second similar explosion hurled another ball of dirty smoke into the hot August air. The fire from the ridge finally began to taper off, and then ceased. Dilger used the pause to reorganize hurriedly his unit. Many horses were down, some men needed medical attention, and several of his guns had been damaged, though not beyond repair.

The respite was brief. A gun flashed from those heights

behind the Rebel lines, then another, followed seconds later by a whole series. Seconds later dull booms were heard; the enemy guns had reopened; shells screamed overhead, tore great clods of earth from the fields, burst viciously in the air over the Ohio men, and brought the Federal gunners back into action. Dilger sent a man hurrying to Sigel; the battery's ammunition was low, and Dilger wanted some help. Wiedrich's and two pieces of Dieckman's German batteries trotted out to relieve the harried Dilger, who was greatly hindered because so many of his horses were down.

On Schurz's front, where a German brigade temporarily got a toehold on that musket-studded railroad bed, the Federals had some temporary success. Hampton's Pennsylvania battery, in reserve till now, trotted across the field and tried to get into firing position on the far side of the woods to support the attack. A wicked cross-fire drove them back. A second time they rushed out only to meet the same fate. At that point Roemer's battery came to their aid with an outburst of counter-battery fire, and under this cover and diversion Hampton moved his weapons into battle.

Two small mountain howitzers, the kind that could be disassembled and carried on mules, were sent to Schurz's aid. Light and relatively mobile, the two little guns were immediately rushed forward to the infantry line.[3] But now the Gray regiments had rallied following the break in the line, and with a roar they lashed out, throwing the Germans back from the railroad bed into the woodland where they had begun. And as the powder smoke drifted lazily upward, there on the slope just in front of the bed stood one of the little mountain howitzers, abandoned — silent evidence that another piecemeal attack had failed.

Meanwhile, in back of Schenck's slowly moving ranks, which had by this time reached the woods where Gibbon's brigade had set up its hospital the previous night, came two regiments and a battery from Stevens's division of the IX Corps. The guns were from Battery E, 2nd U.S., Lt. Sam

Benjamin commanding, and their massive breech quickly identified them as 20-pounder Parrotts, the most awkward of all field pieces then in use. Benjamin soon became the choice target for the mass of enemy artillery on the plateau east of the Brawner house. The Confederate guns now gave Benjamin the same sort of barrage they had delivered before to Schenck's batteries. Schenck saw what was happening and sent to Sigel for more artillery. That request reached the corps commander just as Roemer's battery rolled into line in front of the J. Dogan house, north of the pike, in Schenck's right rear.

Benjamin's position was about 200 yards southeast of the intersection of the turnpike and the Groveton-Sudley Road on a commanding knoll. It gave the Regulars a beautiful view of the Rebel position in that area, but on the other side they also afforded an excellent target for Jackson's gunners. For several hours Benjamin and his crews fought, but when the battery finally pulled back one of its two sections had virtually been obliterated — quite a different story from Benjamin's experience on this same field thirteen months earlier.

By this time John Reynolds's division from the Army of the Potomac had come into line of battle on Schenck's left south of the pike, and the division commander tried to deploy his brigades parallel to the pike so as to strike Jackson's right flank. Reynolds pushed Meade's brigade across the road and gave him Cooper's six 10-pounder Parrotts as support. The concentration of enemy artillery on Jackson's right promptly announced to Meade that he was trespassing in such a telling manner that Meade later remarked that he had stirred up a hornets' nest of artillery.

The Blue regiments came to a halt, and Jim Cooper waved his battery into Action Front. But the ammunition supply in the chests would not stand the strain of a long severe fight. Cooper had to withdraw, his ammunition gone, and another division battery was called up — Ransom's, DeHart's unit of Peninsula days. However, before the new unit could get into position the situation had changed. Reynolds discovered Rebel infantry and artillery moving against his own left flank — Longstreet's corps — though they were not identified by the Union command at that time. Reynolds thereupon began pulling back to high ground southeast of Groveton.

It was now about 2 o'clock; Hooker's division from Heintzelman's corps, which had come on the field about 11 a.m., started relieving Schurz's battered regiments. Other reinforcements were streaming into the battle area: Kearny's division was taking over the right of the Federal line, and the small IX Corps, temporarily under Reno, was also available to Pope.

The two battered armies faced each other, making long-range swipes with artillery flare-ups. At one point a noisy gun duel broke out, and the return fire from the Rebel batteries made a lasting impression on one Yank, who described the shells as screeching 'over our heads, or (plowing) the gravelly surface with an ugly whir, that made one's flesh creep.' [4] About 3 p.m. one of Hooker's brigades, Grover's, suddenly began to move forward toward the Groveton woods in front of the center of Jackson's position. Reverberating hurrahs echoed across the countryside as the lines rolled onward. Then the Gray guns on the high ground behind their infantry turned their muzzles on Grover's men, and sheaves of flame leaped from banks of muskets along the railroad bed.

Grover's charge is one of the least-known attacks of the Eastern phase of the War, but it was one of the most gallant. That one brigade ripped into Jackson's position east of the so-called 'Dump,' splintering the first line, wrecking a second, and giving a third a rough go of it before enemy reinforcements slammed the breach closed and the Blue regiments were driven back. Whooping Confederates, yelling taunts, and pausing to snipe at fleeing figures in Union blue, followed the retiring line. Help for the hard-pressed Yanks appeared in the form of a fresh Federal battery, arriving in reply to a call from Milroy whose own two batteries had run out of ammunition.

The gun crews took one look and knew that there could be

but one loading — canister. The first blast shook the leading wave of advancing Rebels, blowing pulpy gaps in their line. But still the Gray troops kept coming. The Federal infantry began to give way as the charging mass reached the hundred-yard point; Milroy ordered the battery out. More Yankee infantry moving up from the rear rallied the line and the Confederates slid back.

On the extreme right of the Federal line a staunch fighting man was leading his division into assault positions — Phil Kearny and his men of the Red Patch.[5] Some time after 4 o'clock Kearny, supported by Stevens, struck at the Reb left flank. Cheering Yankee infantry found a gap in the enemy line and poured through. The defenders' flank was driven back as Kearny's men stormed down the cut and into the fields beyond, bending Jackson's left back on his center.

Kearny himself stood ahorse near Freeman McGilvery's 6th Maine Battery, which was supporting his attack. McGilvery's men were weary; the day before the battery had been ordered to move by forced marches to join Heintzelman's artilleryless corps. They had left Bealeton Station at 3 a.m. of the 28th and sixteen hours later pulled rein at Manassas, thirty-four miles distant. Ninety minutes later they set out for Centerville, six miles farther, where they arrived at midnight. Now they were in action, having marched another ten miles that morning as they followed Hooker's division from Centerville to the battlefield.

As the gun crews bent to their work, Gen. Kearny carefully observed the result of every salvo they fired. After watching a while he turned to McGilvery and said; 'You are getting the value of your ammunition. Yes sir, you are giving them just what they need.'[6] But the men of the Red Patch could not do it alone, and Confederate reserves were quickly shuttled to the threatened point. It was bullet, bayonet, and gun butt for a few minutes, but the end was inevitable — repulse for Kearny's men.

As the outnumbered Federals fell back, A. P. Hill ordered his Confederate division to counter-attack. The Gray ranks pushed the Federals back through the woods into the fields beyond where there were three Yank batteries. One Rebel brigade changed direction slightly and made straight for a six-gun unit. The fire of all three batteries was turned on the attacking brigade, but grim determination and guts held the men in the ranks despite heavy loss, and the crews at the threatened battery readied a final blow. When the oncoming swarm of bayonets was seventy yards away, the loud command to fire rang out. A cloud of smoke, orange flame, and a thunderous crash shook the ground. With a wild yell the Rebels broke into a run for the gun position, and the crews abandoned their empty weapons to the enemy. An Irish battalion of Jackson's command wrested a 3-inch rifle from another battery, and still another gun was captured before their attack was stopped.[7]

It was nearly sundown. The Union forces had been repulsed in countless piecemeal attacks, and the Rebs had advanced their line to the Groveton woods. Then down the pike, westward past the stone house, puffed the dog-tired men of King's division. These troops had been marched over a good share of the Prince William County since their tangle with Jackson the evening before. They had come up from Manassas about 3 p.m., and now were marching toward the site of their battleground of the 28th. Pope had ordered them to pursue the enemy, which, he concluded, was beaten and in retreat.

Hatch's brigade was in the lead, with Gerrish's New Hampshire howitzer battery as support. The rest of the division batteries trotted over to relieve others on the rise near Groveton. Hatch's regiments were preceded by a wave of skirmishers wearing dark green uniforms — Post's 2nd Regiment, U.S. Sharpshooters. Three-quarters of a mile down the road the advance bumped into heavy rifle fire, and King shook his columns into line of battle across the pike. Gerrish's howitzers went into action, a piece on each side of the road. The leading

regiments snapped up a few surly Gray prisoners, who loudly
boasted that 30,000 of their friends lay lurking in the quiet
woods where King appeared to be headed.

The Blue line moved slowly forward, eyes straining against
the sun's setting rays. The popping of the skirmishers' muskets
grew in intensity, and the green-uniformed riflemen began to
drift to the rear through the heavy Blue ranks as the firing took
on volume; the enemy had been developed and their job was
over. Then everywhere the woods reverberated with the shrill-
pitched Rebel yell. A fierce fight began in the fading light. The
prisoners' boast was true enough. Hood's division of Longstreet's corps, with the famous Texas Brigade leading, collided
with King; Longstreet had slid his divisions into line south of
the turnpike, and Hood had been making a reconnaissance in
force. Hatch fell back. With a new burst of frenzied yelling
enemy infantry rushed Gerrish's battery. The captain gave the
order to retreat, but not in time, as Gerrish himself and one of
his howitzers fell prize to Southern arms. Longstreet was not
yet ready to throw his full punch, though, and the Confederates
broke off contact. An ominous quiet settled over the battleground.

Silently, stealthily, in the 2 a.m. darkness of August 30th,
Hood pulled his men back west of Groveton, leaving the ground
they had wrenched from King's division in the twilight still
and deserted except for bleeding and torn human bodies. One
gun seized from Gerrish rested in an awkward location, so with
no time to wrestle with it, the Rebels smashed the carriage,
spiked the tube, and then left the wrecked remains behind.

At the same time, back by the Henry house — the scene of
Griffin's and Ricketts's debacle of the first battle — Capt. A. J.
Monroe's Battery D, 1st Rhode Island, had been dropped off
from the rear of King's division as it moved toward Groveton.
The battery had reached the battlefield about 3 p.m., fully
expecting to enter into the noisy cannonade then raging be-
tween some of Pope's and Jackson's artillery. Instead, the
Rhode Islanders had remained idle until Capt. Monroe de-

cided to use the time to put the unit through 'cannoneers' hop.' 'The men undoubtedly thought this a most singular thing to call upon them for a drill in the direct presence of the enemy,' wrote Monroe, 'but I wanted to know by experience how steady they could contain themselves with the immediate prospect of coming under fire.' [8]

The battery commander was most impressed by his unit's apparent display of coolness; so it was with a feeling of confidence that he carried out an order received about sundown: namely, to move his battery to a spot between the Stone House and the J. Dogan farmhouse just north of the turnpike. Directly in his rear, though, was high ground, called Bald Hill by Monroe, but actually now known as Chinn Ridge; and on this rise were several Federal batteries busily engaged with Jackson's line to the north and northwest. The Rhode Islanders rammed home their loads and leaped clear as their first salvo crashed across the rolling fields. But Battery D quickly discovered that it was not the enemy who would cause them trouble here, but their own friends atop Chinn Ridge; someone was either cutting the fuzes too short or getting an unusually high number of premature bursts. No matter what the cause, the volume of splattering pellets and fragments was of sufficient quantity to make Monroe hurriedly limber his unit to the rear.

As the battery rolled rearward, Capt. Monroe was accosted by Gen. Sigel, whose corps was occupying this area: 'What you come back for?'

'Your batteries are hurting me more than the enemy,' came Monroe's reply.

'I thought you could not stay there. I saw their shells burst over you,' remarked the old general. With that the captain led his command into position in a less vulnerable area.[9]

When the clear dawn of the 30th came, the tired men of a Union regiment who were camped near the turnpike stirred themselves about in small groups. Wisps of smoke from tiny fires drifted vertically in the still air as the troops boiled their coffee and bit into tasteless hardtack or salty fried pork. The day promised to be hot. The infantrymen sitting about their fires looked up as a party of officers, orderlies, and escorts clattered past. Several of the men recognized one of the officers as Gen. McDowell. The general was making a personal reconnaissance, and what he found he would report shortly thereafter to Pope.

Poor reconnaissance on both ends of the Federal line brought in the following intelligence: on the Federal left where Hood had been encountered at sundown the day before no enemy had been found; despite the fact that a regiment which went out prowling in front of the Federal right came back badly cut apart; it seemed that Jackson had given up ground there too.

The Yankee high command pondered this intelligence. Pope was convinced, as he had been for two days now, that Jackson was retreating. McDowell and Heintzelman agreed. Accordingly, at noon Pope issued a special order providing for the pursuit of the enemy, with McDowell to be in charge of the assumed chase. Porter's V Corps was ordered to push west along the pike with King's and Reynolds's divisions following. Ricketts's division was to swing up beyond Sudley, then turn west via the old Haymarket Road, which roughly paralleled the pike a few miles to the north. The rest of the Army was to be in reserve.

Couriers galloped over the dusty roads, carrying the order to the scattered commanders, and slowly the ponderous Blue mass began to uncoil into marching columns. Porter's veterans swung forward, led by a veritable swarm of skirmishers — in reality a loose attacking line in itself, and limbered field artillery batteries followed in the wake of the marching regiments.

Behind Sykes's division of the V Corps were four Regular batteries: Weed, Smead, Randol, and Hazlett.[10] It was not normal at any time during the war to group Regular batteries together as division artillery in the infantry commands, but there had been no time to reorganize the Army of the Potomac units as they landed. Whatever batteries had been available were tossed into whatever line of march of the division which happened to be marching by at the time. On the right of Sykes, Butterfield was leading two brigades of Morell's division toward the Groveton woods, which screened a part of Jackson's line near the Groveton-Sudley Road (now Virginia Route 622). Behind Butterfield was Waterman's Battery E, 1st Rhode Island. King's division, now under Hatch, was to the right of Butterfield, and supporting it were Battery B, 4th U.S., and Reynolds's Battery L, 1st New York.

As Porter's tramping columns closed on the Groveton woods a vigorous pop-popping stuttered from within the green foliage, and here and there a Yankee skirmisher was felled. More troops came into action and artillery began unlimbering as it became increasingly apparent that Jackson had not backed up an inch and had no intention of doing so. There was then a lag in the action as the Union command adjusted its thinking. Gen. Fitz John Porter, destined to be the incompetent Pope's scapegoat, struggled to get his V Corps swung around to the northwest in position to get a good crack at Jackson. The general grabbed Lt. Charles Hazlett's Battery D, 5th U.S., Griffin's old West Point Battery with its six 10-pounders, and sent it hurrying to a knoll just southeast of the intersection of the pike and the Groveton-Sudley Road; this was a good spot from whence to lay down fire on Jackson's position, though Sam Benjamin and his boys had found it rough going from the same location the day before. Hazlett's orders were to shell the woods in front of the reinforced V Corps until the advance of the Federal infantry lines masked his field of fire; at that point he was to shift to counter-battery fire.

The racket of battle swelled to a roar about 3:30 p.m. as Porter's attack began to roll. Hatch's men, having the shortest distance to go, were the first to collide with the enemy, and Campbell's and Waterman's batteries began pounding away at the Confederate position. By Porter's direct order, Waterman moved down to within canister range, and the nasty pellets rattled through the leaves and branches as Confederate pickets fell back on the main line. Sykes's regiments began the terrible march toward that railroad bed, as Hazlett's battery thundered out in their rear.

Confederate gunfire roared over the crackle of musket fire. Jackson had retained the left group of sixteen guns in position, but he had moved forward eighteen others from the group on his right into the interval between his corps and Longstreet's, where they had a position to deliver flanking fire on any force crossing the open field in front of 'Old Jack's' right. Adjoining his guns were those of Lt. Col. Stephen D. Lee's Reserve Artillery battalion, eighteen more tubes. This was in striking contrast to the Union artillery effort, which would be dissipated in scattered and divergent fire on a protected enemy.

As Sykes's lines marched over the fields, two of his batteries tried to soften the enemy line; the other available unit, Randol's, the general kept in reserve, its four shiny Napoleons remaining in column on the pike. In minutes Waterman's guns found themselves out of the fight as Blue infantry moved into their field of fire. An aide from Porter rode up and commanded them to pull back to higher ground to try to knock out some of the enemy batteries.

The Rebel gunners concentrated on the Blue infantry as it pounded its way across the open, but now smoke- and dust-clouded field. On Porter's right the Union infantry closed with the enemy rapidly, and the Gray batteries soon had to cease firing on that quarter lest they endanger their own infantry. The center and left parts of the assault then caught the full fury of the Confederate artillery fire. The Federal attack had force and it had heart. Lone brigades had broken through yesterday, so there was hope for a reinforced army corps. The leading regiments started up the slope about a hundred yards from the railroad bank. It was now up to the Gray riflemen whether there would be any further advance. The Yanks did gain a bit more ground, but it was in the face of a murderous fire; if the line was to be broken, supports would have to arrive quickly.

On the left of Hatch's brigades came the Regulars of Sykes's division. The dense mass obliqued to the right so as to bring their battle front parallel to Jackson's, then began to press their attack. The center of Jackson's line was already in trouble as Hatch's force was threatening to tear one hole and Butterfield's, another. To the Confederates on the ridge it was imperative to stop any support waves from restoring the force to the Union charge, and to the Rebels on the extreme right of their line Sykes's division appeared to be a second wave coming on in the rear of Hatch and Butterfield, though a little more to the west.

For the first time Stonewall Jackson had to send to Lee for help, and the army commander promptly relayed the request for a division to Longstreet, who had already spotted the danger. Longstreet had also noticed that Confederate artillery fire from that mass of thirty-six guns had a beautiful target in Sykes's masses, and they were already ripping into the Union corps. Under such fire no attack could survive; to make sure, though, that the job would be done thoroughly, Longstreet sent back for two of his own batteries.

While the general waited for his units to come up, the guns of Stephen D. Lee's battalion and those of Jackson's corps under Col. Stapleton Crutchfield found themselves shooting much as the Yanks had done at Malvern Hill. Lee was able to run some of his short range howitzers down to within 500 yards of Sykes's ranks. At this range only the smoke hindered their shooting at the perfect target. Federal counter-battery fire was pitifully weak; the Graycoats reported that only two Yankee batteries took them under fire and these overshot their mark.[11] The weakness was also noted by a Federal colonel who bemoaned, 'Our batteries were unable to silence the enemy's raking concentrating fire. Our loss here was heavy through shot and shell.' Goaded and tormented by the terrible fire which ripped down the length of their line, knocking bodies in all directions, two Blue regiments swung to their left and tried to charge the enemy's line of guns, now distinguishable only by darts of flame through dense clouds of low-hanging smoke. Discharges of canister ended their valiant effort.

By now the first of the two batteries called up by Longstreet had arrived, going into position well to the right of the main mass of Gray artillery. But the Federal attack was stopped before the second unit went into action. The Blue lines wavered on the slope in front of the enemy's railroad bed fortress, the forward elements mutilated by a frightful rifle fire coupled with a barrage of rocks by those whose boxes were empty. Enemy artillery fire made the position of the left flank units and those in rear absolutely untenable. The Union lines began retiring.

At this point Gen. McDowell pulled one of the more appalling blunders in this amazing collection of Union command errors. Reynolds's division had been covering the Army's left, on the south side of the pike, and that officer had confirmed his findings of the previous day: The Confederate battle line extended southward across the turnpike. McDowell, acting as a sort of wing commander for Pope, had received this warning and had told Reynolds to deploy so as to meet such a threat. Then, as Porter's attack began to crumble, McDowell sent a hurry call to Reynolds to pull his division to the north side of the road to bulwark the retiring V Corps — while Sigel's corps waited idly in reserve near the J. Dogan house.

Lt. Charles Hazlett, calmly directing the fire of his guns, was astounded to see Reynolds's three brigades and four batteries marching away from that critical position; Hazlett's, with its six Parrotts, was now the only Federal unit on the south side of the road to cover Porter's left. Porter must be notified, so Hazlett sent an orderly galloping to that general's field headquarters; another rode rapidly to the commander of a small two-regiment brigade of Sykes's division, which was waiting nearby in reserve. The commander of the brigade was Col. G. K. Warren, and the artilleryman's message advised him of that open flank and asked the colonel's assistance in covering his battery and the unguarded left.[12]

Warren, whose quick decision to seize a hill in Pennsylvania in 1863 was to bring him fame, instantly put his two regiments, the 5th and 10th New York, in motion toward the woodland on Hazlett's left. The two units deployed, the 5th on the right and the 10th on the left with several companies thrown out toward Compton's Lane to the west, while in their rear the tail of Reynolds's command was moving off the ridge. At this point Lee gave Longstreet the nod, and some 30,000 fresh Confederates were loosed in counter-attack, and parts of Jackson's jaded and fought-out corps were ordered to cooperate.

Warren's pickets were quickly driven in, and it was not long before the colonel realized that the best he could do in the face of such weight was to try to cover Hazlett's withdrawal. Warren yelled to Hazlett to clear out. Under the circumstances the lieutenant had little choice, for the New Yorkers were between his guns and the fast closing enemy, so he called up his limbers and, with a bold show of guts, which might have cost him his guns, Hazlett walked his battery off the field hoping such an act would have a calming effect on nearby Federal troops. A wide ditch — no doubt Dogan's branch — barred their exit to the road. A spot was found, though, where the unit could cross. Slowly, one at a time, the carriages moved out. Cannoneers dismounted as drivers carefully nursed the teams and vehicles across. As each section reached the other side, cannoneers remounted, and Hazlett, who later died on Warren's seized hill in Pennsylvania, led his battery out onto the choked and cluttered roadway.

Battery D moved slowly and tediously through the mass of men, wagons, and debris which jammed the pike. Shortly Hazlett spotted a piece of high ground that seemed to offer a good position for his guns to go into action again. A wide swing of the arm, and the battery followed its captain up the rise. Some of Joe Hooker's infantry were nearby, and a request for support was granted. Hazlett's battery unlimbered and opened fire again — very near the same ground where the battery had been knocked out in the First Bull Run.

Longstreet's counter-attack, having overwhelmed Warren's little command, swept forward and in the process caught the last elements of Reynolds's division — C. F. Jackson's brigade and Kerns's, Cooper's, and Simpson's batteries — in column headed for the north side of the pike. The brigade and the batteries tried to fight where they were, but they had little chance. In minutes Kerns's battery lost thirty-four men, including its commander and all of its guns; Cooper counted twenty-three casualties and all his caissons gone; only Simpson seemed not to have suffered serious loss of matériel. By the end of the day Reynolds's artillery had lost some eighty men.

On the north side of the turnpike Sykes's division was slowly giving ground. One of his batteries, Randol's, caught in column on the road, barely had time to reverse itself and retire to a hill in rear. Here they unlimbered, but before a round had been slipped into a tube Gen. Porter personally ordered the unit to a threatened point on the left, probably the second ridge east from Groveton. Commands were yelled over the din of battle, men leaped back onto the carriages, and Randol's battery advanced toward the endangered point. Randol strained his eyes in the stinging sulphurous smoke, looking for the best approach to the position. Suddenly he caught sight of something waving on that ground; another look revealed it as a Rebel battleflag waving from the ground he was supposed to occupy. The battery commander thereupon turned his column down the pike toward the Stone House.

Over on the Union center Gibbon's Black Hat brigade, part of Hatch's division, had fallen back from the Groveton woods to a hill where several Federal batteries had formed line. The brigade went into prone position behind the guns, a German New York battery on their immediate left. As the Confederates began to follow up the retiring Federal infantry, the battery commander became excited and rushed up to Gibbon standing nearby: 'Gott in Himmel! General, vhy you no zay schoot by my battery? I vill be disgrazed by New York. By Jesus Christ, vhy you no zay schoot?'

Gibbon looked the man in the eye and snapped 'Go to your battery, Captain, and obey orders when given.'

Minutes passed and then the nervous captain appeared again. A second time Gibbon gave the man an icy stare, then summarily sent him back to his unit, this time to the accompaniment of loud guffaws and cat-calls from the men of the brigade.[13]

Gibbon watched with experienced eye as the Gray line emerged from the Groveton woods. They came a few yards farther, then the former battery commander turned general yelled to the batteries to open fire. Charges of canister sped through the air and slammed into the attacking ranks. An Irish private of the 6th Wisconsin sang out, 'Set 'em up in the tother alley, boys, they are all down on that.' [14]

Waterman's Rhode Islanders picked up some Rebels forming ranks in the woods and opened on them with shrapnel. But the battery's ammunition supply was about gone, and the unit soon was forced to join the sorry parade of batteries headed for the rear. The initiative had passed to Lee. At all points the Gray forces went over to the attack. Confederate batteries quickly limbered and moved forward into the open fields across which the Yankees had charged. As Porter's corps fell back, Sigel's corps tried to restore the situation. Part of Schenck's division was moved forward to the high ground about the J. Dogan house accompanied by Schirmer's New York battery. Dilger's and one other artillery unit were already on the crest trying to beat down the enemy's fire, which one Union officer reported was plastering the whole area.

Earlier, McLean's brigade with Wiedrich's Battery I, 1st New York, had been sent across the road to the Chinn Ridge. This was the high ground immediately west of the Henry house hill and across the Manassas-Sudley Road. Coupled with the Henry hill and the high ground north of the Stone House the area formed a good defensive barrier. If held, this chain of hills would keep the Union line of communications over Bull Run via Stone Bridge open. Now two brigades from Ricketts's division on the Federal right were en route to the Chinn Ridge, with Hall's and Leppien's Maine batteries bumping along as support.[15]

Wiedrich had taken over four 10-pounder Parrotts, leaving his howitzer section on the north side of the pike. The four rifles were unlimbered with two regiments on either side of the battery. The line faced west. Through gaps in the smoky haze that hung listlessly in the still air, the men on the ridge could see, to their right front, fleeing Union troops in red pants — some of Warren's Zouaves. Wiedrich barked the command to open fire on the distant enemy. McDowell, who was nearby, loudly countermanded the order, explaining that there was a friendly battery 500 yards to the right front and Blue infantry to the left front.

The sound of whooping Confederate infantry drew closer. Wiedrich's men grew tense waiting for a target. Suddenly, there they were, and the crisp command to fire sent the four guns into furious action. At first they fired shell, then, as the charging enemy showed no sign of stopping, Wiedrich gave the order to switch to canister. McLean's infantry thereupon let go with thundering volleys of hundreds of muskets fired in unison.

A body of troops appeared out of the woods to McLean's left front. McLean ran to Wiedrich and ordered him to pull a section around and fire at those troops. A staff officer yelled not to fire: Those were Federal regiments. McLean looked hard; their uniforms, though not clearly distinguishable, appeared dark like the Federal blue — perhaps reinforcements moving into the area vacated by Reynolds's troops. Gray infantry pressed McLean in front heavily, and the Blue regiments fought furiously. But then the supposedly friendly troops appeared on the brigade's left rear and McLean hurriedly had to change front.

The Blue regiments, under heavy fire and somewhat shaken, began the maneuver. Suddenly through the smoke came Wiedrich's battery, careening madly to the rear, throwing one wing of the brigade into temporary confusion. Then deep sharp explosions, and orange flashes jarred the air over the harried troops, here and there knocking a man to earth — Confederate artillery fire. Slaughter or retreat were the alternatives, and McLean chose the latter.

When one reads McLean's report of this fight written while the events were still very fresh in his mind, one is able to detect that he was far from pleased with the conduct of Wiedrich's command. Praise he gives to every other commander under him, by name, but Wiedrich's name is quite prominent because of its absence.[16]

To stem the assault Sigel rushed over two more brigades, Koltes's and Kryzanowski's. These units with reckless abandon charged at Longstreet's victory-flushed regiments which had just pulverized Warren's and Jackson's brigades. The Confederates were stung by this blow and in its face recoiled. On the hill of the J. Dogan house just across the road several Federal batteries had been waging a long-range duel with some of Jackson's guns, but, when the roar of violent battle erupted on the Federal left these weapons were swung around. As the enemy's battle lines came into view, the Blue gunners fired everything they could at them.

It is regrettable that history does not give a clear picture of exactly whose batteries were in on this shooting,[17] but one thing is known and that is that Gen. Longstreet appreciated the effect this gunnery was having. Those units had to be neutralized, so the general sent for some of his own artillery to do the job. But soon Longstreet's gunners found themselves enfiladed by other Federal batteries farther to the north. 'This threw more than its proper share of fighting upon the infantry, retarded its progress, and enabled the enemy to escape with many of his batteries which should have fallen into our hands,' wrote the Confederate corps commander. One of these Yank batteries was certainly that of Capt. Hubert Dilger, an officer who became a specialist in fighting rearguard actions during his brief stay with the Eastern army; this was his first demonstration.

The charge of Sigel's two brigades and the fire of those guns momentarily stalled the enemy advance, and Rebel regiment and brigade commanders sent back requests for reinforcements. Under these conditions Sykes's division, with Weed's and Smead's batteries, passed the Dogan farm. Weed's six 3-inch rifles pulled off the road and unlimbered on a neighboring hill; the captain ordered the caissons to keep moving to the rear. Long, ash wood rammers pushed by number one and two men thudded charges down the tubes. Cries of 'Ready' echoed from the chiefs of piece, followed by Weed's terse command, 'Fire!'

Smead's battery was likewise halted near Weed's, and Sykes sent Randol's weapons into battery on the right side of the Dogan house. Randol was no sooner in position than Gen. Porter himself rode up. He pointed to a spot where he wanted Randol's battery shifted. The crews obediently stowed their implements back in traveling position, grabbed the gun trails and swung them onto their pintles, and the little unit started down the slope to the main road. The battery had to force its way onto the pike, a stream of floundering humanity wearing dirty blue. Every kind of soldier and vehicle in the Army was trying to use the road as an exit from that lost field. Randol's drivers booted their teams and yelled at the men in the road. Some gave way without a word, others cursed the artillerymen but moved out of the way of the ponderous hoofs and heavy wheels.

From the pike Randol could see he would have a hard time reaching the designated spot as artillery fire was raking the whole area. Then he noticed men and vehicles leaving the place, and minutes later he caught sight of a waving red banner on the ground. A closer look disclosed a Rebel battle flag. With that Randol had no choice but to go to the rear with the stream until he could find a place to go into battery again. Back near the Stone House, on what was probably Henry Hill, Randol spotted a friendly battery in action. Leading his own command up the rise, the officer then threw it into line beside the other battery, which was Hazlett's.[18]

By now the Rebs had moved into action again, and their attack waves were taking Chinn Ridge away from the Bluecoats. Sigel had to pull the remnants of his corps on the north side of the pike rearward to prevent their being cut off. The evacuation of the J. Dogan ridge began and Capt. Dilger volunteered to cover the retirement. Rebel infantry appeared through the smoke and Dilger fired at them with case and shell. The lines continued to come, so the German went to canister, his four Napoleons making quite a racket. But even those canister blasts failed to stop the enemy's advance, as Dilger plainly saw when the smoke from his discharges cleared. He yelled for his limbers, and galloped back about a hundred yards. Once again he went into action with canister, and this time the enemy stopped, then fell back out of his range.

Dilger then analyzed his position: he was alone — not another Union outfit anywhere near him. So with his job done, a dwindling ammunition supply, and sitting in an exposed spot, Dilger decided to retreat. A weakened gun carriage gave way as he moved off, but with deliberate haste the tube was lashed under a caisson in the manner prescribed in the manual for such eventualities, and the Ohio battery walked calmly from the field.

Capt. A. J. Monroe's Rhode Island battery had been idle all day. That morning, from their position near the Stone House, the men had watched other batteries limber and move out with the weaving columns of infantry which were supposed to be pursuing a fleeing enemy. At last, about 3 p.m., the waiting unit received an order to move up into the fight. The sound of gunfire grew louder as the battery approached Groveton. A staff officer rode up with more orders, and the guns were halted in a field on the edge of the road. For what seemed to Monroe to be a full hour, the battery just sat there, a juicy target for stray rounds.

It was about 4 p.m. when a sweat-streaked officer whipped his frothing mount down the pike. Standing in his stirrups the officer scanned the fields south of the pike, saw Battery D, and jerked his horse's head in that direction. The officer spotted Monroe and brought his horse to a stop beside him, gasped out an order, and pointed to a hill some 800 yards in the rear and south of the road. With that the man left at a gallop. Capt. Monroe called his men to attention and gave the command to counter-march to the indicated ground. Skillfully, the drivers led their heavy vehicles about and followed the captain. At a point about two-thirds of the way down the west face of the intended hill was a piece of level ground; here Monroe unlimbered his guns.

As the crews were rapidly preparing the battery for battle, Capt. Monroe looked over the ground to his front. Directly ahead was a sharp drop which extended for about seventy-five yards and then leveled off to a nearly dry creek bed. On the far bank stood a single line of Federal infantry — two brigades strung out — while some thirty yards in rear was Milroy's brigade.[19] Then away to the west a cloud of dust, which the men had been following from the far distance, had rolled eastward until it hung over a hedge of timber 1000 yards beyond the creek bed. From a piece of high ground near that distant stand of timber there was a flash, then another, and another. Seconds later there was a heavy whirring noise in the air followed by deafening claps of exploding shells. Monroe instantly ordered them to open up on those Reb guns.

The six Napoleons banged out angrily, and Monroe watched anxiously to pick up the strike of his projectiles. The bursts were short; corrections were barked out, and gunners twisted their elevating screws. Again the salvo fell short; the enemy was undoubtedly using rifled cannon, and they were beyond the range of the Napoleons. That was trouble enough, but suddenly the cry rang out that there was Rebel infantry in the woods to the front. Rattling volleys shook the woodland, as Yankee infantry on the far bank pulled trigger, and the Rhode Islanders scrambled to turn their weapons on this more dangerous target. Suddenly a weaving, swaying, irregular line burst from the woods on the run, their yip-yip-yeeing adding the shrill notes to the bass roar of pitch battle. The Blue regiments of the far bank fired one ragged volley, then turned and fled up the slope, around and through Monroe's battery area. The Rhode Islanders were left to face the charge unsupported.

As the enemy ranks poured down the slope toward the creek, Monroe bellowed for canister. Staccato blasts rent the air as the guns tried to beat the attack to earth. Fortunately, the Confederate artillery fire was high, most of their rounds exploding in rear of Battery D's location. The waving hedge of bayonets reached the stream bed, and with that the Yankee gun crews began to load without swabbing, firing at maximum effort, which under these conditions meant two or three shots per minute. Their effort apparently was successful, since the charge stopped at the creek bed.

Confederate Col. Benning, commanding a brigade of Longstreet's corps, reported sending his winded and panting troops prone on the cool sand and mud of a creek bottom in front of a Yankee battery — perhaps Monroe's. The slope gave the Rebels adequate cover from the canister blasts which tore through the air just overhead. A few minutes rest brought the men back their wind. Benning then stood up, called his men to attention, and pointed his sword at the battery, a scant sixty-five yards above them. Again that yell pierced high over the roar of gunfire, and the Gray ranks swarmed from the ditch and trotted forward.

The reorganized Confederate line now lapped Monroe's position on both flanks, so the battery commander quickly swung his two flank pieces to the oblique to protect himself. If ever supporting infantry was needed it was now, so Monroe looked to where he had last seen the wide lines of Milroy's regiments; there was nothing there now in the way of infantry — only Gen. Milroy and a few staff officers. Milroy, according to Monroe's account as well as others, seemed to be in a state of panic. The general was standing atop the carcass of a dead horse making wild gestures, which the captain said would 'have been amusing if the situation had not been so serious.' [20]

Several of the staff, seeking to be helpful as well as gallant, rode forward, dismounted, then clumsily tried to assist the gun crews. The artillerymen found them more of a hindrance than a help, but somehow managed to keep up the volume of fire despite their well-meant efforts. Again, the assault was beaten back, and the enemy survivors retreated to the protection of the creek bed.

The repulse had been much closer than Monroe had realized, as the sergeants reported their canister expended with only a few rounds of solid shot left in the chests. Simultaneously the Rebel commander could be heard exhorting his men to another charge. This was no place for a battery with no canister, so Monroe called for the limbers. The last rounds crashed from the guns just as the foe swept from the creek bed. With perfect timing the limbers pulled up beside the pieces, and away went Battery D — without losing a man amazingly enough.

On the extreme right of Pope's Army, Heintzelman's corps had been equally unsuccessful in following up a retreating enemy. The only difference was that on Pope's right many Federal units, for some unexplained reason, just stood about as so many spectators to the distant struggle by other parts of the Army.

About 5 p.m. Heintzelman, seeing the retirement of the left, gave orders for his corps to conform. But A. P. Hill, by Stonewall Jackson's command, was not planning to let the Bluecoats escape, so he sent more elements of Jackson's corps in for a counter-attack. Part of Ricketts's command with Thompson's Pennsylvania battery caught the initial blow and tried to ward it off. Confederate artillery took the Yankee battery under fire and horses and men went down. Thompson decided to move his unit back, but a sudden rush by the Rebels carried clean into the battery position, and when the melee was over Thompson was retreating as he had planned — only minus five of his guns.[21]

At sundown the Union right had fallen back to the fields about a brown frame Carter homestead a half-mile west of

Bull Run on the north side of the turnpike. Here the remnants of Thompson's battery joined with the other available division battery, Matthews's — Hall and Leppien having been sent previously to the south of the pike — in holding this last piece of high ground left to the Federals. The Chinn Ridge-Bald Hill area had fallen to the Rebels. McLean's and Tower's commands had been driven away, Leppien's battery losing four of its guns in the process. The last high ground south of the pike was the Henry plateau, the scene of the struggle of the First Bull Run. If this terrain fell, the Union line of retreat across the run via the Stone Bridge would be closed. The principal route of escape would then have to be across the poor fords between the bridge and Sudley two miles to the north. These crossing points could handle the infantry, but artillery and plodding wagons inching along in pitch darkness would probably never make it. Pope suddenly took extreme interest in keeping open lines of retreat and began looking to his rear. The two still serviceable brigades of Reynolds's division, Meade's and Seymour's, with Ransom's battery, were hurried up onto the Henry plateau and there they wheeled into line of battle just east of the sunken Sudley Road.

Swarms of Confederates in ragged apparel, faces streaked with black powder and sweat, some barefoot, rushed from a pine thicket across the road. Yelling and shooting, the Rebels came to a halt in the roadway. A volley flashed into the faces of the Pennsylvania troops, who returned an equally vicious fire. The Bluecoats then got the jump, lowering their bayonets and driving the enemy from the road. In the process Meade's men recovered a Federal battery which had fallen into Confederate hands. The battle had entered its final and critical phase.

Shouts, bursts of gunfire, told of Rebel units creeping around the Federal left. Then, with that battlefield luck which was usually the exclusive property of the Confederate Army of Northern Virginia, Sykes's Regulars arrived on the hill in time to prolong the Union left. The enemy kept probing for the end of Sykes's line and Sykes kept extending his front until it was strung out very thin. A Union battery on the right of the Regulars earned the contempt of that crusty old soldier by retiring when the fighting was at its greatest pitch. But other batteries, horses puffing and tugging against sweat-soaked leather, rolled into firing positions between gaps in the Blue line or any place where the battery commanders felt their weapons could do some good. Smead's Regulars had done little shooting so far, but now the unit swung up onto the hill. Nearby, Randol's cannon were booming furiously, and Capt. Weed's battery had shot up everything they had in their limber chests and the captain was searching frantically for his caissons.

Battery K, 1st U.S., had been standing idly in reserve with some of Heintzelman's command all day. Now that corps was pulling back to conform with the left of the Army, Battery K's commander, Capt. Graham, was disgusted. As the guns bumped across the fields, Graham spotted Gen. McDowell, unmistakable in his unusually high forage cap of his own design, and asked whether the general could make use of a good Regular battery? The general, who was apparently convinced that the battle was completely lost, ordered him to keep moving to the rear.

The battery neared the Manassas-Sudley Road. There Graham spied Gen. Fitz John Porter. To him the captain proffered his guns. Porter looked at him for a second, then turning in his saddle and pointing to the Henry hill, replied: 'We are all going to the rear, but if you want to fire off your ammunition, go over there on that hill and experiment on those fellows over there.'

This was all the captain needed in the way of an order. For a battery, especially a Regular one, to have been on the field of battle all day without having fired a shot would have created, in the stiff, unrealistic code of that war, an embarrassing blot on the battery's record and a blow to the morale of the men. So up the Sudley Road went the battery, pounding along in the wake of three of Reno's regiments. Tying in with some of Reynolds's division, the Regulars unlimbered their weapons on the west edge of the road and cut loose at Longstreet's regiments coming in from the southwest.

The racket of deadly battle raged on, but to all intents the decision had already been reached. It was now only a question of whether the Army of Virginia could be saved. Pope sent orders to Gen. Franklin, whose VI Corps of the Army of the Potomac had reached Centerville, to put all troops he could find into the old earthworks about that hamlet and hold them to the last. The Regulars, backed up by a patchwork collection of units from the entire Army, hung onto the Henry hill with the skill and tenacity that has always made the United States Army a force to be reckoned with, and Stone Bridge remained open as an avenue of escape for Pope's Army.

Darkness, the blessing of all Civil War battlefields, began to close about the body- and debris-strewn fields. In the final minutes of twilight Confederate Gen. A. P. Hill's division tried to break the last Yankee defense line north of the pike — the knoll about the Carter house, 'Pittsylvania.' Here Ricketts's division, supported by Capt. Freeman McGilvery's Maine battery, posted close to an oak woods, waited nervously to beat off any attempt to cut off the army from the fords north of Stone Bridge. The infantrymen and the gun crews heard the wild battle yell of Confederate infantry on the attack, and the Maine men leaped for their action posts. In a minute or two smoke and the last fading rays of light threw a hazy cloak about the battery area, but, even so, through the haze crewmen could pick out the indistinct but unquestioned forms of charging Rebel infantry. The cannon went off with quivering concussions. The enemy, in what seemed full brigade strength, was now coming on the dead run, headed straight for McGilvery's unit. Seeing no chance of stopping that rush, the captain wheeled about and yelled for his limbers.

With typical rattle and clatter, the vehicles swung about in front of their respective pieces, and cannoneers hurried to get their weapons secured to the limbers. McGilvery watched anxiously. At last the battery began to move off. No sooner had

the leading team, the right piece, begun to roll than a heavy
crash from a mass of rifles dumped every animal in the team.
Shrieks, screams, flailing hoofs, and raw confusion ripped the
little command. Yankee infantry came jogging forward, and
the line held just long enough to let the battery get away after
losing five men taken prisoner, nine killed or wounded, and
two complete gun sections left in Confederate hands. With that,
complete darkness fell on the field. As Capt. John R. Smead
led his Regular battery off the field, a dull boom of a distant
cannon echoed across the farms, and there was a buzzing noise
as the projectile went through the air. There was a heavy thud
and the Regulars looked down to see the sprawled and partially
decapitated corpse of Capt. Smead.

All night the Union troops retreated eastward across Bull
Run, a steady rain adding to their misery. By way of Stone
Bridge and the fords the beaten Army made good its escape.

The next day the Confederates sent Jackson on another one
of his patented flank marches. But rain and the strain of the
past week had taken a heavy toll of his corps, and at a point
below a hamlet named Chantilly the threat was stopped completely. This success, though, cost the Federals the life of Phil
Kearny — a high price to pay in an army that was not then
overstocked with driving general officers.

The battles of the 29th and 30th had seen the first major-
size Federal use of offensive tactics in the Eastern theater. On
the Peninsula McClellan's strategy had been offensive, but his
tactics had been defensive. Here it had been different; Yankee
troops had been on the attack, and this was the first time their
artillery had been called upon as an offensive weapon, and this
in an army where the artillery lacked even the most basic concept of control by a competent artillery officer. This sad effort
cost the Army thirty guns,[22] not an irreparable loss as it turned
out, but harmful.

It was not then realized that artillery of that era was not as
potent a force offensively as it was defensively. The history

books and sage old veterans of earlier wars spoke otherwise; but they forgot to qualify their claims with the words 'smoothbore musket.' The student of military science in the period between the end of the Napoleonic Wars and the outbreak of the American Civil War read of the undisputable power of Napoleon's cannon: how the Emperor — a former gunner himself — would run his batteries forward to within 300 yards of the enemy's infantry line and blow a gap through which he would throw the *garde*.

If it was so then, why not now? thought many commanders of 1861. But one new ingredient had been tossed into the tactical mix — the rifled musket — which completely upset the balance. Field artillery could no longer unlimber within easy canister range of the enemy's ranks and at the same time be outside the effective range of the enemy's muskets. Instead of having an effective range of some seventy-five yards, as was the case for the old smoothbore, it was now hazardous for artillery to expose themselves at ranges under 500 yards.

The simple fact was that by 1861 the rifled musket had relegated the artillery to a defensive role. The massed batteries were now forced back to positions behind their own infantry, yet called upon to perform the same role as before. True, there had been improvements in artillery matériel and ammunition, but these did not increase the effectiveness of that arm in the same proportion as the rifled musket. While a 3-inch rifled gun could peg an explosive projectile about two miles under average conditions, it was a feeble charge with crude and erratic fuzing. Furthermore, this greatly increased range was of little value, since there was no indirect fire system to take advantage of the improvement; gunners of 1861–65 generally fired at targets visible from their weapons, and after some shooting this range could drop with the smoke to a few hundred yards.

The Second Bull Run could have brought about many tactical adjustments, but these were lost sight of, on the Rebel side, by the glory of whipping the braggart Pope, and, on the Federal side, by personal vendettas, political and military, ensuing from the Union defeat. But one thing did come through clear and sharp to the Federal administration: with Lee headed for Maryland, it was no time for John Pope to command in the East. The Army was encouraged when it was announced that McClellan would resume command of the Army of the Potomac troops and that the Army of Virginia would be absorbed into this body.

IX

SHARPSBURG WAS ARTILLERY HELL

Antietam

OLD BRAINS HALLECK, with a two-line letter to Pope dated September 5, 1862, ended that officer's assignment in the Eastern theater of the war: 'The Armies of the Potomac and Virginia being consolidated, you will report for orders to the Secretary of War.' [1] There was beyond doubt an improvement in morale in the Army of the Potomac as the word spread through the ranks that McClellan was back in command.

The suave little general had never actually been relieved of his command; his troops had just been detached or borrowed from him. Now they were being returned with Pope's as well, and McClellan was called upon by a nervous government to repel this first Rebel invasion of the North — repel it with troops that had been moving and fighting since early August.

The Army of Virginia was absorbed into the Army of the Potomac, according to Halleck's letter. But it took more than an order to make this a fact. The original Army of the Potomac had had its organization rudely shaken during its transfer from the Peninsula; this was particularly true of the artillery. Then came the severe battles about Manassas, in which many regiments and batteries of both Pope's and McClellan's forces had been roughly handled. Clearly there had to be an overhauling, renovation, and integration of Little Mac's augmented Army of the Potomac.

Certainly McClellan would have liked to have had another

nine months, as in the past spring and fall, to prepare his Army
for the field. But Robert E. Lee's men were already splashing
across the Potomac fords into Maryland; the Army of Northern
Virginia held the initiative and did not mean to give it up without a fight. Even McClellan could not stand still in the face of
this threat, the overhauling and repairing would have to be
done on the march. To reorganize the artillery of the entire
Army McClellan elevated Hunt to the position of chief-of-
artillery. Barry moved to a staff job in the War Office, and
Lt. Col. William Hays took Hunt's place as commander of the
Artillery Reserve. Hunt had to learn the exact status of his
command for himself. Still without any staff to assist him, Hunt,
with great personal effort, rode from one part of the Army to
the next, from battery to battery. First he determined how
many guns he had and where and with what commands they
were serving. This done, he ascertained their condition, and
deficiencies and shortages were made a matter of record. His
findings were grim enough.

All of the batteries with the Army had been in the field
steadily since early August, with little or no chance to refit,
and now there were the losses of the recent fighting to be re-
couped. Although Pope had boasted to Halleck that he had not
lost a gun or a wagon, this was pure Pope-ism. There had been
losses; in guns, in horses, in men, and in every variety of
equipment. Hunt found the efficiency of many batteries greatly
reduced; some were completely crippled, and the overall assignment of batteries was in bad need of readjustment. But there
was no time to wait for new levies and to train new units, re-
pairs had to be made.

From the baggage train Hunt seized horses to fill up decimated teams; from the infantry he borrowed men to replace
losses in the guns crews; and from the Artillery Reserve — his
only source — he brought up complete batteries to replace batteries which had been totally wrecked. By juggling and shifting
he tried to restore the desired balance in the divisions of one

Regular to three Volunteer batteries. Here he was least successful, for time ran out. The newly added XII Corps retained all of its batteries grouped as corps artillery, and only Hooker's corps later fought at Antietam with a division artillery set-up resembling that used on the Peninsula.

These steps provided most of the corps and divisions with sufficient artillery support. Preparations had been complicated, however, by the absorption into the Army of the Potomac of a few corps and divisions which, by Hunt's and McClellan's standards, did not have adequate supporting batteries. Again, with no time to look for new units — the Army was already moving after Lee — the only available source was the Artillery Reserve.

As a result of these detachments from the Artillery Reserve — first, to Pope's forces during the recent campaign, and now to repair and augment the line batteries — Hunt's bulwark of massed firepower was reduced to a cadre of its former size. When the Army reached Antietam Creek, the Artillery Reserve consisted of only seven batteries, five of which were 20-pounder Parrott units, four of these manned by New York Germans. Fortunately for McClellan, by the time the Army of the Potomac caught up with Lee at South Mountain, two days before the Antietam battle, Hunt had stroked the artillery of the Army with his wise and firm hand, and it was ready — at least, on an individual battery basis. But the command system was still the same squeaking one born of the smoothbore era. Higher artillery staffs or commands were still not thought necessary, largely because they had not been necessary in the past.

Lee had gone to a battalion organization shortly after he assumed command of that Confederate Army which became known as the Army of Northern Virginia. This step partially offset the Southerners' inferiority in quantity and quality of their matériel. While their batteries were much less uniform than those of the Yankees, with the number of pieces per battery varying from two to six, and usually two different types or

calibers within a battery, their battalion organization gave
them a system with a ready means of centralized control to
shift batteries to threatened points.

The Confederates had witnessed at the Second Manassas the
great power of their own massed artillery, and following this
campaign they strove to put more guns with the divisions. They
realized, too, that having batteries grouped into battalions had
not in itself gained this end. Similarly, having an artillery reserve should not mean a mass of guns rumbling in the rear of
the Army, but it should mean a body under the close direction
of the commanding general, whose wider grasp of the tactical
picture would enable him to throw the reserve artillery into the
point where its effect on the issue would be greatest. The Federals were already making some progress in learning this lesson.

Thus, just prior to Antietam further reforms were ordered
for the Gray artillery. The theory was to attach one artillery
battalion to each of Jackson's four and Longstreet's five divisions, an additional reserve battalion for each corps, and a general reserve for the entire Army. Each battalion, whether divisional or reserve artillery, was to have its own field officers,
and a battalion assigned to a division fell under the command
of the division chief-of-artillery. While these forward steps
were not all completed by the time of the battle, they were
sound moves and anticipated by nine months similar ones that
Hunt was finally able to have the Union high command accept.

Within the Army of the Potomac the only semblance of an
artillery staff were the division and corps chiefs-of-artillery. But
these men nearly always had two functions, the first a useful
one, the second a theoretical and rarely useful one. These two
functions were hard to reconcile, for it was extremely difficult
for a young officer to be a battery commander, putting his own
unit into action and directing its fire, and at the same time be
a division chief-of-artillery, and go looking for positions for
other batteries of his command — even assuming that he had
the authority to order guns to spots of his choosing. Here, as
before, in the Army of the Potomac, the field batteries found

themselves tied down to the very narrow limits of infantry commands, which at this stage of the war all too often meant merely a brigade — at best 1500 men. And the infantry commanders held onto the control of batteries wherever possible. This division of command caused the Union great trouble on its right flank on September 17th.

Ever uneasy about the safety of the Federal capital, and quite uncertain of Lee's intentions, Halleck tied McClellan's forces close to Washington. When the weary Yankee cavalry finally convinced the high command that Robert E. Lee was behind the Monocacy River between Washington and Frederick, McClellan followed in his usual slow fashion. On September 7th elements of the Yankee Army reached the quiet hamlet of Rockville, fourteen miles northwest of Washington. Hunt, now proudly and deservedly wearing a brigadier general's star, discovered that there was a dangerous shortage of artillery ammunition. To the arsenal in Washington he sent orders to make up a reserve ammunition train similar to the one used on the Peninsula and have it join the Army as quickly as possible. As during the Seven Days battles, Hunt's train was finally used to supply ammunition to the batteries of the entire Army.

The Confederates, ill-equipped but in high spirits after walloping the braggart Pope, waded across the Potomac and on September 7th kindled their campfires in the fields outside the quaint town of Frederick. From here, three days later, Lee split his Army; Jackson with roughly half the Confederate strength set out at a typical Jacksonian pace to seize the Federal base at Harpers Ferry, while the balance of the Army marched westward over the mountains toward their fate on a sunken road.

Utterly indefensible in the first place, Harpers Ferry fell on September 15th to Stonewall Jackson. Among the spoils of war the Confederates acquired were seventy-three pieces of artillery, some of it badly needed field artillery.[2] In the meantime Lee's entire plan of action and disposition of his troops became known to McClellan when on September 13th, an authenticated copy of Lee's Special Order 191 fell into Yankee hands. The leading Blue regiments had tramped into Frederick two days after the Army of Northern Virginia had departed westward; on a camp ground used by the Confederates the copy of Lee's order had been found.

Armed with this historic stroke of luck Little Mac sent masses of men in dark blue jackets and sky blue trousers west toward the passes of the Blue Ridge Mountains. The Army of the Potomac was in good spirits, even though everyone now knew that those ragged but deadly regiments that made up the Army of Northern Virginia lay somewhere beyond these hazy peaks and ridges.

Confederate Jeb Stuart's sharp patrols picked up the news of the lost order, and during the night of September 13th a dust-covered courier on a jaded mount slid to a halt at Lee's headquarters, the ominous news in his dispatch case. Time was the key for the Rebels; the passes over the mountains had to be held to give Lee time to reunite his army. Tired footsore brigades were faced about and sent hurrying up the crests of the mountains.

In the misty dawn of September 14th Yankee cavalry started up the east face of South Mountain to see if Turner's and Fox's gaps were clear. A few scattered shots greeted them, then a sheet of flame ripped the top of a rock wall and sent them sprawling in the dust. Blue infantry moved forward cautiously; by noon two whole corps had wormed their way into position to force the gaps.

The outnumbered Confederates fought bitterly, and it took until late that evening, when both flanks of the thin Gray line had been enveloped, for the Federals to secure Turner's and Fox's gaps. Some distance to the south more Bluecoats forced Crampton's Gap, and now McClellan was free to flood his regiments onto the rolling valleys between the mountains and the Potomac River. A sleepy little trading town, Sharpsburg, lay off in the westward haze, just beyond a meandering creek named the Antietam. Yankee cavalry kept up a running fight with Jeb Stuart's troopers, as the weary Rebels pulled back toward the Potomac near Sharpsburg.

On the range of hills immediately across Antietam Creek, with the Potomac at his back, Lee united the greater part of his Army; here he would stand and fight, even though A. P. Hill's division was still absent — Jackson had left it at Harpers Ferry to take care of the surrender of that garrison — and McLaws's and Anderson's divisions were not expected until early on the 17th.

In the sunny morning of September 15th the waiting Confederates caught sight of the leading brigades of the Army of the Potomac as they tramped down the road from Keedysville toward Sharpsburg. Several of the Gray long-range batteries cut loose at the lines as they moved along the hills along the east bank of Antietam Creek. Federal horse batteries returned the fire.

Late that afternoon McClellan turned to Gen. Hunt and asked him personally to select the locations for the guns of position — as the heavier pieces of the Reserve were called. With the break of dawn the next day Hunt and Col. Hays were riding furiously back and forth along the heights just east of Antietam Creek, shepherding the Reserve batteries into line. Heavy iron-rimmed wheels clattered over rock and shale; puffing, snorting teams heaved in the traces as the heavy guns of Taft's, Langner's, Von Kleiser's, and Wever's 20-pounder Parrott batteries rolled onto the ridge between Middle Bridge and the Pry house where McClellan had set up his headquarters.

Confederate gunners spotted the activity and opened fire with their handful of long-range rifles — there were only six 20-pounders in all of Lee's Army. The Yankee gunners ripped the leather vent covers from their pieces and swung into it, replying many times over. One sharp-eyed Confederate crew quickly picked up the range, and as Maj. Arndt, commander of the 1st New York (German) Battalion, and one of the few field grade artillery officers in the Army, walked over to check the sighting of one of his pieces, an enemy round perfectly fuzed mortally wounded Arndt. The noisy duel continued until the Confederates, who had few rifles capable of reaching their target and were worried about their tight ammunition supply, ceased fire. The Union guns then slackened off and finally ceased. A tense night settled over that quiet farm country.

It is difficult to understand how a professional soldier such as McClellan would bring on a major offensive action without a carefully detailed plan. Yet it appears that he fought the battle of Antietam like a rank tyro who had only the vaguest notions of the basic principles of warfare. In his original version of his final report McClellan gives us his 'plan.'

> The design was to make the main attack upon the enemy's left — at least to create a diversion in favor of the main attack, with the hope of something more, by assailing the enemy's right — and, as soon as one or both of the flank movements were fully successful, to attack their center with any reserve I might then have in hand.[3]

When carefully read, the plan said little specifically and was confusing and contradictory; for instance a main effort was also to be a diversion. Small wonder then that McClellan's offensive would be a series of disjointed attacks, each one of which, strangely enough, came close to bringing an end to the Confederacy.

To carry out the plan, on the afternoon of September 16th, Gen. Hooker was told by McClellan to push his I Corps across the Antietam a few miles north of Sharpsburg and find Lee's left flank. Lee saw him coming and sent Hood's division to meet him, with several batteries bouncing along in the rear as support. The prodding Blue columns shoved out for the higher ground between the creek and the Potomac just north of the town. Hooker gained the northern shoulder of this divide, swung his front to its left, and started south.

In an open little glade, which became known as East Woods,

Meade's division, covering the flank of Hooker's corps, collided with Hood, and both sides unlimbered their batteries. One Rebel shell whirred over Meade and finally exploded above Gen. Abner Doubleday, in the process dismounting three of that officer's orderlies. This outburst evoked a snarling answer from Hays's 20-pounders of the Reserve, and three of Meade's batteries began hitting the Confederate gunners hard.[4]

The fight continued viciously until darkness forced the Federals to stop their firing.

The weary Yankee infantry threw their blankets on the ground behind the Poffenberger ridge just north of where they had fought, and fell into exhausted sleep. It rained on and off all that night of September 16th. The troops in Hooker's ranks sought protection under their flimsy oilskins, but cold rivulets seeped through every opening and turned the heavy uniforms into sopping mats of itchy, smelly wool.

Joe Hooker and his staff established headquarters in J. Poffenberger's barn, from which couriers came and went as preparations for the attack of the coming day were made. The general himself finally rolled up in a blanket in a corner of the stone building and snatched a few hours sleep, as outside jumpy pickets of both armies sniped at each other in the black, pouring night.

Just before first light the pelting rain slowed to a drizzle; at dawn it stopped, and a heavy mist hung low over the drenched countryside. The Blue troops were awakened while it was still dark and ate hurried make-shift breakfasts. The I Corps then prepared to smash its way south to seize the high ground three-quarters of a mile away which commanded the whole enemy position.

The land in front of Hooker was rolling and scarred by frequent outcroppings of rock, cornfields, orchards, and stone and split-rail fences. Three patches of woods checkered this front. One of these, North Woods, lay on both sides of the Hagerstown-Sharpsburg Turnpike, a little over a mile north of an unimpressive small white building known as the Dunker

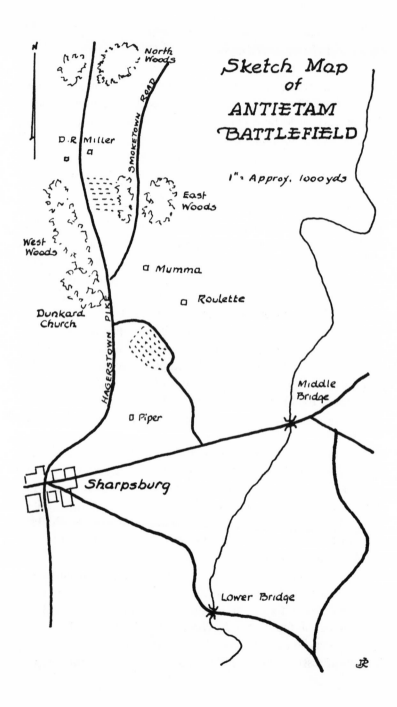

Church. The church stood on the west edge of the turnpike about a mile north of town. The building is gone now but the ruins remain. East of the pike and about a quarter-mile northeast of the Dunker Church was an open glade known as East Woods, and the ground between both of these woods and the church was farm land, partly cultivated with corn. Just across the road was the other stand of open timber — West Woods — whose southern edge curled about the backyard of the little white church.

Directly in front of Hooker as he struck south, roughly parallel to the pike, were the men of Stonewall Jackson, their left flank anchored by Jeb Stuart with a mass of his own and Jackson's guns shrewdly posted on some low hills northwest of the Dunker Church. These guns annoyed the Yankees all day. Jackson's infantry was strung out from the West Woods across the pike into Miller's cornfield with detachments in the East Woods. On his right was the division of D. H. Hill in position along the rise where stood the Mumma and Roulette farm buildings. On Hill's right, swinging south past the town, the few remaining available troops under Longstreet guarded Lee's right. The Confederates were short on men, but they were long on guts and confidence — trumps on this day.

The I Corps lines swept over the top of sheltering hills and started into the muddy plowed fields by the pike, and its left flank, Ricketts's division, headed for the still-quiet East Woods. Doubleday's division, in which marched Gibbon's Iron Brigade, was the right of Hooker's attack, and George Meade's division followed as support.

The first rays of sun could now be seen over the hilltops to the east. The officers and men of Battery D, 1st Rhode Island Light Artillery, one of Hooker's batteries, had not yet received orders committing them to action, though their horses were saddled, teams hitched, and guns in position behind a crest. The captain, J. A. Monroe, and his officers sat in a group on a blanket, as an orderly brought them a pail of steaming coffee and a pan of johnnycakes. Within sight were other I Corps batteries, awaiting the command that would send them into action. Suddenly a bright flash, a deafening clap, and a deadly buzzing scattered the breakfast group; a Rebel shell passed a foot over their heads and exploded just beyond. Monroe, who was also Doubleday's chief-of-artillery, sprang to his feet and bellowed the loud command, 'Action Front!' The Blue gunners ran to their pieces, grabbed the big wheels, and shouldered the guns forward onto the crest. The artillery fight was on.

Into action with the Rhode Islanders went three other batteries of the division. Reliable old Battery B, 4th U.S., took their left, while Battery L, 1st New York Light Artillery, and a New Hampshire battery of 12-pounder howitzers under Lt. Edgell clattered up on their right. Twenty-four cannon banged away in defiant reply. The smoke thickened rapidly, and it was soon impossible for the Federal gunners to determine how many enemy batteries had opened; some of Monroe's men thought three, others two, and a few believed only one.

Actually Confederate Col. Stephen D. Lee had put five batteries of his battalion in a field just southeast of the Dunker Church, and these guns had picked up the I Corps columns in the distant haze. When the Rebel gunners spotted the heavy lines and thick columns, they quickly loaded their pieces, brought on target, and fired. Far over on the Confederate left Stuart's valiant gunner, Pelham, joined by some of Jackson's cannon, began punching at Hooker's right flank. With a terrific crash one of those Gray shells exploded over the 6th Wisconsin of the Iron Brigade, knocking thirteen men out of action — an amazingly high total for one shell of that era.

Hooker's columns found the going slow. A Yankee colonel reported to Hooker: 'The rebels are opening from a battery in the edge of the woods!' 'Let them open,' scoffed Hooker, 'we have as many batteries as they have. Forward!' [5]

Doubleday's men brushed aside some rail fences, swung into wide front, and tramped into a plowed pasture with a cornfield beyond. Confederate skirmishers began firing at them and drifted back to the northern edge of the cornfield, and Ricketts bumped into a murderous fire as his troops moved through the East Woods.

To the rear of John Gibbon's Black Hat boys rumbled old Battery B, ordered forward from its position on the ridge. Enemy cannon on a knoll about halfway between the pike and the East Woods had picked up the range on the cheering Federal infantry. Doubleday sent orders to Battery B to knock out those guns. Capt. Campbell, commanding Battery B, swung his right arm and ordered his little bugler, fourteen-year-old Johnny Cook, to blow the unit into action. The rasping notes ripped over the battle roar, and Battery B wheeled about so that its muzzles were pointing south, and they went into position — in a field nearly abreast of the Miller house which still stands on the east side of Maryland Route 65.

More artillery fire from directly in front harassed the Black Hat boys, and heavy musketry from Confederate infantry covered by a stone ledge on the Yankee right flank inflicted heavy casualties. Gibbon sent for two guns of Battery B to move up, and Capt. Campbell detached Lt. Stewart and his section to handle them. Stewart's cannoneers hurriedly tore down the stone wall behind the Miller house, and the two guns and caissons were rushed through the gap, across the lawn, and out onto the pike. Just south of the house, on the opposite side of the pike, was the Miller barn in a stable yard. Beyond was an open grass field with some straw stacks in a corner close to the stone barn. The barn and the open field stand today, almost unchanged. Stewart led his section a few yards down the road, passed through a gate into the barnyard, turned toward the open field which rose gently to the south. They went through another gate, and when they had gained the crest Stewart yelled, 'Action Front.'

Immediately the lieutenant spotted a large body of enemy infantry a little over 400 yards away. He ordered spherical case, with a one and a half-second fuze. The undulating ground militated in favor of case, the range being overlong for canister. There was a flurry of moving men about the two guns, then the crews stepped clear of the readied weapons. 'Fire!' Stewart's command rang out, and the upraised right arms of the sergeants chiefs-of-piece dropped in signal. The two pieces flamed in unison. The Gray ranks partially broke under the fire, and Rebel troops could be seen running across a hollow in front of the section, crossing to the east side of the pike, and diving into the now-famous cornfield.[6]

Thirty to forty yards in front of Stewart, a fence separated the western part of the cornfield from a pasture. The corn was green and high, and soon it was swarming with Confederate infantry who rose up, took quick aim at the battery, then ducked down to reload. Others crept alongside the stone fence-line by the road. Within minutes Stewart's command was all but out of action, with fourteen casualties. The bodies of the dead and fallen wounded hindered the survivors working the guns. Several of the able-bodied cannoneers hauled bleeding bodies to the shelter of two nearby haystacks, but then saw some of the wounded, delirious with pain, stagger to their feet from beds of straw, only to be struck again and this time killed.

Then there was a loud clattering of wheels and heavy pounding of horses' hoofs, and through the battle smoke came Capt. Campbell with the other two sections and the battery's twelve caissons.[7] Into line on Stewart's left went the other four Napoleons. Campbell dismounted and Johnny Cook came running to be at his side, his shining brass bugle bouncing on his hip. At that instant there was a crash of musketry from somewhere out front and Campbell staggered and started to fall. Johnny grabbed the falling officer, who had been hit in the shoulder and in the side. The captain's horse, pawing ground near his master, was killed instantly by seven bullets. Cook aided the stricken officer to his feet and helped him to the rear till they reached a driver, who took the captain over his shoulder. As he was being carried to safety Campbell retained enough composure to order Johnny to tell Stewart, the only other officer on the field, that he was now in formal command of the battery.

BATTERY B'S POSITION

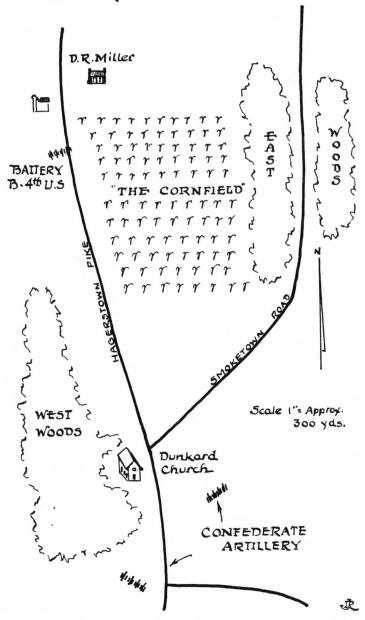

D.R. Miller

BATTERY B. 4th U.S.

"THE CORNFIELD"

EAST

WOODS

HAGERSTOWN PIKE

SMOKETOWN ROAD

N

WEST WOODS

Dunkard Church

Scale 1"= Approx. 300 yds.

CONFEDERATE ARTILLERY

On all sides the vicious crackling of musket fire swelled to an almost unbroken roar, punctuated by the deep crashes of Battery B's six Napoleons. The position being on a rise, the gunners had trouble depressing their muzzles enough to reach the fence line in front from where a sizzling fire was coming. Then an enemy battery on a hill to the right of Battery B added to their troubles by opening fire, but the men had no time to notice the battery, as they were acting as mere automatons in the sweaty work of loading and firing. Crewmen were dropping at every piece, some without a sound, others screaming in pain; Battery B's rate of fire began to fall off, as the survivors had to do double then triple duty.

Johnny Cook, returning from his mission, found the battery a shambles. A dead cannoneer, his leather pouch complete with an unfired round still strapped to him, lay directly in front of the youngster. Johnny was a bugler, but he was first a soldier; without hesitating the lad picked up the fallen man's pouch, stepped over the body, and ran to the nearest gun. The brave young boy stuck with the piece and served it well for the rest of the engagement. For his conduct that day he became the youngest Medal of Honor winner in the nation's history.

The vicious fight about the guns raged on. The air about began to stink from burned sulphur, and the howling missiles continued to inflict death and pain. The smoke became so dense that gunners could only guess where their targets lay, even though the nearest cover for the enemy was a bare thirty paces away. At one time, only a corporal was left standing. Alone, the man grabbed a case round, cut the fuze for muzzle burst, rammed it home, primed, and then jerked the lanyard as a covey of Rebels came streaking toward him. The attackers ducked back to cover.

Federal commanders were working frantically to bring up infantry to protect the guns, but as yet the battery stood alone, and would do so for some minutes more. A sergeant staggered to earth, a bullet through his abdomen. He was hauled to Miller's barn, where he was told his wound was fatal. In agony, his face lined with pain, the sergeant bit his lip, drew his Colt, and shot himself through the right temple.

Pvt. Horace Ripley from the 7th Wisconsin had been attached to Battery B on September 13th as a supernumerary on a gun crew, but on the morning of the 17th he had been given the job of horse-holder for a sergeant. During the early part of the action Ripley helped a wounded gunner over to Miller's barn, which had now been turned into a crude field hospital, rapidly being filled with bleeding humans. On his return to the battery Ripley was given two horses to hold. He had no sooner grasped their bridles when one of the animals was hit in flank and fell dying. Then a sickening splat of a flying Minié ball knocked the bit from the mouth of the second, carrying away the whole under jaw of the beast. A corporal ran over, drew his pistol, and shot the horse.

Casualties were now so heavy that Ripley was called up to serve one of the guns. The slaughter raged on until only Ripley and a sergeant were left on their weapon. Then several of Ripley's friends from the 7th Wisconsin, fighting nearby, saw their plight and aided them in serving the piece.

At this point Gen. Gibbon rode up. The gun in the road had been swung over to play on the enemy, who seemed to be making headway through the cornfield east of the pike. The piece was firing furiously but seemingly with little effect. Then Gibbon saw why. The gunner had allowed the elevation screw to run down, and the rounds were passing harmlessly over the enemy's heads. The general yelled to the gunner but so great was the battle roar that the man never heard him. Dismounting, Gibbon ran to the piece, pushed the gunner aside, and grabbed the screw and began twisting, at the same time sighting along the top of the tube. The muzzle began to drop; there, lined up as it should be. Gibbon stepped clear and motioned to the gunner to take over again. Miraculously Gibbon escaped being hit, even though he wore the obvious trappings of a general officer. Probably only the wispy drifts of smoke saved him from the sights of the Southerners' muskets.

Gray infantry threatened to seize the piece in the road. Double canister was rammed home; the crew stepped clear as a sweaty hand jerked the lanyard. A terrific clap shook the air, nearly stunning Maj. Dawes of the 6th Wisconsin, whose regiment was close by preparing to move forward again. The swath of slugs from the big gun slammed into the fence in front, blowing it into large hunks which arched lazily through the air.

All the pieces now shifted to double canister, as the yelling Confederates closed in. Lt. Stewart was startled to see the loader at one of the cannon, an attached Volunteer, shove two complete canister rounds down the tube. Stewart ran to the soldier and hurriedly explained that double canister meant two of the tin canisters, but only one powder charge; and instructed him to tear the cartridge off the extra round before loading! The man nodded, then proceeded as shown. The lieutenant walked back to his post behind the guns. Reaching his position he turned about; his eyes fell instinctively on the loader. The poor Volunteer was still struggling to pull the heavy tin canister free from the wooden sabot and its attached cloth powder bag. Then the man obviously caught his finger and was struggling to free it. His finger loose, the Volunteer immediately decided he had had enough of this nonsense; thereafter every double canister he loaded went into the tube as it came from the arsenal — with powder bag attached.

For ten minutes more the battery kept up its banging; then, as Hooker moved his men forward to drive back Jackson's now decimated regiments, the battery's field of fire became masked. Lt. Stewart called for cease fire, and the hot, smoke-blackened Napoleons fell silent. As the 6th Wisconsin moved past Battery B's position, the men saw a horse apparently in the process of trying to rise from the ground. The beast's head was proudly erect and its forelegs were set firmly forward. But the animal never seemed to move. As the column passed they saw that the horse was dead.[8]

In fact blood was splattered all over Battery B, and the dead were sprawled about it. With its teams virtually obliterated and forty men out of one hundred present for duty as casualties, the unit had taken a heavy beating, all of it in outright casualties, for there had been no loss of men as prisoners, as would happen when a battery was overrun by the enemy. Few batteries before or afterward would endure such a bloody day.

Hooker's I Corps was now ripping a big hole dead center in Jackson's line — a feat not too often accomplished against that man. The cheering Blue lines drove forward in the haze of drifting gunsmoke. Through the East Woods struggled Ricketts's brigades, as Doubleday's shouldered their way through Miller's cornfield, two brigades of Meade's division following in their wake. Ricketts found the enemy extremely obstinate as he fought through the woods toward the turnpike. His division's two batteries, Matthews's F, 1st Pennsylvania Light Artillery, and Thompson's Independent Pennsylvania Battery, each with four 3-inch ordnance rifles, had rolled forward with the infantry, and when contact was made the two batteries slipped into open ground to bring supporting fire to bear.[9]

In the meantime Hays's big Parrotts of the Artillery Reserve had cut loose shortly after the Blue infantry began moving at dawn, and their heavy projectiles were pounding the whole area in front of Hooker's attack. The dull booms of the big guns sounded as distant thunder over the battlefield. Since their position was almost perpendicular to a good part of Jackson's and D. H. Hill's lines, their fire began to take the Gray regiments in flank — an ideal situation in those days of linear warfare. Jackson found himself in deep trouble and sent a staff officer galloping to Lee for help. That officer later remarked that so severe and furious was the shelling by the Yankee batteries that he believed he would never return from his mission alive. Heavy rifle volleys from front and enfilading blasts of cannon fire were wrecking Jackson's line. Confederate artillery, of necessity ignoring the Yankee guns across the creek, spotted gun flashes and tried to counter the fire of the arc of guns from the fields near the East Woods to the Poffenberger ridge.

A number of Federal batteries from Hooker's I Corps seem

to have been left on the Poffenberger ridge for two reasons: first, as protection for the open right flank; and second, because the ground over which the infantry was advancing was undulating and patched with woods, thus making it no proper place to station accompanying field batteries. But a call for more artillery filtered back to that rise, and Reynolds's Battery L, 1st New York Light Artillery, promptly ceased fire, limbered, and moved forward through the North Woods into the plowed land beyond. As the New Yorkers pulled away, there was a clattering of shod hoofs on dirt and rock, and two fresh batteries rolled into the vacated spot.[10]

Through the fog-like smoke that hung low over the ground, flicks of fire and dull distant booms of an enemy battery in a field beyond the pike gave the New Yorkers a target. The guns peeled from column into action front. With a shuddering roar the six rifles let go, and immediately the Rebels reacted with counter-battery fire.

The Confederates had put a good number of batteries behind Jackson's and D. H. Hill's lines, with a heavy concentration of Col. Lee's battalion on the slope just southeast of the Dunker Church. These presented a conspicuous and tempting target to Hays's Reserve batteries east of the creek; it was one they did not ignore either. With few guns capable of reaching across the Antietam, Lee's batteries had to sit and take the enfilading fire from the 20-pounders while they themselves tried to stop the I Corps infantry or dueled with the closer Yankee batteries.

The fire of the Federal batteries began to have an effect. The guns dueling with Reynolds called it quits and pulled out. Gibbon then shifted Reynolds over to the right, where the sad remnants of Battery B — two guns were all that battered outfit could man — had been retired. Although neither battery knew it then, they would not be in serious fighting again.

The Gray artillery was not the only arm suffering from the crushing weight of incoming artillery fire. Most of Jackson's and Hill's infantry was perpendicular to Hays's guns, and some regiments suffered considerably from their fire, while others though not hard hit, found the fire extremely annoying. At least one Gray commander witnessing the profusion of Yankee shelling concluded that the Federal guns were so far superior to his own in weight of metal, character of guns and numbers, and in such quality of ammunition 'that there was but very little to be gained by opposing ours to it, and I therefore did not renew the attempt after the first experiments.' [11] Two months later Col. Lee, on learning that the talented Gray officer Col. E. Porter Alexander was being transferred to the artillery, told him: 'Pray that you may never see another Sharpsburg. Sharpsburg was artillery hell.' [12]

In the wake of Doubleday's slowly advancing regiments came two brigades from Meade's division. Close on their right was the turnpike, and on their left was the plowed field and an orchard, and beyond this was the cornfield. Into this plowed field bounced Ransom's Regulars — Battery C, 5th U.S., with four shining bronze Napoleons. Ransom opened fire on the enemy infantry and the Gray batteries.

Meade's two brigades reached the cornfield and deployed along a fence line to cover Doubleday's men, who were recoiling in the face of a blistering Rebel fire. Then orders came from Hooker to send a brigade over to the left. Meade obeyed. That left one brigade on the fence line. Instantly powder-streaked Confederate infantry poured toward the gap left by the departed unit. Trigger-tempered Meade saw the danger and galloped over to Ransom. Pointing through the yellowish haze at the advancing enemy, he ordered him to take those people under fire. A shout by the captain, and immediately hands grabbed trail spikes and swung the reeking gun tubes around on the new target. The four pieces boomed away, and Ricketts's infantry caught the spirit and picked up their rate of fire. The enemy halted, held a ragged flaming line for a few volleys, then fell back to the cover of the West Woods.[13]

The tide of battle had turned against Hooker, though. After Jackson's line had been cracked open, Hood's division, with some of the finest fighting regiments in the Confederacy, piled in to seal the break and then punched back in counter-attack. The shock to the I Corps was great, and the exhausted troops began to give ground. At this point the two-division XII Corps, which had crossed the Antietam the night before, at last oriented and deployed itself, and came forward to Hooker's support.

The XII Corps had five batteries, two of which the corps commander had posted before dawn on the hills adjacent to general headquarters. The other three had apparently crossed the creek with the corps that night and during the morning had been waiting idly for the corps infantry to move up. Now the XII Corps was on the field, Greene's division striking southward astride the Smoketown Road, while Williams's marched southward from the North Woods toward Miller's cornfield. Gen. Mansfield, the corps commander, rode out in front of Greene's men, groping for intelligence on a confused field, and was shot down mortally wounded. Immediately Williams, the senior division commander, took charge and ordered forward the other three batteries: Knap's Pennsylvanians, Cothran's New Yorkers, and Hampton's Pennsylvanians from Pittsburgh. The three units dug spur and rumbled down the gravelly roads to where the infantry was prepared to attack Jackson's men in the West Woods.

As the batteries trotted out of the East Woods, a heavy and continuous buzzing began to sing about their ears. The old-timers knew what that meant: They could expect to take casualties now from enemy musket fire. Knap swung his guns into line across the road leading from the woods to the Dunker Church, while Cothran's Battery M, 1st New York Light Artillery, angled off to the right of the road until they were about 650 yards from the church and 450 from the Hagerstown Pike. It was now about 7 a.m. Knap opened fire, and Hampton's guns moved into battery farther to the left, near Greene's division.[14]

The XII Corps, with Williams's division on the right and Greene's on the left, began its attack. Through the ranks of

Hooker's shattered regiments the newcomers marched, and on into the cornfield toward the West Woods. Hood's division fought to hold the field, but the weight of the heavy fresh Blue regiments was too much, and the gap in Jackson's line threatened to reopen. The yelling and hurrahing Yankees kept coming. Jackson had every man who could fire a musket in the fight, but it was not enough, and his line split open wider than before. Greene's men reached the turnpike, swept across to the west side, and gained a fingerhold of the rise about the Dunker Church, but Williams's regiments had all they could do to recover the ground originally seized by Hooker's men earlier in the morning.

All this while the big Parrotts of Hays's Reserve had been giving the Confederate batteries near the church a merciless pounding. Coupled with Hays's fire came that of the advanced Yankee batteries near the cornfield, and undoubtedly some of those on the Poffenberger ridge were firing in this direction. A converging storm of iron slammed into Col. Lee's batteries from front and flank. Wheels were smashed, men knocked down, and horses sent screaming. To stay in that field was to sacrifice units needlessly. Unable to neutralize Hays's guns because of the great range, Lee pulled his battalion back to a crest west of the pike that offered some cover from those big 20-pounders but still gave them a field of fire toward the I and XII Corps.

It seemed to Confederate Gen. D. H. Hill that every time one of his own guns opened fire every Yankee cannon in range would converge its fire on it and blow the hapless gun out of action.[15] One Rebel infantryman described the Yankee shelling as the heaviest he had ever heard. In awe he noted the semicircle of guns which seemed to be planted on every hill commanding the Gray position. 'The smoke rolled backward to the mountains in their rear, but their destructive shot and shell were falling, it would appear, on every foot of land behind us. I doubt not that at one time there was one piece of artillery firing at the hill to every five men we had defending it.'[16]

However, at this point the XII Corps' attack was stopped. The corps was utterly spent, and it had run low on ammunition. During the brief lull in infantry fighting, as the Federals lay exhausted, Robert E. Lee used the precious minutes to hurry more brigades from his right to repair his shattered left. The action fell off to a bitter snarling and snapping of artillery.

It was now somewhere around 9:30 a.m. and at this point Sumner led his II Corps onto the field. The scene which greeted the old man told him the story beyond any mistake. Union soldiers of both the I and XII Corps were streaming back toward the safety of the line of batteries on the Poffenberger ridge.[17] Sumner, the blood rushing in his veins once more with the vigor of youth, could see but one thing to do — attack! So with the only element of his corps then on the field, the infantry of Sedgwick's division, the general threw its columns into line and headed for the West Woods.

The attack was gallant but stupid. With no prior reconnaissance Sedgwick's men tramped into a virtual cul-de-sac. In short minutes the division was virtually destroyed, as the Confederate force shredded it from front, flank, and rear. There was only one place for the few lucky survivors to go — north and east over the turnpike.

One may well ask: where was Sumner's artillery? The corps had a complement of seven batteries, five short of McClellan's ideal for a three-division corps, but the records indicate that in the hurried and haphazard deployment none of these were in position in time to aid Sumner's first attack.[18] Frank's New Yorkers were probably the first to go into action, with that officer reporting his battery in firing position sometime prior to 9 a.m., on the 'right and center' of the line with a Maine infantry regiment in support.[19] Frank's gunners bent to their work, as eager Confederate infantry were trying to make tactical hay out of the near panic of Sedgwick's routed lines. A half-hour had passed when an enemy battery suddenly opened a severe fire on Frank's left front. The captain ordered his guns to switch to solid shot and knock out those guns. There was a flurry of motion as cannoneers grabbed the long hickory handspikes which stuck up at an angle from the end of the carriage trails, and the big mouths of the four Napoleons swung over toward the new target. Frank's upraised arm dropped, and a thundering crash of ten pounds of exploding propellant powder shook the ground.

The New Yorkers had fired only a few rounds when a whirring low overhead, quickly followed by explosions nearby, warned them that a new Gray battery was raking them with a nasty cross-fire from their left flank. But Capt. Frank kept his gunners working on the first battery till it pulled out of the duel; only then did he swing his four Napoleons about, changing front forward on his left piece. The new antagonists proved a bit more tenacious, and it took Battery G fifty rounds of solid and shell before this second enemy unit retreated.

As Sedgwick's beaten regiments fled eastward over the pike, Capt. F. N. Clarke, Sumner's chief-of-artillery, ordered Battery I, 1st U.S., led by Lt. G. A. Woodruff, into an open field about 300 yards from the West Woods and a little to the right of the church.[20] With horses straining in taut traces, the column wound into position. No fire greeted them as they began unlimbering; apparently they had been unnoticed by the enemy. Woodruff called for canister, and as the crews readied the guns the lieutenant looked about for some infantry support. There was none, only disorganized or demoralized regiments streaming rearward in quest of safety. The hope that any of these would stand was nil. Woodruff saw that he would have to stand alone against the pursuing Rebels. So, spurring his horse, Woodruff trotted out in front of his guns. After waving his hands to clear the fleeing troops from his front, he sent his six Napoleons crashing into action at the long, hollering line of advancing Rebel infantry.

Gen. Gibbon, whose own exhausted and depleted regiments were resting on the Poffenberger rise, had seen Sumner leading Sedgwick's division out of the East Woods. Thinking he might be of some service to Sumner, he galloped over to his position.

Knowing that officer's fine reputation as a gunner, the old man
eagerly accepted Gibbon's offer. Sumner asked Gibbon to assist
the corps chief-of-artillery in finding positions for the batteries.
Gibbon tipped his hat brim in salute and rode after Capt.
Clarke, the artillery chief. Finding the captain he advised him
of Sumner's request, got a battery, and proceeded to lead it
toward high ground just beyond the road leading to the Dunker
Church. Before he could get the unit into position, pandemonium broke loose over on the right. Sedgwick's men had
walked into the trap and were fighting desperately to extricate
themselves. Gibbon left the battery and galloped northward at
top speed to rally the broken regiments and be with his own
command should that ridge fall under attack.[21]

As the shaken elements of Sedgwick's command and part of
Greene's fell back into the Miller cornfield, already filled with
dead bodies of both armies, Southern gunners to the south took
them in flank, and Pelham's cannon hit them in their backs.
Every available Yankee gun now came into action. The Poffenberger ridge was aflame as I and XII Corps batteries barked
and snarled in frenzied and defiant reply. As their fields of fire
became uncovered, other guns in the cornfields and plowed
ground in front of the East Woods began to chop up the pursuing Confederates. It was a critical moment for the Army of
the Potomac, and the outcome rested solely on the shoulders of
the Federal artillerymen.

Woodruff's Napoleons were being fired as fast as they could
be worked; the polished bronze barrels grew too hot to touch
with the naked hand; the roar of cannon fire reached a crescendo. The fierce hail of shelling took a heavy toll, and the
Confederates, unwilling to close in the face of a fire which was
both lethal and psychological, were at last stopped. Woodruff's
guns had used about 180 rounds up to this point.

There was a brief pause in the firing. Then Woodruff spotted
other Rebels massing in back of the church. The lieutenant
watched them for a minute or so. Then the Gray ranks started
to move; it looked as if they were going to try and side-slip to

their right into a piece of low ground and take Woodruff on his left flank. Immediately, Battery I started work on them with solid shot. When the smoke parted once or twice the batterymen saw several of their rounds pass clear through the little building and bounce into the enemy position behind.

The Southerners were not easily discouraged, though. Into a low part of the road went the Rebel force, and it headed for the battery's left flank just as Woodruff had thought it would. To change front to meet the enemy troops would expose the battery's right to Pelham's guns. Instead Woodruff pulled his command back about a hundred yards to the very edge of the East Woods,[22] and re-opened fire. One overly zealous Confederate regiment, in its enthusiasm of chasing fleeing Yankees, suddenly found itself out in the open, some 300 yards in advance of the Gray lines and in full view of the mass of Federal cannon. Within minutes the regiment had been hideously cut to pieces; now it fell back to the West Woods to avoid complete annihilation.

That there was confusion among the numerous Yankee batteries competing for the sparse number of firing spaces on the Federal right is indicated by Capt. Owens, commanding Battery G, 1st Rhode Island Light Artillery. His unit had been ordered into action by Capt. Clarke, and Owens had searched for a position. From the extreme right to the center of the long Blue line they wandered, finally reaching the East Woods opposite the Dunker Church. From here Owens spotted a piece of open ground across the pike in rear of the church, and as Sedgwick's columns disappeared into those woods west of the road the battery commander decided to move forward to this open ground. But scarcely had he given the order when Blue figures came running from the timber — at first just a few, then a whole swarm, retreating over a rise, with the enemy in hot pursuit.

Owens swung his arm and turned his column about, bringing it back to a position close to the burning Mumma buildings. Here he found Capt. Clarke again. Owens asked him where he should put his guns. He was told by Clarke that there were more batteries now than could be used. Owens was to put his men under cover for the time being. So Owens led his unit back to a field behind an orchard in rear of the Mumma house. Here they would remain until later in the morning when they would replace a shattered sister battery that was running out of ammunition.

In the meantime, as Sedgwick and Greene were taking their beating, the other two divisions of the II Corps had filed onto the battlefield. But instead of following Sedgwick's path they had diverged more to the southwest. The leading division, French's, rolled into line of battle on the left of Greene's crumbling line, and collided with D. H. Hill's men just beyond the Mumma house. The last of Sumner's corps, Richardson's division, then came hurrying forward on French's left, and a bitter fight was soon in progress in the center of the two opposing armies.

At this point a staff officer from Gen. Sumner rode up to Capt. Tompkins, commanding Battery A, 1st Rhode Island Light Artillery, with orders for it to report to Gen. French. Across fields and over rough farm paths the column trotted, finally reaching French's line near the Mumma house. At this point a hasty buzzing, resembling an aroused beehive, greeted the gunners. A man fell from his horse; then a cannoneer riding on one of the limbers was hit. Minutes later two more went down. Drivers bent low over their horses' necks and cannoneers astride the limbers instinctively ducked down to avoid the whirring missiles. The six black 10-pounder Parrotts wheeled about into line in front of the Mumma place, on a knoll bordering a large cornfield. Directly to the front was a low road which wound eastward from the Hagerstown Pike for about 500 yards before it swung generally south. This was the road which was to become known as 'Bloody Lane.'

The Rebs at this moment were trying to force their way into a gap on French's right, and the Rhode Islanders went to work to try to plug it by means of their shot. Suddenly, at the battery's right front, on a rise not over sixty yards distant from the right piece, a flag appeared, then a hedge of shiny bayonets which instantly swelled into a mass of charging Gray infantry. Tompkins had a rookie Pennsylvania regiment as support. A part of this outfit panicked immediately and fled; others stood fast, many bunched in little groups about the guns. But the ragged Blue line on the right began to give ground, and the Confederates moved forward until they had surged past the battery. Part then wheeled to their right, and an officer pointed his sword at Tompkins's position.

Battery A hurriedly obliqued its pieces to meet this charge and let go with double canister. The deadly balls bit into the oncoming mass, but still the Rebels came. So close were they now that the gunners could clearly distinguish the individual faces. One blast tore into the dense mass and knocked a color-bearer and his flag to the ground. Under conditions such as these, hard-pressed batteries usually stopped sponging between shots, running the risk of a premature discharge in order to get off an extra round or two. But for some reason Tompkins's crews kept sponging. A sergeant commanding a piece urged his number one man, who had a reputation as a very rapid sponger, to hurry up and swab the gun. 'I'll sponge this gun if the Rebs come and take the sponge staff out of my hands,' was the man's confident reply.[23]

At ten paces distance the heavy fire of Tompkins's guns and the scattering of Blue infantry stopped the Rebels — but not all of them. A handful of cheering enemy leaped into the battery position, and it was a free-for-all battle. One six-footer, his musket with bayonet fixed, made a swipe at one of the cannoneers. The man saw the blow coming, dropped his sponge, and ducked under the gun tube. A nearby Blue infantryman clubbed the Southerner over the head with his musket butt, splattering brains all over the hot gun tube. There the slimy mass baked into a hard crust. At the end of the action a sergeant cut this crust off with his knife and kept it as a trophy.

The battery was saved as fresh Federal infantry came bound-

ing into the melee, driving the Confederates back, and claiming
the fallen enemy flag in front of Tompkins's position — a move
for which Tompkins chided them. As calm returned, the men
saw that human bodies and limbs and pieces of equipment littered the ground in front of the battery. Crewmen drew a deep
breath at their close call, but their respite was all too short. Directly ahead an enemy battery opened fire, and seconds later a
second joined in from their right near the Dunker Church.
Tompkins swung his right section about to deal with the enemy
by the church, while the other four rifles tackled the battery
to their front. Sharp fights broke out on both fronts.

Following one salvo from Tompkins's left section, a bright
flash was seen, followed by a heavy boom: they had blown up
one of the enemy's caissons or limbers. A thick mushrooming
cloud of smoke rose lazily upward over the wreckage. The
volleying continued for twenty minutes more, at which time the
Gray guns ceased fire and Tompkins reported the enemy's batteries as silenced. Now Capt. Tompkins became aware of a
commotion in his rear. Turning, he saw that the burning
Mumma house and barn were threatening the safety of his
caissons, which had been parked nearby. The chief of the line
of caissons was now rapidly shifting them away from the
flames.

The II Corps' attack led by French and Richardson stalled
temporarily, as the Confederate division of D. H. Hill was reinforced by a second, and then Hill lashed back here and there
in vicious crisp counter-attacks. Above the racket of thumping
muskets and booming cannon rose the distinctive yip-yipping
of the Rebel yell. Over on Tompkins's left, French's boys lowered their muskets at an enemy charge pounding through a
cornfield on their front. Tompkins yelled to his gunners to take
on the new target. Shell and case were fuzed for two seconds
before they burst from the gun muzzles, then the fuze time was
dropped to one and a half seconds. The firing reached a pitch,
then quickly slackened as the Gray regiments were driven back.

Twice more Hill's troops charged up to the edge of the cornfield, only to be raked by Union fire and hurled back. But the Federal chiefs-of-piece began reporting that their ammunition was running dangerously low. Accordingly, the battery commander sent an orderly galloping to Sumner with this information and a request for orders. The runner returned: the general had stated they would be relieved. Finally, at noon, Owens's Battery G, 1st Rhode Island, the one for which Capt. Clarke had no place, rattled into the line, and Tompkins's tired gunners were finally able to pull off the field.

It is indicative of the technique of fire of that era that Capt. Tompkins proudly pointed out in his official report that, with the exception of shots fired at a battery on his right which was hidden by a ridge, every round was carefully fired at a *visible* enemy. And fire the battery did, reporting an expenditure of 83 rounds of canister, 68 solids, 427 shell, and 454 case — a total of 1050 rounds fired during something over four hours and twenty minutes. The battery left the battle well depleted in other aspects, too. Their casualties had been four killed, fifteen wounded, ten horses down, and three complete sets of harness burned (when the caisson teams got too close to the burning timbers of the Mumma house); their six Parrott rifles were rendered completely useless, with worn and enlarged vents.

If Owens's men of Battery G had felt neglected because it was kept in reserve so long, they would now get more action than they had bargained for. Their six 3-inch rifles were moved into the tracks left by Tompkins's weapons, and immediately the crews began to fire at a Gray battery a mile away. At this long range Owens asked for shell set at eight seconds fuze. The gunners spun their elevating screws till the sights read four and one-half degrees elevation, reported their pieces ready, and started the fight. Once again the exchange lasted just twenty minutes, and once again it was the Confederate guns which stopped firing.

Suddenly, though, the situation changed. A puff of wind parted the smoky haze in front of Battery G, and the pleased artillerymen were stunned to see Federal infantry retreating on the run toward the battery, with the enemy after them in hot pursuit. Battery G quickly decided to join the retreat, and the guns went clattering into the road leading away from that knoll. Just as the whooping Confederates were gaining the rise, the last caisson lurched away from it.

Down the lane the battery's men galloped, giving hurried glances over their shoulder and urging the big team horses to a faster pace. The column had gone several hundred yards when Capt. Owens raised his arm overhead in the halt signal. The command rattled to a halt, and the captain, seeing that they were safe for the time being, ordered the cannoneers to replenish the ammunition of the gun limbers from the caissons. As the men hurriedly transferred chests, Blue infantry came by on the double quick, swung into line, and set out to retake the lost ground. Owens sent one section along behind them for support. The charging Blue ranks retook the ground, only to lose it immediately, Battery G's little section fleeing along with them.

Soon Gen. French straightened his lines once more and pulled Owens up close in his rear. The general ordered him to fire at the corner of the woods near the church. Owens was dubious of the success of such firing but obeyed without questioning the point. He reported his results as poor. And with that Battery G's chance for glory ended. The unit had been in action for only some forty minutes, expending seventy-five rounds at a cost of five men lightly wounded and four horses killed.

The last of Sumner's divisions to reach the fight was Richardson's, which was placed on French's left to prolong the Federal line in a southeasterly direction. Two batteries were assigned to Richardson — Pettit's New Yorkers and Thomas's Battery A/C, 4th U.S. The Regulars swung around into position, the same one occupied by Woodruff; but Pettit did not arrive until later. Thomas's guns were ready, but they did not fire, for there was a lull in the battle. Then the fighting flared up, and the

Yankee left flank began to give ground. The Regulars quickly changed front and cut loose with case shot. The Rebels had momentum and were hard to stop. Thomas gave the order to switch to canister. Still those wide thin lines continued to advance.

The men working Thomas's six Napoleons prepared for the worst; it was too late to get the guns away. Suddenly a heavy crash of musketry let fly from behind the battery, and the Confederates were flung back — infantry from Franklin's VI Corps had wheeled into line behind Sumner. Thomas took no credit away from them either, admitting that his guns would probably have been lost but for Franklin's men.

Now Thomas changed back to his original front and commenced flinging solid shot at a battery in the West Woods. The enemy soon ceased, but a second Gray unit immediately took up the fire, and the Regulars turned on them. The Rebel unit had Thomas's men directly on range, and the Federal battery's horses were soon taking too many hits. Furiously the Regulars fought to gain fire superiority, but it was no use, because their Napoleons did not have sufficient range to reach the enemy. But at that moment a Federal battery of rifled guns trotted onto the rise and unlimbered near Thomas. Feeling that his men would only take more useless punishment if they remained, Thomas withdrew to replenish his low ammunition supply, leaving the argument in the hands of the fresh rifled battery.

So far the Confederates holding the center of their line had been beating off the Federals without too great difficulty. Their grim infantry, with muskets propped on the north bank of that sunken road, had a clear field of fire and smashed several attempts by the II Corps to breach their line. But fate was about to take a hand against the Confederacy. Some Federal infantrymen were able to work their way around the Confederate right and thus completely enfilade a long stretch of that jammed sunken road. The Gray ranks struggled to meet the new threat by refusing their right, but an order was misinterpreted. Instead of an orderly adjustment there was slaughter and pell-mell retreat. The middle of Lee's line now simply disintegrated. Loose groups, intact commands, and scattered individuals fled through the cornfield on the gentle rise south of the road. Past Mr. Piper's farmhouse they ran, toward the weathered brick and board of the town of Sharpsburg.

Confederate D. H. Hill groped frantically for a brigade or even a regiment to stem the rout. But there was no infantry for the job, only an exhausted South Carolina battery resting nearby. With a shout these guns were run up on a rise from whence they could sweep the fields this side of the sunken road, into which Yankee infantry was now pouring. Canister burst from the cannon, but the Blue lines kept coming. Some Federal artillerymen spotted the threat and turned on it. Iron chunks slapped the ground about the Carolinians, churned the air, and made a direct hit on one of their caissons, blowing it up with an ear-splitting crash.[24] A section of another Gray battery galloped into the field, and it too ran smack into the Federal artillery fire.

The battle — indeed, the war — was almost over for the South. Nothing stood between McClellan and the Potomac but a handful of shot-up batteries and a pitifully weak infantry line which had been patched up just in front of the town. One more forward push and it would probably be over.

The final push never came, though. The Confederates gained that desperately needed time. They scraped together every usable gun and man — Gen. Longstreet even turned his personal staff into cannoneers — and poured a heavy converging fire from cannon and musket into the hole in their lines. The effort was sufficient to do the job, but it was in no way comparable to the potential which the Yankees could have thrown into the break but failed to. And this was particularly true of the artillery. The Yankee infantry that seized the sunken road and fought its way down the cornfields toward the Piper house did so with very little close-up artillery support. Meanwhile, those few Rebel guns kept firing while their infantry was regaining composure.

Richardson's struggling division, without any batteries in direct support, had to give up ground under the rising enemy fire — a fire which no doubt could have been greatly neutralized if some of the plethora of jammed batteries on the Poffenberger ridge and the open ground south and southeast of it had been brought forward to the sound of the firing. Instead, these guns were to all purposes in another fight — one which had ended a few hours before.

Richardson's exhausted regiments pulled back to a crest northeast of the Piper house. From here their general pleaded for artillery with which to hammer back at the nearby Rebel guns. The plea echoed from command to command. Even the redoubtable Hunt could offer no help, as all of the Reserve batteries were either engaged or detached or unsuitable for the mission. At last a section of Robertson's Battery B/L, 2nd U.S., came over from the Cavalry Division which, together with parts of the V Corps, was holding McClellan's line due east of town. The two Napoleons under Lt. Vincent went to work in the disciplined manner characteristic of Regular batteries.

Two guns, a mere section, was all that the Federal command brought to bear from an arsenal of nearly 300 cannon on the field. It was here that the Yankee Army reaped the harvest of its antiquated artillery staff and command set-up. This moment represents the nadir in the history of American artillery.

Finally, after all hope of restoring the lost momentum of the II Corps' attack had vanished, another battery from the Reserve came to Richardson's aid. Two Gray guns in an orchard in front had proved extremely annoying, and Battery K, 1st U.S., promptly leveled its barrels on them.[25] The range for the Regulars was 700 yards, quite within the capabilities of Napoleon guns, and in ten minutes the enemy had left the field.

Suddenly two heavy columns of Gray infantry swung out of the tall corn several hundred yards in front and started for Graham. The big guns were ready and chewed them up with case and shell. Gaps began to appear in the enemy ranks, as dead and wounded or just stunned Rebels fell out of line, and determined Federal infantry bit cartridge, rammed, primed, and fired into the marching mass. Rifle bullet and cannon slug did the job, sapping the line of its strength and forcing it back. Next, two enemy batteries with rifled guns took Graham under fire from long range. They quickly moved on target, and wild shrieks of wounded horses gave adequate evidence that Graham was being hurt by their fire.

The Regulars began adjusting their guns for range. Slowly the blackened muzzles lifted higher as dirty hands pulled on the elevating screws under the rear of the tubes. A salvo burst from the Napoleons, and anxious eyes watched through the haze for the tell-tale puffs of smoke or dirt which would show where the rounds had fallen. Then they saw the shots were short. Now the six guns tried more elevation, and there was another stunning series of heavy booms. But once more Battery K's rounds fell short, though several of the explosive rounds burst at the muzzle. Now all of the pieces switched to solid shot as a safety precaution and also to get maximum range. A last try proved no better than before; those flicking flashes from distant black specks were out of range of Graham's Napoleons.

As this gun duel was at its height, one of the strangest incidents of the war occurred. A black two-horse carriage pulled up behind Graham's position. From it alighted a civilian, perfectly calm and apparently oblivious to the Rebel shelling. To the amazement of the sweating crewmen, this unknown soul proceeded from gun to gun generously doling out ham and home-cooked biscuits. Then, refusing to be scared off by more shell bursts, he carefully loaded his carriage with some of the battery's wounded, mounted to the seat, calmly reached for the reins, and trotted the little carriage off the field. But not for long, for soon he was seen trotting his team onto the battery's position. As he drew rein an enemy shell exploded near his carriage, wounding one of his horses, but leaving the man unruffled. The stranger hauled another load of wounded into his carriage, and this time left the scene for good.[26]

Away to the east, at McClellan's headquarters, a number of

the staff and visting foreign officers had watched with admiration the courageous stand of Graham's men. Finally, though, the battery became completely shrouded in the dust and smoke of searching enemy shells. Graham had already been recommended for a brevet for gallantry on the Peninsula, and this day's action won him his second — a full colonelcy.

The one-sided duel provoked Graham to ride to Gen. Richardson. He reported that the enemy was out of range of his guns and asked what the general wanted him to do. He was ordered to pull back his battery, as the general was preparing to advance and wanted Graham's battery to advance with him. At that instant a nearby orange flash and a loud clap made Graham flinch. He turned to see Gen. Richardson collapse with a mortal wound from an enemy case round.

Graham, however, began to carry out the general's last order. He sent his guns to the rear behind a little rise about 200 yards away. His casualties in personnel up to now had not been too severe — four killed and five severely wounded — but, as usual, the horses had taken the brunt of the enemy fire, with twenty-three casualties. Drivers hurriedly patched teams together, and, following the old rule of artillery service, used them to pull off the guns first. By utilizing every horse to the maximum they were able to salvage everything but two caissons. Later, a lieutenant and a sergeant returned with teams and saved the caissons as well, despite a heavy harassing fire.

Remembering Richardson's statement about a new advance, Graham moved rapidly to patch his command. The supply of ammunition in the gun limbers was low, and the captain followed regular artillery procedure by exchanging supplies with the caissons. Then he ordered two caissons to return to the ammunition train for refilling. The division never did make its attack, though, and Graham's Regulars pulled no more lanyards that day.

Back at the Pry house McClellan received word of the loss of Richardson, and a courier sped to Gen. Hancock, then commanding a brigade of Franklin's VI Corps, with orders to take

command of Richardson's division of the II Corps. When Hancock reached his new command, it was early in the afternoon.
Riding hastily along his lines, he found the division still without
artillery, and he saw a dangerous gap yawning between two of
its brigades. The general looked about for guns, but none were
in sight. To every command within reach he made a request
for cannon. The answer everywhere was the same — none
available.

Apparently the generals commanding the Union's right flank
were momentarily expecting another vicious counter-attack
such as had rocked them earlier that day. Recalling McClellan's
ridiculous overestimate of Confederate strength, the generals
nervously watched the West Woods, counted on their fingers,
and kept their hands tightly gripped on every battery within
reach. So while Franklin's fresh VI Corps' batteries were rolling into an uneven line in front of the infantry facing the West
Woods, and the tired I and II Corps' guns still thumped on and
off from the north and northeast of the Miller cornfield, Hancock's cannonless division hung on and waited.

Suddenly movement among the enemy skirmishers and columns of Gray regiments marching across his front caused Hancock to send a frantic message for artillery. This time the plea
got results. Hexamer's Battery A, New Jersey Light Artillery,
from the idle VI Corps, brought its six 3-inch ordnance rifles
over and plugged a threatened point in the smoking line. Fighting broke out on Hancock's right, and Hexamer fired furiously.
And at about this time the stray division battery of Capt. Rufus
Pettit, 1st New York Light Artillery, finally reached the field.

Hancock need not have worried about an enemy attack here
or elsewhere along the long battle line, however. Lee's Army
was utterly spent, parts of it almost completely wrecked, and
the Army was totally incapable of mounting an attack at this
time. For the next two years Union infantry and gunners would
pay a terrible price for their general's failure to press their advantage that morning. Several times the Union commander

had complete victory within his grasp, but his overcautious approach made the Union Army miss the opportunity.

Still another of these instances happened later in the day directly east of the town, about 1200 yards southeast of Sumner's line, on the thinnest part of both armies' line. The road from Boonsboro and Keedysville led down past the Pry house, swung into a sheltered valley, curved to the right, and crossed Antietam Creek at Middle Bridge. Just beyond the road there was a crest, which then fell away into a short valley, only to rise again on the edge of town. In the sheltered valleys east of the creek waited Fitz John Porter's V Corps and the Cavalry Division under Pleasonton. Sometime after Sumner became hotly engaged, McClellan told his cavalry commander to cross the creek at Middle Bridge and stage a diversion to aid Sumner's left. Pleasonton obliged by ordering the rifled Regular battery of Capt. John C. Tidball forward, along with some troopers. A scattering of Gray infantry covered the crossing and its approaches, but they were quickly driven away. Then four Regular horse batteries went racing forward, unlimbering on the hills just west of the stream.

As the cannoneers prepared for action, they could see the spires of Sharpsburg, which were directly to their front, partially hidden by the sheltering hill. The face of this slope was dotted with Confederate cannon of the Washington artillery from Louisiana. The Rebels were firing from positions now occupied by the National Cemetery and the Battlefield Park Headquarters. To their right front Pleasonton's gunners could watch the thick clouds of dirty smoke and hear the staccato bursts of gunfire that marked the bitter fighting in front of the sunken road.

The decision to push these horse batteries onto the heights west of the creek was a shrewd one, accomplished just in the nick of time. Robert E. Lee had seen that he was in great danger and his left virtually wrecked, due in part to the harassing fire of Hays's Reserve command. To avert further disaster, Lee had ordered his chief-of-artillery to bring up his best along this crest in front of Sharpsburg. But before this could be done, the four Regular horse batteries clattered across the bridge, swung into line, and twenty-four cannons began chipping away at the Gray units already on that crest. The fire of these horse batteries undoubtedly helped the II Corps indirectly, for it kept a number of Lee's guns well occupied when they were desperately needed to back up D. H. Hill. It was here too, that some of the Regular infantry sent over as support for the horse batteries spotted the thinness of Lee's line. But no attack was permitted by McClellan, and the day was decided instead on another field south of the town.

While Pleasonton's guns were battering that crest, Hancock's demand for artillery reached the cavalry camp. Pleasonton felt none could be spared and refused the request, but the general agreed to shift the fire of some eighteen of his pieces to play on the enemy facing Hancock. Further, he would advance one section several hundred yards to try to drive off some Gray cannon annoying the II Corps.[27]

The fighting in front of the bridge was largely a long-range, jabbing scrap, enlivened by occasional tangles with small groups of enemy infantry who crept through the corn to snipe at the batteries. Canister and the few protecting battalions of Regular infantry were always successful in driving them off. After two hours of firing, not furious but continuous, the horse artillerymen were running low on ammunition. And since the enemy return fire had slackened quite noticeably, Pleasonton began retiring these guns piece by piece and section by section, replacing them with Randol's and Kusserow's batteries from Sykes's division of the idle V Corps.[28]

Later, about 4 p.m., Pleasonton wanted to shove his guns forward so that they could enfilade the Confederate regiments who were harrassing the IX Corps, which in turn was slowly forcing Lee's right back onto the town. To accomplish this mission the cavalry would need more infantry support, so Pleasonton galloped to Fitz John Porter. But the latter denied the request, and another opportunity to end the day sooner and differently may have been lost.

Having fiddled on three of his bow strings, McClellan now began to pluck at the fourth — the IX Corps. These were Burnside's men, who had acquired some fame by their amphibious operations in North Carolina under that sincere, but militarily limited general. Brought north just prior to the second Manassas campaign, they had fought under Pope in that sad debacle, and then had became an integral part of the reorganized Army of the Potomac. But they never seemed to find a proper place in this proud Army, and they were not with it for long.

The IX Corps had been holding the Army's left flank all that morning, though their activities had been limited to sporadic shelling by the division and Reserve batteries posted along the hilltops east of the creek and south of the Middle Bridge. The infantry remained under cover in the valleys behind the hills. At daybreak the corps' line extended roughly from the left flank of Sykes's division covering the Middle Bridge to a point below the Lower Bridge — the one now known as the Burnside Bridge. To hold this ground the corps had four divisions, backed by eight batteries and a howitzer company of the 9th New York Infantry manning five Dahlgren boat howitzers. All told, the IX Corps had almost fifty tubes,[29] and over and above these a number of the Reserve batteries was scattered along these same hills.

On the corps' right flank, south of the Middle Bridge, in good position to offer direct support, were the Reserve batteries of Taft and Von Kleiser, each with four 20-pounders, and the four 3-inch rifles of Weed's V Corps battery. South of these were Durell's and Clark's batteries of the corps' second division, and below these, opposite to the Lower Bridge, the balance of the corps' guns, including the superb Regular battery of 20-pounders under Lt. Benjamin. This was the same Lt. Benjamin who had been present as a rookie battery officer at First Bull Run. A New Yorker, a graduate of West Point in the spring of 1861, the youngster had learned fast, and by the war's end he won the Medal of Honor for his service.

Early in the morning some of the Gray gunners in front of Sharpsburg caught some sprawling lines of idle IX Corps infantry in the open, and with vicious fire forced them away from the creek. This harassing fire forced Rodman on the corps' right to pull his division further to the rear, and to start Benjamin's 20-pounders banging away in reply.

Benjamin's guns had flung a fair number of rounds on the previous day, and as the hours wore on the lieutenant had replenished his depleted stocks from the ammunition train. Now, as this morning grew toward noon, Benjamin's guns had taken another healthy bite into their stocks; once more resupply from the train was sought. But an alarming situation had developed. So furious had been the firing by all of the 20-pounder units in the Army that the ammunition train was almost out of this caliber. The best Benjamin could do was to bring back forty rounds. His battery would end the day furiously firing blanks, on Burnside's order to give the impression they were still doing damage.[30]

Similarly, Durell's Independent Pennsylvania Battery was run out during the morning to drive away some enemy guns, whose accurate firing was dropping shells into Sturgis's division near the Lower Bridge. Weed's Regulars were already firing from the high bank overlooking the creek, and the Pennsylvanians swung in on their left. As Durell's cannoneers were bending to their task, a small, grizzled officer wearing a brigadier general's star trotted up. In a soft almost girlish voice he cautioned Durell to take his time and to fire slowly and deliberately; rapid fire was a waste of ammunition. Knowing cannoneers whispered to their friends that he was Gen. Hunt. Satisfied, the chief-of-artillery spurred his horse down the ridge toward the next battery in line.

During one of these morning outbursts of firing Durell saw a Confederate officer on a white horse ride out into plain view on a distant plateau. The target was too tempting; the captain ordered a gun turned on him.[31] Over on the enemy side Gen. Lee, along with Gens. Longstreet and D. H. Hill, was riding in rear of Hill's and Longstreet's lines. A courier galloped up to report the Yankees' making threatening gestures, and the three generals turned their mounts toward a nearby rise near the present National Cemetery to get a first-hand look. Lee and Longstreet dismounted, but not Hill. Longstreet joshed that, as long as Hill insisted on riding up there and drawing fire, he would at least give them sufficient interval so they would not be in the line of fire when the Yank guns cut loose. As Longstreet swung his field glasses around toward the Union left, he spotted a puff of smoke from a gun a mile away. Three or four seconds later, the round came whizzing onto the rise and with a passing zip took off the front legs of Hill's horse.[32]

It was to his friend 'Dear Burn' that McClellan first sent word at 9:15 a.m. to cross the creek to ease the pressure on Sumner. Burnside gave the order, and the artillery opened up in support. But one Blue general complained that because of the shape and depth of the creek valley the Federal guns could not reach the enemy positions by the Lower Bridge. And, in addition, the Gray cannon posted on the eastern edge of the town, on the site of the National Cemetery, could enfilade the approaches to the bridge.

The first attempt to rush down from the heights and seize the bridge was easily driven to earth by an ample concentration of Confederate batteries and a handful of infantry. A second try made no better progress, even though the Yankee guns were told to hold down the enemy artillery. By now the corps commander had sent Rodman's division with Durell's and Clark's batteries and the five howitzers of the 9th New York winding along behind the crests toward a ford which was supposed to exist a short distance south of the bridge.

Finally, around 1 p.m., two regiments from Sturgis's division came barreling over a rise and made a rush for the bridge. A light howitzer from Simmonds's Kentucky battery was run forward to a spot where it could fire point-blank on the west end of the bridge. This gun had been taken by the Federals in West Virginia earlier in the war and was carried along as an additional gun by the Parrott-equipped Kentuckians.[33] The little gun sprayed the far side with double canister, and instantly the ridge behind flamed with covering musket fire. Burnside sent word to his batteries to concentrate on the woods above the bridge. Before the startled Confederates could pull many triggers or jerk but a few lanyard, the two regiments reached the bridge, bounded across, and began peeling off to right and left.

This new Yankee move was a serious threat but could be contained if there was no further build-up. A good supply of Gray guns guarded this flank, though their infantry line was paper thin. Every Confederate cannon now within range began to slug away, and more were expected. Lee quickly realized the danger, and he sought help from Jackson. Could the Yankee right be attacked? Jackson would try. But that was all he did. The overwhelming preponderance of Yankee gun strength, about sixteen batteries, was massed here in an almost continuous line, hub to hub, from the Mumma family cemetery north to the Poffenberger ridge.

The Blue commanders saw the slowly rising dust clouds of Jackson's men as they moved to positions, and the Federal infantry was pulled in behind the gun line. Then the cannoneers sprang to their pieces, and an ear-splitting racket broke loose. The ground under the feet of the watching Federals trembled under the terrific pounding of the batteries.

Jeb Stuart had his gunner Pelham try to beat down the Yankee fire, but it was hopeless, and he called it quits after some twenty minutes in view of 'a most terrific fire from a number of the enemy's batteries.' [34] Even the offensive-minded Jackson realized to go further was folly and reluctantly had to advise his chief that he 'found his Federal numerous artillery to judiciously established in their front and extending so near to the Potomac . . . as to render it inexpedient to hazard the attempt.' [35]

While Federal artillery was holding the line on this flank, the Gray gunners on the Confederate right could not by themselves stop the IX Corps. Over came the rest of Sturgis's division, and Rodman's wanderers had found the ford, splashed over, and were lapping the enemy's right. Soon elements of four powerful Yankee divisions were on the west bank of the stream. As the Blue regiments climbed the steep slopes of the creek valley to the rolling hills overlooking Sharpsburg, Confederate cannon fire ripped into them. Rebel batteries which had been shot up earlier in the day and had been withdrawn to refit were now called to battle again. Some were reduced to mere sections but forward they came. In face of this the Federal infantry screamed for their own batteries to come forward.

Reinforcements were delayed because of a jam near the bridge. Sturgis had claimed that he was low on ammunition and that his men were weary and had had them relieved by the corps reserve — Willcox's division. The narrow valley was choked with moving men, going in opposite directions on wagon-width trails. By the time the Yankee generals had untangled the traffic snarl, about half the available corps batteries had succeeded in crossing the Antietam — the balance staying on the eastern crest with covering fire.

Sturgis's two batteries — Durell's, and Clark's Regulars — both armed with Parrott rifles, crossed; Cook's 8th Massachusetts Battery with six 12-pounder howitzers clanked across with Willcox; and part of the Kentucky battery also was on the other side. Left behind were Benjamin's four 20-pounders, Muhlenberg's six Napoleons, McMullin's six 10-pounder Parrotts, the five Dahlgrens of the 9th New York, the rest of the Kentucky unit, and probably Roemer's Battery L, 2nd New York Light Artillery.

As Willcox's division plodded over the bridge, some alert and advantageously posted Rebel gunners opened a sweeping fire down the valley. Blue infantry reaching the plateau just west of the crossing found themselves in a virtual cross-fire from an arc of enemy guns that ran from just east of the village around to the southwest. The Confederates were throwing in every available cannon to try to stop the IX Corps. The Union commanders responded by asking for friendly artillery to come forward.

Behind the tail of Willcox's command moved Cook's battery. As the column came off the bridge, a delay up front forced the weaving stream of Blue to a halt in the road — a dangerous spot, because Rebel cannon were pouring fire down the ravine from the hill east of town. One of Cook's sections wriggled through the stalled column, swung to the left, and heaved its way onto a plateau. From here they could see. There, 200 yards distant, ringed in smoke, were some enemy guns. The section jumped down, swung their two pieces about, and cut loose with canister. Their shots were on target.

With this annoyance neutralized, Willcox moved a brigade ahead again, and Cook's section worked in close unison with it. On an elevation to the right of the road into town was another of those small orchards, and some weary Rebels had drawn up ranks there for a final stand. Willcox brought up the rest of Cook's guns and ordered them to blast out the Rebels. Four 12-pounder howitzers spat at their target, the Blue infantry rushed forward with a roar, and the ground was theirs.

It now appeared that time was running out on the Confederacy. Lee's shattered right was nearly split in two as Willcox's men were at the very edge of the town and Rodman's division, diverging to the west, threatened to break through to Lee's rear. Then the miracle happened.

Every student of this war cannot help but thrill at the oft-told account of Confederate A. P. Hill's tired, dirty, and panting division coming onto the field from Harpers Ferry seventeen miles away. Into line of battle they swung, smack on Rodman's left flank, and with a fierce charge collapsed the Yankee left. The day was nearly over when their attack struck, and when darkness stilled the muskets, the Yankees still held a bridgehead but were definitely on the defensive. The fighting at Antietam Creek was now over.

That the powerful Army of the Potomac had not splintered and smashed the valiant Army of Northern Virginia was not the fault of the Blue gunners or the men who carried the muskets. The Rebels were badly hurt but still willing to fight some more. Never before had the Army of the Potomac had so many batteries under its control, but there had been an appalling misuse of their fire, not by the artillerymen but by the infantry commanders who still controlled them. The basic fault of the Peninsula and of the Manassas fiasco was even more prominent here: the lack of a higher echelon of tactical organization and command. That the Blue gunners had had things on the battlefield virtually their own way despite gallant efforts by the Confederates in counter-battery fire, only points up the possibilities of what might have happened under a better command set-up.

As one artillery veteran of that fight, Brig. Gen. John C. Tidball later wrote, the key to the whole battlefield was the group of knolls and secondary ridges between Hooker's right and the Potomac River. The Rebels had put Stuart out there with a number of guns which had annoyed the Federal right considerably. The veteran Regular believed that the advantages of these positions probably did not come to Hooker's eye, and he had no chief-of-artillery to point them out to him, for his battery commanders could not very well leave their guns to go looking far afield for positions. Hence many of his batteries sat in enforced idleness.

Gen. Tidball felt that the Federal artillery had little opportunity to show what it was capable of doing, though he seems to have overlooked its invaluable service in breaking up enemy counter-attacks which followed the repulse of the I, XII, and II Corps' attacks. He also noted that the quantity of ammunition expended by the Federal guns greatly exceeded the return. This was largely due to brigade and division commanders ordering their guns to fire, regardless of whether the positions enabled the batteries to accomplish anything, and to the fact that the battery commanders were obliged to obey these orders.

Individually the Federal batteries had good right to pride themselves on their conduct, and there is no doubt some truth in saying that they may have saved McClellan's right. The big Parrotts of the Reserve had been handed an ideal situation. In positions virtually immune to counter-battery fire, they had the artilleryman's dream — an enfilade on their enemy. But these big rifles were brittle and cumbersome, and Hunt was beginning to lose patience with them. After Fredericksburg he would try to rid the Army of them altogether.

The day following this bitter fight the two battered armies sullenly watched each other. Of the two, Lee's Army was the more seriously wounded, and that officer must have realized by standard intelligence procedures that Porter's corps had not been committed by McClellan, and that fresh troops — Couch's and Humphrey's divisions — were coming up to reinforce the Federal Army. So after waiting with astounding daring all day of September 18th for McClellan to make a move, Lee decided to give up the field that night. So, for the first time, the Army of the Potomac saw the backs of Lee's veterans as they retreated over the Potomac into Virginia.

X

THERE GOES BATTERY B TO HELL!

Fredericksburg

TWO DAYS after the battle of Antietam, the Army of the Potomac found itself still around the cornfields and woods of Sharpsburg, burying the dead, tidying up the place generally, and trying to get used to the new feeling of remaining in possession of a battlefield after a battle was over. The Army was proud of itself, for it believed it had stopped Robert E. Lee.

But, as the days passed, this elation was blunted by more sober thoughts. The realization that this success, if it were really that, had been attained at a stiff cost in casualties was sobering enough, but the leaders soon saw something even more disturbing. As the facts came in, it was humiliatingly clear that the high command had amateurishly booted away numerous chances to put an end to Lee's Army for once and for all. Such a realization made a portion of the Army look for a scapegoat. McClellan never blamed himself for any shortcoming of the Army, and certainly the corps and division commanders could never conceive themselves at fault. But someone recalled the scream for artillery which had gone up from Richardson and Hancock. Here then was a culprit — the Artillery Reserve!

Since McClellan had first organized the Army of the Potomac, there had been officers who saw no necessity for the existence of the Artillery Reserve, and this situation was made to order for them. The campaign to break up Hunt's special

pride and joy rapidly gained force, as senior colonels and brigade and division commanders came forward to protest that
the blunders at Antietam had occurred because the artillery
was not available when it was needed most; that they had
thought the vaunted Reserve was supposed to provide for just
such contingencies. If they had had control of the batteries in
the battle, it would have been different, they said.

However, these men completely ignored the fact that the
Reserve had already been greatly dissipated by the demands
of the various divisions. Thus, when calls came for artillery
there were no light batteries available, only clumsy unmaneu-
verable 20-pounders. In actuality, virtually all the light batteries had been under division control during the battle. Thus,
their cry was to assign all the light field batteries to the divisions. When a mass of guns was needed, they argued, the batteries could be temporarily detached for this purpose.

In the meantime, McClellan's claims of a great victory were
gladly received by a victory-thirsty nation, but the gaunt man
in the White House realized that Lee had been permitted to
get away, his ever dangerous Army still very much intact. The
President urged his commander to move after Lee. But he was
still dealing with McClellan. It was the Peninsula all over
again: McClellan was outnumbered; he needed time to prepare
his forces; he needed reinforcements. Finally, when Jeb Stuart
rode completely around the Yankee Army untouched, Lincoln
had had enough.

On the night of November 7th an aide informed McClellan
that an officer from the War Office wished to see him. A Gen.
Buckingham entered, followed by Maj. Gen. Ambrose Burnside, until this night commander of the IX Corps, but now, by
virtue of orders in Buckingham's hand, the new Commanding
General, Army of the Potomac. Much more was to change in
the ensuing weeks, as the Army of the Potomac unknowingly
marched toward its own Golgotha — Fredericksburg. By the
time the Army reached the Rappahannock every corps and division would be under a new general officer. And, meanwhile,

Burnside was seriously considering abolishing the Artillery Reserve.

While this assault against his Reserve was gathering, Gen. Hunt was rolling in from the other side with blunt thoroughness to improve the efficiency of his arm. Hunt was a thoroughly dedicated man, convinced that the artillery, if properly organized, adequately trained, and capably led, could be the decisive factor in future battles. And he was equally convinced that so far in the war its force had not been properly utilized. He had argued continually that his artillery should be provided with a modern staff and command set-up, but he could do little about the matter except recommend and plead with his superiors to put his plans into effect. When it came to the conduct of batteries on the field of battle, however, he could do something. On December 4, 1862, he published an order as Chief-of-Artillery, Army of the Potomac, which set forth his ideas.

It had come to his attention, he said, that batteries had been expending 300 to 400 rounds in little brush fire squabbles, which was a preposterous amount. Also, they not only had been firing too much, but too fast — sometimes better than one round per minute per gun. In fact, he had been told that in general engagements certain batteries had been shooting their entire ammunition load — basic load, it would be called today — in something over an hour and a half. Now, Hunt went on, rules and regulations covering this matter had been published in orders of September 12, 1862, and any officer who shot up his ammunition improperly was displaying complete ignorance of the proper use of the arm and had no business commanding a battery. In no case except when using canister at close range should the rate exceed one shot per two minutes per gun, and this should only happen at critical moments when the guns simply could not miss. At other times one round every four to six minutes was adequate.

Further, these rules were particularly applicable to rifled guns, whose principal value was their accuracy. Accuracy, the general said, could only be accomplished by careful aiming, and this took time. Twelve shots per hour at a target over 1000 yards would, to Hunt's mind, produce better results then fifty fired over the same period of time. The campaign allowance of 250 rounds per gun, he wrote, was carefully calculated to suffice not only for a general engagement but for all the little firefights which usually preceded it. Then Hunt threw his bolt: an officer who shot up his ammunition in a few hours rendered himself liable to the dark suspicion that his reckless firing was prompted by a desire to quit the field — the most heinous accusation a soldier of that ultra-honorable era could be accused of.

Hunt now turned his attention to the problem which had plagued the Union Army so far in the war. This was the sight of ammunitionless batteries galloping to the rear, usually at moments when a couple of rounds from a calmly poised line of guns would have proved decisive. In the future, Hunt declared, batteries with empty limbers and caissons would not be permitted to leave the scene of action; guns and crews would stay put while a caisson from each section would go back for resupply. With a final caution that the nation could not stand the constant straining of its resources with excessive demands, Hunt ended his order.[1] It remained to be seen if it would bring the desired results.

One of Burnside's first moves after taking command was to shake up the army by dividing it into three grand divisions and a reserve corps. Old Indian-fighter Sumner was given the right grand division composed of the II and IX Corps; aspiring Joe Hooker commanded the center with its III and V Corps; the left went to Franklin with its I and VI Corps; while the XI Corps under Sigel was the reserve, though it would see no action in this campaign. Having shuffled his command about, Burnside was asked by the President to spell out his operation plans. The major general commanding had his ideas all right, but they differed sharply from the vague ones of McClellan, and were most unpalatable to Lincoln and his ineffectual Chief-of-Staff Halleck. Nevertheless, Burnside wangled a grudging approval from those two to move the Army of the Potomac on Richmond via Fredericksburg, supplying the Army from bases at Aquia Creek and Belle Plain on the Potomac.

Plan as he might though, Burnside was headed for serious trouble. He himself seems to have been a likable person, but his brief career as the Army commander totally lacked one element which always proves essential — luck. And nowhere was his bad luck in greater evidence than at Fredericksburg. Indeed, the very name would make every survivor of that battle recall with smoldering rage the frightful slaughter the Federal forces suffered there. The Army had suffered defeats before, and it would suffer them again, but no defeat engendered the bitterness of Fredericksburg. And the blame for this horrible debacle, wrong or right, the Army laid entirely at the feet of Ambrose Burnside.

Things went badly for the new commander almost from the start. His plan called for a quick move to Fredericksburg, where he would cross the Rappahannock and then sweep behind Lee, thus interposing the Army of the Potomac between Richmond and its defending army. The lock and key to the whole scheme were speed and the river. Burnside ordered pontoon bridge trains sent down immediately from Washington, or so he thought, and at the same time he put his columns on the roads toward the river. As his leading elements drew rein on Falmouth Heights opposite Fredericksburg, it looked as if that city was ripe for an easy crossing and plucking.

Yet, when the Blue columns began to look about for the bridge trains, they were not to be found. Somewhere, amid misunderstanding and incompetency, the pontoons had gone astray, and with them had gone the possibility of an easy crossing into Lee's rear. One of the division commanders wanted to ford the river, but Burnside refused because he knew the Army would need the bridges. By the time the engineers arrived with their spans on November 25th, Lee was ready to dispute the whole idea.

The ground that Lee chose to fight on was close to ideal

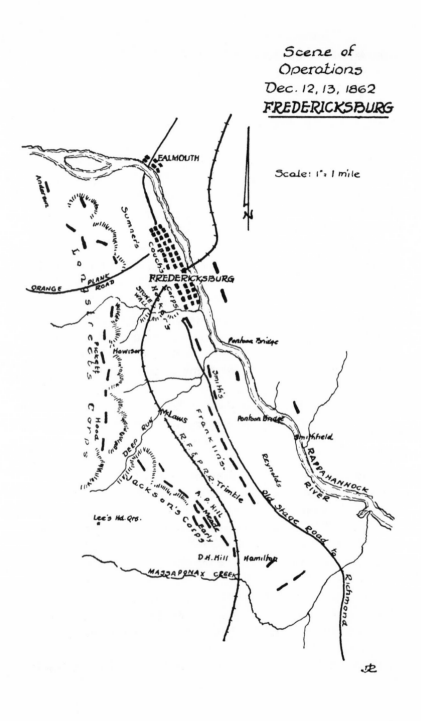

Scene of
Operations
Dec. 12, 13, 1862
FREDERICKSBURG

Scale: 1" = 1 mile

FALMOUTH

Anderson

Sumner's

Couch's

ORANGE PLANK ROAD

FREDERICKSBURG

STONE WALL

Longstreet's Corps

Pickett's Corps

Hood

Howison

Hooker's Corps

Pontoon Bridge

Smith's

McLaws

DEEP RUN

Franklin's

R.F.& P.R.R.

Trimble

A.P. Hill

Meade

Early

Pontoon Bridge

Smithfield

RAPPAHANNOCK RIVER

Reynolds

Old Stage Road to

Jackson's Corps

Lee's Hd. Qrs.

D.H. Hill

Hamilton

MASSAPONAX CREEK

Richmond

from his standpoint. The Rappahannock swings down across central Virginia in a generally southeast direction till it reaches Fredericksburg and then cuts through a series of hills. For a short way it sweeps around to an almost north-south course, leaving the high slopes of Falmouth and Stafford Heights on its left bank and a wide flood plain on its right. The town itself lies on the right bank, with the plain which extends out behind it for about a mile finally rising up to a low chain of hills roughly paralleling the river. It was on these hills that Lee's men dug in.

The position was 'high ground,' always a desirable feature for a defensive line, and the area in front was wide, open, almost flat, and virtually void of cover for attacking lines. The only disadvantage of the position was that it was a considerable distance to the river and to the heights on the other side. With a limited number of rifled guns Lee could not effectively hammer the Yankee columns as they crowded in for the crossing. Thick masses of Blue infantry, helpless in marching columns moving up onto fragile pontoon bridges, would make a lush target for Lee's gunners — if they could see them and if they could reach them.

At this moment, nearly 120,000 Federal troops were crowded into tent and hut camps in sheltered hollows of Falmouth and Stafford Heights, waiting for the bridges to arrive. The air had taken on a crisp December bite, and snow was falling. Finally the lumbering wagons arrived loaded with overgrown rowboats called pontoons, planks for bridging, and barrels full of other engineer equipment. After some confusion over where the troops should cross, Burnside at last decided that Fredericksburg would be the point. When the general had finished riding the length of his line and had observed the many fine artillery positions, he remarked to one of his generals that, '[The] reserve artillery has as yet had no chance to show its value, and I am going to make the crossing here and below, under cover of the guns of the reserve artillery.' But his associate prophetically remarked to Burnside, 'When your army is across your troubles will begin.'[2] During the afternoon of December 10th, countless couriers galloped back and forth over the heights, riding into every camp, searching out commanding officers, and delivering folded orders. The big day was tomorrow.

Gen. Hunt's tent had been bedlam for hours, as the artillery plan and orders were committed to paper. Hunt's command and responsibilities were deemed by at least one contemporary officer as being equivalent to a full corps, yet Hunt had only three colonels, two lieutenant colonels, and two majors to aid him. The job Burnside assigned the long arm was broad: protect the construction of the bridges and cover the passage of the Army. Since five bridges were to be laid over two miles of water, and the flanks beyond the upper and lower bridges had to be held, the Union line was almost five miles long. As Hunt saw it, this meant his guns would have some six missions: (1) to control any enemy movements on the plain; (2) to neutralize the enemy batteries on the ridge behind the town; (3) to command the town itself; (4) to cover the bridge construction; (5) to cover the Army's crossing; and, (6) to protect the Army's left flank, which was more vulnerable to attack from the direction of the Massaponax Creek opposite Lee's right flank.

Hunt saw that the depleted nine-battery Artillery Reserve could never do the job by itself; this meant additional tubes had to be withdrawn from the divisions. And it was now that Burnside saw the folly of abolishing the Reserve, for the wild howls that went up from the division commanders at the mention of their releasing the batteries, for even such a short period as this, was most enlightening. To provide Hunt with the necessary muscle, every division commander was ordered to release all but one of his batteries;[3] the commanders were promised that the guns would be returned when the divisions crossed the river. Hunt took a total of 147 tubes in thirty batteries and split these up into four large groups.[4] The infantry divisions then contained thirty-six batteries and the cavalry commands three more. The total gun strength of the Army present for duty was 325 to 329.[5]

To Lt. Col. Hays went the right group — thirty-four light rifled guns and six 20-pounder Parrotts. These were to line the heights from Falmouth Dam above the town to a deep ravine 500 yards below Falmouth. This group's field of fire was the hills and plain upstream from Fredericksburg. The right center was under the command of Col. Charles Tompkins, and was assigned positions from the ravine on Hays's left to near the spot designated for Burnside's middle bridge. Thirty-eight guns, a mixture of light rifles and Napoleons, was the weight of metal given this part of the line. The group was to protect the throwing of the bridges by neutralizing any enemy fire coming from houses in the town opposite, and by keeping enemy troops from moving down the streets.

The left center group contained the big guns: seven ugly black 4.5-inch iron rifles — big brothers to the light 3-inch ordnance rifles; two batteries of 20-pounder Parrotts; and three of 10-pounder Parrotts, a total of twenty-seven rifled cannon under the command of Col. Robert O. Tyler. This group was to occupy the crests from a point near the middle bridge to a wooded ravine near the center of the ridge facing Lee's position. Tyler's batteries were to command the ground from the left of town — from Hazel Run to Deep Run. They were to keep Lee from reinforcing either flank by moving units over this open ground in front of his trenches.

The last group, on the left, was the largest, with forty-two pieces, eight of which were 20-pounder Parrotts and the rest light rifles. Their ground was from Tyler's left on the high ridge out onto a lower rise which terminated at Pollock's Mill, almost opposite Lee's right flank. Capt. G. A. De Russy was the commander, and he was told to sweep the open ground fronting the lower bridges so that Lee could not swing his right flank around and hit the Yankee left as it deployed on the plain in front of the Confederate right.

Hunt told his group commanders to smash any Rebel guns

or troops that attempted to hit the Federals as they approached
the bridges. The Union guns would then cover the actual crossing, and keep the enemy forces from coming down from the
hills as the Yanks were forming on the plain. Finally, after the
Blue infantry was deployed, they were not to fire over its head
except when absolutely necessary, but they were to aid the advance when the field of fire permitted.

The batteries detailed for the covering force received orders
to rendezvous at sundown December 10th, at designated spots
a few miles in rear of the high bluffs overlooking the river. As
the sun faded away behind the woodlands, captains and lieutenants clustered around their group commanders, bending
over maps dimly lit by candles, fingers tracing routes to positions on the bluffs. When everyone was satisfied as to his location, the groups disbanded. Officers returned to their commands, and the orderly process of moving out began.

The night was cold, and two inches of fresh snow wrapped
the countryside in a winter blanket. The batteries were stripped
to bare necessities — packs and all personal gear were left in
camp — and the men were cautioned against talking loudly or
lighting fires. With trace chains bound by cloth and all loose
equipment firmly secured to insure maximum silence, the big
team horses heaved in their traces, breath frosting from flaring
nostrils in the twenty-five degree cold, and the guns began to
roll out.

Sometime after midnight all the guns were in their new firing positions — an almost unbroken line of batteries five miles
long. Crews began making final checks on equipment and ammunition, then waited in the darkness for the command to commence firing. The men had been permitted to bring their over-
coats and blankets which they now pulled tight about themselves in vain efforts to thwart the piercing cold.

Down below on the river's edge, in the damp cold blackness,
the engineers were manhandling four bridge trains toward the
crossing sites. A few regiments of shivering infantry plodded
along as their covering force. Shortly after 3 a.m. the engineers

began laying the first sections, and for a while everything went smoothly. As dawn came, the bridges were nearing the far bank, and not a single musket had been fired in opposition. Now with first light came a heavy fog which obscured one bank from the other. They could finish the spans without trouble if the Rebels were not watching. But the Rebels were watching, and trouble descended on the engineers in greater quantity than they could handle. The worst of it came opposite the town where the high command had ordered three bridges — two above the center of town and one opposite the lower end. Here Graycoats took advantage of the river-edge building and wall; they poked their long polished gun barrels from windows and over the tops of aged brick walls, leveled them for a moment, then they coughed and slipped back out of sight, only to reappear a minute later. The fire was accurate enough in the fog-clouded dawn to dump a few of the engineers and send the rest scurrying back to shore.

On the high banks the waiting Union gunners took the firing for their cue. But where were their targets? The gray soup obscured the whole far bank. Four batteries of Col. Tompkins's right center group, however, began a slow fire with solid shot in the general direction of the enemy, hoping that their fire, if not accurate, would at least drive the annoyers away. They fired a few rounds and then ceased, and the engineers trotted out onto the nearly completed spans to try again. Once more those muskets thumped, dumping more Blue bodies on the rough planks, and putting a quick end to the renewed effort. The Yankee guns bellowed anew, their deep booms echoing down the river gorge. The fire was directed at the buildings, occasionally visible through the fog. Enemy casualties were few, for the Rebels dove for the cellars as the heavy iron projectiles smacked into wooden roofs, scattered splintered shingles, knocked holes in brick walls, and collapsed chimneys.

The Federals thought their fire had taken its toll, as the bark of Confederate muskets, slackened, then ceased altogether. Confident, the engineers clambered onto the unfinished bridges, one of which was only eighty yards from the far bank. They had barely begun to swing new pontoons into position when the Southerners' muskets once more drove them back. Now the big Federal guns went to work again. But the fog was still too thick for the gunners to sight their targets and know where the shells were hitting. Nevertheless, the guns banged away slowly and deliberately until about 8 a.m. But the tawny Rebel riflemen held their ground, and the uncompleted bridges floated out in the current.

Then some Union commander had an idea. If Napoleons could be brought down close to the river, perhaps their heavy charges of shell and canister would drive the Confederates away. So couriers galloped off with orders from Gen. Hunt for six batteries of Napoleons, which were attached to the idle divisions, to report to Col. Tompkins. Around 9 o'clock the Napoleons began arriving, and Tompkins put three of them on the bank to the right of the Lacy house. Then all of Tompkins's right center group turned loose at the rifle-loaded buildings across the river.

The big 12-pounders were flinging some explosive shells along with solid shot, but occasional brilliant orange-red flashes close in to the guns or just at the river edge indicated some of the shell projectiles were bursting short, thus endangering friendly infantry and engineers. Word was quickly passed to the batteries to fire solid shot only. For one hour Tompkins's gunners constantly fired on the buildings, with some sporadic help from parts of the other three groups. More battered wood and brick was sent crashing into dust and smoke-crowned piles of rubble.

At 10 o'clock the guns stopped firing. Then anxious Federals watched and waited. Had the Confederates been driven off? There was only one way to be certain. Again the engineers gathered up their tools and moved back to their floating bridges. The answer immediately came back to them. Muskets barked at them from the far bank. Lead slugs began ricocheting off the planking, kicking up little spouts of water, putting holes in the pontoons, and injuring some men. With muttered curses the rest of the engineers hurried back. Then someone spotted a column of Gray infantry moving down one of the main streets toward the waterfront. Battery G, 4th U.S., saw them too, and its four Napoleons on the bank to the left of the Lacy house swung onto target, letting go with a crashing salvo that quickly proved it was accurately aimed. The Gray troops fell back from the scathing fire.

However, the enemy in the buildings were quite another problem, and so far artillery fire had not proved an effective way to flush them out. Now Tompkins's batteries cut loose with their full force and gave the river front buildings a steady beating for thirty minutes.[6]

By now the sense of frustration had reached Burnside's headquarters. The Union commander was determined to have his bridges. If artillery could not clear out the Rebels, perhaps an all-out effort to set fire to the place would accomplish more. So Hunt passed the order to flatten Fredericksburg and set it afire.[7]

It was now shortly before noon, and the shapes of buildings became more visible to the Federals as the fog began to lift. Now, the Blue forces prepared to launch their large-scale bombardment. Instead of hit-or-miss shelling there would be a systematic process of destruction, building by building, as the Blue gunners could now see to adjust and shift their fire from target to target.

Up until this point, the big monsters of the 1st Connecticut Heavy Artillery had fired but little. Their commanding officer, Maj. Thomas S. Trumbull, had held their fire down to one round every ten to fifteen minutes to preserve his precious ammunition, for those big twenty-five pound projectiles were not as plentiful and as easily hauled about as the lighter ones. That there were no more than seven of these 4.5 inch rifles on hand for a job made to order for them was not the fault of Hunt or Col. Tyler. These two officers had received permission from McClellan, just prior to that general's relief from command, to form a siege train of seventy guns, forty of which were to have been 4.5's. But the train was never organized, apparently because of Halleck's opposition.[8] If any guns could smash those buildings, they could, and their time had arrived.

It was about 12:30 when Hunt's orders reached the batteries. The hills overlooking the left bank of the Rappahannock opposite the town shortly began to shudder and tremble as gun after gun ranged in on Fredericksburg. The bulk of the fire came from Tompkins's group, now augmented to thirteen batteries, and from the long-range rifled batteries of Tyler's command on his left. The Yankee cannon began a slow but destructive fire. Gunners bent over their pieces and deliberately sighted specific buildings. They rechecked the alignment, stepped back and raised their arms to signify the gun as ready, and then awaited their battery commander's order to fire. All along the heights came the clear loud commands: 'Number one, Fire!' A pause would follow, as commander and crew watched the flight and effect of the projectile. Then, 'Number two, Fire!' And so it went for two hours.

Though the scene on the heights was partially masked to the Confederates below by a thin mist, they could not mistake what was happening. Confederate artilleryman E. P. Alexander, watching from a vantage point near Marye's Heights, saw white clouds of bursting shells appear like exploding puffs of cotton over the tops of the buildings and about the silent church spires. He soon saw three or four columns of thick black smoke from burning buildings rising vertically for several hundred feet in the windless sky.

When the Union guns were stopped about 2:30, Fredericksburg was a mess. Building after building, house after house, were holed, partially destroyed, or completely flattened. When the cease fire order finally came, the Federals themselves could see at least two buildings burning fiercely. It seemed hard to believe that much resistance could remain in that rubble, and the engineers set forth to find out.

This time volunteers were called for, and after considerable persuasion a number of men responded. But it was no different than before. The Federal artillerymen were aghast to see those ominous little puffs of white smoke dart from the rubble of shattered buildings. With the first salvo, the Rebels had dived for the cellars and there they had stayed, almost immune to the Yankee projectiles. Not enough fires had resulted to force them out of their positions.

The Yankee gunners blamed part of their failure on their ammunition. No less than twelve Yankee battery commanders complained bitterly over one type of shell or another exploding prematurely, failing to take the rifling, or failing to detonate. That the complaints were not uniform as to the type or make of shell or fuze is significant, and, were it not that these same failures were plaguing the Rebels as well, one might have suspected sabotage of the Federal ammunition. One Blue officer was so blunt as to report his ordnance-issue shrapnel as being serviceable only as solid shot. It is difficult to account for this failure.

Gunners of both sides also suffered from gun failures. A slew of gun trails and axles broke, and one complete Union battery was forced out of action for these reasons. A 20-pounder Parrott of Benjamin's battery blew up on the second shot — an event which did nothing to change Hunt's low opinion of this weapon — and two big Confederate 30-pounder Parrotts were destined for the same fate two days later.

Whatever the reason, the Yankee cannon failed to do the job. But it was an artilleryman who solved the problem of moving the Union infantry across the river. Hunt himself suggested that the unsecured pontoons — which were glorified rowboats — be filled with infantry and ferried across under covering fire of the Federal guns. The handful of enemy snipers — actually a thin brigade — could then be readily mopped up, and the business of bridge building could begin again. The idea was accepted.

Orders went to the batteries to start hitting the town again. And, as the guns began to boom, volunteers from two infantry regiments jumped into the pontoons oared by the engineers and waited for the shelling to cease. With the final burst the boats shoved off, but the boatmen found their passage hindered by ice. In minutes, though, they had crossed the 400 yards, and as the bows grated on the far banks a sputtering of musketry broke from the nearest houses. The infantrymen jumped from the boats, cocked their rifles, and a swift house-cleaning began.

At the downstream bridge-site, opposite Lee's right, the Blue soldiers had much less trouble, as the ground opposite was more open. Only a shallow twisting ravine and a few farm buildings gave the harassing Confederates any cover. Here the Union engineers had been able to put across all but one section of the pontoons by 8:15 that morning. Suddenly a company or so of Rebels ran out from some nearby farm houses and tossed a volley at the Bluecoats. Six of the engineers dropped wounded, and a number of the pontoons sprouted holes about a half-inch wide. For a time construction was stopped here too.

Back went a cry for artillery, and three batteries of light rifles from Col. De Russy's group came galloping down from the hills to the river bank. Two more Napoleons were detached from nearby waiting divisions, and the five units totaling eight 12-pounders and fourteen 3-inch rifles,[9] set up in position at the river's edge. The guns took aim at the farm buildings which were sheltering the enemy riflemen; the sniping soon halted in that quarter. But when one Yankee general ordered the structures completely destroyed, the guns were less successful. The batteries had done their job well enough to let the engineers continue with their two spans here, however, and by midmorning Franklin was waiting only for the word from Army headquarters to pour his grand division over onto the right bank.

Burnside had his bridges now, and the actual crossings in force of the 120,000 man Union Army began around 4 p.m. By nightfall elements of three divisions were holding bridgeheads. Small skirmishes continued in the town itself, though, until after dark, when Lee finally ordered his harassing forces back to the safety of his lines behind the town.

During the day Confederate batteries had done little firing; there had been the danger of hitting their own men in the town, the lack of long-range weapons to hit the Federals before or in the act of crossing, and stringent orders against wasting precious ammunition in futile cannonades. Such batteries as did venture a round or so provoked a short lopsided pounding in return from the guns of Hays, Tompkins, and Tyler. That the Gray gunners suffered but little from this fire was due to a lesson they had learned the hard way at Antietam — to dig in the guns before arguing with Yankee batteries.

The first phase and the first day of Burnside's attack on Fredericksburg was over. There had been no real test of strength yet, as Lee's resources and the terrain dictated that he not dispute the crossing in force, though it is interesting to speculate what the results might have been had Lee chosen to occupy the town in force and fight Burnside's crossing. Such resistance as there was had been knocked out, not by explosive or solid missiles smashing up buildings, but by men with rifles in their hands. Technological advances to the contrary, things were no different here than they were at Cassino eighty-two years later.

The Confederates now knew, if they had ever had any real doubts over the last week, that Burnside was going to attack here rather than try a side-slip above or below. Thus, the Gray commanders spent that night adjusting their infantry positions and setting up artillery to sweep all the streets that led out of town. With great deftness the Rebel artillery battalion commanders, operating under their flexible system, deployed their batteries along the length of the Confederate line. Well aware that they could not match the Yanks gun for gun, they decided to outmaneuver them instead. Their heavier weapons, the rifles and Napoleons, they put in commanding dug-in positions, but a great part of their ordnance was short-range 12-pounder howitzers and light old 6-pounder guns, which were concealed in protected spots behind the crests. They would be used when the enemy's infantry made its move and came into range. Until that time the heavier guns would carry the brunt.

The night of the 11th passed clear and cold, though when light came a fog again veiled the lowlands. The powerful Federal Army arose from their breakfast fires and marched down to the narrow bridges. Across the bridges to the right bank poured Sumner's and Franklin's grand divisions, and along with them went their artillery, including the batteries that had been jealously loaned to Gen. Hunt.

The division commanders' determination to keep the batteries under their fingers meant that there would be no shortage of artillery for the divisions which crossed the bridges. At the upper bridges, opposite the town, there passed with Sumner's grand division ten batteries of fifty-six pieces plus nine more batteries of forty-eight guns from Butterfield's and Stoneman's corps — a grand total of nineteen batteries of 104 guns. But ironically only seven batteries or parts thereof of this huge mass pulled lanyard in the action which followed.

Franklin's men hauled seventeen batteries over the downstream bridges. These were soon augmented by two additional infantry divisions which brought along five more batteries. He also had two full army corps, the I Corps under Reynolds and the VI Corps under Smith. This meant that Burnside's left, with 55,000 veteran soldiers, had an artillery strength of twenty-two batteries of 116 guns and the further advantage of De Russy's reserve group — still a potent force though somewhat reduced. But since the terrain here was quite open, positions were found for all and only one failed to taste powder.

Burnside, however, had not scheduled an attack for this day, for he was content to cross his men and line them up along the far bank from the town downstream to a point just below the lower bridges. The day then was quiet. A few rounds from Confederate batteries were flung through the mist at the dense Yankee columns, but these outbursts always resulted in a fierce return fire from Hunt's alert gunners. The damage that each inflicted upon the other was paltry, as the Rebel fire was too light and the Federal was hindered by the earthworks protecting the Gray guns.

On the afternoon of December 12th Burnside rode down to Franklin's headquarters. As the Union commanders thought that the weak part of Lee's line was that which fronted Franklin, from Deep Run downstream to where the hill mass terminated at Hamilton's Crossing, it was decided that Franklin would make the main attack, and Sumner's command would make a secondary move on the portion of Lee's line behind the town. On December 13th, however, Franklin received a foggily written attack order from Burnside — an order which left him in doubt as to just what he was supposed to do. The orders were to keep his whole command in position for a rapid movement down the old Richmond Road, and to send out at least one division to pass below Smithfield to seize, if possible, the heights near Hamilton's Crossing.

After pondering this order, Franklin began to carry out what he believed were the instructions — a limited attack. Apparently what Burnside wanted was a seizure of the shoulder overlooking the Richmond Road, which swung around at the crossing, so that the Federals could run Lee's right end and thus force him to leave his advantageous trenches on the heights.

Holding this end of Lee's line, roughly from Deep Run to Hamilton's Crossing, was Stonewall Jackson's corps — packed in thick and deep. His chief-of-artillery had found firing positions for about thirty-seven of the corps' guns; fourteen were massed at the eastern terminus of the ridge overlooking the crossing. On the corps' left nine of the fourteen guns were actually on the Yankee side of the railroad bed, which paralleled Jackson's line. His batteries, then, could almost cross-fire over the plain in front.

Virtually all of Jackson's line was in the woods which extended down the slopes to the railroad. Here the timber stopped except for one spur about a hundred yards on the Federal side of the tracks. Some of old Stonewall's officers, noting this as the weak link of their chain, wanted to block it with some light guns set in these woods; these could cover the area by canister. But the ground was believed too marshy either to be traversed by attacking infantry or to be fortified with heavy gun carriages, so the soft spot in the line remained. It was this projection of woods masking an area some 800 to 1000 yards wide that complicated Jackson's position. The fourteen guns on the Confederate right could not sweep it adequately, and only the more advanced pieces on the corps' left could cover the space by effecting a swing to an extreme right oblique — a move which would let the Union batteries take them in flank.

The Federals had correctly estimated that this flank was the weaker part of Lee's line, though that it was slightly less than impregnable would have been a more correct estimate. By luck the Federals stumbled into that Achilles' heel of Lee's defense line. The move began about 7 a.m. December 13th: Franklin told Reynolds to start forward with his I Corps, and the corps commander told Meade's division to fix its bayonets; Gibbon and Doubleday would support Meade. At 8:30 Confederates peering through the fog caught glimpses of Meade's compact columns swinging down the river, crossing the Smithfield ravine, then wheeling to their right and passing over the Bowling Green Road. Behind his division came Doubleday's, driving parallel with the river to protect Meade's flank and rear. Finding Rebel cavalry in the woods Doubleday unlimbered Gerrish's and Stewart's batteries and began to clear them out. Meade shoved his men into a wide line of battle, one brigade behind the other at a distance of 200 yards. The third brigade of the division trailed along in column covering the left flank. It was between the first two brigades that Meade herded his artillery. The weaving columns moved forward, slowly plodding up a slight rise in the plain about 400 yards from the railroad. At that moment on the left, there was a flash and a puff of smoke, quickly followed by another. Seconds later the dull boom of two cannon reports rolled over the plain and two shells hissed angrily overhead. Federal officers scanned the terrain and spotted Rebel artillery cleverly planted behind some hedges near the junction of the Bowling Green Road and the road which cut west toward Hamilton's Crossing.

There was only one thing for Meade to do: halt his command and find out how much artillery the Rebels had on hand. Even one battery firing down the length of the Blue line, or hitting it in the rear as it advanced, could be demoralizing; if infantry was there in force it could be disastrous. Promptly the third brigade swung into line facing this threat, and Meade's batteries wheeled about and galloped toward the threatened flank.

Meade's division was the one that had been led by McCall on the Peninsula, and still with that command were the battle-tried batteries which had been in the thick of it at Gaines Mill and Glendale (Frayser's Farm) — the Pennsylvania batteries of Cooper, Simpson, and Amsden, plus the Regulars of Ransom's Battery C, 5th U.S. All of these were now at hand except Amsden's — Kerns had been its commander until he had been cut down at Gaines Mill — and it was just about now crossing the Rappahannock following its stay with De Russy.

Simpson unlimbered on the left front of the alerted third brigade, and Cooper and Ransom headed for a knoll on the left of the enfiladed first brigade. As they rolled in the Rebel guns boomed again. Simpson's trails hit the dirt, followed by Cooper's and Ransom's, and eager hands began spinning elevation wheels and pulling handspikes. Quickly the deadly tubes began banging return fire. In minutes the meadows in front were covered with dirty-white acrid smoke. On the east side of the Bowling Green Road Doubleday's men came forward to Meade's support, and Walcott's Maryland battery of that command rapidly wiggled into a position that permitted them to hit the Rebel gunners in flank.

A nasty if somewhat lopsided fire fight had begun. Almost immediately Simpson took a hit which smashed one of his guns.

Then one of Walcott's rounds succeeded in overturning and wrecking one of the enemy's guns — a Blakely rifle. Nevertheless, one enemy piece, a Napoleon, continued its annoying fire. The Gray gun began to shift position to throw off the enemy's aim. When the Yank gunners caught up, it would move again. But these Blue gunners — all solid veterans — kept chipping away at the remaining piece. For nearly an hour the racket continued until the Rebel gun commander, the gallant Pelham of Confederate legend, his crew chewed up and his ammunition almost gone, yanked the weapon out and sent it back to safety.[10]

As this daring shelling by Pelham had shown, the I Corps had an open flank. But Reynolds, the corps commander, pushed Doubleday over on the flank to block any enemy advancement into that quarter. And Burnside used his field telegraph to advise Franklin that all the artillery he needed could be had from the batteries on the bluffs.

Meade, with this threat neutralized, turned his attention to the heights in front. His third brigade, relieved by Doubleday, shifted forward into line with the others, its skirmishers swarming out to front and flank. As his infantry was shuffling into realignment Meade moved Ransom to the left of his first brigade, which was holding the right of his line — a move calculated to protect in case of Federal repulse and retreat. He moved Amsden into battery between Cooper and Ransom. Simpson with his three serviceable pieces was the only one of Meade's batteries left facing the threatened flank. Then the corps commander rode up to the artillery line and ordered Cooper to fire onto the silent heights 1000 yards distant. The four rifles barked for an hour.

Up to now the Confederate batteries on the hills had remained silent, obeying orders to wait for the Yankee infantry. Then, as a Pennsylvania regiment moved out in front of the long waiting line to take up its mission as skirmishers, it was instantly spotted by the Confederates. At least a part of the Rebel batteries on the right flank thought this was the start of the big push and opened a blistering fire.[11] For forty minutes Cooper, Amsden, and Ransom fought with these Rebel pieces.[12] They proved they were not rookies by blowing up an enemy ammunition chest and hitting men, horses, and matériel.

It was close to 1 p.m., and Meade was ready to go after the Rebels in those wooded hills, leafless in the chill December afternoon. There had been little evidence that Rebel infantry was present in force, but now there could be no doubt. To soften up their stubbornness Col. Wainwright ordered Cooper, Amsden, Ransom, and Hall to pound the silent crest, with the four batteries being given equal areas for targets. First one battery began a steady fire, then the second, third, and fourth chimed in, till eighteen weapons were exploding iron over the Virginia slopes. From the far banks of the river came dull thuds followed by the buzzing high overhead of the shells from some of Col. Hays's Reserve. Sam Benjamin was there — still a lieutenant, ably directing the fire of his six 20-pounders. Durell's Pennsylvania Battery, Pettit's New Yorkers, and Roemer's New Yorkers, all with light rifles, took up the fire as they saw targets. But the range was great for these batteries — 2000 to 3000 yards, and Lt. Benjamin doubted the efficacy of his 20-pounders at this range. Actually the Union aim was accurate, shells were hitting home, and batteries were so hard hit that they were later relieved by reserve units with 20-pounder Parrotts. Nervous infantry of both sides peered through the haze of rank burned powder, the Federals watching the effect of the shelling, and the Rebels looking for the Federal infantry to make its move.

In the meantime, on Meade's right, things were happening to one of Gibbon's batteries. Shortly before 9 a.m. Capt. James Hall's 2nd Maine Battery had clattered over the pontoon bridge to join its parent division, Gibbon's, then taking up position on Meade's right. The cannoneers were following the strict rule of the book, which said that in field batteries, in contrast to the horse batteries of the cavalry division where every man rode his own horse, they were not to ride the vehicles except in extreme measures. Actually this rule appears to have been seldom followed in combat, where movements were executed under fire and at a fast pace. Then Hall was ordered to hurry forward, and with the loud command of 'Trot-Hee-yo!' the six rifled gun sections and cannoneers rumbled across the road.

Col. Wainwright, the I Corps chief-of-artillery, ordered Hall to take position behind the crest of a small rise on Gibbon's left. Reaching the designated spot the teams swung about, pointing the gun muzzles at the wooded hills. Cannoneers grabbed the trails, unhooked, and lowered them to earth. The men removed rammerstaffs and water buckets from their traveling hooks on the gun carriages and readied everything for instant action.

The battery's arrival immediately provoked an outburst of firing by some Gray gunners 1600 yards to the right front. The Maine men loaded with shell, and their six 3-inch rifles began biting back. As they worked their weapons the booming on Meade's left came rolling over the plains — Pelham's duel with Meade's and Doubleday's batteries. The men could not determine whether Pelham was actually shooting at Hall or whether they were catching the overs fired at the other Yankee batteries, but they did know a galling fire was hitting them in flank. Hall wanted to swing his rifles about and go after his annoyers — the range was only about 700 yards — but Gen. Reynolds disagreed; there was Federal infantry between the battery and the enemy, and the general did not trust overhead fire by friendly artillery.[13] The 2nd Maine Battery continued its shelling to the front.

All the corps' batteries on the line proceeded to pour everything they had into the Rebels. Ransom, Cooper, Amsden, and Hall set up a thunderous racket. Then Gibbon's second battery, Thompson's Battery C, Pennsylvania Light Artillery, rolled up on his right and joined in. The whole Yankee left flank was a line of gun fire, from Simpson on Meade's extreme left, all the way past Gibbon and on down the seven-odd batteries of

Smith's corps on Reynolds's right. Smith's batteries were in line with and over the Bowling Green Road, forming a large mass of thirty-eight guns designed to protect that flank. Ten additional pieces were emplaced farther to the right. Little if any of Smith's fire, however, aided Meade, as Smith's line was long and part of his batteries were arguing with the Gray guns on the hills directly to their front, those closer to town — Longstreet having turned a part of his artillery loose at 11 a.m. as a diversion to the threatened Confederate right.

Now loud orders of infantry commanders were heard amid the staccato gunfire, and the men rose to their feet. Muskets were loaded, bayonets fixed, and lines dressed. Officers, swords and pistols in hand, moved to their posts in front of the waiting ranks. With a loud 'Forward March!' the advance began, and the 3rd Division, I Corps, Army of the Potomac, began rolling toward the ominous hills. The Confederates reacted instantly. Both ends of Jackson's line came to life as the hitherto silent batteries on his flanks had their leashes cut and were free to snap back.[14] The Gray gunners concentrated on the wide weaving lines of Yankee infantry.

Hall's 2nd Maine battery, backing up Gibbon's division, began to catch return fire. Capt. Hall was sitting on his horse in the rear of his battery calmly watching his gunners at work. About fifty feet away two colonels, one a regimental commander and the other in temporary command of a brigade, sat astride their mounts. Over the deep, almost continuous roar of the guns Hall exchanged occasional words with the two officers. Suddenly, a well-aimed shell from one of Stonewall's guns sizzed through the gap between Hall and the two colonels, and with a stunning explosion slammed into one of Hall's caissons, blowing it into splinters.

The captain steadied his unnerved horse, dismounted, turned the reins over to an orderly, and calmly walked to one of his just-loaded 3-inch guns. Motioning the gunner aside, Hall stepped to the vacated position, leaned over the thick breech of the weapon, and took a sight on the enemy battery he believed responsible for that crippling shot. Two cannoneers grabbed hold of the handspike; the number four jerked the lanyard, and a sheet of orange flame and an acrid cloud of smoke jumped from the muzzle. As the heavy report echoed across the field the gun rolled back in recoil. Hall and the crew watched for the effect. One second, two, three, then a flash directly in the middle of the enemy battery. As the distant thump of the exploding shell rolled back from the slope the Blue artillerymen saw what they took to be a direct hit on one of the Confederate guns. Satisfied, Hall turned and walked back to his horse, remounted, and resumed his post just in the rear of his gun line. An impressed gun crew then rolled the weapon forward into battery from its recoiled position and resumed the shooting. But the hit on Hall's caisson caught Gen. Gibbon's eye; he promptly rode over to Hall, and ordered the captain to send his caissons across the road to cover.[15]

Simpson's Battery A, 1st Pennsylvania, was not so lucky. His line of guns still faced the left flank, and, as such, they were almost perpendicular to the heights. Some shrewd-eyed Rebel saw the juicy target and began a fast and accurate fire upon Battery A, bowling over men and horses. Simpson, realizing the dangerous position of his battery, gave the order to change front — a task which had to be done by hand, as sixteen horses and eleven men were down. Once positioned facing the Rebel line, these Yankees responded with their iron and adopted Pelham's tactic of shifting position in order to confuse the enemy's range.

Under the cover of their corps' artillery, ably controlled by Col. Wainwright, Meade's long weaving lines of blue moved slowly over the intervening plain. Then several of Pelham's guns began firing again from their new position in the low ground just a little to the east of Hamilton's Crossing — on the left front of the advancing Federals. Pelham's fire coupled with that of the fourteen guns firing from the hilltop on the Confederate right tore into the Union masses. Col. Wainwright looked about for more artillery to counter this fire just as Doubleday's batteries came into view. Quickly the colonel put Capt. Gerrish's New Hampshire battery into action against Pelham at 1100 yards range. But, since Gen. Reynolds wanted more weight added to the fire, reliable Battery B, 4th U.S., still bearing the scars of that fight in Miller's cornfield, was put into position near where Pelham had been earlier in the day. Even Hall's Maine battery swung their tubes over at a 1300 yard range. At least twenty-one guns were soon hammering the crest, and fourteen more were shooting at Pelham.

But the show was not one-sided. The New Hampshire battery was severely pounded in this fight, losing its commander and thirteen other casualties, and suffering a smashed-up limber. A well-aimed Rebel round crashed into one of Walcott's guns and completely dismounted it. Battery B was not spared either. They lost a caisson to accurate enemy gunnery and one of its Napoleons was knocked off its carriage. The Battery B men, however, hit an enemy ammunition chest which exploded with a roar and a billowing cloud of smoke.

Meade's men had now reached the projecting strip of woods; the columns on the left obliqued into the timber for cover. They had been hurt by Jackson's guns but not stopped. On Meade's right Gibbon began to advance in support of the attack. But the old artilleryman Gibbon still retained his outdated practice of having field batteries accompany the infantry lines, and Capt. Hall received the general's order to move his battery forward on the division's left flank. At a point 200 yards from the smoky woods Gibbon ordered Hall to put his guns into action.

Gibbon's second battery, Thompson's C, Pennsylvania, had moved up earlier in the morning on the division's right where it had engaged in some sporadic firing with enemy batteries. Beyond Thompson was Smith's corps, which was under no orders to advance or support the I Corps. As such, a wide gap could develop between Gibbon and Smith when the former began his advance. Accordingly, as the division moved out, Gibbon pulled Thompson along to keep a close protection on that flank.

Meade's cheering regiments tramped through the woods, swarmed over the railroad embankment, shoved their way through the gap in Jackson's line, and swept up to the top of the ridge. The Rebels were caught completely off balance. Once more the life of the Confederacy was endangered. It was Antietam all over again as Confederate reserves came hurrying forward to close the gap and bring Meade's men to a halt.

The Federals called for support. But Gibbon, who was to be the support, had been separated from Meade in the heavy woods. The result was that the Rebels had two unconnected attacks to deal with. Though some of the more advanced Gray batteries had retired in the face of this attack, Gibbon was stopped and Meade was forced back as his thinned regiments were hit in front and both flanks. The remnants of both divisions stubbornly fell back toward the open plain where they had started. Further, Stonewall began prodding his men to follow up the Federal repulse.

The Federal batteries which had supported the assaults were now in a dangerous position, particularly those more advanced. One of these, Amsden's, continued to be unfortunate. As the Blue infantry emerged from the woods Amsden concluded that it was no longer safe to fire the two pieces with the snapped axles, and since their ammunition was nearly gone, the captain ordered the pieces off the field. Minutes later an enemy round slammed into a gun of the right section, shivering its wheel and axle. This weapon too was ordered to the rear.

The situation became more confusing when the rest of Battery G misunderstood Amsden's last order to mean that all the remaining guns should retire. Next, Amsden's horse was shot and fell, pinning him to earth. Amsden freed himself, caught up with his shattered command, reunited the sections, and then reported to Gen. Reynolds, who ordered him to replenish ammunition and report back to Gen. Meade. But Capt. Amsden was unable to carry out this command — there was no more ammunition on the trains. The battle was over for Battery G.

Whooping Confederates were spilling down from the heights in an attempt to turn the Federal repulse into a rout, and Hall's Maine battery, still covering Gibbon's left, was endangered when enemy troops, pursuing Meade's across the railroad, suddenly turned on it. At a short range of 200 yards Hall's gunners fired double canister, feverishly reloaded, and jerked lanyard again. Men and colors went down from the frightful blasts, and for a few minutes the battery was safe. As Hall had expended all of his ammunition, he ordered his command to retire.

Quickly the limbers came up and the guns were hooked on. At that instant a loud crash of musketry from the Rebels hit the left gun, knocking down and wounding five horses and twisting the traces. There was no chance to recover the gun; it had to be left behind as the crew fled. As the battery galloped to the rear they met fresh Union infantry advancing to stiffen the Blue line. Only then did Capt. Hall halt and order a party to try to recover the abandoned weapon. Four horses were cut out of one of the teams and six men led them back to pull the rifle off the field.

Although the 2nd Maine Battery again had all six of its guns, it was in no condition to go back into the fray. Twenty-five of its horses were dead, six were badly wounded, sixteen men were casualties, and 1100 rounds of ammunition had been fired. This ammunition expenditure might seem to be high, particularly in view of Hunt's admonition, but Hall had been in almost continuous action from around 9:30 a.m. to 4 p.m. — six and a half hours.

The situation confronting Franklin had become serious, and he had sent Birney's division forward to reinforce the weakened line. These were the men Hall had passed as he retired from the field. As Birney moved up he ordered his two batteries

— E, 1st Rhode Island Light Artillery, and F/K, 3rd U.S. —
to relieve those of Meade's which were running out of ammunition.

The Regulars under Lt. Turnbull dropped their trails on the
right of Meade's men, then the Rhode Islanders under Lt. Jastram — the same officer who had received Kearny's stinging
rebuke after the battle of Glendale — went into position on
Turnbull's left. Both batteries began firing shell and case into
the edge of the woods and the willing Rebel artillery immediately replied. The Blue gunners were firing hard when pleas
came back from their infantry to stop firing fuzed projectiles;
some of them were exploding short!

The Blue infantry fell back, pursued by the enemy to within
canister range of Birney's and Reynolds's remaining batteries.
Here the Graycoats ducked behind a low rise, trying to snipe
through the smoke at the Yankee cannoneers. Jastram's gunners switched to canister, as did Turnbull's. Others followed,
and the Rebels were stopped. More Yankee batteries rolled
into the fighting. One of Dan Sickles's — Dimick's Battery
H, 1st U.S. — started firing at 1200 yards. Sickles's division
was in reserve on both sides of the Bowling Green Road. The
last of Gibbon's batteries, Leppien's 5th Maine Battery, came
out of its reserve position in the road and into the fray. And, as
had been the case so many times in the past, the Federal artillery did its job well, taking up the slack in a sagging line, thus
preventing a possible disaster.

The Confederates paused and surveyed the Union line,
which still looked formidable. There were eight to ten serviceable field batteries stiffening the Blue line in addition to the
guns on the far side of the river. What the Rebels did not know
was that Col. Hays, who had not been able to determine the
exact location of the friendly troops, had greatly curtailed the
fire of his Reserve group. Nonetheless, the Confederate command was in favor of renewing the attack on Franklin. About
4:30 p.m. approximately ten Gray cannon rolled onto the
plain preceding the charge of the Confederate infantry; actually

more batteries were expected to support the charge, but confusion in their staff and disorganization among some batteries prevented others from entering the action in time.

The Confederate cannon roared their fury, but the stubborn Federal batteries bellowed back without respite. Once more, as at Antietam, Stonewall Jackson decided there were too many Union guns to counter-attack. One of his division commanders, whose unit had been in reserve all day, reported that he had suffered only 173 casualties — nearly all from Federal artillery fire.

But the fighting at Fredericksburg was far from over; for much of the Federal infantry some of the worst slaughter of the war started about noon against Lee's line on Marye's Heights directly behind the town. The Union command had chosen to attack the heights on Lee's left where Longstreet's corps with massed artillery were entrenched. The Federal force had to move through the city then across open ground within easy range of the protected Confederates. Burnside ordered Sumner and his right grand division to seize the high ground west of town. Sumner passed the order to Couch, who was commanding the II Corps, who in turn picked French's division to make the attack; Hancock was ordered to support French.

Around 9:30 a.m. staff officers rode furiously to carry orders to the units waiting under cover in the town. The streets were jammed with infantry, trains, ambulances, provost marshal's men, and staff personnel. Division commanders had brought over as many of their artillery batteries as they could. It is not surprising that it took another two and a half hours to ready an attacking force. To get attacking troops into the wide lines required by tactics of that time for such an assault was not an easy job. The deployment was complicated by a canal which traversed the open ground just beyond the city. The canal was about fifteen feet wide and six feet deep — though the Federals opened a sluice gate which lowered the water level to wadable depth.

But Federal commanders refused to deploy on the near side

of the canal, believing the ranks would lose cohesion if they
tried to cross the ditch on a wide front. Instead, they decided
to march the columns out of town via the major exit streets
which had bridges over the canal. On the far side of the ditch
the columns would peel off to right and left to form line of battle. A slight rise just beyond the ditch would offer the deploying
troops some cover.

At 11:30 everything was set. Several regiments marched
from town, crossed the canal bridges, and deployed in a thick
skirmish line. Behind them came the masses of French's division — Kimball's brigade in the lead. On Marye's Heights the
famed Washington Artillery battalion from New Orleans was
ready, the men having slept beside their weapons that night.
Sighting the Yank columns, the Confederates jumped to their
pieces, rammed home the loads, and stepped clear as the guns
boomed.

Farther to the left, three Napoleons of Alexander's battalion
were able to bring their fire to bear on the Yankee columns,
and the artillery of McLaw's division, forty-eight pieces, had
a veritable rabbit-shoot at the expense of Burnside. Just in
front of Marye's Heights the Confederates held a small road
which for a short way ran parallel to the Rebel line and perpendicular to the direction of the Union attack. The road was
partially sunken at the southern end and at the northern end
it was bordered by a fieldstone wall some four feet high. They
also held a second line on the exposed hill just behind the road.
Above the Confederate infantry was their artillery — over
three battalions on line. More batteries were nearby as reserve.
As soon as the Blue columns turned into the exit streets from
town the Gray gunners began to jerk lanyards, bouncing their
iron balls down the narrow streets into the Blue ten-pins.

At first the only reply to the enemy fire came from some of
Hunt's long-range batteries across the river, their heavy reverberations echoing over the town. As the Federal infantry
neared the enemy line many of these batteries had to cease fire
for safety reasons. The bark of close-up artillery support was

weak, however. Eight batteries were assigned to Couch's corps, two to each of the three divisions, and two more in reserve. Five of these batteries, four of them armed with Napoleons, had crossed with the corps. Yet it appears that the only guns in initial close support of French were two rifled pieces — one section of Arnold's Battery A, 1st Rhode Island Light Artillery, which opened fire from a point between two houses at the head of Charlotte Street.

In commenting later about this battle, Gen. Sumner stated that the lack of good firing positions on the Federal right limited the Federal artillery, though the unorganized control over the division batteries was as much the fault. The demand that the field batteries of the divisions cross with their commands should have been resisted. Careful planning would have showed that there was limited space. Instead, some nineteen batteries crossed into the town, jamming the streets and hindering each other. Only seven or parts thereof of these nineteen batteries actually pulled lanyard. Gen. Hunt remarked that, given the proper authority, he could have drawn a hundred idle guns from the town and sent them to Franklin's aid. Then Franklin, supported by two of Hooker's divisions already on the ground, could have struck with his entire corps and no doubt could have smashed Jackson's line.[16]

At Fredericksburg the Confederates had the artillery upper hand. Their dug-in batteries, liberally emplaced along the length of their line, covered the open ground behind Fredericksburg so well that one Gray artillery commander boasted to Gen. Longstreet that when they opened fire a chicken wouldn't be able to cross untouched.

As the leading ranks of Kimball's brigade swung out over the top of the protecting rise beyond the canal, the Gray batteries hit them from the front and from the obliques, flailing away at the Blue masses with cold precision. From across the river some of Tyler's and Tompkin's long-range guns still tried to beat down the Confederate batteries, but the ranges were great — a severe handicap for direct fire tactics of that era; some of the ammunition behaved badly; many of the enemy batteries were well dug-in; and there was the danger of firing too close to their own infantry. Only Arnold's two little rifles kept up a continuous fire, as they had been instructed against the enemy batteries enfilading the Federal infantry.

Some of French's men seized buildings at the corner of Hanover and Fair Streets and began a sniping fire on the sunken road, but the bulk of the regiments were stopped by the combined fire of the enemy's infantry and artillery some 200 yards from their goal. Here the survivors dropped into a crude firing line behind fences and a little swell in the ground. When French's second and third brigades followed they met with the same hideous repulse. Hancock's division shook itself into line and prepared to take up where French's men had failed. Howard's division was recalled from its flanking move to follow French and Hancock.

It was about noon when Burnside decided that his assault with one division supported by a second was not the right formula and decided more men would be needed. Accordingly, a division of Willcox's IX Corps, Sturgis's, received orders to support Couch, and promptly began to move through town. Sturgis had two batteries assigned him; Battery D, 1st Rhode Island Light Artillery, and Battery E, 4th U.S. These were both waiting in the town as the IX Corps chief-of-artillery had not been able to find firing spaces for his units. Sturgis decided to hold the Rhode Islanders in reserve, but he ordered the Regulars under Lt. George Dickenson into battery near a brick kiln on the left of the railroad on the south edge of town. His infantry halted temporarily under cover near the depot.

About 12:30 p.m. Hancock's proud regiments were halted on line with the wreckage of French's command. Seeing this repulse and the near state of collapse of the Federal left here, Sturgis sent Dickenson into action, along with a brigade of infantry. The battery with its four 10-pounder Parrotts trotted forward to a little ripple in the ground, 1200 yards from the enemy guns. Before the first piece was ready to fire enemy riflemen had picked off some of his cannoneers. Although Lt. Dickenson scanned the front he could see only the enemy cannon as they stuck their blackened snouts from behind earthworks on the heights. He commanded his men to fire on the enemy batteries.

The Confederate gunners in turn quickly picked up the exposed Federal battery, finding it a lush target for solid shot. At this moment one of the Regulars spotted some Gray infantry and the battery turned to fire on them. The Gray gunners, having picked up the range with their solid shot, switched to shell and case, and immediately began splattering the whole battery area with fragments. The unit had been in action a bare thirty minutes when one perfectly aimed and fuzed round ended the life of Lt. Dickenson; twelve other men were also casualties. Lt. John Egan, who took command when Dickenson fell, concluded that the mission was futile, their own fire seemed to have no effect on the protected enemy. Gen. Sturgis concurred and ordered Battery E to withdraw from the fight.[17]

At 1:30 p.m. it was obvious to Couch, to French, to Hancock, and certainly to the survivors of their splintered commands, that the attack had failed. There was a ragged Blue line of intermingled regiments hugging the ground behind the little rise 200 yards from the enemy, but it was a fixed line. A man rising from the ground, to advance or to retreat, invited a vicious outburst of firing.

Couch surveyed the debacle of the infantry and the heavy casualties suffered by Dickenson's battery and sent a distress call at 1:30 p.m. to Burnside: 'I am losing. Send two rifle batteries.' [18] The message got immediate attention from Army headquarters. One of Hunt's staff led Waterman's Rhode Island and Kusserow's New York batteries across the river and turned them over to Capt. C. H. Morgan, the II Corps chief-of-artillery. The captain promptly ran both batteries into action on a small ridge near the still-standing historic Kenmore house, where the range to the Confederate infantry was about 1100 yards. The two units began a slow fire to their left oblique.

It was about this time, too, that Capt. Arnold received orders to move forward the rest of his Battery A, 1st Rhode Island, to join his section, which had been supporting the attack since noon. The corps' chief-of-artillery instructed Arnold to fire on the enemy's infantry. The battery swung into battle with case shot. At first their fire was rapid in order to help the advance of the infantry. But when the Blue regiments crumbled and fell away, Arnold slacked off, reducing his firing to occasional salvos.

The Union high command, unwilling to admit defeat, fed in more troops. Burnside ordered Hooker's grand division into the fight from its reserve assignment east of the river. Hooker had discovered the true picture and protested to Burnside against further assaults — to no avail. The attack continued. More infantry was fed to the Confederates as Hooker tried to round up more artillery.

Shortly after 4 p.m. Couch watched still another division break itself apart in a vain attempt to reach the enemy works. At this point he realized that something had to be done to take the pressure off the IX Corps regiments which were trying to revitalize the attack. He decided to send a battery into the open ground behind the infantry in order to try to neutralize the enemy fire. Couch commanded Capt. Morgan to run out a battery. The captain was appalled and protested that it would be suicide — that he would lose the battery. 'I would rather lose my guns than lose my men,' retorted Couch.[19] He suggested running Arnold's rifled guns forward, but Morgan again protested and won his point.

Morgan summoned Arnold's guidon bearer, who was acting as his orderly, and instructed him to advance over the canal to see if the ground there could support horses and vehicles. The young lad touched his cap in salute, turned, and set off on his hazardous mission. The officer watched the rider clatter over the bridge spanning the canal and ride out into open ground in front of the enemy position. Rebel fire, aimed at the stalled Blue infantry, buzzed about the orderly's head as he scanned the ground. After a few minutes he reported to Morgan that it could be done. Morgan then ordered Capt. John Hazard, commander of Battery B, 1st Rhode Island, to limber up and gallop his men to a hillock 150 to 200 yards from the enemy infantry line. Drivers booted their mounts and away the battery went. As the column rode past its sister unit, Battery A, they heard one of those men prophetically remark: 'There goes Battery B to hell!' [20]

The six guns rattled over the wooden bridge, and at a gallop the battery headed straight out Hanover Street toward the hillock. They reached the ridge and the column turned left and then wheeled almost instantly into action right. This put the left and center sections on a rise off the road, while the right moved out thirty yards down the road. Hazard yelled his orders: 'Left and center sections — solid shot — fire at will; right section — shell — fire at will.'

As was the case with Dickenson's battery, Hazard began taking casualties even before the guns were unlimbered. Lt. Adams, commanding the right section, caught hot and heavy fire. As the teams swung about to go into action a searing blast of musketry dropped every horse of one gun. The cannoneers pushed the gun into position and a man stepped to the muzzle to shove in a round. He was instantly shot down. Another tried and he too was cut down, as was a third. But Adams had come to stay and somehow, in the face of that point-blank fire, the gun stayed in action, firing away at the stone wall obscured by the dense gunsmoke.

For three-quarters of an hour Hazard kept his men firing, trying to lessen the attack on the stalled and grounded Federal infantry. Hazard lost sixteen men and twelve horses before he got help from four Napoleons of Frank's Battery G, 1st New York Light Artillery, sent into action by Joe Hooker.

Frank had six Napoleons. Earlier in the day one section had moved to the head of one of the exit streets where it had fired a few rounds without any visible effect. The enemy, however, had the exposed section within easy range of their rifled

pieces and soon drove it to cover. When the captain received
Hooker's demand for the battery, he tried to locate French, his
division commander. Failing to do this and fearing that his
commander would call back for more guns, Frank decided to
leave his right section behind.

Hooker ordered him to unlimber 400 yards west of the town
— left and rear of Hazard's command. The position was under
heavy infantry and artillery fire as he came in. Like Hazard,
Frank split his battery's fire — one section worked with solid
and shell on the enemy's batteries, and the other used case on
their infantry.[21]

It is probable that the Federal artillery support on this flank
reached its maximum effort — which was in effect not much
of an effort, through no cause of its own making — about 4
or 4:30 p.m. It was at this time too that Hooker's command
was getting ready to fight. Of the five available batteries of
Couch's corps — Arnold was still engaged; Frank had two sections in for a short time during this period; Hazard was heavily
engaged; a section of Kirby's battery of Regulars may have
done some firing, but it appears to have been kept as a reserve;
and Thomas's Battery C, 4th U.S., fired from the left near the
railroad for a short while, though it appears he was withdrawn
by Capt. Morgan prior to 4 o'clock. Of the other batteries originally sent to support Couch, the two rifled commands of
Waterman and Kusserow were, no doubt, still in action.

About this time also, Battery E, Massachusetts Light Artillery, under Capt. Charles A. Phillips, was ordered by Capt.
Weed to the lower part of town between the Poorhouse and
some brickyards. Their arrival drew fire from the Rebel cannon and Battery E returned with case shot. One lieutenant of
the battery wrote a letter home that night which expressed the
feelings of the whole arm: 'I do not learn that our artillery was
used to any advantage. . . . The fact is that we have no
general who has shown himself able to handle infantry, artillery, and cavalry so as to make them cooperate together. Malvern Hill is the only battle I have been in where the artillery

was even decently managed, and there the number of pieces was so small that it could not have been mismanaged very well.' [22]

Elsewhere along this part of the Federal line two batteries — Puttkammer's 11th New York Battery with six 3-inch rifles and Bruen's 2nd New York Battery of six Napoleons — had moved with elements of the III Corps to the northern part of the city. They were to protect the approaches to the city from the west and to cover Howard's right flank in that division's flanking move which was later canceled. Four pieces were positioned at the upper end of the city to sweep the flatlands and bridges, and another four went into battery near the upper junction of Charles and Prince streets with Fauquier and Lewis streets to cover the frontal approaches. It is unlikely that either of these batteries, while they may have done some firing at this time, assisted the attacks on Marye's Heights.

That the Federal artillery was doing damage, though, is confirmed by one Confederate battery commander who told of seeing eight Yankee guns move to the edge of town and open on him, forcing him to divert his fire from the Blue infantry. A staff officer suggested he run a gun forward to try to enfilade the Federals. Before he had set the gun up on the forward slope the Yankee gunners had killed one of his men. The Gray gun fired three rounds and had just been loaded for the fourth when a Yankee shell slashed into the gun, disabling it and wounding three men. The Federal shooting was effective but limited.

The V Corps had crossed the river to make the final attack shortly after 2 p.m. Capt. Alanson Randol, now serving as chief-of-artillery of Humphreys's division, crossed his own battery of veterans, which could bitterly recall the vicious fighting around Glendale where it was overrun; and Phillips's Battery C, 1st New York Light Artillery, followed. Randol hurriedly rode forward to find good positions for his batteries, but he found nearly every available site occupied by Sumner's batteries. He found his division commander, Humphreys, and told him his findings, and the general directed the captain to hold

268 _____ *Grape and Canister*

his guns in readiness in case of a repulse of the attacking infantry. Then, as Randol rode back to bring his commands through the town, Gen. Butterfield, the V Corps commander, ordered him to report to Capt. Weed of the V Corps.

In the confusion of retreat brought about by the wounded, and the milling troops, Randol had no success. But he did find Hooker who informed him of the point of attack and ordered Randol's guns into action. Accordingly the captain led his column toward the only unoccupied piece of ground which he could use to support the assault.

As the head of his column reached the spot, a section of Kirby's battery galloped onto it. Randol surveyed the area and concluded that there was room for only one more section, so he shoved in one of Phillips's, holding his own and the rest of Phillips's as a reserve.

Second Lt. William Phillips, commanding Battery C, 1st New York Light Artillery, reported that it was about 4:45 p.m. when his section got into line. He judged the range to the enemy riflemen as 500 yards and to their batteries as 800 to 1300 yards. These ranges were well within the capabilities of his 3-inch rifles so he ordered his section to load with fuzed shell. The two guns cut loose, firing forty-seven rounds before their friendly infantry made its move and Phillips ordered cease fire.

That final charge was made about sundown by Humphreys's division of Butterfield's V Corps. As the division crossed the canal and began its deployment it ran into Hazard's battery. Hazard was ordered to cease fire as the infantry formed, then passed through the intervals in the battery. The Rhode Island stopped further shooting and shortly retired to the city. The V Corps regiments marched to where the battered remnants of the earlier attacks lay. There Humphreys's attack was wrecked, destroying Burnside's chances of beating Lee that day.

As darkness settled, battle-weary survivors of destroyed brigades were relieved and many of the batteries replaced. The entire Army hoped it would never see a day like this again. One Confederate artilleryman proudly noted in his report, written sometime later when he had had the advantage of Northern accounts of the action, 'In the Yankee accounts of the battle it is stated that about one-fifth of the killed and wounded were from artillery.' [23] Another remarked, 'More artillery appeared to be used this day than I have ever known before.' This same officer counted as many as fifty shots per minute.[24]

Lee learned that Burnside planned to renew the offensive the next day. But the Union commander changed his mind and the Confederates waited for the assault which never came. The beaten and dispirited Federal Army re-crossed the Rappahannock the night of December 14th. Fredericksburg was the epitome of failure for the Union Army. One Yankee officer later wrote that the only useful thing that happened was the experience gained in crossing a river in the presence of an enemy. Although the Federal artillery did not lose a gun or a carriage to the enemy, it suffered 170 casualties in thirty batteries, fifty-eight of them in the four batteries of Gerrish, Hall, Hazard, and Dickenson.

Hunt reported that in the handling of the batteries by the various corps chiefs-of-artillery had improved and that the 'expenditure of ammunition was notably reduced when compared with the effect produced and former experience.' [25] There was, however, still the ammunition resupply problem. Hunt still disapproved of the system of keeping the reserve ammunition wagons for division batteries with the division trains. 'Until the ammunition trains were placed under the direct control of the chiefs-of-artillery,' he said, 'resupply would be unreliable.' His warnings, however, regarding useless expenditure of ammunition, had been effective, for only a few units moved to the rear after shooting up their basic load.

In his report of the battle Hunt asked that field batteries be strengthened to a minimum of 150 men for a six-gun unit. Serving a battery in action was exhausting work, and each reduction in the number of men increased the load on the others, resulting in a loss of efficiency. He suggested a special recruit-

ing service for the batteries of each state be established, with
depot units for training purposes. The service would place recruits in veteran batteries, continually strengthening them
rather than creating new batteries. But his suggestion was ignored and the problem plagued the Army for the length of the
war.

Gen. Hunt, who was a persistent and energetic man, did not
give up trying to improve the artillery command structure and
to obtain reward for those he felt deserving. Immediately after
Fredericksburg he asked Burnside to assign officers to him for
artillery duty according to their brevet; this would improve the
arm by providing chiefs-of-artillery of competent rank for the
corps and divisions. He also requested Burnside to ask Lincoln
about conferring the brevet promotions recommended during
the Peninsula and Antietam campaigns. Hunt gathered later
that Burnside had agreed, and following a visit with the President, Burnside told him that Lincoln was in accord, as was
Secretary of War Stanton. But the usual fly in the artillery oint-
ment, Halleck, put the damper on the plan.

The gunners could look back on Fredericksburg and think
that the long arm had performed well enough on the Union
left flank that December 13th. Offensively the batteries had
done about all their capabilities would allow. They had
knocked about some of Jackson's batteries, but not enough to
weaken the Rebel fire so that the ensuing Federal assault could
be successful. Defensively the batteries had once again stopped
an attempted counterstroke by Jackson. The threat of the
heavy Federal artillery strength on both sides of the river was
a major factor in Lee's decision not to attack Burnside on the
14th.

On the Union right, there was little for the Federal artillerymen to view with pride. There had been individual instances of
gallantry by isolated batteries such as Hazard's, but improperly
used forces — a return to the tactics of the First Bull Run —
weakened the Federals. Fredericksburg was no doubt the dark-
est hour in the entire war for the Army of the Potomac.

XI

I CAN'T MAKE AMMUNITION

Chancellorsville

WITH THE debacle at Fredericksburg, active operations in northern Virginia ended until the spring of 1863. Both armies, tired and in need of refitting, went into winter quarters. Burnside had made one more attempt on January 23rd to flank Lee out of his dirt fortresses on the hills west of Fredericksburg. But driving rains turned the roads into impassable, mucky canals, and the abortive 'Mud March' which resulted marched Burnside right out of the Army command.

On January 26, 1863, Maj. Gen. Joseph Hooker, who privately delighted in his unofficial sobriquet of 'Fighting Joe,' at last got command of the Army of the Potomac — a job he had been angling for for some months. For all of his personal faults, Gen. Hooker realized that the Army of the Potomac needed an overhauling. Ordinarily a change in army high command is a remote thing to the man in the ranks — a distant and impersonal change of names. Rarely does it immediately affect the plain soldier, but in this instance it did. Hooker's headquarters may have been a rendezvous for carousers at night, as one sour contemporary wrote, but during the day his subordinates were rejuvenating the Army. Hooker's reforms must have had some success, for one gunner wrote that Hooker eliminated the difference in efficiency between Regular batteries and the Volunteers which had existed in prior campaigns.[1]

271

While much of the Army staff changed with the ascendancy
of Hooker, he saw fit to retain Gen. Hunt as chief-of-artillery.
Hooker must have appreciated, at least initially, the reputation and ability of this man, for shortly after assuming command Hooker issued General Orders No. 6, paragraph II of
which plainly rings of the gospel according to Hunt: 'Hereafter the corps will be considered as a unit for the organization
of the artillery, and no transfers of batteries will be made from
one corps or division to others except for purposes of equalization, and then only under the authority of the chief-of-artillery.' [2] This proved to be only a temporary attitude of Hooker's, however. By the time the Army broke camp in late April,
Hooker had reduced Hunt to the status of an adviser on artillery matters with no personal authority whatsoever. During
the hard fighting around Chancellorsville the Army's chief-of-
artillery was anything but that, and in his after-action report
Hunt was extremely blunt and critical of his commander for
this reduction in authority.

In the meantime, Hooker's 'new look' program, which included more liberal furloughs, began to have a good effect, as
AWOL's and desertions fell off and morale and equipment
improved. While the artillery as a whole was about 3500 men
under strength, as of February 24, 1863, the incidence rate of
AWOL's and desertions appears to have been lower in the
artillery batteries than in the other branches; and the Artillery
Reserve, according to a medical report of March 29th, had
the lowest sickness rate in the Army except for the Provost
Marshal Brigade.[3]

If there was ever any doubt in the Army that the new commander was in dead earnest about his rejuvenation program
that doubt ended with the publication on March 3rd, of General Orders No. 18. This order separated the haves from the
have-nots, for it listed those units which inspection reports
found either above or below acceptable standards. Stunned
men of nine batteries found their unit listed as below par —
with no further leaves or furloughs to be granted and all ab-

sentees to be recalled. Some of these units were veteran batteries which had been with the Army since Peninsula days.[4]

On the positive side, Hooker's inspectors found fourteen batteries to be worthy of commendation, and as such entitled to an increase of 1 per cent in the authorized number of leaves and furloughs. This honor roll was made up entirely of veteran units of the Army of the Potomac, eleven of which were Volunteer batteries.[5]

As spring came and the Army readied itself for the battles everyone knew were coming, there was some justification to Joe Hooker's boast that it was the most powerful army on the planet. Its rolls listed as present for duty on March 31st almost 137,000 men with 74 batteries of over 400 guns, in contrast to Lee's 65,000 with about 220 cannon.[6] On the surface there appeared only one possible weakness: the distribution of artillery. The Federal batteries, despite Hooker's order that transfers of batteries might be made for purposes of equalization of strengths among units, remained unequally distributed as follows:

Artillery Reserve	11
Provost Marshal	2
I Corps	10
II Corps	8
III Corps	10
V Corps	8
VI Corps	9
XI Corps	6
XII Corps	5
Cavalry Corps	5
Total	74

While there was some inequality in the gun strength of the corps, particularly in the Army's newest — the XI and XII — there was less uniformity of battery distribution within the corps. McClellan's system of assigning batteries to divisions was continued, though only in its broadest terms, as some divisions were assigned four batteries, while others had only one. In the II and XI Corps there were even small corps reserves of two and three batteries respectively.

The Army of Northern Virginia, however, having learned its artillery lessons at a heavy cost, now determined to offset its numerical and matériel inferiority. A most obvious method was to provide a means of rapid concentration of gun strength at critical points. Their first step, taken the previous year, had been the battalion organization for division and reserve batteries, but now a further step was taken. All division battalions were placed, at least theoretically, under their two corps commanders' control, with an army reserve under Lee's control. This plan was in sharp contrast to the dissipation of control as practiced by the Union high command, and it would pay off handsomely in the coming action.

During the first week of April 1863, both armies prepared to move and began shedding their winter gear. Tents, stoves, and all extra trappings were bundled up and sent to storage, and troops of each side began to feel a little nostalgic about leaving the crude huts which had been their homes these four months. But even with an army of 130,000 at his back, Hooker was shrewd enough to dispense with any thought of trying to smash through Lee's lines as Burnside had attempted. Instead, he would use maneuver to bypass those mocking heights behind Fredericksburg. The width of the river, the swampy nature of the country, and the difficulty in concealing movements of large forces dictated against trying Lee's right, so it had to be his left.

Hooker's scheme called for a conventional turning movement of his enemy's left, with a holding force opposite Fredericksburg. The maneuver element was to swing wide to the west, fording the Rapidan and Rappahannock rivers, then turn in on Lee's left or rear. The holding force was to slip downstream and force a crossing at Franklin's site of the previous December. This holding element would be of sufficient strength so that it would, it was hoped, confuse Lee as to the true point of attack.

The campaign began on April 13th, when Hooker sent his cavalry trotting off to threaten Lee's communications. Their mission failed because they did not press the attack and because miserable weather made roads and fords impassable for a time. The Blue infantry columns began to march on April 27th; three corps — the V, XI, and XII — shouldered their muskets and set out for Kelly's Ford up the Rappahannock. Another, the II, was to move two of its divisions to Banks' Ford, about midway between Falmouth and Kelly's Ford, to cross when the other three had completed their turning movement. The envelopment was to be fast, the men carrying eight days' rations, the lumbering wagon trains to be left behind. Additional food and ammunition would be carried on pack mules — an unsuccessful innovation of Hooker's.

The three leading corps were restricted to one artillery battery per division, while the two divisions of the II Corps were to have their entire complement — two batteries each — plus the two units of the corps reserve. The batteries which were left behind, including that of the XI Corps, would cross after the turning movement had been completed. The infantry were told to carry an extra twenty rounds of ammunition in their pockets, in addition to the usual combat load of forty rounds in their cartridge boxes, and sixty more rounds per man would be packed on the mules. The artillery only filled its limbers and caissons; carried no extra rounds with them, although an additional 100 to 150 rounds per piece were in the wagons of the main trains.

While the columns of the flanking corps trailed away to the west, the holding force under popular John Sedgwick, consisting of his own VI, Reynolds's I, and Sickles's III, cooked its rations and prepared to make its own move. To cover Sedgwick's crossing, twenty-seven batteries, eleven of which comprised the whole of the Artillery Reserve, were rolled into firing or close reserve positions. The balance of this artillery cover was drawn from the corps themselves: eight of the ten I Corps batteries, four of the III's ten, five of the nine VI Corps units, and one of the five cavalry corps batteries. The remaining twelve stayed under division or corps control to accompany their parent units over the river. These covering batteries were split into three groups. Opposite Franklin's Crossing were eight batteries under the control of Col. Tompkins; near Pollack's Mill another eight under Col. Wainwright; and covering the bridge over Massaponax Creek at Travellers' Rest were three more under the command of Lt. Col. Warner. Nearly all of the guns in these groups were rifles.

Opposite the town of Fredericksburg, on the bluffs near the Lacy house, was a Regular battery of Napoleons, while in reserve near Falmouth Station were four additional Napoleon units. Also available if needed were three rifled batteries with two attached sections; they were waiting near White Oak Church under Capt. Graham, who was temporarily in command of the Artillery Reserve, now that Hays had accepted a general's star in the Volunteer service. There was one other point that would need artillery protection, and that was Banks' Ford. This was an open alley leading into Lee's position which the Confederates were watching closely. On the hillsides south of the ford the Rebels had dug a series of trenches to protect it. This ford also made a tempting route for Lee if he decided to make a quick dash at Hooker, though. To counteract this threat, Hooker ordered the path guarded lest Lee catch him in the midst of his move and raise hob with the Yankee Army. And since it was planned to cross some of the follow-up elements here, Banks' Ford was a critical point in the initial hours of the maneuver. To insure its safety Hooker sent his artillery chief to make a reconnaissance of that point and direct the emplacing of such guns as would be required to command the crossing and neutralize the enemy positions.

Hunt promptly set out for Banks' Ford, carefully studied the terrain there, and made his notes. Necessary instructions to place the batteries and to command in his absence were given by Hunt to his able inspector of artillery, Maj. Alexander Doull. Doull immediately sent two Reserve units — Brooker's Connecticut battery of four 4.5-inch rifles and Blucher's 29th New York Battery of four 20-pounder Parrotts — heading for the ford. To reinforce them he was to use the idle batteries of the II, XI, and XII Corps.

On April 28th the three corps of Hooker's turning force had reached Kelly's Ford. Two days later they had crossed the Rapidan and had moved to the crossroads known as Chancellorsville. That same day the two divisions of Couch's II Corps crossed at U.S. Ford so that by nightfall of April 30th 50,000 Federals with just over one hundred guns were parked on Lee's left rear. Meanwhile, Sedgwick had followed instructions, and on the afternoon of the 29th he forced a bridgehead at Franklin's Crossing. Hooker's Army now seemed to be in a good position to hit Lee's forces, and the Union commander had hopes of seizing a good portion of the enemy's forces.

May 1st, 1863, was a beautiful day, marred only by a heavy fog early in the morning. Contemporary accounts describe the warm bright sunshine, a magnificent cloudless blue sky, and the majestic quiet of the new-green woods disturbed only by the chirping of birds. There was no sign of the Army of Northern Virginia, though. Intelligence was scant on where and in what strength the enemy was at this moment, as Hooker had sent most of his cavalry off on a senseless raid. Nevertheless, Hooker still felt offense-minded, so at 11:30 a.m. he gave the command to seek out and engage Lee's Army. He sent orders to Sedgwick to create a diversion at Franklin's Crossing, while other units probed eastward from Chancellorsville. Unfortunately for Hooker, his message to Sedgwick was not received by that officer until 4:45 p.m. that afternoon.

The Army moved from Chancellorsville by three roads. Meade, with two divisions of his V Corps and one battery, was to take the River Road, while his third division under Sykes, with Battery I, 5th U.S., Lt. Malbone Watson commanding,

would march by the turnpike south of the River Road. Slocum's
XII Corps with five batteries [7] had orders to march east on
the Plank Road below Sykes. Howard's XI Corps was to provide over-all support while the other two corps took position
from Tabernacle Church on the south to Banks' Ford on the
north.

The columns got under way in mid-morning, just as Sickles's III Corps began plodding into Chancellorsville from Falmouth after crossing at U.S. Ford. It looked as if Hooker's
plan would work perfectly. Some 50,000 men with fourteen
batteries were heading or preparing to head for Lee's rear,
while Sedgwick was to pin the enemy down in front. But, as
often happens in warfare, the battle was not to follow Hooker's
well-laid plans.

What Hooker did not know was that by this time Lee had
learned about the strength of this flanking force, and, with
shades of Peninsula days, had determined to crush this isolated
wing of the Yankee Army. Jackson's corps was already hurrying toward the threatened left to augment the blocking force
Lee had put out on the line Hooker's two corps were hoping
to reach — Tabernacle Church to Banks' Ford.

About noon the initial collision occurred, a mile and a half
east of Chancellorsville. Here Sykes's Regulars on the turnpike bumped into the Confederates who had just chased off
a handful of Yankee cavalry. The Federal infantry wheeled
into line of battle in a large open clearing on the east fringe
of that wooded semi-jungle known as the Wilderness. It was
soon evident that the Rebels were there in force; long lines of
deployed infantry were visible, and it appeared that they had
artillery with them. What Sykes did not know was that, while
the Confederates did have artillery in their column — two
batteries up front — the terrain was such that they could get
but two pieces into position to bear on the Yankees.

A dull boom was heard from the Gray line. The shell buzzed
overhead and burst atop the woodland behind the Federals. A
Yankee Captain was heard to remark: 'Twenty minutes past

eleven; the first gun of the battle of Chancellorsville.' [8] Battery I, 5th U.S., under Lt. Watson, was waiting in the road behind the deploying infantry. The call came back for his guns and Watson gave the command: 'Forward, Trot, Heeyo!' Onto a small crest in front of the timber he led his six guns. The trails hit dirt between two brigades, and the gunners swiftly began leveling their sights on the enemy ranks. A furious fight took place between the Regular battery and the two enemy guns. There was a solid hour of shooting, but little damage was done to either side. However, one participant thought that the Regulars' action may have saved Sykes's column.

Sykes was having trouble — in fact, there was even danger of his being outflanked and cut off — and so he sent word to Hooker at Chancellorsville about 1 p.m. to hurry reinforcements to him. Apparently at the same time Sykes asked Hunt, who had arrived at Chancellorsville with Hooker the previous day, to reinforce him with two more batteries — one of rifles and one of Napoleons. But the request found the Army's chief-of-artillery with no batteries under his control, or for that matter with no authority to order any to that point. Hunt did his best, though. He borrowed Arnold's rifled Battery A, 1st Rhode Island Light Artillery, from Lt. Col. Charles Morgan, II Corps chief-of-artillery, and, finding Battery F, 4th U.S., of the XI Corps waiting idly near the Chancellor house, he just commandeered it. Both units were put under Maj. Doull's charge, and they started for the front along with Hancock's division of the II Corps. No sooner had the two batteries begun their march than the XI Corps, situated on the Plank Road, shouted for its guns, and so Battery F, 4th U.S., was ordered to return. Battery A, 1st Rhode Island, continued alone, as Hunt could find no battery to replace Battery F.

Hancock's men hurried forward and formed line behind Sykes. At the same time Arnold's guns turned into the cleared ground on the left of the road and smartly prepared for action. After the Rhode Islanders had fired a few salvos, a courier galloped up with the news that Gen. Hooker had ordered a retirement to Chancellorsville. So under the covering fire of Arnold, Watson, and a section of Cushing's Battery A, 4th U.S., the Federal infantry disengaged and began what the men in the ranks considered a mystifying retreat.[9]

The same general situation prevailed on the southern route, the Plank Road. Slocum's XII Corps had bumped into Rebels in undetermined strength a little over a mile from Chancellorsville and had deployed two divisions. There was some delay in forming the lines, and it was not until 1 p.m. that the battle line began to move. At first Slocum met with some success. Then Stonewall Jackson committed more troops and began feeding in some of the fourteen batteries with his advanced elements. The Federals quickly unlimbered Battery E, Pennsylvania Light Artillery, under Lt. Atwell, and Winegar's Battery M, 1st New York Light Artillery — a newcomer to the Army of the Potomac — and at this point called for Battery F, which Hunt was about to send to Sykes on the turnpike. Capt. Best, Slocum's chief-of-artillery, ordered Atwell to begin action with a slow fire, but before the others could even get set Hooker's recall order reached the field.

Late that afternoon and during the evening Chancellorsville became a center of frantic activity. Thousands of Federal troops were thrown into battle lines in the woods and fields surrounding that place. Slocum, holding the center of this new line about Chancellorsville, was worried about the possibility of the enemy's rolling in on the roads from the south and east which converged here. He ordered Best to set up guns to cover these approaches. Capt. Best was a Regular, a West Pointer of the class of 1847 who had developed into an excellent artilleryman, with a quick mind and a good eye. Best rolled fourteen guns into position to cover the junction at Chancellorsville,[10] and another fourteen on the high open ground a quarter-mile to the west on the plateau known as Fairview.[11]

As the day closed, the Rebels followed the unexplained Federal retreat cautiously, fearing a trap, and, as they neared Chancellorsville, Best's batteries began to thunder away, bouncing solid shot down the roads and shredding the wooded areas with case and canister. The Confederates brought up their own guns and in the fading light both sides swapped blows. Here and there the infantry of both sides collided. Just to the south of the crossroads Federal Gen. Geary became too bold. Pulling away a section of Atwell's battery, Geary pushed it down the road with his infantry and nearly succeeded in losing it.

About 6 p.m. one of these Confederate probing attacks came busting up through the woods just southwest of Chancellorsville. Supporting the attack were four guns of Jeb Stuart's Horse Artillery. As the Gray infantry drove in the Yankee pickets, eight to ten Federal cannon opened a vicious fire on them. These were some of Best's group at Fairview, Winegar's New York battery of six 10-pounder Parrotts and one section of Crosby's Battery F, 4th U.S., which had been admirably posted on rolling ground that partially screened them from the Rebels. Shortly after a second section of the Regulars joined the fire from the ridge west of the Fairview ravine, about 300 yards away.[12] Accurate Federal fire forced the Gray gunners to swing over to counter-battery fire. The two sides took dead aim at each other, and soon a vicious gun duel was raging in the sunset. The Confederates were subsequently to report that this was one of the hottest fights they had ever participated in, but even though Stuart's gunners came off second best, they were not too badly hurt.[13]

As the day closed, the Confederates were still poking about in the attempt to locate the Yankee positions and find a soft spot in the Blue line. By this time the Federals had formed in an arc, beginning northeast of Chancellorsville, where the V Corps stood along a low divide between Mine Run and Mineral Spring Road, with the II Corps prolonging the front south to and curving in front of Chancellorsville. The XII Corps, facing south, covered the southern edge of the Fairview plateau. There was then a gap of about a half-mile before the XI Corps picked up the line again along the turnpike, also facing south.

In reserve behind the Chancellor house was the III Corps, while Sedgwick's VI and Reynolds's I Corps were still in front of Fredericksburg, with elements holding bridgeheads in front of Franklin's Crossing.

Lee was impressed with the Federal position, terming it one of 'great natural strength,' surrounded by woods and tangled undergrowth, reinforced by earthworks, with artillery in position to command the woods and sweep the few narrow roads by which the position could be approached from the front. But Lee was never one deliberately to play into his enemy's strong point; he preferred to hit the flanks, and his troops were already searching these out.

About the time that Hooker recalled his units to Chancellorsville, he became concerned about Banks' Ford. If this ford were seized by Lee, the Rebels would be able to strike behind Hooker and sever his communications with headquarters at Falmouth and with Sedgwick. To prevent this from happening, the commanding general ordered Hunt to Falmouth, where he was to gather up every available battery and take them to Banks' Ford. But Hunt quickly concluded it would be easier to telegraph the message to Falmouth. So he used the telegraph station linked to headquarters at Falmouth. His wire, sent at 2:25, informed Butterfield, the Army's chief-of staff still at Falmouth, that Hooker wanted the twenty-two guns under Capt. Graham at White Oak Church to be sent to the ford. Butterfield was also asked to dispatch two Napoleon batteries, or rifled ones if that was all that was available, from Sedgwick's command, if that officer could spare them.[14]

To add still more beef to the Banks' Ford force, Hunt sent back Battery B, 1st Connecticut Heavy Artillery, with its lumbering 4.5-inch rifles, which he found on the road from U.S. Ford, having just recently left Banks' Ford. The artillery chief then turned his horse toward the ford to take personal charge, as Hooker had ordered. By 7:30 that night Hunt was able to wire Hooker that the guns were arriving, though more infantry would be needed to secure the place.

May 2nd was another beautiful warm spring day. In the

dawn's light the Federal line looked like an inverted question mark with the shank pointing northeast. Directly west of the bottom of the loop, separated from it by a three-quarter-mile gap was Howard's XI Corps — the Army's right. Couch's II and Slocum's XII Corps held the middle and Meade's V Corps the left, with Sickles's III Corps in reserve behind Chancellorsville. While the Army's left, the V Corps, was anchored on the river, Howard's XI Corps on the right was an open flank. It was deployed along the Orange Plank Road until it forked with the turnpike and then for three-quarters of a mile to the west along the turnpike. Almost two full divisions had been placed along the turnpike facing south and southwest, while two small regiments were perpendicular to it as protection from the west.

Of the six 6-gun batteries in the XI Corps three were deployed along the line. At the extreme right, at the point where the two regiments were watching the road to the west, two pieces of Dieckman's 13th New York Battery were placed so they could sweep that road; the other four guns were a quarter-mile east, covering the Orange Plank Road and the open ground south of the pike. Dilger's Battery I, 1st Ohio Light Artillery, probably Howard's best battery, was just on the north edge of the Turnpike-Plank Road intersection, sighted to cover the approaches from the south and southwest. A third battery, Wiedrich's Battery I, 1st New York Light Artillery, the same unit which had disappointed Gen. McLean at Second Bull Run (Gen. McLean was close by this day, too, commanding the right brigade of Devens's division), was southeast of the road junction behind Bushbeck's brigade, which was occupying rifle pits on a little rise east and south of the junction.[15] Someone had the foresight to dig trenches perpendicular to the road at this point, extending north a few hundred yards along a low crest. Behind this readied but as yet unoccupied line facing northwest, the three corps' reserve batteries took position later in the day. Wilderness Church stood in a little grove of trees about 300 yards west of this point.

Lee's later remarks about the great strength of Hooker's position meant he must have been looking only at the head side of the coin. Had he been able to see the tail side he would have spotted a serious weakness. Cluttering the fields and woods around the Chancellor house and by the fords was battery after battery of idle artillery. Hooker's choice of a battle line left no positions for many of Hooker's hundreds of cannon, and so a prominent Federal advantage was thoroughly neutralized. On this morning Hooker's forces had approximately thirty-six batteries of division artillery — about 210 guns. Of this number, all six of Howard's batteries were employed; the XII Corps batteries were split by Best into the two fourteen-gun groups at Chancellorsville and Fairview; five of the eight V Corps batteries were in line on the left; and about three of the III units were scattered along Sickles's part of the front. This meant that the gun strength actually in the line was about ninety pieces, or less than half the total available. And only Best had been able to put together any mass of weapons.

During the night Hooker's corps commanders had reported their positions could be held in the event of an enemy attack, but at dawn the Army commander decided to make a personal tour. One weak spot, the gap between Slocum and Howard, he found had been plugged by Birney's division of Sickles's III Corps. Birney's three brigades had moved onto an open plateau called Hazel Grove about three-quarters of a mile southwest of the Fairview clearing. This grove was really not a grove but a narrow strip of open ground slightly higher in elevation than Fairview and separated from it by a dipping valley through which trickled a marshy creek. As long as this ground stayed in Federal hands Hooker's Army was reasonably safe. But the right flank still lay open, and nothing was being done to bolster it.

Lee was expected to attack Hooker's line either from the south or the east or else retreat. As the Union Army awaited Lee's move, the Confederate commander had already made his decision to attack. At this early hour about 60 per cent of his Army, led by Stonewall Jackson, was already hurrying on a wide envelopment which would bring them up against the weak Union right flank.

To cover Jackson's move Lee's remaining force created a diversion on the east front. Ten rifled guns were promptly pushed forward near the Plank Road to hammer Hooker's men about Chancellorsville. Two of Best's batteries there, Atwell's and Hampton's, snarled back, and the Federals claimed two enemy caissons blown up and a gun knocked out. Then Muhlenberg caught sight of some Rebel infantry on the Plank Road south of Chancellorsville and proceeded to spray them with canister from his two Napoleons. Further south the probings of the Gray infantry led some Union officers to conclude that Lee was conducting a 'rolling reconnaissance' along the Yankee line.

About 8 a.m. Birney's lookouts, sitting in trees on Hazel Grove, spotted Jackson's column on the road to Catherine Furnace, a mile distant. When this news was forwarded to Hooker, the Federal high command concluded that Lee was retreating. At 10 o'clock the enemy was still on the move — infantry, artillery, and wagons in an endless stream. It was too good a target to pass up; Birney sent for a section of Sims's New Jersey battery. The range, 1600 yards, was within the capabilities of rifled cannon, so Birney told the section leader to begin firing. The bursting of Sims's shells, while doing little harm, made the enemy move more rapidly over the exposed part of their route. But more important to the Confederates, the shelling gave notice that their column had been discovered.

Another hour passed, and the stream of the moving Gray column was still in view of the Union line. Reports were continually being sent back to Hooker apprising him of the Rebels' progress. These reports convinced Hooker that Lee was falling back. At one point Hooker seemed to have an inkling of what was really happening, for he sent a warning to his right flank, but he failed to follow it up later. In the meantime, Birney had put all of Sims's guns to work to disrupt what now appeared to be a major enemy move, and he had brought up his other two division batteries, Turnbull's Regulars and Jastram's Rhode Islanders, so they would be close at hand.

Sickles, the III Corps commander, now asked for Hooker's permission to go after the enemy column. But the Army commander, as he pondered this intelligence, ordered him to remain and told Howard to look to his right. (Howard later denied he received such an order.) At the same time, about 2 p.m., Hooker sent instructions to Sedgwick to make a solid attack if there was the least chance for success on that front. Finally, about 3 o'clock he gave Sickles permission to take two of his divisions and go after the Rebels. Birney's men led off from Hazel Grove toward the Catherine Furnace Road. As they closed on the Furnace a Gray rearguard with a battery atop a hill halted them completely. Concluding that he could not advance until the Rebel guns had been driven off, Birney sent a courier to Sims's battery at Hazel Grove. The message reached the corps artillery chief, Capt. George E. Randolph, who quickly concluded it would be easier to send Turnbull's Battery F/K, 3rd U.S., waiting at the edge of the clearing, than to pull Sims out of position.

The Regulars then, with six potent Napoleons, mounted up and prepared to move out. Randolph ordered them to leave their caissons behind, as he did not think they would have much use for them up ahead. When the Regulars accompanied by Randolph, reached Birney, the enemy guns were still banging away from their position near the Welford house. Turnbull scanned the ground for a place to put his weapons, but there seemed to be no open ground nearby from whence he could bring fire to bear. At last he found a narrow slip, and with some difficulty he and Randolph brought the battery in line and opened fire.

Slowly and deliberately the Regulars fired, with undetermined effect. Then the supply of suitable ammunition in the gun limbers began to give out — and the caissons were at Hazel Grove! Randolph sent back for Jastram's rifles, but, by the time the Rhode Islanders came up, the Gray battery had pulled out and Birney was rounding up the stragglers of the Confederate rearguard. Pressure from Lee's forces to the southeast prevented a prompt follow-up of the disappearing Gray host.

It was now late in the afternoon. Over on the far right several of Howard's subordinates had become increasingly worried over reports from their pickets of enemy activity on that front. These reports were duly relayed to Army headquarters but were continually disregarded.

Capt. Hubert Dilger, the intrepid German artilleryman of Howard's corps, decided to take a personal look. In company with an orderly, he rode out to the west. The two had not ridden far when Jackson's oncoming legions fired at them. They fled and Dilger made his way back to Hooker's headquarters at Chancellorsville where he sputtered out what he had seen. His report, like the others, was discounted. Headquarters was still convinced that Lee was retreating, even though as early as 2:30 Jackson's leading elements had reached the turnpike on Hooker's right flank.

The sun was now just over the tops of the tall pines on the west edge of Taylor's farm. Suddenly some of Howard's pickets spotted a handful of Rebel cavalry, and Dieckman's two guns on the pike fired at the prowlers — blasts which Gen. Schurz later reported were unauthorized. Far beyond the sight of the Yankee pickets, grim-faced Jackson watched his 25,000 men deploy and, noticing a number of familiar faces from his school-teaching days at VMI, remarked: 'The Virginia Military Institute will be heard from today!' [16] At 5 o'clock he asked the commander of his leading wave if he was ready, and on receiving an affirmative reply, loosed his last great attack. Like a raging west wind the Confederates swept through the woodland, driving the XI Corps' pickets before them. Some of Stuart's Horse Artillery were leap-frogging each other down the pike, staying with the leading lines and bouncing shot down the road ahead of the Gray infantry.

Devens's division, caught unawares, was overwhelmed and

swallowed up. The gunners of Dieckman's two pieces sprang
to their weapons and fired a few rounds, but it was instantly
obvious that they were facing an attack of tremendous force.
Here and there through the openings in the forest they could
see the extent of the wide flag-speckled line of battle, which
resounded with the shrill piercing Rebel yell. If anything was
to be saved it had to be done quickly. The section leader yelled
for his limbers, and two sets of teams hurriedly wheeled about.
At that instance a heavy crash of musketry fire spilled horses
and men, and the whooping Confederates swarmed the section.

Next in line, Schurz attempted to check the rush by swinging his front about to the west and retiring on the previously
unmanned earthworks north of the road where Bushbeck's
brigade had now taken up position. Dilger's battery, assigned
to Schurz's division, had been posted at the road junction facing south. The captain looked for room to swing his Napoleons
around to meet the foe. The only ground he could see was
back of his present stop, near Wiedrich's New York battery.
With a wave of his arm, Dilger led his command scurrying for
this rise, and here the battery swung about, the big wheels
biting deep into the earth as they turned. Crisp commands
given with a strong German accent called for case shot, and
seconds later the Napoleons were hewing the Rebel lines.

Nearby, south of the road, Wiedrich turned his guns about,
and ordered his men to load canister. Nervously his men
watched the woods, waiting for a clear shot at the enemy. But
it seemed that the only troops that came out wore blue. Finally
there was a pause, and then the Rebel yell was heard quite
near. Suddenly the enemy was in sight — a ragged weaving
line jogging forward. Wiedrich bellowed his command to fire.
Six lanyards were given a quick jerk and deadly canister tore
into the Confederate line. Blue infantry fought hard to stem
the advance, and for some twenty minutes Jackson's forces had
all they could handle. But the Confederates had a wide line of
attack, and when checked at one point they simply enveloped
both flanks and quickly eliminated the trouble spot. When

this finally happened to Schurz, Dilger and Wiedrich had to withdraw quickly.

Like Dieckman before him, Wiedrich ran into trouble immediately. On one crew every man but one was hit, and the piece had to be abandoned. Another gun was part-way off the field when a shredding blast of fire killed four horses, and so this weapon also fell to the enemy. A third gun lost two animals, but by quick work the crew cleared away the dead beasts and got it away. With thirteen men casualties Wiedrich galloped his cut-up battery back to the artillery park at Chandler's to refit.

Dilger, too, had to retreat when the Rebels stormed his flanks. The Ohio men did not escape unscathed either. The captain's horse was shot from under him, but Dilger saved himself from probable capture by riding double with one of his men. Another gun was lost to the enemy as three horses were shot down in a snarl of tangled traces and harness. The crew tried to drag the piece off the field, but to no avail.

Dilger was not ready to abandon the field, though. By keeping one of his Napoleons astride the pike and bouncing shells down the clear straight road he could deny the confederates the use of that avenue into the Yankee lines. He promptly detailed a gun to this duty, sending the remaining four to the rear under a lieutenant with orders to report to the first field artillery officer he met. Dilger then waved them on their way and turned to stay with his lone gun in the road. Under his personal direction the polished Napoleon fired, limbered to the rear a short way, unlimbered, and fired some more. It was a daring piece of rearguard action, and it kept the pursuing Rebs hugging the timber on either side of the road to avoid the lethal blast.[17]

About the same time Dilger and Wiedrich had taken up the fight, a battery of the corps reserve opened fire over the heads of Schurz's men in the hope of landing their shells in the Rebel masses near Hawkins's farm just north of the road junction. Shortly thereafter a second of the corps reserve units found some space on Dilger's left, and the third opened with a roar from a vacant spot in Bushbeck's line of pits.[18] One of these reserve units shortly ran out of ammunition and headed to the rear, and the onward surge of Jackson's infantry caused the others, like Dilger and Wiedrich, to relinquish their ground, with no apparent loss.

When the Confederates forced Bushbeck's line the XI Corps was through for the day as an effective combat unit. A disorganized mass of demoralized and terrified men fled head-long down the Plank Road toward Chancellorsville. Here and there a few units kept their discipline, turning around to shoot at the enemy, taking advantage of the threat posed by Dilger's busy Napoleon.

By a strange freak of nature, somewhat similiar to that which befell the Confederates at Seven Pines, the sound of this firing on the west flank was not heard in other parts of the Federal line. Not until the last few minutes before the mass of retreating Blue forces reached Fairview did anyone notice shells winging in from the northwest, and even then they were somehow interpreted to be coming from Sickles's troops pursuing the Rebel column seen earlier in the day. Not until the wreckage of the XI Corps began to stream past Fairview toward Chancellorsville about 6:30 did the rest of the Yankee Army realize it had been struck by a major attack.

Near Hazel Grove were parked Sims's and Turnbull's batteries of Birney's division of the III Corps and Martin's 6th New York Battery, attached to the cavalry.[19] Also nearby were the three batteries of Whipple's division: Huntington's H, 1st Ohio Light Artillery; Lewis's 10th New York Battery; and Puttkammer's 11th New York Battery. None of these troops knew of the attack on the Union right until the XI Corps collapsed, and the remains of the outfit poured past Fairview.

Seeing this beaten force, Capt. Best rapidly shifted his fourteen guns to cover the woods and the Plank Road on the west, 600 yards distant. Loud commands sent gun and limber wheels crunching on the gravelly soil. Horses snorted and puffed, and iron clanked on iron, as the guns rolled up to the west edge of the plateau. On the right, nearest the Plank Road, Best put the two sections of Crosby's F, 4th U.S.; on the left of the Regulars went Fitzhugh's K, 1st New York; and next to them and just to the right of an old log hut were the guns of Winegar's M, 1st New York — all XII Corps units. Back in the woods between Chancellorsville and Chandler's, waiting in reserve, was Berry's division of the III Corps with its three batteries: Dimick's H, 1st U.S.; Winslow's D, 1st New York; and Barstow's 4th New York Battery.

Now Hooker was finally aware of the danger to his Army. A hurried order to the artillery of Berry's division caught those units unharnessed and the horses being watered. The piercing wail of a bugle's *Boots and Saddles* touched off furious activity. Minutes later, with everything ready, Capt. Osborn, the division chief-of-artillery, led his three units out of the woods onto the road to Chancellorsville. Dimick's Regulars led, followed by Winslow, then Barstow.

As the column neared the Chancellor house, it ran into a string of supply wagons which was trying to evacuate the field after having been under Confederate fire. With loud curses and yells, the officers and noncoms forced a path through the tangle of rattling wagons, threading the batteries up to the junction with the Plank Road. As the column started to turn to the right, they saw a solid wave of fleeing soldiery running wildly toward them — the XI Corps headed for the fords or anywhere that held hope of safety. The panicked masses were choking the roadway; it was hopeless for the batteries to try to use it. The only way was through the open field on the south side, and even here there was some spill-over of fugitives.

After much twisting and weaving, stops and starts, Osborn's men reached the west edge of Fairview overlooking the little valley and the woods beyond. Osborn ordered Winslow to go into line to the left of the road and two sections of Dimick's Regulars to unlimber in the road on line with the other units; the third section of the Regulars led by Dimick himself trotted on down the road still further, finally going into battery about 400 yards west of Fairview, on line with Slocum's infantry which had quickly shifted to a north-south line on the east edge of the woods.

The third battery of this group, the 4th New York, was apparently not thought reliable and so had been left in the vicinity of Chancellorsville. This had been Capt. James E. Smith's battery during Peninsula days, and it had had a troublesome career. The present unit had been formed from some forty-odd veterans of Varian's New York battery which had marched off the field just prior to First Bull Run, when its members had contended that their three months were up. After Fredericksburg the battery had troubles again. The new men said they had enlisted on the assumption that their battery was to be assigned to a New York engineer unit. This meant they would draw $18 per month engineer pay instead of the $13 artilleryman pay. Of course such an arrangement was wholly unworkable, but the men failed to see it that way and carried a grudge that they had been falsely enlisted.

By the time Chancellorsville came, they had had command problems, too. As their commander, Smith, had been commissioned a captain early in the war, he suddenly found himself after Fredericksburg the ranking artillery officer in the III Corps. Gen. Hunt recognized the fact in January 1863 by assigning him as chief of the corps' artillery. At the same time the battery's senior lieutenant resigned, leaving only a lieutenant deemed by the men — and soon after by an examining board — as incompetent. Then, as a crowning blow, two complete strangers — first, a lieutenant from another New York battery, and finally a Regular, Lt. Barstow — assumed command of the battery. The battery regarded this as an insult to sensitive home state pride.

To make matters worse, they refused to comply with an order shifting them from one division to another, since they had seniority and felt they should stay and a junior unit be moved. By today's standards this action could only be interpreted as direct disobedience to orders, and one can scarcely conceive of a present-day unit acting in this way. But, as Bruce Catton pointed out in *Mr. Lincoln's Army,* these Volunteers regarded such actions not as mutiny but the rightful acts of aggrieved men who were expressing a legitimate complaint. Unfortunately for them, their superiors did not see it the same way, for the 40th New York Volunteer Infantry was sent marching to the park of the 4th New York Battery with orders either to move or bury the battery. Now during this crucial action, the Union commanders did not have faith enough in the unit to throw it into the desperate struggle.[20]

Further to the left of the guns on Fairview were the three batteries of Whipple's division, waiting on the north edge of Hazel Grove. These units were supposed to be under the command of Capt. Puttkammer, the division chief-of-artillery and commander of the 11th New York Battery. For some reason that was later deemed unsatisfactory, causing his dismissal from the service, Puttkammer was away from his command when the storm broke. Lt. James F. Huntington, commanding Battery H, 1st Ohio Light Artillery, promptly assumed command and sent the three batteries into action. Apparently at the same time cavalryman Pleasonton ordered Martin's Horse Artillery battery on the south edge of the clearing to swing about to the west and load with double canister. This was the same unit that had been engaged earlier in the spring with Stuart at Kelly's Ford and had killed Confederate gunner Maj. John Pelham.

Huntington had scarcely made his units ready when the woods in front disgorged a bevy of disheveled Blue troops, which were trailed by a clattering array of vehicles from Whipple's division park.[21] The fleeing torrent ran pell-mell across the open ground in front of the batteries and through the gun positions. Instantly the battery horses became startled, and a few anxious moments were passed before the animals were quieted.

Moments later a rattle of Rebel musketry exploded from the

timber in front. The Yankee cannon crashed into action, and the fight at Fairview was on. Soon gunfire slicing in from the woods on Huntington's right warned that officer that he was in danger of being flanked. Looking about, Huntington saw it was possible to shift his units around somewhat and still control this important ground.

Lewis's 10th New York Battery, closest to the woods, received the worst and had no room to change front to the flank in danger. Seeing this, Huntington sent them galloping to a new position to the right rear. Huntington then turned his own battery about to rake the woods. With great roars his six guns ripped into the leafy timberland. The third battery under his control, the 11th New York, was kept in its original position facing west, though a real threat never materialized here.

By now a tremendous force of artillery bristled from the edge of Fairview. By his own report Capt. Best had now put thirty-four pieces into the line across to Hazel Grove, where Huntington and Pleasonton had some thirty-six more, and every gun was now in action. The blasts of orange flame which emanated from the guns danced through the heavy smoke in the fading light of day and made it appear as if the two positions were on fire. At times Winegar's gunners were cutting their fuzes for one second, or cut to burst about 400 yards out, which was daringly close to friendly infantry.

At some time during these closing moments of daylight there occurred one of the most disputed events of the war. This was Gen. Pleasonton's claim, backed up by the reports of his aide and of Gen. Sickles, that a mass of twenty-two guns at Hazel Grove skillfully organized by Pleasonton drove back Jackson's charging infantry at the critical moment and thus saved the Federal Army from certain defeat and probable destruction.

Pleasonton had been waiting with part of his cavalry division and with Martin's horse battery atop Hazel Grove for some hours. When the XI Corps collapsed, the general did go into action. But Pleasonton was in error about some points he made, which were later repeated by Sickles. In Pleasonton's favor, it is true that he exercised a degree of command over a force of some twenty-two guns which were engaged in action on Hazel Grove. But here the accuracy ends. Martin's battery was already on the Grove, parked and waiting, and unquestionably operated under the general's eye. In addition, Pleasonton claimed that Lt. Frank Crosby offered his Battery F, 4th U.S., to the general and that the latter accepted this offer. However, Capt. Robert Fitzhugh, commander of the artillery division of which Crosby was a part, contradicted this view. He reported that Crosby unlimbered on the right of his own Battery K, 1st New York, and that still other units were to his left. It also seems improbable that Pleasonton had any other XII Corps batteries. However, the general undoubtedly did have two of Birney's division batteries — Sims's New Jersey unit, which had been in position on Hazel Grove since early that morning, and at least one section of Turnbull's Regulars, which had returned from their excursion on the Catherine Furnace Road.[22] It is possible that one of Huntington's group, the 11th New York Battery, which had stayed in its original position, may have been close enough to Hazel Grove to make Pleasonton assume he had control over it, but it was actually operating exclusively under Huntington's orders.

Thus, Pleasonton's group was with fair certainty made up of Martin, Sims, and part or all of Turnbull's unit — possibly eighteen guns in all, with the general adding in four pieces from one of Huntington's batteries to get his total of twenty-two. But it appears quite obvious that Pleasonton exerted no command over the initial deployment or subsequent conduct of fire of Whipple's division batteries; this was done independently by quick-thinking Capt. Huntington, who subsequently received Sickles's approval of his dispositions and actions.[23]

Furthermore, Pleasonton's guns did not repel a major Rebel attack, as he later claimed. No major effort was made by any of Jackson's troops against Hazel Grove. Actually the Rebel assault had been slowed in front of Slocum's line in the woods astride the Plank Road west of Fairview. Here the Confederate

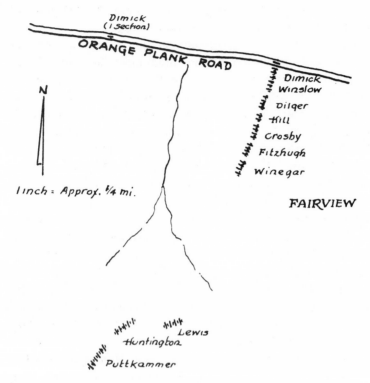

Dimick
(1 Section)

ORANGE PLANK ROAD

Dimick
Winslow
Dilger
Hill
Crosby
Fitzhugh
Winegar

N

1 inch = Approx. ¼ mi.

FAIRVIEW

Lewis
Huntington
Puttkammer

HAZEL
GROVE

Martin
Turnbull
Sims

Probable Alignment
of
Federal Batteries
about 7 P.M. May 2nd
@
CHANCELLORSVILLE

units, badly intermixed and lacking control, paused before taking on the fresh XII Corps.

However, it seems that a small force of Confederates under Col. Winn of the 4th Georgia strayed off toward the grove. This party bumped into the division park near there and stampeded it, along with some wandering Blue infantry, capturing some matériel of a Federal battery. These troops and vehicles were the ones which had fled into Huntington's position and also overflowed into Martin's, upsetting several of his vehicles in their haste.[24] They were soon chased away by the Federals' artillery. This action bore little resemblance to the furious fighting later described by Pleasanton. It was Huntington's, to the south of his command, that was the most hotly engaged artillery force in that region.

About 7 p.m. Jackson's chief-of-artillery, Col. Crutchfield, moved three pieces out on the Plank Road to relieve Stuart's tired horse artillery gunners. From a point half-mile east of Dowdall's Tavern the three cannons opened fire on Fairview. This provoked an immediate barrage from the Federals, including Dimick's section in the road.

As this angry duel began, Gen. A. P. Hill's Gray division was hurrying down the Plank Road to restore momentum to the stalled attack waves. As Hill's regiments moved up the road toward their deployment point, they ran into the hail of fire from the Yankee cannon. The columns broke for the timber on the sides of the road, and frantic pleas went back to Crutchfield to halt this terrible shelling. After some delay, the Confederate guns fell silent, and the Federals, thinking they had silenced the Gray gunners, stopped, too. Hill's troops then began filing into the darkening woodland to try to establish a new line.

Where were the Federals? The Confederates had the impression that the Blue infantry had retired behind that awesome artillery line at Fairview. Actually they were furiously building a line in the woods about 500 yards west of Fairview.

In the clear night air the Rebels could plainly hear the whack-whacking of axes, as the Yanks busily cut logs for abatis and breastworks. An outburst of confused picket firing broke loose on Jackson's right, and for a few minutes little spits of fire darted at each other in the night. Some of the Federals thought the Gray attack was on again. But then the firing died away as quickly as it had started, and the night became ominously quiet.

Some two hours later, about 9 o'clock, Yankee Capt. Thomas Osborn, Berry's chief-of-artillery who was with Dimick's section, was peering out in the moonlight, carefully watching for any movement on the road ahead. Suddenly there was a noise, then voices. Osborn strained his eyes in the silvered darkness. Now the captain saw a body of men about 150 yards away; it looked like the head of a column preparing to deploy. Quickly Osborn snapped the terse order to open fire, and Dimick loaded with canister.

Heavy crashes of the two Napoleons shook the night, their wide flashes lighting up the road with each discharge. Osborn could see the Confederates break for cover as the canister flailed the air about them. Then the batteries at Fairview took alarm at Dimick's firing, and an awesome barrage erupted from the Federal guns — one which Osborn thought was equal to Malvern Hill. Shell and case swished over the heads of nervous Blue infantry. It was a calculated risk for the Federal gunners, but they felt they had little choice if the line was to be held. At one point some Rebels holding a batch of Yankee prisoners saw their area ripped by shells. Soon Gray captors and Blue prisoners alike were diving for the shelter of Slocum's log works to avoid the smothering fire.

When no Rebel attack came, the guns slacked off, and quiet settled over the fields and woods once more. Then at midnight someone pulled trigger, and the racket began all over again. As before, it died out as quickly as it had started, and the exhausted troops fell asleep.

Meanwhile, about the time of the 9 o'clock barrage, the

Confederate cause had been dealt a severe blow. The daring Jackson, starting on a personal reconnaissance north of the Plank Road, was accidentally shot down by some of his own men, who in the darkness mistook his party for Federals. Efforts to carry him from the field had been greatly hindered by that first outburst of Yankee cannon fire.[25] The wounding of Jackson and the resulting confusion in command was unquestionably the reason the Confederates failed to launch an assault again that evening.

Meanwhile, in the dark night, the Federals launched a minor attack of their own. Sickles loosed part of his III Corps in a drive northward from Hazel Grove in an attempt to correct his isolated position and thus straighten out the Union line. Shortly, the left flank of the attack collided with Jackson's men, and the right flank began exchanging confused shots with its own army — men of Slocum's XII Corps. Capt. Best's batteries, unaware that any Union attack was under way, heard the firing out front, concluded the Rebels were attacking again, and began jerking their lanyards. Snarling shells creased the air over Slocum's line and slammed into the woods beyond. The already shaken Confederates hugged the ground and held their breath as the pounding kept up. A. P. Hill, who had succeeded Jackson in command, stopped a fragment, and the Rebels sent for Jeb Stuart.

In this mumble-jumble battle in the dark, some of Sickles's men became completely confused and charged ahead at a battery which was firing in their front. When they were on top of the position, they suddenly discovered that they had seized one of Best's units. The attackers sheepishly returned the guns to their owners.

This terrific artillery pounding, coupled with Sickles's attack, brought a final element of chaotic disorganization to the Confederate ranks and ended any plans they had for continuing the attack that night. Fortunately this shooting, which at times must have been extremely heavy, had done little or no damage to the Federal infantry, for Best reported with obvious pride that for a change there had been no complaints of short rounds — an occurrence which troops of that era as well as later ones looked upon with great bitterness.

Finally, the firing petered out, but the Federal artillery was not to rest that night. Best took a page from the Confederate book and told his batteries to throw up earthworks. Tired cannoneers wearily took up their shovels — in some units they had to improvise tools — and began digging the pits which may still be seen crowning the west edge of Fairview. Toward dawn some engineers plodded in to relieve the exhausted gunners of their digging chores.

Elsewhere in the Union camp there was continued activity, too. To the northwest reinforcements were pouring in under the cased flags of Reynolds's I Corps, making their way to Chandler's via U.S. Ford. Meade's V Corps was shifted to the right, and the reorganized but still shaky XI Corps moved into Meade's old lines on the Federal left, and Hooker's engineers began laying out a new main line of resistance along the Mineral Spring Road to Chandler's, thence northwest along the Ely's Ford Road.

For the Federals May 2nd had not been a good day. One corps had been wrecked and the entire Union line put into confusion. Lee had threatened the Yankee left, but, outside of making it apprehensive and nervous — precisely his intent — he left that flank intact.

As dawn arrived on May 3rd, Hooker's staff was still working out the new defensive line. An order was issued to Gen. Couch to pull back some artillery batteries to the new line from the impromptu second line about Chancellorsville. Couch sent twenty-seven II Corps guns to the rear, all but Pettit's battery and three of Thomas's.[26] In addition, Dilger's unit and the section of Hill's, which had been with Best, were relieved and sent to U.S. Ford. Also departing was the controversial 4th New York Battery, which was later dismounted and scattered among other commands.[27] Furthermore, Fitzhugh's K, 1st New

York, was split up between Meade's new line and Lt. Muhlenberg at Chancellorsville.[28]

Best lost a good outfit when Dilger was taken from him, but received a satisfactory replacement in Hampton's veteran Pennsylvanians. Still remaining on the Fairview plain were Winslow's, Dimick's, Crosby's, and Winegar's commands — or a total of about twenty-six cannon, plus Dimick's advanced section.

As the sun came up, there were a number of changes in the Union lines. The whole position now outlined a tipping pail. The right edge was manned by the XI Corps, running from Scott's Dam on the Rappahannock southwest toward Chandler's; the bottom led northwest to Compback's Mill and contained Meade's V Corps; and the left edge ran northeast to near Todd's Ford and was held by Reynolds's I Corps. Like a big drop hanging from the bottom of the right edge of the bucket, a circular defensive position looped down from Chandler's south around Chancellorsville, took in Hazel Grove and encompassed Fairview, and then turned north to the Bullock Road. Sickles's III Corps still held Hazel Grove, while intermixed parts of the II and XII Corps manned the rest of the loop. Best's wall of guns, still intact, was obviously the strong point around which any defense on the west was based. The other key terrain feature was, of course, Hazel Grove, but Hooker had already given orders to evacuate it as his first step in shifting to his new layout.

On the Confederate side, Col. E. P. Alexander had been scouring the ground all night in search of positions for his guns. For all of his skill, he could place only eight cannon, in two lines of four, astride the Plank Road — the axis of the planned Gray attack. He spotted seven more cannon in the woods and roads leading to Hazel Grove. But he was forced to keep approximately a hundred more guns in idle reserve because he had no place to use them.

As the sun spilled over the tree tops to the east that morning, Sickles began pulling away from Hazel Grove. Immediately after, Jeb Stuart launched his attack. The Confederate troops loping through the woods pierced the quiet morning air with their wild whoops. Soon the deep thundering of Best's guns joined the loud crackle of infantry fire which echoed through the little valley near Hazel Grove.

At the grove itself the Rebels caught the tail end of Sickles's column as it poured off that plain. Only Huntington's battery remained there, as the rest of the artillery had preceded the infantry from the position. The cocky Gray infantry broke out into open ground in front of the grove, and right behind them came one of their batteries which Alexander had stowed away in the woods. The guns immediately went into action against Huntington. More enemy infantry poured from the woods on Huntington's left, and it was soon evident that the two Blue regiments which were supporting him could not stem this sweep on the flank. Huntington was keeping the Rebels in his front at a distance with slashing discharges of shotgun-like canister, but the force on the left was closing in. The support regiment on that flank fought desperately, but had to give ground.

Huntington shot a quick glance rearward, saw the tail of the III Corps winding onto Fairview, and concluded his job was now done. He commanded them to limber to the rear, and eager hands grabbed for the gun trails, while others swiftly stowed implements in traveling racks, as the roar of rifle fire sounded closer. The Rebels concentrated their fire on Huntington's horses to prevent the battery's escape. The horses of one gun were spilled in a milling mass of traces, and the gun was lost. A second piece, then still another had to be abandoned. The rest passed through the gauntlet of fire. Huntington paused briefly on Fairview to see if there was a way for him to recover his lost weapons. However, one quick glance told him that idea was hopeless. Both Confederate and Union fire was raining on the field. Dejectedly, Huntington put his

depleted unit on the road to Chandler's, where he joined Turnbull's and Puttkammer's batteries.[29]

Stuart was now trying, against fierce opposition, to cave in
the Yankee line along the Plank Road. Best's guns, aided by
Jastram's and Sims's batteries of Sickles's III Corps, were keeping up a strong fire against the Rebels. Dimick's four guns still
held the right, and two other guns of his section were far out
front; Winslow remained on Dimick's left. Further left, next to
an old log house serving as Couch's headquarters, Jastram occupied a vacant redoubt. Sims rolled his guns into battery on
the south side of the house. The other III Corps batteries —
Seeley's and Lewis's — occupied the extreme left end of Fairview and the rear of the Chancellor house, respectively.

By giving up Hazel Grove, Hooker discovered he had dis-
carded a crucial trump. Thanks to a smooth-working battalion
system Confederate Col. Alexander was soon running battery
after battery onto Hazel Grove. From here his guns could
slam the Yankee batteries on Fairview almost in flank. In minutes eight Gray cannons crowned that rise. Ten Gray guns in
action along the Plank Road converged their fire with the eight
on Hazel Grove to give the Federal troops a difficult time, even
though most of the Blue units were operating from behind
earthworks. The Federal return fire was of necessity divergent
and therefore less effective.

Stuart was hurling his men at the Yankee line across the
Plank Road, and to the south and east Lee himself was ap-
plying pressure in a major effort against the Army of the Potomac. To stem this drive, the Federals had a powerful force
of guns. The woods west of Fairview shook from the torrent
of exploding shell and case unleashed by the almost forty cannon along Best's line plus Seeley's six on the southern face,
while to the south and east twenty more guns posted about
Chancellorsville added their noise. The din must have been
frightful, even by modern standards. Best's guns at Fairview
must have been firing at least a round every minute and a half,

at times perhaps more. Added to this racket were small arms fire and the booming Confederate cannon.

The struggle reached a climax when two Rebel brigades drove hard at the Yankees near the road. A rookie Maine regiment broke, and a breakthrough threatened. The guns of Dimick's advanced section were soon spitting canister in a desperate attempt to plug the hole. Enemy riflemen replied with such vicious fire that Osborn ordered the two pieces retired. The limbers wheeled about; blackened sweaty hands hurriedly swung the trails up to the pintles, and the two guns began to pull out. But a blaze of Rebel fire cut down a team. Dimick dismounted to help clear the piece and promptly took a bullet through his foot. But the young lieutenant ignored the wound and continued to direct the clearing. Another volley crashed out and Dimick fell mortally wounded, his spine shot in half. The stalled gun was lost, but the horses on the other piece were put at a gallop, and the gun escaped. From the relative safety of Fairview an eager lieutenant saw the lost weapon standing mutely in the road between the flaming infantry lines; he grabbed a limber, galloped back through the heavy fire, secured the weapon, and proudly hauled it back to Fairview.

Winslow, too, was receiving heavy Rebel fire, and was hurling shell and solid shot at them. A Union regiment directly in front began to waver and fall back, with Graycoats in pursuit. Winslow instantly ordered his guns to cease, load with solid shot, and await his signal to fire. Back came the Yankee regiment, slowly giving ground. Suddenly the regiment's commander barked an order for them to wheel to the flank, thus giving Winslow a clear field of fire. Winslow seized his chance; at almost point-blank range he fired his battery. The Confederates paused, then retreated as Winslow's guns reloaded.[30]

The enemy infantry south of the Plank Road was forced back by the slashing volleys of the Federal infantry and the booming guns on Fairview. But north of the road the Gray brigades seemed on the verge of bursting through the Federal line. If they succeeded, the batteries on Fairview would be in danger of being enfiladed. Fortunately at a crucial moment a Blue brigade piled in from its reserve position to protect the infantry. For a time, the line was restored.

Hooker, briefly recovering his skill as a combat commander, loosed French's division in a counter-attack which drove the enemy back, and the Plank Road line and Fairview appeared safe. Capt. Randolph, chief of the III Corps artillery, was of the opinion that if the artillery ammunition had held out and if the Union forces had retained the woods north of the road, they could have beaten their antagonists. But the ammunition did give out, and the Federals failed to hold the woods, so once more the Army of the Potomac had to give up the field.

Shortly before 9 a.m. infantry commanders, as well as the supporting batteries, began reporting that their ammunition was dangerously low. Urgent calls went back to headquarters for resupply; Hooker's answer came back: 'I can't make ammunition!' [31] Some of the batteries thereupon obtained whatever they could from units which still had rounds in their limbers. Sims's New Jersey unit borrowed some rounds, and after firing them were given permission by Sickles to retire from the fight.

In the meantime Col. Alexander continued to feed his Rebel batteries onto Hazel Grove. Behind his guns massed in the clearing were other units, for whom there was no room up front. They were held in readiness as instant replacements for any front-line guns which became damaged or ran out of ammunition. Alexander estimated that he had some forty guns hammering the Federal batteries at Fairview and enfilading several parts of the Blue line.

Hampton's Pennsylvania battery, which had come forward opposite Hazel Grove on the left of Best's line about 3 o'clock that morning, was taking a heavy battering from Alexander's guns, as they were one of the batteries closest to the Rebel line. But they were a stubborn bunch and refused to be driven off. Not until the order came down to evacuate Fairview did they leave, and even then one section left still firing by prolonge. In those last minutes the Gray attack reached a crescendo, causing the Pennsylvanians to have a limber blown to bits and a second disabled. Then a Gray shell exploded beside Capt. Hampton as he was preparing to fire a final round. The flying fragments tore his horse almost in two and severed Hampton's left leg above the knee. By the time the battery cleared from Fairview it numbered as casualties its commander, seven others killed or wounded, and twenty horses. Elsewhere on Alexander's line his gunners were having equal success, and only the failure of their fuzes to respond properly kept them from blowing the Yankee batteries off their crest.

Meanwhile, Stuart was bringing up fresh brigades from the rear. With loud yells, blasts of bugles, and rolling volleys of musketry, the Confederates stormed forward again. Two Gray companies found a hole on the Yankee right and seeped through. Almost immediately the Rebels spotted the rest of Dimick's battery — four big Napoleons astride the road — but before they could seize the guns, the battery quickly pulled back, leaving Winslow's New Yorkers as the right flank battery.

Figures in rag-tag uniform wormed their way toward the flank of the gun line. Some of the more reckless Rebels even dashed up to a point a bare hundred yards from Winslow's cannon, where a color-bearer ran up with his flag and jammed the staff into the ground at the edge of the road. A little knot of riflemen rallied around the fluttering banner and unleashed a ragged volley at the battery. Young Capt. Crosby, commanding Battery F, 4th U.S., nearby, dropped to the ground shot through the heart. Men and horses were falling on every side. Meanwhile, Winslow loaded his guns with canister and barked the command to fire. The six Napoleons erupted with a shivering crash which literally blew the enemy off the road.

The respite was short-lived. Through the smoke the Federals could see more columns of enemy infantry moving to the attack. Winslow saw that unless he pulled back his guns immediately he might well lose all or part of his battery, and so he ordered his men to begin evacuating from the left. The left piece instantly ceased firing, limbered, and pulled away while the other guns provided covering fire. One by one, the guns ceased and pulled out, the last piece firing a final round just seconds before it retired. Only two horseless caissons were left behind, and when Winegar later returned to try to recover them he was captured.[32]

The Union fire from Fairview dwindled sharply, as batteries were sent rolling rearward when they ran out of ammunition, while others were forced into retirement by Rebel infantry. The only saving factor was that as the Blue infantry retreated the Yankee gunners were able to switch to their most effective round — canister. Having lost Dimick and Winslow, Capt. Osborn appealed to his corps chief-of-artillery, Capt. Randolph, for a replacement battery. Puttkammer was sent for, but he never arrived.[33]

North of the road the Blue regiments continued to give ground, and there was imminent danger that the Confederates would soon break the line south of Fairview. This threat and the scarcity of ammunition forced the Federal high command to decide to abandon Fairview. Under cover of some batteries at Chancellorsville, the retreat began. Capt. Best ordered his exhausted units to retire to U.S. Ford, while Randolph sent his III Corps batteries to Chancellorsville, where some of the still serviceable commands joined the few batteries already in action there.

Earlier in the morning, during the flurry to find replacement batteries, one section of Fitzhugh's K, 1st New York, was finally located on the eastern part of the field and told to hurry back to its former position. Lt. Davis commanding the section promptly moved toward Fairview at a fast trot. The little column reached the small Fairview cemetery, which still stands in the open ground 300 yards south of what is now Virginia Highway 3. About a hundred yards ahead was the Federal gun line, but Davis suddenly saw through the pall of acrid smoke that the batteries which had been manning it were all retiring under heavy enemy fire. He quickly wheeled his section about just northeast of the cemetery near a reserve regiment of infantry and cut loose with his two cannons at the awesome Confederate display of artillery atop Hazel Grove. As the section boomed its salvo the last Yankee battery to leave Fairview — Winegar's — galloped past. Davis's crewmen watched twelve of their shells burst amid the line of enemy guns. One round slammed into an ammunition chest, which brought the characteristic thunderous roar and billowing clouds of smoke.

A commotion to the right front, along the Plank Road, caught Davis's eye, and he saw enemy infantry moving out toward Fairview. The two guns were quickly shifted over, and the lieutenant put his men to work with a mixture of shell and case. But two little 3-inch rifles were scarcely the force to hold back this advance, and, as the Gray ranks filed down the valley and swarmed up onto Best's old position, Davis bellowed for percussion rounds at point-blank range.[34] At this point the regiment of Blue infantry which had been lying prone on the section's right rear rose to its feet and tramped off toward Chancellorsville, leaving Davis's two guns alone in the field. There was no choice now but to limber his weapons to the rear. So, under the cover of the fire from the batteries around the Chancellor house, the section retired to the new line near Chandler's.[35]

In the meantime III Corps Battery K, 4th U.S., under Lt. Francis W. Seeley, had been detached from its sister units on Fairview and sent by Hooker's order 600 yards away to the extreme south edge of the plateau. Here it took position in support of Sickles's men swarming in from Hazel Grove. Almost at once Seeley's men became a target of the booming Gray cannon on the grove 500 yards away. As the Rebels found the range, the Regulars began taking casualties. Battery K's position was such that the enemy guns were for the most part in defilade. Still Seeley's left three pieces could get a partial sight on the enemy, and the lieutenant told them to swing around in the hope of neutralizing the destructive fire.

For fifteen minutes the big Napoleons boomed away with case and shell, and the cannoneers could distinctly see their rounds exploding over the crest, behind which lay the Rebel cannon. However, the Graycoats were apparently not being hurt by the fire, so Seeley to save his precious ammunition reluctantly ordered his weapons to cease firing at them. Then Seeley spotted Confederate infantry moving in on the battery's right, and he ordered his right section to shift over to the new target. Rammers gripped by two powder-blackened pairs of hands shoved charges down the yawning tubes; cannoneers stepped clear of the muzzle and the wheels, and both guns went off with a terrific crash. Looking about him, though, Seeley saw no other Blue batteries on the field. Nothing could be gained by staying here, so Seeley gave the welcome order to his harried gunners: 'Limber to the rear!' The order came not a minute too soon, for the Rebel infantry was advancing so rapidly that the battery had to leave its wounded behind as it hurried toward Chancellor house.

At the Chancellor house some of the retiring batteries — presumably those which still had ammunition and a stomach for more fighting — turned about in the fields and prepared to go back into battle again. Lewis's 10th New York Battery rolled into position near and to the east of the house, four of Seeley's guns just west of the house on the south side of the Plank Road, and two of Jastram's Rhode Island guns further along the same line.[36] Already set in position was the group of seven guns under Lt. Muhlenberg which was supporting Hancock's harassed division. Soon Leppien's excellent 5th Maine Battery and Pettit's Battery B, 1st New York, joined the line.[37]

The rest of the Army's artillery was scattered all over the rear and frantic efforts were being made to put them into line. It is not surprising that one contemporary wrote, 'The army had a crazy-quilt appearance.' Gen. Hancock remarked that the woods seemed alive with artillery in a state of confusion!

About Chancellorsville, Hancock's and Geary's divisions were holding the gate open for the retreat of the rest of the Army. As Alexander's guns moved up to Fairview and the Confederate infantry pressed from three sides, Hancock found himself fighting on two fronts and being shelled from three directions. Crushing fire converged on that little hamlet, plowing up the fields, slamming into Union batteries, tearing up the Chancellor house and setting it afire, and knocking Hooker himself out of combat. This artillery battle around Chancellorsville was one of the few times during the war when Confederate gunners were able to put their Yankee counterparts at a decided disadvantage. In this instance it was the Gray gunners who had the superiority of numbers, of position, and of converging fire — in fact, enfilading fire.

The two wings of Lee's Army were by this time in contact with each other, and the Confederate fire ringing Hooker's Army stretched solidly from east to south to west. The Federals fought back desperately, but their artillery was not holding up its part very successfully, for commands had become confused and batteries split up. It was becoming increasingly evident that the Army missed Hunt. Instead of directing the guns, he had been sent back to Banks' Ford by Hooker on a relatively insignificant mission, and no one else had been given the authority to take hold of the galaxy of batteries that roamed the area.

Earlier Hooker, now fully alert to the deterioration of things, ordered Col. Morgan, Couch's chief-of-artillery, to bring up every corps battery which had not been in action. The colonel went in person, but by the time he succeeded in rounding up Cushing's, Arnold's, and Kirby's commands, Fairview was lost and the Federals were fighting to hold the door open at Chancellorsville. Approaching Chancellorsville with his fresh XII Corps batteries, Col. Morgan was appalled at the sight around the burning house. Yankee cannon, everywhere in the surrounding fields, were booming away at the menacing hordes of enemy troops and taking a thorough beating in the process.

'I do not think it [Chancellorsville] could have been held by any number of guns I could have placed in the contracted ground near the . . . house,' wrote Morgan in his official report.[38]

In spite of the disadvantages under which they fought, the Blue batteries did a good job; but it cost them a stiff price. The hardest hit seems to have been Seeley, who had been flung into the scrap again by Capt. Randolph. At one point Seeley loaded his guns with canister and then, with steel nerves, waited until the yelling Rebels were within 350 yards before yelling the command to fire. The sleet of pellets discouraged further advance, and the Confederates rushed for the cover of woods on the battery's left front. Quickly the lieutenant changed to solid shot, and as the enemy dove for the timber his men took great delight in bouncing the solid iron balls into the trees after them.

At the same time Seeley's men were under a devastating pounding from what seemed to be three directions. As usual the battery lost more horses than men, but at one point the crew was so short-handed that Seeley was forced to call on nearby infantry for help in operating his guns. Finally, with his ammunition exhausted, the lieutenant ordered his command to the rear, leaving behind a horseless caisson and five smashed wheels. With fifty-nine horses out of action, many of the vehicles cleared the field with only two or three animals to their team. But the frugal Seeley saw to it that every piece of harness was brought off, though Chancellorsville had cost Battery K, 4th U.S., seven dead and thirty-nine wounded of a strength of 120 men. This was about the same proportion of loss as Battery B, 4th U.S., had suffered in the cornfield at Antietam.

Blasting away on Seeley's right were the two pieces of Battery E, 1st Rhode Island, under Lt. Bucklyn. The section had been sent forward by Capt. Randolph to help hold the door open for the Federal infantry to retire. On receiving the order from his former battery commander, Bucklyn remarked, 'Whoever goes up there will not live to return.' Randolph was in complete agreement, but he said he had to have someone who would chance it. Bucklyn then turned to his section and asked for volunteers; instantly every man stepped forward. With that the little band went bouncing forward.

Out in the field the section was almost destroyed by the heavy Confederate pounding. When Bucklyn finally received permission to retire, enemy infantry were a scant twenty-five yards away, and there were no horses left on his teams. Yet, somehow those determined men managed to spike one gun before abandoning it, and drag the other by hand from the field. Bucklyn's daring resulted in the Medal of Honor.

Other batteries were cut up in varying degrees, but none seemed immune. Pettit's men of Battery B, 1st New York, found themselves being hammered by one full enemy battery at their front, by another on their left flank, and by a third section in their rear. By the time their order to retire was received, the New Yorkers had shot up 600 rounds of case and shell and had had a caisson blown up. The battery considered itself lucky to have lost but twelve men.

Still another hard-hit Federal battery was Leppien's 5th Maine, a I Corps unit. Leppien's orders that morning had sent him in support of Reynolds's corps on the Army's right, but en route he was diverted by Hooker's order to Chancellorsville. The 5th Maine trotted down the road, the men loudly singing one of those morbid melodramatic songs of that era: 'I am going home, to die no more. . . .' Near the Chancellor house the unit reined to a halt amid a blistering fire which was shredding the leaves of nearby trees and ripping away limbs with frightening regularity. While the battery awaited position orders, someone stood up and offered a short prayer for the entire unit, then with a shout drivers booted their teams and the guns went away to their indicated spot — the edge of a circular field 450–500 yards wide near a small orchard north of the house.

As Leppien's men emerged from the woods, they saw Confederates in the field opposite them. Leppien instantly threw his guns into battery amid a wicked reception of enemy firing. Suddenly the Gray ranks wheeled to the flanks, disclosing a line of cannon in partial defilade behind them — no doubt Alexander's guns on Fairview. The Gray artillerymen took aim, and the air about the battery was speckled with exploding case and shell. Even a few balls from an occasional canister round whistled overhead. The Confederates' short rounds were also hurting the Maine unit, bouncing off the hard ground in front and ricocheting into the teams behind the guns. Leppien waved his caissons further to the rear to spare them this punishment.

In the hope of conserving his ammunition and achieving maximum effect from each round, Leppien ordered his men to work the pieces slowly and deliberately. Even so, the supply of rounds in the limbers began to run low. Now a large body of Rebel infantry moving up on the left front caused fresh anxiety. Leaving his right half battery to duel with the Gray guns, the captain shifted his left half onto the threatening enemy regiments. The Maine guns hammered the enemy infantry hard and Federal infantry joined in with a fierce fire, but still some of the Graycoats fought their way to within 150 yards of the artillery before being driven back.

The shelling continued unabated. Then the ammunition in the right section limbers gave out, and there were but three or four left in one limber of the center section. Before these few could be expended, an enemy round scored a direct hit on the chest and blew it and the limber to bits. Then the left section reported its ammunition gone, and a detail was hurriedly formed to bring up a supply from the nearest caisson.

The Confederate cannon gave the harried Federals no respite as it kept plastering the whole area around the burning Chancellor house. And then once more Gray infantry made menacing motions in Leppien's direction. The battery appeared on the verge of total demoralization, as Capt. Leppien was cut down with a shattered leg and the other two officers were also out of action. Gen. Couch, nearby at that moment, looked

about for someone to take command of the battery. Then up
the road came veteran Regular gunner Lt. Edmund Kirby,
riding well in advance of his oncoming battery. When Couch
saw the young officer he yelled to Col. Morgan to put Kirby
in command of the 5th Maine.[39]

Kirby got the order, located the beleaguered Maine outfit,
and galloped over. Presently, when Morgan trotted up to
check, Kirby showed him where his horse had already been
hit just behind the girth. The colonel stayed a few minutes, exchanging a few words with Kirby, and left, satisfied that Kirby
had the battery firmly in hand. But the 5th Maine continued to
be mauled, and Kirby was soon down with a mangled hip. As
the officer fell to earth, his horse, wounded by the same burst,
threatened to trample him; a private saw the danger, quickly
drew his pistol, and shot the beast.

The surviving cannoneers, exhausted and stunned by this
fierce shelling, began leaving their empty guns. Two men lin-
gered around one piece — Corp. J. H. Lebroke and Pvt. John
F. Chase. Finding a few stray canister rounds, the two men
decided to fight a while longer. With Chase sponging, loading,
and ramming, and Lebroke aiming, priming, and firing, the
two soldiers got off a couple of rounds. But their fight ended
when an enemy shell made a freak hit smack on their gun's
muzzle, completely wrecking the piece. Only now did the men
leave the weapon, on direct order of the wounded Kirby. Lebroke promptly ran for help to save the horseless crewless battery. Locating Gen. Hancock nearby, the corporal told him of
the battery's desperate plight, and the general quickly sent
some nearby infantry running across the field to haul away
the threatened guns.

Lt. Kirby, still alive, though painfully hurt, lay on the
ground, refusing all attempts to remove him until the guns
were clear. Only after this was accomplished did he permit
some men to carry him to an ambulance. As Kirby did not appear dangerously wounded, it came as rather a shock when
the Army subsequently learned he died on May 28th. So much

did President Lincoln think of the two officers who commanded the 5th Maine in this fight that he awarded Kirby a general officer's commission five days before the lieutenant died, and Leppien learned on his deathbed of his promotion to lieutenant colonel.

Elsewhere, the 10th New York Battery, under Lt. Lewis had been firing from a point described as near the northwest corner of Chancellorsville and had taken a beating from Alexander's cannon.[40] Then Lewis, too, ran out of ammunition, and the battery commander looked about for someone who might give him the authority to retire. Through the smoke and dust he spotted a mounted officer — undoubtedly a general — surrounded by aides and orderlies. Spurring his horse, the lieutenant rode over, saluted, explained his predicament, and asked permission to withdraw. 'No!' came the quick reply. 'If they see you retire they will advance!' [41] Lewis saluted again, and dejectedly returned to his men; the battery would just have to sit and take it a while.

Lewis was in luck, though, for the order soon came down to start withdrawing, and the artillery was to be pulled out first. The general, who had minutes earlier refused Lewis's request, then rode over to the unhappy 10th New York and dryly remarked to its commander: 'You may now withdraw your guns by hand; your horses would only attract attention.' Before acting on this welcome news, Lewis asked the officer who he might be. The answer came back, 'General Hancock.' [42]

About the time the order to retreat reached the troops, Gen. Meade apparently directed his chief-of-artillery, Capt. Stephen H. Weed, to round up every available battery and swing them into line around Chandler's to cover the retirement. Weed corralled fifty-six guns from a hodgepodge of batteries representing virtually every corps on the field. These he formed in a wide V, 500 yards on a side, the point toward Chancellorsville. Twenty-eight pieces went on the right side, twenty-four on the left, and four held the apex itself.

Of the elements in the Union Army that had seen hard

fighting only the XI Corps was of dubious combat reliability. The rest of the corps were still in fair enough order, and backing them up along the new line were the completely fresh I Corps on the right and V Corps on the left. Reynolds's I Corps infantry had marched onto the field well ahead of its artillery so a few of the XI Corps batteries under Lt. Col. Louis Schirmer were trotted over to support them. When the I Corps guns did arrive, some of the batteries were then diverted to other parts of the field, thus further compounding the artillery confusion. At one point during the day, one or two of these German batteries which had been loaned to Reynolds, their memories still burning from Jackson's blast from the west, apparently panicked again at an outburst of firing and fled madly to the rear. Whether this report was true or not, it eventually made the rounds of the Army, adding to the sad reputation of the XI Corps.

As May 3rd drew to an end, Hooker realized his scattered artillery needed someone to put it back in order. He recalled that Hunt had been sent back to Banks' Ford on the afternoon of the 1st, so he turned the prodigious task of reorganizing the artillery over to Col. Wainwright [43] until such time as Hunt could be recalled. There was little that Wainwright, or even Hunt, could have done to remedy the sad condition immediately. The best that can be said of Hooker's belated move is that he at last comprehended the error of turning his best artillery commander into his glorified orderly.

Under Wainwright's guidance the Federals wheeled about a hundred guns into the battle line, and approximately 140 more waited nearby in reserve. When Hunt galloped up to Chandler's about 10 o'clock that night, he found the Union position bulwarked by three large masses of artillery: thirty pieces under Capt. Randol on the Army's left, forty-eight under Capt. Weed in the center, and thirty-two guns under Col. Wainwright's immediate charge on the right.[44] Giving his approval to the general battery dispositions, Hunt next rode after the rest of the batteries. He found them parked in the open

ground near U.S. Ford and in the woods behind the main line
of resistance. Each unit was queried as to its ammunition supply; those that were low were ordered to fill up their chests.
This done, the general made a few minor adjustments in reserve positions; then everyone waited for Lee's morning attack.

The Gray commander never got a chance to try Hooker's
new works, though, for Sedgwick's activities at Fredericksburg
finally made themselves felt. About noon on the 3rd, just as
Lee was preparing to deal Hooker's Army a finishing blow, he
received word that Sedgwick had driven off Early, taken
Fredericksburg, and was moving on Lee's rear. Lee thereupon
pulled four brigades of Anderson's division from his line and
ordered them to move eastward and block Sedgwick until such
time as Early could recover and strike that Union force in the
rear. The drama now shifted to that quarter.

Upon receiving Hooker's 4 p.m. order at midnight, Sedgwick had put his men under way about 3 a.m. May 3rd. Now
in the dawn's light Sedgwick's VI Corps marched up the Bowling Green Road toward the city. Newton's division, with three
batteries in tow, led the way; Brooks's division followed with
its four batteries. Griffin's division from the II Corps, which
had been left as an ineffective screen on Falmouth, was preparing to cross on a pontoon bridge into the town proper. Griffin rapidly occupied the town, while Sedgwick turned his attention to the Rebel lines on Marye's Heights. Remembering
that December day in 1862, Sedgwick's men knew the job
ahead of them would not be easy. The best hope lay in flanking the Graycoats. It was soon evident that the flanks were
impassable, however, so Newton's division was told to try to
take the Rebel forces frontally with such support as the other
two divisions on the flanks could give.

Loud commands sang out in the cool dawn air, and couriers
and orderlies set off at a racketing gallop on missions. Orders
reached Butler's Battery G, 2nd U.S., McCarthy's combined
C/D, 1st Pennsylvania, and Harn's 3rd New York to move up
in support of Newton. Harn unlimbered on the right of the

railroad tracks near the gasworks, while McCarthy and Butler took position on the left of the tracks, some hundred yards in advance. That awful stone wall stood directly to their front. All three began a slow feeling-out fire.

Similarly, on the left of the line, Howe's artillery, consisting of Martin's F, 5th U.S., and Cowan's 1st New York Battery, prepared to support a drive against the enemy right. In front of the Bernard place, east of Deep Run, Brooks's division and his four batteries shook out their lines, and by 6 a.m. his gunners were already in a brisk fire-fight with a distant Gray battery. McCartney's Battery A, Massachusetts Light Artillery, and Rigby's Battery A, Maryland Light Artillery, located just west of the Bowling Green Road, found themselves the target of four enemy smoothbores dug-in on the hills 1300 yards away. Both Yank units turned their tubes on it, and were shortly joined by Parson's battery in their rear.

At one point, a detachment of Rebel infantry ventured down from the hills into the plain, and McCartney swiftly swung over his left section and blasted at them with canister. The firing kept up for two hours. McCartney felt sure a shot from his right gun had dismounted an enemy piece. Then the puffs from the Confederate cannon stopped. The Federals concluded the enemy had been silenced and allowed their own guns to cool. A few moments passed, then the Yankees saw that the Rebels were trying to replace their smoothbores with rifled pieces. Barked commands instantly sent the Blue batteries back to work, hoping to catch the Graycoats in the open.

The morning hours ticked by steadily as Sedgwick struggled to get his commands set. His artillery roared away in intermittent duels with some of the forty-eight Confederate guns thinly sprinkled along their six-mile line from Hamilton's Crossing to Dr. Taylor's place north of town. It was 10:30 when Newton's regiments finally were clop-clopping from the sheltering streets of Fredericksburg, straight for that open ground of awful memory. Newton's guns — twelve rifled and six Napoleon pieces — received orders to concentrate their fire at a point on that stone wall. The batteries were told to keep firing at that point till the Blue infantry closed; they were then to shift fire to the enemy batteries on the crest behind the wall. The plain behind town shook with the thunder of the Federal guns and the explosions from answering Rebel shells. Actually, the enemy cannon were not proving too effective, as some of their guns were having trouble depressing their tubes to bear on the attack waves. Only two little howitzers planted almost abreast of the Rebel rifle line seemed to be doing any damage. As Newton's men marched into range, the wall rippled in flame. Banks of muskets thumped a deadly fire, and the two howitzers spat canister in angry tones. The assault fell away like a spent wave.

Fortunately for the Federals, though, the battle would not be a repeat of that December debacle. During an unauthorized truce in the firing to permit removal of wounded, Newton's officers spotted the thinness of the Confederate line. With this encouraging piece of intelligence, they ordered another charge, and Newton, aided by Howe on the left, swept forward.

Howe's two batteries, Cowan's and Martin's, began jerking lanyards in earnest as they took dead aim on the Gray batteries on Lee's and Willis's hills; Newton apparently again followed orders and aimed at the wall. This time the Yankee bayonets were successful. At 10:50 the word was on the telegraph to Hooker that Marye's Heights had been carried.

Over the stone wall swept the cheering troops of Howe's command. They captured scores of prisoners, and gleefully seized eight pieces of Rebel artillery. Following closely behind the infantry were the two batteries. One of them, Martin's Regulars, had just reached the crest when a heavy slashing fire from some eight Rebel guns on Lee's and Howison hills to the south burst about them. The Regulars wheeled into action. However, this gun duel was short-lived, for the Confederates realized they could not halt the Federals. Part of the

Rebel force began falling back to the southwest, while other elements on their left under Gen. Wilcox retired down the Plank Road leading toward Chancellorsville. And Gen. Sedgwick left a small force to hold his captured ground and moved to follow the enemy out the Plank Road.

Newton's division, its batteries bouncing along in the wake, again led the way. As the leading elements reached a point about a mile and a half from town, a Rebel battery 800 yards distant burst into action. The first round buzzed harmlessly past, but the second exploded with a crisp bang, wounding a sergeant and killing a horse in the Maryland battery. The Marylanders promptly wheeled off the road, unlimbered, and opened fire on the annoyers. But the enemy gunners were only performing a rearguard action, and as soon as the Blue column was forced to halt and deploy, their job was done, and they speedily limbered and galloped away.

After a pause to allow Howe's and Brooks's divisions to catch up, Sedgwick ordered the column forward, with Brooks's fresh troops now in the lead. Brushing aside a delaying party at the Toll Gate, the Federal advance party collided with the Confederate infantry in a woods just west of Salem Church. Unknown to the Federals, detachments from Lee's command at Chancellorsville had joined Wilcox's group here. The result was that Sedgwick's advance was completely stopped.

The fighting at Salem Church was almost entirely an infantry affair. Brooks had only sporadic artillery support. For a time his forces drove the Rebels back, but the latter committed their reserve at the crucial moment and so drove back the Blue regiments. Only now did the Federal artillery really come into action. Williston's Battery D, 2nd U.S., moved two sections of Napoleons in position on a rise to the left of the road near the Toll Gate and one section in the road proper. Rigby's and Parson's rifled were in open ground on the right of the road. As the Blue infantry fell back from the enemy-held woods, the rifled batteries began a slow overhead fire with percussion shells. A call for help from the left of the Union line caused the left two sections of Williston's command to swing around to aid that quarter.

Williston saw the Rebels driving the Blue regiments across the open ground on the right of the highway. The enemy forces would soon reach a point where guns could hit them in the flank. The gunners looked at him anxiously, eagerly awaiting the command to fire. A few yards more, then Williston yelled: 'Number one, fire!' A case round cut for one and three-quarter seconds sped toward its target and burst smack in the middle of the enemy line. Williston now gave the order to fire at will, and sweating crews unleashed a fierce cannonade.

The enemy ranks, caught in flank, were stunned and thrown into confusion. Their pursuit was halted and they fell back to the left side of the road. Williston followed them with solid and shell, twice knocking down a set of Rebel colors. There was a short pause, then once more the enemy came down the Plank Road, this time making straight for Williston. At 300 yards the two pieces let go, pitching canister square into the faces of the charging ranks. Then the rifled batteries on the flanks came to Williston's assistance. This storm of fire stopped the charge and gave the shaken Federal infantry the chance to reform behind the line of hot smoking guns. Now it was becoming dark, so the two armies followed the practice of the times and called off further action for the day.

During the fighting that day one of the lieutenants of Cowan's 1st New York Battery had a rather hectic experience. The officer had been sent back to camp at Falmouth that morning with a damaged gun; he was to have the weapon repaired, then return to the unit as quickly as possible, bringing with him the gun, plus the battery wagon, rolling forge, and baggage vehicles. At 6 p.m. the lieutenant led his hodgepodge column over the bridge into Fredericksburg. Learning the course of Sedgwick's column, the officer moved his vehicles out the Plank Road. But unknown to the lieutenant, the Rebels were already beginning to close in toward the town to cut off Sedgwick. As the little column trotted to the road they stumbled into a Rebel picket, which for some reason fled without firing a shot. But a Gray battery 600 yards further down the road took the lieutenant's command under fire.

The lieutenant wheeled his column about, and for a minute it appeared as if they had made their escape. Then a well-placed shell burst in the road just in front of a wagon pulled by mules. The shell terrified the normally placid beasts and caused them to upset the wagon across the narrow roadway. The rolling forge and two more wagons now stood behind with no room to pass the wreckage. More shells slammed into the nearby field. The lieutenant quickly decided to save what he could. He gave the order to unhitch the teams and lead them through. One team trotted by, then a second. The lieutenant suddenly discovered that the Negro driver of the next wagon had fled and had left his mules still hitched to the vehicle. There was no time to unhitch them so team and wagon, plus the forge and two other wagons, were promptly abandoned. The Confederate gunners must have taken great delight in shooting at this sad-looking little column as it fled across a mile of open ground. Later the column rejoined its parent unit.

Back at Chandler's the main Federal Army watched the woods and open ground in front of its rifle pits for a move by Lee's Army. But meanwhile the Southern commander had turned his weight toward Salem Church. The only activity around Chandler's was a move by a weak Confederate division toward the fords behind the Federal position. Weed's cannon caught this column on the road and hit them so hard that the Confederates drew back in alarm and tried nothing more on that front for the rest of the day.

The next day, May 4th, was quiet until late in the afternoon when Lee unsuccessfully tried to box in and finish off Sedgwick, who stood with his back to the river awaiting orders from Hooker. A few Federal batteries did some shooting, but the fight here was largely with infantry. However, around Banks' Ford some thirty Union and Rebel guns became involved in an ugly fight. Confederate Maj. Hardaway had moved up with eighteen rifled pieces to a position known as Smith's Hill, and from there he opened a furious bombardment on some of Hunt's batteries near the ford. These Federal guns had been pouring a flanking fire into some of the Gray ranks trying to oust Sedgwick.

Hardaway's fire was aimed primarily at an entrenched group of eight Yankee guns located just in front of an old white-frame house on the north side of the Rappahannock. Four other Federal cannon, two upstream and two downstream, promptly waded into the fight. Iron projectiles were soon whizzing across the river in both directions. Five of Hardaway's guns were out in the open with absolutely no protection, and the Yankee gunners poured a wicked accurate shelling onto these choice targets. For a time the Yanks literally silenced almost all of the Gray pieces. Only Hardaway's personal effort kept his crews in action.

The Confederates were using fuzed projectiles in their rifled guns, but they were not functioning at all. Hardaway immediately checked the rounds and discovered they were equipped with fuze-igniters. This was a little tin concave device that fastened over the nose of the projectile and was supposed to trap the flame of the burning propellant and funnel it into the fuze. The major concluded that his men had been knocking off some of the fuze powder when they were inserting the fuzes. In effect then, the Confederates were throwing solid shot at the Yanks. Hardaway claimed that, in spite of his fuze troubles, his men knocked out six of the eight Union guns directly in their front and chased off the other two.

Nightfall of the 4th found Hooker's lines around Chandler's still intact and Sedgwick's VI Corps still holding its bridgehead south of the river. However, the Confederates had reoccupied Fredericksburg, despite the fire of the Union batteries on the opposite heights. Many high Federal officers hoped Hooker would regain his combativeness and bring on a final knock-down fight the next day. But before dawn Hooker received word that Sedgwick, who had received conflicting orders, has escaped to the north bank during the night. That settled matters for the Union commander. He sent out orders that the Army of the Potomac was to retire over the river during that night.

Hunt, now restored to the command of the artillery, received specific orders on the morning of the 5th to herd all the batteries not actually in the line over the river and then to Falmouth. The rest would take their chances with the divisions. Hunt now showed that shrewd insight into conditions which distinguishes good combat officers. He reasoned that surplus gun batteries would do Hooker no good as they trotted toward Falmouth, but that they could be used advantageously to cover the Army's withdrawal. An army crossing a river by fords and flimsy bridges could be a vulnerable target for harassing enemy artillery.

The main withdrawal was supposed to be carried out under cover of darkness on the night of May 5th, with the last elements getting their protection from the early morning fog. But Hunt did not think it was possible that this immense force could move across the river before daylight, and he knew that an army as capably led as Lee's would certainly attempt to harass this crossing with artillery. Now the artillery commander sent for Capt. Best.[45] Best listened to his senior's instructions. He was to make a survey of the several fords the Army was going to use. Then, as Hunt moved the surplus units across the river, Best was to deploy them in such a way as to command the ground on which Lee could place his batteries to hit the Federal columns. With vigor Best went to work, and eventually he moved forty-four cannon from the I, II, and XII Corps into covering positions on the north bank of the Rappahannock, ten below U.S. Ford, and thirty-four covering the ford itself.

The able Confederate gun commanders were not to be caught napping, though, and, in anticipation of just such a move by Hooker, Col. Alexander had begun digging six pits on the hill overlooking U.S. Ford. At dawn on the 5th one four-gun battery of Napoleons and a section of another were rolled into the partially completed earthworks. Across the river, about 1000 yards distant, were two Yankee batteries, which Best had placed that they could hit the Rebels on the very ground they were occupying. With the first light the Federals spotted Alexander's activity and the shooting began.

Capt. Joseph Knap, commanding one of the Yankee batteries, E, Pennsylvania Light Artillery, suggested to his fellow commander, Capt. James Thompson of Battery C, the same regiment, that the latter fling a round or so every minute to keep the Rebels off-balance. The first gun was loaded and, with a crisp boom that echoed clearly in the dawn air, it caught the Southerners unawares. A short pause, then Thompson fired again; shortly a third, and a fourth. Slowly and deliberately the men fired, and the accurately aimed shells struck the Confederate position.

About 9 o'clock Alexander attempted to counteract the Union cannonading by bringing up seven more guns, including a 24-pounder howitzer. Any advantage the Rebs obtained, however, was almost immediately offset by the ringing crashes from two more Union batteries further to the right. All of the Federal batteries were well dug in and hard to hit, so Alexander had to call off his exposed units.[46] When the command to cease fire went out to the Confederate gunners, the shooting of the campaign of Chancellorsville had all but ended. By midday of May 6th the Federal Army was plodding along the roads back to its camps opposite Fredericksburg.

As Gen. Hunt rode with that beaten Army, he was still smarting under the indirect insult he had received from Hooker. But this was more than a personal rebuff, for the whole Army had suffered from Hooker's mishandling of the artillery. Had Hunt submitted his after-action report while Hooker was still in command of the Army of the Potomac, he would no doubt have been asked to withdraw it or at least modify it. It is probable too, that in view of Hooker's popularity with a large faction of the Republican members, the Chancellorsville defeat notwithstanding, Hunt would have been sacked as a McClellan supporter, had he insisted upon his point of view. As it turned out, he was the only senior officer of the Army of the Potomac who owed his command to Mc-Clellan to still remain in a position of authority at the end of the war.

But whether by design or by fate, Hunt never committed his blunt thoughts to official paper until August 3, 1863, almost two months after Joe Hooker had been relieved from command. Its blistering nature must have raised some eyebrows in the War Department. To the detriment of the service, said Hunt, his command authority, which he had held under both McClellan and Burnside, had been taken away from him; he learned of movements which were of concern to the artillery only when they had been completed; he had received requests for artillery help when the fighting began, and he was utterly helpless to answer them; and at a critical hour he was sent off the field to command at Banks' Ford. In addition, the artillery had been badly hurt by the transfer and promotion of some of the veteran Regulars to the Volunteer service in other arms. This loss was felt most in the division artillery chief slots. Then the limits which the War Office had placed on the number of officers which the four-gun Volunteer batteries might have, plus the lack of field officers, had sharply cut into the artillery's fighting edge.

For the command and management of 9543 artillery officers and men — with 400-odd guns, 8500 horses, and the massive ammunition train — Hunt had but five field-grade officers, and, because of the scarcity of junior officers, staffs were almost nonexistent. Then Hunt concluded his report by condemning Hooker for leaving his artillery, which was engaged in a furious battle, without a commander until late in the engagement: 'I doubt if the history of modern armies can exhibit a parallel instance of such palpable crippling of a great arm of the service in the very presence of a powerful enemy. . . . It is not therefore to be wondered at that confusion and mismanagement ensued.' [47] It was indeed fortunate that under such conditions as these Hooker lost only fourteen cannon and minor quantities of other artillery matériel.

XII

AN ARTILLERYMAN HAS TO FIGHT

Gettysburg, 1st Day

IF THE morale of the Army of the Potomac was at a low point after the battle of Chancellorsville, it was certainly understandable. The Army resembled a good heavyweight fighter who knew he had a knockout punch, but who had been out-maneuvered by a fast-hitting lighter man, simply because a succession of managers had tied his hands in the ring.

In the twilight of the Chancellorsville defeat, the Federal high command attempted to discover why it had been such a fiasco. One of the first things that occurred to Union strategists was that once again the Army of the Potomac had failed to use its tremendous weight advantage — the I and V Corps had scarcely pulled trigger, while the rest of the Army had fought for its life. This fault was not restricted to the infantry. As was well known, the woods had been filled with idle bat-teries, through no fault of the battery commanders; they were simply tied to the coat-tails of the infantry generals.

Viewing the situation superficially, some Union leaders blamed much of the failure on the artillery. Lt. Col. Charles Morgan, chief of the II Corps artillery, had been personally criticized for his artillery's failure to hold back the Gray in-fantry in front of the Chancellor house, and, even though he tried to explain the situation in his official report, he knew there were those among his superiors who would not be con-vinced.

Part of the artillery idleness was instantly recognized as command error, and Hooker had tried, albeit belatedly, to remedy this by restoring Hunt to command. But questions subsequently arose as to whether the Army's artillery organization was still basically sound and whether the Army was accordingly overstrength or below strength in guns. All the artillery people knew consistently that there had been a glaringly weak link — the lack of adequate artillery staffs. But transcending this, there was now the realization that because of attrition the Federal division was no longer the battlefield factor it had been in 1862. Instead, the Army corps was becoming the basic tactical unit. Therefore, if artillery was to be utilized to the maximum degree, it followed that its movements as well as its administration should be tied to the corps. This was the same precept that had earlier dictated the elevation of battery control from regiments to brigades, then from brigades to divisions. Sooner or later it had to come again, so it is not surprising that the Army adopted on May 12, 1863, the artillery brigade organization which tied its batteries to the corps instead of the divisions.[1]

Just prior to Chancellorsville, Hunt had submitted several projects with the aim of equalizing the distribution of batteries, a program which had not been put in effect since Antietam. However, Hooker had opposed Hunt on the flimsy excuse that he did not wish to separate batteries from divisions with which they had served. Gen. Hunt had tried to show the Army commander that such a battle plan had no great validity, since under Pope much of the artillery-infantry team combinations of long standing had been upset, and they had not been reestablished prior to Antietam. Furthermore, Hooker was shown that some of his divisions had one or two batteries, while others had five or six. But 'Fighting Joe' would not change his mind until he was proved wrong in battle.

Finally, after Chancellorsville Joe Hooker was ready to admit his error, and so he sent for Henry Hunt. The artilleryman then received the commanding general's idea for reorganizing the Army's artillery: every division was to be reduced to one supporting battery; all the other batteries in the Army to be lumped together in a huge reserve! Hunt was appalled at this complete reversal of form. Realizing that such complete centralization was probably worse than the current set-up, he countered with his brigade idea and it was accepted.

Under this new plan the Army of the Potomac retained its seven infantry and one cavalry corps, with each infantry corps to have one artillery brigade, the cavalry two, and the Artillery Reserve five. The strengths of these brigades would vary, but generally they were five batteries, and the old concept of putting one Regular battery to leaven each group was retained — no doubt to the distaste of the Volunteers, who now regarded themselves, with some justification, as being every bit as good as the Regulars. These brigades were in effect battalions in the modern sense, equal to Lee's battalions. No doubt the term brigade was chosen by Hunt, who insisted these units were the equivalent to an infantry brigade, and should be commanded by men with greater rank than captain. The commander of each such brigade was to be an artilleryman, Hunt hoped, of rank commensurate to the job, and these men were to be given adequate staffs — their own medics, quartermasters, commissaries, and adjutants.

Hunt had been urging these improvements since the spring of 1862, but even now he would get only part of what he asked, for the officers assigned as brigade commanders would not receive their commensurate rank; instead, veterans with the rank of captain or even lieutenant would lead the new units onto the fields of Gettysburg. And the pressure of Lee's Army prevented much progress in the building of staffs for these officers, beyond the establishment of brigades with their commanders. These changes would definitely improve the combat efficiency of the artillery. However, it was even more vital that something be accomplished about that perennial headache — battlefield ammunition resupply.

What could conscientious battery commanders do when

they sent their caissons rearward in search of division trains and never found them available? The division batteries had been carrying their extra ammunition with the ammunition trains of the division, and as such they were under the control of an infantry officer or some staff officer detailed to the job. Quite often the responsible party was the division quartermaster, since the wagons frequently traveled with the division trains. Hunt was firmly convinced such officers were completely lacking in understanding or sympathy for the artillery needs, and might even jealously guard whatever limited autonomy they had.

Here, too, Hunt proved successful. Paragraph IV of the reorganization order provided for an artillery ammunition train to be formed for each corps and placed under the direct control of the corps chief-of-artillery — the brigade commander. This seemed to alleviate, on paper at least, most of the difficulty; but, in order to make certain his forces would have ample ammunition when the next battle came, Hunt enlisted the support of the Army quartermaster corps. From them he corralled wagons and teams, and into these he stowed for every cannon in the Army, an extra twenty rounds over and beyond the authorized campaign allowance of 250 rounds per gun. Neither Hooker nor his successor, Meade, learned of this until after the fighting at Gettysburg, where this train proved of inestimable value.

It was also believed that this new brigade system would bring such an improvement that the number of batteries could be decreased with no loss in efficiency or effectiveness. Part of such a reduction from the pre-Chancellorsville strength of over 400-odd guns had already been accomplished by the guns of the Rebels. Some of these decimated units, far understrength and unable to find replacements, were combined — as happened with Hampton's and Thompson's Pennsylvania batteries.

For the units which remained intact, it is difficult to ascertain the mechanics of how certain batteries were selected to remain with the corps and others were to go to the Artillery Reserve. It is probable that the corps chiefs were appointed first, on Hunt's recommendations, and then these officers chose the batteries they wished to retain within the number allocated to each.

All infantry corps would have artillery brigades of five batteries each, except for the VI and XII which had eight and four respectively; the cavalry corps was allotted two brigades of five and four batteries; and the Reserve ended up with five brigades totaling twenty-one batteries. In command of these brigades were two colonels, one lieutenant colonel, one major, nine captains, and one lieutenant! Thus nobody was advanced in rank as a result of the promotions in responsibility, despite Hunt's bitter complaints over this injustice. The very competent Capt. Stephen H. Weed left the artillery for an infantry command and its brigadier general's star, thereby adding his name to those of Gibbon, Getty, Hays, Ayres, Griffin, Ames, Graham, and other good artillerymen who jumped to other branches of service where there was some prospect of promotion.

In practice as well as theory, the Federals had at last caught up with Lee's able gunners in the matter of organization. Actually neither the Federal artillery brigade nor the Confederate battalion had any legal basis; they were both merely *ad hoc* creations born of necessity, and the field commanders would not worry about their legality until the job was done.

In terms of actual gun strength the Army of the Potomac would continue to out-number its adversary, though the difference between the two would be about half what it had been at Chancellorsville. This was brought about by the return to Lee's immediate command of Longstreet's absent battalions, plus a slight reduction in the number of Federal batteries. At Chancellorsville the Army of the Potomac had seventy-four batteries totaling approximately 411 guns to the Confederates' 228 pieces. In the weeks following this campaign seven Yankee batteries left the Army's rolls and eight more were so understrength that they were combined into four full units — an overall loss of eleven batteries. However, the addition of four new batteries reduced the loss to a net total of seven, giving the Army of the Potomac a strength of 366 guns [2] with which to oppose Lee's 272 cannon. Both sides would put every tube, with their infantry commands, onto the battlefield, except for the two Yankee Connecticut outfits with the eight big 4.5-inch siege rifles.

When the Army of the Potomac started out on the Gettysburg campaign, the man in the ranks was in a 'show me or else' mood; he had had just about his fill of high command ineptitude. He could not fail to see that a succession of commanders had succeeded only in squandering human lives. One member of staunch Battery B, 4th U.S., wrote after the war that the prevailing idea among the old soldiers, 'and it formed the staple of camp talk — was that the Army was being murdered by inches.' [3]

The men probably would not have been so bitter about their command if they thought they had been beaten under fair conditions, with all their forces committed. But too many instances of lost opportunities came quickly to mind: the piecemeal actions at Antietam, the failure to support Meade at Fredericksburg, the vacillation at Chancellorsville. All were common knowledge to every one in the Army. The man in the ranks was worried that the same pattern would show again in the new campaign.

Even Gen. Hunt was apparently depressed, for he later wrote that he believed the Army of the Potomac was not in good favor with the War Office and government in general. 'Rarely, if ever, had it heard a word of official commendation after a success, or of sympathy or encouragement after a defeat,' wrote Hunt in a rare moment of naïveté. [4] All the Army of the Potomac ever received, said Hunt, were accusations against its leaders of disloyalty and incompetence. A century later, it seems there was considerable justification on each side for its view.

No wonder then that when a gunner in old Battery B, 4th U.S., was heard to say just prior to the opening gun at Gettysburg, 'If we are whipped here, and I pull through it alive, I'm going to make tracks for home, and the provost-guard may be [damned].' [5] Such was the temper of the Army of the Potomac. Yet there were many able officers in that Army, and the high command must have been aware that this would be the crucial battle; the Army had placed its lives on the table once more, and if it were let down again many men would act as the gunner in Battery B and pick up what was left and go home.

So far as the Confederates were concerned, their morale was at an all-time high. Only the loss of Stonewall Jackson muffled their elation. This loss had forced Lee to reorganize his infantry from two corps to three, to be led by Gens. Longstreet, Ewell, and A. P. Hill. In addition, the Rebels shook up their artillery again. Ever aware that they would be operating under an over-all inferiority in gun strength, they had to make certain that every gun got onto the battlefield. Experience had indicated to some of Lee's younger artillery commanders that under their old Army Reserve system there was too much danger of batteries lying idle, in part because their chief-of-artillery was not an aggressive commander like Hunt. Under their new three corps set-up, each infantry corps was allotted five artillery battalions, and Stuart's cavalry received one. The total in the infantry commands was sixty-two batteries of about 245 guns, with five batteries of twenty-four guns assigned to the cavalry.

Strategically it was essential that the South undertake prompt offensive action. Supplies and subsistence were badly needed to relieve its war-torn economy; the growing peace faction in the North needed aid if it were to continue to be a factor; and it was believed that foreign recognition hinged on a successful campaign, particularly one conducted in the enemy's own yard. A number of moves in different theaters were considered, but it was decided that the cocky, competent Army of Northern Virginia carried the best odds for success. As a result Lee immediately began making preparations to invade Maryland and Pennsylvania.

The plan called for the Army to move from its position south of Fredericksburg by stages down the Valley of Virginia and along the western slope of the Blue Ridge, then across the Potomac above Washington. From here Lee would move on Harrisburg, the state capital and critical communications center for the Federals. Leaving A. P. Hill's corps to stall the Yankee Army opposite Fredericksburg, Lee began by moving Ewell on June 3rd.

Hooker shortly suspected something was happening and sent his cavalry to find out what it was. On learning that the Rebs were side-slipping away from Richmond, Hooker wanted to lunge straight for their capital, despite the fact his mission was to guard Washington and the eastern part of the United States. With Lincoln's reminder that Lee's Army not Richmond was the true objective, Hooker put his divisions on the road to shadow Lee. It then became one of those times in a campaign when soldiers do nothing but march and march; it would take almost a month of this tramping before the Army of the Potomac would catch up with its foe.

Life on the march was not always dull, though, as the men of Battery A, 1st Rhode Island Light Artillery, learned. By June 21st, the column of which the battery was a part had reached Gainesville, near the old Bull Run battlefields. While loafing around their bivouac area, some wandering Blue infantry came across an artillery projectile — it appeared to be either a shell or a case shot. Being unfamiliar with such projectiles in their unexploded form, the curious men sought out some Yankee gunners for an explanation. It so happened that the men collared as their instructor a garrulous young cannoneer of Battery A named Pvt. John Tyng — a lad described as always willing to show anyone everything pertaining to a battery and its equipment. Tyng examined the projectile, said it was not a percussion round, but one which exploded by time fuze. To illustrate his point, he carried the shell to the battery forge, where he proposed to break the projectile apart. Taking a sledge in hand Tyng hit a couple of solid licks, but he could not seem to keep the object from skidding as he hit it.

This failed to deter young Tyng, who, seeing an old railroad switch frog nearby, walked over and nestled the projectile in the frog. Again the sledge was put to work, but still the round failed to break. A couple of infantrymen tried their hand at it. Finally a brute of a man from the 1st Minnesota took the sledge and proceeded to give the shell a tremendous wallop. As the sledge struck there was a tremendous explosion, and the shell blew to bits, throwing the sledge a hundred feet or more into the air and showering the men with limbs from a nearby oak tree. There were some fifty men standing about, and miraculously not one of them was injured, though Pvt. Tyng's pride suffered considerably. Ever afterward the rest of the batterymen took great delight in walking up to Tyng with some projectile and asking, 'John, we would like you to explain how this shell is made!'

Similarly, veteran Regular Battery B camped one night near its old battleground, Second Bull Run. As the batterymen were preparing to retire for the night, several of their members, attached Volunteers from the 19th Indiana, stumbled across a skull. The soldiers, seeing a chance for some grim humor, picked up the eerie thing and calmly and quietly returned to the bivouac area. At an opportune time the pranksters slipped the skull to a spot on the ground directly in front of the sleeping face of cannoneer Augustus Buell. Then with a piece of grass they tickled Buell's ear until he awakened. The young lad opened his eyes, and there in the darkness, leering at him, was the bleached skull. Buell later admitted he had been startled, but at the time he regained his composure quickly enough to turn the joke around at the pranksters' expense by remarking that this must be a new recruit from the 19th Indiana.

As the two armies moved northward, Hooker became involved in an argument with the War Office over controlling the garrison at Harpers Ferry. Hooker wanted that post abandoned and its troops assigned to him, but Washington said it must stay as it was. Hooker thereupon resigned. On June 28th then, Maj. Gen. George Gordon Meade, a capable officer with an unfortunately violent temper, became the fourth and final commander of the Army of the Potomac.

As the month of June drew to a close, both armies were scattered across eastern Pennyslvania and Maryland; neither was quite sure where the other one was. About noon on June 30th, Federal Gen. John Buford's cavalry division clattered into a little crossroads town named Gettysburg in search of the Rebs. Buford found the town in an uproar. It was quickly learned that Confederate troops had passed through earlier and that more were reported on the western outskirts of town. So Buford trotted his forces out the Cashtown Road. A short way from town the column met a scattering of rifle and pistol shots which echoed over the quiet farms that dotted the countryside. Here and there the cavalrymen could see lines of dismounted men; closer scrutiny revealed they were infantry, and this clearly spelled trouble. Word of this discovery was quickly dispatched to Army headquarters. Gen. Buford, one of the ablest and most unappreciated officers of the Union Army, had with him two cavalry brigades and Battery A, 2nd U.S. Artillery. His men were tired and the horses jaded, but all night a constant stream of scouting parties moved in and out of town, as the Federals groped for intelligence.

Just west of Gettysburg, starting about a half-mile from town, began a series of ridges and valleys. They were the foothills of the rugged peaks of the South Mountain range, ten miles west of the village.

The easternmost of these ridges was open-wooded Seminary Ridge, so named because of the Lutheran theological school which crowned it. About 500 yards west, across a gentle little valley was a second almost parallel crest, wider, flatter, less wooded, and slightly lower than its eastern counterpart. It was sometimes known as McPherson Ridge. Both of these swells had their northern terminus on an oak-topped knoll about a mile and a quarter northwest of town called Oak Ridge. West of McPherson Ridge was the meandering little stream of Willoughby Run. And cutting across both ridges were two roads and an unfinished railroad bed, all of which led into the west edge of town. The northern-most road left Gettysburg in a northwest direction leading toward Cashtown and Chambersburg, while the second forked from the first short of Seminary Ridge and trailed away to the southwest toward Fairfield. The railroad bed paralleled the Cashtown Road a hundred yards north of it.

The day was only a few hours old on July 1, 1863, when galloping couriers brought word that Confederate infantry was moving east on the Cashtown Road toward Gettysburg. Buford, realizing that this little town — a hub of converging roads from all parts of the state — could be the critical point, was determined to hold on to it as long as he could. He asked for help from Gen. Reynolds, who was approaching the town from the south with his own I and Howard's XI Corps.

Bugles sounded, and Buford's 1st brigade deployed on both sides of the Cashtown Road on McPherson Ridge overlooking Willoughby Run. With the cavalrymen was Lt. J. A. Calef's Battery A, 2nd U.S., the only artillery in Buford's command, and the six 3-inch rifles were trotted forward to back up the line. The troopers quickly dismounted, horses were led to the rear, and the men began checking the chambers of their breech-loading carbines — a weapon with not quite the range of the infantry rifled musket but with the advantage of much more rapid fire. As Calef's guns rumbled onto the ridge, Col. Gamble, commanding the 1st brigade, met the lieutenant, acquainted him with his line, and, with rare understanding of an artilleryman's problems, told him to select his own position.

Calef's independence was brief, however, for as he began rolling his rifles into battery north of the Cashtown Road, Buford stopped him. The general ordered him to put one section on each side of the road and use the third to cover the

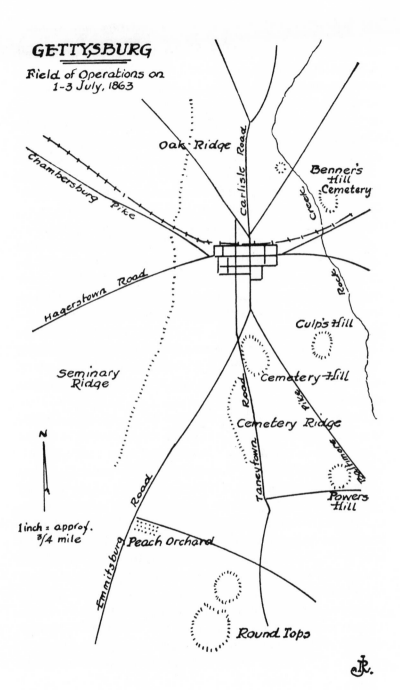

GETTYSBURG

Field of Operations on
1-3 July, 1863

Oak Ridge

Chambersburg Pike

Carlisle Road

Benner's Hill
Cemetery

Creek

Hagerstown Road

Rock

Culp's Hill

Seminary Ridge

Cemetery Hill

Cemetery Ridge

N

Taneytown Road

Baltimore Pike

Powers Hill

1 inch = approx.
3/4 mile

Emmitsburg Road

Peach Orchard

Round Tops

open ground beyond McPherson Woods about 600 yards south
of the road. The lieutenant saluted and promptly pulled his left
section over to the south edge of the rutted dirt thoroughfare,
while the center one trotted off to the indicated position just
beyond the patch of woods that divided that ridge into about
two equal parts.

The battery had scarcely set itself when a flurry of shots
racketed from in front of Willoughby Run; the Rebels had
run afoul of Buford's pickets. Shortly after, a party of mounted
Graycoats, probably staff and orderlies, trotted out on the
right shoulder of the road. Lt. John W. Roder, commanding
Calef's right section guarding that side of the highway, spotted
the horsemen and quietly gave the command to load. The two
crews quickly went through the oft-repeated rhythmic process,
and the gunners took careful aim at the Rebels. With everything ready Roder gave the brisk command: 'Number one —
Fire!' A brief pause followed; then, 'Number two — Fire!' The
two claps of thunder rolled across Willoughby Run — the first
two cannon shots of a battle that was to see the enormous total
of 50,000 rounds of artillery ammunition expended [6] before
it concluded.

Roder's fire was instantly answered by what Calef estimated
as two four-gun batteries, and shortly two brigades of Heth's
Confederate division began shaking out their battle line. It
was now about 8 a.m., and under the cover of several batteries
of their own artillery the Gray infantry came rolling forward
on both sides of the road, preceded by a mass of skirmishers.
On they came at a steady tramp, bright flags speckling the
drab lines. As they neared the creek valley, Calef's men could
hear them whooping and hollering, and their skirmishers began trading shots with the Union cavalrymen. The rate of fire
of both sides picked up, and the air about the Yankee gunners
hissed and buzzed with Minié balls and artillery shells.

Gen. Reynolds's I Corps was at this time moving toward
town from the south. However, when Reynolds received the
call for help from Buford and at the same time heard the rolling

racket of gunfire to the west, he wheeled his columns around to the west and sent them hurrying toward the battle, the general himself galloping ahead to reconnoiter.

For about an hour and a half the cavalrymen fought the Confederates. Making the most of every scrap of cover and being effectively backed by Calef's six 3-inch rifles, they were able to use their carbines to harass the Confederates who were not yet ready to brush the cavalrymen aside. Finally the troopers saw over their shoulders the long meandering columns of Wadsworth's division of the I Corps moving up the ridge to relieve them. And bumping along behind the infantry was Capt. James Hall's 2nd Maine Battery — an outfit that had shown up well at Fredericksburg. Wadsworth had two small brigades, one of which was the stalwart Iron Brigade. Keeping the Black Hat boys temporarily in reserve, the general fed the rest into the fighting south of the Cashtown Road, and Capt. Hall's guns were ordered to relieve Calef's horse battery as the Gray lines now began to push in earnest.

As the tired but still cocky cavalrymen began retiring through Wadsworth's ranks, Gen. Buford reined up beside Calef and ordered him to withdraw his pieces one at a time. First one piece, then the second of the right section cleared with no difficulty. The left section on the other side of the road prepared to move off. As the first gun began to limber up, a searing blast of musket fire cut down four of its horses, and Calef quickly sent a courier galloping to the rear for a caisson limber so that the piece might be saved. But the section was led by a determined sergeant (with only two officers present, the left and center sections were under the command of sergeants), and before the caisson limber could be brought up the sergeant had succeeded in dragging the gun off with the two remaining horses.

With two sections safe, Calef set out for his center section, down past McPherson Woods. On reaching it Calef found the two guns in a precarious situation, enemy infantry, elements of Archer's brigade, were headed straight for them, and the sergeant was holding his fire until the oncoming ranks came within canister range. This was danger enough — two rifled guns firing canister facing a horde of enemy infantry, but Calef noticed that the dismounted troopers had all but disappeared from the crest; so the section would have to fight alone. Further, the patch of woods extended right up from the bank of Willoughby Run to the top of the ridge, and by using this as cover Rebel infantry could move in close to the section's right flank. Calef decided it was foolish to risk staying and so he ordered the section to evacuate without waiting to fire its canister. The two rifles were thereupon limbered to the rear, and it soon joined the rest of the battery in checking its men and replenishing ammunition in the gun limbers from the full caissons.

By now Wadsworth's full division was spread along the battleline, and the cavalrymen were pulled back to watch the flanks north and south of town. As Wadsworth's two brigades took up the fight on both sides of the Cashtown Road, Hall's 2nd Maine Battery clanked up to where Calef had been on the roadside. Here they met Gen. Reynolds, who had assumed command of the field. The general ordered Hall to throw his guns into battery in the open field just north of the Cashtown Road, in order to divert the enemy artillery while the Blue infantry continued to deploy. With that Reynolds rode off for McPherson's Woods and the death that awaited him there.

As the battery turned off the road, six enemy guns cut loose at them from a distance of 1300 yards, but the rounds buzzed harmlessly overhead. Quickly unlimbering, Hall's crews were sent to work exchanging similar rounds with the Rebels — solid shot and shell. The Federals' first salvo forced one section of a Rebel battery to pick up its equipment and seek more sheltered ground.

For twenty minutes Hall and the enemy fought over the position. Suddenly one of his lieutenants ran up with word that the battery was being flanked. He had seen enemy troops firing into the battery's right from a ravine sixty yards distant from that flank. Hall could not believe this information was correct, even though he had had no opportunity to reconnoiter the ground himself before taking up position. No one had told him of any ravine on his flank either. (Actually the 'ravine' was an unfinished railroad bed.)

Hall spurred his horse toward the threatened point to verify the report; he got verification in the form of buzzing Minié balls from Rebel muskets. In fact the lieutenant commanding the right section had already anticipated his captain's next move, for he had swung his two guns around, and crews were already jamming double canister down the blackened bores. The two rifles roared, and the swath of pellets seemed to discourage the Rebels from advancing on the battery. But then the captain was appalled to see the Blue infantry, which was scattered all about the area, suddenly rise up, form column, shoulder their rifles, and move rearward. If, thought Hall, this position is too far forward for infantry, then certainly artillery has no business here.

Without orders, then, Hall began retiring his command by sections. The right section he ordered out first, telling it to move back seventy-five yards and then to open a covering fire for the other two. But so fast did the Blue infantry leave the area that pursuing Rebs ran forward to within musket range and shot down four horses of one right section gun. The dogged crew leaped for the stalled weapon, unlimbered it, and dragged it to the rear as the other pieces tried to keep the enemy at a distance. But, as one witness put it, it was like trying to shoot mosquitoes with a rifle.

With the crippled weapon safe, the second, third, fourth, and fifth pieces cleared the field. Then as the last rifle started to roll off, a burst of fire cut down every horse in its team. Hall jerked the rein of his horse in attempt to return to save his gun, but at that instant doughty old Gen. Wadsworth rode up, collared Hall, and told him to forget that piece and concentrate on moving the rest of the battery back to the hills beyond town where they could cover the infantry's retreat. But Hall would

concede the point only after he had left behind a sergeant and
five men to save the weapon; this done, he trotted the 2nd
Maine toward Seminary Ridge.[7]

As Hall's troops were being smacked in flank by the Rebels
in the railroad cut, a courier reined his lathered horse to a halt
beside Calef's battery, which was replenishing its ammunition
from the caissons near the seminary. The courier saluted and
delivered his message: Gen. Buford presents his compliments,
and would the captain please move a gun up to enfilade the
railroad cut; the general says enemy infantry are moving
through it.

Calef instantly barked an order, and Lt. Roder moved out
his right gun, and sent it galloping across the fields. On reaching a little rise Roder moved to the north a short distance until
he found a position from which he could sweep the cut. There
in the cut, he saw Rebel troops moving straight toward his gun.
The Yankee crew hurriedly unlimbered and in seconds the
long rammer slid down the bore and stopped with a dull thud
as the round hit bottom. Suddenly the Rebels spotted Roder,
and the Yankees plainly heard one of them holler, 'There's a
piece, let's take it.' [8]

The gun went off with a furious crash, and instantly some of
the Confederates swarmed out of the cut and made for the
gun. A cannoneer ran for another round of canister and started
back with it in his hands. A musket barked and the Blue soldier
stumbled and fell, the round still clutched in his hands. An
alert gunner who saw the man fall, ran back and seized the
canister, and hurriedly loaded the weapon. There was a brief
pause as the crew stepped clear, then flame, smoke, lead balls,
tin, and wood splinters spat from the tube and a sharp boom
set the crew in motion again. The smoke rose and the gunners
could see their foe scurrying for the cover of the bank.[9]

The Confederates seemed to be carrying the battle, though,
as Davis's brigade cleared the north end of McPherson Ridge,
driving the Federals back to Seminary Ridge. Then it was
the Federals' turn to go over to the attack. The Confederate

brigade which had advanced north of the road, parts of it using the railroad cut to force Hall from the field, now found itself caught in the flank. Archer's men south of the road — the regiments which had threatened Calef's section near McPherson Woods — also ran into serious trouble. Archer's advance up the west face of the ridge and through those woods brought him squarely up against the oncoming Iron Brigade. The Rebels fought furiously and inflicted frightful losses on the Westerners, but in turn they were almost surrounded and were forced to pull back — a badly shot-up outfit.

As the Federals retook the lost ground, Gen. Wadsworth caught sight of Calef's idle battery, and in the absence of his own guns — Hall's — the Regulars were told to bring back two sections and reoccupy the old site evacuated by the Maine men, covering the division right flank. Grimy, powder-stained hands grabbed gun wheels and handspikes, and soon Calef's four 3-inch rifles were hurling shells at the retiring enemy. But no sooner had their first round hissed through the air than some three Rebel batteries opened on their right front.

A noisy artillery fight now raged across Willoughby Run, and, just to make it a bit more dangerous for Calef's men, Rebel skirmishers kept up a severe harassing fire — the battery's twelve wounded resulted from this fire. After fifteen minutes one of the Gray batteries shifted position more to Calef's right and took up position again, under the cover of some timber. From here the sharp-eyed enemy gunners could take the Regulars partially in flank.[10]

More Confederate cannon entered the fight at various points along the front, from the Fairfield Road on the south to some distance north of the Cashtown Road.[11] Calef now found his battery in such a wicked cross-fire from the west and north that he had little choice other than to pull back and swing his guns about more to the north, using McPherson's Woods as cover for his left flank. Here the Regulars stayed until Reynolds's Battery L, 1st New York Light Artillery, relieved them.

It was now about 1 p.m., and Reynolds was dead from a

rifle bullet; Doubleday had taken command on the field. Approaching were the other two I Corps divisions under Gens. Rowley and Robinson. Rowley was moving toward Seminary Ridge with Cooper's Pennsylvania battery, while Robinson, followed by the remaining three corps brigade batteries under Col. Wainwright, was hurrying out along the Cashtown Road. At the base of Seminary Ridge Col. Wainwright pulled his three batteries off the road, while he rode forward to reconnoiter the ground. Atop the ridge he was met by one of Doubleday's staff officers, who stated that the general wished that Wainwright would place a battery on the far ridge, in the open area just north of McPherson Woods.

The artilleryman immediately sent back for Reynolds's Battery L, 1st New York, and in the meantime he himself rode forward to make a personal survey of the ground. When he reached what he believed was the intended location, the colonel was disturbed: the ground was exposed, and there was no sign of any available infantry support. Since his orders were on the discretionary side, Wainwright rode back and turned Reynolds's approaching battery around.[12]

To the south, however, Rowley's division with Cooper's battery began forming line on the left end of the contested ridge, shoving its skirmishers out under a heavy Confederate artillery fire. Soon Col. Wainwright rode up, caught sight of Cooper's guns twisting up the gentle slope, and led them into an oatfield 500 yards south of the Cashtown Road. As the sections galloped through the swaying shocks of unripe oats, the battery's bugle pierced the deeper racket of gunfire and the six pieces wheeled about. Even before the teams had been brought to a halt, cannoneers leaped from the carriages and began unlimbering their weapons.

Veteran Capt. Cooper spat commands, and with the skill of a well-trained outfit the six rifles opened a steady, rhythmic bombardment on a Confederate battery which was annoying the Federal infantry. After receiving twenty-five rounds, the Gray unit on the far side of the creek moved away. But no sooner had Cooper's people dispensed with this target than more fire opened up from their right flank. Cooper swung around to meet the new threat — Confederates firing from Oak Ridge. One of his guns snapped an axle, but the other three rolled out.

The Confederates had by this time pushed two batteries out on the forward nose of Oak Hill, their initial outburst of firing having caught the Yankees completely unawares. From this dominating high ground their rifles could shoot virtually the length of the I Corps line. The return fire by the Federals, Calef's, Cooper's and shortly Reynolds's batteries, was termed by the Rebs as slow, but one of the Gray batteries nevertheless got a good fire and lost eleven men, and one of the deploying infantry brigades — an Alabama outfit — had to retire a short distance to retain its formation.

The busy Col. Wainwright next appeared a little further up the ridge, where Calef's exhausted crews were still fighting their four guns. The hot sun was full overhead, and the cannoneers looked as if they had been splashed with soupy black paint as sweat and powder dripped from their faces. It was quite obvious Calef needed relief, so Wainwright again sent back for Reynolds's battery. With a rattling and clanking the gun carriages and limbers of Battery L, 1st Now York, bumped up the crest. Into line on the left of the road, slightly in rear of Calef's still snapping guns, went its six rifles. Smoke and battle racket were everywhere as the Federals were using every gun and musket that could be brought to bear.

The Yanks still held McPherson Ridge south of the Cashtown Road, but otherwise their position was none too good. Clouds of dust to the north and south told of more Rebel brigades being fed into the fight on the Federal flanks. The high ground of Oak Ridge was already in enemy hands, as the Blue batteries on McPherson Ridge had found out. And, unknown to the Federals, Confederate corps commander A. P. Hill was preparing to put all of his weight behind a push from the west. Hill had two full artillery battalions with which to launch his

attack. Capt. Reynolds's New Yorkers found this out as they
unlimbered. The lead section had scarcely uncoupled when a
blast of artillery fire from their front hit them, and seconds later
more salvos from the north ripped through both Reynolds's
and Calef's position.

Reynolds tried to bring his guns into full action but the position was a death trap. The ridge here was open, and the Confederate shells were sweeping it like a broom. Caught in this
wicked cross-fire the two Blue batteries were driven from the
ridge, Capt. Reynolds being severely wounded in the process.

The Confederates clearly outnumbered the defending Bluecoats, and slowly but steadily the Gray line was extending itself more to the north and east as Ewell's advance elements
came down the west face of Oak Ridge to take the Yanks in
flank. Old Wadsworth saw things slipping and looked around
for more artillery to hold back the Gray masses. There were
now no Yankee batteries in action on the north end of the
Union line, and they were badly needed. The general recalled
that Hall's unit had been in action and was probably still available somewhere in the rear. He ordered one of his aides to find
Hall and bring him through the railroad bed.

The officer caught Hall's unit as it was nearing Cemetery
Hill, a commanding rise south of town, and delivered the order.
With muffled curses about the high command's lack of ability
to make up its mind, the drivers turned their teams around.
Following the general's order, the staff officer led Hall out of
town via the railroad bed just north of the Cashtown Road. The
battery trotted along the road bed until the route gradually
turned into a cut as it traversed Seminary Ridge. As the column
reached the top of the cut, they were immediately visible to
the enemy, and suddenly Hall's men found themselves the
choice target for some Rebel gunners in a position to shoot
down the length of that slash through the ridge.

Hall was trapped. The banks on both sides were steep and
high, so there was no turning off; the bed was narrow, so there
was no chance to turn around — the only thing to do was

keep going. The command was given, and drivers hooted and yelled at their teams. Gradually the column picked up speed, and cannoneers grabbed the seat handles. For 1200 yards the battery went at a full gallop, finally emerging from the cut miraculously unscathed. Here, on the south end of the prolongation of Oak Ridge, Hall looked about in vain for someone to tell him where his guns were needed. Parking his unit behind the sheltering hill the captain trotted forward to look for a position.

Just then Hall bumped into one of Wadsworth's staff officers. From him the captain learned his battery was wanted on McPherson Ridge. Returning to his unit Hall waved the column forward, and the 2nd Maine cleared the rise, passed across the valley in front, and began the ascent of McPherson Ridge.

Suddenly a Federal orderly rode by, frantically waving his arm and shouting to Hall that he was moving straight into the Rebel lines. Hall was puzzled and halted his column. To confirm the orderly's warning he rode forward for a closer look; the zip-zip of passing bullets immediately made it clear to him that the soldier knew what he was talking about. Rapidly turning his battery about, Hall led it galloping back to Seminary Ridge. Here they met Col. Wainwright who hollered to Hall that his lost gun was still standing unclaimed in the field of the morning's action. This was a challenge Hall could not refuse. Cutting out a limber and taking a sergeant with him, Capt. Hall galloped back to McPherson Ridge, recovered the weapon, and gleefully hauled it back past Wainwright's admiring eye. The column then resumed its twice-interrupted march for Cemetery Hill.

On Cemetery Hill the serviceable remnants of the 2nd Maine Battery — three undamaged pieces — were emplaced by Gen. Howard's order, in position south of the cemetery. In the day's fighting Hall had lost eighteen men wounded and four captured; twenty-eight horses killed and six wounded; one gun useless and two badly damaged with broken axles — a considerable amount of wreckage for about two hours of actual fighting.

The Federal I Corps had its hands full with Rebels pushing them from the west and the north. Robinson's division had entered the battle on the right of the line to try to stem the threat to that flank. In addition, Howard's XI Corps, bearing the Army's cross of Chancellorsville on its back, had finally reached the field. One division, Von Steinwehr's, was held out as a reserve on Cemetery Hill, but the other two were hurrying through town for the open ground beyond.

As A. P. Hill's brigades put on the pressure from the west, the Yankee high command became more anxious about the high ground south of town. If Seminary Ridge was lost, it would be bad enough, but Cemetery Hill, south of town, had to be retained if Lee was to be stopped. Accordingly the order was given that, in the event the Federals were forced from the ridges west of Gettysburg, they would rally on Cemetery Hill, which had to be held at all costs.

Col. Wainwright, the I Corps artillery commander, happened to hear this warning given to Gen. Doubleday, but the colonel knew nothing of the existence of Cemetery Hill and assumed they were speaking of Seminary Ridge. Wainwright promptly made ready to have his guns defend Seminary Ridge to the last means. Riding forward Col. Wainwright located Cooper's battery and sent it scurrying back to the ridge to take up position near the school buildings. Another I Corps battery, Leppien's old 5th Maine, now commanded by Capt. Greenleaf T. Stevens, was pulled from reserve to a point about 200 yards east of the seminary, replacing Battery B, 4th U.S., which was then dispatched to help Robinson's division.

Battery L, 1st New York, which earlier in the day had been forced to retire some 500 yards to escape an enemy cross-fire, was then moved up to the open ground south of McPherson Woods. A call from Wadsworth for artillery to cover the left flank of the line dictated detaching one of Battery L's sections under Lt. Wilbur. The lieutenant went into position with two

3-inch rifles in an orchard, with a few farm buildings to cover his right — flimsy shelter, but at least something to hide him from the Gray guns west of Willoughby Run.

These dispositions had just been completed when into view on the Cashtown Road came a dense column of Confederate infantry. It shortly turned off the road to the right, and thus gradually extended the Gray line well beyond the Yankee left. At that point the column wheeled into double line of battle. Another short pause and the lines began to move; Battery L had begun jerking its lanyards as soon as the Rebs came into sight, but some odds and ends of Federal infantry, milling about in front of their position, hindered the battery's efforts to shoot. In fact, Col. Wainwright could see no formal Blue infantry line at all on that ridge. When the steadily advancing Rebel ranks reached a point 200 yards away, the colonel sent the battery galloping back to Seminary Ridge — the ridge he thought was to be held at all costs.

It was about this time that cocky Battery B, 4th U.S. — supposedly a Regular battery, but with its ranks about half-filled with detached Volunteers from the rugged Iron Brigade — joined the fight. The Union generals, caught earlier in the day by their failure to cover the railroad cut, now figured to block this avenue with Battery B's Napoleons. The battery's commander, Capt. James Stewart, split his troops into half-batteries, or two groups of three guns each, and he himself led the right half to a site on the north side of the railroad bed. The left half, under Lt. Davison, unlimbered in wide interval just west of Mrs. Thompson's house south of the cut about a hundred yards east of Stewart's group. Davison lined his guns directly west so as to take the Cashtown Road at a slight angle, his caissons under cover of the Thompson buildings and the slope in rear.

One cannoneer, noticing the abundance of Federal infantry in their rear behind the crest and in the cut, facetiously remarked that these were placed there to shoot down any faint-hearted recruits on the crews. Battery B was a tough outfit,

and most of its members did not take kindly to any disparage-
ments of its fighting qualities — even if such remarks came
from one of its own members. A grim-faced corporal thereupon
looked the man square in the eye, and told him to see that he
himself behaved as well as the recruits.[13]

The guns were all on fairly high ground, and the crews could
see the infantry battle rising in fury. It began as a bitter snapping between skirmishers, but then the main Gray battle line
began to roll. At first just the tops of their flags were visible,
then the glint of bayonets, then their heads, and over the far
ridge they came in steady cadenced step — a yelling battle line
almost a mile wide.

On this hot day Battery B's crews, their jackets off and
their shirt-sleeves rolled up, heard the terse commands: 'Load,
double canister!' Rammers seated the rounds with a wisp-
thump. And chiefs-of-piece raised their arms with cries of
'Ready.' The wide battle line came on. Davison waited a
few moments more; then his order to fire brought the big
Napoleons into action with shuddering concussion. The clouds
of canister cleared the road in front, while the zip-zip of bullets about the gun crews rose in intensity. Lt. Davison personally stopped two bullets.

While the Confederates were being denied the use of the
road and of the cut by the storm of canister from Battery B,
they were able to make progress on Davison's left flank. The
lieutenant, badly wounded and staying on his feet only with
the assistance of one of the men, yelled for the left piece to
shift about from its position almost in the road. This done,
the three Napoleons now faced south, dead on the flank of a
long wavering line of charging Confederates trying to crash
the Federal ranks in front of the seminary.

For about five to ten minutes Battery B was in as vicious a
fight as it had been in the cornfield at Antietam. At close
range, with no cover for either antagonist, muskets banged
singly and in ear-splitting volleys, and bright jets of flame

leaped like lightning from the mouths of the Napoleons. Every cannoneer worked at utmost effort, his motions coming as reflex actions born of hours of practice; there was no skulking for anyone, as one man later wrote, for each gun crew was an interlocking team with every man in plain view of the other, which meant 'an artilleryman has to fight.' [14]

Double canister tore gaps in the Confederate ranks, and wounded units on the Rebel flank wheeled about to hit back. The Gray regiments originally in front of Davison's three pieces — now on their flank following the guns' change of position — took advantage of the diversion to slam volleys into Davison's right. All that saved the unit was two Union regiments, which scrambled over from the north side of the cut and waded into the caldron of flying lead and iron.

To the south of the road the leading Rebel wave was gored, then stopped, but their fire line continued to blaze away from a hundred or so yards in front. By now Lt. Davison had collapsed from his wounds, and a sergeant had assumed command of the three guns. At this point a second line of Confederate infantry was spotted moving up to the attack. With his ammunition low and casualties heavy, the sergeant ordered the guns limbered to the rear, a move which his captain was already performing on the north side of the railroad bed.

Around the seminary grounds proper the rest of the I Corps artillery was also finding the day a rough one. Gathered together in a tight group with a bare five yards between wheels was one mass of eleven guns — Cooper's three serviceable 3-inch rifles; six Napoleons of the 5th Maine Battery on Cooper's right; and the two rifles of Lt. Wilber's section of Battery L, 1st New York, which had fallen back from McPherson Ridge. And somewhere nearby was the balance of Battery L. As the Confederate attack which had threatened Battery B rolled toward Seminary Ridge, these guns threw out a curtain of case and shell. At some points the combined Blue infantry-artillery fire beat the advance back, at others the bounding line kept advancing. As it closed, the batteries switched to canister, and from across the road Davison's three Napoleons took the line in flank.

It was touch and go for awhile, and, though the Union line held, it was obvious it would be just a matter of time before the whole position would have to be abandoned — distant booming of cannon and swirling clouds of dirty smoke told of heavy fighting north of town. There the unhappy XI Corps had been thrown in to stop Early's division of Ewell's corps arriving from York and Harrisburg.

Just before 4 p.m. the decision was made to evacuate Seminary Ridge and retreat through town to the chain of hills of which Cemetery Hill was a part. The order went down to the infantry to fall back, but somehow Col. Wainwright never received the order. The first he knew of it was when he saw the 5th Maine limber up and start for the road. On questioning Capt. Stevens, he was told that Gen. Wadsworth had given the retirement order. Puzzled, but still under the impression he was on the hill which was to be defended to the last, Wainwright ordered the other batteries to stand fast.

For some reason the Confederates were not pressing their attack at that moment, otherwise most of the I Corps guns would probably have been seized. Instead, Wainwright spotted the long twisting ribbons of Blue infantry descending to the fields west and south of town. Convinced now of his folly, the colonel limbered his batteries and moved them at a walk down the Cashtown Road.[15]

Only as the column of rolling batteries neared the town did the Confederates threaten them. Numbers of them ran pell-mell down Seminary Ridge across the fields until they were within musket range of the column. At this point they opened a galling fire on the rearmost units, and they were soon supported by a couple of pursuing Rebel batteries, which opened a hurried fire from the captured ridge. The Blue units quickly broke into a fast trot, but it was too late to save everything. It was the usual story: The Confederates shot down horses right and left, and Battery B had to abandon three caissons, while a fourth took a direct hit and blew up, and Lt. Wilber had to abandon a teamless gun. When Col. Wainwright finally took stock, he found his brigade had lost about eighty officers and men and an equal number of animals during the day.

What had actually precipitated this retreat from Seminary Ridge was the collapse of the Union position on the north side of town. When it was learned that Confederate units in considerable strength were approaching Gettysburg from the north, the Federals had tried to spread their thin I Corps line to cover the threat. Then, as the XI Corps marched into Gettysburg, two of its divisions were hurried to the open ground north of town. However, Confederate Gen. Ewell, bringing Rodes's division along the Mummasburg Pike, had spotted the value of Oak Hill — the northern terminus of both McPherson and Seminary Ridges — and had instantly planted some of his artillery on it. His infantry then formed on both sides of the hill and moved south to strike the Federal right. It was about 2:30 p.m. when this attack finally started rolling.

The two XI Corps divisions, Barlow's and Schimmelpfennig's, were originally to prolong the I Corps line onto Oak Hill, but Ewell's seizure of that ground forced the Bluecoats to form line in the generally flat farmland short of the ridge within easy range of the Confederate batteries on the forward slopes of Oak Hill. The XI Corps had barely shaken its brigades out of column, Barlow on the right and Schimmelpfennig on the left, when the Confederate attack came booming down on them. The Germans cocked their muskets and let fly, determined this would be no Chancellorsville.

Gen. Schurz, commanding the XI Corps after Howard replaced the fallen Reynolds, had sent forward three of the Corps' five batteries, retaining the other two with a division as reserve on Cemetery Hill. One of the batteries sent forward was Capt. Hubert Dilger's. As the deployment was underway, Schurz indicated to the captain that the corps' line would be between the Mummasburg and Harrisburg Roads, and he ordered Dilger to unlimber wherever he thought advisable — a rare exhibit of confidence in an artilleryman's ability. Dilger scanned the terrain, and then sent one of his sections forward on the left to help hold a small rise of ground on the north edge of town. No sooner had the two Napoleons reached the place than a Confederate battery spotted them and opened with such fury that Dilger had to commit his other four guns to keep the section from being blown to bits.

Offsetting this reinforcement, the Confederates thereupon rolled out another battery, bringing some eight pieces into action against Dilger. But the German was a redoubtable gunner, and odds of eight to six carried no weight with him, even if the range was 1400 yards — about the maximum for his Napoleons. Fourteen guns raged and bit at each other. One eager Rebel captain moved two of his pieces forward to within 1000 yards of Dilger. But the Germans seem to have had the better aim, with Dilger claiming five enemy carriages disabled before the Rebels decided to give up the duel.

A new threat quickly arose, though. The Confederates had trotted out some rifled guns, and it was not long before the earth about Dilger's position began to show ugly furrows from the elongated projectiles which were tearing into the ground. Under these circumstances, the German asked for help from Capt. Osborn, chief of XI Corps artillery. That officer quickly dispatched Wheeler's 13th New York Battery, formerly Dieckman's outfit, with orders to place themselves under Dilger's command. As Wheeler's column rattled out of town, they found the road extremely rough, and there was a brief flurry of commotion as two caissons broke down under the strain. But Wheeler waved his four rifles forward, figuring to recover the damaged vehicles later.

Wheeler's battery raced across the open ground, and, spotting Dilger, swung into line on his right. Dilger pointed out the target, and Wheeler's gunners began ranging in on the Gray cannon. As soon as the distant flashes and puffs of smoke of exploding shells showed they were on target, Wheeler gave orders to 'pour it on.'

With the enemy fully occupied by Wheeler's fire, Dilger saw the chance to move his own Napoleons forward to within effective range. With shouted commands the six guns limbered up and forward they went — 400 yards closer to the enemy. At one point Dilger had to halt his unit, under the enemy's fire and some shorts from Wheeler's guns, while a ditch that barred his way was shoveled in. At last, in a green wheatfield the Ohioans dropped their trails and opened fire on Oak Ridge.

Now it was Wheeler's turn. Following Dilger's route and covered by its partner's fire, the 13th New York galloped into the wheatfield and unlimbered fifty yards to Dilger's right. The two batteries then drenched the air with their crashes and clouds of sulphurous smoke.

Ewell's attack had some initial success, but a solid Yankee counterpunch rocked the Gray line and sent parts of it sprawling back in complete rout. At this point, though, another of Ewell's divisions came pounding down the Harrisburg Road headed smack for the flank and rear of the XI Corps. But colorful Yankee general Francis Barlow decided to move his division onto a low knoll that would take his name, and here to anchor his right.

In support of Barlow atop this knoll was Battery G, 4th U.S., under the command of Bayard Wilkeson, a nineteen-year-old lad who had been appointed a lieutenant in the Regular Army in the fall of 1861. His father, a war correspondent for the *New York Times,* was at this hour at Meade's headquarters, unaware that that night he would have to write his son's obituary. Peeling off a section to cover the Harrisburg Road and the corps right flank from a position just northeast of the county poorhouse, Wilkeson took his other two sections up onto the knoll 600 yards further north. Immediately the unit became embroiled in a fire fight with the Rebel batteries.

Wilkeson's pieces had barely shot their first salvo when the young lieutenant collapsed to earth, an ugly wound in his right leg from a Rebel shell which had mangled his horse as well. The command fell to Lt. Eugene A. Bancroft, as Wilkeson, mortally wounded, was carried from the field by four of his men. That night, according to one account, the young officer lay in the poorhouse, then serving as a crude field hospital for the wounded of both sides. In his dying moments Wilkeson asked for some water; a canteen was brought, but as he feebly reached for it a wounded man next to him pleaded for a drink. Wilkeson thereupon passed the untouched canteen to the soldier, who drained every drop. The lieutenant watched quietly, smiled, turned slightly, closed his eyes and died.[16]

The arrival of Early's division astride the Union right gave the Rebels the advantage for the day. Putting Jones's battalion of twelve guns in action east of the Harrisburg Road, Early then moved his infantry out under this covering fire to try and crack Barlow's line. By 4 o'clock, the Gray attack had begun to close on Barlow. The fire of Jones's battalion raked part of the Federal line and gave Bancroft's two sections a particularly bad time. Only by constantly shifting position could the Regulars stay in action. Some of Jones's fire spilled over to Dilger's and Wheeler's positions, in the gap between the left of the XI Corps and the right of the I Corps, and added to the discomfort they were already feeling from Carter's guns on Oak Hill.

Both Dilger and Wheeler were taking casualties. Wheeler, being on Dilger's right, swung his own right section about to see if he could slow up the Rebel barrage. Shell continued to whoosh into the wheatfield, and one of them put a Napoleon of Dilger's out of action. Horses and men in both units went down under the heavy rain of iron. Dilger, a determined fighter, never liked to quit a field because of lack of ammunition, so all afternoon he had been shuttling three caissons up to his gun limbers to keep up the supply. In spite of this, he nearly ran out twice, and in addition, the fuzes were working poorly. Nonetheless, the German kept his guns snapping back.

Early's attack forced cracks in the Union line north of town.

The Germans had been determined this would be no Chancellorsville, but once again they were outnumbered and caught in flank. There was only one thing to do: fall back on Cemetery Hill. To cover the retirement, Capt. Heckman's Battery K, 1st Ohio Light Artillery, was hurried down from the cemetery and put into position on the north fringe of town near Gettysburg College. From here they were able to throw shells at the distant Rebel line as it slowly forced the XI Corps back.

The 5th battery of the XI Corps was Wiedrich's I, 1st New York, and, along with Heckman's and Von Steinwehr's infantry division, it had been wisely left in reserve on Cemetery Hill. Wiedrich had been waging a sporadic long range sparring with Early's batteries until the distant Blue line began to withdraw toward Gettysburg. At this point Wiedrich shifted his fire to the Rebel infantry, and it appeared to the German gunners that their shells were bursting right on target. But it would take more than Wiedrich's six 3-inchers to halt the growing momentum of the Rebel sweep into the town.

On the XI Corps left, Dilger and Wheeler began pulling back, once again using their successful leap-frog tactic to cover each other's withdrawal. It did not prove altogether foolproof, though, for a Rebel shell plowed into one of Wheeler's rifles, completely dismounting it. The captain instantly had its crew sling the tube under a limber by use of ropes, in accordance with the procedure set forward in the manual, but the heavy piece of iron refused to stay secured and was finally abandoned.

At the edge of town Dilger cut out a section of his own battery and one from Wheeler's, and sent the balance of the two units trotting toward Cemetery Hill. With these four remaining guns Dilger opened a furious covering fire for the retreating infantry. The last of the Blue units finally passed Dilger's smoking weapons, and Dilger immediately waved Wheeler's two rifles off the field, as, at the point-blank range which now existed, he considered these guns useless. After a few more rounds of canister from his two Napoleons, Dilger limbered the guns and galloped back into the streets of town. He found the road choked with hurrying troop columns, artillery, ambulances, and stragglers. At a street corner his forces met a section of Wilkeson's guns, which was apparently prepared to fight a rearguard action right in the town. There was not much hope of moving through this jam, so Dilger swung his column of two guns to the left at the next intersection and galloped clear around town, finally rejoining the rest of his unit on Cemetery Hill. Taking stock of his losses, he found fourteen men casualties, twenty-four horses disabled, and one gun out of action.

Heckman's Ohio battery had had a close call, too. The unit had held on until the last minute, throwing canister as fast as the crews could load and shoot. For thirty minutes they stood firm, expending in that time 113 rounds — most of it canister. By the time Heckman received the order to retire, it was almost too late, for while they were limbering their guns, jubilant Rebel infantry waded into them. The Ohio battery attempted to wiggle clear as the rifle troops cut and hacked at each other, yelled and screamed, and shot at close range. Finally Heckman extricated two of his Napoleons, but the other two were irretrievably lost. The remnants then clattered through Gettysburg. Heckman's losses turned out to be moderate — fifteen men casualties, nine horses dead — yet apparently the battery was now considered of questionable combat reliability, for it was sent to the rear and fought no more at Gettysburg.[17]

The day was now lost for the Federals. As the retiring Blue columns hurried through the streets of Gettysburg, there was much milling and confusion: units lost their way, stumbled into dead-end streets, or made wrong turns and ran back into the pursuing Rebels. Losses in captured infantry ran quite high, but miraculously there were no further artillery losses for either the I or XI Corps — a rather amazing occurrence since the batteries were among the last Federal troops off the battle ground, and since they were clumsy units to move through choked streets. While the pursuing Rebels contented themselves with nabbing the straggling and lost Yankee troops in the streets of Gettysburg, the two shaken Union artillery corps withdrew to the environs of Cemetery Hill. Here they were quickly deployed to protect the height from an expected follow-up attack which never came.

Ewell's failure to pursue Lee's 'if practicable' order for continuing the assault against Cemetery Hill that evening has been a leading source of controversy among people writing about the Civil War. Authorities have argued over what would have happened if Ewell had attacked, and they have attempted to fix the location of the respective forces to support their position. However, there seems to have been little attention to a crucial consideration: how much ammunition was available to the Federal troops who would have had to withstand such an assault. Five divisions of Yankee troops, regardless of their size, would have been of little consequence if they had had no ammunition, or enough for one meager volley and no more. Not only how much artillery did the Federals have to repel an attack, but how much ammunition was available?

The Federals had put eleven batteries into the day's fighting, five each to the two infantry corps and Calef's to the cavalry. This was a total of sixty guns. Of the five I Corps units totaling twenty-eight cannon, seven had been either disabled or lost, and there had been some eighty personnel casualties — about 15 per cent of their strength. Then, too, chances are that all the I Corps unit had quite thoroughly depleted the ammunition stocks existing in their limbers and caissons. Cooper reported an expenditure of 400 rounds; Hall fired 635 for two days, though most of it no doubt was shot on July 1st; and Stewart, in addition to being heavily engaged, lost four caissons, so his ammunition was undoubtedly low. Data on the expenditures for the 5th Maine and Reynolds's L, 1st New York, are not available, but both units were hotly engaged for times during the afternoon. However, Col. Wainwright was astute enough to look into this question almost immediately, and even though his own I Corps train had not arrived, he was able to have his batteries replenish their stocks from Maj.

Osborn's XI Corps wagons, which were on the field. In effect, then, the I Corps batteries were probably in fairly good condition.

In the XI Corps the story was pretty much the same. Of their five batteries of twenty-six pieces, four were lost or disabled. Though Heckman's two Napoleons had been sent to the rear, they could have been used in an emergency, making a total of twenty-two cannons available. While Dilger, Wheeler, and Wilkeson had been in hard fighting, they were all still very much ready for combat, even though they had suffered from 10 to 15 per cent casualties — only half of what is generally considered the critical breaking point for unit effectiveness. With the corps' ammunition train readily available, too, the XI Corps batteries could probably have hurt any Rebel attack waves badly. And Calef's battery, which had helped the I Corps for part of the morning, had now been returned to the cavalry command and was watching the Army's flank.

In summary, had Ewell's troops charged that hill, they would have faced forty-one guns, all well-sighted. About half this number were deadly Napoleons — the ideal gun for this type of 'close in' defensive fighting. Chances are Ewell would have suffered considerably from their fire and, if his forces had faced equally determined resistance from the Blue infantry, the attack might have been beaten off. In any case, it certainly would have been no walk-in for the Rebels.

XIII

DON'T LET THEM TAKE MY GUNS AWAY

Gettysburg, 2nd Day

BY SUNDOWN of July 1st, Confederate troops were in possession of all the ground formerly held earlier in the day by the I and XI Corps, and the battered brigades of these two commands had retired through Gettysburg to Cemetery Hill. There they were met by Gens. Howard and Hancock, who had hurriedly rigged them into a battleline on the heights. Units from the I Corps were planted astride Cemetery Ridge, with detachments garrisoning Culp's Hill to the east; between these two points, along East Cemetery Hill, the XI Corps was placed. All batteries of these corps, except for Heckman's Ohio outfit, were spotted along the high ground. Some of the batteries were not in top condition, but all of them were frantically patching their wounds, replenishing ammunition, and digging in their guns.

Early that evening Gen. Hancock, in Meade's absence and at his direction, looked over the ground; Hancock liked the set-up and promptly advised Meade that this was a good spot to stand and fight. Actually, because of urgent calls for help from the battleground during the day, four Union infantry corps were by nightfall either at or approaching Gettysburg; it remained only for Meade to order up his other three, and this he did later that night. On the Confederate side of the field, two of Ewell's divisions were holding the line north of town, with his third expected shortly. To the west was A. P.

Hill's corps; Pender's division was astride Seminary Ridge; Heth's division was regrouping on Herr Ridge, and R. H. Anderson's was hurrying east from Cashtown. Lee's other corps, Longstreet's, was bringing up the Army's rear in the vicinity of Chambersburg.

While the Confederate commander had reached the field around 3 p.m., Meade did not arrive until about midnight. He then opened his headquarters in a hollow just east of Cemetery Ridge. In concert with Gen. Hancock and the Army's engineer officer, Gen. Warren, Meade ordered a line organized from the two high knolls three miles south of town called the Round Tops, northward along a low broad crest called Cemetery Ridge, to the higher ground of Cemetery Hill; from here the line would swing eastward to take in the elevations of East Cemetery Hill and Culp's Hill — the now famous 'fish hook line.' The weary troops of the other corps plodded on the field and were quickly moved into position along the widening Union lines. By the following morning only the V and VI Corps and the Artillery Reserve had not reached Gettysburg.

However, during the night of July 1st, the Federal artillery commanders had done a good job of putting strength where it was needed along the line. Col. Wainwright, the I Corps chief-of-artillery, had dug his corps' guns in on the hill north of the Baltimore Pike — seventeen pieces in all.[1] The XI Corps batteries under Maj. Osborn were planted further to the west, in the cemetery proper — fifteen guns. Later that morning when Gen. Hunt inspected the lines, he felt the XI Corps front was undergunned, so he reinforced Osborn with the three-piece remnant of Hall's 2nd Maine and with five batteries from the Artillery Reserve. This brought the total gun strength along the center of the loop to forty-six tubes.[2] Another weakness the artillery chief spotted that morning was a yawning gap between Slocum's XII Corps, which had taken station on Culp's Hill, and the I Corps elements on East Cemetery Hill. Gen. Hunt promptly adjusted some of the XII Corps batteries so that part of their twenty pieces could sweep that opening.[3] And midway between these and Wainwright's guns, Stevens's 5th Maine Battery had been plunked down on the face of a little knoll from which they could bring an oblique fire on the east face of East Cemetery Hill.

As the sun climbed over the eastern horizon that July 2nd, the Union command was in some doubt about what their next move should be. The Confederates were believed to have superior strength, yet at one point Meade considered attacking Ewell with just the V and XII Corps. On the advice of his chief engineer, Gen. Warren, he soon abandoned this plan. It was decided instead to await Lee's next move.

Sometime during the morning a disturbed Meade rode up to Hunt with the report that the entire artillery ammunition train of one of the corps had been left behind. Some of the others did not appear much better off, either. The commanding general was most concerned that the heavy expenditures of the day before would not leave artillery ammunition to carry the Army through a heavy battle. What was Hunt's opinion? Hunt was ready with an answer. Earlier that morning when he had sent for the Reserve he had instructed Gen. R. O. Tyler, commanding that body, that no matter what else he had to leave behind he was to bring forward every last round of ammunition in his trains; and it must have been now that Hunt told Meade about the twenty-extra-rounds-per-gun which he arranged for. The artilleryman thus assured his commander that there would be ample ammunition on hand, but, he cautioned, 'none for idle cannonades, the besetting sin of some of our commanders.'[4] Reassured on this point, Meade continued his preparations to stand and fight.

All went according to plan, and the troop deployment continued unhindered until early afternoon. At that time Gen. Dan Sickles, commanding the III Corps, nearly upset Meade's plans. That officer had been told to throw his men into a line from the Round Tops northward across a stretch of lower ground until his right linked with the left of Hancock's II Corps on Cemetery Ridge. However, dissatisfied with the terrain, Sickles moved to higher ground crowned by a peach orchard 800 yards in front of his assigned position. He then rode to Meade's headquarters to get approval.

Sickles was pleading his point with Meade at the time that Hunt had been making the check of the Federal artillery positions — a task which Meade had asked Hunt to do and which the artilleryman interpreted as a re-recognition of his command of the Army's artillery. When Henry Hunt returned to headquarters, he found Sickles still deep in discussion with Meade. Turning to the artilleryman, Meade announced that Sickles would like to have Gen. Hunt inspect the line that officer had occupied with his III Corps; Sickles explained the location originally assigned him placed the III Corps artillery at a distinct disadvantage, because it would be dominated by higher ground in front.

Hunt thereupon rode out with Sickles to the peach orchard. The artillery commander instantly saw that Sickles had a point, even though the new position created a sharp salient. If, thought Hunt, such a line were held in sufficient strength and tied to the Round Tops on the left and to Hancock's II Corps on the right, it would be acceptable. But Hunt probably realized that the III Corps alone was not strong enough to man such a front, and he probably questioned whether Meade had enough troops to reinforce Sickles adequately. Another factor which Hunt called to Sickles's attention was that there was a heavy wood directly west of the angle of the proposed line. If the Rebels controlled those woods, they could make it extremely difficult for Sickles to hold or strengthen the angle. Would it not be a good idea to find out if the enemy were there? Sickles agreed and called for prowling parties.

As the two officers awaited the results of this reconnaissance, heavy gunfire erupted to the north, and Hunt now felt obliged to return to Army headquarters. As he turned to leave, Sickles spoke out to ask whether the III Corps should be moved out to the new line. 'Not on my authority,' retorted Hunt, though he agreed to acquaint Meade with the layout. With that he trotted off.[5] Now, a crisp outburst of riflery from the woods being reconnoitered gave Sickles his answer: The Confederates held that crucial ground. But the corps commander, pondering reports that came back of enemy troops massing to the southwest, finally took it upon himself to push his III Corps out to the new position — occupied woods and sharp salient notwithstanding.

As a result of Sickles's action, one of his divisions, Humphrey's, went out to the Emmitsburg Road and formed line of battle facing west, its left near the peach orchard. Birney's division prolonged the line from the orchard southeast to the rugged rocky area now known as Devil's Den. This was the longest part of the corps' line and therefore the thinnest; eventually a brigade would be hauled over from Humphrey's front to stiffen it. Sickles now had his high ground, but in getting it he had opened a gap between his right and the II Corps, as well as creating a salient whose faces could be enfiladed, and had also left unmanned the crests of the dominating Round Tops.

Sickles's artillery chief, Capt. George E. Randolph, was delighted with the chance to get his guns on higher ground, and immediately the captain began shifting his batteries forward. Smith's 4th New York Battery, the same unit that had caused a dispute over its officers during the Chancellorsville campaign, was placed on the extreme left of the line, just west of Little Round Top, atop a rocky ledge where its rifles could by an oblique fire command the open fields in front of Birney's regiments. Northwest of Smith, beyond Devil's Den, in 'The Wheatfield,' surrounded by woods, Capt. Randolph placed Winslow's Battery D, 1st New York. It was a tricky spot with timber all about, but the captain believed his six Napoleons would offer good support to the Blue infantry in front of them. Further west of Winslow, in a larger wheatfield, was Clark's Battery B, New Jersey Light Artillery, with six 10-pounder Parrotts. All three of these batteries faced south or southwest, the direction from which a Confederate attack was expected.

The west face of Sickles's angled line near the orchard was backed up by Battery E, Rhode Island Light Artillery — six Napoleons, under Lt. John K. Bucklyn, the same officer who had held a section in the road near the Chancellor house covering the retreat from Fairview. Bucklyn's guns were disposed along the Emmitsburg Road about fifty yards north of the peach orchard.

Actually, part of this posting had been done under the eye of Gen. Hunt who had ridden up as some of the batteries were trotting across the fields. The artillery chief, after determining that nothing serious seemed to be in the making on the north end of the line, had become anxious over Sickles's proposed position and decided to return to that area. As he rode up, Capt. Randolph spotted him and galloped over to ask the general's approval of some gun locations in the orchard suggested by Sickles. Dismounting, the two officers walked into the grove; Hunt paused a moment, looked the ground over, then remarked that, as long as Sickles had ordered guns placed in this general area, the spot was as good as he could find. However, Hunt noticed that Randolph did not have enough firepower in the corps artillery brigade to cover the front properly. To make up the shortage, Hunt immediately sent to Gen. Tyler commanding the Artillery Reserve for two batteries, one of Napoleons and one of rifles. At the same time he sent word to Gen. Humphreys to call for batteries from the Reserve as he needed them.

Around 3 p.m. Lt. Col. Freeman McGilvery, commander of the 1st Volunteer Artillery Brigade of the Reserve, trotted in with three batteries in tow: Bigelow's rookie 9th Massachusetts, and two veteran outfits, Phillips's 5th Massachusetts and Hart's 15th New York Battery — all from the 1st Volunteer Brigade.[6] Hunt and McGilvery promptly began filling out Birney's front by running the two Massachusetts units into the wheatfield to sweep the open ground west of the woods on Winslow's right flank. Hart, at Hunt's direction, set up command on the left edge of the orchard facing south, one of his

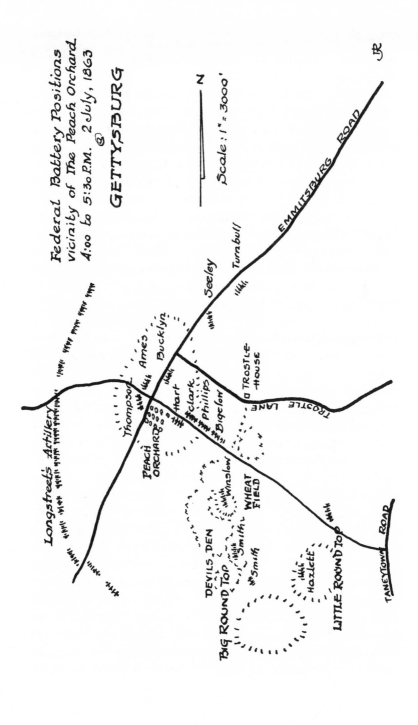

Federal Battery Positions
vicinity of The Peach Orchard
4:00 to 5:30 P.M. 2 July, 1863

GETTYSBURG

N

Scale: 1" = 3000'

Longstreet's Artillery

Thompson

Ames

Bucklyn

Seeley

Turnbull

EMMITSBURG ROAD

Hart

Clark

Phillips

Bigelow

TROSTLE HOUSE

TROSTLE LANE

PEACH ORCHARD

Winslow

Smith

WHEAT FIELD

DEVILS DEN

Smith

BIG ROUND TOP

Hazlett

LITTLE ROUND TOP

TANEYTOWN ROAD

JR

two sections about a hundred yards in advance of the rest of the artillery.

Up until this point there had been only one short outburst of firing, about 2:30 p.m. At that time Clark's New Jersey battery near the peach orchard had spotted the start of the Confederate deployment across the Emmitsburg Road. The range was quite great — 1400 yards — but Sickles ordered him to fire his 10-pounder Parrott rifles. Clark's gunners eagerly went through the orderly process of loading their weapons. When all was set the captain gave the command: 'Number one — Fire!' Down the line, one by one, the black tubes let go a shuddering boom, their rounds buzzing through the air like great birds. The Yankee officers watched for the bursts of their first salvo as crews rapidly reloaded. The first piece fired again, but at that point the Gray column disappeared from view and Capt. Clark ordered a cease fire.

Then, shortly after 3 p.m. the Confederate gunners received their fire orders, and the battle for Meade's left began. Hunt studied the Rebel lines carefully with his field glasses and saw them roll out more guns directly south of the road. There seemed little doubt that Lee was preparing a major assault on this end of the line. Hunt thereupon sent back to Tyler for still more reinforcements — rifled guns he wanted, as range and accuracy were needed to knock out those distant Gray batteries.[7]

While he waited, Hunt listened for the answering bark of Capt. Smith's 3-inch rifles atop the ledge in front of Little Round Top. Not hearing their reports the general galloped over to investigate. As he reached the Devil's Den area he found the rocky footing treacherous for his horse, so he dismounted and tied the animal to a nearby tree. Up the slope he climbed till he reached the rough shelf where Smith had just then succeeded in manhandling four of his rifles. So narrow was the opening and so studded with huge boulders was the knoll that the captain had no room for his other two pieces or the limbers for any of the guns. The remaining two guns Smith had spotted on the low ground slightly to the rear where they could enfilade the gorge — Plum Run Gut, in front of Little Round Top. The captain explained to Hunt that he was concerned about his left flank and had tried unsuccessfully to get infantry protection. Just then the air about them began to sizzle with flying iron as Confederate gunners took aim at the position.

Smith's attention was immediately concentrated on conducting the fire of his four guns lest he be knocked off the face of that hill. The fire of the 4th New York's Parrotts converged with that of batteries to their right, covering an enemy artillery position with a cloud of bursting shells. For a time the Confederate fire ceased. Hunt raised his glasses again; more batteries were rolling out on the far side of the Emmitsburg Road, and Smith was told to shift his trails and put the Rebel guns under fire. These gun's promptly answered Smith's fire, and a hideous racket boiled up from this rocky knoll, as Smith's rifle barks were answered by the crash of incoming shells.

Gen. Hunt watched for a few moments. When he saw that Smith was at least drawing off fire from other less sheltered parts of the Union line, he started for his horse. As he left, he told the battery commander that he would try to find him some infantry support, but the hope was slim; if the Rebels struck around the base of the hill Smith would probably lose his guns. As the general scrambled down the slope, he became concerned that he would find his horse either a casualty or driven wild from the torrent of bursting shells. But he instantly found himself in a situation which would have been ludicrous if it were not so potentially dangerous. He was smack in front of a herd of panicking horned cattle who were swirling about in the narrow valley between the hill and Little Round Top. The flying enemy shells were taking a toll of the herd, too. A projectile exploded inside one poor animal, scattering flesh all over the gorge. Terrified beasts ran from one side to the other frantically searching for safety — and Hunt's horse was tethered on the far side of the gorge. The general had little choice other

than to run, and luckily he escaped, though 'badly demoralized,' as he facetiously put it. Finding his horse safe, Hunt
mounted and set off through the woods. He passed Winslow's
battery, which was still unengaged because of its restricted
field of fire. Beyond, however, the general found Bigelow,
Phillips, and Hart in a heavy fire fight with the Confederate
batteries.

Confederate Col. Henry's battalion of ten guns was busily
engaged in trying to clear the way for Hood's first line to move
forward by knocking out the batteries in the wheatfield and
Smith's rifles perched on that commanding ledge. As the bitter
dueling continued, Col. Alexander, in command of all the
Gray artillery on that flank, had been forced to run out still
more firepower, ordering up two additional battalions opposite the orchard. The weight of these three commands, Alexander felt, would be sufficient to do the job. In moving guns
into action, the Rebel batteries apparently rolled in progres-
sively from south to north, bringing an increasing enfilading
fire on the Union batteries south of the peach orchard.

The Federals lashed back with terrific fury. For Bigelow's
9th Massachusetts Battery, located astride the lane running
from the Taneytown Road to the orchard, fifty yards beyond
the woods bordering Winslow's right flank, this was the first
fight. The battery was armed with six Napoleons, and they
had joined the opening fire on the Rebel batteries. Bigelow
singled out a cluster of enemy cannon firing from the partial
cover of a few farm buildings and a little patch of woods; the
range was far for Napoleons — about 1600 yards — but the
big guns went to work.[8]

Phillips's 5th Massachusetts had started from the Reserve
park behind Cemetery Ridge about 3 p.m., galloping down
the dirt lane leading from the Taneytown Road to the orchard
and the Emmitsburg Road. So rough was that ride that one
man broke his arm when he was thrown from a limber. At last
the 5th Massachusetts unlimbered in the open field to the left
of Clark's already engaged New Jersey outfit. As their six

3-inch rifles rolled into line abreast, an outburst of enemy shelling slammed in all about them. Capt. Phillips ordered his guidon, which was almost as large as a regimental flag, stuck in the ground on the right of the battery.[9] Instantly it seemed as if the Rebels were using the bright flag as an aiming point, for the shots now came thick and fast. The very first round plowed into the wheel horses of the right gun and splintered the limber pole.

The 5th Massachusetts was firing from relatively lower ground than its companion batteries on its right flank, and as such Phillips's targets were the Gray batteries more to the south. But this meant they caught many of the overs fired by Alexander's battalions, out of their sight to the west, aimed at the Blue cannon about the orchard. This flank fire was extremely annoying, and Phillips wished he had been able to see his tormentors and answer them. Instead he just took it, trying to stay ahead of the damage to the teams by cutting out stricken horses and replacing them with spares as long as the supply held out.

On Phillips's right, atop higher ground, was Clark's New Jersey battery. When the Rebs had started this fight, Capt. Randolph galloped over to Clark, pointed out a cluster of enemy guns near a house on the Emmitsburg Road, 1400 yards range. Randolph ordered them knocked out. For the second time in thirty minutes Clark's cannoneers dipped into their chests for shell and case shot to feed their Parrott rifles. The heavy racket of an artillery battery in action swelled up about the command, as gun after gun went off with a thundering boom, and the sharp calls and commands of officers and noncoms pierced the din. Then there was a pause in the enemy's return fire, and again Clark believed his job done and ordered cease fire.

However, it was just the lull before the storm. The Confederates had paused to let their infantry move past their guns, then those ominous, seemingly harmless little puffs of smoke showed on the horizon again, and more little puffs further to the right showed Clark that additional Rebel guns had entered the battle. The New Jersey unit immediately leaped to their weapons once more, with Sickles ordering them to 'hold this position while you have a shot in your limbers or a man to work your guns.' Over close to the peach orchard, Hart's 15th New York Battery waded into the contest with the growing line of enemy guns. Estimating his range at 900 yards, Hart swung his tubes over to his right front and opened a heavy counter-battery fire with solid and shell. The New Yorkers whooped with pride as they thought they saw one Gray unit pull out.

That sweeping fire from Alexander's guns was making it extremely hot for every Yank battery in the wheatfield and orchard, though. While Alexander would later bemoan that his batteries had little cover, neither did the Federals. Futhermore, every Blue battery there was subject to at least a partial enfilade as well as direct fire from Alexander's batteries, which crowned the apex of the angle in Sickles's line.

Closest Federal battery to the enemy was Ames's Battery G, 1st New York, an Artillery Reserve unit loaned to Sickles earlier in the day. Ames had been waiting idly behind a stone barn (probably the Trostle barn), in the rear of the battle line. As the fighting became heavier, Randolph sent for them, and across the fields they went, headed for the orchard. They were to take on some of the guns which were shooting up the Federal line from a point 850 yards southwest of the orchard. As the New Yorkers headed across the open ground, they were spotted at once. The Confederate officer directing the fire on the advancing battery must have been a solid veteran, for he pegged the range to perfection; shells struck everywhere in and around Ames's column, but by sheer luck the only damage was two horses killed.

As his column neared the orchard, Ames had to call a halt — a rather unnerving experience in view of the heavy volume of incoming fire — for two rail fences barred the route. Some cannoneers leaped from the limbers, threw aside the rails, and jumped back on the limbers as the heavy vehicles bumped past. Ames led his guns forward into the orchard, and let fly a torrent of case and shell. Muzzles flashed and smoked as the New Yorkers poured it on, and after thirty minutes Ames thought he saw an enemy battery pulling out. But before the New Yorkers had a chance to feel smug about their alleged success a fresh Rebel unit — a four-gun battery, Ames thought — swung into action a bare 500 yards west of the Emmitsburg Road. Now Ames was caught in a perfect cross-fire. The New York captain did the only thing he could do under the conditions of battle. He swung his right section about almost ninety degrees and put it to work against that flanking battery, while his remaining four guns continued to contend with those further to the south. To the west the fire of Smith's four rifles on the knoll near Devil's Den had picked up the same Rebel batteries, and their shells crossed with Ames's and Clark's in a wicked converging fire. The men of Ames's command plainly saw, even through the swirling clouds of smoke, one enemy piece knocked from its carriage.

A little distance north of the orchard, aligned on the edge of the Emmitsburg Road, was Bucklyn's Battery E, 1st Rhode Island. Their initial target had been two enemy batteries behind a low stone wall to their left front. But as they exchanged salvos with them, the Rhode Islanders became a target for the guns due west. Bucklyn then did as Ames had done, and detached a section to handle the annoyance.

While this cannonading was in full fury, an enemy shell swished into Clark's position and exploded, tossing two batterymen twenty feet into the air. The men fell beside each other, a mass of blood and dirt. Amazingly enough, one of them, a man named Ellis H. Timm, instantly stood up and looked down at the other, a lean Irishman named William Riley, and asked if he were badly hurt. 'By jimminy,' spat Riley, 'I don't think they could touch me without taking a limb, and now, d'-em, they have taken half the meat I did have.' Timm looked closely and saw to his horror that the

shell had cut away all the flesh from Riley's right hip, exposing
the bone. In spite of his gaping wound Riley then stood up.
Not realizing the man's condition Lt. Sims bellowed at Riley
about why the soldier was not helping on his gun crew. At
that Riley spun around presenting his mangled side to the lieutenant's eyes, and bitterly answered, 'Lieutenant, if your hip
was shot off like that, what the bloody h--l would you do?' The
young Irishman was sent off the field.[10]

The volume of Union fire that roared in on Alexander's
Rebel batteries, on the other hand, was equally great. To get
maximum effect Col. McGilvery rode from battery to battery
ordering them to unite their fire on one Gray battery at a time
until it was driven from the fight. McGilvery rather naïvely believed this practice knocked out five enemy batteries.

As can be best determined from the dissimilar reports, by
4 p.m. the Federals were opposing Longstreet's attack with
eight or nine batteries totaling thirty-eight to forty-four guns.
Certainly all five of the III Corps batteries were in line, but it
appears that Seeley had not yet opened fire, and two of Smith's
rifles in the gorge were idle. The III Corps alone then was
shooting with twenty-two guns. Supporting these units were
three, perhaps four, batteries from McGilvery's Reserve brigade. This was a minimum of sixteen tubes, and if Thompson's
C/F, Pennsylvania Light Artillery, was in action by this hour,
the number of guns should have increased by six.

Against the Federals the Confederates had in action some
forty-six pieces: thirty-six guns in Cabell's and Alexander's battalions west of the Emmitsburg Road, concentrating on the
peach orchard and the wheatfield, and ten tubes in Col. Henry's
battalion east of the road firing on Birney's line. In reserve
close by, Col. Alexander had another ten cannon.

This was probably the most evenly matched and vicious
artillery duel since the war's beginning. The ranges of fire were
relatively close for the most part, both sides reporting them
predominantly from 500 to 800 yards; only Henry's battalion
appears to have been at ranges of over 1000 yards. The units

on both sides were on open ground; and at these intermediate ranges both rifled guns and smoothbores were quite effective. At times the firing was so heavy that at least one unit had to cease to allow the thick smoke to blow away so that pieces might be relaid.

In this scrapping the Confederates apparently received the worst of it, though the Yankee batteries would find themselves in deep trouble later in the day at the hands of the Rebel infantry. One of Alexander's units had two of its four 12-pounder howitzers knocked from their carriages and also suffered the loss of forty men as casualties; another was soon so reduced in strength that it could man but two of its four guns. Still a third unit, equipped with heavy 24-pounder howitzers, was located on a slight slope, and the work of hauling these monsters up the grade after the recoil of each discharge eventually exhausted the crews and necessitated their augmentation from nearby infantry, some of whom died at the guns. 'Our losses both in men and horses,' said Alexander, 'were the severest the batteries ever suffered in so short a time,' [11] and since Alexander was commanding the Gray gunners in this action, he was in a position to know.

As the fighting spread, Humphreys's men along the Emmitsburg Road began receiving heavy fire in front and on the flank from the busy Rebel cannon. The damage this shelling was causing was slight, but it was miserably annoying. To reduce some of this harassing fire Humphreys brought up Seeley's Battery K, 4th U.S., which had been placed at his disposal earlier in the day, to a position on his left near a farm dwelling. With much cheering the Regulars zeroed in on a Confederate battery due west of them, and Seeley made the invariable claim that fills artillery reports of both sides — the enemy was silenced and driven off.

To fill the gap on the division right, which Seeley had left, Humphreys called on the Artillery Reserve for help. Shortly the answer rolled up in the form of Turnbull's F/K, 3rd U.S., accompanied by Capt. Dunbar Ransom, the commander of the

1st Regular Brigade of Tyler's Reserve. Ransom was one of the Army's veteran Regular battery commanders. He had attended West Point but was not a graduate, though he had been appointed a Regular second lieutenant in 1855, and had been with the Army of the Potomac since the Peninsula days. Ransom now took personal charge of positioning Turnbull's unit. Suddenly a thunderous clap of an exploding shell over the battery made the men flinch, and Ransom dropped from his horse badly wounded.

For approximately an hour the fighting had been exclusively an artillery affair. Then around 5 p.m. the Confederate infantry made its move. At first the Federals could make out only a long gray pencil-thin line across the horizon as smoke and distance merged the Rebel infantrymen into this wavy blur. Hood's division headed straight for Birney. The Yankee gunners scrambled to their handspikes and elevating screws to readjust their sheaves on the new target. The Confederate wave split, a portion veering away from the Emmitsburg Road toward the Round Tops — Devil's Den area of the field. The rest headed for the wheatfield.

Smith's 4th New York Battery saw them coming beyond the ring of woods, and the battery tried desperately to break up their line with case shot. The famous Texas brigade felt the sharp bite of Smith's four rifles, and so annoying did Law's brigade find this incessant fire that the 44th Alabama regiment was given the specific assignment of putting Smith out of the fight. While the Rebels suffered some casualties from this shelling, it failed to stop them. The Gray regiments overwhelmed the Federal infantry and pushed them back. Part of the Gray left flank was exposed to the fire from the orchard area, though, and had to pull back.

A swarm of musket-carrying Rebels swept out of the strip of woods and closed on the base of the rocky ledge on which Smith's four rifles were perched. The New Yorkers ran for their canister and began shooting for their lives. The Graycoats reached the protection of the rock and boulder-littered slopes, and Smith's troops had trouble depressing their tubes to reach them. Then, too, 10-pounder Parrotts, like other rifled cannon, were not the best canister weapons on the field.

If his guns were to be saved, Smith needed infantry protection, and he needed it quickly. The captain himself ran rearward until he discovered a nearby New York regiment, the 124th, and he pleaded with them, 'For God's sake, men, don't let them take my guns away from me!' [12] At this point the 124th, along with some others, rose up with a cheer and charged down the rugged slope. The bounding, yelling blue figures quickly masked what field of fire remained to Smith, and from that moment on the fate of the 4th New York rested on the efficiency of the infantry's muskets and bayonets.

The Federals had made some last minute attempts to strengthen this end of their line by running in some elements of the V Corps, but it was not enough. Benning's Confederate brigade found the gorge between the New Yorkers' hill and the two Round Tops and began to push their way through. The Rebels' right crossed the face of Big Round Top, and, finding it vacant, they pushed toward the smaller rock a few hundred yards down the gorge, curling around the east base of the hill crowned by Smith's battery.

Meanwhile, other Gray regiments repulsed the charge of the Union infantry, drove it back, and began inching up the rocks toward the Parrott rifles. By now Smith had only three guns left; the fourth was disabled, and the captain had run it off down the back slope. The 4th New York's position was now critical. Smith's left was almost isolated, and the thin line in his front was collapsing. Pleas for help brought no results, only urgent requests to hold on another thirty minutes when aid would arrive. But Smith's forces would be lucky to last another ten!

The captain debated ordering his guns manhandled to the rear. Such a task would be no easy job, even with no one shooting at them; instead, reasoning that help should arrive shortly and they would then be saved, he decided to leave the three weapons. To make sure that the guns would harm no one in the meantime, Smith ordered his men to remove all the firing implements. Then the men of the 4th New York ran down the back crest to their other section in the gorge a few hundred yards in rear. The Confederates immediately rushed up the slope and proudly seized the abandoned weapons. The next day these guns were shooting at their former owners.

Down in the gorge the Graycoats who had curled around Smith's left, next came in view of the two rifled guns nestled against the east base of the hill opposite Little Round Top. Smith promptly threw these two weapons into the fight, their blasts of case and canister sweeping obliquely down the gorge.

The picture was bleak for the Federals at this point. However, in the nick of time the Army's chief engineer, Gen. Warren, had spotted that Little Round Top was unmanned. Quickly that officer diverted some V Corps infantry and Hazlett's Battery D, 5th U.S., toward that dominating hilltop. By herculean efforts Hazlett's six 10-pounder Parrotts were dragged by the batterymen and some nearby infantry up the back or east face of Little Round Top. While that face does not have the cliff-like steepness of the opposite side, it was still no small feat to haul these awkward masses of wood and iron up a heavily timbered incline.

The Confederates were slowly pushing up the ravine as the guns were shoved out on the edge of the west cliff. Hazlett immediately ordered canister. The officer knew there was too much cover for his fire to accomplish much, yet he believed his fire would have a psychological effect on the enemy as well as on the hard-pressed Union infantry. From their rock and boulder shelters below, the Rebel infantry now turned a stinging fire on Hazlett's position. Standing near Hazlett was Brig. Gen. Stephen H. Weed, now a V Corps brigade commander, formerly a battery commander. Without a sound Weed dropped to the ground mortally wounded. Capt. Hazlett immediately bent over to hear something the general was trying to tell him, and took a bullet in the brain himself. Lt. Rittenhouse then assumed command of the battery and kept its guns barking loudly.[13]

By now more V Corps units were rushing forward to seal off the threatened rupture in the line, and Capt. Frank C. Gibbs's Battery L, 1st Ohio Light Artillery, was thrown into the battle. As the column neared the area, Gibbs quickly discovered that horses would be of little value to him, so he unhitched his teams and had his men push the guns the last few yards. The V Corps commander, Gen. Sykes, a solid and stubborn fighter, was nearby as Gibbs rolled up. Following the general's directions, the lieutenant tried to place his weapons to sweep the ravine in front of Little Round Top. One section he placed on the northwest face of the hill, just to the right of Hazlett's smoked-up position; another section he planted at the base of the hill; the third he kept in reserve.

As soon as the Ohioans caught sight of the fleeting forms of Rebel riflemen sniping from behind the shelter of rocks and gullies, they sent their four guns crashing discharges of case and canister at them. At one time a ragged line of Rebel troops rose up with a yell and attempted to charge, but Gibbs's two sections blasted them with double canister, firing so rapidly that the tubes became too hot to touch. Racked by these blasts and the bite of the Blue infantry muskets the shattered line retreated into the cragginess of Devil's Den.

This quick securing of Little Round Top by Warren probably saved Meade's position. So furiously did the Federals react to all attempts to advance in this quarter that the Confederates were forced to the defensive. But elsewhere, in the wheatfield and orchard area, the Confederates were having much better success. Hood's regiments had waded into Birney's line along the wheatfield. The clash developed into a see-saw battle down the full length of the front, as one side charged and drove the other only to be counter-charged and driven in turn. Finally, the Blue line had to give ground.

Further to the Confederate left, opposite the peach orchard, McLaws's division received orders to move out and support

Hood's attack, and some of Alexander's guns temporarily ceased fire to allow the infantry to pass to the front. As Mc-Laws advanced, two Federal batteries annoyed him immensely, one near the orchard and the second 200 yards beyond — probably one of the units in the wheatfield. While the fire of these guns did no great damage, it did hinder the enemy's efforts to maintain his lines. To obliterate this annoyance, part of Kershaw's South Carolina brigade was wheeled about and sent charging after the bothersome Federal batteries.

The first Blue unit to tangle with Kershaw's troops was Hart's advanced section. The lieutenant in command of the two guns saw them coming headlong through the smoke, straight for the section. There was one chance, as the lieutenant saw it, to save his crews, and that for them to fire a final blast of canister and then flop to earth immediately and feign casualties. Onward came Kershaw's regiments, and the crews of the two pieces stood ready with loaded canister. The lieutenant bellowed the command to fire; the guns crashed, and under cover of this fire and the accompanying smoke the men hit the dirt.

Hart's canister volley did damage, but not enough. The Rebels halted, fired a volley, then charged. Through the now-silent and apparently obliterated section streamed a horde of charging Confederates, bent on seizing the rest of the batteries about the orchard. Federal infantry rose up; the remaining guns spat canister; a Blue counter-charge hit the enemy, who then retired in face of this onslaught and confusion of orders. Back past Hart's section they went, into the wheatfield beyond. The crews of the two pieces thereupon leaped to their feet and with the aid of prolonges hurriedly dragged their weapons rearward to the safety of the main gun positions. This little episode, however, had cost the section seven men and eleven horses.

Clark's New Jersey gunners also spotted the long dun-colored lines as they moved across the wheatfield. Quickly shifting targets, they began spewing forth generous portions of case and shell. A steady fire swished from Clark's guns, and it seemed that while their shells appeared to chew gaps in the Gray ranks, the enemy regiments would not be stopped. The firing was first by gun, then by section, then by half-battery, and once or twice the entire battery was ordered to fire in volley. Ammunition began to run low so the battery commander sent back for resupply. Incoming artillery fire continued to slam into Clark's position, and one burst knocked a soldier named Hanyen unconcious. Another Irishman — the battery seemed to be recruited from Dublin rather than New Jersey — bent over his prostrate companion wailing tearfully, 'Mike, shure you're not kilt entirely, for 'tis I would be lonesome without you.'

As he watched the enemy advance, Capt. Clark calmly walked from gun to gun, encouraging his men to keep up their cool fire, while an old noncom strolled behind the captain with a long stick in his hand. With each gun discharge the fellow cut a notch in the stick, and grumbled when a shot was off target. 'Keep cool, keep your shirts on!' he kept telling the crews.[14] On came the yelling Confederates. Part of the force headed for the woods to Winslow's right, and Clark's Parrotts continued to hound them. Loadings were switched to canister. As one cannoneer handed the canisters to another to be loaded, the second crewman remarked, 'This is the stuff to feed them; 'tis good for them'; and turning to Timm, who had resumed his post on his crew, spat out more of his feelings, 'Timm, mow them down, Timm.' The gun coughed hard and another cannoneer yelled loudly, 'D--- them, we are paying off for Riley now.'

From the cover of the woods on the east edge of the field Confederates began a deadly sniping at the crews of the other Yankee batteries dotting the open ground between the woods and the orchard, with Bigelow and Phillips apparently receiving the worst share. One lucky sergeant of Phillips's 5th Massachusetts had a rifle bullet enter the front of his jacket, freakishly zip around through the lining, and come out the middle of the back. Then, as the man stooped over to sight his gun, another slug struck the top of the weapon and glanced off right through the sergeant's cap.

The New Yorkers of Hart's battery likewise had picked up the thick Rebel masses, but Hart was running precariously low on ammunition, and, in addition, some unauthorized person had moved his caissons to an undisclosed place away from the unit. Reaching to the bottom of their limber chests, the batterymen pulled out the few remaining rounds of case shot and promptly flung them at the enemy. When that was gone the nearly exhausted supply of canister was tapped, and with these the Gray charge was temporarily halted. There was a short pause, then the long, weaving ranks began to roll again, this time a part of the Graycoats moving into the wheatfield about 400 yards to Hart's left front. The last few rounds of canister were delivered to the left piece, which promptly flung them at the men in the wheatfield, and with this Hart pulled out.[15]

In the meantime Winslow's guns became deeply involved. Since some of the Blue infantry were fighting from behind a stone wall in front of the battery, Winslow wisely used solid shot in overhead fire, aimed so that it bounced around the trees in the woods where the Confederates were massing. As Capt. George E. Randolph put it, 'Such use of solid shot always [was effective] when troops are engaged in woods, the moral effect being at least equal to the physical.' As the Rebels forced Birney back, Winslow began dropping his range. Finally the thin Blue line retired to the north edge of the timber in his front, little more than 400 yards from the cannon muzzles. There the line held for a short time, but another push by the enemy forced the Union troops to pull back through the timber on both sides of the field. Winslow now sought to deny the enemy any easy advance across the open ground in front by switching loadings from solid to case shot. The bursting of the New Yorkers' shells may have had some effect, for the Graycoats made no immediate move on the battery.

Gen. Birney was having trouble on either side of Winslow, though. Through an aide he advised that battery to watch the infantry movements carefully and to look for a ready avenue of escape should the situation dictate his retreat. Winslow thereupon rode through the belt of trees on his left, perhaps 200 yards wide. Obviously this was not the way out, for here he met Union infantry falling back into the timber. Returning to his unit, the captain noticed that the Blue ranks had followed him through the woods, and even though his guns were firing, the shaken infantry began crossing the field in front of his crashing cannon. Winslow had no choice but to shut off the fire lest some of those people get hurt.

The Federal position was obviously deteriorating rapidly, but Winslow still was not ready to quit the field. Suddenly, musket fire crackled from the woods on his left; the Rebels had come into rifle range of the battery. Winslow loudly barked orders for the left section to move to their right rear and to take on this new threat. Before this could be done, a slashing volley ripped into Battery D from the timber on the right, bowling over men and horses. The time had come, Winslow reasoned, to heed Birney's advice and leave as quickly as possible. Accordingly, the battery began withdrawing by piece, in succession from the left; the remaining guns continued to fire to hold off the Rebels while the evacuation went on. The horses of one limber crumpled in heaps before another volley, leaving the piece immobilized. Fortunately Winslow's caissons were nearby, and grabbing one of their limbers he saved the guns; the caisson was hauled off by two stray horses that had wandered into the area.

As the unit cleared the field, they passed Gen. Sickles and Capt. Randolph, and Winslow was told to move to the rear and repair as much damage as possible. The ten horses they had lost might be replaced, but ten wounded men and eight missing were another matter. The battle of Gettysburg was over for Battery D.

Luckily for the hard-pressed Federals, Hunt's request for

more firepower had reached Gen. Tyler commanding the Reserve, and that officer was sending up batteries as soon as they could be readied. Thompson's combined Battery C/F, Pennsylvania Light Artillery — the F part was Hampton's old command — arrived and was thrown into the roaring hell of battle. As the battery rolled up, Col. McGilvery yelled to Capt. Thompson to take position in the peach orchard facing south. It was instantly obvious to Thompson that he was going to have to do what Ames and Bucklyn had already discovered — fight in two directions. He plunked down two of his 3-inch rifles with their muzzles pointing west, while the other four pieces were shoved into battery on their left facing southwest.[16]

Ames's command, spread out along the front part of the orchard, was in a bad corner. For approximately an hour they had been exchanging fire with Rebel batteries to front and flank. Then the Gray infantry made its first move in the battery's direction, and Ames, too, found his ammunition running low. As a column of Rebels went wading into the wheatfield to the battery's left front, the left section was allotted all the case rounds remaining in the battery limbers; these the two Napoleons liberally showered on the 'Johnnies' in the field; but it did not prove enough. When the supply of case gave out, the section leader put his men under every scrap of available cover until advancing Confederates come within good canister range. In the meantime the other two sections were keeping up a slow but steady rhythmic fire with solid shot against Alexander's hammering battalions. Then a relieving battery arrived, and Ames retired to the Reserve park to refit.[17]

It was now somewhere close to 6 p.m., and time had just about run out for Sickles. Pressure on the angle increased. At last McLaws's troops caved in a part of the Blue line. Thompson's right section was engulfed in a swirling fight waged with rifles, gun-butts, pistols, rammers, and any instrument men could lay their hands on, and for a few minutes the Rebels held one of the guns. Minutes later, Blue infantry slashed into the Confederates and retook the gun. However, Thompson could see, as he looked about, that this success was only temporary; the Yankee infantry was giving ground on all sides. Thus, he gave the order to clear out, which his forces did, losing a horseless gun in the process. Clark's New Jersey unit saw the situation the same way, and also withdrew.

A little further east, the men of Bigelow's 9th Massachusetts Battery had also been drawn into the fight with the enemy's infantry. They had dueled, quite successfully they thought, with some Rebel artillery earlier in the afternoon. They had next spotted a large mass of Rebel infantry forming in the environs of a farmhouse 500 yards to the south. A slight hillock interfered with the line of fire of the battery's left section as it tried to sight in on the new target, so Bigelow shifted it to the other end of his front. From this point the section had a clear field of view and quickly joined the rest of the battery in shooting at the Gray infantry.

So far as the men at the guns could see, their rounds — case and shell — were exploding right on target. Quite visible was one mounted Rebel who rode out slightly in advance of the mass. Suddenly the Federals saw the flash of a shell burst apparently right under the horse, and beast and rider were thrown to earth.[18] More infantry suddenly appeared moving toward the battery from the area of the peach orchard. The Blue gunners hesitated for a moment before turning their fire on them; it was possible they might be some of Sickles's troops. Then their flags became more visible and doubt vanished. These were more troops of Kershaw's command, and the 9th Massachusetts raked them with scalding blasts of canister. The enemy lines became confused and their attack failed to gain momentum. The only portion of this mass which would continue to bother the battery were snipers in the woods on Bigelow's left front.

Col. McGilvery watched the Blue infantry give ground and realized that if the batteries did not pull back immediately they might well be overrun. Quickly he ordered the remaining units in the wheatfield-orchard area to retire about 250 yards, there to set up a new base of fire.[19] Clark and Hart, completely out of ammunition, pulled off the field altogether, but the two Massachusetts batteries, Bigelow's and Phillips's, still had the will and the wherewithal to hurt the enemy, and these two units prepared to execute McGilvery's command.

Capt. Phillips decided to cover his own withdrawal by fire from one of his sections. While the other two sections began limbering, the right one received the order to fix prolonge and fire retiring. The crews of the two guns grabbed for the ropes that lay coiled between two hooks on the tops of the gun trails, one toggle being fastened to the lunette or towing ring of the piece, and the other to the pintle on the limber. With such an arrangement the crews would still be able to load and fire the pieces as they were being dragged rearward.

Before the Massachusetts men could complete the operation, the Rebels found a hole in the Blue line and streaked toward the battery. Phillips changed his mind in a hurry and ordered his last section to clear the field. Drivers of the limbers began hitching their teams to the guns. Suddenly a burst of enemy small arms fire dumped both the horses and drivers of one gun. Phillips grabbed for the still-fastened prolonge of that piece and with the help of its crew pulled the weapon to the rear. The remaining piece was finally limbered, after a lieutenant had dismounted and with the aid of a cannoneer had lifted the trail to the pintle. The lieutenant then saw the driver of the lead team shot out of his saddle and a driver take a shot that broke his arm. Seconds later a rifle bullet went clean through the lieutenant's face, passing through both cheeks without touching a tooth.

The 5th Massachusetts Battery left the field then by dribbles. Three serviceable pieces finally ended up beside Dow's 6th Maine Battery near the Weikert house. The other three guns were commandeered by Capt. Hart of the 15th New York Battery, who did not think there was any officer over them and so took the three units rearward with his own — a feat which displeased Phillips.

Just as the other Massachusetts battery, Bigelow's, got the order from McGilvery to clear out, they came under fire from Confederate infantry advancing from the captured orchard area as well as from the woods. Federal infantry was now nowhere to be seen, so Bigelow instantly realized that if the battery ceased firing to limber up it would give the Rebs a clear invitation to rush his helpless outfit. As long as the big mouths of his six Napoleons kept booming though, there was always a chance to beat off an attack.

Bigelow thereupon asked McGilvery for authority to use his prolonges and shoot his way back. The colonel agreed, and there was a flurry of activity around the sections as the prolonges were hurriedly fastened to gun and limber. While this was being done Bigelow shot a quick look toward the orchard area on his right where Barksdale's Mississippians were showing themselves, 200 yards distant. Their line was almost parallel with the Emmitsburg Road, and it stretched to the north as far as Bigelow could see. This meant the battery would probably have trouble retiring; the exit hole in the stone wall surrounding the field where the battery stood was near the Trostle house, 400 yards in the rear — and these 400 yards were almost parallel to the enemy's line of battle. With no friendly infantry anywhere in sight, and enemy troops on front and flank, chances of escape for the 9th Massachusetts looked slim. However, there was little more advantage in remaining there under heavy fire, so Bigelow started his slow withdrawal. The left two guns lashed out at Kershaw's men with canister, while the other four bounced solid shot toward Barksdale's men. Each discharge was a punch thrown at the enemy in hopes of keeping him off balance and at a distance; in addition, each recoil took the guns that much closer to safety.

Lt. Erickson, commanding the center section, had taken a bullet through a lung earlier in the fight but had refused to leave the field. He was still shepherding his two pieces across the open field, though a bloody froth dripped from his mouth. Then one of the guns seemed to be lagging behind too far for safety and Erickson rode over to speed up its pace. No one heard the specific crack of the individual musket that hit, but a Minié ball thudded into Erickson's head just as he reached the gun, and before his lifeless body could hit the ground it was riddled with bullets. On another gun a cannoneer was shot just as he was going to pull the lanyard of his piece; a second cannoneer leaped forward and grabbed the rope, and he too was instantly cut down, as was a third man. Not until the fourth gunner stepped up did the weapon get fired.

Shot by shot, yard by yard, the 9th Massachusetts slowly retired across the field, at heavy cost in men and horses. Finally they reached an angle in the stone wall at the Trostle house. A slight rise fifty yards to their right gave temporary cover from Barksdale's regiments, so Bigelow gave the order to limber up in a hurry. It looked as if the battery would get away after all. But before the unit could start filing through the gate, Col. McGilvery reined a lathered horse to a halt beside Bigelow. McGilvery ordered him to put his battery in action at this point. The colonel pointed out that behind the 9th Massachusetts, for a distance of 1500 yards between the Round Tops and the left of the II Corps, there were absolutely no Union forces! Bigelow was told he must hold here until McGilvery could move a line of guns in across that gap. With that Col. McGilvery booted his tired horse into a gallop and left the lone battery to its seemingly hopeless task.

This was one of those times when the outcome of an entire battle depended upon the guts and determination of one small unit of men. Bigelow and his crews were the thumb in the hole of the dike, and they no doubt realized this in view of McGilvery's hurried briefing. Bigelow looked about; it was a terrible place to emplace a battery. They were shut in by the stone wall. Along the wall to the battery's left were some of Kershaw's riflemen; along the other side of the angled wall and to the unit's front Barksdale was advancing. In addition, the battery had left a trail of casualties, human and equinine, as it retreated across the field, and not much ammunition was left in the chests.

Few batteries ever entered such a critical action in such poor shape as Bigelow's. Nevertheless, the fate of an army rested on its guns, and Capt. Bigelow began issuing orders that would put the 9th Massachusetts Battery into one of the most frenzied single unit actions of the war. Crews quickly began unlimbering the six Napoleons; the enemy was closing in rapidly now. Seeing that space was extremely tight because of an abundance of boulders, Bigelow ordered the left section under Lt. Milton to clear out. Loud commands set the first piece in motion, and the team clattered its way through the gateway in the wall. As the gun wheels entered the gap, one of them snagged a rock and the gun turned over. Furiously the crew struggled to right the weapon, a veritable shower of bullets hindering their efforts. Lt. Milton dismounted and put his weight to the effort, and at last the big gun was righted, and away it went.

The other piece of Milton's section was driven headlong into the low stone wall, the horses clambered over it, and with much huffing, puffing, and snorting, dragged the weapon over and through the wall, the iron tired wheels bouncing over some rocks and tumbling others from the heap to the ground. Amazingly enough, the gun cleared the barrier safely, and Milton led his two weapons off the field. The remaining four pieces were already in battery, and every last round of ammunition had been removed from the limbers and piled beside the gun muzzles — a dangerous expedient, but one which would permit maximum rate of fire.

No sooner were the crews set than the enemy appeared over the little rise fifty yards in front. Both sides crashed into action. The Confederates wisely refrained from rushing the battery ahead. Instead, under the cover of a heavy fire from the front, the 21st Mississippi began slipping around toward Bigelow's right flank. The four guns in the meantime roared and boomed,

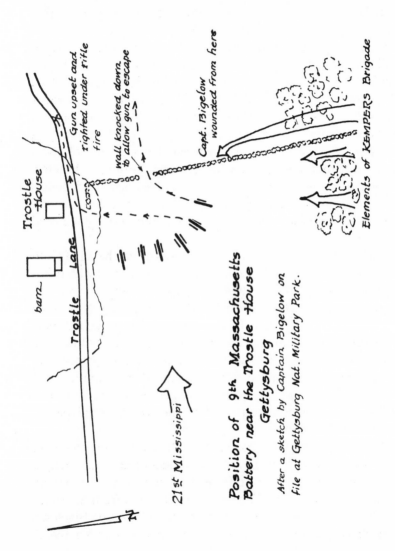

Trostle House

barn

Trostle Lane

21st Mississippi

N

Gun upset and righted under rifle fire

wall knocked down to allow gun to escape →

corn

Capt. Bigelow wounded from here

Elements of KEMPERS Brigade

Position of 9th Massachusetts Battery near the Trostle House Gettysburg

After a sketch by Captain Bigelow on file at Gettysburg Nat. Military Park.

churning the air in front with swarms of canister pellets, keeping the enemy at a distance.

About this time some of Kershaw's men began to edge in on Bigelow's left, and the captain realized his position was becoming increasingly precarious. If that gap in the wall were widened a bit and cleared of tumbled rocks, perhaps he could send away another gun or two, saving them from what now appeared as inevitable capture. Bigelow urged his horse over to the wall in the hope of corralling some stragglers from Milton's section who could be put to work clearing the passage. The crews on the four guns still in action were so reduced that it would be impossible to detach anyone from that quarter. As Bigelow reached the gateway, his bugler, who was riding beside him, suddenly pulled his horse back on its haunches. To their left front six Rebels were taking deliberate aim at the two riders. Muskets cracked, and two slugs ripped into Bigelow, two more felled his horse. A nearby cannoneer immediately helped the wounded captain to his feet.

Even in his injured condition Bigelow could see that the situation had suddenly deteriorated. The 21st Mississippi was charging into his battery from the right rear. Already some of the Graycoats had climbed atop the limbers and were taking pot shots at the surviving gunners. Several of the more reckless Rebels made a wild dash into the position itself. One Gray soldier tried to spike a gun but was summarily killed on the spot. Another collared a stunned gunner and started to drag him off, but a friend rushed to his aid with a handspike — an implement which could be a wicked weapon, being the approximate size and texture of a modern baseball bat. The Yank soldier swung the handspike and knocked the capturing Confederate sprawling. A third Confederate was brained with a rammerstaff. Glancing to the rear, Bigelow thankfully saw in the distance a group of guns unlimbering across the feared gap. His thirty-minute stand, then, had not been in vain, and he was free to save whatever he could of his shambled command.

Turning to his orderly, Capt. Bigelow told him to send the survivors to the rear.

The 9th Massachusetts had gone into action about 4:30, and it was around 6:30 when Bigelow gave the order to leave the wreckage about the Trostle house. The cost had been frightful: Four guns had been lost. Among the battery's four officers, one was dead, one was mortally wounded, and a third seriously wounded. Of some sixty men on the gun crews twenty-eight were casualties; sixty horses were dead and twenty disabled out of a total of eighty-eight on the field. During the action the battery had expended all but four of the ninety-six rounds of canister its limbers contained — indicative of the sustained fury of its close-range fighting. Sustained by a gulp of whiskey from a fellow officer's flask, and helped by one of his men, Capt. Bigelow led his diminished and exhausted little band rearward until they reached the safety of the gun line Col. McGilvery had now strung across the fields about 500 yards to the rear.[20]

Meanwhile, the collapse of Birney's front put the Federal troops along the Emmitsburg Road north of the orchard — Humphreys's division — in difficult straits. As the roar of combat drifted closer to the orchard, Bucklyn's Battery E, 1st Rhode Island, began to take a second look at its position. The general view of its situation can be gathered from the remark of a battery man later: 'We began to fear that the Army of the Potomac would have to resume its habit of retreating.' [21]

The Gray batteries south of Bucklyn were still pouring in shells to which Bucklyn could make no reply, being masked by the retiring Federal infantry. To the west Confederate General A. P. Hill added his guns to the battery's troubles. As Barksdale's Gray infantry brigade stormed in from the west, the gun crews began losing men from musket fire. Soon, almost 30 per cent of the unit and half the horses were out of action.

Seeing he could do no further good by staying, Bucklyn decided to try and shift his position to his right rear — extremely welcome news to the men of the sixth gun in the most exposed position out on the road. Nearby was Capt. Randolph, the corps artillery chief, and he instantly sized up the precarious spot Bucklyn was in. Rushing over to some Pennsylvania infantry, Randolph urged them to save the battery. The troops promptly responded and charged forward colliding head-on with advancing Rebels. A pitched battle flared up around Bucklyn, as he tried to prolonge his guns rearward. This section of the Federal line suddenly collapsed as the battery's individual pieces fled the field, hurriedly scattering in all directions in their haste to get away. So confusing and headlong was Battery E's retreat that not until the afternoon of the next day would the scattered segments be reunited as a unit.[22]

Toward the closing stages of the fight for the orchard and the angle, someone in Sickles's command set off in panicky fashion to scour the area behind the lines for every available battery. It so happened that two V Corps batteries — Watson's I, 5th U.S., and Walcott's 3rd Massachusetts — were posted in rear of Cemetery Ridge awaiting orders. When at last the V Corps sent for its guns, they were gone — appropriated by someone on Sickles's staff who contended he had the authority to commandeer every gun in sight! [23] The result was that, besides depriving the V Corps of its artillery, Watson's battery of Regulars was almost commandeered into extinction. Without any support, Battery I rolled its four 3-inch rifles into firing position about 400 yards east northeast of the Trostle House, about 150 yards north of what is now United States Avenue. This was the extreme left end of McGilvery's second line. For twenty minutes the men waited, then the yelling victory-flushed Rebel line marched into view, some 350 yards away, the setting sun at their backs. Watson coolly ordered his weapons into action with shell.

Unlike Bigelow's men, though, the Regulars could not stop that ominous line, as it kept coming through the battle haze, accentuated in the fading light. Some of the Confederates crossed little bush-bordered Plum Run directly in front of the battery and opened an accurate fire on the Regulars. Lt. Watson was spun around and knocked to earth by one of those heavy musket slugs, and the command fell to Lt. McConnell. The new commander thereupon changed loadings to canister, blasting away at the Confederates by the creek. The thin black rifles spat flame and defiance in rapid order, and, while they did some damage, it was not enough. Twenty rounds of canister were thrown in the Confederates' faces, but the long muskets of the Gray infantry — that 21st Mississippi again — rippled flame and shot the Regular battery to pieces. The survivors of Battery I had two choices: either stay and become casualties or prisoners, or run. Being normal, they ran, leaving their guns silent in the green field.

Just a little to the north of Watson's position was another battery, whose designation Col. McGilvery was never able to learn; also three pieces of Phillips's 5th Massachusetts; and two stray guns from Thompson's Pennsylvania battery — McGilvery's patchwork second line. They were shortly reinforced by Dow's fresh 6th Maine. These units had been pouring out a desperate fire at the enemy regiments in the captured fields 800 yards to the west and at several of Alexander's gun battalions, which had advanced with their infantry to the peach orchard. Alexander's artillery pounded the Yankees vigorously, and under this covering fire Confederate infantry made a rush for the creek bed from which other Gray infantry had sniped Watson out of action. Dow's 6th Maine and the three pieces of Phillips's outfit opened a blistering defensive fire with the deadliest round in their limber chests — canister.

Flame from the gun muzzles flashed in the sunset, and crashes rolled like thunder across the fields under dense billowing clouds of battle smoke. A road leading into Meade's rear lay just to the left, and the artillerymen knew if the Rebels obtained a toe-hold there, the day might well be lost. Behind the guns Meade was rapidly pulling units from the right and center to stiffen the shaken left. But time was needed, and the Federal gunners fought like men possessed.

Meanwhile, Humphreys's division, which had been holding Sickles's right along the Emmitsburg Road, had become heavily engaged. As the angle at the orchard was pushed in, Humphreys's left locked bayonets with the sweeping Southern advance. Bit by bit, more and more of the division became embroiled, as the last elements of Longstreet's troops were fed in, and Anderson's division of A. P. Hill's corps rolled out to support Longstreet. The pressure built up so fast and so powerfully that Humphreys had to call on Hancock's II Corps for help.

At the same time, Seeley's Regular battery was turned from the Gray artillery onto the enemy's infantry. Soon Turnbull's fire was added, while Humphreys bent his left back to cover the break on that flank. Seeley's men hit the Confederates with solid shot, shell, and case. They were shooting at a part of the line that reached a little hollow west of the road. Since field artillery of that era was not capable of high-angle fire, Seeley ordered his guns to cease. Figuring the Graycoats would come swarming into view again in a minute or so, the battery commander ordered his weapons loaded with canister. No sooner had he given this command than he went down badly wounded.

Just as Seeley had figured it, the Gray waves rolled into view again, coming at the double, and the Federal line gave ground before them. Lt. Robert James, who took over command of the battery, fired some of his canister before everything collapsed around him. The lieutenant then sent his unit galloping a short distance toward his right, hoping to get in position to enfilade the charging Confederates. As fast as cut-up teams could drag the guns, James moved the battery 400 yards to the north, then bellowed the command to go into action again. Scarcely had the crews cleared the guns from their limbers than out of nowhere Rebel infantry rose up on the battery's right rear, not thirty yards distant, and rushed the guns.

Once more a Federal battery had to fight in the nastiest of all combat — hand-to-hand. Federal infantry rushed into the melee, and with their help James finally extricated his guns and galloped rearward. Finally reaching and joining McGilvery's line of guns, the Regulars set up position again defending the road leading into Meade's rear.

Another Reserve battery came rolling forward from Cemetery Ridge — Lt. Julian V. Weir's C, 5th U.S. The Blue infantry was already falling back on the left when his guns began unlimbering. Wier immediately cut loose with solid shot, then switched to case, and when this failed to slow the Gray charge, he went to canister. The six Napoleons made short work of the supply of this round, and, when this had been shot, Wier determined to pull back lest he be overrun. As he was furiously limbering, Federal reinforcements reached the fight and for a time made the enemy give ground. Weir saw a chance to stay where he was, and yelled to his crews to stand fast. The fighting swirled in determined fury as Weir's men watched for the outcome. But some of the Rebels had spotted the battery, and soon horses and drivers began dropping at a dangerous rate. The combat spilled back into the battery position, and before he realized it Wier had only three guns left to extricate.

On all sides Humphreys's forces were pushed hard, though they gave ground with extreme stubbornness. Turnbull's battery received a solid whacking as it fought to cover the retirement toward Hancock's ranks atop Cemetery Ridge. But Hancock was also having his troubles. One of his divisions had already been pulled away to aid Sickles's left, and this had widened the gap between Hancock's left and the right of the III Corps. To cover this, Gibbon's brigade extended its front with two regiments, and Brown's Battery B, 1st Rhode Island, moving forward to a small crest near the Codori farm. As Humphreys fell back, these regiments and Brown's battery tried to cover his open right flank.

The battle had now spread northward and had embroiled all that was left of the weakened II Corps. Gen. Gibbon, the former captain of Battery B, 4th U.S., fell heir to the II Corps, as Hancock replaced the wounded Sickles. Gibbon put the II Corps batteries to spitting solid shot over the heads of their friendly infantry. Soon the smoke became so dense that Gibbon had to direct some of the guns to cease firing so as not to endanger their own troops.

Brown's first target was enemy artillery — probably some of Hill's batteries. So deeply engrossed in this gun fight did the Rhode Islanders become that they scarcely noticed infantry closing in on their left front. The air was full of battle smoke, its clouds hanging low over the battlefield like a dense mist, and through this haze it was hard to distinguish friend from foe. Some of the artillerymen saw the approaching infantry, but were sure they were Federal regiments, and continued to concentrate on the cannon flashes of A. P. Hill's batteries on Seminary Ridge.

Then it happened. Like Griffin at Bull Run and Wiedrich on the same field a year later, the approaching infantry halted and raised muskets; a streak of fire ripped the smoky air, as the men of Wright's Confederate brigade let go a volley and charged. Forward they came, the piercing scream of the Rebel yell rising over the racket of gunfire, bright flags dotting their front. Lt. Brown instantly swung his battery to the left oblique, but this shift permitted only the left and center sections to bear on the charging Rebels. Crews quickly shoved in case shot cut for three seconds; the enemy was closing fast and the fuze cuttings dropped to two seconds, then one. Finally canister, then double canister, burst from the hot cannon, and still the charge swept on.

Friendly Blue infantry nearby shouted to the battery to clear out before they were overrun, and Brown apparently was in full accord for he ordered his men to limber to the rear. Under a heavy fire the battery began clearing the field, losing horses as they went. Backward across the field Brown led his guns toward a low stone wall which had been breached at one point to a width sufficient to allow one vehicle at a time to pass through. One, two, three guns got through, then the fourth moved up. Suddenly two horses on its team stumbled and fell from enemy fire. The gun was immobilized in the snarl of panic-stricken horses. The fifth piece rolled through the opening; then the last one suffered the fate of the fourth, and Battery B left two weapons behind as it clattered up Cemetery Ridge. Thirty horses and ten men were left behind.

Actually, it was on this part of Meade's line that the Confederate attack enjoyed the most success. The Rebel brigades of Anderson's division had buckled Humphreys's right, and one of them, Wright's, even had planted its feet atop the ridge, smack in the middle of the Yankee line.[24] Part of this attack from the west had found a gap on Gibbon's left and had raced through. Gibbon quickly sent the 1st Minnesota Infantry regiment which had been supporting Thomas's Battery C, 4th U.S., to the charge. The sudden impact turned the flow, and Thomas's guns sprayed the Gray ranks as they sought a new route. Yet, this Confederate assault had been so heavy and had had such momentum that the three Gray brigades of Anderson's command alone claimed over twenty-two Federal cannon overrun and temporarily captured, with Wright's outfit — the one which actually reached Cemetery Ridge — claiming to have taken eleven.[25]

By stripping his right, Meade was able to launch vicious counter-attacks all along his center, and by sundown these attacks had recovered most of the ground lost in front of the II Corps, though the high ground by the orchard, the wheatfield, and Devil's Den remained in Confederate hands. The danger which had developed with the collapse of the angle further to the south had been marvelously negated by Bigelow's sacrificial stand, and by the searing blasts from McGilvery's second line of guns behind Plum Run. Even so, it had not been easy. Thompson's guns had run out of ammunition; Watson's outfit was capable of only limited effectiveness in its shot-up condition; the unidentified Volunteer unit had suddenly picked up its trails and left the field; and Battery B, 1st New York, had fired only a few rounds before it too departed.[26] Partially offsetting these losses had been the arrival of Seeley's Regulars, still grimy from their struggle with enemy infantry. So cut up was this battery, though, that it could man but four of its pieces, the other two being sent to the rear. These four had swung in line beside Dow's Maine battery and, with the help of Phillips's three guns, McGilvery had kept the door slammed on the face of Longstreet's potent infantry until Willard's brigade of the II Corps came over and drove the Rebels back across Plum Run. Col. McGilvery must have personally felt that he had used up all his luck. His horse had been hit in the body four times by rifle fire, once in the leg by shellfire, and once on the hip by a spent solid round before it died. But not a shot had touched the colonel.

When the Federals took stock of their artillery losses in this region that night, the casualties must have staggered them. Among the eighteen batteries which had participated on this front, there were at least 230 officers and men casualties, and about 340 horses had been killed. Four units had seen over forty of their animals hit, and Bigelow's battery alone reported forty-five killed and fifteen wounded.

However, if the Yankee artillery on Meade's left had had a rough time of it, some of the batteries on the right of the line had also had hard going. The Confederates' original plan for this July 2nd attack was to support Longstreet's assault against the Union left by simultaneously having Ewell advance against Meade's right. But the Gray high command went at the attack haphazardly. The result was a series of piecemeal attacks on the right which failed to do anything except kill and wound a great number of men, with the artillery of both sides especially hard hit.

About 4 p.m. one of Ewell's artillerymen, Maj. J. W. Latimer, received orders to prepare for action. The only ground Latimer was able to find was atop Benner's Hill, 1400 yards northeast of Cemetery Hill and almost due north of heavily wooded Culp's Hill. Space was extremely limited, and the young major was concerned over the lack of cover for his teams and caissons. Nevertheless, he planted fourteen pieces on that rise and, on another little knoll behind, stationed two 20-

pounder Parrotts plus a battery from the Reserve. Opposite Latimer, atop Cemetery and Culp's hills, was a mass of Yankee cannon, so placed by Gen. Hunt and Col. Wainwright that it brought within easy range every parcel of ground that the enemy could possibly use for its artillery. Over on Culp's Hill Slocum's XII Corps had available its four batteries of twenty guns; on the east face of Cemetery Hill were four batteries under Col. Wainwright — seventeen pieces in all; and midway between these two groups, at the head of the valley separating the two hills, were the six Napoleons of the 5th Maine Battery. Further to the left, on Cemetery Hill proper, were three XI Corps batteries, backed up by five Reserve units, judiciously posted there by Hunt — the whole under the command of Maj. Osborn, the XI Corps chief-of-artillery.

When the twenty-year-old Latimer gave his battalion the order to commence firing on the Yankee right, he presented an ideal target to this massed Federal power. For awhile the Gray cannoneers made a fight of it with surprisingly accurate gunnery — the most accurate Col. Wainwright had ever seen from Rebel artillery. This fire was instantly answered by Wainwright's thirteen rifled guns — Battery B's four Napoleons being kept out of this long range fight. Then Stevens's 5th Maine Battery added its heavy coughs to the deluge of shells that plunked in on Latimer. At the height of this raging fight three pieces of Atwell's Pennsylvania [27] and a section of Kinzie's Regular batteries opened a blistering fire on Latimer.[28] The projectiles from these five cannons buzzed angrily across the valley and slashed into the left flank of Latimer's center battery. The Gray gunners held gamely, but they were being badly hurt by this concentrated fire.

After an hour and a half of this firing, Latimer's forces were weakening. Men and horses were being hit, and two of his pieces had run out of ammunition. Then a XII Corps gun splintered one of Latimer's caissons. At this point Latimer sent a sergeant galloping to headquarters for authority to withdraw the battalion. Since Latimer had a well-based reputation as a most willing and determined fighter, the Confederate command respected his judgment and authorized his withdrawal. So all but four pieces went rolling rearward, two of them hauled off by hand, the Federals later claimed. The remaining cannons were retained in position to deter any Yankee infantry attack. After the battle was over and the Federals had a chance to examine Latimer's position, they found twenty-eight dead horses and three dismounted guns.[29]

This withdrawal was followed by a natural lull in the cannonading, which lasted until about 7 p.m., when Ewell's infantry at last began its move on Culp's and Cemetery hills. During the lull, some Confederate infantry had begun to harass the Federal gun positions by sniping at the men from the windows of houses, buildings, and church steeples on the near edge of town. From a small brick house, a gabled affair with two windows on each story facing Cemetery Hill, one Rebel nicked a gunner in Regular Battery B. The Regulars put up with this annoyance as long as there were no casualties. But now the situation demanded action. Sgt. Mitchell ordered a gun loaded with case shot cut for 600 yards.

The piece which the sergeant selected was a new gun, being issued to the battery soon after Fredericksburg to replace one of the old model Napoleons which had a scored and worn barrel. The new weapon had been fired the day before for the first time, so she was probably as accurate as a smoothbore gun could be. Sgt. Mitchell gave orders to hit that gabled house, and the battery's gunners took perfect aim at the target. The big gun fired, and bounded rearward in recoil. The smoke cleared quickly and the men watched for the effect. Some two seconds later they saw bricks fly between the two windows of the second story and the shell explode inside the building. There was no more trouble from snipers in this area for the rest of the day.[30]

Similarly, this sniping was worrying the Germans of Wiedrich's New York battery on the east crest of the hill. They, too, decided to take a hand in ending this annoyance, and,

spotting some Graycoats shooting from atop a steeple on the
edge of town, they promptly put one of their rifled projectiles
into the structure. Like the Regulars, the Germans were bothered no further.

Toward sundown the swarm of dozing Yankee cannon on
the hills facing Ewell suddenly came angrily alive again. Latimer had put his four remaining guns into action once more.
Again the Union artillery replied, this time killing Latimer.
The Blue crews now had Rebel infantry to contend with — a
factor which much experience had dictated should never be
slighted. In addition to Latimer's four pieces on Benner's Hill,
other Rebel guns of Ewell's corps suddenly came to life, with
Cemetery Hill as their target. By now a good portion of A. P.
Hill's artillery was hard at it, too, a fair share of their fire
being aimed at the Yankee batteries studding the hill.[31]

This shooting immediately brought the batteries under Osborn's command into action. Some of these units had done
some sporadic dueling during the day with Rebel guns north
and northwest of town, so that by 5:30 at least one battery,
Wheeler's, had run low on ammunition. Taft's big 20-pounders
of the 5th New York Battery, the only guns of large caliber the
Federals would have on the battlefield during these three days,
went to work about 5 p.m. From their centrally located position on Cemetery Hill, Taft's gunners had a clear view to the
north and west, and four of the big Parrotts joined one of
Bancroft's Regular sections and Norton's Ohio battery in taking on Ewell's troops, while Taft's other two guns slugged
away at Hill's batteries to the west and also inflicted some in-
cidental damage to nearby Gray infantry. Edgell's New Hampshire battery spotted some of Hill's guns banging away from
a position on the Chambersburg Pike near the seminary, and
the New Englanders' six 3-inch rifles discharged 105 rounds
of time and percussion shell at ranges of some 2000 yards.[32]

Over on Culp's Hill the XII Corps, weakened badly by detachments to aid the harried III Corps, lost some ground to
the attacking Rebels. By grim determination, though, the Un-

ion forces were able to hold most of the hill, while Atwell's battery, which had shifted during the lull to Slocum's Hill, and Winegar's M, 1st New York, on a second rise 400 yards to the east, covered a big gap in the XII Corps front. Toward Cemetery Hill, a little to the west, more of Ewell's infantry was storming the Yankee lines. Riflemen in dirtied blue uniforms lined the front crests of the hill and volleyed into the faces of the charging Confederates, whom the 5th Maine Battery had begun harassing at 1500 yards range with the aid of a crude but apparently effective range finder called a French Ordnance Glass — the only instance the author uncovered of the use of such a device.

As the Rebels tried to rush the east face of the hill, part of their line was almost perpendicular to the gun tubes of the 5th Maine — a bare 800 yards away. Six Napoleons slashed and cut at the length of the exposed line with shell and case. The battery's fire must have hurt, but it failed to stop the advance, for Stevens soon had to grab for canister. Little did the men of the 5th Maine believe they would run out of canister, as they had anticipated there would be much close-in fighting, and had repacked their limber chests with upwards of forty-six rounds of this deadly stuff. But they did run out before the attack ended. With this considerable help from Stevens's cannon, the lean Blue infantry line on the right face of Cemetery Hill held fast.

On the other quarter of the rise though, things were not going this well. For a time the fire of the Federal infantry and the plunging shells from the batteries on the northeast crest held back the Confederate attack. Then the enemy's right, Hays's brigade of Louisiana troops, plus a North Carolina brigade worked up through the fields east of Gettysburg, and came booming out at the charge.

Just as the Gray regiments bounded onto the open crest in front of Ricketts's battery, a cannoneer of that unit, pale and trembling, presented himself to Ricketts with the plea that he was sick and would like to go to the rear. Even if such a plea had honest justification, Ricketts knew that one man running toward the road in their rear could trigger a panic. The captain drew his big Colt, pointed it squarely at the poor lad's head, and then dryly remarked, 'If you don't take your place, I'll make you sicker!' [33]

A Federal brigade fired a few volleys and was then overwhelmed. Dead ahead of the whooping Graycoats stood the Yankee batteries, still firing, but badly handicapped because of fading light and difficulty of depressing tubes. Beyond the batteries was the Baltimore Road and the rear of Meade's line on Cemetery Ridge, and the Southerners may have sensed they could have victory if they reached that last 200 yards. The batteries on the western part of Cemetery Ridge heard the crash of fighting in their rear, and some were turned about to cover that threat.

Astride the pike stood Battery B, 4th U.S. Its four serviceable Napoleons had been pointed down the road into town. They had been loaded with canister, as the crewmen had anxiously watched for any movement by the enemy via this route. When the racket of the Rebel charge swept toward Wiedrich's and Ricketts's commands, Battery B instantly swung around forty-five degrees, and Lt. Stewart bellowed the command, 'Fire by piece! Fire at will!' The hoarse roars of the four guns shook the ground as the Regulars fought to hold the foe. For all the viciousness of this scrap the battery's historian reported that, compared with the fighting of the day before, 'the second day seemed a rather trivial affair.' [34]

Up the hill they came, whooping, yelling, and heading straight for Wiedrich's Battery I, 1st New York — a German XI Corps outfit temporarily detached to the I Corps artillery brigade. A panting, rushing mass of about a hundred Rebels burst into Wiedrich's position, and for a few minutes the Germans disputed matters fiercely. But pistols in the hands of a few noncoms, rammers and makeshift clubs in the swinging grasp of others, were not the means of repelling a determined infantry attack. In the semi-darkness Wiedrich's cannon fell into Confederate hands, and the surviving gunners retreated to the other side of the Baltimore Road.

Similarly, the battery on Wiedrich's right, Capt. Ricketts's F/G, 1st Pennsylvania, caught the same charge. This unit had just come into position there, replacing Cooper's battery which had suffered some in the duel with Latimer.[35] Ricketts had poured out canister when the attack on the hill first began, and, as Hoke's brigade appeared, the battery fired the last canister rounds in their limbers. Quick-thinking Ricketts had one trick left that might work. He ordered case shot fired with no fuzes inserted. This meant that the rounds would be exploded while they were still in the tubes, which gave a sort of canister effect. The captain ordered his guns loaded in this manner.[36] The Pennsylvania guns pierced the dusk with their orange flashes, as the unit fought to keep back the sweeping tide of enemy riflemen. One source stated that Ricketts's rate of fire now reached four discharges a minute.

The capture of Wiedrich's position, though, had completely compromised Ricketts's position, for it enabled the Gray troops to spill into the gap between the two units, utilizing a stone fence on the Rebels' left as partial cover. From a point about opposite the battery's left piece, a group of the enemy stood up, took deliberate aim, and wrecked the gun detachment with a slashing volley. With that they leaped the low wall and waded into what was left of the crew, relying on bayonet and gun butt to complete the job. In no time the entire detachment was made casualties, save three who were lucky enough to be taken prisoner.

Having taken care of one gun, the Confederates quickly turned on the others still firing to the front, their decimated crews augmented by officers and drivers. The battery guidon waved from one low earthwork protecting a gun. A Rebel lieutenant spotted it and made a rush to seize the little banner; as his hand reached out, the battery guidon bearer spotted him, quickly cocked his pistol and fired, dropping the officer. A flurry of return shots then cut the guidon bearer down.

The Graycoats were now in the midst of Ricketts's position, and a wild melee swelled up in the near-darkness, making it difficult to tell who was friend and who was foe. Once again it was handspike against bayonet, pistol against musket, rammer against gun butt. In the dim light a battery officer saw a Confederate reach down and pick up the fallen guidon. The officer reached for a handy rock and hit the Rebel. As the man fell, the officer seized his musket and shot him with his own weapon. The guidon was returned to its proper owners.

By now light was virtually gone from the field, and this factor, together with the discovery that the mass of Union artillery across the road could hit them from front and flank, caused the Rebels not to attempt any further advances. If they held what they had it would give them a lever for the next day.

Fortunately for the Army of the Potomac, Gen. Hancock became concerned over this boiling battle, and scraped up a brigade from his front, and sent it jogging toward East Cemetery Hill. This outfit collided with Hays's troops there, and finally drove the wearied and battered Gray regiments down the hill, thus restoring the Union line. The second day of fighting at Gettysburg was now over. While the artillerymen of the Army of the Potomac may have wondered what tomorrow would bring, there was too much repair work to be done to permit them much time for idle conjecture.

XIV

THE BIGGEST HUMBUG OF THE SEASON

Gettysburg, 3rd Day

By MIDNIGHT of July 2nd the soft peaceful sounds of night replaced the harsh racket of war. In the darkness of the evening both armies began looking to their wounds, and the Army of the Potomac wondered what the next step would be. If the pattern of past campaigns was any measure, they would be pulling back to some point; in fact Meade had already sent for his generals to discuss this matter.

The two armies had suffered about equally heavy losses of infantry in the battle on Meade's left, though of course neither side knew this about the other. The Confederates knew the extent of their own losses; they also knew that one brigade had shoved a foot into Meade's front door, and that other brigades had obtained levers in both side doors. On the Federal side, Meade knew his casualties, too, and he was aware his troops had thrown the enemy back without having had to commit all of his big VI Corps. In effect, then, the picture did not look too bad to either commander.

At some time during the fighting of July 2nd, however, approximately forty of the Army of the Potomac batteries had pulled lanyard. Fifteen of the nineteen Reserve units had been committed, and guns from every corps except the VI had been in the shoot. A number of units had been hit hard, and brigade and battery commanders were already struggling to patch the damaged batteries. In some cases this meant that they had to reduce battery strength from six to four guns in order to field full crews.[1] Several batteries had lost so heavily in men, horses, and/or matériel that there was no hope of repairing them in time to be ready for duty on July 3rd. Bigelow's, Watson's, and Smith's units were in this category. And there was Buck-lyn's Battery E, 1st Rhode Island, which was so scattered that it would spend all night and most of July 3rd in gathering itself together again. In the matter of officer casualties, the artillery was hurting where it could least afford to hurt — in top command. Of the three officers killed and sixteen more reported wounded, ten were battery commanders and two were brigade chiefs.[2]

Another factor which needed immediate attention was ammunition. In many commands the supply had been totally exhausted; in others it was in varying stages of depletion. With Lee's Army only several hundred yards away, no battery commander in his right mind would face the dawn with anything but full limbers. As a result, Lt. Cornelius Gillett, the ordnance officer of the Artillery Reserve, spent a hectic night. From early evening till dawn a seemingly endless stream of caissons queued up to his ammunition train to replenish their loads. Many of the vehicles came from the various corps batteries, whose spokesmen were asking for ammunition, claiming their own train was unavailable. Gillett's men dutifully doled out seventy wagons full of artillery ammunition in answer to these pleas. All told, over 10,000 rounds were issued to other than the Reserve batteries.

Battery B, 4th U.S., a I Corps outfit, was among those which drew on the train of the Artillery Reserve. Their ammunition detail left the guns at 6 p.m., and the journey of this group left a vivid impression on the memory of at least one of that detail. As the party moved south in quest of the Reserve park, their route was directly in the rear of the II, III, and V Corps lines, and human wreckage of the afternoon's fighting was deposited in every field and farm building along the way. Innumerable groups of wounded lined the roads in all stages of misery and suffering, and the pitiful groans and cries were hideous to hear. Some screamed for water, others moaned for brandy or whiskey, some pleaded for the surgeons, or in delirium called for relatives or friends. A few were even begging for someone to shoot them so as to end their torture. It was an unnerving experience for even the most hardened gunner, so it was with relief that Battery B's detail at last reached Gillett's train. The men took their place in the long line of caissons, and as they sat waiting they could plainly hear every battery, as its turn came, call for the same type round — canister! Not until 2 a.m. of the 3rd did the detail get back to the battery position, and only then were the exhausted men able to flop down on their blankets for a few short hours of sleep.

While the Federal artillerymen labored to have their units ready by morning, the high command of the Army had held a war council to decide the course of action for the coming day. For the second time in twenty-four hours the Army commander, this time backed up by the vote of his generals, determined to stand and fight. In addition, Meade decided that at dawn of the 3rd the Confederates were to be thrown out of the XII Corps' captured trenches on Culp's Hill; the job was to be done by the XII Corps, which had its borrowed units returned from the Army's left. But, by coincidence, the Confederate commander had also decided on a dawn attack by elements of two divisions of Ewell's corps to complete the capture of Culp's Hill and gain entry into Meade's rear.

In the dark hours between midnight and dawn, then, the XII Corps began to slip into jump-off positions for its attack, and two of its batteries — Kinzie's K, 5th U.S., and Muhlenberg's own F, 4th U.S., were hauled up to high ground overlooking the valley of Rock Creek which intersected the corps' line. Both units were run into battery parallel to and southwest of the Baltimore Pike. Directly in front, between 600 and 800-yard range were the enemy-held trenches in the woods. In addition to these units, Winegar's New York outfit remained in position on Powers Hill and Atwell's battery waited on a little rise about

400 yards more to the east; both commands could easily bring
fire to bear on the contested ground.³

Brig. Gen. A. S. Williams, now commanding the XII Corps
while Slocum acted as a wing commander, gave orders for a
crisp fifteen-minute artillery preparation for the attack which
was to start at daybreak. Following this, Geary's division was
to attack from the corps' left, while the right of the corps' line
created a diversion by making noise. At 4:30 a.m., with the
first streaks of light breaking over the eastern horizon, the four
battery commanders barked their orders: 'Number one —
Fire! Number two — Fire!' For the prescribed fifteen minutes
ten rifled cannon and ten Napoleons lashed the still dark woods
with a blistering concentrated shelling. The woodland shook
with the crash of exploding shells; splintered tree limbs came
tumbling to earth; and flying hunks of iron hurtled through
the air. Two Rebel regiments in forward positions near a stone
breastwork suffered a bit from this pounding, as did part of
the famed Stonewall Brigade waiting in reserve. All in all,
though, the damage was light, and shortly after, the Graycoats
were clinking their bayonets into place on gun muzzles preparatory to moving out against Culp's Hill itself.

At 4:45 a.m. cries of 'Cease fire' rang out from the Federal
gun commanders. For a few minutes all was quiet, and then the
Blue infantry rose up and prepared to move out. But, meanwhile, the Rebels stole a march on the Federals and stormed
forward into Geary's amazed regiments. This was the start of
a bitter fight which would rage for some seven hours to determine which side would own Culp's Hill.

At 5:30 a.m. the XII Corps batteries reopened in support
of the hard-pressed Yankee infantry. The corps' batteries were
soon joined by Rigby's Battery A, Maryland Light Artillery, a
Reserve outfit loaned to the XII Corps the day before. The
unit had been put in position 500 yards west of the Baltimore
Pike a mile south of Gettysburg, and this was the first chance
of the campaign the Marylanders had had to do any real shoot-
ing.⁴ On and off during the morning the Union batteries ham-

mered away at the woods in the rear of the Confederate assault
waves in an attempt to break up reinforcements and to chop
up any Rebel units who showed themselves within the fields of
fire. It was a duck shoot for the Yankee gunners; the Rebels
had found the ground too rough and broken to permit them
to bring forward any of their own batteries, so the Federals
had the field to themselves.

Despite their lack of artillery support, the Confederates gave
the XII Corps a difficult time. Meade was forced to rush over
reinforcements, including a brigade from the fresh VI Corps.
Even Capt. James M. Robertson's artillery brigade from the
cavalry corps was sent hurrying over to the Reserve park to
be ready for any eventuality. By this time the Reserve had been
depleted, since twelve of its batteries were already sitting along
the battle line.[5] Finally, about 10:30 the exhausted and decimated Confederate regiments, stopped in front and threatened
on their left, were driven yard by yard down the east face of
Culp's Hill and back into their former lines east of Rock Creek.
Bit by bit the cannon fell quiet, hot powder-fouled muskets
got a chance to cool, and a heavy stillness slid in over the whole
battlefield.

About the time the fighting on Williams's front was drawing
to an end, Gen. Hunt set out on an inspection of the artillery
along the length of the Federal line. He started with the XII
Corps, and, finding things there were now in hand, he turned
his horse toward Cemetery Hill. As he rode along the Union
right and center, Hunt found that there had been very few
changes in the battery line-ups. North of the Baltimore Pike,
Wainwright still had his five batteries in position — twenty-
four guns, ten of which were Napoleons.

As he inspected the I Corps units Hunt noticed that Regular
Battery B, 4th U.S., was still manning only four of its pieces,
the other two having been disabled two days before. He reined
to a halt and asked the acting commander, Sgt. Mitchell, about
ammunition status, casualties, and horse losses. When informed
that the unit had only fifty men present for duty and barely

enough horses to pull the remaining four guns and two caissons, Hunt remarked that had he known the true state of their condition he would have replaced them early that morning with a unit from the Reserve. The sergeant respectfully requested that the general not relieve them, and Hunt smilingly nodded agreement and rode off toward Osborn's guns across the road.

South of the Baltimore Pike, in the cemetery, rested Osborn's batteries, forty-three guns, of which six were 20-pounder Parrotts, eighteen were Napoleons, and the other nineteen light rifles.[6] On the left of the cemetery were the II Corps batteries of Capt. John G. Hazard. This block contained five batteries of twenty-six tubes, two less than the day before, as Brown's Rhode Islanders were down a section. Ten of Hazard's group were Napoleons, the rest light rifles. And just to the left of these units was a battery from the Reserve, Lt. Evan Thomas's C, 4th U.S., whose six Napoleons had done good work in protecting Hancock's center the day before.

As Hunt trotted down the long line of the II Corps, he came to the open lower ground at the southern end of Cemetery Ridge. Here was the reinforced Reserve brigade of Lt. Col. Freeman McGilvery. Present were five Reserve batteries which had been in the fighting of the day before, plus a fresh Connecticut outfit and an attached section from a new Pennsylvania battery.[7] This collection of Reserve batteries was made up of eleven light ordnance rifles, sixteen Napoleons, and the four James rifles [8] and two 12-pounder howitzers of the Connecticut battery.

Passing McGilvery's line, Hunt reached the extreme left of Meade's position — the environs of Little Round Top, held by the V Corps. Here were the six 10-pounder Parrotts of Rittenhouse's Battery D, 5th U.S. — still resting on the forward face of the knoll where Hazlett had put them before his death. Nearby on lower ground to Rittenhouse's right were six Napoleons of Gibbs's Battery L, 1st Ohio Light Artillery, but due to their relatively short range, Gibbs's guns would not pull lanyard on the 3rd. Backing up this end of the Federal line (but they would not become engaged) were two more V Corps batteries, Barnes's C, 1st New York, and Walcott's C, Massachusetts Light Artillery.[9]

The Army of the Potomac, then, had in readiness nearly 180 cannon almost equally divided between light long-range rifles and the heavier Napoleons.[10] Of this awesome collection of artillery Hunt estimated that seventy-five guns could be brought to bear on any attack made against the center of Meade's line; it was possible, though, that by a minor shifting of positions by the batteries on Cemetery Hill, the number of pieces that could cover Hancock's part of the front might be raised even higher.

Gen. Hunt was well pleased with what he found. All the batteries seemed to be in good condition and all had replenished their ammunition. In addition, Hunt could draw on the eight completely fresh batteries of the big VI Corps.[11] If worse came to worse, these might have to be called upon, since the Artillery Reserve had already loaned away almost all of its units. All that remained to the Reserve command in the way of serviceable batteries were Weir's C, 5th U.S. (which had recovered its lost guns during the night); Parsons's A, New Jersey Light Artillery; Fitzhugh's K, 1st New York; and Cooper's B, 1st Pennsylvania, which had been exchanged for Ricketts's battery the night before — a grand total of twenty-two guns. However, Tyler's command still had the visiting brigade of three batteries from the cavalry corps under Capt. Robertson.[12]

However, there was one point in the Union position which worried Gen. John Newton, now commanding the I Corps. This was the open area to Hancock's left. Here was the ground Sickles's corps was to have manned the previous day but abandoned in favor of the peach orchard line. Late in the afternoon of July 2nd elements of the I Corps had been hurried over to reinforce the threatened collapse on this part of the field, and one small I Corps division, Doubleday's, still remained here. By hurried patchwork measures on the morning of July 3rd,

Newton filled up the breach with intermingled detachments of the I and II Corps, and then the battered III Corps lined up its troops in rear of these, giving Newton a feeling of reasonable safety for this part of the front.

Artillery support was hard to obtain, though. Newton's own I Corps batteries were all committed on the north end of the line, and Hancock's were likewise all deployed. Therefore, Newton applied for and received authority to call on the Artillery Reserve for help. The only immediate aid which came to him was Capt. Andrew Cowan's veteran 1st New York Battery, detached from the VI Corps. This unit trotted up about 10 a.m., but Gen. Doubleday decided there was no immediate need for the guns at the moment and told Cowan to park in reserve somewhere nearby.

At some point in Hunt's ride, probably while he was atop the west face of Cemetery Hill, his attention was called to the movement along the Rebel line on Seminary Ridge and its southern prolongation. Scanning its length with his field glasses, the general could see battery after battery being pulled and shoved into position, their muzzles pointing at Cemetery Ridge. Hunt could not tell what this maneuver meant. It could be merely a defensive move by Lee, but on the other hand that Confederate commander was known more as an attacker. If that were to be Lee's game, thought Hunt, it certainly appeared that he would move against Meade's center. Hunt therefore began cautioning battery and brigade commanders to reserve their fire if the enemy's guns open up. They were to save their ammunition for the infantry. Only after the Rebel batteries had been firing for ten or fifteen minutes were the Union guns to reply, and then they were only to direct a slow return fire against the more obnoxious batteries.

If Lee was going to hurl regiments at Meade's center, Hunt foresaw a beautiful opportunity to whiplash the Graycoats with a devastating cross-fire, as soon as they showed themselves. But this barrage, together with the frontal shelling the Union batteries would launch, would require plenty of ammunition; thus his caution to husband the supply. If everything worked as Hunt hoped, the Rebel attack would probably never reach the Federal line.

What Hunt suspected might happen was already in preparation. Pickett's division of Longstreet's corps, reinforced by Pettigrew's from A. P. Hill, was getting ready to make a lunge for the center of the Yankee line — at the point where Wright's Rebel forces had wrested a foothold during the twilight hours of the previous day. To pave the way for this attack, the Confederate artillery was to lay down a concentrated shelling. To accomplish this, the Rebels were juggling their artillery about in order to put as much weight as possible into their gun line. This was the maneuvering which Hunt had spotted and could not explain. Col. Alexander, in charge of Longstreet's batteries, rolled seventy-five pieces into line along his front; on his left, Col. R. L. Walker, A. P. Hill's chief-of-artillery, had sixty guns under his control; and prolonging the arc of cannon around from the seminary to Benner's Hill were twenty-four rifled guns of Ewell's corps under Col. Tom Carter. Besides these, there were two of the weird breech-loading Whitworth rifles sitting on Oak Hill a mile north of the Cashtown Road. This represented virtually all of the available effective gun strength of Longstreet's and Hill's corps, except for a small number of short-range 12-pounder howitzers left undeployed. However, Ewell failed to make use of all this artillery strength, thus giving the Federals an unexpected break in the crucial fighting ahead.

The Confederate battle plan suffered from one grave misjudgment — one which Col. Alexander would later admit. With a line that would permit them to enfilade the center and right center of the Yankee position, the Confederates chose to put almost their entire effort hub to hub along Seminary Ridge in direct parallel to the Federal ranks on Cemetery Ridge. Only A. P. Hill seemed to give any thought to the possibility of raking the Federal lines with fire, rather than blasting them straight on, and the only action Hill took to carry out his views was to position the two Whitworth rifles north of the railroad cut.

Sometime between 7 and 8 a.m. on July 3rd, five Rebel guns on Seminary Ridge cut loose, at Hill's direction, against the right flank of the Federal II Corps. The salvo of shells came whizzing across the mile of open fields and slammed into the caisson line of Battery A, 4th U.S., a unit commanded by a promising West Pointer, 1st Lt. Alonzo H. Cushing. This officer was just two years out of the academy, and he had already received brevets for gallantry in action at Fredericksburg and at Chancellorsville; he would win his third one here — posthumously. One shell of that salvo tore up Cushing's ammunition supply. It made a direct hit on the number two limber, which exploded with a shuddering crash and instantly set off two nearby limbers, which shook the ground with their explosions. The terrific shock wave from the almost simultaneous explosions of the three limbers was felt in the next unit over — Battery A, 1st Rhode Island. It knocked a Rhode Island driver from his horse, twisted up the teams of a gun limber, and sent another team off in driverless panic across the open fields west of Cemetery Ridge. When the Rhode Islanders last saw their limber, it was headed straight into the enemy lines.

The Federals lashed back to counter this annoyance. A Rebel artillery commander quickly rode over to see what had triggered off this exchange; finding his five guns getting much the worse of this unnecessary duel, the commander immediately ordered them to desist.[13]

About 11 a.m. a strange quiet settled over the entire battlefield. The sudden silence was so overpowering that the men of Battery A, 1st Rhode Island, could do nothing but just stare at one another. When someone did speak he unthinkingly talked in a low tone, as if afraid the vibrations from his voice might set off a new explosion. Gradually the Federals began to relax and move about. The Rhode Islanders, for example, used the lull to break out their cooking gear, for the men had not eaten since the evening before. With their stomachs full, they checked their ammunition again, saw that the sponge buckets were filled with water, and made certain the battery was ready for instant action.

The hot noon sun beat down on Gettysburg as 150,000 men literally sweated out the waiting. Then, at 1 p.m., from the lower end of the Gray line, there was a tiny gun flash, and seconds later the shell buzzed over the Federal line on Cemetery Ridge. It exploded in the midst of a group of 19th Massachusetts Infantry men, who were having lunch, and killed a lieutenant. A brief pause followed; then there was a second flash from the same area, and another shell came buzzing over the same Yankee position and smashed into a stack of muskets.

Union veterans interpreted these shots as coming from signal guns, and, before anyone had a chance to dispute their claim, the Confederate gun battalions proved the point. As if someone had put a match to an exposed powder train, a flurry of distant flashes ran the length of Seminary Ridge, growing in intensity. The first salvos screamed toward a little grove of trees near the center of Meade's ranks on Cemetery Ridge, which had been mistakenly assumed by Longstreet's chief gunner to be the town cemetery.

These first crashes of exploding shells sent the Yankee artillerymen running for their action posts. But the Federal gunners heeded Gen. Hunt's caution about being drawn into a needless artillery duel and so ducked low behind their pieces and waited. Capt. Phillips and Lt. Frederic A. Lull of the 5th Massachusetts Battery had been resting under a pup tent when the bombardment began. Both men immediately scrambled out and ran for the cover of a nearby dirt pile. Their decision was most wise, for minutes later an enemy shell plunged into the flimsy little tent and completely shredded it.

The racket of exploding shells reached an ear-ringing pitch as some 140 Confederate guns swung into action. Capt. Phillips later estimated that at least a hundred shots a minute were fired by the Confederates during the next hour and a half. (The actual number was probably nearer 60 to 75 shots per minute.)

The din was constant and quite overpowering. Longstreet's and Hill's battalions on Seminary Ridge were firing fuzed projectiles, but many of the batteries of Ewell's corps had had so many fuze failures that they were hurling only solid shot. The fields about the formerly peaceful little village were quickly blanketed in billowing clouds of dirty-white smoke, and the din of cannon fire and exploding shells rose to a roar described by one Yank artilleryman as 'rivaling the angriest thunder.' Fortunately for the Federals, though, a good part of the enemy projectiles were passing clean over the ridge and exploding in the hollow just beyond. Here their damage was confined to killing and wounding some of the horses of Meade's staff, blowing up a number of Reserve's caissons, killing Gen. Tyler's horse, and causing Meade to seek safer ground for his command further east.

As Hunt had instructed, the Union gunners just sat and took it. After some fifteen minutes, Gen. Hancock, whose II Corps was absorbing the bulk of this pounding, galloped over to Capt. Hazard and shouted for him to put the II Corps artillery into action. The captain obeyed his corps commander. Further south, McGilvery's batteries were not being hurt in the least by this awesome cannonade. Most of the enemy projectiles screamed by twenty to a hundred feet over their heads. Mc-Gilvery's men seemed quite safely sheltered behind the low dirt and rail parapets which their commander had ordered erected that morning in front of every gun; indeed, some of the men even seemed to enjoy the noisy display. On his part, Capt. Phillips of the Massachusetts battery later wrote disdainfully of his enemy's effort: 'I don't know what the Rebels expected to do, but it was certainly a very foolish performance.' He remarked further: 'Viewed as a display of fireworks, the Rebel practice was entirely successful, but as a military demonstration it was the biggest humbug of the season.' [14]

This horrendous barrage from the Confederate guns caused Gen. Newton to call for artillery. Cowan's New York battery quickly mounted up in response to the request. Leaving his

caissons behind, Cowan sent his guns up the slope at a brisk
trot and wheeled into battery in support of Doubleday's I
Corps division. Tops of limber chests flew up, implements
were snatched from their traveling positions, and the 1st New
York Battery began a slow counter-battery fire. Newton's call
also reached Capt. James Robertson, who had temporarily
assumed command of the Reserve when Gen. Tyler had collapsed from heat prostration. Newton's request was for rifled
guns, so the captain answered it by sending up one of his horse
artillery outfits, Capt. J. J. Daniels's 9th Michigan Battery,[15]
which, like all cavalry artillery, was armed with 3-inch rifles.
Daniels immediately ordered his men into their saddles and
onto the limbers, and away he galloped to Newton's support.
As they reached the position, the general waved them into line
and yelled at Daniels to beat down the enemy fire.

While the Confederates' avowed purpose was to silence the
Yankee artillery in general, they were concentrating much of
their effort on the area closest to their intended objective —
the area centered by that little patch of trees. Just in rear of
these were the three II Corps batteries of Rorty (Pettit's old
command), Brown, and Cushing, and these outfits received
a thorough hammering.

Gen. Gibbon, in charge of the division commanding this
part of the line, had been involved in some furious battles before, including the cornfield at Antietam, but even he was
amazed by the volume of the Confederate fire. With the trained
eye of a former artilleryman, he watched the sky and could
plainly see the round smoothbore projectiles as they curved
down in trajectory; the rifled ones he could spot only when
they upset in flight and tumbled through the air. Exploding
shell and case shot shook the air overhead and threw fragments
in all directions, some of which struck the ground and tossed
dirt and rocks about, thus creating as much danger as the fragments were in themselves. Gibbon said it was 'the most infernal
pandemonium it has ever been my fortune to look upon.'[16]

The Union general tried to learn how his infantry was faring under this noisy rain of iron, but very few men were in sight; those he could see through the haze of smoke were taking advantage of every scrap of cover, a number crouching behind a low rock wall some twenty-five yards in front of the booming corps batteries. The only moving creatures Gibbon saw on the ridge proper were the artillerymen, and smoke obscured all but their legs. As he watched the batteries, he became entranced with the apparent lethargic attitude of the horses. Even when a shell struck down several in a team, the rest would stand by stolidly. The general's eye then came to rest on Cushing's battery. A cannoneer was standing in the rear of one of the limbers when a shrieking shell swept low over the ridge, passed clean under the limber, and almost severed a leg of the man standing behind it. The poor soldier somehow arose, and Gibbon watched him hop rearward on his good leg, the other was dangling uselessly in shreds.

Brown's Battery B, 1st Rhode Island, also knew that not all of the Rebel shells were missing the low crest. One of their pieces was being loaded when an enemy projectile made a direct hit on the front part of the tube. The number one man, who was waiting to ram a new load home, had the left side of his head blown off, and the number three, who was in the act of inserting the new round, died soon after; his left arm had been torn from its socket.

Quickly clearing away the physical and human debris, the gun commander and the rest of his crew tried to resume loading. The new round was again pushed into the mouth of the Napoleon and the rammer seated against the ball. The men gave a shove, but the charge scarcely moved. Again and again they heaved and strained on the rammer, even slamming the opposite end with an axe, all to no avail; the dent on the top of the muzzle caused by the enemy hit was too great. As the gun cooled, the partially loaded round became firmly wedged in the mouth, and the command reluctantly reported the piece out of action. This particular gun had been abandoned on the field in front of Cemetery Ridge during the fighting of July 2nd, and it had been recovered that night. In addition to the hit which put it out of action on the 3rd, it was struck twice more by enemy shells and thirty-nine times by bullets. It was withdrawn from the field after the fighting, and eventually returned to the state capital, where it became Rhode Island's famous 'Gettysburg Gun' monument.

On the extreme right of the II Corps, in the front skirt of a heavy cluster of trees, stood the excellent Regular outfit Battery I, 1st U.S., Lt. George A. Woodruff commanding. This was the same outfit Ricketts had led up to the Henry house hill in July 1861, and it had fought hard for the Army of the Potomac in every campaign from the first battles of the Peninsula through to Gettysburg. Behind this was an illustrious Mexican War record, so that the battery was rightfully proud of itself. Woodruff's battery was receiving heavy pounding from the Rebels. Time after time the crews had to interrupt their firing to clear away large branches of trees which Rebel shells brutally ripped off and dumped atop the thundering cannon. A caisson was hit and exploded with a deafening crash, the concussion jarring the ground all about the battery. Horses went down in every team, and men, too, were being hit. Lt. Tully M'Crea, commanding a section of Woodruff's battery, was not too impressed with the Rebel barrage which was crashing onto Cemetery Ridge and the slope behind, though. 'If their artillery had been as good as their infantry,' said M'Crea, 'our loss would have been very much greater.' [17]

Gen. Hunt was visiting Rittenhouse's battery on Little Round Top when the enemy turned on the bombardment. After determining its scope, the artillery chief galloped back to where the Reserve park had been. He was prepared to order fresh batteries and ammunition up to Cemetery Ridge as soon as the enemy shelling ceased. But, on reaching the spot, the general found nothing but a shell-swept plain littered with dead horses and debris from a dozen blown-up caissons. For a moment he was puzzled; then several mounted soldiers rode up to advise him that the Reserve had been moved to safer ground. They had been detailed to this most unhealthy location as guides and messengers.

Following the messengers' lead, Hunt rode over to the new park and alerted the units there to be ready to move up at a moment's notice. Then he set off to report to Meade. He was unable to do so, for the commanding general had left his battered headquarters building for safer ground atop Power's Hill. The artilleryman then decided to ride the line himself to observe the results and replace disabled batteries.

As Hunt trotted onto the ridge, Hazard's II Corps guns were in full fury, and some of Osborn's batteries on Cemetery Hill were adding their crashes to the interminable roar of battle. From their elevated position on Little Round Top, way to the left, Rittenhouse's long-range Parrott rifles had earlier began an annoying and damaging fire on the batteries of the Rebels' Washington Artillery battalion on the Emmitsburg Road.[18] Col. McGilvery's Reserve batteries, however, were following Hunt's instructions implicitly, and had remained silent.

As Gen. Hancock rode along his front, now obviously the enemy's chosen point of attack, he spotted three idle batteries on the left of his line — Phillips's, Thompson's, and Hart's. These were the right-flank units of McGilvery's command, but Hancock gave them pre-emptory orders to cease their idleness and commence firing. Capt. Phillips was disgusted with Hancock's order, which he interpreted as utter ignorance by an infantry officer of artillery techniques. 'The Rebels were not doing us any harm,' said Phillips later, 'and if they wanted to throw away their ammunition I do not see why we should prevent them.'[19] But what line captain would dare disobey a corps commander? Therefore, all three batteries promptly went into action.

Col. McGilvery quickly spotted this outburst and galloped over to see who had authorized this firing contrary to the orders of Gen. Hunt and himself. He was told Gen. Hancock had done so. However, the colonel was not a man to be intimidated when he thought himself in the right, so he promptly ordered the three units to cease fire immediately and to tell their men to take cover again behind the low parapets. Any order to open fire would be given by Hunt or himself.

The enemy shelling continued in unabated fury, the bulk of it pouring down on the center of Hancock's line, and losses began to mount. On Cemetery Hill some of Osborn's batteries were catching some damage, as the Rebel projectiles whistled into the cemetery and beyond at a rate which astounded Osborn; the volume convinced the Yankee major that the Confederate guns outnumbered the Federal by two to one. Osborn's position was not only being hit from the west and northwest, but some of Ewell's batteries to the northeast on Benner's Hill were flinging their projectiles down the length of Osborn's line on the west face of the hill. The enemy shooting was deadly accurate, raking the line of Osborn's guns, bowling over men and horses, and blowing up caissons. One projectile, probably a solid shot, went through six horses standing side by side.

Osborn instantly reacted to this vicious fire by turning Taft's big 20-pounder Parrotts and Norton's 3-inch rifles on the enemy guns. These two commands were located on the northern edge of the cemetery, so it was relatively easy for them to get a line on the Gray batteries. After a few minutes of this counterbattery fire, the Confederate guns ceased. They reopened a little while later, but this time their aim was poor and they did no harm.

The cannonade had been under way perhaps an hour when Col. McGilvery finally cut the leashes holding his batteries in check. Once again telling his gunners to concentrate on single enemy batteries, which were the plainest targets, he sent every one of his units into action with a slow deliberate fire.

For over an hour more the terrific bombardment continued. Observers described it as surpassing anything they had ever seen. As it continued, the Confederates became a little disheartened, for there seemed to be little if any reduction in the Federal return fire, and time was running out, as the Rebel attack was set to begin about 2 p.m. The Union's counter-battery fire was equally impressive to its own side: Capt. Phillips of the 5th Massachusetts was as enthusiastic about the Union fire as he been unenthusiastic about the Confederate display: 'I never saw artillery so ably handled, or productive of such decisive results. It was far superior even to Malvern Hill.' [20]

The situation began to worry Col. Alexander, who was in over-all charge of Longstreet's artillery. The Yankee fire was cutting up some of his batteries, but more alarming was the rapidly diminishing stock of ammunition. Confederate planning of resupply in this action was miserably inadequate, and battery after battery tried unsuccessfully to find the trains to replenish its fast disappearing supply. So long as rounds remained in the chests, though, the Confederates continued to pour it on.

By 2:30 many of the Federal batteries, particularly those of the II Corps, were beginning to have the same ammunition problem. Attempts were made to use wagons and caissons from the Reserve to bring up fresh supplies, but crossing the shell plastered plain behind Cemetery Ridge was extremely hazardous for those heavy vehicles. Some of the enemy's shells had even reached the Reserve park, killing a mule, and making the others so nervous and unmanageable as to threaten the train with wholesale stampede.

Phillips's Massachusetts battery suddenly saw their luck changed as Rebel guns bore in on them. Near the gun limber of one piece driver John Canty was kneeling on his right knee, his right arm behind one of his horses forelegs, the reins in his left hand. Close by was a corporal assisting a number five man in serving ammunition. Between his knees on the ground, the corporal held a Schenkl combination shell, trying to turn the cap to set the time fuze. Before anyone could duck, there was a sudden whoosh, and a Rebel projectile cut the horse's leg off above the knee, severed Canty's arm above the elbow — he died shortly after from the wound — and hacked the horse's right hind foot off above the ankle, tearing the shoe clear of the hoof in the process. The shoe flew through the air and caught the corporal on the left wrist, disabling him as well. Looking down at his feet the shaken corporal saw the now inert but still unexploded Rebel projectile; the man reached down, picked up the deadly thing, threw it away, and lived to tell the tale.

Throughout the closing hour of the bombardment Gen. Hunt was roaming all over the field. With no staff to help him, the artillery chief was called upon to do everything for himself. In view of the man's tremendous ability and energy, perhaps it was just as well for the Army of the Potomac that he was forced to do so much in person. As the general checked with his gunners, he learned about the declining supply of ammunition and the difficulty of resupply under heavy fire. Realizing that such a condition should be brought to Gen. Meade's immediate attention, Hunt set off for Cemetery Hill, where Meade was said to be. Hunt was prepared to recommend to Meade that the guns be ordered to cease firing, so that the balance of their supply could be saved for the anticipated infantry attack.

Up onto the hill he rode, but Meade was nowhere in sight. Spotting Gen. Howard, Hunt advised him of his proposed cease fire, and Howard concurred. With that the artilleryman swung his horse about and galloped down the ridge, instructing the batteries to gradually slacken their rate of fire and then to stop altogether. Shortly after, one of Meade's aides galloped up to Hunt to say that the commanding general wanted the artillery to stop firing, so Hunt received retroactive approval for his unilateral decision.[21]

By the time Hunt's instructions reached the II Corps guns, they were already at the end of their supply of long-range rounds — only canister remained. Also, these batteries had taken a good pounding and could stand relief. Cushing was apparently in the worst shape; three of his gun limbers had been blown up earlier, and, although these had been replaced by caisson limbers, he was minus three chests full of ammunition. Several wheels had been shot off his guns and replaced by the extras from the caissons. Casualty figures are unavailable for the batteries at this point of the battle, but it seems quite certain that the three II Corps batteries behind the clump of trees had been hurt rather severely, both in men and horses. According to one source Cushing could man but one gun. Gen. Webb, commanding the brigade between Brown and Cushing, noticed the battered condition of these two units and sent back a request that they should be replaced.[22] But Hunt had spotted the need and already sent back orders to the Reserve for every available gun to be moved forward.

By coincidence, as Alexander on the Rebel side neared the end of his ammunition, Capt. Hazard's Federal guns had fallen silent. To the Confederates peering through the haze of battle smoke which crowned Cemetery Ridge, it appeared that the Yankee cannon had finally been knocked out. Vehicles could be seen moving rearward — the Rebels thought they were guns — and Alexander sent a message urging the Gray infantry to make its move. It was now or never he said.[23]

Gen. Pickett, in command of the assault force, extracted a reluctant go-ahead from Longstreet, and the word to move forward was hurriedly passed down the line of waiting Brigades. From their sheltered positions in the wooded slopes behind the artillery, regiment after regiment of Southern troops rose up, formed, dressed their lines, and with loud cries of 'Forward!' emerged into open ground. Altogether, there were 15,000. The Confederate cannon fell silent while their infantry regiments passed through them. A number of batteries were supposed to accompany the attacking force, but the combination of low ammunition supplies and the damage done by the Yankee counter-battery fire left only a couple of thin battalions available for such support. These were now limbered and moved forward along the wide battle line. From the Washington Artillery battalion only five guns from three batteries were in condition to obey the order.

The Federals spotted Alexander's slackening of fire as the Gray infantry moved through his guns, and realized that the enemy was deploying for his big move. Hurried last-minute efforts were made to strengthen the obvious point of attack. There was almost a mile of open ground to be crossed by that Rebel battle line, so it meant the Yanks had some twenty minutes to get ready, and during this period it was up to the Blue artillery to break up the assault before it even reached the Union line.

As the Gray infantry moved forward, the Confederate artillery resumed shooting with all the fire power they could muster. Once more Cemetery Ridge trembled under the holocaust of bursting shells. The harassed II Corps batteries began suffering casualties again. But help was on the way. Through this curtain of fire came Capt. Andrew Cowan's fresh 1st New York Battery. Gen. Webb waved him into position just to the left of the clump of trees. Cowan, however, found space so cramped that he had to shift his right gun over to the other side of the trees close to Cushing's left. Cowan had already done some firing from his position further down the ridge in support of Doubleday, but, when the enemy infantry was spotted forming, the battery was sent rolling up the crest to back up the center of the II Corps line. As Cowan unlimbered just behind Brown's battered Rhode Island unit, the Rebel skirmish line was already flushing the Federal skirmishers out of the fields west of the Emmitsburg Road. Cowan's guns roared out, and the chopped-up Rhode Island battery was withdrawn.

Every gun in the Federal line that had solid, shell, or case shot in its chests now cut loose, and the shriek of flying shells filled the air above the Codori farm. Only the II Corps guns were silent; all they had left was canister — useless until the enemy came in close — so they just had to sit and take it. The pall of smoke covering the fields south of Gettysburg became so dense that the sky overhead darkened as if a monstrous thundercloud had blotted out the sun. Much of the shooting on both sides was now by sheer guesswork, with gunners having trouble seeing their targets.

Then loud shouts and the racket of galloping horses added their clatter to the din, as the last three batteries of the Artillery Reserve came careening up the gentle east slope of the ridge. Hunt waved them into line behind the low stone wall seventy-five yards to the left of the copse of trees. Fitzhugh's Battery K, 1st New York, was put on the right; next to it went Parsons's A, 1st New Jersey. Nearby Weir's Battery C, 5th U.S., began unlimbering.[24] Lt. William Wheeler's 13th New York Battery, an XI Corps unit which had not been engaged, charged onto the ridge, was collared by Gen. Hancock, and flung into line to the left rear of Capt. Rorty's New York outfit.[25]

With the center of the position now strongly reinforced, Hunt raced down the front in search of Col. McGilvery. Finding him, the general yelled over the racket of gunfire and exploding shells to swing his weapons over and rake the Rebel right flank as it angled across his batteries toward Hancock's center. McGilvery quickly relayed the instructions to his gunners, and battery by battery the blackened snouts of the cannon began shifting to the right oblique. Gunners quickly lined up on the awesome spectacle of 15,000 marching men, three lines deep, and stretching across the entire plain opposite Hancock's corps. Thirty-three guns barked violent destruction at the dense target, as it moved slowly but inevitably toward its objective. The Blue artillerymen could plainly see the flashes of their shell-bursts in the target area, and here and there the enemy lines wobbled a bit, as casualties dropped out and the ranks closed up. But still the enemy kept advancing.

Back to Hancock's front galloped Hunt. Here every available gun of the II Corps was being loaded with canister. Lt. Cushing, Sgt. Fuger, and a couple of surviving crewmen were pushing one of the battery's 3-inch rifles down to the stone wall directly in front of the position.[26] Steadily, relentlessly, despite the converging fire of the Yankee cannon, the surviving Rebels kept coming. Men went down; ranks weaved, broke, and re-formed; gaps closed; the left of the Gray line began to crumble away; but still the rest advanced.

Atop Cemetery Ridge the men of the thin II Corps line peered out at this fantastic sight, half in admiration and half in trepidation. An officer of Woodruff's battery, watching that mass moving on his position, concluded that his chances at that moment for a trip to Kingdom Come or Libby Prison were indeed very good. Blue officers could now be heard cautioning their men: 'Steady! Stand fast!' As the Gray ranks neared the Emmitsburg Road, a rustle of clicks ran the length of the II Corps infantry line: musket hammers were being brought to full cock. Behind the thinly spread regiments of Hancock's first line which crouched behind the low rock wall, the corps' batteries waited, their tubes pointed through gaps between the Blue regiments.

The leading wave of Rebels crossed the road and moved into the field a bare 300 yards from the top of the ridge. At that instant, regiment after regiment of Federal infantry blazed away in slashing volleys, and then with fierce ear-ringing crashes Capt. Hazard's batteries at last got to pull lanyard again. The Confederates halted, muskets lowered, and volleys of return fire ripped back. Then they let loose their wild yell and charged for the wall.

Further to the right, nearer the cemetery, Woodruff's Napoleons coughed hard, and six wicked rounds of canister ruptured their tin containers, the balls flying in inverted wedge shape toward the foe. The guns were furiously reloaded with double canister and again laid on the charging mass, which was Pettigrew's division. 'It was impossible to miss,' said one of the Regulars. The battery had forty rounds of canister per gun, an unusually high supply, but by the time this battle was over almost all would be expended. Visible gaps were hewn in the enemy lines. Men went down like ten pins before the devastating blasts of canister and double canister. Federal infantry was pouring in volley after volley, but the ragged lines would not be stopped.

Lt. Woodruff watched their fantastic advance; suddenly he noticed a body of them heading toward a dirt lane that ran up from the Emmitsburg Road past the battery's left. In order to plug that entry route, he gave the command for Lt. Egan's left section to move over further to the left and cover the lane. The limbers moved up, and the two pieces were fastened on. Spurs dug into horses, and the teams began to move. Woodruff now turned to go back to his post behind the other guns. Suddenly a dull thud of a bullet's hitting flesh made Lt. Egan turn in his saddle; young Woodruff was holding his side and painfully struggling to dismount. Egan hastened to his commander's aid and helped him to a sheltered place on the ground behind a tree. But the wounded man, while appreciative of Egan's help, insisted the lieutenant hurry his section to the threatened point. With a last wish of good luck to the mortally wounded Woodruff, Egan led his section along the crest. He had moved only a short distance before Gen. Hays rode over to him and informed him that Cushing's battery was in bad shape and needed his assistance. Seeing a piece of open ground to the right of the threatened battery, Egan waved his little column forward.

The furious flanking fire of Rittenhouse's and McGilvery's batteries had had the effect of pushing the Confederate right in on the center, making the target mass that much easier to hit from the front. One Confederate brigade, Garnett's, felt the bite of the Yankee guns ripping into its flank. Up to now their losses had been very light — about twenty during the pre-assault shelling — and very few had been hit during the advance to the road. But here the pattern changed. Yankee cannon fire from the heights of Little Round Top and McGilvery's line slammed into them, one shell taking down ten men at a clip.[27] By the time the enemy broke into a run up the front face of Cemetery Ridge, their line was scarcely a line — the survivors were just a charging mass of men. Garnett's brigade, for example, was reduced 50 per cent.

North of the clump of trees, opposite Woodruff's battery, Pettigrew's regiments were for the most part stopped cold, as Woodruff's guns and Osborn's units in the Cemetery worked in concert with the cutting volleys of Union infantry. Opposite Cushing, though, others, wild-eyed with battle fury, rushed for the wall where Cushing's lone gun stood. The piece boomed its last round of canister, Gray muskets cracked in return, and Lt. Cushing slumped into Sgt. Fuger's arms, his spine cut in two.

Over the wall the Rebel mob swarmed. It soon overwhelmed the handful of Federal infantry which tried to halt it. Confederate Gen. Armistead, his hat on his sword, could be seen cheering and leading his men on. The line of Blue cannon on the crest of the ridge just beyond, now let go wicked blasts of canister. Then it fell silent as Blue infantry, which had been waiting behind the ridge, came charging forward. The enemy was now pouring into Cushing's position and was shooting at everything in sight. Every officer in Cushing's battery was down; only Sgt. Fuger was left of the commissioned and non-commissioned staff, and he gallantly led what remained of his unit in bitter hand-to-hand brawling over the guns. Even Gen. Hunt got into the vicious fighting. He galloped past the break-through, firing his pistol into the compact mass and tried to rally the broken Federal infantry. A sharp-eyed Rebel rifleman spotted the general, raised his musket, and shot Hunt's horse out from under him, dumping him boot over head to earth.

Further down, by the copse of trees, more Confederates poured over the rock wall and turned on Rorty's guns. In a desperate effort to stop their charge one crew jammed triple canister down the bore of their Parrott rifle. The gun went off with a shivering roar; the force of the recoil was so great that, instead of just rolling rearward, the gun was uplifted and over-turned. Rebel soldiers crumbled to the earth under the charge, their bodies shattered by the heavy canister balls, but others swept into Rorty's position. One tall wiry Reb planted a flag on one of the guns shouting, 'This is ours!' A Yankee sergeant yelled back, 'You lie!' and seizing a handspike whacked the man full across the forehead, killing him instantly. A flurry of shots riddled the sergeant. Then Capt. Rorty fell mortally wounded; others went down about him, and for a few brief

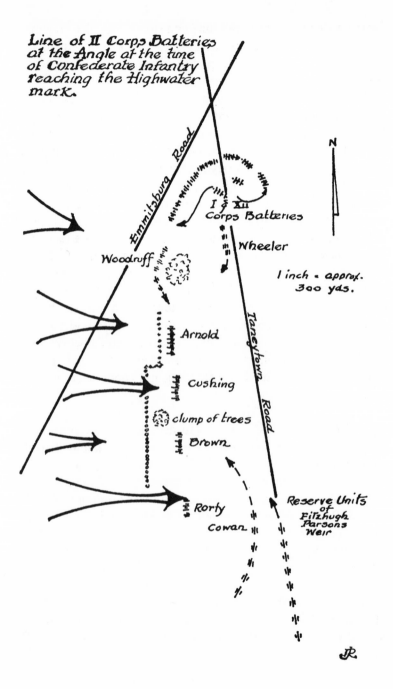

Line of II Corps Batteries
at the Angle at the time
of Confederate Infantry
reaching the Highwater
mark.

N

Emmitsburg Road

I & XII
Corps Batteries

Wheeler

Woodruff

1 inch = approx.
300 yds.

Taneytown Road

Arnold

Cushing

clump of trees

Brown

Rorty

Cowan

Reserve Units
of
Fitzhugh
Parsons
Weir

moments — the only time in the battery's history — the enemy had control of its guns.[28]

Cowan's 1st New York Battery also felt the hot grasp of enemy hands. The Federal infantry that had been covering the battery suddenly rose up and wheeled to the right of the trees, and through the gap created by this shift poured Rebel infantry. Running low through the smoke, some of the Graycoats spotted Cowan's guns. One of them, a young major, shouted, 'Take the guns!' The crews were in the midst of reloading, and, seeing the precarious position of his guns, Cowan shouted to drag the pieces rearward after the next discharge. Lt. Wright, who was standing nearby, prepared to carry out the order, but before he could open his mouth he was shot down, and another bullet from the same volley went through Capt. Cowan's coat. By this time the weapons were loaded, and the crews leaped clear. The 3-inch rifles cracked sharply, and double canister chewed at the attackers. All of the available battery officers were down by this time except Capt. Cowan.

When the smoke cleared, the enemy had retreated. Left behind was a pathetic mass of human wreckage. Right in front of the guns lay the body of the young Rebel major, sword still in hand, surrounded by dead and wounded of his command. That evening the dead Confederate officer was buried near the spot where he fell, and Capt. Rorty of the 1st New York Light Artillery was interred on the major's right. The major's sword was retrieved as a trophy; Capt. Cowan returned it to some of the enemy survivors on the same spot twenty-four years later.

Over on the right of the breakthrough point, at the back end of an angle where the stone wall turned east-west for a short distance, was Battery A, 1st Rhode Island. The Federal line here was some twenty yards in the rear of the point where Cushing was overrun, and the Confederates charging this segment had to come up the ridge that much farther before they could cross bayonets with the Federal infantry. Holding the line here with the Rhode Islanders were Connecticut and Delaware infantry regiments. The momentum of Pettigrew's Rebel charge here carried almost to the wall. At this point a number four man of one of the double-canistered Rhode Island guns stood with lanyard in hand, seemingly paralyzed by the sight. A sergeant bellowed at the man, 'Pull! Pull!' And finally the entranced soldier gave a jerk on the rope, and the gun went off with deadly effect. With that, Yankee infantry rose up and slammed volley after volley into the Gray troops. The charge disintegrated in smoke and blood.

On the south flank of the Confederate penetration, Stannard's I Corps brigade, which Hancock had ordered to wheel on its right flank and enfilade the Rebel waves, was bringing tremendous pressure to bear. The struggle inside Hancock's line near the clump of trees still lasted some fifteen to thirty minutes, though. Finally Union reinforcements surrounded and crushed the small band of Confederates who had burst into the Yankee position.

The main body of the Gray artillery had ceased fire when their infantry closed with the Federals. The guns which had gone forward with the Confederate attack tried to support the advance by laying down an enfilading fire on Stannard's brigade from the peach orchard and the nearby fields. Fifteen to eighteen pieces were all the Rebels had been able to send forward, and these few pieces soon found themselves in the more common predicament of Confederate artillery — outgunned and overwhelmed. One cluster of guns had unlimbered a bare 200 yards to the left front of Col. McGilvery's mass of cannon. For a while the Yankee colonel ignored them, concentrating his fire on the Rebel infantry. When his guns became masked by the proximity of the two lines, however, he deftly swung four batteries around, pointed out the enemy cannon, and told his men to 'clean house.'

It took about ten minutes for the Union guns to execute the order, according to Capt. Phillips of the 5th Massachusetts. At the end of this time he could not see a moving soul about the enemy guns; he assumed they were all casualties or had fled. And indeed the deserted and muted Confederate battery stood in the field all afternoon like an eerie monument. Phillips's impression of the punishment the Confederate guns received was later verified by a letter one of the Gray battery commanders wrote to Col. Alexander after the war. This officer told his old commander that the Yankee fire quickly wrecked several of his weapons and disabled a number of his men and horses. It was soon obvious to the Rebel batteries that they were engaged in a hopeless job. As their limited supply of ammunition ran out, the officers began sending their gun detachments from the field. One group of four cannons promptly had two of its number put out of action as it attempted to withdraw. It was indeed a dismal day for the Confederate soldier.

As the Rebel forces retreated from Hancock's front, Hunt began directing the repair of the wreckage the assault had heaped on his artillery. Rorty's, Arnold's, and Cushing's decimated batteries were withdrawn, and other units which were still combat-effective were put in their places. Where necessary, commands were sent galloping to the trains to refill empty chests; and, this done, they hurried back to their positions on the crest.

Assured that the center of the line was being adequately repaired, Hunt trotted toward the left to initiate the same action. En route he was startled to see another smaller force of enemy marching toward McGilvery's part of the line. This was Wilcox's small brigade, which, through miserable mismanagement, was belatedly moving to support Pickett's now non-existent right flank. Hunt scurried after Col. McGilvery, found him, and told the colonel to blast the Rebel brigade. Thereupon he wheeled his horse about, and when he reached the ridge behind Hancock's troops again, he flung every available battery — mostly Reserve units — against Wilcox's left flank. His orders were instantly answered with heavy crashes and rolling echoes of Union cannonfire.

This was more than the Confederates had bargained for. Wilcox's troops soon realized how hopeless their situation was made by this powerful enemy barrage. They halted their advance, and then turned and marched swiftly back to Seminary Ridge. Now, to all intents and purposes the battle of Gettysburg was over.

The only separate piece of fighting that day was a clash between cavalry elements of both armies. Hoping to coincide with a Confederate breakthrough on Cemetery Ridge, Jeb Stuart put 5000 troopers in motion to sweep into Meade's rear from the northeast. The Confederate column was spotted about noon moving north of town, and Yankee cavalry commander Gen. Alfred Pleasonton — the self-styled savior of Chancellorsville — received the alert. About 1 p.m., the Gray troopers popped up in front of Pleasonton's skirmish lines some three miles east of Gettysburg. Like their 'coffee boiler' brothers atop Cemetery Ridge, the Blue cavalrymen beat off the enemy attacks, with grateful assistance from Pennington's and Randol's Regular batteries, and the final threat to Meade's position was thwarted.

The results of Gettysburg were many-sided. More than any other battle fought between the two armies it opened a wealth of controversy involving senior officers of both sides. For the Confederates, Stuart, Ewell, Longstreet, and even Lee himself became the center of these disputes. On the Federal side, Sickles was criticized for his unauthorized change of position, and Meade for his failure to counter-attack on the 3rd. Still another less-publicized disagreement arose between Gens. Hunt and Hancock over the conduct of the artillery on the third day. The dispute between the two men began that very night.

Maj. Gen. Winfield Scott Hancock lay painfully wounded in a corps field hospital; he had been shot down as Pickett's men broke into his lines. Despite his wound, the general was able to send off a short terse message to Meade in which he advised his commanding general that unauthorized tampering with his II Corps artillery had almost cost the Federals the day. 'I . . . found that the twelve guns on my salient had been removed by someone,' wrote Hancock, 'whom I call upon you to hold accountable, as without them, with worse troops, I should certainly have lost the day.' [29]

Actually no guns were withdrawn from Hancock's line until Cowan replaced Brown's battered outfit. Thus, there was an augmentation of firepower, not a detraction. And it appears that any other wrecked II Corps batteries were removed from the field only after Pickett's troops had been driven back. It may be that Hancock had only witnessed the charge from the left end of his line. Under such circumstances he might have assumed that since the batteries beyond the clump of trees were silent they had been removed — as Col. Alexander had done. But at this stage of the fight the II Corps guns were silent by necessity, not by choice — nothing remained in their chests but canister. It is true that earlier in the action Gen. Hunt had instructed not only the II Corps batteries but all other batteries as well to hold their fire. Hancock shortly overruled Hunt's instructions to the II Corps gunners, and he endeavored to bring part of McGilvery's weapons into play as well. This action prompted Hunt to go on record to say that, if his original orders had been followed, the Confederate attack would never have reached Hancock's line in the first place.

On the face of it one might assume that a corps or division commander had complete tactical authority over all troops assigned to him for a specific occasion. Therefore, Hancock had the right to scream about who had ordered his guns out of action without his consent. However, the case was not quite so clear cut; it was inexorably involved in the Army's custom and practice and lack of clarity in Army regulations and orders. In the Army of the Potomac it had been common practice to allow division commanders almost complete tactical control of artillery assigned to them. But the position and authority of the Army's chief-of-artillery had been accepted by custom as being supreme in artillery matters — that is, until the tenure of Hooker. Barry and Hunt were both respected artillerists, and few officers, at least in the early part of the war, felt qualified to question the judgment of either of them.

When the Army of the Potomac was first organized by Gen. McClellan, Barry's job as chief-of-artillery was to handle purely administrative duties, unless directed otherwise. When Hunt succeeded him in September 1862, Gen. McClellan informed him personally that Hunt was to have absolute command as well as the administration of all the artillery in the Army, and McClellan would hold him responsible for it. No written order to this effect was ever issued, however. At Antietam Hunt operated exactly in this manner, controlling both the division and the Reserve batteries. When Burnside replaced McClellan, Hunt and the new Army commander agreed to a continuation of the same duties for the chief-of-artillery, but again it was an informal decision unconfirmed by written order.

Then came Hooker, who defined Hunt's duties as being purely administrative — a situation Hunt considered anomalous. Hooker carried this change even to the point of issuing orders to the artillery through the Army's adjutant general. Hunt was not even to be directly informed about his command's movements. When his troops went into combat, Hunt was just supposed to hang about Hooker. Only after Hooker's battle was lost and his artillery in a mess, did he restore Hunt to the command of that arm.[30]

The Army was on the road when Gen. Meade inherited it, and in the press of the hours Hunt did not have the opportunity to get an interpretation from Meade about what Hunt's duties were to be. But the assignments that Meade gave to Hunt on the night of July 1st and the morning of the 2nd convinced the artilleryman that he was once again the commander of that arm.[31] Furthermore, Meade restored Hunt to the list of those designated to receive copies of all orders which had bearing on the movements of the artillery. Such authority and treatment was above that which Joe Hooker had accorded this senior artilleryman, and more in keeping with his former status.

As it turned out after Gettysburg, Meade reaffirmed Hunt's assumption. The command of all artillery not attached to troops was given to Hunt, as well as the management and re-

sponsibility of the movements, equipment, training, etc. of that
arm, which were attached to other troops. 'In fact,' Hunt told
the Congressional Committee, 'it amounted to giving me the
command of the whole of the artillery, as in other armies.' [32]
As a matter of record, though, Hunt had previously defined to
the committee that his command authority, prior to Hooker's
time, involved 'the control of all the troops not attached to
corps or divisions and under the immediate command of other
officers at the time.' [33] Therefore, if this latter statement was
the true bounds of his authority, then Hunt had no right to
interfere with any troops under the control of Gen. Hancock.
But it had been a tradition established by McClellan and perpetuated by Burnside that Hunt could step in at any point on
artillery matters, and McClellan had told him that, if necessary,
he could use the name of the commanding general if Hunt ran
into a dispute with anyone who outranked him. Custom and
practice, then, had given Hunt carte blanche in handling the
artillery of the Army of the Potomac.

Hancock, for his part, had seen the fiasco in the woods and
fields around Chancellorsville caused by artillery which had
not been under proper control. In fact, he had been one of
those who remarked bitterly about it. Therefore, Hancock must
have recognized the necessity of such a position as chief-of-
artillery carrying some command authority. But how far he
was willing to acknowledge this authority was another matter.
It is clear from his message to Meade that he regarded his own
corps' batteries as being outside the sphere of the chief-of-artillery.

In the situation which arose on the third day at Gettysburg,
Hunt undoubtedly believed that he knew better what Hancock's
artillery could do under the circumstances than Hancock did,
when the latter ordered it into action, and Hunt probably felt
there was not time to locate Hancock to obtain agreement to
his, Hunt's, command to hold fire. Thus, Hunt felt justified in
using his carte blanche authority to tell Hazard to hold his fire
and later to replace his broken units. Hancock, who was un-

aware that Meade had confirmed Hunt's order, quite naturally regarded the whole affair as pure usurpation of authority. But he must have learned the true facts before long, since his testimony before the Congressional Committee omitted this point completely. In fact that body heard testimony from Gen. Meade that he personally had halted the Federal guns.

Hancock also took issue with the Army's artillery on a second point — the lack of ammunition. In his official report he remarked that his corps' batteries were 'imperfectly supplied.' Though admitting that his corps had brought up but half its ammunition train, and was therefore 'somewhat' dependent on others, Hancock complained that the train of the Artillery Reserve was not able to resupply his batteries to the extent desired. While not making a major issue of the point, in either his report or testimony, it was a back-handed slap at Hunt which was not justified. Hunt had no control over Hancock's ammunition train. That it did not reach the field was no fault of the Army's artillery chief. On the other hand, Hancock (as well as all the other corps commanders) should have been thankful for Hunt's foresight in once again providing their guns with ammunition, even if not to the extent they desired.

The whole affair was unfortunate, but luckily for the Army it never erupted to the point where it interfered with the cooperation between the two men in the remaining campaigns. Not until the mid-1880's did the affair gain much publicity. At this time Hunt reiterated his views in an article on the third day in *Battles and Leaders*. By this time Hancock had died, so Brig. Gen. Francis A. Walker wrote in rebuttal for him, stating that Hancock commanded the battle line on that part of the front and thus commanded *all* combatant troops then in action.

Hunt, in rejoinder, stated that the Army regulations, while suffering from lack of precise wording, still implied the traditional concept that the chief-of-artillery was just that. In addition, Hunt took no stock in Walker's contention that only Hancock was capable of determining the morale consequences if the friendly artillery ceased its fire; Hunt wrote that he was well aware of the morale tone of the Blue riflemen, and he respected their capabilities, otherwise he would never have ordered the cease fire. In any event Meade must have agreed completely with Hunt's decision, for the matter was never brought up in charges nor were any disciplinary measures taken against Hunt.

After the battle of Gettysburg, both sides knew they had been in a tremendous fight. Each artillery's matériel losses were rather light. The Confederates had six pieces lost or disabled, but had captured seven Yankee cannons. Battle casualties were another story. The Federal artillery, for example, suffered some 759 losses — roughly 10 per cent loss of the men committed to action. The Confederates lost somewhere between 580 and 610 — approximately the same ratio as the Federals, but a correspondingly greater bite because Lee's Army was considerably smaller.

According to Gen. Hunt, the Yankee guns shot some 32,781 rounds, which was approximately one-third of the Army's supply of 97,740 rounds (270 rounds per gun for 362 guns). Col. Alexander estimated the Confederate expenditures as 22,000 out of an approximate total supply of 40,800 rounds (150 rounds per gun for 272 guns), or about half their entire supply. For the Confederates this ammunition factor was quite serious not only in the last minutes of the pre-attack shelling but also after Pickett's repulse when a counter-attack was feared. Many of the Rebel batteries sat facing the Yankee lines with empty or nearly empty chests, hoping desperately that Meade would not move on Seminary Ridge. By the next day, though, the Confederates had rounded up their strayed and misplaced ammunition trains and had discovered that they had enough left for one more day's good fight.

However, the Federal batteries, while expending only one-third of their supply, were probably in fairly bad shape, too. Reports do not show which corps brought their trains forward, but indications are that most trains did not reach the front until some time on the 3rd, if they came forward at all. Thus, the Blue guns may not have had much on hand in the way of ready supplies on the afternoon of the third day. In fact, Gillett reported his Reserve had issued 19,189 rounds and had only 4694 more remaining in his trains.

Gillett's statement indicates that the Reserve opened the campaign with some 24,000 rounds, which seems to be a very low amount. For the 110 Reserve guns at Gettysburg there should have been 56,700 rounds — if they were supplied as Hunt said they were. Of this total, no more than half would have been with the batteries, leaving 28,350 to be carried by the Reserve train. Then there was the extra twenty rounds for every other gun in the Army, which should have made another 4800 rounds on hand for the Reserve. Since Hunt's instructions to Tyler and his reassurance to Meade indicate that the Reserve brought everything forward, it is difficult to reconcile Gillett's figures with what the proper figure should have been. Given the internal errors and disagreements within the ordnance reports, the best assumption is that Gillett's figures were incomplete.

On the theoretical side, the significant point was that Hunt's new artillery brigade idea had paid off. This was a great personal victory for the general after months of frustration and humiliation. At Gettysburg the Federal artillery functioned as it never had before. Even in the first day's fighting, really a series of meeting engagements, the Yankee batteries seemed to have been used better. Certainly the advantage of control at corps level was seen in the closing hours, when Col. Wainwright and Maj. Osborn were able to say where their batteries should go on Cemetery Hill. In the fighting on the second and third days, there was no question that the corps system, backed up by the Army's Artillery Reserve, was superior to anything either side had used before. Col. Alexander had good reason to praise the Federals' handling of artillery, and he explained that only the Confederates' lack of guns had dictated that they had no army reserve backing up their corps' battalions.[34]

The key to the Federal system was that it countered the old

tendency to dissipate the artillery among too many units; at the same time there was no over-centralization, and the retention of the Reserve gave a means of quick reinforcement. Further, the artillery brigade commanders seemed to have been granted greater authority and discretion in the handling of their batteries under this organization, and they all seemed to use these advantages well. Hunt's officers had given him valuable help during the battle. The best proof that this system was a success is that there would be no further changes in the line for the rest of the war.

The ironic part of the saga, though, is that just when the Federals found a system which permitted them to make the most of their great superiority in artillery firepower, they would have no further opportunity to make full use of it. Gettysburg was the last battle of the two armies to be fought in open country; from now on the struggle would be a different type of warfare. Never again would the two armies mass against each other with hundreds of guns in line on open ground. In the Wilderness, the artillery would fight with small groups of batteries or even single battery actions. At Petersburg, field cannon would become siege artillery, joining the big mortars and guns of position in fixed fortifications, with chests removed from limbers and caissons, and all vehicles and horses sent to the rear. But all of this was of course unknown to the Army of the Potomac, as on July 5th its first elements began a slow cautious pursuit of the wounded but still deadly Army of Northern Virginia.

XV

LIMBERS AND CAISSONS, PASS YOUR PIECES!

Fall Operations—1863

LIKE Antietam nine months before, Gettysburg left the Union Army in charge of the field; though again like Antietam, the Yankees had been badly hurt. But if the Army of the Potomac had suffered heavy losses, the Army of Northern Virginia had suffered far more grievously, for good Southern soldiers could not be easily replaced. The North's advantage in manpower was making itself increasingly felt after every succeeding battle, and especially was this so after Gettysburg.

According to its reports, the Army of the Potomac had suffered about 760 artillery casualties — about 10 per cent of its gunner strength. But, over-all, only four or five of the sixty-five-odd batteries which had been present on the field were incapable of further action on the three days after the battle proper. The Union Army's main shortage in those days was ammunition, and records indicate that, even so it had more on hand than its opponent and was much closer to its source of supply.

By July 14th, Lee had moved his bruised army across the Potomac and slowly moved down the fertile Shenandoah Valley to feed and recoup. Once more a Union general — this time Meade, rather than McClellan — had let Lee escape, and he received the wrath of Congressmen and other people at home for his failure. But by the end of July, Meade too had crossed the river with his Army. Lee thereupon moved east of the valley and into position near Culpeper. The Federals now lined up opposite the Rebel Army on the familiar ground north of the Rappahannock.

Here the two armies sat for several weeks, content to watch each other and to tend to administrative details. During these weeks troubles elsewhere forced Meade to give up troops. Detachments were hurried to riot-torn New York City; more were pulled out for duty in South Carolina; and losses due to expiration of two-year and of nine-month regiments further reduced the Army. Fortunately for Meade, Lee had given up Longstreet and two of his heavy divisions for duty in the west, while the ill-starred Pickett took his depleted division to Petersburg.

Lee's losses, however, were proportionately greater, and, when Meade gained this intelligence, he shrewdly decided to pursue the Confederates. No sooner had he laid his plans than the clicking telegraph brought word from Washington: The XI and XII Corps were to be relieved on October 3rd from duty with the Army of the Potomac and sent to the West. So now the numerical table turned back in Lee's favor, and the Southern commander, after learning this fact, promptly set out after Meade. On October 9th the leading elements of the Army of Northern Virginia crossed the Rapidan. Thus began a period of nearly two months which would see the opposing armies march and maneuver without one being able to put the other in a situation where it could launch an all-out attack.

The brunt of this campaign fell on the veteran II Corps, now commanded by the freshly promoted Maj. Gen. G. K. Warren in place of the wounded Hancock. The action occurred when Meade, finding that Lee had turned his right and was apparently headed for Warrenton on his rear, ordered his Army to fall back along a line following the Orange and Alexandria Railroad to the heights of Centerville. On October 14th, Warren's II Corps, with its six battle-tried batteries, was bringing up the rear of the retiring army and had reached the vicinity of the practically extinct hamlet of Auburn [1] on Cedar Creek after dark on the 13th. Warren brought his column to a halt; all the fords over the creek in that vicinity were choked with the men of French's III Corps. The one thing Warren could do was rest his men south of the run.

As he watched the troops of the III Corps splash through the shallow water toward the Greenwich Road, Warren became increasingly uneasy about his own situation — with good reason. He was still south of Cedar Creek and knew of no other available crossing point; his command was alone and isolated, jamming three miles of road on the enemy's side of the water barrier. If Lee's Army had reached Warrenton five miles distant (as it had), it would be possible for the Gray commander to hurl an overwhelming force against the vulnerable II Corps. Since the III Corps ahead of him had already run afoul of Rebel cavalry, it was safe to assume Lee had the intelligence on the Yankee columns — not a comforting thought!

Before dawn of the 14th the fords were clear, and so the II Corps shook itself out of its blankets and hit the road. When the sun did rise, the Blue soldiers found themselves wading through a pea-soup fog so thick they were able to see no more than a hundred feet ahead. The first division to cross was Caldwell's. It was directed to take position on a high hill on the left spur of the road covering the approach from Warrenton. With the division was Capt. Bruce Ricketts's Battery F, 1st Pennsylvania, in possession of its six 3-inch rifles, which Ewell's Confederates had briefly owned at Gettysburg. As Caldwell's infantry stacked arms and sat down on the hilltop to boil coffee, Ricketts rolled his guns into line in their front and pointed his tubes down the road from Warrenton. The smoke of myriad little fires covered the whole hillside as the rest of the corps began filing off on the right spur toward Catlett's Station.

Suddenly there was a brilliant flash in the sky over the heads of Caldwell's resting troops. A split second later, a shivering crash told the battle-wise soldiers that Rebel artillery had found them. A dim flash and a distant thump from a hill 800 yards to the east announced the location of the Rebel gunners. The Confederates now let loose a powerful barrage; one Gray shell took down seven men. Caldwell sent his infantry scrambling for the shelter of the west face of the hill while Ricketts's battery immediately executed 'Action Rear.' The battery commander barked his commands, and the six cannons lashed out in counter-battery fire.

The Federal generals had foreseen the possibility of being hit from the west, but no enemy had been reported or suspected in the east, which was where this Rebel barrage was coming from. The corps was in danger of being boxed in! However, in actuality this surprise shelling came from only seven guns of Jeb Stuart's Horse Artillery which the Gray cavalryman had hidden in nearby woods that night along with two brigades of horsemen. Gen. Warren had little way of knowing that such a small force was harassing his men, though. The stream of shells pouring onto Caldwell's hill, later dubbed by the men 'Coffee Hill,' indicated a much larger force. Warren now sent out Hays's division to poke at the unknown force in their front.

Back at the ford at Auburn, Capt. William A. Arnold's Battery A, 1st Rhode Island Light Artillery, had just crossed when the shelling broke loose. He was ordered to throw his guns into action beside Ricketts atop Coffee Hill. A III Corps battery, Capt. Nelson Ames's G, 1st New York Light Artillery, was also sent clattering up the slope. The Rhode Islanders swung into battery on Ricketts's right and added the sharp cracks of their six 3-inchers to the crisp little fight, as Federal infantry pushed in Stuart's skirmish line. Fortunately for Warren and his corps there was nothing beyond the thin line of Gray cavalry, and Stuart soon realized that he was engaged in an unequal fight. Yankee infantry began reaching out for his flanks, and Ricketts's and Arnold's guns were causing him trouble. Before long Stuart was compelled to withdraw his artillery, then mount up his troopers and abandon his position.

Even though the immediate threat was gone, Warren's II Corps was still in a potentially precarious spot. The corps was

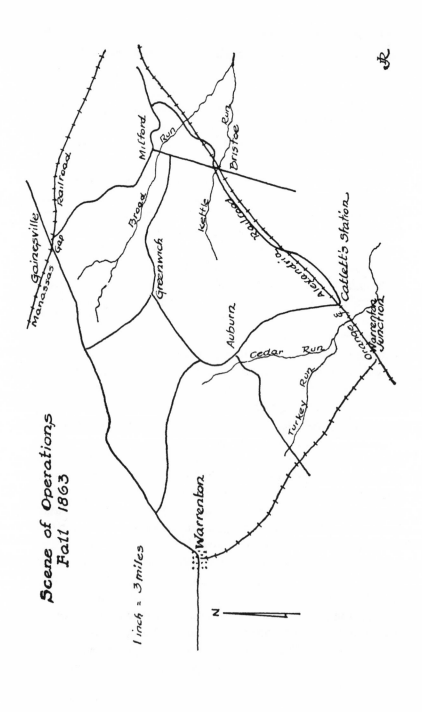

Scene of Operations
Fall 1863

1 inch = 3 miles

N

Warrenton

Gainesville

Manassas Gap Railroad

Milford Run

Broad Run

Greenwich

Kettle

Bristoe Run

Auburn

Orange & Alexandria Railroad

Catlett's Station

Warrenton Junction

Cedar Run

Turkey Run

JR

still split between the two sides of the stream; it was encumbered by a huge wagon train; and there was ominous news from the west — now the Union rear. Reports from that sector warned that an enemy column in overwhelming force — actually Rhodes's division of Ewell's Corps — was advancing on the fords from Warrenton. The II Corps speeded its movement across the stream and prepared to meet the forward elements of the Rebel assault.

As Ewell's Confederates approached Auburn, they spotted the Union gunners atop Coffee Hill. They immediately realized that the two or three Yankee batteries on the almost clifflike perch on Coffee Hill had a magnificent field of fire over the open lower ground to the west and that they would have to chase those batteries over that height if they expected to catch the straggling Federal corps. Col. A. L. Long, commanding Ewell's artillery, quickly gave orders to deploy three of his five battalions in such a manner as to take the Yankees under cross-fire. This was a time-consuming process, though, for the batteries had to be pulled out of column and suitable firing positions had to be found. Finally four guns of Col. Carter's battalion were brought into position on the left of the Halsey house, off to the right of the Warrenton Road.

By now the fog had burned off and the Federals on the hill had a clear view to the horizon. At the moment the Confederate batteries were deploying, several men of Arnold's Rhode Island unit, still faced east, happened to glance to the rear. There, unlimbering in plain view in a field 1500 yards distant, was a Rebel battery. Most conspicuous was an officer riding about on a pure white horse. The men hollered to Capt. Arnold and pointed toward the enemy unit. Instantly the battery commander bellowed 'Action rear! Limbers and caissons pass your pieces!' Gen. Caldwell, who happened to be nearby, took prompt issue with Arnold's order, contending these were Federal troops. Scarcely had he uttered his dissension when the first salvo from Col. Long's guns came screaming past the Rhode Islanders, one of the projectiles cutting the knapsack from the shoulder of gunner John Tyng (the same garrulous Tyng who had attempted the crude autopsy of a live shell) without breaking the skin. Another slammed into the number six gun, shivering its carriage and rendering the weapon unsafe to fire; it was quickly but gently limbered off the hill. But the carriage had been too badly damaged to stand the strain, and the gun collapsed. While their comrades above prepared to take on the Rebels, the crew of number six piece began the process of slinging their tube beneath its limber.

As the Confederates struggled to bring up more pieces, Ricketts and Arnold hurriedly reversed their weapons and began firing at the Rebels. Despite the fact that Col. Carter finally moved four more Gray guns into line to add to the firing, these two Federal batteries proved so effective in their fire that they held their own with the superior Rebel force. Then eight rifled guns — two of them 20-pounder Parrotts — were added to the Confederate fire. Finally about 11 o'clock elements of the third Gray battalion reached a point off to the Confederate left and prepared to enter the fight. However, by this time Warren's troops were clear of Auburn, and the danger, for the moment anyway, was past.

While Caldwell's gunners and some cavalry delayed Ewell's advance, the rest of the corps, with its sprawling wagon train, moved swiftly eastward toward Catlett and then along the road, north to Bristoe and Centerville. The corps' batteries atop Coffee Hill were gradually pulled out, their place was taken by a section of Martin's 6th New York — a battery from the fast-moving cavalry command. Arnold's was the last of the batteries to leave, and, as it reached the road to Catlett, Lt. Peter Hunt's section was detached to stay with the rear of the column as a rear guard. To make sure the Rebels did not press the column too eagerly, Hunt unlimbered his two weapons and fastened on the prolonges. He then began a slow methodical spraying of the woodland to right, left, and rear, rolling a few yards to the rear after each discharge. An hour of this activity brought the rearguard near Catlett, and it was only then that

Peter Hunt felt his charges were safe enough for him to stow the implements and limber up.

In the meantime, Arnold's damaged gun, which had been hauled from the field, missed its parent unit as the column began the march to Catlett. Instead the men fell in with some Yankee cavalry. However, the horsemen were going north via another road, by way of Wolf Run Shoals, as they were convoying the Army's army of train wagons. It turned out to be a hectic trip for the little gun detachment.

At least ten times during the day and the next night the horse column was halted and orders quickly passed back to prepare to destroy everything lest the Rebels capture it. Finally the troops reached Wolf Run, and in its turn the gun detachment began the descent of the bank. Suddenly they were stopped; an officer yelled that the awkward tube slung beneath its limber was a menace — it would block the ford — and he ordered the men to dump it in the creek. A crewman protested, claiming his team could easily get through. The officer agreed to let them try.

Down the bank slid the six big horses; the limber with its ponderous appendage pushed against the rumps of the snorting animals. Suddenly the vehicle came to a halt; the teams heaved but something was caught. A glance under the limber showed the gun caught in some brush; it looked as if the officer had been right. The crew decided to try once more; they booted their teams and yelled at them. With a sudden lunge the gun came free and the limber rolled down the bank, as the horses struggled to hold their footing. 'That's the best artillery team I ever saw,' yelled the watching officer, as the detachment happily splashed across the ford toward the rest of the battery.

At Catlett, Warren tightened his columns and started them toward Bristoe and Centerville — the ultimate destination twelve miles distant. The troops were to follow the tracks of the Orange and Alexandria Railroad. Webb's division was to lead, with two batteries on the left side and Hays on the right; then would come the wagon train, and Caldwell's infantry would again cover the rear. Warren now felt rather safe. Ahead, near Bristoe was Broad Run, another water barrier, but he had been assured that Sykes's V Corps would be in position there to cover his crossing, while the left of the II Corps was being screened by Gregg's cavalry. There seemed little chance for trouble.

About 2 p.m. the leading elements of Webb's division emerged from a strip of woods just a mile or so southwest of Bristoe. Suddenly a reconnoitering officer galloped up to Webb with the disconcerting news that he had spotted a Rebel Battery unlimbering to the left front of the advancing Federals. Skirmishers were quickly thrown out in that direction, and they soon returned with word that a strong enemy force of two columns was moving on the left. Where was the V Corps? A careful scanning revealed the tail end of a Federal column (actually the V Corps) disappearing into the woods beyond Broad Run. The II Corps would have to go alone again.

Webb saw that the corps was in a dangerous predicament. Looking about, he spotted some high ground west of the run and south of the railroad, and at once ordered his troops to occupy it. Lt. Fred Brown's Battery B, 1st Rhode Island, backed them up. It was Webb's hope that he could still press forward by side-slipping to the right, and orders to this effect were passed down to the brigades. Brown's gunners were to cover the movement designed to tie in with the rear of V Corps, and the rifles began to spit at the Gray lines with case shot.

Soon Webb's leading brigade reached the run and crossed over. Brown was told to limber up and follow them. But on reaching the creek the artillerymen saw that the path used by the infantry was unsuitable for heavy horses and weighty vehicles of an artillery battery. Instead they had to move some distance down the bank; finding a passage the battery sloshed over. Once across, the artillerymen looked about for their infantry. To their utter astonishment they saw that the portion of the infantry which had crossed was now pouring back to the south bank; Gen. Warren had galloped up and recalled everyone. Brown shot a quick glance back over the route his own unit had marched. It was no longer open; the Graycoats were in full command of the path. If he stayed there, Brown would be keeping a valuable part of the corps' firepower idle when it would probably be badly needed.

Brown looked around him. Some 200 yards up the railroad he spotted a good rise of ground from which his rifles could enfilade the Rebel line swinging in from the northwest toward the II Corps. He ordered his men there. With loud urging the Yankees booted their teams up the slope and threw their six rifles into action from there.

Actually things were again not quite as the Federals thought. The Confederates were there in force all right; they were from A. P. Hill's corps and had come down the road from Greenwich in pursuit of the III Corps. They had reached the high ground west of Bristoe just in time to see Sykes's V Corps leaving the area, but the eager Graycoats had not seen Warren's II Corps. Warren's alert advance, though, had spotted them. By the time A. P. Hill realized this, it was too late.

Hill threw two good Confederate brigades in line across the Greenwich road and backed them with a third plus a battery — the one Warren's troops had spotted. By so doing Hill hoped to catch what he thought was the end of the III Corps as it fled northeast across Broad Run. Just as the Rebel battle line prepared to swing across the stream, Warren's troops, who thought the attack was directed at them, wheeled into line of battle south of the railroad bank. From here they cut loose a scorching fire almost into the right flank of the unsuspecting enemy. The Graycoats were hurt, stunned for a moment, then began to wheel around to meet this unexpected attack.

At this point Fred Brown's 3-inchers on the far side of Broad Run sent their shells screaming into the flank of the left Confederate brigade as it swung toward the railroad. Then two sections of Arnold's battery came pounding up at a dead gallop. The shrill rasp of the battery's bugle topped the crackle of musketry, Arnold waved his arm, and the guns went into line. They were farther down the line and in a beautiful position to hit the right Confederate brigade hard. As the roar of guns rose along the railroad bank, Capt. Ricketts's battery joined the battle in position on a hill near the railroad bridge over the creek. The Pennsylvanians began slinging out full doses of case and canister at the now-wavering Gray lines. Then one gun from Ames's New York battery was run out a hundred yards to Arnold's left front, close to the railroad, and joined its fire to that of the other three Yankee batteries already in action.

In order to give his ambushed infantry some help A. P. Hill ordered up more artillery; the one battery the Graycoats already had in action was having a miserable time trying to cope with the hard-shooting Yankee units. Shortly five rifled guns came into the fight on the hill behind the Rebel line; the railroad bank was a bare 500 yards distant. Arnold's men suddenly found themselves the unfortunate target for Hill's gunners, as the Rebel projectiles sizzled lengthwise down their gun line. While the damage from this fire was remarkably light considering the range, one Federal cannoneer described it as 'the most spiteful firing I had ever witnessed,' [2] and Capt. Arnold reported it as 'a very spirited one on both sides.' [3]

The two Confederate brigades, though, proved no match for the powerful Union force — about half a corps in strength. After reaching almost to the railroad bank, the Gray regiments were literally blown apart by the vicious fire which poured in from front and flank. Recoiling in the face of this holocaust the remnants fled rearward, with a number preferring to be captured rather than to try to escape through that drenching rain of death and pain. The Confederates went back, sweeping past the battery of five rifles which had tried to cover them. A heavy line of Yankee skirmishers swarmed across the railroad in hot pursuit and quickly overran the unprotected guns. They gleefully sent them as prized trophies back to the railroad line.

On the north side of Broad Run Lt. Brown's battery continued to fire away. Realizing that there was no organized body of Federal infantry on this side of the stream near enough to come to their support, a young bugler, John F. Leech tried to scrape up some sort of infantry protection for his unit. Drawing his saber Leech speedily collected thirteen stragglers, described as being from every division in the Army, and these he threw into a tiny skirmish line on the battery's right. No sooner had Leech completed his task than a thin wave of Rebel skirmishers waded cautiously across the little creek. Little puffs of smoke rose over the brush on Brown's right as Leech's riflemen tried to stall the Graycoats. The Rebels swung their own muskets to shoulder and began shooting back. Then they began to inch their way forward. An eager Graycoat shinnied up a tree, and from his high perch got a good view of Bugler Leech riding up and down behind his newly acquired infantry command. The man cracked down on Leech but missed; three Yankees instantly spotted the culprit, and their rifles dumped the Confederate to earth.

Unknown to Brown or his men, their Gray skirmish line was clearing the way for a full brigade. The Confederate regiments actually crossed the run, but, like their foe minutes earlier, they were summarily recalled to assist in the fighting south of the stream. But Leech and his comrades became thoroughly convinced the straggler-formed line had saved the battery from capture.

The Confederate repulse at Bristoe Station was a thorough and costly one, and it brought upon the impetuous A. P. Hill a torrent of official censure. This defeat was caused largely by the effective fire of the Yankee artillery, and the Confederate reports are replete with comments to this effect. This was to be Lee's last major chance to hack off a chunk of the Army of the Potomac, but his lieutenants had let him down. As a result, Meade was able to move his divisions back to good defensive ground at Centerville and so frustrate Lee's attempt to find an opening in his lines. With winter fast approaching, the Gray commander had to content himself with tearing up the railroad; then he turned his Army about and marched back to winter quarters south of the Rapidan. As Lee withdrew, Meade followed slowly until he reached Warrenton, and there he halted the Army while the destroyed supply line — the Orange and Alexandria Railroad — was rebuilt. The Army could now turn its attention to pressing administrative problems.

As early as the end of August Gen. Hunt had put the Army's artillery back in solid shape. He had had to do some minor juggling of assignments in order to restore balance; three batteries and a section had left the Army's rolls, but three rookie outfits had come in as replacements. The net difference then was a lone section. However, there was a slight drop-off in gun strength — 355 pieces instead of 374 — with the difference appearing because of the reduction of some batteries from six to four guns.[4]

Some of this reduction was brought about through losses in matériel in the Gettysburg campaign and the realignments made by Hunt to restore balance to the commands. But no doubt part of the decrease in gun strength was occasioned by the drop-off in personnel. On November 2nd, Hunt advised the Army's adjutant general that the artillery was short some 3000 men. Most of this shortage was in the New York and Regular Army units, since over half of the Army of the Potomac's batteries were from these two sources. In so far as the Volunteer batteries were concerned, it was a matter to be turned over to the various states which would bring in replacements. Theoretically this was a simple job, but in practice experienced replacements were not forthcoming; raw untrained units usually came instead.

The Regular Army batteries had an even more difficult time. The inherent handicaps the Regulars suffered in trying to compete with Volunteer units for recruits still remained; in fact, they had been magnified by increased state bounties and grants, as well as by the Federal Government competing against itself in granting bonuses to all comers. The practice of filling up Regular batteries with men detached from infantry regiments had not proved very successful. Some bad feeling had been encountered on the part of some regiments; needed men were often recalled to their parent commands at inopportune times; the loaned men were not trained artillerists; and this practice presented regimental commanders with a wonderful opportunity to rid themselves of their shirkers and trouble-makers. Hunt suggested that the Regulars be sent drafted men, which the states were now using to fill out their quotas. However, nothing much came of this idea. For the remainder of the war, the Regulars would continue to find their replacements through catch-as-catch-can methods.

During these early fall weeks Hunt continued his ceaseless efforts to improve the efficiency of his artillery. Still plaguing the general was the old ammunition trouble. Now he had a new plan for solving this problem. He wrote to the Army's quartermaster, Brig. Gen. Rufus Ingalls, and pointed out that the practice of hauling the Army's ammunition in wagons had proved impractical. Instead, Hunt urged that the proper vehicle for the job was a caisson. He reminded Ingalls that ever since Malvern Hill the division ammunition trains were forever getting mixed up, tangled, lost, or blocked by the baggage and supply wagons. He had asked Ingalls's predecessor to provide black tarpaulins for the ammunition wagons so they might be readily spotted, but the suggestion was not accepted, and the trouble persisted. On the other hand, said Hunt, caissons were instantly recognizable for what they were. Furthermore, time would be saved. Under the present system the ammunition was hauled in boxes which had to be broken open and the contents then restored in proper compartments in the caissons; often critical moments were lost by this procedure. In the proposed system a quick shift of teams would be all that was required.

One of the objections the quartermaster general might be expected to raise to such a plan was where extra drivers could be obtained. A wagon team used four to six horses, required one driver, whereas an artillery caisson on field duty was equipped with six horses in pairs, the left horse of each pair being ridden by a driver. Hunt advised Ingalls that, since train caissons would not be called upon to execute intricate field maneuvers, one driver would be adequate. If this was not acceptable, the old-style Gribeauval caisson requiring one driver might be substituted. As matters turned out, Ingalls thoroughly approved of Hunt's idea, added his strong endorsement, and forwarded the proposal to his boss in Washington — where it apparently died a bureaucratic death.

Hunt had a further idea for improving the effectiveness of the Yankee artillery. It had come to his attention that the current issue canister was not doing the damage it should; this had been very noticeable at Gettysburg, and the horse artillery batteries which had been skirmishing constantly since then had complained bitterly of its ineffectiveness at close range. The artillery commander now wrote to Gen. Barry, promoted to inspector of artillery in Washington, proposing that the current model canister, consisting of twenty-eight 7-ounce balls, be replaced by sixty to eighty balls of two to three ounces. These would make a much more deadly round under 200 yards.

At Meade's new headquarters the rebuilding of the railroad was progressing rapidly. Intelligence available to the Federal commander showed that Lee had scattered his two corps in camps south of the Rapidan, and it seemed to Meade that the enemy's right flank was vulnerable. If the Federals marched hard and fast, crossed the river at the lower fords, they might be able to chop up the Rebel Army. This was the purpose behind Meade's Mine Run campaign.

The staff machinery began to turn, and soon orders went down for the Army to begin moving — fast and light. Hunt's orders provided for the Napoleon batteries to carry one hundred extra rounds; everything else would stay behind until called for. D-day was dawn of November 26th. It was a smaller Army of the Potomac that moved on Lee this November. Since October 3rd it had only five corps; the I, II, III, V, and VI. The departed XI and XII corps had taken their organic batteries with them — a total of nine, comprising 45 guns; this left Meade with an army of some 80,000 with 310 guns to oppose Lee's 47,000 and 174 guns. This was Meade's first offensive blow at Lee, but it added nothing to the stature of the Union commander. From the very moment the troops began to march, everything went wrong. Some columns were slow in getting underway, others took wrong roads, and the timing of the whole advance was thrown into a mess. Lee, with plenty of warning, brought his Army together behind formidable works, so formidable that engineer Gen. Warren took the responsibility of calling off Meade's planned assault — and was immediately backed up by the Army commander.

The third season of campaigns was over, and victory for either side seemed a long way off.

XVI

SEND NO MORE ARTILLERY

Wilderness, Spotsylvania, and Cold Harbor

THE WINTER of 1863–1864 and the ensuing spring brought about many changes in the Army of the Potomac. Enlistments ran out, and men left the ranks for home; new faces appeared in fresh units, and recruits and consignments of draftees arrived to fill vacant slots in old commands. But none of these had the effect of the arrival on the scene in March 1864 of Lt. Gen. Ulysses Simpson Grant as commander-in-chief of the wide-spread Federal armies. For the first time, these scattered Union forces were to have effective direction and coordination of their efforts. While Grant could have made his headquarters anywhere he pleased, he chose to pitch his tent with the Army of the Potomac. One reason for his decision was that this army, still under the actual command of Gen. Meade, faced the deadliest weapon of the Confederacy — the hardened, devoted fighting men who comprised Lee's Army of Northern Virginia.

Pvt. Frank Wilkeson of the 11th New York Battery noticed an immediate tightening of discipline with the coming of Grant, and throughout April the little tent villages showed an unusual hustle. There was a constant rumble at the railheads. Trains rattled in, tooted whistles, unloaded, and rattled out again. White canvas-covered wagons choked the roads into bivouac areas as units took on stores, equipment, and provisions; it was soon evident the Army was about to move. Old soldiers who had seen thousands of men and lots of reputations melt away before the battle-fire of the Army of Northern Virginia re-marked stoically, 'Well, let Grant try what he can accomplish with the Army of the Potomac. He cannot be worse than his predecessors; and, if he is a fighter, he can find all the fighting he wants.' [1]

Grant's plan was simple enough: apply pressure at every point and keep pushing, no matter what the consequences. Realizing the inherent weaknesses of the Confederacy, he knew that under such pressure something would have to give. In the east this meant that Meade's Army would hammer at Lee, while another Federal Army under Gen. Butler would threaten Richmond from south of the James River. Meade now drew up his plan to move rapidly across the Rapidan early in May, turn Lee's right, and destroy that Confederate Army.

What neither side realized at the time was that Grant's new strategy would bring about a drastic change in the pattern of the fighting. Heretofore the two armies had locked in fierce combat, only to break off, recoup, and rest before beginning again. From now on, though, the fighting — sometimes in major actions, sometimes in relatively minor skirmishes — would continue almost without interruption until the war was ended at Wilmer McLean's house at Appomattox almost a year later. The opening phase of this final year of war, beginning on May 5, 1864, is known as the Wilderness campaign.

Earlier that spring, the Army of the Potomac had undergone a major reorganization. This had been occasioned by the re-duction and consolidation of the forces into three large infantry corps of roughly 25,000 men each — the II under Hancock, the V under Warren, and the VI under Sedgwick — and a cav-alry corps of 12,500 men under Sheridan. Accordingly, there had been a concurrent realignment of the artillery. Hancock's II Corps artillery brigade was expanded and placed under Col. John C. Tidball, a Regular artillery captain, who had until recently been commanding a horse artillery battery. Like so many other Regular officers, Tidball had joined the Volunteers, specifically the New York heavy artillery. Hunt respected him

highly, and when he returned to the Army of the Potomac Hunt
quickly put him in charge of the II Corps brigade of nine batteries, comprising thirty Napoleons and twenty-four 3-inch
ordnance rifles manned by forty-six officers and roughly 1400
men. The V Corps received eight batteries: twenty-four Napoleons, eighteen 3-inch rifles, and six 10-pounder Parrotts;
forty-four officers with 1470 men manned them. In command
of this brigade was the familiar face of Col. C. S. Wainwright.
Maj. Tompkins's VI Corps brigade was identical to the V
Corps in number and type of weapons, though he had fifty-five
officers and 1170 men. Sheridan's cavalry brigade consisted
of twelve batteries, eleven from the Regular Army, with forty-
six 3-inch rifles and sixteen Napoleons and totaling forty-three
officers and 1714 men under the command of Capts. Robertson and Ransom.

In addition, there was Hunt's prized child which had come
into full manhood at Gettysburg — the Artillery Reserve. Now
commanding that splendid body was a newcomer to the Army
of the Potomac — Col. Henry S. Burton, a classmate of Hunt's
from West Point. Though Col. Burton had had no Mexican
War experience, he was one of the few field grade artillery officers in the Army prior to the First Bull Run, and during the
past summer he had been promoted on the Regular Army rolls
to colonel of the 5th Regiment of Artillery. The Artillery Reserve likewise had been reorganized. It was formed into three
organic brigades, with two more detached to Sheridan's cavalry corps. The first of these brigades was composed of heavy
artillery troops. The other two brigades comprised twelve batteries, eleven of which were Volunteer, containing twenty-six
Napoleons, eighteen 3-inch, twelve 10-pounder Parrotts, and
six 20-pounder Parrotts — a total of sixty-two guns. Fifty-
seven officers and 1571 men was the strength of the two commands.

Since McClellan's Peninsula campaign there had always
been a smattering of heavy artillery troops with the Army. On
the Peninsula Tyler's 2nd Connecticut Heavy Artillery had

been brought down to man the Army's siege train; however, there was little opportunity to use them. Two companies of this regiment had been kept with the Army, and they had been of some help at Fredericksburg, but in campaigns of maneuver they could not play much part. The rest of the regiment had therefore been returned to join the outfits manning the plethora of little forts ringing Washington, D.C. The two Connecticut companies were now supplemented by three New York heavy artillery regiments — the 4th, 6th, and 15th — which were the forerunners of dozens of such units that Grant would root out of comfortable garrison slots, arm with Springfields, and convert into infantry regiments. On this occasion, each of the three corps artillery brigades were given one battalion of the 4th New York, which was armed as infantry and was to provide escort, protection, and field construction work for the brigades — a role not unlike present-day engineer combat battalions. The other two heavy regiments, except for a detachment of the 15th New York, were assigned to the first brigade of the Artillery Reserve in a similar role.

Burnside's IX Corps was present too, though not an organic part of Meade's Army. This body operated under the direct control of Gen. Grant until May 24th, and after that date it was assigned to Meade's Army. But during the entire campaign, regardless of assignment, it operated with Meade and as such should be counted as part of the Army of the Potomac. This means that an additional 20,000 men with approximately seventy-two guns (estimated) in fourteen batteries should show in the totals of forces opposing Lee. Thus the total army available to Meade consisted of over 100,000 men with about 346 guns.

In the matter of the force's armament, the number of rifled guns slightly exceeded the total of Napoleons, and there were only twelve light and six heavy Parrotts still with the Army. Hunt disposed of the six 20-pounders in mid-May; the brittleness of these cast guns had earned his contempt. One old Regular gunner expressed the Army's opinion: 'If anything could justify desertion by a cannoneer it would be an assignment to a Parrott battery!' [2]

At this stage in the war, there was no visible difference in combat efficiency between Volunteer and Regular batteries, though the Regular soldiers of old Battery B found it hard to understand how their friends in Mink's Battery H, 1st New York, could call their captain 'Charley,' and be allowed to argue with their officers. But the Regulars had great respect for the New Yorkers' fighting ability.

Nearly all the present batteries were veterans. The Volunteer batteries had been, for the most part, brought up to strength by recruiting and the key positions were filled by men who had experienced fire in previous campaigns. For many Regular batterymen Gettysburg had a further significance. Before that battle most of the 'new' men — those who had enlisted in the Regulars since the start of the war — had stood in awe of all their officers. Now, however, they thought of themselves as old 'pros' and approached the officers on a friendly — respectful but not servile — basis. The Union's long arm was cocky and in excellent condition for the battles ahead. After the Wilderness campaign, Gen. Hunt declared his forces had never been in such condition before an action. The only point which had given him concern was the ever-present lack of general and field-grade officers.

Opposing this formidable force of over 100,000 men, Lee had some 61,000 men. As always, his artillery was heavily outnumbered in every aspect. However, Lee now followed the historical pattern of generals whose infantry strength was diminishing by attempting to hold onto his artillery strength. Even so, according to Lee's chief-of-artillery, the Army of Northern Virginia could count on no more than 213 guns during the campaigns that May.

Formal word on the impending advance was given to the Federal troops at parade on the evening of May 3rd. Regiment after regiment, battery upon battery, formed an immense mass of dark blue on the spacious fields. Bugles rang, drums pounded, and trumpets carried melodies over the fields; adjutants strutted forward and read the march orders. Suddenly a unit burst into wild cheering, and their chorus was quickly picked up by adjacent commands. To the men the orders meant an end to monotonous camp routine and perhaps to the war itself.

That night every man in the Army of the Potomac began packing up all unnecessary clothing and personal effects, some to be mailed home, other items to go with the trains. In some instances old soldiers took rookies under their wing, advising them what to take and what to discard. A newcomer in a Reserve battery was counseled to cut his gear down to a change of underclothing, three pairs of socks, a spare pair of shoes, three plugs of tobacco, a rubber blanket, and two wool blankets. In addition, the rookie was told not to pick up anything on the march except food and tobacco; he was advised to get hold of all the food he could, even if he had to steal haversacks from the dead. 'Let your aim be to secure food and food and still more food. . . . Do not look at clothing or shoes or blankets. You can always draw those articles from the quartermaster.' And also: 'Don't straggle; fill canteens at every stream, and never wash one's feet until the day was over to prevent blisters.' ³

Fully aware that he was greatly outnumbered, Lee hoped to make Meade move at him through the wilderness, where dense brush and intertwined thickets would neutralize part of the Yankee preponderance. So when Lee's cavalry brought him the word that the Army of the Potomac was splashing through the Rapidan fords, he put his Army on the move with the intention of catching the Federals as their forward line was strung out along narrow roads in miserable terrain.

The Union order of march was by two columns screened by cavalry. Hancock's II Corps, followed by the Artillery Reserve, crossed at Ely's Ford and headed for the old battleground of Chancellorsville. The V Corps, leading the way for the VI, crossed at Germanna Ford and marched toward Old

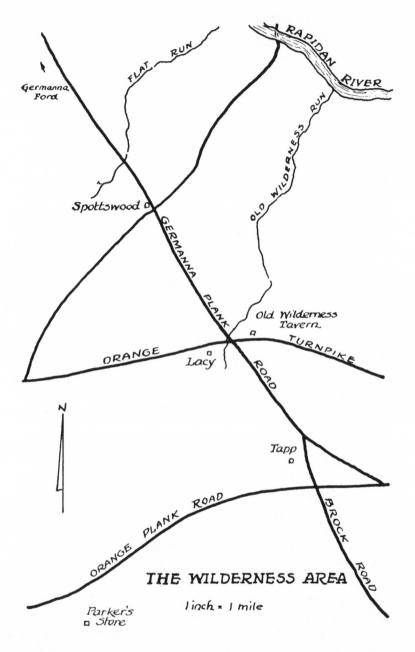

THE WILDERNESS AREA

1 inch = 1 mile

Wilderness Tavern on the Orange-Fredericksburg Turnpike, a mile west of where Jackson had deployed his divisions for their flank attack on Hooker.

The artillery of Warren's corps started forward at 1 a.m. on May 4th. Strict orders had been issued to the Army to lighten their baggage; for the artillery this meant no knapsacks or personal gear of any sort were to be strapped to the carriages — the trains would carry them. However, the men of one battery did not take the order literally; as in the past, they heaped their packs, blankets, mess kits, rubber ponchos, and other possessions onto the vehicles. At the very moment, just after daybreak, the unit was temporarily halted at Germanna Ford, the corps chief-of-artillery, Col. Wainwright, rode up to the column.

Looking slowly down the length of the stalled battery, its limbers and caissons piled with all sorts of forbidden baggage, the colonel turned to the lieutenant in command: 'Lieutenant, what is this you have here?'

'Why General [sic] this is Battery ——, 1st ——'

'Oh, thank you for the information, Lieutenant; I couldn't quite make it out. You carry too many guns for a baggage-train, and too much baggage for a battery!' [4]

By noon of the 4th the V Corps had reached the burned ruins of the Chancellor house. Here the men were subjected to a sickening sight; in plain view in every field were scattered bones and skulls. The men of Sleeper's 10th Massachusetts Battery, wandering through one of the patches of woods near the house, counted fifty bleached skulls on the surface of the ground within an area of ten square rods. Even though a year had passed since Hancock's division, its ranks facing in three directions, had fought here, there was still an abundance of broken muskets, cartridge boxes, belts, buckles, canteens, pieces of uniform, and other debris littering the area. Crude shallow graves had been uncovered by animals and the elements, leaving exposed whole carcasses or dismembered parts — legs still cased in moldy, dirty army blue, and shoes still covering remnants of feet. Some men of a New York outfit found the exposed remains of one of their sergeants, identifying him by his false teeth and the tattered uniform which still covered his skeleton. 'It was one of the dark, horrible pictures of war,' declared one battery historian.[5]

The 4th of May passed without a collision between the two armies, though Lee was fully alert to Meade's advance and was pushing Ewell's and Hill's corps eastward along the Orange-Fredericksburg Turnpike and the old Orange Plank Road. Longstreet's corps, the most distant of the three, was following generally in Hill's wake. That night Hancock's II Corps was at Chancellorsville, Warren's V at Old Wilderness Tavern, and Sedgwick's VI strung out along the Germanna Ford Road between the tavern and the river. Burnside's IX Corps was in the Army's rear, closing on Germanna Ford north of the Rapidan.

It was near Old Wilderness Tavern that the infantry of the two armies exchanged the first shots of this furious campaign. During the evening of the 4th, Warren had pushed Griffin's division out a mile to the west on the turnpike to protect his approach, and it was up this road that Ewell's corps was advancing. With Griffin was Winslow's Battery D, 1st New York Light Artillery, which had been with the Army of the Potomac on the Peninsula and the year before had distinguished itself in the wheatfield at Gettysburg.

Soon after dawn the next morning, Griffin's advance units bumped into Ewell, and word was rapidly passed back to Army headquarters that enemy infantry was present in force. Both Meade and Grant came forward in a hurry. They quickly saw that here was the chance to destroy a major part of Lee's force before the rest could save it. Orders went out to halt further southward movement, and Warren was told to tear into Ewell; the attack to be supported by some of Sedgwick's troops on the right.

Meanwhile, Hancock's II Corps halted in obedience to orders near Todd's Tavern several miles to south. To give

Hancock's front some sort of artillery support, two batteries — Dow's and Edgell's — were run into the woods seventy-five yards in rear of Mott's division south of the Brock Road. Troops went swiftly to work cutting an opening in the front so that the guns would have some sort of field of fire. Other troops struggled to cut a path to the rear toward the Plank Road, where Rebel infantry had been reported. Now Getty's division on the corps' right flank called for a battery, and Ricketts's Pennsylvanians trotted off in answer. The other six corps batteries were, at Hancock's direction, put in position on a solitary piece of relatively high open ground, a ridge about a mile in rear of the II Corps battle line known to some of the troops as Poplar Neck Ridge.

Warren's attack got rolling about noon, but it was almost exclusively an infantry show. Lee's scheme of fighting in the Wilderness paid immediate dividends, for Col. Wainwright's V Corps artillery was hard put to find firing positions. The best that could be done was to mass four batteries in a line atop a low crest, to the right of the Lacy house, commanding the valley and road southwest to Parker's store. While the infantry combat raged to their right front, Wainwright's gunners had to content themselves with shooting at some enemy columns passing over open ground 2700 yards away. The colonel put the four units to work harassing the marching Rebels.

The sporadic shooting gave the colonel a chance to compare the relative merits of 3-inch ordnance and 10-pounder Parrott rifles. His finding, following an afternoon's shooting by Rittenhouse's Battery D, 5th U.S., with Parrotts and three Volunteer batteries with wrought iron rifles, was that at this range the elevation each type required was the same, as was their accuracy. As for ammunition, he estimated the Hotchkiss shell to be slightly superior to the Parrott and ordnance issue.

In the meantime Capt. Winslow and his command ran into trouble. Supporting Griffin's attack, which at first swept Ewell's leading elements before it, one section of the battery was run down the road with the charging Yankee infantry. The two-gun detachment trotted across a small road junction onto a little rise just beyond, unlimbered, and began bowling 12-pounder solid shot down the turnpike. Suddenly Winslow, who had accompanied the section, discovered that he had apparently outrun the Blue infantry — at least on the right flank. Thereupon the captain pulled the two guns back across the open clearing, and the section went into action again on slightly lower ground. But only a few shots had left the tubes before Winslow realized he was in deep trouble; Confederate infantry was counter-attacking and flanking the Union right. Suddenly rifle fire ripped into the section, killing and wounding the teams, and then cutting down Capt. Winslow with a severe wound. The Gray riflemen charged the guns with piercing yells, and then the section leader fell wounded into enemy hands along with his two Napoleons.

The two armies were locked in savage combat throughout both May 5th and 6th. Thousands of muskets rattled; pistols cracked through the din; bitter hand-to-hand skirmishes extended along the line; but absent from the battle was the resonant boom of supporting cannon fire. It was as if a band had suddenly lost its bass section. One gunner of an idle reserve battery guessed that at one time he saw at least a hundred guns parked in view. This was to be the pattern for the Wilderness campaign, and one can imagine Hunt's frustration as he watched his splendid batteries sitting idle on the roadsides, or in shallow clearings. The Artillery Reserve was actually moved to the rear, where, with the exception of the foot artillery brigade, it stayed during the entire Wilderness fighting. A few corps batteries became involved in heavy fighting, but such encounters were the exception. The few available roads were narrow, and the terrain where the fighting took place was virtually inaccessible to artillery.

On May 6th the Federals struck again — Warren and Sedgwick against Ewell, and Hancock against Hill. A devastating charge by the reinforced II Corps nearly succeeded in achieving Grant's goal of catching the Rebel Army. Only a chance clearing near the Tapp house studded by Rebel artillery and the opportune arrival of Gray reinforcements saved Lee. To the north, as Warren's infantry struck at Ewell, the men of the supporting Battery B, 4th U.S., felt a deep sense of uselessness. On all sides there was the continuous crash of musketry. But 'we could do nothing,' wrote one of them, 'because no horses could have pulled a gun through the brush in which the infantry were fighting.' [6]

Later that afternoon Lee hit back, routing Hancock's veteran regiments, while at the same moment Ewell's troops curled around Sedgwick's right. Hancock's first line was driven back on his second, where Dow's Maine battery stood. From his post behind his unit Capt. Dow saw a party of Graycoats plant a set of colors on the Yankees' lost position. He promptly threw his guns into action, bursting shell and case over the enemy ranks. Five times the flag was shot down and five times replaced. Just when everything was under control, Dow spotted a Confederate column swinging in toward his position through the woods on his right front. He bellowed for double canister, and the gun crews scrambled to load and get on target. As one section was slightly detached, the captain was able to set up a fierce cross-fire, which checked the enemy advance until fresh Blue reserves stabilized the line. At the height of the battle the tinder-dry logs which had been thrown up as breastworks in front of the guns caught fire. And some of Dow's rookies, instead of detaching the powder cartridge from the extra canister as they took it from the limber, separated it as the round was loaded, dropping the powder bag on the ground and on the smoldering logs under the gun muzzles, where several of these bags flared up, giving a number of the men nasty burns.

Up on the Plank Road Ricketts's two sections had been bouncing solid shot down the planked surface, chipping off splinters which were as deadly as bullets. Then one of the guns burst, and a Gray counter-attack overran and for a while retained still another.

During the day Pvt. William H. Phinney, of Battery E, 1st Rhode Island, had an unnerving experience. Having been detailed for duty with the ambulance corps, Phinney spent an exhausting day as a stretcher bearer, and as the day closed he found a chance to drift off into the woods and flop down for a few hours sleep. It was morning when he awoke. As he stretched out, then sat up, he discovered another man in blue uniform apparently asleep beside him. Thinking the man would probably want to be awakened so as to rejoin his unit, Phinney reached over and gently shook him. The man failed to respond. Looking closer Phinney discovered the soldier was dead! Then, as full consciousness returned to Pvt. Phinney, he realized that he had been sleeping in a row of some thirty dead Federals. They had been laid out here during the night by other stretcher bearers, who apparently had assumed Phinney to be a corpse. The private quickly leaped to his feet and fled the area.

By nightfall of the 6th the Confederates had regained their lost ground, but had failed to deal the attacking Federals a crushing blow. The infantry in both armies had suffered brutal casualties. However, the Union artillery had only negligible losses: eleven men in the II Corps brigade, all in Dow's and Ricketts's units; another eleven in V Corps, eight from Winslow's battery; and none at all in the VI or IX Corps or the Artillery Reserve.

The past two days had shown Grant that the reputation of Lee as a general and of the fighting qualities of his men were well founded. It was obvious that Lee's force could not be taken frontally, so Grant ordered Meade to search for Lee's right flank. By the time Meade found it, the two armies were near a quiet little farm settlement with the small white-columned Spotsylvania courthouse. The terrain around Spotsylvania differed from the Wilderness proper only in the increased number and size of clearings which existed in the midst of the vast ocean of woods. As a result, the artillery would have a little more room in which to maneuver.

Warren's V Corps, preceded by cavalry, led the way out of

the Wilderness via the Brock Road and ran into trouble at about three miles from Spotsylvania courthouse. Two infantry divisions and four batteries were passed through the cavalry to restore movement. Gradually a Federal battle line began to build up slightly south of the Alsop house. Five V Corps batteries found positions commanding open terrain. Stewart's Regular Battery B, 4th U.S., took up line in a little salient, and, in concert with Walcott's Massachusetts guns, it promptly tangled with a couple of Rebel batteries entrenched in front of the Spindler house 600 yards away. A slight rise of ground actually hid the two sets of guns from each other. The men of Battery B would have liked to move to the higher ground on either side, but they then would have been easy marks for Rebel muskets. Deciding to stay put, the batterymen loaded case into their guns and set two-second fuzes so that the projectiles would graze off the crest of the enemy front 600 yards away.[7] No sooner had the first rounds whooshed across the open ground than return fire came sizzling back.

Lt. Thomas Goodman, the only Volunteer officer serving with Battery B, was struck in the head by a fragment from one of the first salvos. The officer staggered some ten feet, then collapsed; naturally those nearby thought that Goodman was either dead or seriously wounded. However, before anyone could get to the fallen officer, Goodman regained his feet; though bleeding about the head he appeared not to be badly hurt — the ball apparently had just grazed the skull. A sergeant picked up the lieutenant's cap and handed it to him, noticing as he did so that the little metal crossed-cannon insignia on the cap top had been driven through the crown. As he placed the cap on his head, Goodman remarked, 'It's only a scratch, but it was a close call.' No sooner had he uttered these words than he dropped unconscious. Several days later he died.

Battery B knew that the Rebel gunners were on target. One shell exploded almost in the face of another gunner, knocking him to earth by its concussion, killing a second and wounding several more. Another shell took a Blue cannoneer's head clean off at the neck. Through this storm of missiles, Lt. Stewart, limping from a slight injury, hobbled from gun to gun, instructing and praising his men in a display of courage that won him a brevet captaincy. At the end of the day Stewart looked on this action of May 8th as the finest hour in the battery's service. Heretofore Battery B had won applause in rough-and-tumble, close-quarter fighting in the Antietam cornfield and on the railroad cut at Gettysburg. This was the first opportunity for the men to show their skill in precision shooting. Stewart was most pleased with the results.

During the rest of the day musket fire racketed and echoed through the clearings and over the treetops of the area two miles northwest of Spotsylvania courthouse. Sedgwick's corps came upon Warren's right, and Hancock swung into line on his right. Similarly Lee fed his Army into strong defensive positions astride the principal roads in front of the courthouse.

The 9th of May was another day of movement for the Blue troops. Hancock prepared to cross the Po River to hit Lee's left. In the process a section of Brown's Rhode Island battery and Edgell's veteran New Hampshire gunners wheeled into position on a bluff on the north side of the river. It was about noon, and as the units were swinging into battery the men suddenly noticed a target slowly moving into view to the south. It was a sprawling Confederate wagon train, and it was within range of the guns.

At this moment the batteries were joined on the bluff by the Army's top brass — Grant, Meade, and, shortly after, Hancock. The commanders ordered Brown to turn his guns on the Rebel train, and seconds later the two 3-inch rifles cracked into action. As everyone watched, two orange flicks of flame and cottony puffs of smoke directly amid the wagons showed that the gunners had the correct range and deflection. Immediately the lumbering wagons began to pick up speed and peel off into fields to escape the Federal fire. Then a Gray battery came into view and instantly swung into action. Soon innocent-looking flashes told the Yankees that the first rounds were on the way.

And, like the Bluecoats' first shots, the Rebel artillerymen put theirs dead on target. Under the cover of this accurate fire Lee's trains cleared the harassed road, whereupon the Union high command told Hancock to take his corps over the meandering little stream and hit Lee's left or rear.

The Federals suffered a serious loss in the death of one of their most beloved commanders, Maj. Gen. John Sedgwick. His VI Corps had filled out the left of Meade's line in front of Spotsylvania. About 9:45 that morning a section of Capt. McCartney's Battery A, 1st Massachusetts, pulled up to relieve two pieces of Mink's A, 1st New York. Nearby on a cracker box sat Gen. Sedgwick. The zip of passing Minié balls was making some soldiers duck, and the general stood up to josh one of them, saying that the Rebels could not hit an elephant at this distance. No sooner had he uttered the sentence than one of those Minié slugs killed him.

On the same date the Army of the Potomac's arsenal was supplemented by a weapon which was to have great significance in the months ahead. Eight 24-pound brass Coehorn mortars were attached to the Army and placed in the charge of Company F, 2nd Battalion, 15th New York Heavy Artillery. These were short-barreled, dumpy weapons, looking not unlike a short piece of conduit pipe, with no handle which had been cast solid, with only a relatively small hole in its center. The Coehorn mortar range table was figured on a fixed angle of fire, forty-five degrees, with the range variation regulated by the powder charge; a half-ounce threw its seventeen pound shell twenty-five yards while a maximum charge of eight ounces could hurl a shell 1200 yards. The weapon weighed only 164 pounds and was mounted on a wooden block with handles permitting two men to move it about easily. These little mortars provided the Union artillery with a light mobile weapon capable of high-angle fire, something the regular field guns and howitzers were not designed to do. Its great drawback was that, when metal friction primers were used to discharge the mortar, the blast of the propellant drove the fragments of the primer out of the touch-hole, often into the faces of nearby crewmen.[8]

On the morning of May 10th, Hancock pushed his corps southeastward in the wake of the now-vanished wagon train. The force crossed the Po River, but soon after found themselves facing the river again, for near Spotsylvania it turns from an east-west to a southerly course. Beyond the stream here was Rebel infantry, obviously in force, protected by field fortifications. Hancock accordingly decided his best course was to hurry one of his brigades on a wide swing around the enemy's left.

While Hancock's brigade went tramping off to the south, violent fighting flared up in the center of the Union line. Watching this struggle, Meade decided that Lee's position, which had a prominent salient, called by the Rebels the Mule-Shoe, could be broken at that point. Meade then ordered Hancock to suspend operations across the Po and send two divisions to make the proposed assault on the salient. This meant that all of the II Corps had to be pulled back north of the river. As the corps moved back, the alert enemy immediately spotted it, erroneously concluded that they had forced the withdrawal, and began pressing the II Corps vigorously. Gibbon's division broke off contact with little difficulty, and Birney's and Barlow's followed. It was now about 1:30 p.m.

With Birney was the new Massachusetts battery of Capt. J. Henry Sleeper, a Boston outfit raised in the fall of 1862. It had been broken into action during the spring and summer of 1863 by various dull but necessary guard-duty jobs in Maryland and Virginia, finally joining the Army of the Potomac early in the fall of 1863 in time to pull a few lanyards in the Auburn-Bristoe affair. In the withdrawal now, Sleeper's battery was marching leisurely across the Graves's farm in rear of the infantry, with the cannoneers walking beside the vehicles. Suddenly a rattle of shots shattered the quiet, and soon the Confederates were piling into the rear of the retreating division.

Sharp orders sent cannoneers leaping for seats on the limbers and caissons, and the column immediately picked up its pace. Somewhere off to the flank a Gray battery apparently spotted the column, for a shell whizzed overhead and crashed into nearby trees; a second exploded directly but harmlessly over the unit. It was the artillery's job to neutralize this fire, so Sleeper quickly hunted for a position. Spotting a small clearing off to his left, the captain led his unit toward it. But the Rebels had them in range, and, as the unit moved across, a shell ripped away the lower jaw of a caisson swing horse and killed a driver. By now the battery had reached the clearing, but Sleeper discovered to his chagrin that his guns could not be put on target from that point, so the retreat continued.

Providing support for Barlow's division were two sections of guns — two Napoleons from Brown's Battery B, 1st Rhode Island, and two 3-inch rifles from Arnold's Battery A, 1st Rhode Island. Col. Tidball was struggling to mass the rest of the corps batteries on the north bank of the river in order to cover the retirement over the stream. Arnold's section was sent to the right flank and the men were told to unlimber in the back edge of an open field facing the Shady Grove Road, with a thick pine woods to their rear. Combat-wise crewmen promptly noticed that there was no route of escape directly in their rear. Commands to unlimber, however, drove these thoughts from their minds, and the men began an anxious watch to their front. Very soon the whooping Rebel battle line wheeled into view. Some of Barlow's infantry halted, faced about, and opened fire, and the Rhode Islanders joined in.

For thirty minutes Arnold's men worked their weapons for all they were worth. Bit by bit the Blue infantry pulled off the line, and Arnold momentarily expected to receive the order to clear out, but it never came. Having concluded that his position was rapidly becoming untenable, the captain ordered the guns loaded with canister, the horses turned around and limbers backed up close to the pieces, and the crews to lie prone; he would give the enemy one final scathing blast of canister before leaving. The captain and his section commander, Lt. John

T. Blake, nervously watched for the Rebels to make their move. A couple of Gray guns took them under fire, but no hits were scored. Then the enemy appeared, their shrill cry carrying over the battle noise. Arnold bellowed the commence fire!

The Rhode Islanders' rifled cannon, not nearly as effective as Napoleons for delivering canister, seemed to be effective, for the Confederates declined to press the attack. At this moment Gen. Francis Barlow rode up to Arnold: 'Why don't you get out of here?' he inquired. The general was told there had been no order to that effect. 'I have sent three men to you, to tell you to get out,' exclaimed Barlow. Without a moment's pause towing rings began clinking over pintles, and with Arnold's loud cry of 'Forward hyo. Trot, hyo,' the section headed for a little path through the woods Arnold had spotted not far off. The column had just swung into it when they discovered that Graycoats had curled about the patch of timberland and held the other end of the trail. Their only chance was to try to work their way through the woods to open ground.

Almost immediately the lead piece became caught between two trees; the driver of the wheel team scrambled from his saddle, seized an axe which the crew carried on the limber chests, and with a spray of wood chips cut the gun free. The column started again, only to have the last weapon hung up in exactly the same manner. Arnold, Blake, and both detachments went to work to free the trapped gun, while the other, under the care of a sergeant and three drivers, was waved on.[9]

Word of the desperate plight of the stalled gun reached a nearby infantry brigade commander, who promptly halted the retirement of his command and rode toward the scene; the II Corps had a proud tradition at stake, since it had boasted the corps had never lost a gun to the enemy. En route the general met Capt. Arnold, who sadly announced the gun was hopelessly stuck and that his crews had had to leave it. Under the circumstances, there was nothing for the infantry commander to do but put his brigade in motion again toward the Po River.

Meanwhile the other gun detachment was literally threading

its way through the timber. In thirty minutes it had arrived at the top of a very steep hill. The hill was apparently between the lines, for the men could hear the unhealthy whine of bullets flying in every direction. They knew the place was unsafe for them, so they started down the other side of the hill. Cannoneers leaped from the vehicles and slid lock chains through the wheels to brake the momentum as the carriages started down the incline. Even so, the grade was so steep that the vehicles were still skidding forward at a dangerous rate. Fortunately a fallen tree trunk caught the wheels, and both gun and limbers were slowed down enough so that they reached the bottom of the slope safely.

Now the detachment paused to rest the horses before pushing forward to the Po River, which, it was assumed, lay dead ahead. To reach it another hill would have to be climbed; soon spurs were put to the horses, and the ascent began. As the detachment eased into the crest, they were treated to the unwelcome sight of a Confederate battle line coming in their direction across a stretch of open ground. The detachment's only hope lay in speed, so drivers laid on the spurs and gun and limber ran away, with Rebel shots falling all around them but luckily not hitting anyone.

At the end of this run the crew found themselves at last opposite one of the Yankee bridges over the Po. They saw engineers already in the process of dismantling the bridge and frantically yelled and waved to them as they trotted toward the weakened span. The engineers stopped work and looked at the oncoming gun detachment. As the weapon neared the south approach, the engineers waved back at the crew with the warning that the span would not hold. But the four men who had brought the piece this far did not intend to leave it on the south bank, and the sergeant led his horse onto the wooden structure; the limber and gun followed. The span creaked under the weight and water gurgled up between the planks; as the vehicles moved into the middle the wheels were hub-deep in the stream, but the bridge held, and they crossed.

The detachment's feeling of pride and of relief at having saved the gun was short-lived, though. An officer immediately ordered them into line with the rest of the Federal cannon dueling with the Rebels from the north bank, despite the fact they had no cannoneers with the piece and that their sponge staff and bucket had been torn loose and lost in the furious retreat. Orders were orders, though, so they rolled forward to be a helpless target. Fortunately for them they passed unscathed through the firing, which ended with darkness.

Col. Tidball had built up a quite strong line of cannon to cover the retreat over the Po. In a front line he had Brown's Rhode Island battery; Roder's K, 4th U.S.; and a section of Gilliss's C and I, 5th U.S.; Gilliss's other two sections were parked nearby as reserve. In a second line were Edgell's New Hampshire, Sleeper's Massachusetts, the balance of Arnold's Rhode Island outfit, and Rittenhouse's V Corps battery. The colonel's scheme called for the front line to do all the damage they could, and then, if the Rebels persisted in closing in, the front line would retire by the right flank, uncovering the second tier of guns, which would then take up the fight.

About 4 p.m. Rebel infantry came in range, and Tidball's front line crashed into action with solid shot, the iron balls whirring through the air over the heads of retiring Blue regiments. A Gray battery suddenly opened fire from the side and began to hit the Blue guns partially in the flank. Rittenhouse promptly went over to counter-battery firing, and minutes later Edgell came forward to give him aid. Edgell found a spot in a row of entrenchments which ran perpendicular to the river, yet faced the enemy's main works, which were atop high ground to the left some 1500 yards distant. The New Hampshire gunners immediately trained their guns on the annoying Rebel battery, which was approximately 700 yards away. They found the range at once, blowing up a caisson or limber and forcing the Graycoats back, even though they were persistently bothered by the Rebels' small-arms fire.

While this was happening, Sleeper's battery thought they

saw an opportunity to hit back at the enemy. As a column of
Blue infantry closed in on the river an outburst of Confederate
artillery fire gave it a well-aimed salvo and sent it scurrying for
the protection of the river bank. Sleeper saw the enemy fire,
yelled firing commands to his men, and the heavy crashes of
his guns rolled across the river valley. Before the second salvo,
though, a courier jerked his horse to a skidding halt in front
of Sleeper. He carried orders to cease firing. The battery was
endangering Federal infantry!

The Massachusetts men obeyed the orders and spent a horrible hour; Rebel artillery had located them in turn and were
raking their line. The first Rebel shell roared into the left flank
of Sleeper's unit; its fragments swept along the battery front
and cut down the two lead horses of one team. More shells exploded in the position and brought down two additional horses,
along with a driver. Another crash, and another driver casualty. 'To this grim kind of music we [were] compelled to dance
attendance in our exposed position, with positive instructions
against letting our [guns] "talk back," ' the battery historian
later wrote. They moved the teams farther to the rear in an
attempt to cut down on casualties. The gun crews flopped beside their weapons, and whenever they peered out they could
see the Gray cannoneers taking dead aim at them. Finally the
welcome order to pull back came.[10]

Meanwhile, over toward the center of the Federal line a
young colonel was about to take an immortal place in the history of the Army of the Potomac. He was Emory Upton, a
brigade commander of the VI Corps. Earlier in the afternoon
the two divisions of Hancock's corps, which had been pulled
over from their positions on the right, across the Po, tried in
vain to break the Confederate line at the salient. Upton had arranged the twelve regiments of the attacking mass in a dense,
unorthodox column. To prepare the way for Upton's charge,
three VI Corps batteries — Cowan's, McCartney's, and
Rhodes's — were ordered to open up at 5:50 p.m. with a ten-
minute pasting of Upton's objective. At 5:51 these units ex-

ploded into action.[11] Now Upton's thick formation began to
move, with the storm of projectiles from eighteen supporting
guns shrieking over the troops. As the Blue mass closed on the
salient the supporting guns lifted their fire, and Upton's regiments swarmed over the Rebel parapets and completely shattered the Gray line. Initial success was great. But, as the penetration was on a very narrow front and was not properly
supported, the breakthrough was only temporary, and the Confederates restored their line by nightfall. Upton's unorthodox
attack had made an impression, however. It had also won
Upton an immediate promotion to general.

The two armies had now been fighting for five straight days.
Not since the Seven Days campaign before Richmond two
years before had these two armies remained in contact with
each other for so long. While it had cost him heavily, still Lee
had been able to thwart every Federal attempt to crush his
Army. The wide stands of scrub oak, pines, and vines which
made up the tangled woodlands around him had been Lee's
best ally for these five days. On the Union side the main problem was that the artillery had been of little use in the fight so
far. Grant was fully aware of this situation; for on the morning
of May 10th he wired Halleck in Washington, 'We want no
more wagons nor artillery.' [12]

The following day, the 11th, was relatively quiet. Both sides
were patching their wounds in anticipation of the bitter fighting
they knew lay ahead. It was on this day Grant wrote his famous
letter to Halleck stating his 'purpose to fight it out on this line
if it takes all summer.' [13] Grant immediately put his words into
action.

Thursday May 12th started with a dismal rain which continued into the dawn hours. In the soppy darkness before first
light Hancock's II Corps was shifted over from the right of the
line to jump-off position 1200 yards from their assault point,
which was the Mule-Shoe salient. But no one, not even the
commander, knew anything about the salient!

In the drenching rain Hancock, following Upton's plan, put the four solid brigades of Barlow's division into massive assault formation. On their right was Birney's division, and Mott was to support Birney, with Gibbon's division held in reserve. At 4:30, with a faint glow of pre-dawn seeping through the wet fog, the proud II Corps rose to its feet and formed ranks. Using a crude compass direction as their only scrap of intelligence about the enemy's position, the attack waves began to roll. It would be an infantry show exclusively in the early hours; for security reasons no preparatory fires were scheduled, and no batteries were to follow in the wake of the infantry for close support.

Hancock's mass caved in the Confederate first line as if it were a brittle egg shell. In the process the troops seized some twenty Rebel cannons which had reoccupied positions they had abandoned early that night in the salient. In fact so many Blue regiments poured over the Rebel works that they got in each other's way, and lost cohesion in their assault. By the time the attacking wave reached the enemy's second line across the base of the salient, Lee had had time to bring forth troops to stop their charge. Now, with his reinforcements in hand, the Confederate commander turned loose a counter-attack. Shooting and charging with a grim ferocity born of the knowledge that their army's life hung in balance, the Gray regiments flung the Yankees back to the captured first line. Here Union resistance stiffened, as Wright's VI Corps came into battle on the II's right. The savage battle of the Bloody Angle had begun.

It was not long before Hancock called for artillery in order to hold the seized ground. He wanted some batteries planted on the rise in front of and to the right of the Landrum house, 300 yards in rear of the almost face-to-face battle lines. From here the guns were to lay down fire on the area just behind the Angle to prevent the enemy from bringing up supporting columns. About the same time Col. Tidball, commanding Hancock's artillery, received a request for help from the VI Corps on the

right. He sent forth Gilliss's Battery C and I, 5th U.S., and told
Gilliss that Col. Tompkins, the VI Corps artillery chief, would
show him where to go.

On reaching the front Gilliss discovered that Tompkins
could only furnish the battery with a not-too-well-briefed orderly as a guide. The battery commander finally ended up
guessing at the intended location; he put his unit into line, and
opened with solid shot at 1000 yards range, pegging the projectiles blindly over the top of a wooded area as instructed by
Col. Tompkins. Such firing seemed utterly wasteful to Gilliss,
for there was no way for him to tell whether his shells were
plowing into Rebel ranks or falling harmlessly into some field.
In addition, the wet ground made the gunners' work twice as
hard, for the men had to shove their pieces back through the
mud into battery after each discharge.

While thus engaged Gilliss received three urgent messages
from Gen. Upton to send one section of Gilliss's Napoleons up
to the right flank of the bogged-down VI Corps brigade. The
battery commander promptly took it upon himself to comply
with Upton's call without wasting time to clear it through
higher channels, and he relayed the message to Lt. Richard
Metcalf. 'Limber the guns, drivers mount, cannoneers mount,
caissons rear,' came Metcalf's staccato commands, and away
went the two Napoleons. A staff officer, who was leading the
section to its new position, was promptly shot from his saddle
by Rebel guns. This was the forerunner of a veritable blizzard
of rifle fire which engulfed the little column as it rode forward.
The fire was so severe that whole trees, some twenty inches
thick, were cut down by it.

The two guns were unlimbered just back of a gap in the
corps' line. At this point the Confederates were a bare 300 yards
away, a fair range for canister. Metcalf gave the order for canister, and the ponderous Napoleon discharges crushed the air
around the Angle and sent a stream of lethal pellets into the
enemy lines. Instantly a swarm of Confederates — a Mississippi regiment, Metcalf thought — stormed into the heavy fire

and came screaming toward the Federal line. They fearlessly bolted clear to the top of the breastworks which the Yankees were manning, only to be cut down by a withering blast of double canister. Graycoats tumbled off the mounds of earth like ten-pins. Now the Blue infantry recovered its momentum, and turned about and slammed volleys of rifle fire at the enemy. The Confederates grimly retired to the other side of the earthworks.

Thinking that his canister had disorganized the Rebels, Metcalf decided to press his advantage by putting his guns forward into the Blue infantry line. His two Napoleons were booming away there, but Rebel muskets began taking a steady toll of crews and drivers. Soon there were not enough men available to man the weapons. Metcalf called for his limbers to haul away the two guns. The drivers lashed their teams forward, but the big artillery horses were juicy targets for the potent Rebel rifle fire. The limbers were soon rendered useless by the casualties to the horses, and Metcalf finally had to call upon infantry help to remove his weapons from the field. The limbers were not picked up until the next day.

As Metcalf's weary men moved rearward, they were able to see what a fierce battering they had taken. The equipment showed it as clearly as the casualties.[14] The gun carriages and wheels looked as if generations of worms and termites had been working on them. The limber chest lid of one piece had been hit no less than twenty-seven times in the course of being raised and lowered as ammunition was issued. The crewman who had operated the chest had been wounded numerous times in the neck and face by fragments of wood and lead. Even the sponge bucket of one piece had nine holes through its one-eighth-inch wrought-iron.

As Gilliss's pummeled section was withdrawn, Col. Tidball detached another Regular battery — Lt. John W. Roder's K, 4th U.S. — for action at this point. The fresh section raked the enemy lines 400 yards distant with solid shot, case, and shell. Meanwhile, Tidball had been bringing up reinforcements.

Ames's and Brown's batteries were placed on either side of the Landrum house, and Arnold's command was placed where it could give them close-up support.[15] Dow and Ricketts moved into the works on the second line thrown up by the 4th New York Heavy Artillery. Sleeper waited nearby as a reserve. Also, by this time some of the twenty enemy guns, which Hancock's men had captured, had been hauled to the rear. Three or four of them, complete with ammunition, were dropped off near Ames, who thereupon formed additional gun crews from his command and put the guns into his line.

Arnold's battery was constantly changing position during the subsequent fighting. Finally it stood on the reverse side of the enemy's breastworks inside the abatis. One crewman remarked that it was the worst spot they had ever been. The men could not move the caissons anywhere near the position, and had to resupply their weapons by exchanging limbers while under heavy rifle fire. They operated this way about four hours before Roder's K, 4th U.S., relieved them.[16]

Over on the extreme left of the Union line, Burnside's IX Corps had been contributing strong fire power. Although the corps failed to take any ground from Lee, it still engaged a large number of Rebel troops who otherwise would have been used against the Federals on the right and center.

The savage fighting about the Bloody Angle raged until midnight. Then Lee drew back his exhausted first line to the strengthened second line across the base of the salient. Hancock's success had had a good effect upon the morale of the Yankee Army, but the cost to the infantry had been high. Some of the artillery, too, had been heavily engaged. Col. Charles H. Tompkins, commander of the VI Corps artillery, headed his report for May 12th: 'The hard fight.' [17] One of his battery commanders observed: 'Battery was moving continually from one position to another, from right to left, near Spotsylvania courthouse.' [18] Another corps' battery said: 'At 8:20 a.m. opened fire, which was continued with two hours intermission (caused by failure in supply of ammunition) until 4 p.m. Number of rounds expended, 910.' [19] Another added: 'Battery opened at 5 a.m.; continued firing until 3 p.m., expending 873 rounds of ammunition. Moved at 6 p.m. to the rear.' [20] The pattern continued; another corps unit reported an expenditure of 2000 rounds over the three days, a third of which was used in counter-battery fire. But even though these brigade reports show that some batteries were heavily engaged, the batteries as a whole did not see much action at Spotsylvania. The same lack of maneuverability which hampered them in the Wilderness existed here.

The tactical employment of artillery during these days can be accurately seen in Gen. Hunt's report: 'From the 8th to the 16th the Coehorn mortars were employed wherever circumstances would permit of their use, and always with good results, and the caissons of the Reserve batteries kept up the supply of ammunition to the corps batteries in action. The Reserve itself moved its position from day to day, being generally encamped between the trains and the Army, furnishing guards for the train and pieces to command the roads and approaches.' [21]

Now there came down a significant order from Gen. Grant. Recognizing the limited role artillery was playing in the war of movement, Army headquarters on May 16th abolished the Artillery Reserve, and the batteries were to be returned to Washington. This was a bitter dose for Gen. Hunt to swallow, and he fought it. He argued that to ship off men and units which had been a steady dependable part of the Army for the past two years would have a bad effect on the morale, both of those leaving and those remaining. The general quickly came up with a scheme which apparently satisfied everyone. Every six-gun battery in the Army of the Potomac was ordered to reduce to two sections of four guns. The one exception to this order was Taft's battery of six 20-pounder Parrotts, which was dispatched in its entirety to Washington.[22]

The Artillery Reserve per se was broken up, but its batteries were reassigned to the brigades of the three organic infantry corps, thus raising each brigade to a total of twelve batteries of forty-eight guns each. By this scheme Grant reduced the organic elements of the Army of the Potomac by some eighty-two weapons. A short time later the IX Corps was reincorporated into the Army of the Potomac; five complete battery units were sent to Washington, and forty more guns were eliminated. Col. Burton, who was now deprived of his new command, was assigned to Army headquarters as inspector of artillery, and the other field officers of the defunct Reserve, with the exception of Lt. Col. McGilvery, were ordered to the artillery brigades of various corps. McGilvery was put in charge of the Reserve's ammunition train, which was to remain with the Army, and of a battalion of the 15th New York Heavy Artillery. Hunt had won a partial victory, but the role of his artillery would remain unchanged for the next month or so. The saved batteries would mainly tag along in the wake of ever-marching infantry columns.

The experience of the twelve days before Spotsylvania brought the conviction to every man in the Army that the position, as defended, was, in truth, impregnable. Grant in particular recognized this fact, and he abandoned, for the present, his plan to smash Lee by massive frontal assaults. Instead, he ordered Meade once more to attempt to move around Lee's right flank. The Army of the Potomac was soon on the march again.

By the morning of May 23rd the Union Army had reached the left bank of the North Anna, twenty-five miles north of Richmond. Lee was aware of Meade's maneuver and met the Federals there in force. Meade kept slipping to the left in search for an opening. The Army of the Potomac now found itself back close to where it had started its career two years before. The Confederates manned fresh defensive lines south of the Totopotomy Creek within sight of the spires of Richmond.

On May 30th, Meade pushed his commands out toward Hanover courthouse and Shady Grove Church in an attempt to develop Lee's position. Warren's V Corps, moving toward

Shady Grove Church, was brought to an abrupt halt by Ewell's corps, and, as the Union corps commander probed the force in his front, Ewell began to slip regiments to his own right with the object of catching Warren on his open left flank. Learning of this threat, a brigade of Pennsylvania troops from Crawford's division was rushed over the Mechanicsville Pike, the road the Confederate flanking column was using. The Union brigade had scarcely reached the vicinity of Bethesda Church when Rodes's Confederate division stormed into the Yankees from the flank. For a few minutes the Federals made a good fight of it, but it soon succumbed to the weight of force and started retiring toward the Shady Grove Road, with Rodes's men hot on their trail.

On learning of this action, the rest of the V Corps swung onto the defensive. Lt. Lester I. Richardson, commanding Winslow's old outfit — Battery D, 1st New York — recieved the order, minutes after he heard the firing, to move his battery, one section at the trot and the other at the walk, toward the trouble spot. In the outfit were men who had come down to the Peninsula with McClellan, when the battery was under the command of Capt. Osborn; some of them had volunteered to man Webber's abandoned guns in front of Williamsburg when that unit had panicked and fled. Many had been with the battery at Fredericksburg, at Chancellorsville, when Winslow had become its commander, and in the wheatfield at Gettysburg. The battery was now under its third commander in three weeks. Winslow had been seriously wounded in the Wilderness campaign, the next in command badly hit during the North Anna skirmishing, and Richardson had just stepped into the command of the unit. It was lucky for Warren that he had such a dependable battery close by a critical spot.

At a point designated by Maj. Fitzhugh, assigned to the corps' artillery brigade when the Reserve was abolished, Richardson unlimbered his right section. After the gunners had flung two rounds of shot at the enemy, Gen. Griffin, a V Corps division commander, rode up and ordered the guns 150 yards forward. As the section reached the designated spot and wheeled into battery, they could see the enemy marching in tightly packed company front parallel to their two guns. The gunners had an ideal target, and the two pieces were soon hurling iron missiles at the dense target. The Confederates reacted instantly by moving by the flank into a sheltering ravine, and Richardson hounded their movement with overhead fire.[23]

Up to this moment Richardson had not heard from his other section. Worried about its whereabouts, the battery commander sent his orderly in search of it. Shortly the man returned with word that some general had sent it and all the battery's caissons to the rear 'out of the way.' Instantly Richardson told his orderly to bring it forward again. But when the missing section did come up shortly after, it did not rejoin Richardson, but took a post some distance to the right rear of his guns.[24] Meanwhile, Richardson had also requested the orderly, on his trip back for the other section, to ask Mink's New York battery to send forward some ammunition, since Richardson was running low. Even then, the Confederates were bringing new pressure to bear on his section. Some Rebel artillery pieces were firing at them, and snipers soon added to their troubles. At this point Capt. Mink heeded Richardson's request; the ammunition arrived, and the battery commander was able to redress the balance for a short while.

The situation was really quite hopeless. Rebel case and shell were exploding about the harried section, and the men lost four horses in as many minutes. Richardson swung his two pieces around for counter-battery firing, but it was soon apparent to him that he was merely wasting ammunition in trying to dislodge the Rebels from what was a superior position. The lieutenant barked orders to cease fire and told his crews to take cover. 'I never saw the enemy's artillery used to better advantage than here,' he later reported.

Richardson rode back to his division commander to inform him that the section's teams were down to four horses per gun and that he had lost three men so far. The lieutenant requested permission to move the forward section back to his other section's position, thereby uniting his command. His request was denied; he was ordered to hold the line at all cost. Richardson asked for men to help him carry ammunition up to the guns, but this, too, was refused. The lieutenant thereupon saluted and turned his horse back to the forward section, though his 'respect for a general officer made out of a physician [Brig. Gen. S. W. Crawford] was not augmented by the incident.' [25]

After a time the enemy shelling let up, but this was accompanied by word that Gray infantry was massing on the right front in preparation for an attack on this part of the Federal line. Soon the wild Rebel yell was heard across the fields, and then a wave of Gray troops came into view. Richardson kept his section in check until the Gray regiments reached a range of 200 yards; then his two guns began spewing canister into the Rebel ranks. Their cracking was shortly bulwarked by the loud thumps of his other section nearby. At this point an aide from the division commander reined up beside Richardson with orders for him to withdraw immediately because he was in danger of capture! The lieutenant yelled that it was too late for that now. He did not have enough horses, and besides, the enemy ranks were at that moment a bare fifty yards away.

The air was split with piercing noise as the Federal infantry doubled its fire to stop the Rebel charge. Richardson's two guns boomed again and again. Then the lieutenant ordered one of the pieces limbered to the rear. A shivering crash of a heavy infantry fire accompanied the blast from the remaining gun. The Confederate attackers were sent sprawling, and the advance slowed. Another crash and the charge was over. The withdrawn piece had moved only ten yards to the rear when the assault was broken, so Richardson quickly collared it, had it unlimber again, and, in concert with its twin, blasted at the shaken Rebel ranks with case shot.[26]

In later years Richardson described this action, which the Army called the battle of Totopotomy Creek, as 'the hardest fought of any the battery had then been in,' [27] a strong state-

ment, considering the action the unit had seen. Oddly enough
no other battery fired a shot in this scrap, as none seemed to
be immediately available. Gen. Griffin complimented Battery
D highly for holding that crucial road until sufficient infantry
strength could be brought forward.[28]

As a result of the day's probings it was discovered that Lee
was astride a very strong position covering the approaches to
the Chickahominy River. To force a crossing would obviously
entail another bloody frontal assault against dug-in Confederate infantry, and Grant promptly rejected the idea. Once
again the Army began slipping to the left. Their objective was
a crossing further downstream near Cold Harbor — a point
remembered by veterans of the Peninsula campaign and destined to play an even greater role now.

By noon of June 1st the VI Corps and the XVIII Corps,
which Grant brought over by water from Butler's bottled-up-
forces south of the James, had reached Cold Harbor. There
they found that Longstreet's command had dug in strongly on
the edge of a wood behind Cold Harbor. That afternoon the
blood bath of the battle of Cold Harbor began. For three days
the conflict raged, as Grant hurled division after division at
Lee's defensive line. Here ground cover at last gave the artillery
the opportunity to see some concerted action.

On June 3rd Griffin's division of Warren's V Corps held the
extreme right of the Union line near Bethesda Church. The
three brigades of the division were massed about the church
and dismounted in column in the Mechanicsville Road just behind the building. About 3 p.m. clouds of dust a mile to the
north on the Shady Grove Road told Griffin that the enemy
was moving troops toward his right; these clouds were shortly
augmented by additional ones on the Mechanicsville Road to
the west. Griffin quickly wheeled his brigades into a battle line
to meet the threat. To stiffen the northern end of his front,
Griffin rolled out two batteries newly assigned to him — Richardson's D, 1st New York, and Phillips's E, Massachusetts
Light Artillery — while he kept Stewart's Battery B, 4th U.S.,

in reserve near the church. Soon the crackle of skirmishers was heard along the Mechanicsville Road, and the Confederates began to push at the center of Griffin's line.

The most severe pressure came against Bartlett's brigade, which was facing west on the north side of the Mechanicsville Road. As the infantry of both sides came into collision, a wide cloud of dust twisted into the sky beyond the woods a half-mile to the west. The Federal officers about the church plainly saw the cloud as it rose over the tops of the trees, and it was quickly evident to the battle-wise that the rolling cloud of dirt was being made by an artillery battery coming forward at a gallop. The Union officers watched a Rebel battery burst into view on the near side of the woods. Turning to its left, the column swung into a clearing or recess in the timber line and promptly unlimbered with the speed and deliberation of a veteran unit. Seconds later, discharges of canister streaked toward Bartlett's infantry; the men instantly hit the ground and began scraping up little mounds of dirt as low breastworks.

Bartlett's men were in a bad spot, and Griffin acted instantly to help them. As in the cornfield at Antietam and the railroad cut at Gettysburg, Stewart's Battery B got the call. Griffin gave the lieutenant a hurried briefing, then asked Stewart: 'James, can you go in battery under that fire?'

'Yes sir; where shall I unlimber?'

'Suit yourself about that,' came Griffin's answer, 'but keep an eye to your supports. I would like to see that [enemy] battery silenced.'

'I will shut it up, sir,' Stewart said confidently, and ordered his unit into the saddle.

As the command started forward, Stewart rode well to the front, his eyes straining to cut through the smoke for a suitable firing position. Just past the church the ground dipped toward a shallow depression where Bartlett's infantry was pinned; Stewart quickly decided against unlimbering on the back face of the slope, as the range to the enemy guns would be over a half-mile, and fire would have to be delivered over the heads of

Bartlett's regiments. Instead he made the bold decision to run his command all the way down the slope, pass through the Blue infantry, and go into battery beyond — on the other side of the little valley a bare 1500 feet from the flaming Gray cannon! [29] Stewart gave the command, drivers yelled, whips cracked, and the big team horses pounded down the slope.

As the column spread out along the road bugler Johnny Cook booted his white bob-tailed horse, facetiously called 'The Ghost' by his friends, to the run and took post behind his galloping commander. In the boy's pocket this day was his discharge; his enlistment had run out. Stewart had tried to make the lad and his conspicuous mount stay to the rear; too many good men had been killed while fighting overtime. But little Johnny insisted on finishing out the day — and he was lucky, he survived.

Down the soft slope raced Battery B, past the prone Blue infantry, and onto the open ground just north of the road. Into battery swung the four Napoleons, to the accompaniment of Stewart's shouted orders: 'Right section load solid shot and case alternately. No. 1, left section, load common shell. Cut fuzes one second. — "Old Bess" [the left gun], give 'em double canister!' The crews, veterans of some twenty-odd engagements, had already begun to ram in their loads when the battery commander put every gun on its own: 'Fire by piece! . . . Sock it to 'em!'

The Rebel gunners were now on target, too, though, and a torrent of canister rattled among the guns and wheels and whizzed into the places where the crewmen were stationed. Before the Regulars could fire their first salvo, ten or eleven crewmen were down. Battery B did not panic under these conditions, however. Its *esprit de corps* was superb. In the unit was a handful of the old Regulars whose enlistments would expire in the next few weeks and about forty survivors of the Iron Brigade.[30] Their answer to the Rebel salvo was four ponderous crashes from the polished Napoleons which shook the ground underfoot. Seconds later four more staccato crashes, then a third round. Now the smoke was so thick gunners could not see the target. The crews used the well-defined tracks of the gun wheels in the first recoil as an aiming guide for direction and kept a stream of fire pouring from their weapons. Lt. Stewart, usually a calm man in action, was yelling and cheering on his men, who were handling their 1200-pound weapons as if they were Colt pistols.

Three minutes later, the Rebel fire had diminished, but the Regulars kept pouring it on. Seven minutes later, the Gray fire had ceased altogether, and Stewart thereupon quieted his own weapons. Tired, breathless men waited for the foul smoke to lift from the field. As the smoke lightened, they saw an amazing sight in the field in front of them. Standing silent and deserted in the field was the wreckage of a Confederate battery. The rear wheel of the right gun was smashed; the number two piece of the right section was knocked almost sideways; the number one gun of the left section was dismounted from its trunnion caps and its muzzle pointed into the air; only the fourth gun, which was some distance to the rear, seemed undamaged. Even the Gray infantry had pulled back into the timber, and the din of battle had slipped back to the sporadic snapping of infantry muskets.[31]

On June 1st, 2nd, and 3rd, Grant and Meade hurled Federal fire at the entrenched Confederates at terrific cost and with little success. The Confederates would certainly have been overwhelmed had it not been for the efforts of their artillery. No less an authority than Meade's chief-of-staff, Humphreys, pointed out that it was the Rebel artillery who swung the biggest axe in the chopping apart of the Blue assaults at Cold Harbor. Federal infantry commanders protested that new attacks could not be undertaken until the enemy's enfilading artillery was neutralized. Union artillery, scattered along the line without enough suitable firing positions, could not supply the Blue infantry with proper support. Cold Harbor reaffirmed again how artillery could be the decisive factor in a defensive operation. The Army of the Potomac had learned the lesson several years earlier when it was the attacked rather than the attacker.

As one reads the Union artillery reports for the Cold Harbor fighting, in comparison with those for earlier battles of the war, one notices a change in tone. Now the Union Army was fighting offensively, and the field batteries were being called upon to support infantry attacks on a wide front. It appeared, the brigade organization notwithstanding, that the Army of the Potomac had slipped back a year tactically. It was not massing fires against critical parts of the Confederate position, but had returned to the practice of scattering its batteries all along the line.

Entrenching had become standard procedure for both sides. This fact was important, since the low-order bursting charge of Civil War field artillery shells rendered them impotent against such works. In addition, there was no indirect fire system in use, and few weapons available were capable of high-angle fire. Field artillery was incapable of rendering much lethal offensive support.

Capt. Edwin B. Dow of the 6th Maine Battery summed up the artillery's role at Cold Harbor: 'We replied every few minutes throughout the day. About the same time as on the night previous they [the Confederates] opened another tremendous fusillade from artillery and infantry, but without leaving their works. At night we built embrasures and made our position doubly strong . . . June 6, 7, 8, 9, 10, and 11, remained in that position, having built bomb-proofs for the men and ammunition and rendered the works almost impregnable.' [32] One can see in the haze of Cold Harbor the dim outlines of World War I's trench warfare.

The key artillery weapon in the coming nine months of the war would be the Coehorn mortar, which had recently been attached to the Army of the Potomac. One section, New Yorkers, had been moved up to the II Corps front and emplaced in a hollow behind a belt of trees some 800 yards from the enemy lines. Enthusiastic reports came back from the infantry in front of them. They reported that the mortar shells were exploding perfectly over the enemy trenches and were scattering Rebel soldiers in every direction.

At 10 p.m. one night the entire battery of six Coehorns was ordered to move right up into the Blue trenches, 150 yards range from the Confederates. By dawn every weapon was ready. Then the Rebel infantry stood up in their breastworks and leveled a wicked storm of musketry at the Yankee line. The Federal regiments promptly returned the fire, with the mortars joining in. They spewed forth a trail of burning fuze sparks which sent shells in graceful parabolic arcs toward the Gray lines. According to the watching Federal troops, the shells seemed to be causing great havoc in the Rebel ranks. So impressed were two Federal generals that they came over directly to compliment the battery.

The Gray infantry must have demanded that their own artillery do something about those miserable mortars, for at 11 o'clock that same morning the Southern gunners turned loose a tremendous bombardment, primarily from 12-pounder guns, on the mortars' position. However, the good Virginia dirt which the mortars' crews had heaped up around their weapons protected the battery perfectly and made the Southern bombardment futile. The enraged Rebels were setting down a murderous musket fire, though. Gray snipers were so effective that it became sheer suicide for a Yank to show his head above the lines; indeed, in many places along the Federal line it was unsafe to move about in other than a stooped-over position. Now the Blue infantry in turn hollered for help, and the mortars were pressed into action again to drive off the sniping Rebels. Gibbon's division alone lost 280 men to this harassing fire between June 3–12. The era of 'friendly enemies,' with the exchange of newspapers and the passing of gossip back and forth between the two lines, was now over for good.

The Confederates, appreciating the capabilities of mortars and, having none of their own, resorted to the expedient of propping up a 24-pounder howitzer behind their lines. The big gun began dropping shells into the Yankee trenches with good accuracy, and Ames's Battery G, 1st New York, was given the job of neutralizing the pesky piece. It was now the morning of June 8th. The Rebel gun had been located. Ames's four Napoleons stood ready with solid shot, waiting for some sign of activity at the suspected place. Suddenly a dull thump and a flash came from the target area; the Rebel crew had manned their weapon. 'Fire!' barked Ames, and the four Napoleons let go with a shivering crash. Another load was slammed in and a second salvo crashed into the enemy position. Whatever the reason, Federal infantry was not bothered by that howitzer again.[33]

The full significance of the mortar as a field weapon was not lost on the brilliant Confederate artilleryman, Col. E. P. Alexander. Witnessing at first hand their tremendous potential that officer promptly submitted a request about June 10th to the Confederate Ordnance Bureau for a supply of them.

The bloody repulses at Cold Harbor forced Grant to make the boldest move of his campaign; that it did not pay off in complete victory was largely the fault of his subordinate commanders. After an intentional delay in further offensive moves, designed to assist Union operations elsewhere, Grant issued orders for the Army of the Potomac to slip across the James River, turn Beauregard's defensive lines there, and move on Richmond from the south. The movement began after nightfall of June 12th; and with it began the final phase of the war in Virginia.

XVII

THE SADDEST AFFAIR I HAVE
WITNESSED IN THE WAR

Petersburg to the End

SUBSEQUENT to McClellan's unsuccessful try for Richmond in the early summer of 1862, the Confederate high command had become keenly aware of the inadequacy of their defenses around the capital and its rail center, Petersburg, twenty miles south. As a result, the Gray engineers had instructed their men to dig entrenchments around both cities. Those covering Petersburg extended some ten miles in a big flat U, both ends of which rested on the Appomattox River. They were now to be tested.

The shifting of the Federal Army across the Peninsula to the James River began on the night of June 12th. Lee, of course, detected the move, but the sheer audacity and magnitude of Grant's scheme, coupled with a skillful feint by Warren's V Corps, misled the Confederate commander into believing the Union forces were still trying to get into Richmond, this time via the Charles City Road just north of the river.

Gen. W. F. Smith's XVIII Corps, which Grant had borrowed from Butler's inactive Army of the James, was the first Union force to cross the Appomattox River. Its arrival on the south side the morning of June 15th triggered the long, dirty, monotonous struggle for Petersburg.

It was a tired Yankee Army that marched for the James; its ranks had been greatly thinned by the two months of continu-

ous fighting. Some of the losses had been made up by draftees
and new outfits — which immediately became fair game for
the veteran outfits.

One such unit, a 100-day regiment from Ohio, learned its
first lesson from the 12th New York Battery when the latter
passed through the sleeping ranks of the exhausted Ohio unit
during one of the nights the II Corps moved up to the Petersburg lines. The hungry veterans instantly saw that the rookies
had provided them with a good chance to get fresh rations.
The Ohio boys had removed their haversacks and merely
dumped them beside themselves on the ground. Like professional pickpockets the New Yorkers quietly exchanged their
own empty haversacks for the heavily stuffed ones left so care-
lessly on the ground. The rookies learned the hard way that
when a soldier goes to sleep he makes certain his haversack is
either under his head or attached to his person in some way.

Grant's offensive began to show smoke about 7 p.m. on
June 15th. The XVIII Corps guns opened up on the northeast
face of the Petersburg line, and heavy Union assault waves
wrested away over a mile of the Gray defenses. Gen. Beauregard, commanding the meager Confederate forces around the
city, found his situation rapidly becoming desperate and pulled
his left back behind Harrison's Creek.

Daylight of June 16th brought a renewal of the Union hammer blows, and more of the Confederate defense line fell into
Yankee hands. Beauregard pleaded with Lee to send help,
but that old warrior, for the first time fooled by his enemy,
could not believe that the Army of the Potomac was making a
major effort against Petersburg. Although Lee finally released
some troops to Beauregard, the 'Hero of Sumter' had a mere
14,000 men to face the 90,000 Federals then already south of
the river.

The next day there were more blows. During the night of
June 17th Beauregard pulled back again — a mile closer to
the city. Here the Confederates dug in, anticipating another
ponderous Federal attack. An attack had been set up for the

18th. It was to include every Federal corps on the line. At daybreak the Blue batteries erupted in pre-assault bombardment, and then the infantry moved out. However, Beauregard's readjustment of his lines upset the Yankee timing. The II Corps made contact almost immediately, but the IX and V Corps plodded forward about a mile before bumping into the new Confederate defense position.

Terrain favored the Graycoats, and they fought tenaciously. Then Lee, at last convinced of Grant's intention, hurried his veterans down from Richmond. These troops poured into the trenches to augment Beauregard's exhausted commands. By sundown it was Cold Harbor all over again.

As the Union line advanced, some of the fifteen batteries of Col. John C. Tidball's II Corps displaced forward with the infantry to provide close support. One of these, Dow's 6th Maine, soon found itself looking directly into the muzzles of entrenched Confederate infantry at 200 yards range. Federal regiments tramped past Dow's guns and headed for that last thin line of enemy defenses. At fifty yards distance from Dow's position the Rebels let go a shivering blast of fire, and the Yankee attack recoiled. The Maine gunners were recipients of Gray canister balls and Minié slugs. The battery's 1st sergeant (still serving in that capacity though a new commission as 2nd lieutenant was in his pocket) and a cannoneer fell dead, and eight others went down wounded.

On the V Corps front Col. Wainwright had assigned roughly three batteries to each of the three attacking divisions, keeping three or four more in reserve. In the initial successes the batteries had displaced forward with the infantry, but as the Blue waves were finally stopped, three of these batteries — Mink's H, 1st New York, Bigelow's 9th Massachusetts, and Paddy Hart's 15th New York — found themselves within easy canister and musket range of the enemy pits.

Though the Union attacks had carried nearly to the enemy's trenches, the Federals could at no point break through. Despite his heavy casualties, Grant still intended to try another end sweep to flank the Confederate commander out of position. This time he hoped to slip around Lee's right and sever the rail lines which kept Petersburg and Richmond breathing. On June 21st orders went to the corps commanders 'for extending the Union lines' around Petersburg to the Appomattox River west of the city.

Pursuant to this order the II and VI Corps marched out the next morning for the Weldon Railroad, the first objective. About 3 p.m. a gap occurred between the two corps. The Confederates slammed into the opening, rolling up Barlow's and Mott's divisions of the II Corps and sweeping the left of Gibbon's division, which had been the pivot for the whole projected Federal movement.

Supporting the left of Gibbon's line, in a crude redoubt, was Capt. George F. McKnight's 12th New York Battery. About noon an outburst of enemy artillery fire from the right front hit the division line. McKnight, whose embrasures faced only to the front, ordered his men to grab shovels and dig openings in the direction of the enemy batteries. By 2 o'clock the work had been completed, and the New Yorkers opened up on the harassing guns; the Rebels instantly answered with what McKnight estimated as eight pieces. Their range and fuzing were perfect; a din of rifle fire rose across the whole front and blazed across Gibbon's line.

This bickering continued at a distance for about an hour. Then suddenly McKnight's men noticed that friendly infantry on their left were being hit from the left oblique — A. P. Hill's men, the ones who had buckled Barlow's and Mott's commands. Instantly the crew of the left gun grabbed shovels and tore away more of the embrasure in order to permit fire to the left front. Minutes later the gun coughed, and a cloud of canister swished toward the oncoming Confederate ranks. Federal infantry poured on the fire, and McKnight's gun continued to bang away with canister. The Rebels, failing to break their opponents' line, momentarily fell back. They recovered on the support waves and returned to attack the left flank of Gibbon's line. McKnight looked for a way to get his other three weapons into the scrap, but the position would not permit it; if the Rebels were to be stopped, it was up to the Yankee infantry and that one gun.

Sweaty, powder-streaked Federal infantry began to drift back toward the battery, yelling to the gun crew that the left of the line was broken and they had better retreat. But the crew continued to fire the gun which spewed canister across the field, and when canister ran out they resorted to the old trick of slamming case shot down the bore without a fuze in its hole. It was to no avail, though, for the wave of Gray kept eating away more and more of Gibbon's left. The Yankee units fled, leaving McKnight's unit to its fate. The Rebel infantry swarmed over the flank of the earthen fort and drove off the crew of the left piece.

Capt. McKnight yelled to the crews of the other weapons to prolonge their pieces to the rear. The 1st Minnesota Infantry, on the battery's immediate right, wheeled around and fired one shaky volley, then fled. A lieutenant managed to rally a few of them, and these joined Capt. McKnight, his first sergeant, and a couple of crews in trying to save the right gun. An enemy volley instantly killed the sergeant and two men; a call to the survivors to surrender followed. McKnight ignored the challenge and ordered them to fall back. While the Rebels were furiously reloading empty muskets, the Federal soldiers fled the little dirt fortress. They left behind four 3-inch rifles and their four limbers. This was one of the few instances in the history of the Army of the Potomac when the artillery arm lost a full battery to the Southerners. The exuberant Rebels promptly swung the captured guns about and taunted the fleeing Federals to an even hastier retreat with shells from their own cannon.

Grant was stopped on the 22nd by A. P. Hill's timely countermove. He succeeded only in sending a small cavalry force through to the Weldon Railroad to tear up some of the track. Large-scale operations against the Confederates had now come to a halt, and the Union commander pondered his next move.

In the meantime, on June 13th the Confederates maneuvered to take the pressure off Richmond-Petersburg. They threatened the Yankee capital, as Jackson had so often done, by marching a corps down the Shenandoah Valley; this time one of Jackson's lieutenants — Jubal Early — was leading. Such a threat no longer carried the terror it had in the early days of the war, but, as Early approached the capital on July 10th, Grant did feel compelled to detach most of the fine but small VI Corps, and sent it by water to Washington.

The key to Grant's thinking was revealed in his order to Gen. Hunt of June 27th placing that officer in charge of all *siege* operations against Petersburg. In addition, he had instructed Col. Henry L. Abbott, in charge of a siege train recently operating with Butler's Army of the James, to bring his iron monsters to the south side of the Appomattox River.

Back in April, before the Army broke camp for the last time, Gen. Meade, confident that his force would fight its way to the gates of Richmond, concluded the Army of the Potomac would need more power than 3-inch rifles and 12-pounder Napoleons to overcome the known defenses around the Confederate capital. To prepare for just such an eventuality, Hunt was told to make suggestions for a proposed siege train.

The artillery commander wrote that such a train should have no less than forty 4.5-inch rifles, including the eight such weapons of the old 1st Connecticut Heavy Artillery, lately returned to the Washington defenses, ten 10-inch mortars, twenty-inch mortars, and twenty small 24-pounder Coehorns. In addition, ordnance should have a stand-by plan to furnish some 100-pounder Parrott rifles, should the need for them arise. The trains of the Reserve plus those of the brigades would handle the ammunition supply. The stocks should contain 1000 rounds for each siege gun, 600 for each large mortar, and 200 for each Coehorn. Of this quantity 200 rounds per piece should be placed beside the weapon before fire is opened, the balance at some spot convenient for prompt resupply.

Further, it was Hunt's opinion that the train should be formed at Washington so that it could readily move by water to a strategic point. The general proposed that at the point of disembarkation the teams of the two Connecticut batteries, plus those of the Artillery Reserve and additional mule teams, provide the transport to the line of operations. Hunt even invaded the Navy's sphere of operations by suggesting that these weighty giants be moved down to the Peninsula on barges, double-decked ones if possible, such as were then used to ship flour on New York's Hudson River; such vessels drew only five feet of water — about the draught needed for operations around the Pamunkey River.

Since the capable former siege train commander, Brig. Gen. R. O. Tyler, had been wounded at Cold Harbor, Hunt suggested that Col. Henry L. Abbott, then commanding the 1st Connecticut Heavy Artillery, be entrusted with the organization of the proposed train.

Col. Abbott's assignment came in the form of a memo from War Office Chief-of-Staff Halleck, dated April 20th. It instructed Abbott to organize the train and get it afloat without delay.

By May 15th, with the exception of sixteen Coehorns and some of the ammunition, the entire train was on the way to join Butler's Army of the James; the other Coehorns joined the force a month later. Between mid-May and mid-June Abbott's big weapons thundered at the Rebels from behind Butler's fortified line across Bermuda Hundred, expending some 2000 rounds in the process. By nightfall on June 20th three 30-pounder Parrotts, borrowed from original batteries on Butler's old Bermuda Hundred line, were in position with the XVIII Corps holding the right of the Union line threatening Petersburg. From then until July 29th there was an almost daily build-up of siege armament facing Petersburg, and 'from the time of going into position until the explosion of the mine [July 30th] the fire of most of these batteries was incessant.' [1]

It was on the 25th of June that Lt. Col. Henry Pleasant's

regiment of Pennsylvania miners began digging the famous Petersburg mine. Four days later Gen. Hunt received an order to furnish powder and fuzes for the explosion.[2] On July 3rd, Grant, through Meade, called on Hunt and the Army's chief engineer, Maj. James C. Duane, to make a thorough examination of the entire enemy position to determine if any offensive operations from the lines then held by the Army of the Potomac were practicable. Specifically, they were to look at the Confederate positions immediately in front of the mine, where Burnside proposed to attack.

Three days later, Hunt and Duane recommended to headquarters that this salient which flanked the works in front of the IX Corps should be seized before any other operation along that front commenced. Their reconnaissance revealed that the Rebels had greatly beefed up their defenses; they had a system of redoubts filled with cannon and infantry parapets connecting one with the other, and the ground in their front was studded with abatis and entanglements of all types. In view of this Hunt and Duane judged an assault impracticable. Regular siege tactics would have to be employed. The two officers correctly foresaw that such a siege would probably be a long one, as the Rebels would have a second line behind the first and would continue to dig others so long as they had enough ground on the ridge to do so.

Three days later, the Army of the Potomac was officially informed that operations against the entrenched Confederates defending Petersburg would be regular approaches-siege warfare. Construction of such works would be under the charge of Maj. Duane, and plans relating to the employment of artillery would be prepared jointly by Gen. Hunt and Maj. Duane.

The next day, July 10th, Hunt and Duane published their plan. They prefaced their scheme with an estimate of the situation, reviewing the enemy's position and the terrain. The Confederate works ran roughly north-south, from the right of the IX Corps to the left of the V; at that point, near the Jerusalem Plank Road, the front turned west, making an obtuse angle in their defenses. The line was studded with indentations and artillery positions which permitted heavy flank as well as frontal defense; and at the point where their positions turned west a redoubt stuck out, permitting a virtual enfilading fire across the IX Corps front.

In order to destroy the works in front of the area of Burnside's projected attack, the IX Corps artillery would have to be stationed so that they would have a field of fire directly to the front of and bearing on the salient facing the V Corps and on the batteries facing the XVIII Corps on Burnside's right. The V Corps guns would also have to cooperate closely. Since it was possible too that the crest of the ridge behind the Confederate line proper might be crowned with batteries, a vigorous infantry attack to gain this crest should follow the breaking of their forward positions.

Twenty-four hours later Meade approved the plan, and operations against the salient and the battery facing the IX Corps began.

Hunt's first objective was to bring enough firepower to bear on the Gray batteries flanking the fields over which the assaulting Federal infantry would have to cross. It was a job which had to be done suddenly, with no preliminary shelling, lest the enemy be alerted. The job was obviously more than conventional field batteries could handle, since the Confederates, like the Federals, had been continually digging, piling up dirt and logs, and generally making their gun positions safe from anything but a direct hit through an embrasure or by a perfectly placed mortar shell.

The artillery chief sent back for some still-unemplaced mortars of the siege train — ten 10-inch and six 8-inch mortars. Coehorn mortars were distributed along the line so that virtually all parts of the enemy's position would be subjected to a vertical fire. The construction of the works for these weapons was placed under Maj. Duane, who drew the labor from details furnished by each corps.

The build-up of Federal artillery was steady and awesome.

By July 29th Abbott's siege train had set up eighteen 4.5-inch rifles, ten 30-pounder Parrotts, twenty-two Coehorns, twenty 8-inch mortars, ten 10-inch mortars, and the famous 13-inch mortar 'dictator.' [3] Of the total of eighty-one large guns and mortars, twenty-eight pieces were on the left of the line with the V Corps, sixteen were backing up the IX Corps holding the center, and thirty-seven were spotted along the right with the XVIII Corps. The weapons were manned by eight companies of the 1st Connecticut Heavy Artillery, and three from the 4th New York Heavy Artillery.

Planning for the proposed mine explosion and follow-up attack moved more slowly. Burnside's IX Corps was to make the main effort supported by the V Corps on its left and the XVIII on its right; Hancock's II Corps was to be sent to the north side of the James as a feint. Only the fine VI Corps — Sedgwick's old command — was missing, having gone north to counter Early's threat to the capital. D-Day was set for July 30th, H-hour at 3:30 a.m.

On the evening of July 29th, about twelve hours before H-hour, the ranks of the IX Corps were in confusion. The Army high command had suddenly decided not to accept Burnside's assault plan, in which the attack was to be led by a fresh, briefed, and rehearsed Negro division. Instead, the IX Corps commander was told to lead with one of his depleted and combat-fatigued white divisions.

While the infantry was thrashing about to readjust to the change in plan, the corps' artillery prepared with a minimum of interference. Commanding the corps' guns was Lt. Col. J. A. Monroe, one of the former Rhode Island battery commanders. Under his control were twelve field batteries, four of which were old units familiar to the Army of the Potomac: the 2nd Maine Battery, which had acquired fame at Fredericksburg and Gettysburg under Capt. Hall, now led by Capt. A. F. Thomas; Durell's Battery D, Pennsylvania Light Artillery; a borrowed VI Corps unit, Battery E, 1st Rhode Island, which had gained a solid reputation under Capt. George E. Randolph

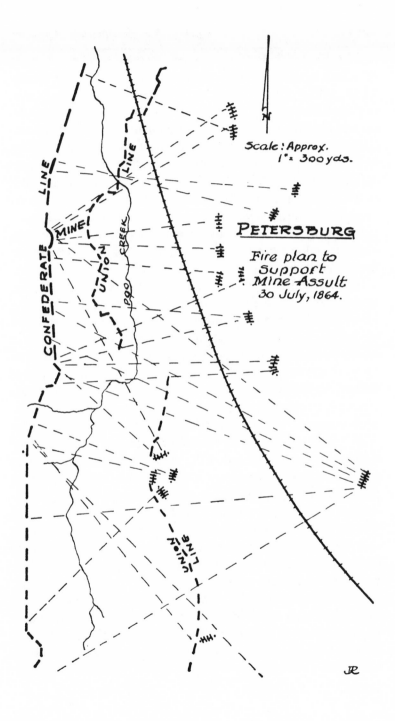

N

Scale: Approx.
1" = 300 yds.

PETERSBURG

Fire plan to
Support
Mine Assault
30 July, 1864.

CONFEDERATE LINE

MINE

UNION LINE

POO CREEK

UNION LINE

JR

and Lt. Pardon S. Jastram, now commanded by Capt. William
B. Rhodes; and Lt. A. N. Parsons's Battery A, New Jersey
Light Artillery, also a borrowed VI Corps unit. In addition
the corps had an organic battery of six Coehorns manned by
men of the 2nd Pennsylvania Provisional Heavy Artillery.

Under the new scheme of attack Burnside's 1st Division —
Ledlie's — would lead out, followed by Potter's 2nd Division
on the right and Willcox's 3rd on the left. Ferrero's 4th Division — the Negro unit — would be the reserve. The plan was
to sweep forward in two columns through the anticipated break
in the enemy's line caused by the mine, and peel off to the right
and left, taking the two halves of Lee's pierced position in
flank and rear.

To give added support to the fire of the four siege mortars
and twelve 4.5-inch rifles of the siege train along the IX Corps
front, Col. Monroe committed eight of his field batteries and
his Coehorn unit into the line; the other four he held in reserve
to run forward to the crest behind the Gray line as soon as
Federal infantry had it in their possession. On the V Corps
front Col. Wainwright had at his disposal fourteen field batteries — of which four were on loan from the absent VI Corps.
These units the brigade commander deftly deployed across the
corps' front so as to cover known or suspected enemy battery
positions which commanded the zone of assault, and also to
sweep the crest immediately to the rear of the Gray salient,
the intended objective.

Col. Wainwright reported he had available twenty-eight
rifled and twenty-four Napoleon guns in position for the attack, and a battery of five Coehorn mortars. Also, there were
sixteen big siege mortars, six 4.5-inch rifles, and six more Coehorns from the siege train.

On Burnside's right was the XVIII Corps artillery commanded by Col. Alexander Piper — the same officer who as a
captain had been appointed Pope's chief-of-artillery in 1862.
Behind the corps were thirty-seven pieces of siege artillery,

ranging from Coehorns to the big 13-inch mortar on its railroad car. Meshed into this net were some thirty field pieces
from about five corps batteries; the balance of the organic artillery was to be kept available, should the need arise.[4]

On July 29th Gen. Hunt circulated written instructions to
his artillerymen in which he revealed that the signal to open
fire would be the explosion of the mine; target of first priority
would be enemy batteries commanding the point of assault,
and the guns that would show themselves on the salient or on
its flanks looking toward the IX Corps. The Federal guns in
Fort Hell and in a small redan nearby were not to fire on the
forward tip of the objective because of the danger of hitting
friendly infantry; instead, they would direct their fire against
the face so that any overs would strike the crest directly to the
rear. After sufficient time had elapsed to allow the attack waves
to gain the crest, the guns were to shift their fields of fire farther to their left so as not to strike the town — which it was
hoped would fall at the first nudge.

The artillery on the more distant XVIII Corps front received special instructions to insure that it opened with the V
and IX Corps, and it was particularly stressed that the weapons
on the left of that corps were to be brought to bear on any Confederate artillery which could harass the IX Corps assault columns. Commanders were cautioned to watch the progress of
the attack closely — a rather difficult task in that era of non-
smokeless powder — so that friendly troops would not come
under their own fire and so that the enemy would not attempt
to bring in reinforcements. The Federal weapons were to stop
with the Confederate guns, and to reopen only to silence renewed enemy outbursts.

By nightfall of July 29th there were, along the V and IX
Corps front, ten 10-inch mortars, ten 8-inch mortars, seventeen
Coehorns, eighteen siege guns, and eighty-six field pieces. Near
the Hare house, bearing on the enemy's line opposite Burnside's right, were six 8-inch mortars, eleven Coehorns, and six

field guns. This made a total of 110 guns and fifty-four mortars,[5] the heaviest concentration of firepower in the history of the Army of the Potomac.

With the approach of H-hour gun crews were awakened, weapons were loaded, and officers and men made last-minute checks on their matériel and gear. Soldiers glanced anxiously at pocket watches and peered in the blackness toward the area of the mine — at some points a bare 300 feet from the Federal trenches. The seconds ticked by; with minutes to go primers were slipped into vents and lanyards hooked on. Number four men stood waiting, the long ropes clenched in their hands. The time came, and muscles tightened in anticipation of the thunderous explosion; nothing happened! Five minutes passed, ten, fifteen, a half-hour, and men began wondering what had gone wrong. Had the mine failed to explode?

Actually, because the fuzes furnished by the Army's ordnance officer had not been of sufficient length, Pleasant's men had spliced pieces together in order to get the needed distance. At one of these splices the fuzing had failed. At about 4:15 a.m., the fuze was relit.

At approximately 4:42 a.m. an orange glow burst from the earth under Elliott's salient, and great masses of dirt, logs, and debris rose hundreds of feet into the air. Then a low muffled thundering rolled toward the watching Federals, followed seconds later by a shuddering crash as the sound wave of 8000 pounds of exploding black powder shook the Union line. The Federals saw human bodies rise in awkward arcs, then fall to the earth. Two cannons from Pegram's battery occupying the redoubt went tumbling through the air. As tons of earth and rock came hurtling down, many of the Rebs who had survived the initial blast were crushed under the falling avalanche. At least 278 Confederates were estimated to have been killed or wounded by the explosion.

Within seconds after the blast some 164 Yankee artillery weapons crashed out in another roar of violence and destruction. After ten minutes of this bombardment, Burnside's infantry began climbing out of its trenches. The Confederates reacted furiously after the first shock. As the dust subsided, the Graycoats spotted the Federal regiments swarming into the reeking crater while a rain of Union artillery fire threatened the section. A Gray battery was in a redoubt about 400 yards south of the crater; one piece of this unit was in an ideal spot to chew directly into the left flank of the oncoming Yankees. Anxious Rebels looked toward that quarter expecting momentarily to see it active. But the battery remained silent, deserted by its officer and crews in the shock of the mine's exploding. An alert Confederate staff officer, realizing this, rounded up some men and put his most advantageously situated gun into action.

The bark of this lone gun to the south of the crater became a focal point of the battle. To the Federals it was a thorn to be removed. To the Confederates it was a burning symbol of defiance and hope. Its blasts of canister added to the fire of Confederate Capt. Wright's battery of four pieces emplaced to the north and rear of the crater — probably the first enemy artillery unit to return the Yankee fire, which poured into the right of Burnside's assault waves. A half-dozen small Coehorn mortars were planted in several ravines to the rear of the broken line. These shells, lobbed into the mine pit jammed with yelling Union soldiery, augmented the fire which kept the Federals pinned in the pit.

While Hunt reported that the Union guns fired slowly and deliberately as befitted his doctrine, a number of the Blue battery commanders admitted that they poured it on for hours. One captain frankly stated that by direct orders — whose he did not say, probably a division commander's — he fired at a furious rate for two hours. The force of the mine explosion had torn a 170-foot-wide crater across the front of the Confederate works held by Maj. Gen. B. R. Johnson's division, and the Army of the Potomac, with 55,500 men poised in four corps, was as close to demolishing Lee's Army as it had ever been. But like Malvern Hill, Antietam, the left at Fredericksburg, and other lost opportunities, the follow-through failed. In this case it was a combination of miserable command planning and inept leadership, a grim determination on the part of Confederate infantry, and the power of Civil War artillery in defensive operations.

Men of the 14th New York Heavy Artillery who served that day as infantry were among those caught in the crater. Seeing two undamaged guns of Pegram's battery on the south tip of the wrecked salient, the New Yorkers rushed over and dragged them to a spot closer to the crater. Sensing that there was no doubt a magazine near the gun's former position, one of the officers sent a sergeant and some men searching for it. The prize was found and the 14th New York promptly put both captured weapons to their own use; one piece opened on the Rebel gun, while the other was sited to the front to protect against the expected countercharge. The gun, however, was well protected from much of the Union fire, and those batteries, which might have had the best opportunity to knock it out, were hindered by a stand of timber which masked their fire. This wood had been scheduled for cutting, but to avoid any suspicions by the Confederates, Burnside had reversed the order. These same trees also prevented some of the potentially more effective batteries from bringing down fire on Wright's guns, which were giving Potter's division of the IX Corps a very bad time. The Union reports are replete with comments on the terrific artillery cross-fire and mortar shelling which the handful of Rebel weapons then in action laid down across that salient.

Some two hours after the mine had gone off, the Negro division was thrown in; the idea was to try to take the crest beyond the crater. But like the commands which preceded them, they were led straight into the already overcrowded crater — with the exception of one part of the division, which did swing around the rim and start for the crest.

To some observers it appeared as if the attack might get rolling again, but the Confederates had two surprises in store.

One of these was the two brigades of Mahone's division, which hurried over from their right and formed a line of battle in a ravine beyond the crest; the other was Col. Haskell's artillery battalion, consisting of one six-gun battery and another battery equipped with nine mortars. Directly to the rear of the mine, about 600 yards distance, was the Jerusalem Plank Road, the bed of which had been cut by years of iron rimmed wagon wheels until it was well below ground level. Ten days before, artillerist Col. E. P. Alexander had placed Haskell's battalion in this sunken road well out of sight of prying Yankee eyes. No earthworks or telltale signs of occupation had been permitted, and the sixteen guns had remained discreetly silent and undetected by the Federals, awaiting the precise moment to show themselves. That time now arrived.

The charging mass of Negroes led by white officers ran headlong into Haskell's fire; they suffered hideous casualties and recoiled in the face of it. One private, his musket at a high port, continued to advance straight toward the smoking gun tubes. Reaching the road before the Gray cannon could be reloaded, the Negro leaped for one of the pieces and was skulled with a rammerstaff.

The attack was broken, and as the shattered segments retired, they carried along with them parts of other commands. Mahone's Confederates now stormed forward, recovering part of the lost line, and it became evident to all that the Federals had bungled themselves into a cul-de-sac. A costly and humiliating repulse was well under way. On the extreme right of the Union line the artillery of both sides raged angrily at each other in an attempt to prevent the shifting of reinforcements. However, it seems that with the exception of sporadic outbursts by Wright's and Haskell's batteries, the lone gun, and the mortars, Confederate artillery opposite the V and IX Corps was relatively quiet. Col. Wainwright's right flank batteries soon found themselves with nothing to shoot at; the enemy guns which were firing were all more or less masked to the V Corps. Many of that corps' weapons fell silent, for they were cautious about shooting at enemy infantry so close to the crater.

As long as the Blue infantry tried to maintain some sort of a line to the front of the crater the Federal gunners were prevented from even shooting at the crest or at Haskell's battalion. But by noon Union leaders had banished all thought of offensive maneuvers. While others had retreated all the way back to their original line, too many of the poorly led Union troops had taken refuge in the crater. The Federal artillerymen began pouring fire on the back crest, as Mahone's Confederate infantry came charging toward the ragged ditch. The enraged Rebels, undaunted by the shelling, recovered more lost ground.

Actually, as soon as the first assault waves dove for the assumed cover of that pit, it was obvious that their attack was a failure, and by mid-morning the Union high command ordered the withdrawal of the beleaguered troops. The shaken, partly demoralized troops were ordered to retire across that short but open plain. In broad daylight this meant inviting wholesale slaughter.

All in all, though, it had been quite a shoot for the Federal artillerymen, and it was certainly not their fault that the attack had been a failure. Abbott's siege weapons had dumped on the Confederate works nearly 1300 big rifled projectiles, 1500 large mortar rounds (which for the first time included spherical case type projectiles), and 1000 Coehorn shells. The IX Corps batteries had pegged some 750 solid, 750 case, and 2100 shell into the enemy area; the XVIII Corps batteries had fired 155 solid, 361 shell, 161 case, and 6 canister; and while totals for the V Corps are not available, two batteries reported expenditures of 370 and 563 rounds. Estimating, then, an average of 460 rounds for each of the twelve V Corps batteries, this would give a total of 5600 rounds, a grand total for the Army of approximately 13,670 rounds of all types.

No wonder then that Grant remarked: 'It was the saddest affair I have witnessed in the war. Such opportunity for carrying fortifications I have never seen and do not expect again to have.' [6] It might also be said that this affair was quite indicative of the ineffectiveness of Civil War artillery on the offensive.

This was Grant's last attempt at a frontal assault on Robert E. Lee's earth-burrowing soldiers until the final week of the war; from that July until the following spring, Grant concentrated on tightening the cord about the Confederate lifeline. Bit by bit he cut the flow of supplies to Lee's Army and the Confederate capital.

On August 17th Grant made the first of these moves — another try at cutting the Weldon Railroad. The task was assigned to Gen. Warren's V Corps. He was also to consider his mission as a reconnaissance in force. The V Corps, supported by elements of the IX, moved out of its trenches on August 18th and marched unopposed westward until it was astride the Weldon Railroad. At that point Warren formed front to the north and began ripping up the rails. By morning of the 19th, however, the general had become worried over his open right and began extending it through heavy thickets to connect with a thin skirmish line thrown out by the IX Corps — now the left of Meade's Army in the trenches.

About 4:30 p.m. of that day the Confederates confirmed Warren's fears and ripped into that weak right flank. Part of the Gray battle line was in the woods, but their left, which projected beyond that cover some 300 yards into open ground, began to pivot around on the Confederate right so as to strike the V Corps line in flank and rear. Seven of the V Corps batteries, which were close at hand, were disposed in a line from east to west; while three were posted facing east, all about 600 yards in rear of the infantry. As the Confederate attack — two brigades — swung left and came around through the open fields, it found itself exposed to Col. Wainwright's fire.

The Blue commanders wheeled some of the infantry around, and soon heavy crashes of rifle volleys joined the cannon booms. The charging ranks came to a halt, then began drifting back. As the retirement continued, about 200 Federal infantry, apparently acting on their own, moved after the Confederates, and in so doing masked the fire of Wainwright's guns and forced them to shut down their fire abruptly. It was good luck that this happened, as the Rebel attack, succeeding against the weak right, had wedged between the Union center and Wainwright's batteries. As the guns had opened up, some of the overs had landed in the area of Crawford's division. The colonel's quick 'cease fire' cooled the guns before any serious damage had been done.

At daybreak of August 21st, Warren pulled his corps rearward about a mile to the vicinity of Globe Tavern. The new position was open ground. Shortly before 9 o'clock Union pickets spotted enemy columns forming in the distance and passed the word back. Minutes later some two dozen Confederate field pieces erupted into action, half of them about the Davis house firing south, and the others over to the west on the Vaughn Road pegging their projectiles east — a neat crossfire on the V Corps batteries.

The Yankee cannon promptly took up the gauntlet, and as the Gray infantry came into view the Blue batteries shifted their fire to this primary target. Two New York outfits, both old hands with the Army — Hart's and Mink's batteries — caught some of the Rebels coming down a road near the Flower house, and the New Yorkers were convinced their fire drove this column back.

All day long Confederate Gen. A. P. Hill flung his brigades at Warren's line. Several times they appeared near the Flower place, at one time even running a battery in there. But four V Corps units — Hart's, Mink's, Anderson's, and Phillips's — dumped a concentrated fire on the area which no doubt helped the Blue infantry drive off the enemy.

All along the V Corps front the story was the same — combined Federal artillery and infantry fire had broken up most of the attacks before they had gained much momentum. Over on the right Confederate prisoners told their captors that their battle line had been three ranks deep, but the first had been smashed by the Yankee artillery before it cleared the woods and the second rank was able to get no farther than 300 yards when the discharges of canister and case in a furious cross-fire from about twenty-six V Corps guns disposed of it. At the other end of the corps' line the Rebels did succeed in entering the left rear of Warren's divisions, but they soon found themselves the trapped ones, as heavy masses of Blue infantry caught them in the cross-fire. Three of the corps' batteries poured in heavy doses of canister. Then a fourth battery, Barnes's, tried to seal off the Rebels by laying down fire on the woods directly in the enemy's rear. Such a volume of fire ripped into the Confederates that some of the Federals thought the trapped enemy had surrendered, and cries of 'cease fire' rang out all along the front. Before the error was discovered, the enemy brigade escaped.

The day ended disastrously for the Confederates. It was a day Col. Wainwright described as one 'in which the artillery on our side bore a more prominent part than in any other action of this campaign.' [7]

On August 25th, four days after Warren's affair, Hancock's II Corps was pulled around to the Union left and put to work tearing up more Weldon track near Reams Station, south of Warren's position at Globe Tavern. Confederates, after skirmishing with the Federals all morning and most of the afternoon, hit the II Corps solidly just before sundown.

It was about 4:30 p.m. when the Union pickets first reported the enemy advancing against the corps' right, close to a small swamp 600 yards distant. Capt. A. Judson Clark, temporarily commanding the corps' artillery, had deployed four batteries across the road in shallow rifle pits: the 10th Massachusetts and combined A/B, 1st Rhode Island, were west of the railroad and parallel to it, to the left of the station in order to hold a road running off to the west; the 12th New York and Battery C, 1st New Jersey, were to the right of the station, east of the tracks, and nearly perpendicular to them.

When word of advancing enemy columns reached the artillery, they immediately opened fire, the 12th New York pegging its shells in one direction of assumed enemy advance — though the actual target was masked from view by a woods. Blue infantry then made contact, and the battle for Reams Station was on.

About an hour later a mass of Confederate artillery broke loose with a furious shelling of the Yankee infantry from the cover of a small scrub pine woods directly on the Federal front. Clark's batteries instantly crashed out with counter-battery fire, and under the cover of this gun duel the Rebel infantry began to roll forward. Such of Clark's batteries as could sight the advancing Graycoats switched targets and tried to break up their lines with a rain of shell and case. One piece of the 12th New York had been sent farther to the left by a general. But neither the fire of the Yankee infantry nor the pounding by Clark's guns seemed to phase the oncoming waves of bayonets, and the artillerymen began ramming in the old standby — canister.

A corporal with a detached gun put his weapon on canister, blazing away until the enemy was atop the earthworks just in front. Too late he tried to retire the piece; and just as the big gun was limbered, Minié slugs dumped a wheel horse to earth, tangling up the traces and immobilizing the piece. Quickly cutting loose the other horses, the corporal and his men fled rearward, leaving the gun to the enemy.

The other guns of the 12th New York were also having a rough time. Lt. George K. Dauchy, commanding the battery, had even pulled his drivers from their teams to help run canister from the limbers to the guns. When the Rebels broke through the Union lines, Dauchy pulled his left piece out of its work into cleared ground to the left and opened with double canister across the face of some abandoned Union works further down that flank. This fire kept the Rebels back from that stretch of trench. Any advance would be smacked in flank by double canister — not exactly the best method of keeping a unit combat-effective.

But in rear of the 12th New York's position was a wood, and some alert Confederate officer, seeing the threat posed by Dauchy's weapons, swung his infantry through the timber toward the thundering guns. Someone in the battery saw them coming, and Dauchy yelled for the limbers. Drivers ran for their teams, swung into saddles, and urged the animals up to the guns. By this time the Johnnies were within rifle range. Two limbers lost their horses before they could move; the limber of the third piece was hooked to the gun and the unit was able to advance until an enemy volley spilled the team; the fourth gun fell into Rebel hands.

Other artillery, too, was running into difficulty. The 10th Massachusetts Battery had been firing off and on all day. About 1 p.m. some of the enemy moved in from the west close enough to wound the battery commander, Capt. Sleeper, and from a cornfield 300 yards away kept up a constant sniping at the battery. One after another, Rebel riflemen picked off the horses until by 5 o'clock not one remained standing.

Then the Gray regiments rushed the battery's right flank. They were driven back bleeding and broken before they had gone halfway across the field. Another pause followed, and the Confederate artillery fire which had lashed at Clark's batteries across the track exploded ominously. Some twelve pieces, the Bay Staters estimated, hit their part of the line, and solid columns of infantry in regimental front moved forward under this protective fire. The proud II Corps lines, no longer filled with eager young Volunteers who had broken the charge at Gettysburg, buckled at numerous spots, and only pressure from the unit commanders kept the units reformed and lines repaired.

At about 6 o'clock the Confederates gave one more concerted push, and the Yankee ranks just to the right of the 10th Massachusetts Battery snapped. Lt. H. H. Granger, now commanding that battery, whirled his right piece around and started to slash at the menacing columns with canister. But there was such weight and determination to this attack that it could not be beaten off. As that mass of bayonets kept coming, Granger abandoned the right gun and relied on the next one to its left. After firing a few rounds from this weapon, it too was abandoned, and a third took over. Only when the picture looked hopeless did the lieutenant abandon all of the weapons. By evening three lieutenants, forty men, and one caisson were all that remained of the 10th Massachusetts Battery.

The gallant and famous Rhode Island batteries, A and B — now combined as one unit because of personnel losses and expiration of enlistments — also shared the same fate. Lt. William S. Perrin, commanding the unit, lost his leg in a Rebel cannon shelling, and with the other two officers of the unit, fell prisoner when the enemy overran the Rhode Islanders' position and captured all four guns and their caissons. When darkness ended the fighting, the II Corps listed 2000 men as casualties — ninety-nine of which were from the batteries — and nine guns with eight caissons were in Southern hands. This marked the last time the Army of the Potomac was to lose guns permanently to the Army of Northern Virginia.

All through the fall and winter the miserable dirty siege continued — the same general type of warfare their grandsons would fight fifty-three years later on the Western Front. In October, and then again in February, Grant made more moves to outflank Lee's line. Finally the Gray commander's 57,000 men were spread thinly along a thirty-five mile front. But with the coming of spring Grant planned to unleash his forces in major offensives which would end the Confederacy. However, Lee, in a move characteristic of a superb commander, again stole the march on his adversary.

In the pre-dawn hours of March 25th the Army of Northern Virginia made its last offensive strike. It was a desperate gamble designed to cut Grant's huge Army in two pieces and tear into his supply base at City Point — not unlike the German Ardennes counter-offensive of December 1944. Lee's last offensive — like the Ardennes strike — despite initial success, lacked the strength to carry through the objective.

The attack was made by Gordon's corps, reinforced by two brigades of Ransom's. The battle plan called for a detachment of carefully picked men to slip forward in the night and clear lanes through the Federal barriers, then overpower the Blue pickets. Gordon's assault columns would rush Fort Stedman and Battery 10 on the forward Federal defense line. From that point Confederate units would peel off to widen and deepen the break. Confederate artillery was to support the assault by opening on the Federals from the Appomattox River on the Gray left clear down to the Plank Road. Picked gun crews were to accompany the attacking units so as to put all seized artillery into immediate use against the enemy.

About 4 a.m. the Rebels launched their bolt. In most places the Yankee pickets found themselves prisoners without having fired a single shot in defense — some Federals claimed this was done by deceit rather than by stealth, the Graycoats gaining access by claiming to be deserters. In any event, the men of the 14th Massachusetts Battery and Battery K, 1st Connecticut Heavy Artillery, manning two 3-inch and four 8-inch guns, and three Coehorns of Battery 10, were never warned of the approaching storm.

With whoops and yells the attacking Rebels advanced toward the parapets of Battery 10. Sleepy gun crews scrambled to reach their posts, and the right gun of the Massachusetts battery crashed its load into the darkness; seconds later the second piece fired. Before the smoke had risen from the muzzles, dark figures bounded over the parapets of the right gun and shot and clubbed the frustrated gun crew. More Rebels scrambled over the works about the second piece, which had been hurriedly reloaded. Before the primer could be inserted, the crew found themselves surrounded, and the lieutenant shot dead.

In the next section, the men of Battery K, 1st Connecticut, had no chance to bring their mortars into action. They had rushed to their weapons and found them surrounded by Rebels with lowered bayonet-tipped rifles. Rifle and pistol fire cracked in the faint light, one of Battery K's lieutenants dropped dead, and the captain was badly wounded. The surviving officer rallied the remnants of the unit and fought it out of the fallen redoubt to the eventual safety of Battery 4, a short way to the north.

Over in Fort Stedman the crews of the 19th New York Battery knew that trouble was in the wind when they heard the outburst that accompanied the Rebels' sweep for the works protecting the battery on its north flank. The guard in Fort Stedman leaped for the four Napoleons in the fort, which were always loaded with canister, and four shivering claps of cannon fire shook the night air. Within minutes the guns of the two battery sections which occupied this fort were splitting the hazy dawn with their sharp flashes. After some ten or twelve shots had been hurled blindly toward the Rebel lines, it became evident that Battery 10 was in enemy hands. Without opposition Graycoats streamed over the north face of Fort Stedman just as the New Yorkers were heaving one of their weapons out of its embrasures to bear on Battery 10.

The Bluecoats never had a chance. Seeing the dark silhouettes leaping into the fort from three sides, Lt. Michael Long, commanding the two sections, yelled to his men to run for it. Long, another lieutenant, and twelve men failed to make it and were taken prisoner. The remainder of the detachment — sixteen men — got away; three of the gunners with the breech sights to their weapons — thus the efficiency of the guns would be reduced when they fell into enemy hands.

Close by was Battery 12, which housed two big 8-inch mortars and four Coehorns manned by Battery L, 1st Connecticut. As soon as the racket broke out around Battery 10 and Fort Stedman, this redoubt had joined the shooting. Shortly after the mortars began erupting, one officer came running into the works to report that Battery 11 some one hundred yards northward had just fallen to the Rebels and most of the command had been taken prisoner. With that the commander of Battery 12 ordered his mortars to pour fire into the fallen fort.

At this point the beginnings of Federal counter-efforts became evident. An infantry officer came running up to the battery commander and ordered him to cease firing. He was going to retake number eleven with his men. No sooner had the weapons ceased when two lines of Rebel infantry — about 1000 men total — appeared, moving rapidly on Battery 12 from the rear. To remain would have been suicide, so the battery commander pulled out his men and fled to the next work down the line — Fort Haskell.

In Fort Haskell were four Napoleons of the 3rd New Jersey Battery and four Coehorns of Battery L, 1st Connecticut. As soon as the shooting broke out, the men of these units were hurried to their pieces, where they nervously awaited developments. They did not have long to wait. Through the mist the Blue artillerymen spotted the body of troops moving toward them in column, inside the Federal line of breastworks. Everyone strained to pick up their identity; they appeared to some to be Federals retreating from Fort Stedman. Not until the mass was about a hundred yards distant were they identified as Rebels!

Some of the attackers rushed for the Yankee rear, while others opened a cracking rifle fire on Fort Haskell from the cover of nearby huts and bombproofs. The Rebels were already too close for the Connecticut men to bring their mortars into play, so the lieutenant in command shoved his men onto the parapet to fight as infantry with rifles and pistols. At this point enemy mortar and artillery fire began dropping on Fort Haskell. Although the Yankee mortars were masked, the Napoleons of Capt. Christian Woerner's 3rd New Jersey Battery had a clear field of fire, and the thunder of its gun rolled through the dawn air. Soon the attackers broke and fled back toward Fort Stedman, giving Haskell a momentary respite.

The Southerners, however, had not given up the idea of

owning Haskell; a second wave of them was spotted forming in the rear of Stedman. As the Federals watched, the Gray ranks wheeled into wide line of battle and, with red banners waving, moved toward Fort Haskell. Capt. Woerner pulled a Napoleon over to the extreme right corner of the fort where it could sweep the open space between there and Stedman. Rounds of canister were hurriedly stacked up beside the weapon, which then began to bite viciously at the attacking lines. By this time the Federals were beginning to recover from the initial shock and heavy masses of Union infantry were hurried forward from their reserve positions. Faced with such odds the Confederates' second assault on Fort Haskell petered out, and broken segments streamed back to Stedman or their own lines.

North of Battery 10, where the Confederates had first broken through, the pattern was about the same. Battery 9, which had three Coehorns of Battery K, 1st Connecticut, and two Napoleons of Battery C/I, 5th U.S., had rushed to their posts when Fort Stedman and Battery 10 were hit. It was about 5:15 a.m. before the command to start firing came. At 400 yards range Rebel infantry was spotted moving on the battery, and the five weapons went into action. The build-up of Federal fire had reached a heavy roar, and the charging ranks were hard hit. The Gray left rested nearly on their own lines, while their right was inside the outer line of Union earthworks. The Regulars poured on case shot. Immediately a heavy fire began to land on the battery from the front, from Fort Stedman, and from the right flank and rear, and a terrible ruckus began which shook the ground for several hours.

The Rebel infantry advancing on the fort was stopped in a narrow ravine and held there by blasts of canister from Battery C/I's Napoleons. Until about 7 a.m. the Rebels sweated out their predicament. Then one of the officers wiggled his way to within calling distance of Battery 9. From here he yelled that he wanted to give himself up; the man was told to come forward, was disarmed, and immediately questioned by

Lt. V. H. Stone commanding Battery C/I. The Confederates astounded the Federals by stating that some 200 to 300 Gray troops would surrender if Stone would cease his fire. Stone ordered the cease fire. The racket of gunfire subsided, and anxious Federals watched the front as over 300 Rebels with hands overhead came streaming toward the fort. With their capitulation all attempts to take Battery 9 ended.

Combat-wise Yankee units had by now recovered their composure and were taking up blocking position independently, until the higher commands could tie things together. The ground in rear of the breakthrough point began to fill up with powerful fresh regiments of infantry, and field batteries, which had been in reserve behind the line, began to drop their gun trails on the hill crest in rear of the break. The sun burned away the early dawn haze and gave the Yankee artillery a clear view of its targets. Every gun, from Battery 4 on the north to Fort Morton on the south, poured it on the Fort Stedman area in a terrific cross-fire, and, with the Blue infantry, completely sealed off the break. Lee's last offensive strike — a faint replica of his devastating efforts of 1862–63 — was finished. By 9 a.m. the Federals had recovered all lost ground, and Gordon's cut-up brigades had paid with 4000 lives.

After the failure of the Fort Stedman operation, there were few Rebels who were not aware that the offensive power of the Army of Northern Virginia was gone — left in a welter of casualties on the trampled battlefields from Gettysburg to Cold Harbor and Petersburg. The only hope of restoring that power lay in uniting Lee's depleted Army with that of Joe Johnston's in the Carolinas. This was Lee's next move.

Now spring had come, though, and the roads were once more passable. Grant was also planning to unloose his huge blue anaconda and stretch it farther to the west to complete the encirclement of Petersburg. Actually, two rested, powerful armies — Meade's Army of the Potomac and Ord's Army of the James, now under an energetic commander (the incompetent Ben Butler had finally been relieved) — had begun to flex their muscles the day before the Rebels struck Stedman. A pugnacious little Irishman named Sheridan had brought the cocky, well-trained and victorious cavalry corps down from the valley. He was operating with Warren's V Corps, and, in the later afternoon of April 1st, he proceeded to Five Forks, some seventeen miles southwest of Petersburg. The undefended Southside Railroad, the last rail link Lee had to the South, lay just ahead.

Undoubtedly the Gray commander realized that there were few pages left in the book of the once potent Army of Northern Virginia. The Yankee artillery opened up on the evening of April 1st in a heavy preparatory fire for the general assault set for dawn the next day. The ground must have really trembled under the fire that Hunt loosed on Lee's lines. The siege train alone totaled 188 pieces, which ran the gamut from 100-pounder Parrotts to Coehorn mortars. Then there were 202 guns and 12 Coehorns in the corps' field batteries. Capable Hunt had made sure that every gun in the Army had 270 rounds of ammunition on hand.

Prior to this final campaign the Artillery Reserve had come back into existence. Ever since the Wilderness campaign it had been relegated to inactive status; only its valuable ammunition train continued to serve with the Army, and apparently only in an unofficial capacity. However, with the trench-type warfare that characterized the Petersburg campaign, many corps' field batteries had become surplus to the needs of their commands — Abbott's huge siege guns and mortars being given the starring role. These field batteries had remained inactive behind the lines, where they simply grew into an Artillery Reserve.

This Artillery Reserve was further augmented in the March 29th shake-up of the Army's field artillery. In preparation for what was expected to be the last campaign, the II and VI Corps were reduced to six batteries each, with five allotted to the V and five to the IX Corps. Since the II and VI Corps were to be the maneuver elements in the coming offensive, this reduction, to be effective immediately, left the field artillery of the Army of the Potomac with twenty-three batteries with a strength of ninety-two guns. The surplus batteries were to be either left in position in the present VI Corps lines or sent to Gen. Tidball commanding the IX Corps artillery. All the batteries which could not be placed were to revert to the Artillery Reserve at City Point.

Lee's thin right was ripped apart by the haymaker punch of the VI Corps as it jumped off about 7 a.m. on April 2nd. Then the Confederate lines broke at other points, and Lee telegraphed his President that Richmond would have to be evacuated that night. The best hope for escape lay in crossing to the north side of the Appomattox River, heading for Amelia courthouse forty miles west, and from there to Lynchburg and the Carolinas. Every Confederate effort on the afternoon of April 2nd was directed toward that objective. Under cover of darkness that night Lee's Army began evacuating the Petersburg-Richmond lines, unaware that the Federal high command has scheduled another assault on the final enemy defense positions for dawn of the 3rd. But by 3 a.m. of that day the Confederate troops had skipped town. Shortly after 4 a.m. Yankee infantry marched into Richmond.

On the IX Corps line facing Petersburg was Battery C/I, 5th U.S., led by Lt. V. H. Stone. At 3:30 a.m., as Stone was watching the fire lighted city, he saw infantry clambering over the breastwork of an enemy fort on his immediate front. Thinking it was Rebel infantry evacuating their lines, Stone commanded his gunners to open on the infantry with case.

The first round appeared to explode dead over the target — fortunately without damage, as a chorus of protesting Yankee yells told the artillerymen to stop shooting at their own people. Young Stone then concluded that this was the Federal skirmish wave moving out. He eagerly asked the brigade commander he was supporting for authority to advance a section. The officer gave Stone the go-ahead, and, without losing a moment, the lieutenant sent back to his camp for his limbers. Minutes passed, and his vehicles did not come. Another orderly was sent galloping back to camp. Then Stone himself rode to the camp a mile distant and led the limbers back to the lines.

An engineers' party cut a path through the outer defenses, and the section of Battery C/I, 5th U.S., headed for Petersburg. At 4:15 a.m. Stone and his two guns reached the city. Cautiously the lieutenant moved toward the center of the deserted city, where he was relieved to find a waiting column of IX Corps infantry. But at the same time another column came into view from the opposite end of town carrying VI Corps flags.

Determined that the IX Corps would take the lead after Lee's Army, Lt. Stone galloped his section down the street and swung his column around the corner of a road that seemed to lead toward the bridge over the Appomattox. He believed he had reversed the positions of the VI and IX Corps units, thus placing his IX Corps in the lead — the first to occupy the city.

It was now just a matter of time. Exactly one week of life remained for the harassed Army of Northern Virginia. Lee crossed to the north of the river and led his little Army, now scarcely larger than one of Grant's corps, westward. Grant instructed his two Army commanders to press the enemy hard.

For the Federal field artillerymen the war had changed. No longer were they watching for those thunderous charges by ragged lines of Confederate infantry which had overrun so many Yankee batteries. With the fall of Richmond and Petersburg the bulk of the Federal cannon had recoiled for the last time. Only on April 6th, at Sailor's Creek, about two-thirds of the way from Petersburg to Appomattox, did the Yankee gunners do any notable shooting. There the VI Corps, aided by Sheridan's cavalry, trapped the hodgepodge corps of Gen. Ewell.

As had been ordered, the VI Corps artillery brigade had been stripped to five batteries: Brinckle's E, 5th U.S.; Harn's 3rd New York Battery; Allen's H, 1st Rhode Island; Adams's

G, 1st Rhode Island; and Cowan's 1st New York Battery. There seemed to be a bit of poetic justice that Cowan's battery should be included among those in at the end. This unit had been one of the first Federal batteries of McClellan's newly created Army of the Potomac to exchange fire with the Rebels at Lee's Mill, as the Blue legions marched up the Peninsula in April 1862. While Cowan was no longer leading the battery, he was present as the VI Corps artillery brigade commander.

At Sailor's Creek Cowan threw his five batteries into action from commanding ground and poured fire into the Gray ranks. Confederate resistance and even a few local successes were finally overcome, and Ewell's corps surrendered — some of the prisoners remarking that the shelling laid down by Cowan's guns was the most terrific they had ever experienced.

The Federal pursuit continued westward at a furious pace. The roads were muddy, and the combat columns were outstripping their supply trains. This pace was hard enough on the men, but it was too much for the artillery horses. For some reason the allowance of forage for animals during the winter months had been severely restricted, and the hay ration was cut to three or four pounds a day. So the artillery teams which started forward that April were not well-fed animals. In the 10th Massachusetts Battery of the II Corps, three horses died April 3rd, another April 4th, one more on the 5th, two on the 6th, two on the 7th, four on April 8th. The terrific rate continued even after the surrender — until a total of thirty-four horses were dead! The only reason that the brigades could remain operational was that Gen. Hunt ordered fresh teams forward from the Army's idle Reserve batteries.

On April 9th it was all over. As soon as Lee's surrender was confirmed, Brevet Maj. Andrew Cowan ordered his old unit — the 1st New York Battery — to fire a thirty-six gun salute, and the thunder, the last discharges of the field artillery of the Army of the Potomac, was soon heard over the field.[8]

In the hours immediately after the surrender Brevet Brig. Gen. Hunt, Chief-of-Artillery, Army of the Potomac, ran across

a former pupil of his old army days — Brig. Gen. Armistead
Lindsay Long, late Chief-of-Artillery, II Corps, Army of Northern Virginia. Lt. Long had served in veteran Capt. Hunt's
mounted battery in the years following the Mexican War, when,
for economy reasons, only two batteries of each of the then existing four regiments of artillery served as mounted field batteries;
the others rotated duty as infantry, or manned seacoast garrisons in order to learn about field artillery procedure. Long had
taken his tour under Hunt.

Now, in the quiet of Appomattox, Hunt remarked to his
former pupil that the conduct of the Confederate bombardment at Gettysburg — which Hunt understood was under
Long's general control — was not in keeping with the principles he had imparted to his student officers. There had been
no convergence of fire on the point of attack, as Long had been
taught; instead, the effort was scattered over the whole field.
Long smiled at the observation and then answered, 'I remembered my lessons at the time, and, when the fire became so
scattered, wondered what you would think about it!' [9]

One can never measure precisely how much of this dearly
bought victory was the individual responsibility of the Yankee
field batteries; nor should this be possible, since artillery, then
as now, is a supporting arm. The fact remains, though, that the
Union could have had no greater asset in the initial campaigns
of the war than the Regular Army artillery. It was an effective
force in being as well as an invaluable school and model for
the eager, but totally untrained, Volunteer batteries which
swelled the Army's ranks.

When McClellan began his Peninsula campaign, the field
batteries of the Army of the Potomac were far superior in
quantity and quality of matériel to their opponents, and the
men who manned these batteries had been forged into well-
trained teams. With anything less, McClellan's Army might
have succumbed before the powerful blows dealt it at Gaines
Mill, Glendale, and Malvern Hill.

On the Peninsula the frightful effectiveness of field artillery defensive fires no doubt saved the Blue Army. The Confederates proved the point at Second Bull Run, where their massed batteries played a major role in destroying Pope's desperate attack of August 30th. If Pope had had McClellan's artillery organization and Henry J. Hunt, the outcome might have been different. Assuming Pope would have listened to Hunt's advice, that artilleryman would have undoubtedly employed a host of guns in counter-battery fire. While unable to use canister at such ranges, solid shot, shell, and case shot would have been effective against this line of guns, limbers, caissons, and teams — a target about as deep as it was wide.

At Antietam and at Fredericksburg the threat posed by the magnificent artillery of the Army of the Potomac caused the redoubtable Jackson to advise Lee against making his proposed counter-attacks. The picture of advancing lines being hewn apart by scathing blasts of canister from masses of cannon was still fresh in his mind.

The Blue Gunners had given Meade at Gettysburg a full measure of their value to his Army, for with less capable artillery the result here, too, might have been different. In the campaigns that followed Gettysburg the Union Army took on the offensive role; much of the fighting in the spring of 1864 was in thickly wooded country; and at Cold Harbor and at Petersburg trench warfare supplanted open field maneuvering. With these changes the Union field batteries became less of a factor, as the North's grip tightened on the gasping throat of the Confederacy; the limitations of the matériel, the terrain, and tactics were all responsible for this diminution.

Napoleon Bonaparte had made field artillery the dominant weapon on the battlefield, a position it retained until 1861. Then, in the years 1861–65 casualties attributed to artillery were only some 10 per cent of the total battle casualties (89 per cent were caused by the rifle and musket, with 1 per cent from all other causes). It would take another fifty years for artillery to regain its former position. In World Wars I and II, and in Korea, upwards of 75 per cent of the battle casualties were caused by artillery and mortar fire.

An American tradition of an artillery arm second-to-none began in 1776. The gunners of 1861–65 perpetuated and enhanced this tradition, and they set the pattern whereby American infantry never lacked superior artillery fire support. Indicative of this is a letter written by a Northern soldier to his mother in 1863: 'There is one thing that our government does that suits me to a dot. That is, we fight mostly with artillery. The rebls fight mostly with infentry. They fight as though a mans life was not worth one sent or in other words with desperation; or like Gen. Lafeyet said to Washington, ther is more *dogs* where them come from. Our Generals are careful of there men.' [10] The letter might well have been written from Europe in 1944 or Korea in 1951.

No less an authority than Confederate Gen. D. H. Hill gave his side's opinion of the value of the Federal artillery when he wrote that Confederate infantry and Yankee artillery together need fear no enemy in the world.

Technical Data

AMMUNITION TYPES

Ammunition for field batteries of the Civil War was of four general types for all guns, whether rifled or smoothbore. These were: solid shot, shell, spherical case or shrapnel, and canister.

The solid shot were just what the name implies — a solid piece of cast iron, which was generally a favorite round for use on cavalry, troops in column, infantry lines caught in flank, or any target where a bowling ball-type effect could be expected. This was supposed to be the most accurate projectile, and those guns which took a weight as part of their name, i. e. 12-pounder gun, it was the weight of the solid round that determined it.

Gibbon's *Artillerist's Manual* stated that solid shot should not be fired at infantry at ranges over 1000 yards or cavalry over 1200 yards, unless the ground was suitable for ricochet firing and the enemy in dense masses, as vision beyond those ranges precluded accurate fire.

As an example, a 12-pounder Napoleon gun used two and a half pounds of powder as a propellant, and, using this charge with an elevation of five degrees, the Napoleon could hurl its solid shot approximately 1680 yards.

The 10-pounder Parrott and the 3-inch Ordnance rifle had a theoretical range of about 6200 yards at thirty-five degrees elevation, but actual practice limited them to about 2400 yards maximum.

The establishing of exact ranges for the various types of ordnance and ammunition is a difficult thing, as no two range tables that the author has used seem to agree, though their

differences are not really too great. I have used Benton's West
Point textbook *Ordnance and Gunnery USMA*, John Gibbon's
Artillerist's Manual, and the several editions of the semi-
official manual *Instructions for Field Artillery* by Barry,
French, and Hunt.

A second common type was explosive shell, or shell as it
was usually called. This was the forerunner of the modern and
far more potent HE round. It was a hollow projectile with
the cavity filled to about 90 per cent capacity with black
powder — or seven ounces in the case of that for the Napoleon
gun. The charge was exploded by means of a time fuze which
was ignited by the flame of the burning propellant charge. Due
to the inadequacies of black powder as a military explosive
the frangibility of the shell was very poor. The large number
of fragments which the author has collected from many battlefields indicate that a 12-pounder shell exploded into about
four or five large pieces. A greater number of smaller pieces
traveling at a higher velocity, as is the case with the modern
HE shell, would have produced a much greater lethal ex-
pectancy per round. Civil War shells used the velocity of the
shell itself as the principal source of its energy, which, for the
12-pounder Napoleon, was only 1400 feet per second at the
muzzle.

However, for all of its ballistic weaknesses the shell round
had definite psychological advantages over solid shot, as it
could unnerve men and horses by its noise and the flash of its
explosion, as well as by its casualty producing effects.

The wall of a 12-pounder shell was about three-quarters
of an inch thick, and the propellant charge used in the Napoleon with this projectile was two and a half pounds. It could
be timed to burst from zero to five seconds by means of a time
fuze, and at an elevation of three degrees and seventy-five
seconds a range of 1300 yards could be attained. Shell rounds
were used primarily on field fortifications and bulky targets
such as enemy artillery. Their use on personnel was less than
case or canister.

12-pounder Shell

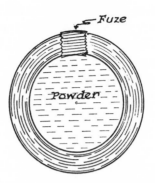

Spherical case or case shot was a form of projectile invented by Gen. Shrapnel of the British Army. It was sometimes referred to by its inventor's name, but more frequently was termed case shot or case.

It was hollow like shell, except that the walls were not as thick — a half-inch for the Napoleon round. Within the cavity was a number of round balls held in a mass of melted sulphur or resin. Again using the Napoleon as an example, the cavity was filled with about seventy-eight balls the size of a marble. The round was fuzed in the same manner as shell and contained a bursting charge of one ounce of powder and was propelled by two and a half pounds of black powder.

Case shot was primarily an anti-personnel round and was used at ranges beyond the maximum effective range of canister or over 400 yards. The manuals of the day said that it should be fused to explode fifty to seventy-five yards in front of the target and fifteen to twenty feet above it.

The only really effective round of the Civil War was canister. This was an elongated tin can containing iron or lead balls in sawdust. Upon the explosion of the propellant, inertia forced the balls to shatter the face of the container as it hurled down the tube, and the effect was that of a huge shotgun. The canister for the Napoleon contained twenty-seven balls about the size of a golf ball. This charge was rarely used at ranges over 400 yards. But when enemy infantry closed under that range artillery switched to canister, and if the attack threatened to overrun the position double canister might be used.

It was a defensive round almost exclusively, as artillery on the offensive in this war seldom if ever moved forward to

12-pounder Spherical Case

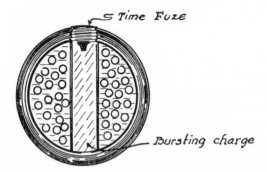

within canister range of the enemy infantry. In the defensive it was a fearsome charge for attacking infantry to face. Closely packed lines of men, rushing to come to close grips with the enemy was typical of the Civil War and made to order for the scathing blasts of Napoleon guns firing canister.

The author has used a bit of poetic license in titling this

Canister

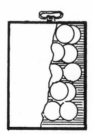

work *Grape and Canister,* for the use of grape in field guns had been discontinued in the United States service for a number of years. It had been considered that for field pieces the size and number of balls in a canister were large enough, and that canister possessed the advantage of potentially striking a greater number of targets at one discharge than the nine large balls in a round of grapeshot. There was also the advantage of reducing the types of ammunition that had to be supplied to and carried by the field batteries.

However, in reading through the *Official Records* one will continually come across references by *infantry* commanders to the fierce storm of 'grape and canister' that their commands had to endure. But careful reading of *field artillery* reports will show that grape was not used. The author has never found a reference by a field battery commander that he had fired grape. Further, the manuals of that time do not make any provision for its use by this type battery, nor is it listed as a standard item of issue in the ammunition chests. But 'grape and canister' was a catchy phrase born decades before, and though now inaccurate would die hard.

Grape actually was issued to the heavier siege and fortress guns. It consisted of nine balls of a size appropriate to the caliber, held in three tiers of three balls each, between two rings and a plate at each end of the stand connected by a metal rod. The frame was shattered by the explosion of the propellant throwing the nine large balls, most frequently about the size of a baseball, in a modified shotgun-like blast.

An interesting story concerning the use of grapeshot appears on page 15 of the unofficial history of Battery B, 4th U.S. Artillery, *The Cannoneer.* The story takes issue with the alleged remark of Gen. Taylor to Capt. Bragg during the Mexican War about 'a little more grape, Mr. Bragg.'

Battery B's historian was of the belief that this phrase could not have been originated by an artilleryman, but was a campaign slogan. In *The Cannoneer* Gen. Pleasonton is quoted as giving the true version of this incident. At the time Pleasonton was a lieutenant serving as an aide to Gen. Taylor, and the general in company with several others rode up to Bragg's battery just as it was opening fire. Taylor watched the effect of the first round, turned, and asked Bragg what he was firing. The reply was canister. Was it single or double? Single. 'Then double it and give 'em hell,' Pleasonton reported Taylor as saying.

Grape-shot

In Civil War terminology there appears the word 'windage,' but it had an altogether different meaning from the present-day usage. In that era of muzzle-loading weapons, both rifled and smoothbore, and fouling black powder, there had to be a difference in diameter between the gun tube and the round to permit loading. This difference was called 'windage,' and for most field pieces was one-tenth of an inch.

FUZES

The explosive type rounds, shell and case, were set off mostly by means of a power train fuze that screwed into the face or nose of the projectile. Earlier devices, such as wooden and paper fuzes cut or manufactured to burn a given time, had been outmoded by this time, and the basic time fuze of the Civil War was a form of Boarmann fuze.

This was a metal disc, threaded on the sides, containing a covered powder train. The cover to the train was soft metal and graduated in quarter seconds up to five seconds. When readied for use the soft face was gouged away at the proper second mark with a sharp instrument, thereby exposing the train to the flame of the burning propellant.

Care had to be taken in loading smoothbore guns that the fuze was on top and toward the mouth of the gun, or the force of the propellant explosion would drive the fuze itself into the round and perhaps detonate it while still in the tube. If properly loaded the flame of the propellant passed over the top of the projectile by means of the windage gap and lapped the face of the round. This style fuze was designed for and most successfully used with spherical rounds or those used with smoothbore guns.

Boarmann-type Fuze

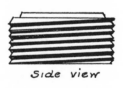

Crude time fuzes were designed for the rifled gun projectiles, which were elongated after the modern manner; and similarly, crude concussion and percussion fuzes were designed for the spherical rounds. However, these were dangerous for the smoothbores and not widely used.

The fuze most successfully used by rifled guns was a percussion type. This was often in the form of a musket cap on a plunger device in a sleeve in the nose of the shell. The force of striking an object forced the plunger and the cap forward violently detonating it against the nose cap in the face. Its great weakness was that the angle of impact had to be such that the point with the fuze in it had to strike with sufficient force to jar the cap forward. A round which ricocheted rarely detonated in this war.

A Type of Percussion Fuze

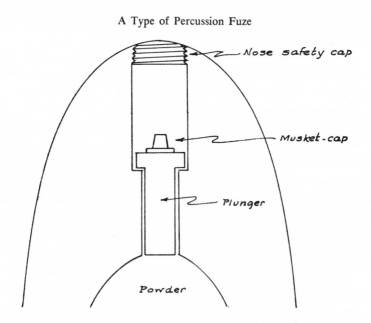

However, the 1864 edition of the *Manual for Instruction* states that for rifled guns firing case shot a 'time fuze' and a 'combination fuze' combining the principles of time and concussion were then in use, and a modification of the Boarmann fuze with a full twelve-second time range was on trial with promising results.

PACKAGING

Ammunition for field batteries was carried in wooden chests especially built for the purpose and divided into compartments for the various types of rounds. Each limber carried one chest and each caisson carried two; the chests were detachable from the vehicles so that they could be unbolted when empty and full ones replaced in their stead.

When full chests were issued the ammunition for the smoothbore guns came 'fixed' as a complete round. Fixed rounds meant that the ball was fastened to a wooden disc called a sabot by means of thin metal straps. The powder bag, which was either silk or wool — for the most part the latter — was then fastened to the other face of the wooden sabot. In the case of rifled guns, projectiles and powder bags were separate from each other. The chests were olive drab in color as were all of the wooden parts of artillery vehicles, though they frequently bore white letters indicating the caliber ammunition contained therein.

The number of rounds carried per chest varied with the caliber of the gun. The chest for the old 6-pounder gun, for example, carried fifty rounds of all types; the 12-pounder chest contained thirty-two; and the 3-inch rifle and 10-pounder Parrott chests held fifty. Additional ammunition was available in the trains and usually brought the total rounds to about 400 per gun. Thus each gun section of a 12-pounder Napoleon battery theoretically carried into action 128 rounds.

It has been stated that the Federal artillery fired five million rounds during the entire war, an average of four rounds per gun per day.

RIFLING SYSTEMS

Civil War artillery was almost exclusively muzzle-loading. While the Confederates employed a few breech-loading British Whitworth guns, the Federals, except for a trial with Whitworths on the Peninsula, stuck to the others wholeheartedly. The author has heard an unconfirmed story that the state of New York raised a battalion of field artillery and equipped it with Whitworth guns. However, the story goes, the Federal government refused to accept the battalion, and it saw no field service. There are, no doubt, isolated cases where breech-loading pieces were experimented with by the Union forces, but these are so rare as to be unimportant for the purposes of this story.

Since Civil War artillery was muzzle loading, the problem of employing rifling in gun tubes had to be met by rather crude methods. Black powder, the basic propellant of that era, left a heavy film in the tubes after firing. Therefore, after each discharge tubes were swabbed out to clean some of this debris away and also to extinguish any loitering spark. But as firing continued some fouling accumulated in the tube, and the process of ramming home a new round was made a little harder as the windage was decreased.

This windage then served two purposes: it permitted a round to be rammed home with a minimum of difficulty, and it also provided a space through which flame from the burning propellant could pass to ignite fuzes.

Rifling, on the other hand, required that a projectile fit snugly into the lands as it sped down the tube. Therefore, a system was devised which permitted the insertion of a round which was slightly smaller than the bore, yet when fired would expand and bite into the rifling. A number of schemes or systems were developed, but they all had the basic concept of a part of the projectile which expanded when fired.

One of the most common projectiles was that developed by Maj. Dyer of the United States service in 1857. The Dyer shell had a cast iron body (a) and an expanding cup of soft metal of lead and antimony (b). The pressure of the burning propellant gases forced the sides of the cup to expand outward — or into the rifling. Of course this process decreased the possibility of flame passing along the length of the projectile to light a fuze. Thus the most successful fuze in all rifling systems was the percussion fuze which fired on contact.

Another very common system used widely by both sides was that of Capt. Parrott. His projectile had a cast iron body (a) and a brass ring (b) cast in a rabate at the base of

Dyer Projectile

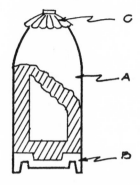

the body. Gas forced the ring to expand outward in a manner similar to Dyer's. A later Parrott shell had a wrought iron expanding cap attached to the base — a modification of another system, Reed's.

Parrott Shell

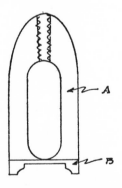

The Schenkle projectile was a third type of commonly used rifled projectile. Here the cast iron body of the shell (a) was fitted with a papier mâché wad (b) which was forced onto the cone-shaped base of the body, causing the wad to bite into the rifling. The wad disintegrated as it left the bore.

Another common type was the Hotchkiss. This design had

Schenkle Projectile

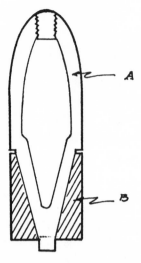

three parts: the cast iron case (a), an expanding ring of soft metal (b), and a cap (c). The cap crowded the soft metal ring and forced it into the rifling.

Hotchkiss Projectile

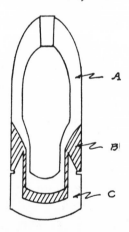

There were other types too, Reed, Sawyer, etc., all of which worked on the basic idea of an expansion ring or device.

PRIMERS

Artillery of 1861–1865 required the use of primers — a device to carry fire from the exterior of the gun to the propellant charge in the bore. Primers were inserted in a hole at the top of the back end of the gun tube called the vent. In the earliest days this took the form of pouring fine grain powder into the vent and lighting this by means of a slow burning wick. Quite often this wick was wound about a heavy wooden stick called a linstock.

Friction Primer

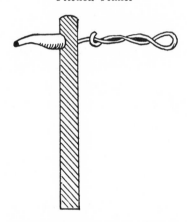

By the time of the outbreak of the Civil War a new type primer had been developed called a friction primer. This device consisted of two small brass tubes soldered at right angles to each other. The upper and shorter tube contained fine grain powder called friction powder, and through its center ran a piece of wire with a roughed end. The other tube was filled with rifle powder, and this tube was inserted into the vent of the piece.

The other end of the wire was twisted into the form of a loop through which the lanyard hook was attached. To fire the piece one had only to jerk the lanyard which pulled the burred end of the wire through the fine powder generating enough heat to ignite it, which in turn lit the rifle powder. As the powder bag of the round was seated, one step in loading required that a wire be run down the vent puncturing this cloth bag, thereby exposing the propellant powder to the fire from the tube in the vent. However, the texts stated that the force of the flame in the tube was sufficient to burn through several thicknesses of cartridge cloth.

TYPES OF ARTILLERY FIRE

Terminology of that era stated that when a projectile hit its target before striking an intermediate object such as the ground it was 'direct fire,' while 'ricochet fire' was a very broad term that had several specific sub-categories. Generally it meant that a shell struck the ground at an angle small enough to permit it to continue to move in a series of bounds or ricochets. A ricocheting ball made a furrow in the ground, and each time the angle of departure from the earth was greater than its angle of entry.

A form of ricochet fire was 'grazing fire' where the projectile rose very slightly from the ground and struck it at a very small angle, making a large number of ricochets at the end of its trajectory.

'Horizontal,' 'parallel,' or 'rolling fire' was where the axis of the piece was horizontal or parallel with the ground. The line of sight struck the ground about seventy-five yards in front of the gun, and the projectile again hit the ground at a very small angle causing a number of ricochets, but never passing at a greater distance above the ground than the muzzle. The textbooks said that this method of fire was more efficient in striking a remote target than direct fire, but theoretically very firm hard ground was necessary — a condition not too often found on battlefields.

Another type was 'plunging fire.' Here the projectile hit the ground at a large enough angle to bury itself in the ground. This type fire was rarely used by field batteries.

SPECIFICATIONS AND MARKINGS OF FIELD GUNS

Type	Weight of Tube	Bore diam.	Length
12-pounder Napoleon	1227 lbs.	4.62 in.	63.6 in.
3-inch Ordnance rifle	820 lbs.	3.00 in.	65.0 in.
10-pounder Parrott rifle	900 lbs.	2.9 and 3.0 in.	70.0 in.
20-pounder Parrott rifle	1800 lbs.	3.67 in.	79.0 in.

MARKING LOCATIONS

Foundry number of gun and inspector's initials — on face of muzzle.

Initials of founder and foundry — on right trunnion end.

Year of fabrication — on end of left trunnion.

Weight in pounds — end of right rimbase.

Block letters U.S. — on upper surface near end of reinforce.

NOTE: Benton's text states that cannon which were modified in 1861 had all their marks on the face of the muzzle.

WEIGHT OF 12-POUNDER, LIMBERS, AND CAISSON COMPLETE FOR FIELD SERVICE

Gun		Caisson	
gun tube	1227 lbs.	body less wheels	432 lbs.
carriage less wheels	736	two wheels	360
two wheels	392	two ammo chests	364
limber body less wheels	335	packed ammo	980
		limber less wheels	335
two wheels	360	two wheels	360
ammo chest	182	ammo chest	182
implements	89	packed ammo	490
ammo packed	490	implements	254
tarpaulin	54	tarpaulin	54
	3865 lbs.		3811 lbs.

WOODS USED BY ARTILLERY

White oak — artillery carriages
Beech — fuzes, mallets, plane-stocks, and other tools
Elm — felloes and small naves
Hickory — handspikes, tool handles, wooden axle-trees
Black walnut — stocks of small arms
Poplar — sabots, cartridge blocks, and linings of ammunition chests
Pine — arms chests and packing boxes
Cypress — sea coast and garrison carriages (good qualities of heat and moisture resistance)
Basswood — sabots and cartridge blocks
Dogwood — mallets and drifts

TECHNIQUE OF SPIKING A GUN

When forced to abandon a gun a good artilleryman always saw to it that the weapon was rendered useless to his enemy. The simplest and quickest way was to drive a spike or frequently a rat-tail file into the vent and then clinch the point of it with the rammer inside the bore. A weapon so spiked required removal from the field and reboring before it could be used again.

Other methods called for complete destruction, such as blowing the barrel apart by firing it with the tube obstructed with sand, gravel, etc. But this was risky business for the man who had to fire the piece in this condition and was not used to any extent by field batteries.

APPENDIX II

Gettysburg Artillery Data

ARTILLERY BRIGADE COMMANDERS

I Corps — Col. Charles Wainwright
II Corps — Capt. John G. Hazard
III Corps — Capt. George E. Randolph
V Corps — Capt. Augustus P. Martin
VI Corps — Col. Charles P. Tompkins
XI Corps — Maj. Thomas Osborn
XII Corps — Lt. E. D. Muhlenberg
Cavalry Corps —1st Brigade, Capt. James M. Robertson
    2nd Brigade, Capt. John C. Tidball
Artillery Reserve —1st Regular Brigade, Capt. Dunbar Ransom
    1st Volunteer Brigade, Lt. Col. Freeman McGilvery
    2nd Volunteer Brigade, Capt. Elijah Taft
    3rd Volunteer Brigade, Capt. James Huntington
    4th Volunteer Brigade, Capt. Robert Fitzhugh

UNITS, ARMAMENT, AND COMMANDERS

ARTILLERY RESERVE:

1st Regular Brigade

H, 1st U.S. (Eakin)	6 Napoleons
F/K, 3rd U.S. (Turnbull)	6 Napoleons
C, 4th U.S. (Thomas)	6 Napoleons
C, 5th U.S. (Weir)	6 Napoleons

1st Volunteer Brigade

5th Mass. Battery, including 10th New York (Phillips)	6 3-inch rifles
9th Mass. Battery (Bigelow)	6 Napoleons
15th New York Battery (Hart)	4 Napoleons
C/F, Pa. L.A. (Thompson)	6 3-inch rifles

553

2nd Volunteer Brigade

B, 1st Conn. H.A. (Brooker)	4 4.5-inch rifles
M, 1st Conn. H.A. (Pratt)	4 4.5-inch rifles
2nd Conn. Light Battery (Sterling)	4 James rifles; 2 12-pounder howitzers
5th New York Battery (Taft)	6 20-pounder Parrott rifles

3rd Volunteer Brigade

1st New Hampshire Battery (Edgell)	6 3-inch rifles
H, 1st Ohio (Norton)	6 3-inch rifles
F/G, 1st Pa. L.A. (Ricketts)	6 3-inch rifles
C, W. Va. L.A. (Hill)	4 10-pounder Parrott rifles

4th Volunteer Brigade

6th Maine Battery (Dow)	6 Napoleons
A, Maryland L.A. (Rigby)	6 3-inch rifles
A, New Jersey L.A. (Parsons)	6 10-pounder Parrott rifles
G, 1st New York (Ames)	6 Napoleons
K, 1st New York (Fitzhugh)	6 3-inch rifles
	Total: 21 batteries with 118 guns

I CORPS ARTILLERY BRIGADE:

2nd Maine Battery (Hall)	6 3-inch rifles
5th Maine Battery (Stevens)	6 Napoleons
L, 1st New York (Reynolds)	6 3-inch rifles
B, 1st Pa. L.A. (Cooper)	4 3-inch rifles
B, 4th U.S. (Stewart)	6 Napoleons
	Total: 28 guns

II CORPS ARTILLERY BRIGADE:

B, 1st New York (Rorty, Sheldon)	4 10-pounder Parrott rifles
A, 1st Rhode Island (Arnold)	6 3-inch rifles
B, 1st Rhode Island (Brown)	6 Napoleons
I, 1st U.S. (Woodruff)	6 Napoleons
A, 4th U.S. (Cushing)	6 3-inch rifles
	Total: 28 guns

III CORPS ARTILLERY BRIGADE:

B, New Jersey L.A. (Clark)	6 10-pounder Parrott rifles
D, 1st New York (Winslow)	6 Napoleons
4th New York Battery (Smith)	6 10-pounder Parrott rifles
E, 1st Rhode Island (Bucklyn)	6 Napoleons
K, 4th U.S. (Seeley)	6 Napoleons
	Total: 30 guns

V Corps Artillery Brigade:

C, Mass. L.A. (Walcott)	6 Napoleons
C, 1st New York (Barnes)	4 3-inch rifles
L, 1st Ohio (Gibbs)	6 Napoleons
D, 5th U.S. (Hazlett)	6 10-pounder Parrott rifles
I, 5th U.S. (Watson)	4 3-inch rifles

Total: 26 guns

VI Corps Artillery Brigade:

A, Mass. L.A. (McCartney)	?
1st New York Battery (Cowan)	6 3-inch rifles
3rd New York Battery (Harn)	?
C, 1st Rhode Island (Waterman)	?
G, 1st Rhode Island (Adams)	?
D, 2nd U.S. (Williston)	?
G, 2nd U.S. (Butler)	?
F, 5th U.S. (Martin)	?

Total: Reportedly 48 guns

XI Corps Artillery Brigade:

I, 1st New York (Wiedrich)	6 3-inch rifles
13th New York Battery (Wheeler)	4 3-inch rifles
I, 1st Ohio (Dilger)	6 Napoleons
K, 1st Ohio (Heckman)	4 Napoleons
G, 4th U.S. (Wilkeson)	6 Napoleons

Total: 26 guns

XII Corps Artillery Brigade:

M, 1st New York (Winegar)	4 10-pounder Parrott rifles
E, Pa. L.A. (Atwell)	6 10-pounder Parrott rifles
F, 4th U.S. (Rugg)	6 Napoleons
K, 5th U.S. (Kinzie)	4 Napoleons

Total: 20 guns

Cavalry Corps:

1st Brigade

9th Michigan Battery (Daniels)
6th New York Battery (Martin)
B/L, 2nd U.S. (Heaton)
M, 2nd U.S. (Pennington)
E, 4th U.S. (Elder)

2nd Brigade

E/G, 1st U.S. (Randol)
K, 1st U.S. (Graham)
A, 2nd U.S. (Calef)   6 3-inch rifles
C, 3rd U.S. (Fuller)

Attached: H, Pa. H.A., 1 section of 3-inch rifles under Lt. Rank.

Total: 50 3-inch rifles
Grand Total: 67 batteries plus 1 section

NOTES

CHAPTER I — FIRST BULL RUN

1. Hains, P. C., 'The First Gun at Bull Run,' *Cosmopolitan* (August 1911), p. 389.

2. *The War of the Rebellion: A Compilation of the Official Records of the Union and Confederate Armies* (Washington: Government Printing Office, 1880–1901), Ser. I, Vol. II, pp. 348, 362, 365, 366 (hereafter cited as *O.R.*); *Cosmopolitan, supra,* pp. 390–91. The exact position of the gun was apparently on the north shoulder of present Route 29 and and 211, just west of the crest of the hill three-quarters of a mile east of Bull Run.

3. The time of the first shot is variously put from 5 to 6:30 a.m. Hains made no official report, though he wrote in 1911 that it was a little after 6 a.m. However, three other artillery officers who were nearby all put it precisely at 5 a.m.

4. *O.R.,* II, pp. 361–6; *Battles and Leaders of the Civil War* (4 vols., New York: The Century Co., 1887–8), I, 205 (cited hereafter as *B.&L.*). This was a section of Latham's battery.

5. *B.&L.,* I, 231; For an interesting comment on 'Portici,' see Freeman, Douglas Southall, *Lee's Lieutenants: A Study in Command* (3 vols., New York: C. Scribner's Sons, 1942–4), I, 66n (hereafter cited as *L.L.*); Lossing, Benson J., *Pictorial History of the Civil War* (3 vols., Vol. I, Philadelphia: G. W. Childs, Vols. II, III, Hartford: T. Bellnap, 1866–8), I, 598. There appears a sketch of a house labeled 'Portici.'

6. *B.&L.,* I, p. 232; *O.R.,* II, p. 489; 'Imboden's Report,' *Richmond Dispatch* (July 26, 1861). Imboden's position is currently marked with a National Park Service sign; and a visitor, after reading the above three sources and then visiting the scene, can readily see and appreciate the ideal spot Bee had selected, as the ground remains unchanged from that day, the little protecting rise just wide enough to give a 4-gun battery some protection.

7. *O.R.,* II, pp. 315, 328, 345–6. The two howitzers had been borrowed from the Washington Navy Yard.

8. *O.R.,* II, p. 384. Initially there was only one piece — one 6-pounder gun of Davidson's battery, set up near the Robinson house lane. Imboden's battery came into position near the Henry house about 10:15 a.m. At about 12 o'clock Imboden had shifted position twice, and by this time had gone to a spot about 400 yards northeast of his first post. Shortly, additional Confederate batteries began arriving on the hill, reinforcing Imboden who was soon relieved.

9. U.S. Congress, Joint Committee on the Conduct of the War, *Report* (3 vols., Washington: Government Printing Office, 1863), Vol. II, pp. 168–77, 242–6 (cited hereafter as *C.W.*). Griffin initially put all five of his pieces on the left of Ricketts's battery, subsequently moving two or three pieces to the right of Ricketts. Ricketts's testimony before the Committee on the Conduct of the War makes reference to minor shifting of pieces on the hill. However, the testimony of Lts. Charles E. Hazlett and Horatio B. Reed, while a bit confusing, gives evidence that Griffin's original position on the Henry house hill was just north of Mrs. Henry's house. Griffin's testimony says that there were eleven pieces side by side when the volley of the 33rd Virginia hit them. But a lieutenant commanding a section stated his two pieces had not shifted, since one had no horses left and the other had a smashed wheel. A forward movement of Ricketts's battery on the hill is mentioned in the unofficial history of the regiment. See Haskin, William L., *The History of the First Regiment of Artillery* . . . (Portland, Me.: B. Thurston & Co., 1879), p. 505 (cited hereafter as *Haskin*).

10. *O.R.*, II, pp. 345–58; *Southern Historical Society Papers*, XXXIV (1906), 363–71. While Barry specifies the range to the 33rd Virginia at 60 to 70 yards, Griffin and Ricketts made no specific estimate of the range at which the volley was fired. Griffin, in his testimony before the Committee, stated that the rail fence over which the enemy regiment climbed was 200 yards to the front. The regiment then moved 50 yards toward the woods, probably Griffin's right flank, then marched 40 yards toward the batteries.

11. *C.W.* (1863), II, p. 216.

12. Ibid. p. 169.

13. See Muster Rolls for D, 5th U.S., and I, 1st U.S. (July/August 1861), on file in The Civil War Branch, National Archives.

14. *O.R.*, II, pp. 556–7, 569; *B.&L.*, I, 190–91; *C.W.* (1863), II, 168–77 (quotations, 169).

15. *Cosmopolitan* (August 1911), p. 395. The spot was probably Mrs. Spindle's, sometimes called Mrs. Spinner's, a house which stood on the north edge of the highway about one mile east of the Stone Bridge.

16. Ibid. p. 398.

17. *Haskin*, p. 53; *O.R.*, II, pp. 357, 364; *Cosmopolitan* (August 1911), pp. 398–9. The 30-pounder with its ammunition was moved from Manassas down to a small fort overlooking the Potomac, where the Southerners used it to harass Federal shipping. Its whereabouts after the spring of 1862 are not now known.

18. These losses coupled with those of Carlisle's four pieces and Hains's 30-pounder, made a total loss of 27 guns — the same number the Confederates reported capturing. See *O.R.*, II, p. 571.

19. Ibid. p. 481. Jackson's comments in his official report indicate that he believed the loss of the Federal guns was occasioned by Griffin's shifting of his position.

20. Ibid. p. 753. At 1 a.m. on July 22, Gen. Winfield Scott had telegraphed McClellan regarding the disaster at Bull Run, but ordered him to '. . . remain in your present command . . .' It is probable that the telegram ordering McClellan to Washington was dispatched shortly thereafter, following consultation with Lincoln and/or Secretary of War Simon Cameron.

CHAPTER II — AN ARMY IS BORN

1. This manual, issued in 1861 (Philadelphia: J. B. Lippincott Co.), was entitled *Instruction for Field Artillery.*
2. McClellan, George B., *McClellan's Own Story* (New York: Charles L. Webster and Co., 1887), pp. 114–15 (hereafter cited as *McClellan*); Birkhimer, William E. and J. J. Chapman, *Historical Sketch of the Artillery* (Washington, D.C., 1884), p. 81 (hereafter cited as *Birkhimer*); Barry, W. F., and J. G. Barnard, *Barry's Report: Peninsular Campaign Army of the Potomac* (New York: Van Nostrand, 1863), pp. 105–6.
3. An armament committee composed of Gen. Barry, Col. Hunt, and Capt. Rodman, in 1861, recommended that light or field batteries be equipped with eight pieces, and horse batteries serving with cavalry be equipped with six guns. All cannon of each battery should be of the same type and caliber. These officers further recommended that the light batteries be armed with either the 12-pounder Napoleon or the 3-inch ordnance rifle; the horse artillery batteries would have the latter weapon exclusively.
4. Tidball, J. C., 'Artillery Service in the Rebellion,' *Journal of the Military Service Institute,* 1891–3, XII, XIII, XIV, pp. 697–733 (hereafter cited as *Tidball*). At the outbreak of the war all but eight of the 48 artillery companies, as they were then called, were acting as foot artillery or infantry in the seaboard and western garrisons. Officers were theoretically rotated from the foot companies to the mounted ones, of which there were but two in each of the four regiments. The mounted companies at the start of the war were: K and I, 1st Regiment, A and M, 2nd Regiment, C and E, 3rd Regiment, and B and G, 4th Regiment.
5. *McClellan,* pp. 114–16; *Barry's Report,* p. 109; *Tidball,* p. 700. The latter gives the number of guns as 39.
6. Hunt, Henry Jackson, 'Our Experience in Artillery Administration,' *Journal of the Military Service Institution of the United States,* XII (1891), p. 216 (hereafter cited as *Hunt*).
7. *Barry's Report,* p. 110. Barry stated that the number of batteries which embarked for the Peninsula, March 15th to April 1st, 1862, was 52, comprising 299 pieces. Later Franklin's division with 4 batteries of 22 guns in all, and McCall's division with a similar number were added to McClellan's forces, making a total of 60 batteries of 343 tubes.

Chapter III — WILLIAMSBURG

1. *O.R.,* XI, 1, pp. 430–32, 446. The manual prescribed that each limber would carry one chest of ammunition and each caisson would carry two chests. Three caissons would then have carried six chests. One additional chest was abandoned, probably from a limber, giving the Confederates their haul of seven chests. Brig. Gen. Paul A. Semmes, C.S.A., reported these chests as being filled. Since each chest for 3-inch rifle ammunition theoretically carried 50 rounds, the total Federal loss was some 350 rounds — about 100 more than the battery had fired in the fight.
2. See Appendix I for a description of a friction primer.
3. *O.R.,* XI, 1, p. 471; *New York at Gettysburg,* III, p. 1294; Smith, James E., *A Famous Battery* (Washington, D.C.: Lowdermilk Co., 1892), pp. 58–9. In the last of these sources the number of pieces Smith brought forward is put at five. It appears, however, that in any event only four were engaged.
4. Ibid. pp. 58–9; Hebert, W. H., *Fighting Joe Hooker* (Indianapolis: 1944), p. 86.
5. *O.R.,* XI, 1, p. 472. My evaluation is that the Confederates actually captured and carried off five guns — four of Webber's and one of Gibson's, and destroyed four of Bramhall's pieces, and possibly the other two, one of which had not been in the main battery position.
6. *New York at Gettysburg,* III, p. 1221. This cook was a former restaurateur and was paid from a fund raised by the voluntary contribution of twenty-five cents per man per month, with the officers making up any deficit.

Chapter IV — SEVEN PINES AND FAIR OAKS

1. Webb, Alexander, *The Peninsula Campaign* (New York: C. Scribner's Sons, 1908), pp. 100–101 (hereafter cited as *Webb*); *O.R.,* XI, 1, pp. 874, 914–15, 918–19, 922. Keyes uses the term 'masses' in describing the enemy formations. Naglee says 'closed columns' from which great gaps were torn by his artillery and infantry fire.
2. Ibid. pp. 918, 923. Naglee states that Fitch was ordered out first, then Hart, and Regan was to cover the withdrawal.
3. Ibid. p. 919.
4. Ibid. pp. 883, 885. Maj. West states that the purpose of the first change of position of the batteries under his control was to give incoming infantry reinforcements room to deploy. This may have been a factor, but it is more likely the increasing proximity of Confederate infantry was the deciding factor.
5. Ibid. p. 887. The standard loading as specified in the manuals for 12-pounder ammunition chests called for twelve rounds of solid shot, twelve rounds of spherical case, four of shell, and four of canister. All

rounds came fixed — that is, the projectile was fastened by thin metal strips to a wooden sabot, and the cloth powder bag was fastened to the other face of the sabot. The whole charge could thus be loaded in one motion. It appears that as the war progressed the number of solid shot was decreased and the number of spherical case rounds was increased.

6. Ibid. p. 883. Maj. West reported that the 'order was given to retire beyond the woods' with no indication as to who gave the order. Capt. Flood reported the order was given by Gen. Heintzelman, though the latter makes no mention of this in his report.

7. Ibid. p. 935. The Confederates generally claimed ten pieces of artillery captured by them.

Chapter V — MECHANICSVILLE AND GAINES MILL

1. Details on total rounds expended are lacking for all the batteries; total for three was 1548–1648 rounds. By interpolation one could allow 600 rounds for two of the other three batteries and 50 for Edwards, who came in the fight late. Breakdowns of types of rounds fired were given by Smead and Amsden; canister fired was given as 'some' and '16' respectively.

2. A careful reading of Confederate reports clearly shows that their infantry suffered extremely light casualties in their approach. Not until they neared the ravine did they begin to take heavy losses, and this was canister range.

3. *L.L.*, I, pp. 533–5; *O.R.*, XI, 2, pp. 622–6; Curtis, Newton M., *From Bull Run to Chancellorsville* (New York: G. P. Putnam's Sons, 1906), pp. 121–4. It is impossible to completely reconstruct which units captured what batteries or elements thereof in this action. However, it appears in this instance that one or two sections of Edwards's battery were seized by the 20th North Carolina Infantry, held about ten minutes, and then retaken by the 16th New York Infantry. Dr. Freeman stated it was Hayden's section of Edwards's battery. See *L.L.*, II, p. 151n.

4. *O.R.*, XI, 2, pp. 271–8, 281–3; *B.&L.*, II, pp. 333, 344–6. The question of the results of the cavalry charge was the subject of much controversy. It appears that the results were as given in this narrative.

Chapter VI — WHITE OAK SWAMP AND FRAYSER'S FARM

1. *O.R.*, XI, 2, p. 465; *New York at Gettysburg*, III, pp. 1219, 1230. By June 10th Wheeler was down to 53 men fit for duty. A draft had been made on several of the infantry regiments to fill up the battery ranks, but these men were still untrained. The practice of pulling replacements from the infantry ranks was a frequent, but not very satisfactory, method.

2. *O.R.,* XI, 2, p. 465. Ayres stated that Cowan was 'quite in rear of any position where he could open with any advantage.'
3. Ibid. Capt. Mott resigned after Malvern Hill.
4. Ibid. pp. 57–8. The railroad iron was probably exaggeration, since such projectiles would have scored the bore of any field gun.
5. Goss, Warren Lee, *Recollections of a Private* (New York: Crowell Co., 1890), p. 64.
6. *O.R.,* XI, 2, pp. 264–5, 551. The Confederates reported only two 20-pounder Parrotts captured; *L.L.,* II, p. 196n, erroneously stated that two 20-pounder guns were carried off the field by the Federals.
7. Alexander, Edward P., *Military Memoirs of a Confederate; A Critical Narrative* (New York: C. Scribner's Sons, 1907), p. 155 (hereafter cited as *Alexander*).

CHAPTER VII — MALVERN HILL

1. *B.&L.,* II, pp. 417–18; *O.R.,* XI, 2, p. 314. Both of these batteries had lost heavily at Gaines Mill and had not been refitted.
2. *O.R.,* XI, 2, pp. 627–8; *B.&L.,* II, p. 391.
3. *L.L.,* I, p. 597; *O.R.,* XI, 2, p. 629.
4. *New York at Gettysburg,* III, p. 1237. This was Frank's Battery G, 1st New York Light Artillery. They turned in Parrott rifles and were re-equipped with Napoleons.
5. *B.&L.,* II, p. 394.
6. Ibid.

CHAPTER VIII — SECOND BULL RUN

1. Buell, Augustus, *The Cannoneer* (Washington, D.C.: *National Tribune,* 1890), pp. 30–31 (hereafter cited as Buell); Rufus Dawes in his *Service with The Sixth Wisconsin* (Marietta, Ohio: E. R. Alderman and Sons, 1890) (hereafter cited as *Dawes*), also makes reference to this incident, but places the time as August 30th. The battery account was selected as being the more probable in its timing.
2. Sumner, G. C., *Battery D, 1st Rhode Island Light Artillery in the Civil War* (Providence: Rhode Island Printing Co., 1897), pp. 15–18 (hereafter cited as *Sumner*). This may have been Pelham's section which came into battery over on Jackson's right flank.
3. *O.R.,* XII, 2, pp. 266, 299. The morning report of July 31st 1862 for Sigel's corps shows a 'Mountain Howitzer Battery' under Lt. Roland Rombauer as present with a strength of one officer and 59 men. The battery was shown as being with Schurz's division, though a 'Mountain Howitzer Detachment' of one officer and 15 men is shown with Von Steinwehr's division. A copy of the report is on file in the Civil War Branch, National Archives, Washington, D.C.
4. Commager, H. S., *The Blue and the Gray* (Indianapolis: Bobbs-Merrill Co., 1950), I, pp. 177–80.

5. Kearney is generally accepted as being the father of the distinctive unit patch, having created a red cloth diamond patch which the men of his division proudly wore on their forage caps. The wearing of such patches became general in the Union armies by 1864.

6. *O.R.,* XII, 2, p. 419.

7. Ibid. pp. 666, 698. Efforts to identify the losing units have been unsuccessful. The amount of data on artillery in this campaign is extremely scarce in contrast to other campaigns of the Army of the Potomac.

8. Monroe, A. J., 'Battery D, First Rhode Island Light Artillery at the Second Battle of Bull Run,' *Rhode Island Soldiers and Sailors Society,* Ser. IV, No. 10, p. 19 (hereafter cited as *Monroe*).

9. Ibid.

10. *O.R.,* XII, 2, p. 482. Hazlett's battery had been detached by Porter and placed on the high ground south of the Warrenton Turnpike — now U.S. Highway 29 and 211, the hill now called New York Hill, with the 14th Brooklyn Regiment marker thereon.

11. Wise, Jennings C., *The Long Arm of Lee . . .* (2 vols. Lynchburg, Virginia: J. P. Bell Co., 1915; reissued New York: Oxford University Press, 1959), I, p. 272 (hereafter cited as *Wise*); *O.R.,* XII, 2, pp. 577–8. While it cannot be proven, it appears that S. D. Lee's batteries had actually done the job before Longstreet's two batteries came into full play. Longstreet's control over Lee's battalion seems to have been remote at this time of the action.

12. *O.R.,* XII, 2, pp. 469, 470. The credit for this move is generally given to Warren, but Hazlett was on high ground with an excellent view of Reynolds's departing troops whereas Warren was probably in defilade. It seems logical that Hazlett, as he says, saw the danger first, but credit for things of this nature usually goes to the senior officer in the vicinity.

13. Cheek, Philip and Mair Pointon, *Sauk County Riflemen* (privately printed, 1909), pp. 42, 43.

14. Ibid.

15. *O.R.,* XII, 2, pp. 286–7, 304, 341, 384; *New York at Gettysburg,* III, p. 1246. The author has come across several references to the effect that DeBeck's Ohio battery went with McLean's force to Chinn Ridge. While this unit had been working with this brigade earlier in the campaign, it was now under the command of Lt. George B. Haskins and that officer reported the battery as not engaged on August 30th.

16. *O.R.,* 2, pp. 286–7, 304–5; Remington, Cyrus K., *A Record of Battery I, First New York Light Artillery* (Buffalo: The Currier Co., 1881), pp. 12–13. The exact events surrounding Wiedrich's departure from Chinn Ridge are obscure. McLean was obviously miffed with the battery, but the unofficial history quoted above, as well as Wiedrich's official report, makes no reference to any misconduct or loss of matériel, nor is there any attempt to justify alleged misconduct. The unofficial account merely mentions that the unit was hard hit — thirteen casualties. And, though

the unit got off the field, they had only one serviceable piece. It is not clear whether the other five guns — the battery had four 10-pounder Parrotts and two 12-pounder howitzers — were lost or out of order. The former seems to be more the case.

17. Evidence indicated that these may have been at varying times Dilger's, Schirmer's (Blume's), Smeed's, and Weed's.

18. *O.R.*, XII, 2, pp. 486–7. This position was probably the Henry house hill. The original spot where Porter intended the battery to go was probably Chinn Ridge.

19. *Sumner*, p. 21. Monroe's exact location is not clear. In his account in the Society papers, he says he was on a hill near the 'Lewis House' as he erroneously called the Henry dwelling, with a sunken road in his immediate front. The sunken road was of course the Sudley Road. In the unofficial unit history by Sumner, the battery position is carefully defined as being on Bald Hill — actually Chinn Ridge, 700 yards west of the Henry hill, with a little creek bed some 60 yards in front — which could have been either Chinn or Youngs Branch. However, McDowell reports that Monroe joined Sykes's Regulars atop Henry hill.

20. Ibid. pp. 20–23; *Monroe*, pp. 24–5.

21. *History of the 97th Regiment, New York Volunteers*, Hall, Issac (Utica: 1890), p. 75. Bates, S. P., *History of Pennsylvania Volunteers* (Harrisburg: Singerly, 1869), I, p. 960, gives the battery's matériel loss as three guns. Thompson makes no mention in his official report of any loss of guns — a common omission in Civil War battery reports since there was a stigma attached to such a loss no matter how justifiable the cause.

22. The author spent many hours trying to determine the matériel losses of the Federal batteries. The Confederates claim approximately 30 guns captured, but official Union reports do little toward verifying this figure. From the *Official Records* it can be ascertained that McGilvery lost two pieces, Kerns lost four, Weed abandoned two in the retreat, Gerrish had two of his howitzers seized, and at least one mountain howitzer fell into enemy hands. However, from the report of the adjutant general of Maine for 1862 the loss of Leppien's four guns is confirmed, and from unofficial histories it appears that the following units suffered losses: Thompson's battery, according to one account, lost three guns and by another account the number was five; and Matthews's battery is likewise said to have lost three of its weapons.

CHAPTER IX — ANTIETAM

1. *O.R.*, XII, 3, p. 813.

2. The number of pieces of artillery surrendered to the Confederates by the Harpers Ferry garrison is usually put at 73. See *O.R.*, XIX, 1, p. 981, for A. P. Hill's report which puts the figure at 70. Maj. A. B. McIlvane, chief-of-artillery of the garrison, reported turning over 47 pieces, of

which 7 were spiked; see *O.R., XIX,* 1, p. 548. None of these guns reached Lee in time to see action in the Antietam fighting; see *O.R., XIX,* 1, pp. 951, 955, 960–62.

3. *O.R., XIX,* 1, p. 30.

4. Ibid. p. 269. Cooper's Battery B and Simpson's Battery A of the Pennsylvania Light Artillery and Ransom's Battery C, 5th U.S., were all engaged in support of Meade. Records on file at the Antietam Park headquarters state that all of Hooker's batteries crossed the creek. However, the writer has uncovered no evidence that any batteries except these three were engaged.

5. Hebert, *Fighting Joe Hooker,* pp. 140–41.

6. *O.R., XIX,* 1, pp. 229–31. Actually there were a number of cornfields on the battlefield but *the* cornfield was D. R. Miller's, just south of his residence and northeast of the Dunker Church.

7. *Buell,* p. 33; *Instruction for Field Artillery* (Philadelphia: J. B. Lippincott Co., 1863), p. 7, states that on a war footing a battery should be equipped with twelve caissons. However, it appears that this was not followed out in practice. This secondary account is the only instance the author has come across of such a practice. Similarly, the manual prescribed that each carriage be drawn by eight horses, but the evidence is that this too was never carried out.

8. *Dawes,* p. 95. See also Noyes's comments on the majestic grandeur of this horse, even in death, in the *Report of the Ohio Antietam Battlefield Commission* (Springfield, Ohio: State Printers, Springfield Publishing Co., 1904), pp. 9–10. Noyes wanted a statue erected on the spot portraying the horse's final pose, but such was never done.

9. *O.R., XIX,* 1, pp. 259, 262, 266. It appears that Thompson took position in the plowed field just northeast of the famous cornfield, with Matthews close by.

10. *O.R., XIX,* 1, p. 227. Monroe, the division chief-of-artillery, merely states that Reynolds moved 'through the woods' into plowed ground. From their prior position it could only have been the North Woods. The call for artillery appears to have come from Gibbon. The two batteries which replaced Reynolds are unidentified, but may have been either Matthews and Thompson or Simpson and Cooper.

11. Ibid. p. 858.

12. *Alexander,* p. 247.

13. *O.R., XIX,* 1, p. 270. The Texas regiments of Hood's division claim to have seized temporarily a Federal battery during a charge to seal off the break in Jackson's line. It may be that Ransom's guns were the ones, but there is no evidence to substantiate the fact. However, the Antietam Battlefield Board Maps (14), 1904, Troop Positions, by Gen. Carmen, show that one of Hood's units had reached the middle of the northern edge of the cornfield. A rush by some of these troops may have been responsible for the threat to Ransom's guns.

14. *O.R., XIX,* 1, pp. 477, 482. Hampton's position and time of arrival are

difficult to establish. The corps' chief-of-artillery and Hampton disagree in their reports. I have used the report of the corps' chief in putting Hampton in on Knap's left.

15. Ibid. p. 1022. This is undoubtedly the source of the legend, which the writer frequently heard, that Hunt deliberately ordered the Federal batteries to concentrate on a single Confederate battery and knock it out before proceeding to the next. I have found no such evidence to support this legend other than Hill's statement which of course was supposition and exaggeration.

16. Wood, William N., *Reminiscences of Big I*, Bell I. Wiley, ed. (Jackson, Tennessee: McCowar-Mercer Press, 1956), p. 38.

17. A number of accounts refer to a mass of guns of both corps being concentrated on this ridge. Hooker claims he ordered this concentration from his spare batteries. See also Doubleday's and Howard's reports for similar statements. Actually it appears that this mass of guns was started by a nucleus of Hooker's batteries which had gone into park there the night before.

18. Of the seven corps batteries, Tompkins's Rhode Island and Woodruff's Regular batteries were assigned to Sedgwick. Tompkins reported that he moved forward about 8 a.m. and reported to Hooker, who put him in position in front of some burning ruins, no doubt the Mumma buildings; he opened fire about 9 a.m. In a more detailed postwar account he stated that he had been sent to aid Gen. French about 9:30, and as they moved onto the field Mansfield's troops were going into action. Tompkins could have mistaken Sedgwick's troops for Mansfield's. Woodruff reported, and the unit's unofficial history agrees, that he came up as Sedgwick was retreating along with some of Greene's troops. Of the other batteries, Owens's G, 1st Rhode Island Light Artillery, Thomas's Battery C, 4th U.S., Hazard's D, 1st Rhode Island Light Artillery, and Pettit's B, 1st New York Light Artillery, the reports are vague, but indicate that they all came into action later on in the day.

19. *O.R.,* XIX, 1, pp. 325, 406. Frank states that the regiment was the 6th Maine of Hancock's brigade. This was the leading element of Franklin's VI Corps, and it reached the field about 9 a.m., going to Sumner's support as he was being repulsed.

20. The lieutenant's official report states his position as 300 yards from the woods, while a later version published in the unofficial regimental history says it was 150 yards distant.

21. Gibbon, John, *Personal Recollections* (New York: G. P. Putnam's Sons, 1928), pp. 82–3 (hereafter cited as *Gibbon*). This battery may have been Owens's Battery G, 1st Rhode Island Light Artillery, whose account appears on pages 207, 211–12.

22. Woodruff's official report says that he retired 200 yards while the unofficial history says 75 yards. See *O.R.,* XIX, 1, p. 309; *Haskin,* p. 158. The most famous Brady pictures of the Dunker Church were taken from the southeast; these show gaping shell holes through the upper

portion of the south end of the church. It is probable that these were made by Woodruff's guns.

23. Aldrich, T. M., *History of Battery A, 1st Rhode Island Light Artillery* (Providence: 1904), p. 141 (hereafter cited as *Aldrich*).

24. It is impossible to state exactly which batteries were responsible for this firing, but due to the positions it is most likely that the fire came from either the Reserve or the Cavalry Division batteries.

25. *O.R.,* XIX, 1, pp. 59–60. Graham's position is marked on the battle-field. It is located at the foot of the present observation tower on Bloody Lane facing the Piper cornfield.

26. Ibid. pp. 343–4. The identity of this man has been lost, with no records on it other than this report. Historian Louis Tuckerman of Antietam National Battlefield Site believes that because of this man's demeanor, frame of mind, and black carriage, he was probably a local Dunkard.

27. Ibid. pp. 211–12. Pleasonton says the section which he advanced was one of Tidball's.

28. Ibid. The slackening of Confederate fire was probably due to their shifting of batteries and of fire to meet the new threat posed by the crossing of the IX Corps below the town.

29. The *O.R.*'s indicate that batteries were assigned as follows: to Sturgis — Durell's Independent Pennsylvania Battery and Clark's E, 4th U.S.; to Wilcox — Benjamin's E, 2nd U.S. and Cook's 8th Massachusetts Battery; to Rodman — Muhlenberg's A, 5th U.S. and the cannon company of the 9th New York; to Cox's Kanawha Division — Edwards's L/M, 3rd U.S., Simmonds's Independent Kentucky Battery, and McMullin's 1st Ohio Independent Battery. Antietam Park records, however, indicate that several other batteries were in positions nearby and may have rendered additional support. One of these may have been Roemer's L, 2nd New York Light Artillery.

30. *O.R.,* XIX, 1, p. 436. McClellan wired the War Office that night to force some 20-pounder Parrott ammunition to him immediately. The able Assistant Secretary of War, P. H. Watson, answered by telegraph the next morning saying that 2500 rounds had been sent by rail with arrangements to run the train at express speeds. At the time of Watson's message the train was at Harrisburg and should have reached Hagerstown by that noon.

31. The narrator of this incident failed to disclose the number of pieces which took the officer under fire, but it is probable that it was only one. Cuffel, Charles A., *Durell's Battery in the Civil War* (Philadelphia: Finley Co., 1900), p. 77.

32. *B.&L.,* II, p. 671. There is no positive evidence that this was Durell's gun, but the two accounts seem to blend quite easily. Another version quoted in a footnote attributes this shot to Capt. Weed's battery posted on Durell's right. The shot could have come from either unit.

33. Ibid. pp. 649–53. The Park records show this battery as being armed with four 10-pounder and two 20-pounder Parrotts.

34. *O.R.*, XIX, 1, pp. 1009–10.
35. Ibid. p. 957.

Chapter X — FREDERICKSBURG

1. *O.R.*, XXI, pp. 827–8.
2. *B.&L.*, III, pp. 129–30.
3. *Hunt*, pp. 221–2. Hunt stated that he had set forth certain conditions which would have to be met, one of which was that he would have the services of all of the Napoleon batteries of the divisions.
4. *O.R.*, XXI, p. 181. Hunt may have ordered the release of all division batteries but one. However, he actually utilized initially only 21 division batteries, leaving some 39 more with the infantry and cavalry divisions.
5. Ibid. pp. 49–61, 325–9. This figure includes Tidball's A, 2nd U.S., which may not have been available, and an estimate of four to six guns per battery on four units whose actual strength the author was unable to ascertain.
6. Ibid. pp. 182–3, 191; *B.&L.*, III, p. 113. Couch states that only the right center and left center groups could bring fire to bear on the town.
7. *O.R.*, XXI, pp. 183, 191. The actual order to burn the town does not appear in Hunt's report; *B.&L.*, III, p. 113. Couch mentions that the order was to set the town afire.
8. *O.R.*, XXI, pp. 838–9. Halleck apparently believed that such a train would have to be formed from ordnance comprising the Washington defenses, thereby dangerously stripping that city's protection.
9. Ibid. pp. 183, 203, 214, 216, 514, 517. Simpson's report seems to indicate that only one section of his command went down to the bank.
10. *L.L.*, II, p. 349; *Wise*, I, pp. 382–3. It is possible that some of DeRussy's guns may have participated in this shelling. See *O.R.*, XXI, pp. 448–52.
11. *O.R.*, XXI, pp. 482, 511, 515. Cooper said four or five pieces opened from the edge of the woods opposite him. Col. Wainwright, the I Corps chief-of-artillery, implied that there was considerable firing by both sides. Confederate Col. Walker admitted two of his batteries were firing prior to the Union attack.
12. Ibid. pp. 511, 515–16. Jackson's chief-of-artillery had instructed his battery commanders to wait for the Federal infantry, and to fire on the Union batteries only if they advanced with the infantry in direct close support. The shifting of the Federal batteries was probably mistaken for an advance.
13. Ibid. pp. 457–61, 483–4. The range given is Hall's estimate, but it appears that he underestimated.
14. Ibid. pp. 649–50. The Confederate accounts, which state that their batteries held their fire until the Union ranks were within 800 yards, seem to be slightly exaggerated. It appears that they opened fire as soon as the Blue lines began to move.
15. *O.R.*, XXI, pp. 483–4. Normally batteries kept their line of caissons a

few hundred yards to the rear, in a protected area if possible. The guns used the ammunition in the limber chests which when emptied were exchanged as described earlier. The road here was the Bowling Green Road which had high banks at this point.

16. Ibid. p. 183; *Hunt,* pp. 221–2; *C.W.* (1863), pt. 1, p. 689. In his testimony before the Congressional Committee Hunt revised his estimate of idle guns he could have withdrawn from 60 to 50.

17. *O.R.,* XXI, pp. 315–17, 318–19, 187. Battery E had had the misfortune of losing all of its officers at Antietam, and Dickenson had been handpicked to reorganize the unit.

18. Ibid. pp. 117, 184. Couch apparently figured smoothbore Napoleons would have to get into position in that plain to be effective, and the prospects of doing this were not very good. Rifled guns could operate at a greater range with slightly better accuracy.

19. Walker, Francis A., *History of the Second Army Corps* (New York: C. Scribner's Sons, 1887), pp. 177–8.

20. Rhodes, J. H., *History of Battery B, 1st Rhode Island Light Artillery* (Providence: Sorow and Farnham, 1894), p. 139.

21. *O.R.,* XXI, pp. 185, 189. Frank's estimate of the range was 600 yards, which, if correct, would have put him some distance in rear of Hazard, and would have accounted for the light losses suffered by the New Yorkers.

22. Appleton, Nathan and others, *History of the Fifth Massachusetts Battery* (Boston: Cowles Co., 1902), p. 497.

23. *O.R.,* XXI, pp. 584–7.

24. Ibid. pp. 612–13.

25. Ibid. p. 188.

CHAPTER XI — CHANCELLORSVILLE

1. *New York at Gettysburg,* III, p. 1179.

2. *O.R.,* XXV, 2, p. 51.

3. Ibid. p. 240. A spot check of battery strengths for this period indicates very few unauthorized absentees. These strength returns are on file in the National Archives, Washington, D.C. It is interesting to note that in the Army of Northern Virginia this was also true, even toward the end of the war when the Army was being riddled with desertions. Wise, in *The Long Arm of Lee,* attributes this to the high type of personnel and the superb morale of the field batteries.

4. Ibid. pp. 119–20. These were Pettit's B, 1st New York; Bruen's 10th New York Battery; Puttkammer's 11th New York Battery; Barnes's C, 1st New York; Snow's B, 1st Maryland; Hexamer's A, 1st New Jersey; Johnson's 12th Ohio Battery; Hampton's 3rd Pennsylvania Battery; and Langner's C, 1st New York Battalion.

5. Ibid. The commended batteries were: Leppien's 5th Maine; Arnold's A, 1st Rhode Island; Hazard's B, 1st Rhode Island; Osborn's D, 1st New

York; Randolph's E, 1st Rhode Island; Martin's C, Massachusetts Light
Artillery; Harn's 3rd New York Battery; Blume's 2nd New York Battery;
Taft's 5th New York Battery; Brooker's B, 1st Connecticut Heavy Artillery; Seeley's K, 4th U.S.; Hazlett's D, 5th U.S.; and Braham's K,
1st U.S.

6. Bigelow, John, *The Campaign of Chancellorsville* (Yale University
   Press, 1910), pp. 49, 499–504 (hereafter cited as *Bigelow*). My own
   research led me to conclude that the Army took the field with 411 to
   419 guns; Bigelow's figure is 412. Wise put Lee's gun strength at 228.
7. *O.R.*, XXV, 1, pp. 512, 524, 525, 546, 674; *Bigelow*, p. 240. Waterman's C, 1st Rhode Island and Randol's E/G, 1st U.S. went with Meade
   but saw no action. Apparently only two batteries went with the XII
   Corps.
8. Ibid. p. 245.
9. *O.R.*, XXV, 1, pp. 309, 545. The section of Cushing's battery apparently came forward to cover the withdrawal.
10. Ibid. pp. 674, 721–7, 771. These were the Pennsylvania batteries of
    Knap, Hampton, and Muhlenberg's section of Crosby's Regular battery,
    with six, six, and two guns respectively.
11. Ibid. These were the other two sections of Crosby's and the two New
    York batteries of Winegar and Fitzhugh, with four, six, and four guns
    respectively.
12. Ibid. pp. 675, 723, 725–6, 1049. Breathed, the Confederate battery
    commander, stated he opened fire initially at 1200 yards. Lt. J. D.
    Woodbury, who wrote the report for Winegar's unit, stated they were
    hit by 18-pounder [sic] shot and shell — no doubt meaning 20-pounder
    Parrotts. The author found parts of a 20-pounder shell on this ground,
    but Stuart's Horse Artillery was not armed with this weapon, so the fire
    must have been coming from some other part of the field.
13. Ibid. p. 1049. The Confederates had one gun disabled, an officer killed,
    five men wounded, and three horses put out of action. The Union ac-
    counts make no mention of any losses in this duel.
14. Ibid.; Bigelow on p. 267 of *The Chancellorsville Campaign* is in error as
    he failed to recall this group as being the twenty-two guns Hooker
    wanted.
15. *O.R.*, XXV, 1, pp. 647, 650–51, 628–9. It appears that four of Wied-
    rich's guns were on the right with two detached for a time. These two
    later took position in rear of Bushbeck's line.
16. *L.L.*, II, p. 554.
17. *O.R.*, XXV, 1, p. 657. Dilger was awarded the Medal of Honor for
    his conduct on the field this day. See U.S. Department of the Army,
    The Medal of Honor (Government Printing Office, 1948), p. 124, for
    the short citation.
18. *O.R.*, XXV, 1, pp. 630, 657; *Bigelow*, pp. 300, 303. The author's
    attempts to identify these units have been unsuccessful. It appears that
    the corps reserve batteries were committed on the personal order of

Gen. Howard, who had ridden to that part of the field from Schurz's headquarters when news of the attack reached him.

19. *O.R.*, XXV, 1, pp. 786–7. Birney's batteries were probably parked with the division trains which were apparently along a narrow road northwest of Hazel Grove.

20. Smith, James E., *A Famous Battery*, pp. 93–7. According to this narrative, the transfer was to have been from Berry's to Birney's division, yet at Chancellorsville the 4th New York was still assigned to Berry's division and served with it. Therefore, the unit either won its point or Smith was confused as to time and units. Smith shortly resigned his commission and accepted a new one with a later date so as to stay with his battery rather than to move up a slot. Smith and his battery fought with some success at Gettysburg, then Secretary of War Stanton had enough of the complaints of this outfit and discharged it.

21. *O.R.*, XXV, 1, pp. 504, 970. It appears that some wandering Rebel units came across Whipple's trains and also caught some artillery resting there — probably Turnbull's battery — and seized a gun and caisson, routing the rest of the park in panic.

22. Evidence indicates that Turnbull's unit was resting with the division trains west of the grove, and, as previously mentioned, lost one or two guns and a caisson. The third battery of the division complement was Jastram's Rhode Island outfit which had replaced Turnbull on the Furnace Road; they did not return until later that night.

23. *O.R.*, XXV, 1, p. 504; *B.&L.*, III, p. 188; *New York at Gettysburg*, III, pp. 1305–6. In the last of these references Capt. Lewis stated he never saw or heard of Gen. Pleasonton during this day's action.

24. *O.R.*, XXV, 1, pp. 404, 970. Capt. Huntington in a letter to W. L. Goss stated that an assertion by Pleasonton that some guns of the XI Corps joined the latter's command is false.

25. *Bigelow*, p. 318. Here Bigelow stated that Dimick's section opened fire on a party of officers and men who had come out to aid the fallen Jackson.

26. Ibid. p. 343. Couch was under the impression that these units were sent to the rear to be cannibalized in order to repair other shattered batteries.

27. Ibid. p. 485. The 4th New York may have been temporarily unhorsed, but it was intact at the start of the Gettysburg campaign and served in that battle.

28. Ibid. pp. 721–2, 726–7, 729. Muhlenberg stated that he was made chief-of-artillery of the 2nd Division during the night. He now had his own section, one section of Lewis's battery, three of Thomas's guns, and by morning Fitzhugh's two guns under Lt. Davis joined him.

29. *O.R.*, XXV, 1, pp. 405, 504–5, 925; *Alexander*, p. 346. Col. Alexander's and Gen. Archer's accounts state that the Confederates seized four guns of this battery, though in falling back from the Federal fire they abandoned one piece. Some Federal accounts mention that the

Rebels turned these guns around and fired them at their prior owners.

30. *O.R.,* XXV, 1, p. 488. Apparently the Confederates were not deployed in line, but were in column, dictating Winslow's choice of solid shot.

31. Walker, *History of the Second Army Corps,* p. 242.

32. *O.R.,* XXV, 1, p. 488; *New York at Gettysburg,* III, p. 1265. Winegar seems to have escaped or was exchanged shortly, for he was back in command of his battery at Gettysburg two months later.

33. *O.R.,* XXV, 1, pp. 405, 485–6. Randolph commented that Puttkammer's 'disgraceful' conduct was already known to his corps commander, so he would comment no further on the subject.

34. Ibid. pp. 444, 721, 722, 724. The records fail to tell why Davis at this point did not use canister as the range was probably not over 350 yards. It may be that he had none, or in view of the lesser effectiveness of rifled weapons using this load, he believed percussion rounds would have more effect physically and psychologically.

35. Ibid. Fitzhugh stated the covering fire came from nine guns under the direction of Lt. Muhlenberg. Actually that officer's command had now been reduced to seven guns as he had lost Davis's section earlier.

36. Ibid. pp. 405, 505, 726–7. It appears that the 10th New York was still operating with only two sections, its third being still detached, with Muhlenberg.

37. Ibid. pp. 309, 310, 350, 505. It is impossible to determine the exact alignment of batteries at this time; there was considerable confusion in command as the records reflect. As best the writer could determine, it was as follows: facing south and southwest — Leppien with five guns, Lewis with four, Seeley with four, and Bucklyn with two; facing east and south — Muhlenberg's group consisting of his own two pieces, O'Donahue's three from Thomas's command, and two guns under Lewis's lieutenant. Pettit had originally been with Muhlenberg, but because of a masked position he had been sent to Chandler's. From here he was recalled and joined the other units about the house. One source stated that the 11th New York Battery was also engaged on the right of the Plank Road and suffered from the heavy enemy fire, but this could not be confirmed.

38. Ibid. pp. 309–10.

39. Ibid. pp. 306–7, 310; Beyer, W. F., and Keydel, O. F., eds., *Deeds of Valor* (Detroit: Perrien-Keydel Co., 1907), I, p. 157; *Haskins,* p. 162. One source states that it was Hancock who put Kirby in command of the 5th Maine Battery, but the evidence indicates strongly that it was Couch.

40. The activities of this battery are most hazy, though it appears that Lewis had only four of his six guns in battery at the time.

41. *New York at Gettysburg,* III, pp. 1305–6.

42. *O.R.,* XXV, 1, p. 314.

43. Ibid. p. 250; 2, p. 360. Hunt reported this as being done on the 2nd,

but he was in error. Wainwright, I Corps chief-of-artillery, was the senior artilleryman present, and no doubt Hooker selected him on this basis, though he apparently sent for Hunt simultaneously.

44. Ibid. 1, p. 250; *Bigelow,* p. 378 and Appendix 16, Hunt's figures are probably based on some period that evening, but are in error, as they include Martin's F, 5th U.S. This unit was still with Sedgwick's forces.

45. Heitman, *Historical Register and Dictionary of the U.S. Army* (Government Printing Office, 1903), I, p. 215. Best held the temporary rank of Assistant Inspector General of Artillery as of May 15, 1863, but his promotion to major did not come until 1867. As Assistant IG, Best held the temporary rank of lieutenant colonel; and he received a brevet majority for his conduct at Chancellorsville, a brevet lieutenant colonelcy for his services at Gettysburg, and a brevet full colonelcy as a reward for his over-all war record.

46. *O.R.,* XXV, pp. 726, 821-2. The writer has been unable to ascertain the identity of any of the Union batteries involved. It appears, however, that the last two units to open fire on Alexander were Woodbury's and Pettit's New Yorkers.

47. Ibid. p. 252.

Chapter XII — GETTYSBURG, 1ST DAY

1. *O.R.,* XXV, 2, pp. 471-2. The order stated the reorganization was necessary because of the Army's reduction in infantry strength. Some 58 regiments left the Army — their time of service having expired.

2. The batteries missing from the rolls after Chancellorsville were: 2nd New York Battery (Jahn); 29th New York Battery (Blucher); 30th New York Battery (Voegelee); 32nd New York Battery (Kusserow); C/D, 1st Pennsylvania (McCarthy); B, 1st Maryland (Snow); and the 12th Ohio Battery (Johnson). Those combined were: F/G, 1st Pennsylvania (Ricketts and Amsden); C/F, Pennsylvania (Thompson and Hampton); the 10th New York Battery was attached to E, Massachusetts; and the 11th New York Battery was attached to K, 1st New York. The new commands were: 9th Massachusetts (Bigelow); 2nd Connecticut Battery (Sterling); 9th Michigan Battery (Daniels); 6th Maine Battery (Dow). Another addition which did not affect the totals was the assigning, to Battery B, 1st New York, of the officers and men of the inactive 14th New York Battery. Gen. Hunt submitted a tabulation dated June 30th 1863, giving the Army's artillery total as 69 batteries of 362 guns. However, these figures vary slightly when compared with other internal evidence. See Appendix II.

3. *Buell,* p. 60.

4. *B.&L.,* III, p. 256.

5. *Buell,* p. 61.

6. *O.R.,* XXVII, 1, pp. 241, 927, 1030-31; 2, pp. 446, 612. The Federals,

according to Hunt, expended 32,781 rounds, and it is quite safe to assume that the Confederates used up close to 20,000 since two corps alone fired 13,000. The gun that opened the battle is now one of the four tubes mounted at the base of Buford's statue, located on the approximate site of Roder's position.

7. Ibid. pp. 277, 359–60. The six men left behind were either casualties or prisoners, but the gun was later recovered.

8. Ibid. pp. 277, 359–60.

9. Ibid. p. 1031. The report does not indicate exactly where Roder's gun was placed, nor does it state that the incident occurred at the same time Hall was struck. However, it seems quite likely that the two units were engaged about ten minutes apart. The troops Roder fired on were no doubt the portion of Davis's brigade which entered the cut east of Hall's position and were shortly caught in the cut and wrecked by the 6th Wisconsin Infantry. From careful reconnaissance of the ground, the most probable position for Roder's weapon was on the right edge of the rise just west of Mrs. Thompson's house — now called 'Lee's Headquarters,' on the Chambersburg Pike near the railroad cut. Lt. Davison's half-battery of Battery B, 4th U.S., shortly went into action on this same ground. Calef's report also leads one to believe that Roder's gun stopped the enemy advance singlehanded, making no mention of any Federal infantry aid — a quite frequent failing of artillery reports in this war. It is quite probable that the 6th Wisconsin arrived minutes later, preventing further firing, as Calef's report indicates Roder fired only one or two shots but was not driven from the ground.

10. Ibid. p. 1032; *Wise,* II, p. 619.

11. Ibid. pp. 618–19. This source says that two battalions were in action on Hill's front, and there were four more waiting in reserve. It is likely that this fire was coming in part from Ewell's guns on Oak Ridge.

12. *O.R.,* XXVII, 1, p. 355. The exact location is not clear but it was no doubt Hall's and Calef's old site on the forward face of McPherson Ridge.

13. *Buell,* pp. 65–7. The site of Davison's half-battery is now marked by a bronze tablet and two Napoleons.

14. Ibid. p. 72.

15. *O.R.,* XXVII, 1, p. 357. Why the batteries moved at a walk is without explanation unless it was to allow time for the infantry to clear the town and to allay panic, though congestion may have played a strong part.

16. *B.&L.,* III, p. 281. One version puts the time Wilkeson was wounded as later in the action, with Confederate Gen. Gordon stating that he could not advance until Wilkeson and his unit were dispersed. The two batteries fired on Wilkeson until he was down. However, from the *O.R.* it seems that the young officer fell early in the action.

17. *O.R.,* XXVII, 1, pp. 748, 755. Osborn seems charitable in saying that

the unit was too badly damaged for further use. The 6th North Carolina Infantry claimed to have captured two Napoleons north of town; these may have been Heckman's.

CHAPTER XIII — GETTYSBURG, 2ND DAY

1. *O.R.*, XXVII, 1, pp. 231, 359. All of these were from his own corps except for Wiedrich's I, 1st New York, attached from XI Corps.
2. Ibid. pp. 232–3. Osborn was so impressed with his position that he says that he suggested to Hunt that more artillery be placed there.
3. Actually Slocum was aware of this gap, and had asked Meade to rectify it. Meade in turn told Hunt to take a look and make the necessary adjustments.
4. *B.&L.*, III, p. 300.
5. *C.W.* (1865), 1, p. 449.
6. *O.R.*, XXVII, 1, pp. 234–5, 872, 881; *C.W.* (1865), I, p. 450. Hunt stated that he sent for two batteries, but three arrived. McGilvery's and Tyler's reports differ in minor details as to which units were the first to arrive.
7. Ibid. p. 235. The Emmitsburg Road here angles to the southwest, and it is hard to determine which enemy units Hunt actually saw moving in.
8. Ibid. p. 886; Bigelow, *The Peach Orchard — Gettysburg* (Minneapolis: Kimball-Storek Co., 1910), pp. 52–3 (hereafter cited as *The Peach Orchard*). The enemy guns were no doubt of Henry's battalion, but the range estimate seems excessive.
9. *History of the Fifth Massachusetts Battery*, p. 635. Artillery guidons of the Civil War era were swallow-tailed miniatures of the national flag.
10. Hanifen, Michael, *History of Battery B, 1st New Jersey Artillery* (Ottawa, Illinois: 1905), p. 72 (hereafter cited as *Hanifen*).
11. *O.R.*, XXVII, 2, p. 429; *Alexander*, pp. 398–9; *B.&L.*, III, pp. 359–60.
12. Smith, James E., *A Famous Battery*, pp. 103–4, 138.
13. *O.R.*, XXVII, 1, pp. 236–7, 659; *B.&L.*, III, p. 309. Gen. Warren was also wounded, though slightly, by this fire.
14. *Hanifen*, p. 75.
15. *O.R.*, XXVII, 1, p. 887. Hart's official report made no mention of an advanced position of one section. This data is contained in the account of Lt. Knox's action there which won him a Medal of Honor.
16. Ibid. pp. 235, 881, 887, 890. According to Hunt's report, Thompson relieved Hart; but McGilvery intimates that Thompson and Hart were in action simultaneously, with Hart being the left battery. Thompson stated he was engaged here about an hour, which tends to confirm McGilvery. However, Hart stated when he retired that only Ames remained on his right. The unit history of Hampton's battery does nothing to clarify the point.
17. Ibid. pp. 235, 584, 882, 901. Ames stated he was relieved by Watson's battery. This is repeated by Hunt and Randolph. However, McGilvery's

report clearly shows that Watson went into action further to the rear nearer the Weikert house, as part of a second line of guns which McGilvery subsequently built up in that area.

18. *The Peach Orchard*, p. 53. Capt. Bigelow later identified the enemy infantry as Semmes's brigade and the building as Rose's house. He further stated that after the war one of Semmes's officers told him that one shell disabled 30 of 35 men in one company, and that Gen. McLaws was reported to have credited artillery fire with incapacitating one-third of the 50th Georgia. Such casualties as 30 men to one shell were possible, but the writer believes this to be highly improbable.

19. *O.R.*, XXVII, 1, p. 882. Apparently Capt. Randolph had been wounded by this time and carried from the field with no one assuming immediate command of the III Corps batteries.

20. *The Peach Orchard*, pp. 60–61; *O.R.*, XXVII, 1, p. 886. The four guns were subsequently recovered. However, casualties listed in the battery's official report were: 8 killed, 17 wounded, and 2 missing with 60 horses killed and wounded. See Miller's *Photographic History of the Civil War*, II, p. 247, and IV, p. 103 for photos of Bigelow's wreckage. Bigelow wrote in 1910 that the fallen stones from the smashed wall still lay where they had been scattered, with the gap filled by a young tree.

21. Lewis, George, *History of Battery E, 1st Rhode Island Light Artillery* (Providence: Snow and Farnham, 1892), p. 208.

22. Ibid. p. 221; *O.R.*, XXVII, 1, p. 590. Lt. Bucklyn was wounded during the withdrawal and relinquished command.

23. *O.R.*, XXVII, 1, pp. 235, 660. It seems logical that this was McGilvery who was then trying desperately to build up a second line; and Watson in the end was under McGilvery's command.

24. *O.R.*, XXVII, 2, pp. 623–4. Wright stated that he had been under the sustained fire of more than twenty guns, but overran almost all with comparatively little loss.

25. Ibid. pp. 608, 618–19, 623, 631. It is impossible to determine which Federal batteries were taken by what Confederate command. Battery commanders were always reluctant to mention they had been overrun, unless it was necessary to explain loss of matériel. If the unit's guns were retaken shortly afterwards, there is little or no mention of the fact in their official reports. It seems quite certain, however, that several II Corps batteries were temporarily overrun and lost where Wright broke in. Gibbon casually remarked that the overrun batteries were retaken.

26. Ibid. 1, p. 883. Actually Battery B, 1st New York was a II Corps unit; and its moves were being governed by Hancock, then Gibbon, in conformity with the situation on the II Corps' front.

27. This battery had formerly been Capt. Knap's command and was known as Knap's Battery. By this time Knap left the service, though, he apparently commanded a battery of Pennsylvania 90-day militia called

up during Lee's invasion of the state. The unit, however, was not at Gettysburg. See *O.R.,* XXVII, 2, p. 215.

28. *O.R.,* XXVII, 1, pp. 234, 862, 863, 870. The XII Corps batteries were not initially deployed across their corps' front, due to the wooded terrain; instead, they were held in reserve behind the lines.

29. Ibid. pp. 358, 363. Confederate accounts, however, do not confirm the abandonment of any guns.

30. *Buell,* pp. 91–2. The narrator of this account stated that they were later told this shot killed one sniper and wounded another.

31. *Alexander,* pp. 408–9. Thirty-two of Ewell's guns on the left of A. P. Hill's corps and 55 of A. P. Hill's participated — a total Confederate gun participation of 87 pieces, most of which were fired at extreme ranges.

32. *O.R.,* XXVII, 1, p. 892. Gen. Tyler commanding the Reserve reported that, in addition to those already mentioned in this narrative, Hill's Battery C, West Virginia Light Artillery, and Eakin's Battery H, 1st U.S., were engaged.

33. Minnigh, L. W., *Gettysburg: What They Did Here* (Gettysburg: Meligakes, 1924), p. 150.

34. *Buell,* p. 82.

35. *O.R.,* XXVII, 1, pp. 233, 358, 365. Cooper's battery was badly hurt, according to Hunt and Wainwright; but Cooper's report gives no such information. Another source states that a 20-pounder shell exploded under a gun, killing two and wounding three men, but no other damage to the unit is mentioned.

36. Ibid. p. 894. At Fair Oaks a section of Federal artillery used the same technique. Since the bursting charge of a 12-pounder case shot was only one ounce, this seems certainly within the capabilities of the tube.

Chapter XIV — GETTYSBURG, 3RD DAY

1. Those reduced to four guns were Brown's Battery B, 1st Rhode Island and Phillips's 5th Massachusetts. Gen. Hunt stated that Rorty's battery was also reduced to this number, but other evidence strongly indicates that this unit operated on July 2nd with only four pieces.

2. The brigade chiefs were Capt. Dunbar Ransom of the Reserve and Capt. George E. Randolph of the III Corps; the battery commanders were Capts. John Bigelow, James Thompson, Patrick Hart, Lts. M. Livingston (commanding Turnbull's battery), C. E. Hazlett, T. Fred Brown, John Bucklyn, Francis W. Seeley, Malbone F. Watson, and Chandler P. Eakin.

3. *O.R.,* XXVII, 1, p. 870. Winegar's unit was apparently split, with one section on Power's Hill and the other on a small rise in the corner of an apple orchard of the McAllister farm.

4. Ibid. pp. 237, 899. The battery had fired a few rounds at Latimer on

the afternoon of the 2nd; but as the range was 2500 yards they soon ceased fire.

5. Ibid. The figure twelve is Tyler's, but it appears quite certain that fifteen of its batteries were then deployed.

6. Ibid. pp. 238, 748–9. Gen. Hunt's total as given in his report failed to include Norton's Ohio and Edgell's New Hampshire units, as well as Wheeler's New York battery waiting in reserve.

7. Ibid. pp. 238, 883. McGilvery's command consisted of: Thompson's five 3-inch; Phillips's four 3-inch; Hart's four Napoleons; Ames's six Napoleons; Dow's six Napoleons; Sterling's four James rifles and two 12-pounder howitzers; and two 3-inch rifles served by the men of Battery H, 3rd Pennsylvania Heavy Artillery, under Capt. William D. Rank. McGilvery's report errs in stating that a New Jersey battery was with him, since of the two units with the army, Parsons was in the Reserve park until 2:30 p.m. when he reinforced Hancock, and Clark stated that he was unengaged on the 3rd. McGilvery also placed Dow's strength at four Napoleons whereas other evidence strongly indicates the unit employed six. Likewise, in *B.&L.*, III, pp. 400, 437, it is stated that Rank was with the cavalry on July 3rd. While this unit does appear on the cavalry rolls as contained by the *O.R.*, it seems fairly certain that he was detached to McGilvery on the 3rd, or in reserve near the Philadelphia brigade.

8. James rifles were an off-breed type of rifled gun of bronze that had proved unsatisfactory for general field service. Most of these weapons had been relegated to state arsenals or storage for emergency use only. Two guns of this type now mark the location of Sterling's battery on McGilvery's line.

9. *O.R.*, XXVII, 1, pp. 238, 661. The other V Corps battery was Watson's, but it had been wrecked on the 2nd, and was not available for duty.

10. Of the 180 pieces, 82 were Napoleons and 2 were 12-pounder howitzers; of the rifled weapons there were 62, 3-inch ordnance guns, 4 were James, 24, 10-pounder Parrotts, and 6, 20-pounder Parrotts. See Appendix II for a detailed analysis of the armament.

11. Cowan's battery was detached about 10 a.m. and sent to Doubleday's division of the I Corps covering Hancock's left.

12. *O.R.*, XXVII, 1, p. 1021. Robertson is not too clear, but indicates that he had three batteries with him including the 9th Michigan Battery, which was one of the five batteries organic to his brigade.

13. Ibid. 2, p. 674; 1, p. 478. Capt. Hazard stated that the firing began at 8 a.m., and that little reply was made except by Woodruff. Woodruff, according to Hazard, opened fire eight different times during the morning, and a lieutenant in Woodruff's command later wrote that he estimated the number to be between eight and ten. See *Haskin*, p. 169. Maj. Osborn's official report; *O.R.*, XXVII, 1, p. 870, also confirms this sporadic firing. Alexander, however, magnified this outburst to an ammunition-exhausting duel involving much of Hill's artillery. The

official reports of Hill and his artillery commanders do not bear out Alexander's contention. See *Alexander,* pp. 420, 431; *O.R.,* XXVII, 2, pp. 608, 610, 614, 650, 653, 673, 675, 678. Federal infantry accounts mention that some buildings were seized in the 'forenoon' and enemy snipers were driven out. This foray triggered some Rebel artillery action which, the writer believes, is the incident referred to above. See *O.R.,* XXVII, 1, pp. 465, 467.

14. *History of the Fifth Massachusetts,* pp. 652, 655.
15. *O.R.,* XXVII, 1, p. 1021. Robertson wrote that this was all that was available, and placed the time of the request at noon. This is puzzling since Weir, Parsons, Cooper, and Fitzpatrick were not brought up from the Reserve until about 2:30 p.m., and the latter three units were also equipped with rifled guns.
16. *Gibbon,* pp. 147–8.
17. *Haskin,* pp. 169, 544.
18. *O.R.,* XXVII, 1, p. 239; 2, p. 435. Hunt stated that the Federal guns on the extreme right and left of the line opened fire early in the action — presumably Osborn's and Rittenhouse's batteries.
19. *History of the Fifth Massachusetts,* p. 652.
20. Ibid. p. 653.
21. *O.R.,* XXVII, 1, pp. 239, 750; *C.W.* (1865), 1, pp. 333, 451. Gen. Meade, in his testimony before the Committee, stated that he ordered the batteries to cease to save ammunition and to deceive the enemy into believing the Union guns had been disabled and thus bring on their assault. Maj. Osborn reported that he ceased fire on his own initiative. Hunt, though, obviously anticipated his commander's wish.
22. *O.R.,* XXVII, 1, pp. 428–9, 480. So great were the losses in the II Corps batteries — 149 officers and men — that on July 4th the remnants of Cushing's and Woodruff's units were combined into one battery as were Brown's and Arnold's units.
23. *Alexander,* p. 423. Alexander stated that Confederate practice had permitted the withdrawal of batteries or the cessation of fire in order to conserve strength; but up to this point of the war the Federals had never practiced this. As a result he was completely deceived.
24. *O.R.,* XXVII, 1, p. 880; *B.&L.,* III, p. 374; *Aldrich,* p. 217. In the last quoted source it is stated that Weir went into battery between Cushing and Arnold. Some accounts state that Brown and Arnold withdrew as these units came up. Brown did, but Arnold stayed on.
25. *O.R.,* XXVII, 1, p. 753. Wheeler reported that he received the order to move up from Maj. Osborn. No doubt Osborn was only the channel for a request from Hunt for every available battery.
26. The dispute as to how many of the battery's pieces were actually pushed down to the wall raged for years, with various 'eye witnesses' and 'participants' ranging the number of pieces from one to all six. The author concludes that one gun was moved down to the wall by battery survivors, perhaps aided by some nearby infantry. This con-

clusion is supported by Dr. Harry Pfanz, Park Historian, Gettysburg National Military Park. The writer has failed to uncover any positive evidence as to why the weapon was moved to the wall. A logical explanation, though, is that Cushing wanted to get the gun even with the advanced infantry line, so he could open with canister without fear of endangering friendly troops. See G. R. Stewart's *Pickett's Charge*, pp. 166–7, for another version.

27. *O.R.*, XXVII, 2, pp. 385–6. This report mentions the fire as coming from Little Round Top, but undoubtedly McGilvery's guns were doing most of the damage.

28. *New York at Gettysburg*, III, pp. 1183–4.

29. *O.R.*, XXVII, 1, p. 366.

30. *C.W.* (1865), 1, p. 92.

31. Ibid. p. 448. Specifically, Meade told Hunt on the night of the 1st to select positions for all of the artillery, and the following morning Hunt was told to take such measures as he felt necessary to plug the reported gap in the XII Corps' line.

32. Ibid. p. 449.

33. Ibid. p. 92.

34. *Alexander*, p. 370.

Chapter XV — FALL OPERATIONS

1. At that time, according to one account, Auburn consisted of a mill and the ruins of four or five houses which had burned down. A visit by the author in 1958 revealed the ruins of the old mill and its race. There was no store or town, only a cluster of three or four houses and a church nestled in a valley.

2. *Aldrich*, p. 251.

3. *O.R.*, XXIX, 1, p. 308.

4. Ibid. 2, pp. 119–31. The departed units were: 2nd Connecticut Light Battery; Battery I, 5th U.S.; Battery C, 5th U.S.; and Rank's section of the 3rd Pennsylvania Heavy Artillery. The newcomers were: the 4th Maine Battery; 10th Massachusetts Battery; and the 12th New York Battery.

Chapter XVI — WILDERNESS, SPOTSYLVANIA, AND COLD HARBOR

1. Wilkeson, *Recollections of a Private Soldier*, pp. 36, 38.

2. *Buell*, p. 147.

3. Wilkeson, *Recollections of a Private Soldier*, pp. 39–40.

4. *Buell*, p. 155.

5. *Durell's Battery in the Civil War*, p. 182.

6. *Buell*, p. 164.

7. Ibid. p. 177. This account fails to make clear why this method was thought to be any more effective than normal overhead fire.

8. Benton, J. G., *A Course of Instruction in Ordnance and Gunnery* (New York: 1866), pp. 188–9. Gen. Hunt stated that the mortars were used for the first time on May 8th, but other evidence indicates it was May 9th.

9. *Aldrich*, p. 306.

10. Billings, John D., *The History of the 10th Massachusetts Battery* (Boston: 1881), p. 171.

11. *O.R.*, XXXVI, 1, pp. 755, 765, 770. The original time of fire was apparently scheduled for 5 p.m., but was delayed about an hour. Cowan says he opened up at 5 p.m., and kept shooting until 6:10 p.m. Rhodes puts his time of opening at 6 p.m.

12. Ibid. p. 3.

13. Grant, U. S., *Personal Memoirs of U. S. Grant* (New York: 1885), II, p. 226.

14. Metcalf reported his loss as one killed and 9 wounded; the unofficial version was 8 killed and 16 wounded.

15. *O.R.*, XXXVI, 1, pp. 509, 514, 525, 533. Apparently some of the VI Corps batteries were also coming into line here as well.

16. *Aldrich*, pp. 316–17. Arnold thought Roder, who took over his position, got a bad pounding. However, Roder's report does not reflect this at all. There is a possibility of error, since part of Roder's command relieved Gilliss in the front line; it is not clear if Roder relieved both Gilliss and Arnold.

17. *O.R.*, XXXVI, 1, p. 756.

18. Ibid. p. 762.

19. Ibid. p. 772.

20. Ibid. p. 771.

21. Ibid. p. 287.

22. Ibid. Some secondary sources have stated that the reduction was made only in rifled guns, the smoothbores having been retained. This, however, was not the case; it was a straight across-the-board reduction.

23. Ibid. p. 653.

24. Ibid.; *New York at Gettysburg*, III, p. 1212. There is no indication as to who was responsible for this separation of sections.

25. *O.R.*, XXXVI, 1, p. 653; *New York at Gettysburg*, III, p. 1212.

26. *O.R.*, XXXVI, 1, p. 653.

27. *New York at Gettysburg*, III, p. 1212.

28. *O.R.*, XXXVI, 1, p. 653; *New York at Gettysburg*, III, p. 1212.

29. *Buell*, pp. 208–10.

30. Ibid. pp. 210–12.

31. Ibid. pp. 213–16. The Confederate unit was apparently one of two from Pogue's battalion ordered forward by Gen. Heth against Pogue's advice. Both batteries were horribly cut up by Federal artillery and infantry fire. Phillips's 5th Massachusetts Battery claimed to have

knocked out the 4th Georgia Battery, finding 10 graves and 20 dead horses on the ground the next day.

32. *O.R.,* XXXVI, 1, p. 516.
33. Ibid. p. 524. Confederate accounts, though very incomplete, make no reference to this instance. There is also fragmentary evidence that the Confederates were using more than one 24-pounder.

Chapter XVII — PETERSBURG TO THE END

1. *O.R.,* XL, 1, p. 658.
2. Ibid. p. 279; *C.W.* (1863), I, pp. 99, 115. There was apparently a lack of co-ordination between those charged with constructing the mine and Gen. Hunt; for the testimony of Col. Pleasants before the Congressional Committee was that the fuzes furnished were not long enough, and arrived too late to make proper adjustments. Pleasants did concede, however, that fuzes of the length he wished were hardly ever required.
3. Ibid. pp. 658, 672. The 13-inch mortar had been part of Butler's department; reportedly, at that officer's suggestion, it had been mounted on a unique railroad flat car.
4. Ibid. pp. 726–7. The line-up of guns along the XVIII Corps' front is confusing. Gen. Hunt's totals included only those weapons emplaced as far north as the vicinity of the Hare house, and as such, he omitted the 13-inch mortar and approximately ten 30-pounder Parrotts from his total. Col. Piper's totals are much greater than either Hunt's or Abbott's, and are hard to reconcile; but in view of the fact that he was the corps' chief-of-artillery, it must be assumed that his is the most reliable total.
5. Ibid. p. 280. These figures for weapons about the Hare house differ, as previously mentioned, from Abbott's and Piper's.
6. Ibid. p. 17.
7. Ibid. XLII, 1, p. 542.
8. Ibid. XLVI, 1, p. 1011. The salute was apparently completed, or almost so, before the order against such celebrations was received from Army Headquarters.
9. *B.&L.,* III, pp. 373–4.
10. Letter of Pvt. William W. Edgerton, Co. A, 107th New York Volunteers, to his mother, dated near Kelleys Ford, Virginia, 'On the Rappahannock, Aug. 4, 1863.' This quote was furnished through the kindness of Dr. Bell I. Wiley, who noted it as being in the possession of Dr. Jack A. Haddick, University of Houston.

INDEX

Abbott, Col. Henry L., 506–7
Adams, Capt. George W., 265; *see also* Rhode Island troops, 1st Regt. Light Arty., Btry. G
Alexander, Brig. Gen. Edward Porter, 121, 201, 242, 260, 301, 303, 305, 311, 372, 374, 376–7, 382, 417, 419, 426, 427, 428, 437, 444, 500
Ames, Brig. Gen. Adelbert, wins Medal of Honor, 14; mentioned, 332; *see also* U.S. troops, 1st Regt. Arty., Btry. I, *and* 5th Regt. Arty., Btry. A
Ames, Lt. Nelson; *see* New York troops, 1st Regt. Light Arty., Btry. G
Ammunition, campaign allowance, 30; types used, 39; canister, 39, 53, 85, 411, 460; case-shot, 39, 85, 243; shell, 39, 85; solid shot, 39, 73, 85, 384; capacity of chest, 71; standard chest loading, 73; fixed, 73; expenditures, 78, 85, 130, 211, 231–2, 257, 269, 340, 361, 410, 431, 443–4, 518; supply, 231–2, 269, 275, 330–31, 365, 410, 416–17, 426, 442–4, 446, 459–60, 489, 506; poor quality, 243
Amsden, Capt. Frank P., 256–7; *see also* Pennsylvania troops, 1st Regt. Light Arty., Btry. G
Antietam, Md., battle of, 181–228
Aquia Creek, Va., 139
Army of the Potomac, organized, 28; status of artillery, 34; growth of artillery, 40–41
Army of Virginia, organized, 138; artillery organization, 146–8
Arnold, Capt. Richard, 7, 23; *see also* U.S. troops, 2nd Regt. Arty., Btry. D
Arnold, Lt. William A., *see* Rhode Island troops, 1st Regt. Light Arty., Btry. A
Artillery Reserve, created, 30; criticized, 229–30; status on July 3, 1863, 413, 415; idle in Wilderness, 472; abolished, 489–90; returns to Army, 530
Atwell, Lt. Chas. A., *see* Pennsylvania troops, Btry. E, Light Arty.
Auburn, Va., engagement at, 447–53
Ayres, Brig. Gen. Romeyn B., 6, 19, 55, 104, 332; *see also* U.S. troops, 3rd Regt. Arty., Btry. E, *and* 5th Regt. Arty., Btry. F

Bailey, Col. Guilford D., 63, 67
Bancroft, Lt. Eugene, 404; *see also* 4th U.S. Arty., Btry. G
Barnes, Capt. Almont, *see* 1st Regt. N.Y.L.A., Btry. C
Barry, Brig. Gen. William F., mistakes identity of Confederate troops, 15; chosen as chief-of-artillery, 28; promoted to colonel, 29; principles for organization, 29–30; recommends use of Regular Army artillery, 33–4; transferred to War Office, 182; mentioned, 9–11, 13, 24, 146, 439–40
Benjamin, Lt. Samuel N., awarded Medal of Honor, 222; mentioned, 146, 153–4, 221–2, 251
Benson, Capt. Henry M., *see* 2nd Regt. U.S. Arty., Btry. M
Best, Capt. Clermont, corps artillery chief, 280; mentioned, 280–81, 284, 290, 294, 299–301, 303, 305
Bigelow, Capt. John, wounded, 393; mentioned, 389–94; *see also* Mass. troops, 9th Mass. Btry.
Black Hat Brigade, *see* Iron Brigade

583

De Russy, Capt. G. A., commands group, 237; mentioned, 244, 246, 249

Dickinson, Lt. George, killed, 263; mentioned, 262–3; *see also* U.S. troops, 4th Regt. U.S. Arty., Btry. E

Dieckmann, Capt. Julius, *see* New York troops, 13th Indep. Btry.

Diederich, Capt. Otto, *see* New York troops, 1st N.Y. Bn., Btry. A

Dilger, Capt. Hubert, 146, 152, 169, 171, 287, 289–90, 356; *see also* Ohio troops, 1st Regt. Light Arty., Btry. I

Dimmick, Lt. Justin E., killed, 304; mentioned, 298, 301; *see also* U.S. troops, 1st Regt. Arty., Btry. H

Dorries, Lt. Fred, *see* Ohio troops, 1st Regt. Ohio Light Arty., Btry. L

Doull, Maj. Alexander, inspector of artillery, 277, 279

Dow, Capt. Edwin B., 498; *see also* Maine troops, 6th Me. Btry.

Duane, Maj. James C., 508–10

Durell, Capt. Geo. W., *see* Pa. troops, Indep. Light Btry. D

Eakin, Lt. Chandler P., *see* U.S. troops, 1st Regt. Arty., Btry. H

Easton, Capt. Hezekiah, 93–4; *see also* Pa. troops, 1st Regt. Light Arty., Btry. A

East Woods (Antietam), 188, 191, 199, 206, 207

Edgell, Lt. Frederick M., 192; *see also* New Hampshire troops, 1st Light Btry.

Edwards, Capt. John, 4; *see also* U.S. troops, 3rd Regt. Arty., Btry. L, L/M, *and* 1st Regt. Arty., Btry. G

Egan, Lt. John, 362, 432; *see also* U.S. troops, 1st Regt. Arty., Btry. I, *and* 4th Regt. Arty., Btry. E

Elder, Lt. Samuel S., *see* U.S. troops, 1st Regt. Arty., Btry. K, *and* 4th Regt. Arty., Btry. E

Erickson, Lt. ——, 389–90

Ewing, Lt. Wm. A., *see* Ohio troops, Btry. H, 1st Regt., Light Arty.

Fair Oaks, Va., *see* Seven Pines, Va.

Fairview (Chancellorsville), Va., 284, 292, 301, 304–5

First Bull Run, battle of, 3–25; Federal matériel losses, 19, 21–3

Fitch, Lt. Butler, *see* New York troops, 8th Indep. Btry.

Fitzhugh, Maj. Charles L., brigade commander, 295, 491; *see also* U.S. troops, 4th Regt. Arty., Btry. C/E

Fitzhugh, Capt. Robt. H., *see* New York troops, 1st Regt. Light Arty., Btry. K

Flood, Capt. Edward H., *see* Pa. troops, 1st Regt. Light Arty., Btry. D

Frank, Capt. John D., *see* New York troops, 1st Regt. Light Arty., Btry. G

Frayser's Farm (Glendale), Va., battle, 109–19; Federal matériel losses at, 116, 117, 119

Frederick, Md., 185, 186

Fredericksburg, Va., battle of, 229–70; artillery mission at, 236; shelled, 240–42

French, Lt. Frank S., *see* U.S. troops, 1st Regt. Arty., Btry. E/G

Fugger, Sgt. Frederick, 430, 433

Fuller, Lt. William D., *see* U.S. troops, 3rd Regt. Arty., Btry. C

Fuzes, 56–7, 243; ignitors, 323

Gaines Mill, Va., battle of, 86–102; Federal matériel losses, 94, 98, 100, 121

Gerrish, Capt. Geo. A., *see* New Hampshire troops, 1st Btry.

Gettysburg, Pa., battle of July 1st, 328–62; battle of July 2nd, 363–408; battle of July 3rd, 409–45; Federal artillery organization at, 330, 444–5; Federal gun strength at, 333; Confederate gun strength at, 333–4; ammunition expended at, 340; Federal matériel losses at, 361, 399–400, 409–10, 414–15, 443; artillery casualties July 2nd, 401

'Gettysburg Gun,' 422–3